Mission with LeMay

Mission with LeMay

MY STORY

BY

General Curtis E. LeMay

WITH

MacKinlay Kantor

GARDEN CITY, NEW YORK

DOUBLEDAY & COMPANY, INC.

1965

to Helen
and all other courageous Air Force wives who
have forever given comfort and strength to
their men

FOREWORD

IT COULD be that I have put my name to some inaccuracies in this book. I tried not to.

Possibly there exist some men with infallible memories but it so happens that I have never met one. You hear a lot of talk about people having what is termed *total recall*. In the interest of accuracy I should amend this to read *partial recall* or *pretty good recall*.

Wherever it was possible, every statement regarding a date, a name, an organization, a speed, a type of bomb, a delivery of explosive force— Individuals, grades, times over target, hours and minutes of rendezvous, varieties of ordnance— Types and models of aircraft and missiles— These have been checked with existing records in file, and with data discovered in archives, and with data unearthed elsewhere.

To my satisfaction I was pleased to discover that my memory for events of the past was better than I had thought it might be. For example, I would say that something happened in 1933. Then we would check and discover that actually it occurred in 1934. But I didn't say 1923 or 1943 or 1953. If occasionally I was only one year off in recounting details of a crowded military career extending well over thirty-five years, I held this to be fortunate.

Offhand I would give the amount of dollars as $481,000,000. Consulting the records, we'd find that correctly it was $491,000,000. Or I would say, "It happened when I was flying an O-2-H," and eventually we would discover that I was flying an O-2-K. Still I think that this is a pretty good batting average. I didn't say $503,000,000, and I didn't say that the aircraft was a Keystone or a B-24.

In a complex recounting such as this (in which the reader will accompany me on varied flights and missions, and become familiar with scores of different procedures, and encounter hundreds of individuals) there exists an assemblage of detail which cannot be checked with existing records because none is available. They have disappeared down the labyrinthian corridors which extend back to each war and each operation. Figuratively or literally they have been poured into wastebaskets, bound into bales of wastepaper, stored or marketed; or often made into a wastage beyond redemption or identification.

In such cases I have depended on my own recollection.

It is one man's memory. Another man's memory may offer a version quite remote from mine, and even in some cases—minimal, I hope—a contrary version.

Remember, it has been a long time since many of the events related herein occurred. Also the Air Force is a good place to learn about new things because constantly there appear so many new things to learn about. This mass and weight of fresh awareness can crush down upon the structure of the past, and bend it out of shape in a person's mind.

What I shall say without fear of challenge is not, "This is the way it was," but only, "This is the way I remember it."

I have indeed bombed a number of specific targets. They were military targets on which the attack was, in my opinion, justified morally. I've tried to stay away from hospitals, prison camps, orphan asylums, nunneries and dog kennels. I have sought to slaughter as few civilians as possible.

CURTIS E. LEMAY

CONTENTS

ILLUSTRATIONS

Those photos not credited are courtesy of General LeMay's personal files, now in the Library of Congress

BOOK I

Pre-Flight

. . . 1963

(1906 – 1928)

Thirty-odd years ago I walked or ran to my military work in the morning; later I rode a bicycle or a motorcycle, or sometimes drove a car; during World War II there was a jeep or a staff car.

During World War II there wasn't any such thing as a time to go on duty in the morning. We were all part of the job, day or night. Time didn't mean anything, except for the way it was set forth in flimsies of Instruction and Procedure. Then time meant everything.

On this Monday of 25 February, 1963, my limousine was picking me up at the door of our quarters (Quarters Number 7, over at Fort Myer on a Virginia hill above the Potomac). We lived at Fort Myer during my latest days in the Pentagon, when I was Vice Chief of Staff and finally Chief of Staff of the United States Air Force.

It is a red-brick gingerbready kind of place like so many ancient Army posts. Structures on the old officers' row at one-time Fort Crook, Nebraska, later Offutt Air Force Base, looked a good deal like these houses among the bare winter elms of Fort Myer, except that they were smaller. Smaller also were more modern homes over at Bolling Air Force Base across the river and farther south. That was the reason we couldn't live on an Air Force base nowadays: no adequate quarters at Air Force bases in the Washington area.

A Chief of Staff has multiple social responsibilities and needs a large house in order to fulfill them. Often I would have been just as glad not to enjoy any social responsibilities. They can interfere with a man's work, and tire him out in a way that work never does—at least that's so in my case. I'd rather be active, doing almost any demanding interesting thing in the world, than participating in social activities.

I would rather be flying and at the same time handling the controls. One portion of my brain likes to run ahead or go back . . . and plan for the future, construct a solid platform on accomplishments of the past, and avoid those treacheries which might be built into the structure if one didn't also review the mistakes of the past.

Most of all, I guess, I would rather be doing that than anything else: commanding actively—in the field, as one might say—even with no declared war in progress.

Next to that I'd rather be out hunting somewhere—maybe Africa or Alaska, or in the Montana Rockies. Next, driving a sports car. Next, maybe it would be fishing. Next— I don't know. But not socializing . . .

except with a few intimates, those with whom I can share a reverence for the past, and an awareness of challenges to come.

So I walked out of the front door of our quarters (really a side door leading down into a curving driveway with no porte-cochère built over it). The driver was there and an aide was there. A sergeant emerged from the house behind me, carrying a bag which I had to take to the office.

Helen came out in her pretty flowered housecoat, to kiss me goodbye as she always did when I was home and going to the Pentagon. She kissed me just like that when we were second lieutenants on our initial duty, after our marriage in 1934.

I got into the limousine and looked at the telephone directly in front of me after I sat down. Briefly, flickeringly, like a dark flak-burst brushing past the Plexiglas blister of a bomber, I wondered about commanders in the old days. They didn't have telephones where people could reach them in a split second from any point on the face of the Earth or in the air above that Earth . . . or telephones in automobiles. In the real old days they didn't have any automobiles. But then they didn't have airplanes either. The course of History moved less rapidly then, than it does now.

In other decades I had commanded a squad, a section, a single aircraft, a single crew, and then later a squadron or a group; more than that later on. In this February of 1963 I had responsibility for the eight hundred and seventy-one thousand, five hundred and twenty-eight officers, cadets and airmen of the United States Air Force.

But on my way to the Pentagon, and on this morning, there was no leisure for me to be considering such items or cogitating about them. So I didn't ruminate. Just reviewed the testimony offered during two intense days of the preceding week, and wondered if I had gone wrong anywhere. Hoped that I hadn't.

We were asking for $363,700,000 to be restored to a procurement law in order that we might accomplish properly the initial stages of our program for a new reconnaissance strike aircraft, formerly the B-70, and redesignated as the RS-70.

. . . You can see the white tombstones of Arlington from our quarters . . . see them in the winter when leaves are gone from the trees; you can't see them in the summer because of thick foliage. You drive down the hill on the most direct route from Fort Myer to the Pentagon. On your right hand along the last northerly ravine of the great cemetery, the little white slabs are rigid in their ranks.

I recall being in Washington long before, back in 1934 when the Air Corps had to take over the flying of the U.S. mail. That year a friend of mine, long since vanished in a smashed aircraft, told me about enjoying a picnic with girls and all, there at Arlington. He described the tomb of the Unknown Soldier, and the Lee mansion, and the fighting top of the battleship *Maine* arranged as its own monument, and other historical sights. It all sounded interesting. As an eager young man I thought that I should like to go there as soon as there came an opportunity. History fascinates me and always has.

. . . My lieutenant friend told me that they all drifted over to those hillsides north of the cemetery, to wander at will. The girls picked violets; after that they sat down to enjoy sandwiches and deviled eggs and soft drinks.

. . . Now that entire woodland and everything north of it, up to the very edge of Fort Myer, is solid with graves. Fifty-two hundred and sixteen funerals for one year alone. About as many funerals in a single year as there are feet in a mile. . . . Fort Myer furnishes a continual cadre for burial details, and has for a long time. That's where the caissons, the gun-carriages are kept, and white gloves for the men to wear, and blank cartridges which are fired in volleys over the graves.

Often the President of the United States and I had sat beside each other during the two years since his inauguration. I suppose if on that chilly February 25th morning some soothsayer had said grimly to me, "Nine months from now, to the day, one of you two—either President Kennedy or yourself—will be buried in Arlington—" I suppose if the soothsayer had said that with all authority, and still refused to tell whether it would be President Kennedy or General LeMay, probably I would have thought that it would be myself. Not that I ever lost any sleep over the possibility of lurking assassins; I'm sure the President didn't either, right up to the moment the bullets struck him. But I did fly a lot, and always have, even after becoming Chief of Staff. The President also flew frequently, as we know; but you might say that we flew under somewhat different conditions.

It would have seemed weird and unforgettable to witness, in precognition, the vast weeping procession and the people watching it.

Occupied with no gloomy forebodings or even sentimental reflections on the dead already stowed in Arlington, we drove past, following the swift sure route to the Pentagon down the river. Usually it is more simple for those of us who approach by private limousine to go around to the south, swing back to the north and go into the garage area which is below the steps of the River Entrance.

. . . No time now for consideration of the Air Force at large, of Fort Myer and Arlington with their history, of the President himself. Fact is, I was engaged in a protracted struggle with the President's appointee, Secretary McNamara of the Department of Defense. We were diametrically opposed in policy. Our contention, easily recognizable in 1962, had emerged again almost a year later in testimony before the House Armed Services Committee.

I went into the Pentagon and stood before the blank elevator door and felt for my key. (We get in by means of the key; no one without a key can operate that elevator.) The elevator can take you down to the Command Post, far underneath the ground. That's a bomb shelter supposed to be proof against any violent explosion up above. But I had no need to go down there at the moment, so I pressed the button for Up.

The elevator brought me to the fourth floor and to my office suite adjoining. Offices of all the Chiefs of Staff and Secretaries included in the DOD (Department of Defense) lie in a given portion of the Pentagon, but on different floors. So this whole arrangement is as convenient for one as for another.

I hadn't spent the bulk of the years since World War II in reorganizing any vast business for the purpose of pulling it from the red side of the ledger to the black. True, I had reorganized and built up a vast business, the Strategic Air Command; but its mission was not to make a profit for stockholders. Its mission was to serve as deterrent against the enemy—a deterrent against nuclear warfare—a striking force so efficient and so powerful that no enemy could, in justice to his own present and future, attack us—through a sneak assault or any other way.

I had not been in the financial and organizational side of the automobile business. I had been active in the airplane business, in crowding the maximum performance from all equipment and personnel I commanded.

Thus it may be believed that Secretary McNamara and I would hold different views on the matter of manned aircraft.

In the official report which came before the public in March, 1962, it was noted that the House Committee had rewritten the Pentagon's major authorization bill in strong language.

Such language had not been used previously in any directive of the sort.

To quote from the report: "It means exactly what it says; i.e., that the Secretary of the Air Force, as an official of the executive branch, is directed, ordered, mandated, and required to utilize the full amount of the $491 million authority granted 'to proceed with production planning and long leadtime procurement for an RS-70 weapon system.'"

Sounded good, but in the end it really didn't mean a thing. President Kennedy himself intervened before the whole project came to a vote in the House. The President got the House to withdraw the language which derived from this recommendation by the House Armed Services Committee, and which would have made it mandatory for Secretary Zuckert to go ahead with the RS-70 plans.

We were not only up against the President. We were up against his Secretary of Defense as well—his appointee, Robert S. McNamara, formerly of the Ford Motor Company. McNamara said flatly that funds authorized for the construction of further RS-70's would not be used, even if voted by the Congress.

Ethics and good soldiering demanded that I state my case to the Secretary. If ruled against—as I was—I could appeal to the President. I did this, and lost.

When a thing like that happens to you, good soldiering requires further that you get to work and carry out *their* orders *their* way. Emphatically this was what I had done.

However, Congress has stern responsibilities in the Defense field. I was required by law to give information to the Congress, and also my opinions when these were requested. It was the only place where I, as Air Force Chief of Staff, and as a subordinate of the Commander-in-Chief, could oppose the Secretary of Defense and the President of the United States after they had made their decision.

Secretary McNamara had his own beliefs and his own attitude. These did not coincide with the beliefs and attitude of the majority of the Joint Chiefs of Staff. All of us excepting a recent appointee, General Maxwell D. Taylor, were in favor of the RS-70 program as I recited it in testimony before the Committee.

Other people might think it rather surprising that those traditional rivals of the Air Force—the Navy and the Marine Corps—would agree to our program; and that it would be supported by the Chief of Staff of the Army as well.

Again, only an especial member of the JCS, brought from retirement by the President to serve as his military advisor, and then appointed by him to the chairmanship of the JCS, was against us.

On the previous Thursday and Friday, hour after hour, the battle had been waged in the Committee hearing. Testimony was rendered, up until five-thirty on Thursday afternoon, and until four o'clock on Friday afternoon. Now the testimony was in: it was Monday morning. Within the matter of another hour or two the Committee would meet, minus the presence of those of us who had appeared to give expert testimony in our fields. And the Committee would vote.

I managed to go through routine motions at my office. An aide came in with details of the day's arrangements: where I should be, at what time. The manuscript of my next talk at the War College was presented. . . . There were courtesies to be paid to a member of Congress who for years had been a friend of the Air Force, and was soon to be leaving the political scene. . . . The regular Monday session of the JCS would be held early that afternoon. Here was a résumé of matters to be discussed. . . .

But it is strange how one can proceed with a given mechanical task and at the same time entertain capable recollection of the problems which have occupied him during recent days, and which still persist. Such challenges surmount the ordinary activity of an office or a command, and—thanks be!—do not appear every day in a commander's life.

If they did, there would be no more commanders. No one could ever stand the strain.

This was really sweating it out. The Committee might finish deliberations and put the matter to a vote by eleven o'clock or so.

I looked at my watch and kept pacing the floor.

It was as if I could hear the words of the Secretary of Defense, hear him actually uttering his opposition.

. . . *I submit to you that it would be a serious waste of this Nation's resources to proceed to deploy the RS-70 as the Air Force and its Chief have proposed.*

At even so early a stage of the game, I should like to make clear to the reader of this book that I have never quarreled about civilian control *per se*.

We know in America that, under law and by tradition, we are commanded by civilians. We are a nation composed chiefly of civilians. So we in the military, at the time I'm talking about, did not raise a blanket objection to being overruled. Sincerely we wanted to play on Secretary McNamara's team.

What we did object to was the Secretary's saying, "No," to something the military wished to do, and giving *a military reason* for his action. Palpably thus he and his coterie were setting themselves up as military experts.

. . . If a Secretary of Defense says, "No. You cannot have this system because we cannot afford it," or if he says, "You cannot have it because it should be deferred to await—" (certain economic developments, perhaps)—

If a Secretary of Defense confines his reasoning to the field of his experience and understanding, we accept his decision.

But if he says, "You can't have your system because *my system is best*," his attitude is resented deeply by those who have spent their lives in the business of preparing for defensive warfare and/or waging defensive warfare.

A wise Secretary should abide by his knowledge of the political and economic fields of national endeavor. It is incumbent upon him to do so. (Although at least some of us military people are not complete dummies in those fields either.)

But if a Secretary should point his finger at you, and say, "You don't know what you're talking about!" his attitude would be met with bitterness. It would be resented in any other profession—legal, medical, educational, religious—the same way.

Ever since I first stood in a gawky Thin Cadet-Blue Line on the Ohio State campus over forty years ago, I have sought to be as honestly obedient a soldier and airman as I could be. Often the columnists have given the public an image of a growling rebellious LeMay who in fact never existed.

Here is what happened: In Congressional committee hearings, behind closed doors and with no press representatives anywhere around, I stated my views as sworn and required. If certain persons felt impelled subsequently to reveal testimony which originally was unavailable to the public, I cannot accept the blame for this.

Now it was my own voice which I heard in memory.

Ever since I have been in the Air Force, there have been people who said that the airplane could not penetrate. And they had arguments to substantiate this. . . . We have operated our offensive systems against all the air defenses of the world, and they can be penetrated. And I think they always will be penetrated in the future.

I had gone on to give Classified testimony regarding our future tactics, weapons, counter-measure systems and other aids which would take our RS-70's within striking distance of their targets—aids which would help to get them in, and get them back out. And I had told the Committee before I closed: *I sometimes think that we have given the defense systems too much credit.*

I believed that the day of the manned bomber was far from done, and was certain that the Chairman of the House Armed Services Committee agreed with me.

. . . I heard in my mind the voice of Congressman and Committee Chairman Carl Vinson, the veteran Democrat from Georgia:

It is a deep and abiding belief of the Armed Services Committee that manned systems should continue to be a major part of our military force.

There is no doubt that our missiles, particularly our intercontinental ballistic missiles, are a major part of our arsenal. Neither I nor the Committee members would for a moment think of minimizing their importance, or cutting back on the missile program.

But the Committee sees a growing tendency on the part of the Department of Defense to place more and more emphasis on missiles, and less and less on manned systems. This is a dangerous course and one which the Committee intends to do everything in its power to stop.

So I went to the window and stood looking out at the cars and figures hurrying there, with winter hunting them still, and a spring unseen as yet, unwilling to melt and warm.

. . . Sweating it out. You could say that again.

I kept thinking, "We ought to get the verdict today. God knows whether my testimony had any pronounced effect on the Committee at the hearing."

I kept thinking of the time when I'd ordered a change in tactics when we were going to hit St. Nazaire, late in 1942. It was the first time in the Army Air Forces' European Theater experience that a large formation of heavy bombers had ever approached a target without using evasive action in an attempt to avoid the enemy's ground-to-air shellfire.

I led that one, so I didn't have to suffer and wonder, off somewhere in the distance. I suffered and wondered right there, twenty-two thousand feet above St. Nazaire.

. . . Or the time when, after anxiety I'd not wish to experience again, I decided that our B-29's should attack Tokyo from an altitude of five to seven thousand feet, instead of their customary twenty-five or thirty thousand feet: just about five miles lower than the usual level over the target. We might lose over three hundred aircraft and some three thousand veteran personnel in this attack. It might go down in history as LeMay's Last Brainstorm.

But I didn't think so. If I had, I wouldn't have ordered the operation to be flown as it was flown.

Trouble was: they wouldn't let me lead that one. I had to send Tommy Power instead. I was relegated to walk the floor at 21st Bomber Command headquarters. It was no fun, walking that floor.

Here's what happened. We ordered three hundred and twenty-five planes to that job, and eighty-six per cent of them attacked the primary target. We lost just four-and-three-tenths per cent of all the B-29's which were airborne. Sixteen hundred and sixty-five tons of incendiary bombs went hissing down upon that city, and hot drafts from the resulting furnace tossed some of our aircraft two thousand feet above their original altitude. We burned up nearly sixteen square miles of Tokyo.

To quote General Power (later he succeeded me as commander of SAC, and was the man who led this operation in person): "It was the greatest single disaster incurred by any enemy in military history. It was greater than the combined damage of Hiroshima and Nagasaki. There were more casualties than in any other military action in the history of the world."

So we had done that from low level, just as I thought we could. But I had to remain on Guam. I owned too much knowledge of future operations—atomic bomb, etc.—to be permitted to fly, the way I had flown missions constantly before.

(Actually I preferred to fly in the left-hand seat. But I did fly a lot of other positions, especially when still a colonel commanding the 305th Bomb Group. I flew as co-pilot on occasion; and then maybe the next mission I would take the flight engineer's job . . . in addition to his dials he had the top-turret guns. Sometimes I would go around and visit the bombardier or navigator or radio operator, or one of the gunners' positions. It was my purpose in so doing to learn whether there were any procedures which were being done wrong—whether there were basic improvements which could be made in the performance of the men flying these positions. I think it did a lot of good. I was able to find places where the work could be improved by the introduction of new practices. Discovered an interesting thing: the best way to lead a mission was to stand between the pilot and co-pilot. You got a good view there, and had no immediate manual task—nothing to do in the aircraft you were flying in—nothing to do except control the entire formation.)

It was not easy to stay home at the base at Guam on that 9th–10th of March, 1945, when Tokyo burned. I would rather have gone.

. . . Behind me one of the telephones calls me to alert. There are a number of telephones in the private office. One of them is red; you can guess about that one. There are others: direct lines leading here and there. And the telephone which is ringing now— It will relay the report of someone who stands near the Committee room.

I answer, and a voice says, "They've voted, sir."

I look at my wristwatch. The hands stand at 1108 hours. It is likely that the Committee session adjourned at eleven o'clock. The news is coming in fast, good or bad, the way I wished it to.

. . . As if it's a gray grim November in 1942, at Chelveston, and one by one crews with jingling chute harnesses are crowding through a door, and flopping down on rough pine planks with Intelligence officers leaning close. Interrogation . . . that's a big deal. . . . How did we do, how did we do? How soon can we see the strike photos? I'm standing there still wearing my Mae West and feeling the damp dirty raw rim of coveralls along the back of my neck, and thinking: "So we went straight in on the target, the way they've never done before. No evasive action. . . . Yes, I know we lost some airplanes. But how many to enemy fighters, and how many to defending batteries on the ground? And what are our bombing results?" . . . Finally the reports are coördinated, and they're all I could have hoped for. Not one B-17 from our 305th Bomb Group (H) has been knocked down by flak over St. Nazaire. We tally some losses to enemy fighters only, which would have occurred in the same ratio whether we'd used evasive action or not. But the 305th, proceeding on our new straight run instead of weaving all over the sky, has placed more than twice the bomb tonnage squarely on the target that any other Group has placed that day.

. . . I take my cigar out of my mouth and maybe I am gripping the telephone more tightly than necessary. My own voice seems to crack a little.

"Well. How was the vote?"

"Thirty-one to five."

. . . Again it's an April morning twenty-nine months later (strangely enough. Let the numerologists look into this one: instead of B-17's we are using B-29's). The place is the limestone-and-coral isle of Guam instead of a tired bomber base on the Bedfordshire-Northants border in England. And I've been pounding that floor until my feet are ready to crack at the ankles. But good news is beginning to mount up. . . . Here comes Tommy Power—he's stooged around for two hours after completing his bomb run, taking pictures of the destruction of Tokyo. We will examine those photos while they're still wet. We have never seriously wounded the largest city in the world before, but this time—

In a few hours, and operating from the seemingly suicidal altitude of only five to seven thousand feet, we have burnt the belly out of Tokyo. We know that we have shortened the war by many months. Each of those fourteen crews who went down on that mission have saved American lives, perhaps by the scores of thousands. We don't pause to shed any tears for uncounted hordes of Japanese who lie charred in that acrid-smelling rubble. The smell of Pearl Harbor fires is too persistent in our own nostrils.

. . . I say, "Oh. Thirty-one to five. In whose favor?"

"In favor of the extension of the RS-70 program. In favor of the JCS majority decision. In favor, sir, if you will, of your testimony."

I say, "Oh," again . . . then manage to thank the caller, and to conclude the conversation quickly.

It's impossible to do anything else for a while except to go over and look out through curtains at the cold Potomac and the distant domes of public buildings beyond.

This is the second time that those Congressmen over on the Hill have supported the expressed Air Force policies, as opposed to those of McNamara. There rises a mighty warmth and I think a pardonable exultation, in realizing that we have the confidence of our law-makers.

. . . Of course McNamara does not have to spend that RS-70 money for that purpose, and has sworn he will not do so. Certain people in the press, ardent Air Force advocates, have spoken and will speak again of "the application of IBM reasoning instead of the application of experienced military advice." I do not exactly concur in this. I don't think it's wise to belittle one's opponents.

Consciences of the Joint Chiefs of Staff, in majority, are clear. And so will be the consciences of the Committee on Armed Services.

I can very nearly prophesy what they will say in their report to the Congress. And I will be correct.

"HOUSE OF REPRESENTATIVES. 88th Congress. 1st Session. Report No. 62. . . . Mr. Vinson, from the Committee on Armed Services, submitted the following REPORT (To accompany H.R. 2440)—

". . . By no stretch of imagination would the Secretary's program develop a fighting machine. . . .

"The concern of the committee stems from the growing tendency on the part of the Department of Defense to place more and more emphasis on the missiles and less and less on manned strategic systems. The committee considers this to be a most dangerous course of action and one with which it disagrees. . . .

"The current strategic bomber force provides . . . that essential element of flexibility which spans the gap between limited war capabilities and the pushbutton war of long-range missiles.

"It embraces that highly essential element—the judgment of man."

2

I REMEMBER the first airplane I ever saw. I'm not sure what kind of airplane it was, nor am I certain about the date. It must have been during the winter of 1910–11 or the year or two following. I couldn't have been much older than four or five. It was winter, because I had a red stocking-cap on.

I was out in the garden alongside our home in west Columbus, Ohio. That was a neighborhood of small houses, gray houses, brick stores on the business corners were rather shabby. It wasn't by any means a slum, but it wasn't the rich side of town either.

Don't know exactly what I was doing out in the garden—probably some sort of little chore, like picking up sticks for kindling—something of that sort.

Suddenly, in the air above me, appeared a flying-machine. It came from nowhere. There it was, and I wanted to catch it. It would be a wonderful thing to possess—that mysterious fabrication which was chortling through the sky, its few cylinders popping in a way far different from any automobile or truck which went past our place. . . . I can't tell you whether the aircraft was military or civilian, although I strongly suspect the latter. (Military aircraft were few and far between in those days. It was in 1911 that the first bomb was dropped from an aircraft; it was in 1912 that a machine-gun was fired first from one.)

Children can muster enormous strength in ideal and idea, in all their effort to grasp the trophy they desire. And nobody was holding me back, no one was standing close to say, "Look, you're just a little child. That airplane is away up there in the air, and no matter how fast you run you can't keep up with it. You can't reach high enough to seize it." I just thought that I might be able to grab the airplane and have it for my own, and possess it always. So I lit out after it.

. . . Ran as fast as I could, across neighbors' lawns, across gardens and vacant lots, sometimes on the sidewalk, sometimes in the street. But the airplane was getting ahead of me. Try as I might I kept falling behind. It had been directly overhead; now it was far ahead, losing its strange crate-shape in the smoke of midwinter, in a ragged horizon of chimneys and roofs.

Then it was gone. Its wonderful sound and force and the freakish illusion of the Thing, a Thing made of wood and metal, piercing the air: those were gone too.

I set out for home in tears. I stamped resentfully along paths where I had skimmed in glee when there still existed a chance of winning out, of catching that critter in the air. It seemed to take seconds as I raced seeking the prize, but it took hours to come back.

. . . I had lost something unique and in a way Divine. It was a god or a spook, or a piece of a god or a spook, and I had never seen one before. I wanted it, and hadn't been able to catch it, and was filled with a sense of exasperation and defeat.

Yet there was the thought of tomorrow. It just could be that another one of those Things might throb through the air next day. Perhaps I would be more fortunate in a future try.

I wanted not only the substance of the mysterious object, not only that part I could have touched with my hands. I wished also in vague yet unforgettable fashion for the drive and speed and energy of the creature. Also I needed to understand and possess the reason and purpose for this instrument—the Why of it as well as the What.

(I could not have spoken of these matters to anyone; yet they formed and circled in my mind like misshapen small aircraft of my own invention.)

Never have I been able to turn my back completely on the tender and the trivial. Sometimes when younger I felt this to be a weakness within myself, but not any longer. The very composition of human life springs from tenderness and frequently from triviality as well. Thus I have never erased from recollection the spectacle of that child in Ohio, trying to chase the aircraft and have it for his own. He stayed with me and sped beside me many times, later on, when it seemed often that I was trying to catch up with something which moved faster than I could run.

3

MY MOTHER and father came from farm families in southern Ohio. My father, Erving LeMay, was born in Union County near the village of

Wadkins. Mother was born at Great Bend, down on the Ohio River in Meigs County. They met when my father's family bought a farm in that same county, and moved down there.

Mom's people, Carpenters and Boyds, had come across the river from Virginia in the early days. Pop's family was, as the name suggests, of French ancestry. A few years ago some LeMay published, in French, a book about the tribe bearing our name, and I have a copy now. In fact, they were kind enough to put me in the book, where I appear along with a great many fine-looking Canadian policemen and a great many fine-looking French nuns.

Maybe my father heard about my mother soon after moving into that neighborhood, before he even met her. He couldn't have missed because of the name. Names always seemed remarkably important in our family. My grandfather Carpenter said he didn't want his daughter to have any ordinary name, so he named her Arizona . . . because he had never heard of a girl named Arizona, and thought it a pretty name. Through all her long life, Mom says, she has never encountered another woman named Arizona. She's met a couple of Zonas, that's all.

Erving LeMay and Arizona Carpenter were married in Meigs County on the 25th of November, 1905. Shortly thereafter they moved to Columbus where Pop had been able to get a job on the railroad. He felt drawn toward working with steel and iron, working with metal tools and structures. But something happened: he lost his railroad job early in the game. Then he took all sorts of work: odd jobs, carpentry, house-painting. Like many men in his category and time, he was subject to whims and pressures of regional and national economy. Sometimes a construction job was there, sometimes it wasn't; sometimes a job wasn't even there, but away off some place else. Then he had to go find it.

During my early childhood we moved like nomads. We lived at four different addresses in Columbus; we lived in a village called Lithopolis, near Winchester; we lived in Pennsylvania, lived in Montana, lived in California. The children kept coming along, but Pop never balked at pulling up stakes and moving the whole caboodle of us almost overnight if a better situation seemed to be promised.

I was the eldest, born on the 15th of November, 1906. Most women had their babies at home in those days instead of at a hospital. I was born in a cottage with a very steep roof which stood next door to a little grocery store, at the corner of Atcheson and Twentieth Streets on the middle-east side of Columbus. It is predominantly a colored section nowadays but wasn't then . . . it is still a calm area with lots of trees. But we didn't live there long enough for me to grow up and enjoy the peace and quiet and generally picturesque quality. Before my brother Lloyd was born we had moved to Lithopolis. My first memories are of that town and place. We must have lived there several years.

. . . We had a screen door on the front of the house, and I owned a puppy dog, and the dog tore the front screen. He loosened it at one of the lower corners where it had been tacked firmly before, so there was a flap of screen: the pup could go in and out through that flap. So could I. Lloyd was just a tiny baby, but I was two and three and upwards, so I was able to get out and go places. I ran away all the time.

It wasn't that I wasn't well treated at home or that I didn't receive affection from my mother. Usually we had enough to eat, we had things to play with. But still I wanted to run away. Something seemed to tell me that I had to get up and go, and invariably I yielded to that command. In after years my mother has said that my truancy bordered on mania. Guess she was right. Clearly I can remember waiting my chance and then dashing away the moment any opportunity offered.

Once Mom was ailing for a while, and Pop treated her to a luxury in the shape of a hired girl. (She was a full-grown woman, no mere mother's helper.) We weren't used to having anyone like that around the place, and I was more dedicated to running away than ever.

Nothing could be done about these demented flights of mine. I was hell-bent on going and that's all there was to it. I'd be found clear across town; then I'd be brought home by well-intentioned neighbors or sometimes by the town marshal; then I'd be punished. Pop had a strong hand and arm because of his steel work, and he could really paddle, but it didn't make any difference. Gone again next day.

. . . Mom and Pop were going downtown . . . and I recall that the flap on the screen door had been boarded back into place. Pop had done it himself, he was taking no chances. Also he had fixed a strong hook on the door, very high up, where a child couldn't reach. What with the newly repaired screen and the new hook the folks thought my journeyings were at an end—for the time being, anyway.

So they went to do their errands or go to church or pay bills or call on somebody, or whatever it was they were going to do— They went away, and I went to the door. The dog hadn't been able to make any headway against the repaired screen. I tried to reach the hook and couldn't.

The hired girl cautioned me. "I know all about you. Your folks told me that you were apt to run away, and I'm not going to give you a chance to do it."

I said, "Please open the door."

"No, I'm not going to open that door, and there's no use asking me to. You'll run away if I open the door, and I'm not going to—"

I said, "Open the door."

"Well, it won't do you any good to ask me. And you can just yell or scream all you want to, but that door *stays hooked*."

Simultaneously I started a physical attack upon the screen, and a verbal attack upon the horrified domestic. I called her every name I could think of, and already I had picked up some pretty good names. (Little boys always learn those things first instead of something that would serve them better.) Whatever epithets, profane or obscene, had been circulating among the youth of Lithopolis—these I had picked up. Now I used them to good advantage. Or bad.

At the same time I was tearing away, kicking my feet and striking at the screen with my hands, and then hurling my body against it. I went through with a crash. Can't remember whether the dog came along or not. But I was out and gone, with the wails of the temporary housekeeper sounding behind me.

My folks came home to find that the hired girl had dragged down a suitcase and was packing her things. She was in tears.

"I won't stay with that child another minute!" she cried. "No one has ever talked to me like that before and no one can talk to me like that now. No, I won't stay!" But she was a good woman and a great help to my mother in a time of need, so Mom managed to persuade her not to go, and she stayed for a while.

Eventually I was caught and dragged home, and got the licking of my life.

But I still wanted to run away. I had to grow older and be burdened with a lot of responsibilities, and begin to nourish ambition— I had to do these things before I could manage to control my temper and discipline my activities.

Sometimes after I grew up I tried to explore the infantile motive which had bossed me, and discover why my unruly addiction persisted in the face of every obstacle, and with severe punishment following.

It seems to me now, as I attempt to recall how I felt so long ago, that it was as if someone had told me of some complex and dangerous yet still wholly attractive activity which was taking place somewhere beyond the horizon . . . just where, I did not know.

It was as if I went in search of a charm and a challenge of which no one else was even aware. It was a mystery which cried for me to penetrate it.

There were a lot of actual difficulties in my life, certainly: I didn't have to go in search of imaginary ones.

Forever changing schools—that was a real complication. It meant a different set of books; a different crew of teachers; a different assemblage of friends, rivals, or enemies. I'd just get all set at one school in Columbus—say, when we lived on Dana Avenue or perhaps on Guildford—and then, bang, we'd have to move out of town.

Being the eldest I was aware of this problem first and longest. New children appeared in the LeMay household every few years. There were seven in all, though one little boy died at birth. We survivors are evenly divided as to sex. My sister Velma followed Lloyd by a few years, then there came Methyl; then Leonard, the third boy, some years after that. Then there came the baby who was lost at birth, and finally after some more years my youngest sister Pat. She was born when I was in Ohio State University, when I was not yet twenty-two. 1906 until 1928—that's a long span of childbearing for any woman. But Mom was healthy and serene about the whole thing, and so she remains serene today.

A while ago I mentioned this strange business about names in the LeMay and Carpenter families. People think that I might have been named after some relative or family friend, but such is not the case. Mom just picked out the name Curtis, she drew it out of thin air. Also friends have suggested many times that she must have been influenced or particularly stirred by the writings of Ralph Waldo Emerson, and in this way she gave me my middle name, Emerson.

Not at all. Mom says placidly that she just liked the sound of the name Emerson.

As for my youngest sister, Pat, I named her myself.

Just to demonstrate how legends get built up in this world (family legends or international, it's all the same) here is Mom's account of the naming of Sister Pat.

Mom declares that neither she nor my father had made up their minds about what to call the baby, and none of the rest of the family came forward with any ideas. According to her, I arrived home from college classes and said, "I've got the baby's name."

"What is it to be?"

"Vernice Patericha."

"Patericha? Don't you mean Patricia?"

"Nope. Vernice Patericha."

"Well, where did you get that name?"

"I just got it. Don't you like it?"

"Yes," everybody said—but some as if they doubted that they really did like it. So, Mom relates, that remained the baby's name.

Now for my version: I named her Patricia, and that was that. I don't remember anything about the Vernice Patericha nonsense, and don't believe it ever happened that way.

4

THERE ARE many valuable forms of discipline in this world, but some are complicated and not realized to be benefits at the time they occur.

First and foremost of course everyone will think of poverty, and they'll be right.

Trouble is, you can't simulate poverty. If you grow up amid the confused ignominy of the very poor and insecure, and if you are sufficiently tough in spite of this, poverty can prosper you. I have heard too many people confess to an angry stimulation which such circumstances gave them, and have observed too many cases myself, and have felt my own case sufficiently, not to believe that this can be true—not invariably true, but often.

But if you try to manufacture that situation for your own child, it just can't be done. It's all a combination of position and a prank of Fate. It either happens or it doesn't happen. When people try deliberately to fabricate such an existence for their young, they look just plain silly. I know of such a case. Can't tell you the name of the family because that might merely embarrass some people needlessly. But it happened in the case of one of America's richest families, in which there were several sons. These boys were sent off to school, and the very wise people in their home, those who controlled the purse-strings large and small, thought that they would discipline the boys by cutting away down on their pocket-money.

Maybe other boys in their class had from two to five dollars per week pocket-money—somewhere in that ball park. These students from the exorbitantly wealthy family were kept on twenty-five or fifty cents apiece, per week. Result was that they never felt a part of the scheme of things, never felt on a par with their schoolmates. The other kids could go down to the corner, and trade sodas and Cokes and sandwiches and things like that; the rich boys had to stay back in their dormitory, and make excuses. They just couldn't hold up their end.

It would have been impossible to keep from these boys the knowledge that when they were twenty-one or thirty or thirty-five, or whatever, they would inherit scores of millions of dollars apiece—come into control of the whole works. But in the meantime, which was more to the point, they were treated to a needless cruelty and crippling. Instead of feeling part of the world in any way, they were cut off from it—far more by the fake poverty inflicted upon them than they would have been if they had appeared in their normal natural role, as rich sons of a rich family.

Seems to me that you can learn a lesson from this and carry it on into about any other realm of human activity. It doesn't do any good to fake a thing, to fake an ill or a benefit. We have to face the facts the way they are, not the way we wish they were. If we start with a false situation, then we're getting off on the wrong foot to begin with. A clear concise awareness of the exact condition, the exact problem which faces an individual, is his best weapon for coping with it.

As I pointed out, we LeMays dwelt in a number of places during the first years which I can remember; and suddenly we moved out West. I was seven or eight when we made the change. Pop had lost his construction job and we were in a pretty sorry situation at home. But Pop had a sister out West whose husband said that a job could be found there in Montana. So away we went. This was about 1913 or 1914.

As I recall, I was perfectly ready for a big adventure, although this sort of thing wasn't particularly unusual, at least in a small way. Forever we had been moving from this house to that, just as Pop moved from this job to that one. But on this particular journey we were going faster and farther than we had ever gone before.

We had the usual day-coach-train-trip of that era, all the way from Ohio to Montana: crowded straw suitcases, squashed and wrinkled pillows, the lunches packed in shoe-boxes with as much food as possible taken from home to start with (and as little as possible to be purchased along the way). There is a memory of people chewing peanuts and children throwing shells around, and babies wailing; and the car was either too hot or too cold; and the smell of a crushed banana when somebody stepped upon it; and the whizzing air and sound of wheels roaring up through the toilet when you sat upon it in that smelly little jolting compartment at the end of the car . . . the news-butcher coming through with a great big square basket filled with all sorts of goodies: wonderful candies, and sacks of nuts, and fruits and bottles . . . beautiful things which we children longed for, in vain.

Well, here was Montana, and the air was spicy silver, spicy blue and very cold. We hadn't known cold like that back East: a high dry splintery cold which seemed to take your breath after you bit into it for a while.

First off we occupied a tenant house on the ranch where my father went to claim his promised job. But that didn't last very long. I don't know whether Pop got fired or quit; but anyway we made another move. This time we children were put into a wagon and bundled up as well as possible with straw and old quilts. We were headed for a sportsmen's club, of all places; but it was a sportsmen's club for fishing only. None of the sportsmen was around in the winter. The place was away south of Butte City.

Never shall I forget that ride in the open wagon. A snowstorm lashed us most of the time. It was a long way to travel, too: to a three-lake string called the Nez Perce. When we ended up there we were twenty-five miles from the nearest neighbor. So no more school for me, as there had been during the period when we dwelt at the ranch.

I think the club people were looking for somebody to take charge of the place, winter and summer. When it came to summer, my father, with his construction background, needed technical help while hatching out the fish. But once you put the eggs in, and got them fertilized, it was just a matter of keeping the water running over them at the proper temperature, and waiting for eggs to hatch. Once they were hatched out, you had to get the fish into the proper pond until they were big enough to put into the stream.

All in all this was a swell place for little boys to be, and I made the most of it. I fished, winter and summer. At the start I learned that the hatchery portion of our area was Off Limits: you didn't go casting a fly or dangling bait in those domains. But there were three lakes on different levels, and a flume took water from the stream and fed into the lakes. The region of the flume didn't freeze in winter, so there was always fishing, at least my style—eight-year-old style. The surrounding steep wooded slopes were exciting and beautiful. This Montana experience strengthened the abiding love I've always had for the out-of-doors: a desire to be in woods and immerse myself along with the wild things, take my chances with them; and let them take their chances with me.

I didn't get to see any airplanes while we were in Montana. I saw other great flying things—bald eagles from the crags, hawks which soared over our valley; but the sight of a certain airplane and a certain flyer—this was waiting for me in the next year to come, when we walked into an extravaganza which none of us could ever have imagined ourselves as being in.

Pop got a job in Emeryville, California, and the whole gang of us were hauled away from the lonely fish hatchery just as fast as the change could be made. Pop's first Emeryville job was in a cannery. Can't remember what came next.

. . . I have a queer habit of making comparisons in my mind, translating other facts into Air Force facts, so to speak; and viewing other things as I might look at them if they occurred within the Air establishment. Thus I have been accused and still am accused of possessing a single-track mind. Guess they're right. Maybe it's not a bad idea for one in my kind of business.

Well, anyway. Suppose we had an Advance Warning and Control Center, a remote little radar outfit stuck on an iceberg off in the Arctic somewhere, and people never seeing anyone except the helicopter which flew in to bring them supplies once in a while. If you took a kid from an outfit like that and stuck him down suddenly in the middle of Times Square on New Year's Eve, it might be a comparable situation to what befell us.

Because this was 1915. And in 1915 the year itself was synonymous, in the United States of America, not with the European war but with the Panama-Pacific International Exposition. That great Fair was held in San Francisco to celebrate the completion of the Panama Canal.

(It's likely that if any fellow American had said that the day would come, in less than half a century— The day would come when the United States would agree not to fly its flag, even in our own Canal Zone, unless the Panamanian flag floated beside it, on the same level— We would have suspected that man to be a traitor. And we would have called him a damn liar.)

Our whole Country had been hearing about the Panama-Pacific Exposition for several years. A lot of money had been contributed by the Government, and tax levies were voted in California. The vast sum of seven and one-half million dollars was actually gotten together by San Franciscans.

The papers said that the cost of the whole Exposition exceeded fifty million dollars. That may be a commonplace figure, as mentioned in the press nowadays; but it's certainly not hay. Translated into buying terms of the modern dollar, it would probably represent enough to put some newly emergent so-called republic in Darkest Africa on its feet—for at least a week or so, until the Cavalry had to be sent for.

Nowadays you can't tell where Emeryville ends and Berkeley or Oakland begins. But fifty years ago Emeryville was just a little place, and children could run around and operate with perfect freedom, as if they lived in a rural village somewhere.

. . . What was happening just across the Bay? Everything, everything—lights, noise, fireworks, towers, palaces, bands and rockets and explosions.

And something else was happening, something which seemed to hold a peculiar fascination for me.

Coming from the utter isolation of the Nez Perce fish hatchery, away up yonder, an isolation increased and intensified when winter fell, we were absolutely dizzied by the spectacle taking place almost in our front yard. The Exposition site covered six or seven hundred acres over on the San Francisco waterfront, barely inside the Golden Gate. I can't believe that modern children, surfeited as they are with all the sights and sounds which can be brought to them through the media of motion pictures or television, could possibly be as thrilled by an exposure to the New York World's Fair as were we by the sight of everything going on there at the Exposition. And we did get to visit it. People made their way clear across our Continent or from other corners of the Earth to see that thing; and we, dwelling in Emeryville, weren't going to be disappointed.

Furthermore there was a lot that could be seen for free. It didn't cost a fortune to go to the Exposition . . . the ferryboat ride over there, and whatever admission may have been charged for people to just walk around. I don't remember too much about the Arch of the Rising Sun or the Arch of the Setting Sun, or the Court of Abundance, or the Court of the Four Seasons. (Sound like Japanese geisha houses.) And there was the Court of the Flowers and the Court of Palms and the Tower of Jewels, and I don't know what all.

Two things stick out in my mind. One was the business of having our pictures taken. There is a photograph included in this book which shows us in our Exposition elegance. It was taken in front of one of those special sets which the photographer had for the purpose. This was a novelty, getting a fancy picture from a professional photographer, and even being aware of it while it happened. . . . There had been a little kodaking in our neighborhood, back in Columbus. I remember that a man brought a little donkey around, and he would get children to sit on this donkey, and he'd take their pictures for so much a throw. I was lucky and got in on that, and I liked sitting on the donkey. But here at the Exposition we were embalmed for posterity in front of a set showing the actual Exposition buildings. And more than that: if you look close you can see a couple of airplanes.

. . . The aviator's name was Lincoln Beachy, and his was the first aircraft I had seen since I went chasing after that flying-machine in Ohio. From the week the Fair opened in San Francisco, this "aeronaut" had been shoving his biplane through skies above the Golden Gate. We heard with awe that he was paid one thousand dollars per week to make those fantastic loops and Dutch rolls. (This was in a time when an experienced schoolmarm would have to teach for a year and a half to earn a thousand dollars.)

But it wasn't the dough that excited me the most. It was the sight of that plane, the appealing gush of its engine—the energy and beauty of the brute. Any realization of what the handsome young pilot (he was twenty-seven or twenty-eight) had done, was enough to set your spine a-tingling. He was the first flyer to circle the Nation's Capitol in a heavier-than-air machine. He looped and rolled above Niagara Falls. True, he had brought death and injury into one idolatrous throng who gaped at him: he'd lost control of his aer-o-plane for a fatal moment. Repeatedly, too, he had been censured for buzzing only ten feet above the heads of other crowds.

But, according to the *San Francisco Chronicle*, Lincoln Beachy "resented being called a 'fool-flyer' and said that his feats were merely to demonstrate the capability and practicability of the aeroplane."

Maybe so. Although sometimes he flew while dressed as a woman. His publicity didn't diminish as the result of such antics. And, only the previous autumn, he allowed himself to be clad in Stanford crimson, and had bombed the U of C football field and fans, over at Berkeley— bombing with a football, of course.

Professional cut-up or not, he was a skilled flyer. Many years afterward I saw a lot of fighter-pilot types who had the same kind of eyes, same sort of grin.

You have to remember, too, the ancient adage about "there are old pilots, and there are bold pilots, but there are no *old bold* pilots."

There was a bright Thursday in March when Beachy climbed into a new yellow-and-silver Taube and cranked up its eighty-hp Gnome engine—or motor, as it was called then. The engine was a monovalve, the aircraft a monoplane. Everything went fine during preliminary flights in the machine. But Glenn Martin—he'd built the biplane which

Lincoln Beachy flew during previous exhibitions—said darkly that the Taube was too flimsy for the demands which stunts put upon it. Only a single set of stay-wires, etc.

Without the pilot strapped in the seat, old Yellow-and-Silver weighed in at 525 pounds. Or so the accounts stated.

He took her up to five thousand, next Sunday afternoon, and proceeded to tear the wings off of her when he was still about three thousand feet above the Bay.

Beachy barely missed a couple of Naval ships when he hit. He went in between them. He was still in one piece when they pulled him up from the mud a couple of hours later. Some of the doctors said he was dead on impact, others thought that he had died of drowning.

Net results were the same in either case.

It seemed strange to us boys in Emeryville, who had looked up and seen Beachy overhead so many times. I remember thinking about it, and looking up again, and wondering. I wondered a little where he had gone; but mostly I wondered how he felt when he was alive and flying.

A human being can take only about so much excitement at a time, or even in a given lifetime; then it begins to pall on him. We could take about only so much San Francisco Exposition, and I could take about only so much Lincoln Beachy. Then we had to revert to the normal practices of ordinary folks in a small community.

Here was where I earned my first money—I mean where I first hired myself out with whatever skills I could possess or demonstrate, in order to earn a wage or reap a profit.

Don't know how I got to be a good shot; but one way or another I'd gotten to be one. I guess it started with bows and arrows, and throwing darts and things like that when we were little. Then of course there were BB guns circulating around. But what occupied my interest now was the existence of the BB caps. These were a form of .22 ammunition which is manufactured still. They are smaller and less powerful than .22 shorts, but actually are fired by a powder charge, and there is a tiny bullet attached to this infinitesimal cartridge. I don't remember the cost of these things in 1915, but it seemed like an awful lot. Could have been fifteen or twenty cents a box.

There was an old lady who lived down our street a little way. She had a cat, and the cat was agèd and infirm, but also fat and hungry; the cat liked to eat sparrows. This old lady hired me to shoot English sparrows for the cat. I was shooting for the pot, so to speak—at least the cat's pot. The rifle actually didn't belong to me. It was a beat-up single-shot .22 which was brought into the crowd of neighborhood little boys by some other fellow, and kind of shared by all of us. The proceeds had to be shared too, and I considered this an imposition. I did the shooting and paid for my ammunition, but still I had to divvy up a certain proportion of my spoils. This was because I didn't own the rifle involved. It was a pretty good lesson, too. Everybody ought to own his own weapons and not depend on others to furnish them.

I got five cents for every sparrow, and I could shoot a lot of sparrows with the ammunition contained in a box of .22 BB caps. My elderly patron was in funds, at least when measured by nickels; she never tried to make me shoot on credit. Only trouble was, the cat's appetite couldn't quite keep up with my willingness and ability to supply the English sparrows. A lot of the time I had to sit around and cool my heels, waiting for Puss to get hungry again.

I resolved that I must acquire a .22 of my own, just as soon as humanly possible. Did, too.

Whatever vein of economic ore it was that Pop had been mining in Emeryville— Whatever it was, it played out the next year, and we trekked back East. There was a brief stop in Columbus again; then we moved to New Brighton, Pennsylvania. That's in the industrial region at the west end of the State, not far northwest of Pittsburgh.

New Brighton stands out in my mind because that was the first place where I ever went into business, not just on my own but working for someone else. I wasn't any longer in the Tomcat Poultry Supply business or whatever you want to call my Emeryville activity. I didn't have to figure out how many cat-er-idges I was going to use. (That's what we all called them, instead of cartridges: cat-er-idges. Funny thing— I always say cat-er-idge even today, unless I stop and think. Sometimes a man can be more concerned with getting the deed done, whatever it is, than in trying to pronounce *cartridge* the right way. Main thing about a cartridge anyway isn't how to pronounce it; it's how it will work. Most people can pronounce them, but not everyone can shoot a qualifying score.)

My New Brighton job was the usual boy's thing: paper route. We must have lived there some two years and I had that route all the time. The First World War was banging and thundering, off somewhere in the East; but I was too small, it didn't mean much to me. Probably if I'd been a teen-ager I would have thought about running away to war; but at eleven or twelve I was just too young. They didn't need any drummer boys, and furthermore I couldn't drum. I kept on delivering papers until after the end of the war.

That came with the hullabaloo common to the occasion, common to America on that day. It was November 11th, 1918, and nobody worked, of course. Everything was pandemonium in New Brighton and all the way back up the river to Pittsburgh. I don't remember everything that happened that day, but I do remember the main event: an impromptu parade through the heart of town. I was on a truck along with my father and Lloyd, and a lot of other boys and workmen. Some of the older men had sons over in France, so they were especially excited. Even if we LeMays didn't have anyone at the Front, we grew pretty excited too.

Everybody had old dishpans or tin cans of some sort, and we beat on those crude drums with railroad spikes or whatever we could grab. Made quite a noise . . . with all the people in the trucks beating and yelling, and lots of citizens trooping alongside, making the same sort of sounds. "Wheeee," kids were yelling, "the war's over! The Kaiser's licked!" Then folks alongside, or maybe girls riding on nearby trucks, would break into some popular songs of the time, like *Over There* or one of the Liberty Bond songs. "The war is *over* . . . war is over! The Kaiser's licked!" Then we'd pound on our dishpans again.

That was the way I spent Armistice Day, 1918.

It was a little different as World War II roared to its close, in 1945. Then I was commanding all the Superforts in the Pacific, including the ones which dropped the atomic bombs.

5

WE RETURNED to Columbus in 1919. Within the year we moved into a house at 511 Welch Avenue. This is the place where we lived longest, of all the time spent in the Ohio capital. The house is still there, looking not too unlike it did forty-odd years ago. It is a narrow building, high-roofed and covered with a shingle trim. The last time I saw it it was white above and red below; but that might have been changed.

Lloyd and I occupied the back room on the second story, and later Leonard moved in with us, on another bed. Lloyd and I fought all the time. It wasn't a very harmonious roomful.

That block was sedate in those days and still is: small families going about their own business, and children playing from yard to yard. There were steps which led up from the sidewalk to our yard, with a concrete curb or embankment along the front, and then a few more steps to the porch itself. Four doors away to the east is Ann Street, with a huge empty cindery lot beyond, four blocks long. Ran all the way from Newell up to Markinson. Years and years ago, folks said, that area was dedicated as a park. As late as 1964 the City Fathers hadn't yet gotten around to making a park out of it.

At the other end of the Welch Avenue block, toward the west, is Parsons Avenue with many shops and much traffic.

While we halted temporarily in residence on Mound Street, before coming to Welch, I sold newspapers at the corner of Mound and High. This job lasted several months, and then I acquired a route. I had to earn money for school, that's all there was to it. I had to buy books and clothing: by this time I was in the seventh or eighth grade, and our family was feeling the pinch of so many children in school. So I went to the *Columbus Dispatch* office and applied. Maybe I wore the man's resistance down by coming back again and again. When a route came open I got it.

There were three papers in town: *Ohio State Journal, Columbus Dispatch, Columbus Citizen.* So I didn't dare content myself with selling or lugging just one paper. Had to keep my eyes open and see if there might not be a better opportunity on one of the others.

By the time I got into high school in 1920 I was at work for the *Citizen* instead of the *Dispatch*. You might say that I was a junior executive. It was a good job, a demanding and exacting one. I bought the papers wholesale, in bulk, and I distributed them to each of the carriers. On Saturday, when the carriers made their collections, they paid me for their papers; then I had to go to the office and settle my accounts. I guess there were maybe between two and three thousand customers on those routes which I served. I don't know what the circulation of the newspaper was, but the population of Columbus at that time was close to a quarter of a million.

Of course a responsibility like this kept me on the jump. There wasn't much chance for extracurricular activities. I couldn't play on any team or have much to do with school clubs. Each day at four o'clock I had to be on hand, waiting for those big bundles of papers to be dumped down on the sidewalk; then I divided them up, counting out the proper number to each carrier boy.

At this age I was proud to buy my own clothes and school things, and pay all my own expenses otherwise. Sometimes I was able to give money to Mom as well. I kept thinking about college, but didn't get far enough ahead financially to save up very much. Then in the summers, while still small, I worked at whatever sort of jobs I could find.

I shouldn't like to give the impression that I worked every moment when I wasn't studying. Few boys could or should do that. But outside activities were limited by the number of hours I could spend at them.

We weren't very active church people, although we called ourselves Methodists, and I went to the Methodist Sunday School. But a great excitement blossomed after we had moved back to Columbus from New Brighton, while I was still in junior high. I joined the Boy Scouts of America.

Our troop met in a church—not our Methodist one, but a Lutheran church. That was up north of Welch, much closer to the business district, a block away from the courthouse on Mound Street.

On the whole it was a good troop, although if we advanced in grade
or accomplishment we had to do it on our own: there wasn't much of
a program for tests, merit badges, things like that. Everybody thought
well of the Scoutmaster: he was conscientious and, I'm sure, did his
best. He worked right up to the boundary of his limitations; that's all
you can ask of anyone. His name was Oscar Grumlich.

Like any eager participant I had ambitions to be an Eagle Scout,
with a whole sash of merit badges draped across my body. But in fact
I didn't quite make Star Scout. I think I had all the merit badges I
needed except one, but this was a slow accumulation, because of the
scanty amount of time I could spend. Oh, we did have a lot of fun out
of doors; I joined in it whenever I was able. There were overnight
hikes, trips up the Olentangy River or along the Scioto. After I got
through with the demands of my paper route sub-station, I could pack
up a bedroll at home and hurry to join the other boys in the woods.

Long before, I had saved money to buy the coveted .22 rifle. Used
to go down the railroad tracks. I liked to plink tin cans, and gradually
progressed into a somewhat better shot than I was even when I served
as the Great White Hunter of English sparrows. There was a good
place down the Chesapeake & Ohio tracks, where there was a kind of
dump with plenty of target material lying around. It was safe, too:
only about a hundred yards from the river. There lifted a railroad
embankment behind you and a steep bank in front, so no danger about
ricochets. You could shoot down over the bank and know where your
bullets were going.

Later on, my father gave me another gun. But I couldn't use it—too
high-powered. I would never say that Pop was the most practical man
on Earth. He had presented me with a 30-caliber rifle. It was beautiful,
it was new, it was expensive; and I just about fainted when I saw it.
It took a 30-40 cartridge. That was the Army cartridge used during the
Spanish-American War. My new gun was a Winchester, Model 95: a
sporting rifle, lever action.

I still have it.

Those were the regular 30-caliber slug bullets, same cartridge used
by the Krag. Pop gave it to me for a birthday present, and where on
Earth was I going to shoot a rifle like that? I needed it about like I
needed a hole in the head. It was only after I got out of college and
into the Air Corps that I ever went hunting with it. There were some
farms where I could go; I remember lugging the big rifle down there,
but on extremely rare occasions. Members of the Scout Council at the
Mound Street Lutheran church were a very solid group of typical Columbus southside Germans . . . some of them owned farms, and we
Scouts had been marshaled to various of these farms for overnight
hikes or Sunday tests and adventures in groves and ravines. I managed

to presume on this acquaintanceship and tote my gun out to one of those farms. But, as I say, very very rarely indeed.

Ammunition was fearfully expensive. At that stage of the game I would rather have saved my money for constructive purposes. Nor did I confine my labors to the paper route solely. There were other things to be done and other things to be acquired. I saved money, bought a second-hand bicycle; then I was really equipped to earn more money. I delivered telegrams for both Western Union and Postal Telegraph.

Remember, the *Columbus Citizen* didn't come out until about four p.m. There were all those hours which could be put to a productive use on Saturdays. Also, after I had distributed my papers on weekdays.

. . . I worked for some gal uptown, a woman who ran a delivery service. She had a contract with various department stores, to deliver their packages, and so the store packages would come in quantity to this woman's depot. There were a number of us delivery boys who had routes going out in every direction. We were equipped with those huge canvas bags which go over the wearer's neck (head sticks out at the top, and you have a big pouch in front and a big pouch behind. You can carry more packages on a bicycle that way than you might think). Of course you had to be on your guard and ride your bike carefully, or you'd take a spill and smear up the packages and yourself too.

We got paid by the package. The more packages the merrier.

I had an extra job as well, delivering for some candy manufacturers. These people owned a little place: sort of a Fanny Farmer shop, with their store out in front and the manufacturing room at the rear. There were about half a dozen employees there, all making candy like crazy. It smelled awfully good. I would deliver candy to the drug stores and confectionery shops which retailed it all over town.

. . . If you were a high school boy and wanted to fool around with some kind of radio set, this was one way of getting your materials. I certainly liked to mess with a crystal set. In those days most kids my age were going through the same stage. I grew even more ambitious: I started to build one of those variable coupler things, but in the end it was too expensive. Still, I could swing a crystal set financially. Some of my high school friends built a lot bigger sets. We all shared information and experiences, and it was stimulating.

I remember when the first vacuum tube came out. One of the boys was the proud possessor of one of those vacuum tubes. Was he a big shot in the community! Imagine—he could build a radio set with a vacuum tube in it!

I envied him, so did others. But there wasn't any use in sitting around being eaten up with envy. I took what I had, the tiny set I'd already built, and tried to see how far I could reach out and snare a radio station. Did all right, too, just fooling around with that thing at night. I preferred the crystal set to going out and hanging around drug stores, or maybe chasing girls. The girl stuff cost money—sodas, sandwiches and all—and I thought my personal cash would be better expended in some other direction—something really valuable, say, like a crystal set. I got KDKA in Pittsburgh and WLW in Cincinnati. Those were the big things you really worked for.

But just the same I couldn't go hog wild and break out in a complete rash of radio sets. I had to ration my time. There was too much work to be done in the outside world, in order to either keep myself and others, or to advance myself. Also I had to ration my expenditures. When the man stands there asking for his rent, or when the grocer hesitates about putting that latest basket of groceries on the bill, then you'd better be ready to come up with cash in hand. Very early in life I was convinced bitterly of this necessity.

Out in a long-ago 1914 Montana winter my father was perfectly willing to sit with his socked feet up against the shiny stove fender, while the frost snapped and crackled outside. The larder was a vague mystery which Pop didn't bother to penetrate. He figured that somehow, from somewhere, Mom would be able to conjure up a meal out of thin air. Often he was right.

But it seemed to me, even when I was only eight or so, that if a job needed doing it had better be done, and the sooner the better. (I suppose a lot of shiny-eyed Liberals and permissive philosophers of these middle 1960's would consider this an alarming concept, perhaps dangerous to the National leisure . . . in a day when labor unions howl for a twenty-hour week, and God knows what fringe benefits besides.)

. . . Fish were out in one of those three Nez Perce lakes beyond the house, and there was only one way to transfer them to Mom's skillet. Of course trout wouldn't take flies in the winter; so I'd grab a scrap of raw meat, impale it on a hook, and go out through the cold and let that hook down into open water where that flume ran into the lake and didn't freeze. Quite a few large trout used to change their residence from the lake to the top of the LeMay kitchen stove by such means. I remember catching one that was so big I had quite a time dragging him up to the house through the snow.

The family would look up—more or less approvingly, I guess—and Pop would move his feet to a new spot on the stove fender. But I didn't stay for long; just got warm for a few minutes, and then hustled back to try to catch another fish.

As I say, there wasn't much opportunity for happy little tinkerings and workshop experiments when I was young. I've tried to make up for that since I grew older. I can accumulate the raw materials more readily nowadays but it's still a question of finding the time. Oh, often I've rebuilt guns or fishing tackle; and sometimes have constructed some of my favorite sports equipment from the ground up. I like to load all my own ammunition: seems more dependable that way. If ever a round should misfire at a crucial moment, I'd have myself to blame, not some anonymous factory employee up in New Haven or Bridgeport. And, like most sports car enthusiasts, I've torn down plenty of automobile engines, and then rebuilt them to suit myself.

Several years ago I did manage to put together a stereophonic system, in consoles rigged up from existing cupboards, etc. I'm quite proud of this. It takes hi-fi tapes, electric organ—everything could or can be fed through this machine. I rigged amplifier cabinets at various other points in our high-ceiled old-fashioned quarters. Made for a good balance of sound, and a faithful projection of whatever musical impulse was desired.

My wife might tell you that I can build anything and everything. Not true. I haven't tried to build everything—yet. The next-to-the-last winter I was on the job as Chief of Staff, I did fabricate for us a color TV set, right from scratch. Helen says that I built it in two months, working on whatever evenings and Sundays I could grab. I think it took a little longer than that. Works real well.

6

In Columbus, in the early 1920's, South High School was in a building now known as Barrett Junior High, at the southeast corner of Deshler Avenue and Bruck Street. That's a few blocks west of the more modern South High School, on Ann Street.

My class graduated in 1924, so it was only the last year of our high school careers that we spent in the new building. To the majority of Americans of approximately my generation, and who grew up in medium-sized or large American cities, our old South High School building would appear perfectly familiar. It was built in 1900, and looks just like the ones built in the Eighties and Nineties: steep stairways, lofty ceilings, a fanlight above big front doors.

It is a common human experience to have enjoyed, during school years, the companionship and encouragement of some particular teacher—maybe a science teacher or a faculty advisor, or a librarian who discerned an ambition in the young person and tried to direct and nurture it. Folks who have such incidents in their backgrounds are fortunate. I don't remember anything of that sort occurring to me. I don't recall coming into contact with any individual on the faculty who waved a flag of inspiration. Chances are that there were people of that sort right there in the classrooms—teachers whom I met every day in the school year. But it never occurred to me to ask anyone to be my encourager or sponsor, and I don't recollect that anybody ever volunteered.

Same thing at home. There was a kind of general air of *laissez faire:*

one LeMay didn't butt into another LeMay's business. If he did, there was trouble. . . . I was able to give money to my mother at times when she needed it; and there were occasions when she did the same thing with me. She used to go out to work all by her lonesome, when conditions were bad, when Pop was out of a job. Then Mom would go out and do housework.

But she didn't burn a candle in the window for me and crouch behind it, muttering incantations about her boy going to college or else. At home the attitude which prevailed was, "Well, if Curt wants to do something like that, let him go ahead." There was never any resistance nor, on the other hand, any fervent cheers being raised. I don't think anyone gave it much thought or cared whether I would get through, or flunk out, or what. The notion seemed to be rather, "As long as he is doing all right, O.K., go ahead. Commendable achievement," etc.

I did more reading in high school—outside reading—than I ever had time to do in college, or later after I joined the Air Corps. I enjoyed historical novels very much indeed—also biographies of men and women who had led explorative and eventful lives; and books of travel. Once again, there were probably eager souls who were just dying to advise an earnest reader, and would have done so if I had had enough sense to ask for advice; but I never did. I just went ahead on my own, either to the school library at South High, or else to the Columbus Public Library. You could take books out of the school library (which it seems you cannot do in some schools) and take them home. Also I was glad to have a card at the Public Library, and used it.

. . . Would have been less than human if I hadn't had a sense of being more or less cut off from normal life. There's a lot of social activity in high school and college, very thrilling to the young . . . kids going out on dates, planning parties and stuff. But I had to spend my extracurricular hours earning money to maintain myself at the time, and also to store up whatever cracked little nest-egg I could for the years ahead. There may have been nights when I looked up into the darkness and held to the opinion that I was carrying a load which not many other people were carrying. Usually however I was too tired to lie there and grieve about what I was missing out on: I'd go to sleep instead, and get the benefit of needed rest. I felt, "It would be nice if I could do these things, too, like some of the others. But such activities are not for me."

. . . It's just that I knew sometimes when boys and girls were arranging a party or a picnic or some such merrymaking. I became aware that they were saying in effect, "Shall we invite Curt? Hell no. No use inviting him because he has to work."

When I was invited I would go if I could. I wasn't essentially a lone wolf, nor was I a social outcast.

There were other students who had to work. Maybe some of them

worked longer hours than I did, outside school. If so, I didn't happen
to know any of those.

All I can say now is that I would have appreciated having had some
time to participate in activities . . . going out for teams, joining clubs
and things. And the boy-and-girl stuff, too.

During the summer, a couple of years, I worked at structural ironwork. I joined the union and got on with the business of being an ap-
prentice.

In that capacity the main thing was to stay out of the way, and help
the rest of the people as much as you could. You were supposed to be
learning the trade; and just about anything you could do to make yourself useful was welcomed. Normally you carried tools around, and
watched; and you kept your eyes and ears open and your mouth shut.
Anybody wanted anything, you'd be there on deck to get it for them.
I wasn't exactly hot-and-bothered at any prospect of spending my life
in structural ironwork; but this wasn't a bad job. And it did help me out
later, when I got into something more advanced.

It was during one of those summers— I think it was a Sunday afternoon, with no work to be done, when I first got off the ground.

Another fellow and I pooled our resources. We put in two dollars
and fifty cents apiece. The barnstorming pilot had said, "Five dollars
for five minutes." The aircraft was a Waco three-seater, so we both
could go (after we talked it up to the pilot a little bit). Ordinarily he
just wanted to take one passenger. I guess he was as eager to get that
five dollars as we were to have the ride.

Couldn't have been more so, though.

The place was called Norton Field. It's not where Port Columbus is,
the regular commercial airport there— It wasn't quite so far out east
of town, and was on the other side of Broad Street. That's a region of
subdivisions and supermarkets now. But in those days there was still
enough grass for an old Waco three-seater to get up and get down
again. We had walked around the biplane admiringly for quite a while,
before I got up enough nerve to approach the pilot with our proposition.

There were two seats in front, side by side, and the pilot sat in the
third seat behind us.

It was all over so quickly that I was more or less bewildered. There
was this business of *Switches Off* and *Contact* and the prop being
pushed around; then suddenly the grind and roar and sputter as it
caught. Next thing, we were taxiing and then bumping on takeoff . . .
the ground went away as if it had sunk in an elevator. We were bucking in some drafts, and I was trying to feel and look and hear all at

once, and making a bad job of all three things. Then I was seeing familiar places all squeezed into a more miniature form, and seeing them from such an angle that they didn't look familiar at all; yet I could recognize them. Then they all started going off at a different angle, and then they came back and lay ahead of us and under us once again, and grew larger . . . we were bumping on grass. My two dollars and a half: gone and done. So was my first airplane ride.

I remember thinking afterward, planning: "Some day I'm going to go up in an airplane . . . I'll be flying it. I'll just ride around wherever I want to go—fly wherever I please, stay up as long as I want to, and just have fun. Have a joyride in an airplane."

Come to think of it, don't believe I've ever realized that joyride ambition yet. Every time we got airborne I've always had something that I had to do, and was kept busy doing it.

It was the fall of 1924. Can't recall how much I had to plank down for tuition in order to get started at Ohio State, but I had saved enough at least for that. Also you had a matriculation fee, and then there were various other fees, depending on the courses you were taking. It varied back and forth. I think I figured out that six hundred and fifty dollars a year would see me through school. So I didn't have the six hundred and fifty to start, but thought I could get hold of the rest of it from time to time. I would work while I went to school, and work summers, too, just as I had before.

My first ambition was to get a degree in civil engineering.

Initially I lived at home, but then the family left. They moved to Youngstown. Pop's new job had a long-term aspect, so the folks all went up there—at least the ones who were still at home. I had joined an engineering fraternity, Theta Tau. I felt rather bemused with the idea that I was now a fraternity man; but principally it was an engineering fraternity, not a social one. Still, they did have a house and you could live at the house. Cost me a little more than it would have cost to live at home, but it wasn't prohibitive.

I thought that belonging to Theta Tau would be a part of my education, and was worth the investment. Couldn't have been more correct. I got a great deal out of it. All the rest of the members were fledgling engineers, and we were able to study together. Some of the upper classmen were especially generous with their advice and direction. They had a habit of bringing in occasional lecturers to speak to us at our meetings. It was a real professional program.

Aside from that, there was the obvious value of the social side . . . not *much* socially, as I pointed out; but the small contact there was what I needed more than anything else. Actually, having been of such single purpose during my four years of high school, I had never attended a dance until I got initiated into the fraternity at college. It was one of the things I had to do; and they were so right in compelling me to do this.

They said, "LeMay, you will have to go down to a dance studio this afternoon, and take a dancing lesson, and go to the big dance which is being held here at college this very evening."

Well, I'd never done anything like this before; but now was the time. If ever I was going to accumulate a degree as Bachelor of Civil Engineering, one route to that degree was through the tender offices of Theta Tau. So it never occurred to me to rebel; I did exactly as directed. I went to that dance studio, took the single dancing lesson, and put in my required appearance at the dance that night. Got by all right, too.

First week on the campus, I'd joined the ROTC. It all looked pretty good to me. I couldn't see anything wrong with a Government's or a university's requiring young men to have a little military training. This whole concept about "millions of patriotic Americans springing to arms overnight," on which a lot of tradition and a lot of flim-flam had been nourished, didn't seem very sound. It was only six or seven years since America had had a hell of a time enlisting a few million men and training them so that they would be any good at the Front. If it happened suddenly that a lot of Americans were needed to serve their Country again, it seemed reasonable that they'd make a better job of it if they had a little training to begin with.

That was the way I felt. There were others on the campus who didn't feel the same way.

Their war cry, if you can call it that, was *Ban Military Training*. There used to be a group like that in almost every college or university town in those days. Inevitably they included among them a few ex-Servicemen who cherished unpleasant memories of slogging through the mud, being bullied by a cruel Chief Petty Officer, or getting bad food in the mess at Ft. Gila Monster, New Mexico. Then too there were the intellectuals, the inveterate pacifists, dreamers and idealists. . . .

(I number now among my intimate friends a man who is entitled to wear a pretty good gong or two among his ribbons. He admits that he was an ardent member of a pacifist group elsewhere in the Middle West, about the same time that the Columbus pacifists were getting into our hair there at Ohio State.)

Also there was a fellow student named Milton Caniff, better known in the present day as the creator of Steve Canyon and all his pals. Millions of Servicemen will remember his *Male Call* in publications during World War II. But back in the Nineteen-twenties the future cartoonist was a hireling of those who believed firmly that the soft answer turned away wrath, and that the nation which did not have a loaded shotgun behind the door had better prospects for Peace than the nation which did.

The pacifists engaged Milt to paint anti-military-training posters. Paid him five bucks a throw. Like myself Milt was working his way through school, and a good old-fashioned long-dimensioned green five-dollar bill with an Indian on it looked prettier to him than any reproduction of Leonardo's. He declared recently that he would have been willing to design posters defaming Heaven and the state of the angels, in order to get caught up on his rent and tuition and board bill.

Not that he was keen on the ROTC. Claims that it was in an abysmally run-down condition on our campus. Caniff calls to mind the time when no less a person than Phil Cochran came scooting into formation in a pair of black-and-white sports shoes. Guess this was after I left college. I never met Phil Cochran until years later, at Langley.

I don't buy this—about the bad state of the ROTC, etc. Our instructor was one First Lieutenant Chester Horn—slim, bow-legged—totally bald at thirty-five—a real artillery type and a very fine officer.

One night the lieutenant saved the pacifists from getting beaten up, and saved some of the rest of us from making damn fools of ourselves.

The pacifists were having a meeting, and we Scabbard and Blade boys held an indignation meeting of our own. I don't recall exactly who our chief rabble-rouser was; I know it wasn't me; I never did care much about making speeches (although I've had to make a lot of them. Occupational hazard).

Well, we got all steamed up, and finally the chief Hotspur among us cried, "Let's go over there and clean out that gang of pacifists!"

Away we went, fiery-eyed and bushy-tailed. Halfway across the campus our advance elements skidded to a sudden halt, and the rest pushed forward to see what was holding them up. The holder-upper was Lieutenant Horn, fortuitously encountered at that moment.

"Where on Earth," he asked, "are you gentlemen going?"

We blurted out our determination to pulverize the anti-military-training boys, since we counted them as Public Enemies of the yellowest stripe.

Our lieutenant grinned through the darkness, and proceeded to lecture us.

"You may or may not be correct in this," he said. "But let me tell you something: History is a great leveler, and Time wields a pretty well-honed smoothing-plane. In other words, everyone gets whittled down to his proper size eventually. Now, if you adherents to, and loyal participants in, the ROTC program of our college are wrong in your belief, Time will emphasize that—not only to you but to everybody else.

"On the other hand, if these other people are wrong, that will be proved as well.

"But if you go over there tonight and start a brawl, don't you see

what you'll be doing to yourselves and to your cause? You'll merely
be making martyrs out of those pacifists. The public who might support
you conceivably in your attitude, will turn against you. Those other
guys will be the heroes, not you. And you will have only yourselves to
blame."

. . . Horn's words had fallen on pretty receptive ears. We went slink-
ing off in this direction and that, by twos and threes. The mob was
broken up effectively and never formed again.

I see by the papers, however, that Steve Canyon is still in good
health, and busy as an Air Force bee. Also I'm glad of the fact that the
ROTC program is still around.

Far as ROTC is concerned, I did get to shoot a little in college—small
bore on the target range. We had some of that sort of training. I fid-
dled around and thought I'd go out for the rifle team, but I wasn't quite
up to caliber. (Pun unintentional.) Might have been, if I had had the
leisure in which to practice. But every time I started, I needed to rush
off to work in a few minutes. There just wasn't any opportunity.

. . . I had wangled a job at the Buckeye Steel Casting Company.
Jobs were relatively hard to find. A friend who worked down there
for the Buckeye told me that the employment manager had worked
his own way through college, and was extremely sympathetic with
people who were trying to do the same thing. That was all I needed.
I moseyed down there to the employment office, and went in and saw
the manager. Told him I needed a job, that I was going to Ohio State,
and how about it?

There wasn't any job open at the moment, but the first time there
was I went to work. Thirty-five bucks a week. That was a lot of dough
in those days.

Six afternoons a week I went to work at five o'clock p.m., setting
cores in the foundry. Usually I finished up about two or three a.m.
Yes, it was hard work, but I liked it. Only trouble was that I needed
more sleep than I was able to manage.

Most people don't know much about foundries. Well, in a foundry
you have a mold; this particular company was making truck-frames at
the time, for railroad cars—the heavy portion underneath the car,
which the wheels are attached to. These frames are all cast. They'd
have a big mold, which they'd put a frame over, and then you packed
molding sand in there with air hammers; then you'd roll it over, and
that would leave these mold frames—just one big mold. Then you had
to set sand cores in there, so when you poured the metal around it, the
frame would be formed. The core was an insert into the mold.

Maybe this explanation won't make much sense to anyone, except those who already know about such things. Guess it doesn't really matter.

What matters in my story is that I went to school at nine every morning like Robert Louis Stevenson's "arrant sleepyhead." I was just dead on my toes. My nine o'clock class was entitled, "Railroad Curves." This embraced engineering (had nothing whatsoever to do with blondes riding the Chesapeake & Ohio). The class was taught by Professor Wall. He was a fraternity brother of mine, too; but that didn't prevent him from flunking me. Which he did. Two semesters in a row.

Didn't seem to be much I could do about this. By sleeping in one class I managed to stay awake through the rest of the day and be fit for work at night. It was just that little margin of sleep which I needed; and slumber would claim me, willy-nilly, Professor Wall or no Professor Wall. But, by golly, I needed that thirty-five bucks a week, and as long as I could keep my job down at the Buckeye, I intended to hang onto it.

My program required a little expenditure, but it was in a good cause; so I became a plutocrat. With an automobile. I put aside twelve dollars and fifty cents for the purpose, and hunted around for somebody who wanted to be a fifty-per-cent pardner in the car enterprise—someone who had another twelve-and-a-half which I didn't have. I knew of a pretty good car which could be bought for twenty-five dollars.

I found the partner, and we made the buy. He could use it daytimes and Sundays; I used it from late afternoon until classtime in the morning.

Having an automobile available cut down a lot on the time which I spent traveling back and forth. Ohio State University is away out in the north end of town and Buckeye Steel Casting was away down at the south end. Moment I got out of school in the afternoon, I jumped into my half-owned 1918 Ford touring car, an old Model-T: crank job, magneto, battery (old-timers will remember this one). I leaped into the car and high-tailed it down there, to get into my work clothes and go to work. When I finished, perhaps at three o'clock in the morning, I'd drive back home and collapse in bed for maybe four hours before I had to get up, grab a bite of breakfast, do some hurried studying, and rush to that nine o'clock class—and, damn it, go to sleep once more under the appraising gaze of Professor Wall.

He may have flunked me those two semesters because of my snores. But I didn't fail in anything else, and before the year was done I got another few dollars ahead, and I bought my car partner out. Now I owned the vehicle all by myself. I felt as my radio-minded boy friend might have felt, years before, when he waved that vacuum tube before our eyes. The 1918 Ford touring car looked like a competition Ferrari to me then. Still does, in recollection.

Professor Wall may not have thought that I was an enthusiastic devotee of higher education because I used his class for my morning bedroom. But I encouraged my brothers and sisters, insofar as I was able, urging them to continue in school at all costs. I provided every sort of assistance which could be managed, though my purse wasn't very hefty. The smaller children stayed in school; but Lloyd quit and went to work about this time, and Velma married and moved into a home of her own. As I say, part of my college home life was with the family on Welch Street, the rest up there at the fraternity house.

The job with the Buckeye Foundry wasn't the only thing I did during those years. One summer I worked for a surveyor. I got this job partly on the strength of my civil engineering course at the college, and partly on strength of the experience I had had down there with Buckeye. It was a good job and I enjoyed it. By this time I understood enough about the business to be able to be on the transit as much as my boss needed me to be. Also I got a thrill out of working out the calculations. This wasn't just school theory, it was real surveying.

I worked also as general flunky to a contractor. Did a few design jobs for him. He was a kind of fly-by-night type, but still this additional experience was beneficial.

There had been vague aspirations toward the military, even while I was in high school. . . .

But let me put something straight now. For years a rumor has circulated to the effect that I tried to get into West Point but was turned down. That is incorrect. I never did take the examination for the Academy, or come close to taking it.

During high school years, whenever I thought about West Point, I thought automatically of a congressman. I didn't know our local congressman, and didn't know anyone who did know him. Now I realize that the sensible thing would have been to go and see him anyway, and apply. I just didn't have sense enough. Probably I thought that a real live congressman would bite my nose off, if I so much as stuck my nose inside the door of his office.

While this was going round and around in my head, I discovered that they had ROTC at Ohio State. *Well, maybe this is just as good a way.* So I dropped the whole West Point notion and aimed for Ohio State.

I had that yearning for airplanes right from the start. With me it was flying first and being in the Service second. You had to go into the Service to really learn how to fly. Weren't any civilian flying schools around, at least not in the Columbus vicinity, or any place else that I knew of.

During college years came the Lindbergh flight, followed closely by all those other transatlantic crossings or attempts: Chamberlin, the German baron with his monocle, the Irishman who went along for the ride, Amelia Earhart, all the rest. There were people who made it all the way across, people who went down in the drink, people who were rescued by ships at sea. Newspapers and magazines reeked with pictures of airplanes and pilots.

That's one of the reasons why, when I concluded my fourth year in 1928, there were already three thousand applications for the United States Air Corps flying school. And they were only taking a hundred or so in each class. Seemed like I wasn't the only one: a lot of other boys were getting itchy in the place where their future wings might grow.

(I have no way of knowing if any of those others chased the first airplane they ever saw, and tried to catch it. Very sentimental, I suppose, to consider that . . . but sentiment can be stirred up with other ingredients to make a valuable addiction.)

I watched and listened. When it came to the Army it seemed to me that reports in the papers were awfully meager. I would have appreciated reading more about the Army Air Service than I was able to read. The summer after I was a sophomore the Air Corps Act was passed by Congress. This law abolished the term "Air Service," changing it to the new designation; and put into the works an expansion program, striking out for new equipment and more trained personnel.

Things like this I read and absorbed to some degree, but they were impersonal: I didn't realize yet that I would ever become a part of them. For instance, I saw that a certain Major Carl A. Spaatz had flown from Bolling Field, in the District of Columbia, out to Rockwell Field in southern California. Vaguely I was fascinated . . . I read and re-read the newspaper account. But my crystal ball wasn't working at the moment. I had no idea that I would ever serve directly under Tooey Spaatz, or that he would become eventually the first Chief of Staff of the United States Air Force—once it achieved its autonomy as a separate Service—and that in time I would be the fifth Chief of Staff. There weren't any gypsy fortune-tellers around. If there had been I doubt that I would have wasted any money on them.

I just knew that I felt more determined than ever to fly. And in order to fly I was going to have to get into the Army.

. . . They roared directly across Columbus—six United States Army de Havillands. I gunned my Model-T right along after them, looking up whenever I was able, and getting a line on where they were going. If you are going to chase airplanes, I recommend a Ford rather than shank's mare.

The traffic in our Ohio capital thirty-five or forty years ago wasn't as hefty as it is now. Of course there were no throughways or freeways; but it was possible to trail those olive drab airplanes to their temporary lair without bowling over any pedestrians or smacking into any other cars. The Army flyers were going to spend the night with us. There wasn't too much soaring around in the dark in those days.

A big pasture stretched alongside the main highway west of town, and that's where the planes settled down.

A few of my ROTC brothers were present. We students hung on the outskirts, yet also clung as close to the Army people as we could, watching every move they made, every gesture . . . listening to every word. We tried not to get in their way too much. There were just about a million questions I wanted to ask any of those intent serious-faced young men, whenever one walked near. Yet I was tongue-tied. Couldn't have asked them the first question, let alone the hundredth.

We did hear this: we heard what time they were going to take off in the morning.

I stayed there until the last dog was hung.

Next morning at the appointed time there was a pretty good-sized crowd out there—cars parked all along the fence. Word had gotten around. Army flyers were a novelty in our neck of the woods.

. . . So they warmed up their engines; so they packed up their few duds, and climbed aboard, and took off. Every time I closed my eyes for a long while afterward all I could see were leather flying helmets and goggles; all I could hear was the sound of those Liberty engines. One after another they went bumping away; one after another clouds of dry grass and dust and leaves and gum-papers and Lucky Strike wrappings blew in the wind.

Then they were gone, lifting, circling, pressing farther and farther into the west. Cars along the fence began to start up, and people backed out and drove off to Columbus or to their farms close by.

I stood watching the airplanes. No one had told me then that it was considered bad luck to watch an airplane completely out of sight. I strained my eyes as long as I could.

My corporeal body remained there on the ground, and eventually went back and cranked up the Ford, and went off to work—whatever job it was that I had at the moment, and was behind-hand in getting to. But that was the corporeal portion: the rest of me buzzed along with those DH's, away off in the sky somewhere. I wasn't good for much until I disciplined that astral body and spanked it back into my carcass again.

Lieutenant Chester Horn, our military instructor, told me about the Honor Graduates. No one was quite sure what priority they'd have in the struggle to enter flight training, but it was a hope. I was glad that I'd gnawed the bone of ROTC work from the start.

But it turned out that there just weren't any vacancies in the Army for ROTC Honor Graduates. So no appointments could be made after I finished up the school year, in 1928.

I didn't graduate from anything except ROTC. There was that less-than-a-quarter's work to be made up in engineering (due to my own private course in "Advanced Slumbering" under Professor Wall) before I would receive my regular degree. But I explored every avenue of information, in order to learn ahead of time whether or not that appointment to the Army might be managed. In May I found out that it was No Soap. The next best thing to do, then, was to become a flying cadet; and just how I was going to wangle that I didn't know.

The line of reasoning ran something like this: I had completed my four years of ROTC, and was an Honor Graduate, but wouldn't receive a degree in engineering until I went back and finished up those fifteen hours. I was the proud possessor of a Reserve commission dated 14 June, 1928, but could receive no Regular Army commission until Heaven knew when.

Reserve officers were down about seventh in priority, when it came to getting into flying school.

. . . But look, what was this? National Guard was *second* on the priority list. It was right behind the Regular establishment. The first priority, after Regular officers, was for enlisted men in the Air Corps. But here was the National Guard *in second place*.

No longer was I the timid high school boy who didn't apply for West Point because he didn't know any congressmen. I was experienced and wise in the ways of our local military—at least I thought so. The commander of the Sixty-second Field Artillery Brigade, Ohio National Guard, was a nice old brigadier-general named Bush. He had graciously submitted to the rather dull ordeal of being initiated into our Scabbard and Blade Society, up at college. His office was right across from the State House, so I scooted down there. By this time, with my long-cherished-Honor-Graduate-Regular-Army-commission dreams all tangling in wreckage around my feet, I was becoming pretty frustrated. Never did take kindly to frustration. Don't yet.

General Bush sat comfortably before his roll-top desk. I thought that he was just about as elderly as God, and just about as militarily sophisticated as Napoleon or the Iron Duke.

I managed to get the words out. "Sir, I would like to enlist in one of your batteries, in case you have a vacancy."

He looked me over slowly. "Why all the eagerness to enlist in one of my batteries, son?"

Seemed like it was best to come to the point without any stalling around. "Sir, the reason I want to— I want to get up on the eligibility list, to get into the Air Corps flying school."

General Bush smiled. "Well, that's putting it pretty bluntly. But, after all, the hours when people rush in here and express themselves as being in a perfect frenzy to enlist in one of my National Guard batteries— Those are few and far between. Tell me this: weren't you in the senior class which graduated from Ohio State in June? Didn't you receive a Reserve commission?"

"Yes, sir."

"Didn't you get a commission in the Field Artillery?"

"Yes, sir. But *still* in the Reserves. And the Reserves are seventh on the priority list for the United States Army Air Corps flying school. The National Guard is second in priority."

"I guess," said General Bush, "that there's some method in every madness. I've got a vacancy on my staff right now— I need an ammunition officer. Why don't you take that?"

"Sir, I should—should feel honored. But actually I'd be perfectly satisfied just to enlist, in order to get up on the priority list. Because I'm—" It all came out with my last blast of breath. "—*determined* to go to flying school."

He said, "All right. We'll fix it up."

There was now a kind of mist in front of my eyes; but through that mist I could see General Bush slowly pulling down the top of his old-fashioned desk. I remember following the sound as the little round pieces went smoothly down through the twin curved grooves. He reached for his campaign hat.

"Come on."

We walked across the street, stopping every now and then, waiting for a car to pass or turn. We walked into the State House; and I was commissioned in the Ohio National Guard as a Second Lieutenant, Field Artillery.

Talk about red tape. I had to resign my Reserve commission in order to accept the National Guard commission. In no time at all I *got another Reserve commission back*, as a result of having this National Guard commission. And, again, if finally I was accepted as a flying cadet, due of course to the new priority established, I would have to resign my National Guard commission.

Let me jump ahead chronologically, just for a moment, and recite that it was only because of old General Bush that I didn't take the full step. He didn't know very much about flying or flying schools; but he knew what he had heard and what he had read, and he was wise in the ways of the Service.

"Look, son, you might go down there and wash out. They wash 'em out like flies. I have a suggestion: why don't you just take leave—go on leave from the National Guard for three months or so? And see whether you make it or not?"

Good advice. I took it when the time came. In fact, when the time came, and after I was in flying school, I was always extending my leave by three months, time after time. It was technically proper, although it does sound rather weird.

My application as a National Guard officer applying for admission to the Army Air Corps flying school went in just as fast as it could be processed. Then ensued the deadly business of waiting.

I was working, of course, so I could keep soul and body together without any trouble. But nothing happened, and nothing happened, and nothing happened. I was realizing for the first time how Washington in general, and the War Department in particular, could seem like a great hopper into which you fed material; and someone back there was stubbornly slow about turning the cranks; maybe they turned them, but nothing came out. Whenever I could grab a few moments I went over and hung hopelessly around Norton Field. That was the place where the other boy and I had paid two-and-a-half apiece, in order to have our five minute journey in an aircraft.

By this time there was a new Reserve station at Norton. They had one Regular Air Corps officer and a few airplanes. Several Reserve officers in the area, who were so qualified, flew there. It had become a sort of Reserve training establishment.

One of these Reserve officers took pity on me, so I got off the ground for the second time. He gave me a ride after he found out that I was hell-bent on going to flying school. Actually the ride was about half an hour long, and I was considerably set up. I thought that this would be invaluable when, if ever, I got out to March Field.

Of course it wasn't any help at all. As soon as you made the first turn on your first trip, out there at March, you were lost, lost, lost, just like everybody else.

In the early autumn of 1928 I was beginning to get awfully scared. There were still those fifteen hours of work to be made up; and as far as registration at Ohio State was concerned, you had to sign by late September—the 28th or 29th, somewhere along in there. Assuredly I didn't want to register and pay my fees if I was going to enter flying school with the November class.

All summer long I heard not a word. Here it was September, and I was up against the wire.

Wire, thought I. A synonym for *telegram.*

I rushed off an expensive Night Letter to Washington and spilled the whole story. I just *had* to know. Was I going to be appointed to the November class?

(This taught me another lesson: there are times when you have to take the bull by the horns. Not just sit around counting your toes.)

A message arrived from the War Department—in the affirmative, thank God. "This authorizes you to enlist as a flying cadet at the nearest Army station." Guess I was pretty lucky that my request for information didn't lie unattended on somebody's desk for endless weeks. Won't say that I was trembling all over, but I was trembling inside. Telegram in hand, I cranked up the Ford and headed for Fort Hayes: it was an Army post, right there at Columbus. Perhaps they had a battalion . . . not very much, even in those days. But it was the only Regular Army post anywhere around.

I dashed into the office and told them that I wanted to enlist. Strangely enough the term "flying cadet" didn't mean anything to those folks at Fort Hayes. Promptly they enlisted me all right; but the joker was that they wanted to keep me there, just like any other character joining the Army. You couldn't blame them very much. A college boy was a real Sergeant York in comparison with the run-of-the-mill volunteer recruits they were getting in those days. Average recruits were really something: all the dead-beats on the street, a lot of poolroom drunks . . . once in a while some fairly decent characters—from the country, usually—farm boys who were eager to get away from the binders and hay-rakes. Otherwise it was a good deal like the ancient English army: a catch-all for people who had been dodging the sheriff or the bailiffs or an angry wife, perhaps—or the even angrier father of a pregnant daughter.

I kept reiterating doggedly, "No, sergeant, no! I want to go *home*. I don't want to stay here at Fort Hayes tonight. There's no point in it. I'm going to flying school," and again I'd wave my telegram from Washington.

Well, the sergeant got hold of a lieutenant and the lieutenant got hold of a captain; at last it was all straightened out. They put me on leave until the date when I was to report to flying school.

I hustled back to the college. Several of our ROTC people up there had been interested in the possibility of getting on as flying cadets. There were a couple I knew who had gone over and taken the physical examination, and didn't make the grade. But I didn't know until later that one Francis Hopkinson Griswold had passed the exam and was sweating out the word from Washington, just as I had done. (He was "Grizzy" to all of us. After we got in flight training his name gradually changed to "Butch.")

. . . Got back up there to the campus and ran smack into Griswold. I didn't know him very well; he had been in the infantry phase of the training at college, and I was in the field artillery. Also he was taking a business course in commerce and journalism; and with my engineering activities, about the only time we'd ever see each other would be at the Officers' Club, or rarely out on the drill ground.

Naturally I was oozing with soldierly pride and the realization that now actually I was in the Army, awaiting my orders to go West. And here was Grizzy—he hadn't heard a thing. I told him about the bull-by-the-horns, so off went his wire to the War Department. Wasn't any time at all until he got the same kind of answer I had received. I escorted him out to the Army post.

By this time the military at Fort Hayes realized that there did exist such an animal as an enlistee designated to be a flying cadet. We had Griswold fixed up in short order. Then it was just a question of waiting around for orders and transportation.

Of course we were terribly revved up about the whole business. I used to wake at night and think about washing out. Just twenty-five per cent of the would-be cadets were making it at that time; the standard wash-out rate was seventy-five per cent. (Our 1929 class, next year, would be the first to graduate fifty per cent.)

Griswold and I were due to report at March Field, at Riverside, California, to enter with the November class. So there came a happy day when it was back to Fort Hayes once more; we picked up our orders and our transportation. The Army was very generous. They awarded us a single upper berth—one upper for the two of us, I mean —to go West and grow up with the country.

But we weren't too downhearted; already we had gathered the notion that a soldier or an airman has to learn to talk his way into things and out of things. Soon as we were aboard the train, and more or less squared away, we talked to the conductor. . . . Here were a lot of other upper berths going to waste, and look at us! Neither of us was a midget. We didn't know whether we'd have to sleep with my feet in Grizzy's ear, or his feet in my hair. . . .

We did a good job on that conductor. Two upper berths from that moment forth, instead of one.

Funny business: there we were that first night, finally parting company and going off to our upper berths, one of them bought by the Government and the other one conned out of the railroad company. I suppose Grizzy found it difficult to go to sleep, just as I did.

And no crystal ball was included in my meager luggage, so I didn't have any glimpses of the future . . . and Griswold and myself studying and flying and yakking, and working our way into that same future. It was all ahead of us, but we didn't know.

We graduated from flying school together; we both received our first duty assignments at Selfridge; later we were together at Wheeler Field in Hawaii. Then, when I went to Langley, back in the States, pretty soon Butch Griswold showed up at Langley . . . except that I got into bombers, and he stayed in fighters. Again we split; then came the time when we both served in England. I had the 305th Bomb Group, to begin with, and Butch was Chief of Staff of 8th Fighter Command.

After World War II there was a period when I was commanding SAC, and Butch served as my deputy commander. That was the time when Tommy Power left SAC, and went to command Research and Development. Then I had Griswold in General Power's place.

Butch's last tour of duty, while I was Chief of Staff, was commanding the National War College.

. . . But it's late October, 1928, and the years are unprovoked and irresponsible, not posing any threat to us. We are on a black sooty passenger train which plows its way toward Chicago in the nighttime, and bangs across switches, and fills the Pullmans with a bitter smell of coal smoke. And we are two kids, jolting along in our respective upper berths, clinging instinctively to the bed-clothes when the train swerves on a fast curve. *Railroad Curves.* . . . No fortune-tellers, no gypsies anywhere around.

We are young, and we go back to sleep.

BOOK II

Air Corps

(1928 – 1936)

1

In Chicago we picked up two or three more characters, and then some others as we went farther West. By the time we reached California there were eight of us on the train, and we all ganged together for meals and constant gab-sessions.

The train didn't get to Riverside until about five-thirty on the second morning out of Chicago; but that didn't matter—we were all too excited to sleep anyway.

Train was on time, and we got off at the station and looked around hopefully. Vaguely, I believe, we thought that we would be met by an intelligent-looking efficient Air Corps type who would say, "How do you do, gentlemen. Allow me to introduce myself: I am Sergeant-Major Propwash. This is Corporal Aileron, and this is Private Rudder. Private Rudder, please take their baggage. . . . If you gentlemen will be so good as to allow me to check your travel orders— Ah, thank you— Now, this way, please! The limousines are waiting yonder—" Or words to that effect.

There wasn't any Sergeant-Major Propwash or anybody else. Not a living soul around that station, anywhere.

None of us had an idea where March Field was. And we didn't know what we were supposed to do, or where to proceed, or how to live, or —I guess—how to breathe the clear California air. In Riverside in those days the sidewalk was still rolled up when dawn came. But we started walking on it.

We wandered down the main street, scraps of luggage in our hands, and at last we came to a place where there were a few electric lights burning and some moderate activity. It was the U. S. Post Office.

We gathered together on the sidewalk and held a consultation. Griswold had an extra nickel—he usually did. He didn't know whether they'd charge him for the call or not, in there at the Post Office; but he was willing to spend his nickel to telephone. After all, the Post Office was a Government agency, and thus remotely related to the Air Corps and March Field and all the rest of it. So Grizzy was elected, since he was the capitalist. In he went to telephone, while we waited and wondered outside.

He got March on the phone, and didn't know exactly whom to ask for, but he finally got hold of the Officer of the Day.

OD says, "Where are you?"

"Sir, we are at the Riverside Post Office."

"That's fine," says the OD. "Our mail truck from March will be in there at nine-thirty a.m. After he gets loaded, you get on the mail truck and come out."

We decided that the Air Corps must be a kind of queer place. But an order was an order. We scratched around, managed to raise enough money between us to get some sandwiches and coffee; and later on that forenoon, when the official mail truck rolled in through the gates of March Field, it carried eight dodos ensconced grandly on top of the mail sacks. We didn't know yet that we were dodos; but we found out in a hurry.

A new class came in every four months. We were a small percentage of the November 1928 class. There would be a hundred and ten to start. We knew that half of us would wash out before we ever went to Kelly, and that maybe some might be killed.

This was driven home to us right off the bat. It was one unexpected element of an initiation which would continue just as long as we were dodos.

We started to draw equipment, and filed into the big supply room. We arrived simultaneously with the departure of a class which was leaving March to go to Kelly Field in Texas for their advanced work. Cadets in the other group were turning their equipment in.

There was an argument between a supply sergeant and one of the departing class.

"Look here, Cadet Longeron, you're short one pair of coveralls."

"Hell I am."

"Hell you're not. Here's the check list right here. . . . Take a look: you're short one pair of coveralls."

"Oh, those."

"Well, what about them?"

"Well, see, sergeant— It was like this: I loaned those coveralls to Cadet Radius a couple of weeks ago. He had 'em on when he put that damn thing down over there on the desert. You know—the one that didn't burn?"

"Sure. I remember Radius. They had to get a block and tackle to lift the engine off of him—"

"Well, see, he was wearing my coveralls when he was killed, and I didn't want those old bloody things back. Someone brought them to me; but I just threw them away."

"Listen, Cadet Longeron. That doesn't make much of an impression on *me*. I want a pair of *coveralls*, and I want them right now, when you're turning in your equipment—"

And so on. I suppose the guy was charged for them.

We greenhorns passed on through, with new equipment being tossed out to us. I don't know what the rest were thinking about, but I was thinking about that pair of coveralls.

There is an old encyclopedia which describes dodos on the island of Mauritius, as observed by travelers in the sixteenth and seventeenth centuries before these creatures became extinct. It is told that some of the birds were brought alive to Europe and "descriptions are confirmed by several more or less rude drawings, preserved in various European libraries and museums. These represent a bird . . . of a very heavy and clumsy form, and a corresponding gait . . . the wings so short as to be of no use for flight. The birds were easily killed, being wholly unable to fly."

It's unlikely that any of our incoming class had read this exact description of a dodo; but very soon we were taught just what a low form of life we represented, extinct or no. First off there weren't enough barracks to go around, so the dodos had to live in tents during the period of their dodo-hood, which lasted until a new class entered four months later.

Three times a year a new bunch appeared, hopeful and eager. Then the inevitable washouts would occur, and a primary-graduating class, reduced enormously as to numbers, would entrain for Kelly Field at San Antonio. Simultaneously the old dodos became cadets for their second four months of training there at March. Four months as a dodo; four months as a cadet, still at March; and four months of advanced flight training at Kelly.

Tents were of the pyramidal type with wooden floors and sides, and they were kept warm by means of the old sheet-iron Sibley stoves. We were due to be in the tents for the four chilliest months of the year, November through February. When we saw those tents we knew that we weren't going to lack for fresh air at night. You never saw such hole-y tents. We wondered whether someone had been using them for fishnets. You could sit on your cot and eat an apple and just throw the core over your shoulder, and be sure that it would go out through a hole someplace.

We learned the explanation for the holes: it was due to the Sibley stoves, and smoke-stacks leading out at the top of each tent. Every stove-pipe was supposed to have a fine screen fastened across the top of it, to keep sparks and live coals from bursting through and floating around to start fires. Nice little theory; but the trouble was you had to clean the screens off every few hours when you had a fire going. Because, if you didn't, you got no draft through the damn stove (which wasn't much good to begin with).

So everybody would get tin-snips and climb up and remove the screen—when nobody was around to report the deed—and cut the center part out of the screen. If you looked at it from the ground, there seemed to be a screen on the stove-pipe, all well and good . . . with screening removed we had plenty of draft . . . sparks would go soaring gaily. When one lit on a tent it didn't burn with a flame; it just smoldered, and the hole got bigger and bigger.

First month of that training was just about the longest month I ever spent in my life. It was all ground school: drill, physical training, aero-dynamics lectures—engines and fuel systems—all that sort of thing. And here was a gorgeous row of white-and-golden PT-3's sitting almost alongside of us, and we were dying to get in them.

Not a chance.

Clean up the place, march out for Physical Training, march to weapons school—all the basic stuff. Every man was thinking, "I didn't come here to do this! Why, I could do this stuff if I just enlisted in the Army in the ordinary fashion! But I became a flying cadet so I could learn how to *fly*. And now look at me: walking-my-post-from-plank-to-plank with a Springfield, or policing up the parade ground, or—" It was a long month.

Might have helped, too, if the mess had been any good, but it wasn't. And cadets received a substantial ration allowance at that time: one dollar per day. Take an enlisted man's ration in the Army: about twenty-eight cents. Here we were with that allotted dollar, which really meant something in 1928 and 1929. Plenty of food, yes; but the cooking was bad and the presentation was bad.

One thing, though—it may have redounded to the satisfaction of the future Air Force and to an improvement in the lives of airmen yet unborn. It made me very mess-conscious, and I swore that I'd do something about bad messes, if I ever got in the position to do so.

Got in that position, and I did do something. After going on active duty and reporting up at Selfridge Field in Michigan, one of my first jobs was that of Mess Officer. Perhaps I didn't astound anyone by my brilliance that early in my career: never went to the cook-and-baker's school, as some of the rest did. But I worked on it, and I learned a lot from the mess sergeant we had up there.

Same way when, many years later, I came to command SAC. The moment I got on the job, one of the first things I did was to bump up the messes. It worked, too. I'll tell about that later.

(At least we had a happy contrast eight months afterward, when our class finally arrived at Kelly. The Kelly mess was so good that no cadet on a weekend pass would stay in San Antonio. Never! The Sunday morning breakfast was something to write home and dream about, and every character off on a weekend pass—he came back to Kelly to eat, Sunday morning. Ought to be a good lesson for young wives somewhere in this.)

The hazing which we underwent at March was persistent, but in the main not too dreadful. I fail to recall that anyone was driven to seek the psychiatrist's couch because of it, or committed suicide, or became a professional sadist. At least it kept us on our toes. As I pointed out, a dodo was merely a kind of probationary cadet; technically a cadet, but actually a dodo.

The hazing eased off toward the end. It was an educational process which we were bound to go through, and I think almost everyone realized that.

It got to be quite a contest between the upper classmen and the lower classmen. Upper classmen of course reserved the right to come around for inspection, any time. You never knew when they were coming. As soon as they came along and kicked on the tent—the equivalent of a knock on the door, for we had no door— They would kick the tent frame, and we were supposed to jump to Attention.

What these characters would do would be to get back and run like hell for the door, smiting the tent frame as they sped through. Simultaneously with the thud they'd be inside; and if you weren't standing at Attention the moment they were in there, they counted you as being slow on your feet, and were prepared to mete out appropriate penalties.

In retaliation for these tactics we maintained a constant watch. We tried to keep someone always on guard duty. In addition to which, we all had our ears cocked for the sound of stealthy feet approaching the tent. A dodo would look out through a hole and see the imminent advance of an upper classman. He would give the signal in a split second; everybody jumped to Attention. Then here's your upper classman diving for the door, kicking on the tent-frame as he came through; and what does he find? Everybody standing at Attention.

That's *if* our guard and detection system was functioning one hundred per cent. Very often it wasn't.

Our basic thirty days came to an end at last, and we started to fly. Actually fly in an airplane—the thing we had come to do. Here were these beguiling PT-3's, and how we had longed to climb into the cockpits. They were the common type of primary trainer then in use: built by Consolidated. Wright Whirlwind engine.

No matter how handsome the airplanes looked, my doom was just about spelled. I drew an instructor by the name of Peewee Wheeler. He was an excellent pilot but he *couldn't teach anybody anything.* He just didn't have the knack for teaching. It is a sad fact that many people in this life are able to exhibit particular skills—to excell in such skills sometimes to a degree almost beyond belief—and yet remain unable to communicate their understandings and procedures to another.

. . . Uncle Wat can shoot a gun, bring down a deer every time. "How do you hold your gun, Uncle Wat? How do you sight?" "Just take the rifle and draw a bead. Allow a little for wind and distance." "How much?" "Not too much."

Or— "Pete, you make the best biscuits of any guide I ever had.

Please tell me how." "Sure enough. Just take a big pan and put some flour in it, and a little baking-soda and sour cream—" "But how much of each?" "Mind you don't get too much flour." "But how do you put it together with the sour cream?" "Just do it real slow. Don't use too much cream or too much flour—"

I must go on record, however regretfully, and say that Peewee Wheeler was an Uncle Wat or a Guide Pete of the purest stripe. At least he couldn't teach *me;* and I guess he couldn't teach anybody else. There were five students allotted to each instructor. The other four students in my group under the tutelage of Peewee Wheeler all washed out. Left me alone with him.

Then Wheeler got three more students, and *they* washed out.

I was dying to ask for a new instructor, but was afraid to. It might look like a dreadful confession of failure or ineptitude on my own part.

Finally it came time for our basic check, in which we were to proceed, it was hoped, from PT's to DH's or the new O-2's.

There were three or four check pilots who specialized in this work. Instructors would all send their students up for a check with a regular check pilot. This would confirm the instructor's estimate as to whether you were ready to go on, or whether you were recommended for a wash out. That was it: one way or the other—either wash out or stay.

You had the right to appeal to the Board if you were going to be washed out. You met with the Board, and the Board's decisions were final.

As in most activities of this nature, word goes around through the organization that Sam Sparkplug is a pretty good character to have for your check ride, and Frank Fuze is a son of a bitch.

The evil genius in this case was supposed to be Red MacKinnon, a first lieutenant. He was a real tough character. It was rumored—in fact it was more than legend, it was part of the gospel faith among dodos—that anyone who got their check ride with Red MacKinnon was in for a bad time.

He was the one I drew. Lucky me.

. . . We started out. First off he took the airplane. Says, "I'll fly it." We flew a while, and the next thing I knew we were right down on the deck. (In old AC parlance, that doesn't mean we were actually *on* the ground; it means merely that we were still flying, but too close to the planet Earth for comfort.)

MacKinnon says, "O.K. Take it." So I took it.

In about thirty seconds he cut the throttle. Here we were, away down on the ground, and he cut the throttle! Well, I looked around in momentary agony, and saw a field. I banked the airplane and headed for the field.

MacKinnon threw up his hands and began to shriek. "God damn it, that's all wrong! Give it to *me!*"

So he took the airplane.

Once more he said, "O.K. Now *you* take it."

So I took it again, and we went along, and Lord help us if he didn't cut the throttle again.

I looked around, and there was another field, and I turned to get into the field.

That man almost leaped out of the cockpit. He jumped up and down and really tore his hair. Then, with appropriate screams, he took control of the aircraft and we went away from that little field which I had picked out so carefully.

There are plenty of old flyers who will read this and probably award their sympathies to Lieutenant Red MacKinnon.

Here is the actual dope on the situation: at low altitude, if you lost your engine, you were not supposed to try to make a turn, because you might stall and spin in. You haven't got the altitude to do it. You are supposed to crash your aircraft straight ahead. That is what he wanted me to do (or least to pretend to do, before he started the engine rolling again).

Always, of course, there are variations to a situation like this. The interpretation of low altitude depends on a variety of factors, such as the type of aircraft which we had then, how powerful the engine, and so on and so on. Generally speaking, in the underpowered airplanes with not too much lift, if you tried to maneuver with a dead engine, the chances of getting into a spin were really good. Or a stall, trying to turn at low altitude. That was what killed you. Whereas, if you went straight ahead you could fly into a brick wall, and the chances were that you might get away with it all right.

In the case of my ordeal with the formidable MacKinnon we had achieved a pretty good air speed, and I thought that I *could* make the turn in order to get into the field. Actually we did it O.K. I did make the turn, and we were all set to go into that field.

But the principle was what Red MacKinnon was trying to teach me.

And Peewee Wheeler had never told me this—not one word of the whole circumstance I've just related. No one had ever told me that you weren't supposed to do this, or why.

I was explaining all this not long ago, in reminiscence to a friend. He laughed and said, "The way you're telling it now, any damn fool could see the whole thing in a couple of minutes."

Guess that's true. But I have been a teacher, often, in my professional life. For instance, I'm a good navigator, and I've taught a lot of other people how to *be* good navigators. You either have the knack or you haven't. Peewee Wheeler didn't have it.

(He'd raise hell if you *didn't* get into a field. That's the thing he impressed on me: always have a field in mind.)

Well, let's go back to that horrible flight with Red MacKinnon once more. After he got through jumping up and down and tearing his hair, we went up and did regular maneuvers. Some of them I did all right, and some I didn't do so well. Then we got into acrobatics. He says, "Do a snap roll."

I could do a snap roll to the right, and now I did it with the greatest of ease. I was really proud of myself, and felt a self-congratulatory warmth.

Then, said MacKinnon, "O.K. Do another one."

I did another one, still to the right.

Then came the fatal words: "All right. Do one to the left."

Now that's how good I was at acrobatics at that stage of the game. I could do a snap roll to the right and come out of it smelling like a rose; but I couldn't do one to the left, to save my neck. I'd tried it again and again. Never could get it.

"Go ahead. Proceed, proceed! I told you to do a snap roll to the left."

"Can't do it."

He signaled that I should go in for a landing. Away I went for that landing, with my heart in my throat. It was a very windy day: one of those dismal days on the desert when the wind thrashes about in gusts, lashing like a whip, this way, that way.

So I misjudged the wind and the glide, and we landed long. Altogether it wasn't one of my better days, shall we say. And I knew it. I could just hear that train tooting dismally through the mountains and prairies once more, carrying a brand new washout with it, back to Columbus, Ohio.

Finally we taxied up to the line, and Red MacKinnon got out. He stood there and looked at me and shook his head.

"Well, son. By Jesus Christ. I don't know whether to wash you out, or give you a chance and send you on."

He considered for a moment, while I sat there not able to breathe.

"I guess," said MacKinnon slowly, "that I will send you on, after all. But I'll keep my eye on you, and see how you do."

You might say that lots of times I have rather imagined that I felt his eye upon me, through the years which followed.

2

IN FLYING school I began to smoke. Hadn't ever done so before—felt neither the need nor the desire.

Many other young fellows have done their first smoking when confronted with a new and demanding situation in their lives. They subscribe to the notion that they can rest their nerves this way. It is partly a desire to demonstrate a quick attainment of full maturity; and mingled with that undoubtedly is the inclination towards conforming, of being one of a gang doing the same thing.

Cigarettes never attracted me. They were expensive, too—something I could readily do without. Cigarettes just weren't interesting, they tasted like nothing at all. A pipe was what I wanted, so I went and bought one; gradually acquired several. Pipe smoking is the cheapest thing a-going, if you don't develop a taste for high-priced imported tobacco. At that time I settled for Half-and-Half.

You might think that a flying cadet wouldn't worry much about the cost of things, but it was a little different in my case. I had to send money home. Always had to send money home. Flying cadet, captain, colonel—whatever my rank, there were folks who needed to be assisted, so it was up to me.

I was in four-star grade, on active duty, the longest of any general in the history of the United States. I was a general officer for nearly twenty-two years, a four-star general for over thirteen years. Nobody else has ever remained so long on active duty in that grade, be it in the Army, Marines, or Air Force. I don't know about admirals.

A private or a corporal supposes that all generals are rich, and maybe some of them are. Trouble is, I never had the opportunity or the time to do anything on the Outside which might make me a pile of dough. Actually I don't yet own a house of my own—we've always lived in quarters. In retirement I hope for the chance to do what most men do when they are young, and that is to acquire a house of my own. Would like nothing better.

. . . So enlisted men and subordinates think that generals are rich, and enlisted men and subordinates in the Air establishment for years have been convinced that I was born with a cigar in my mouth. Negative. I didn't get in the cigar habit until late during World War II, when we moved to the island of Guam.

Oh, I'd sampled cigars from time to time; but the habit wasn't there nor the satisfaction. I loved pipes and had acquired a small arsenal of them. I liked to experiment with tobaccos too. Friends were always giving me pipes, and wanting me to try special brands or blends. I enjoyed the good healthy satisfaction of the perennial pipe smoker.

But out on Guam there was a tropical humidity with which I hadn't grown familiar. No joy in that. Overnight my pipes turned into masses of mildew; also, even more unfortunately, my tobacco would be covered with the stuff. If there was penicillin in that crud on my pipes or tobacco, then it wasn't doing me any good. Every time you'd pick up a pipe in the morning, you'd have to scrape off a moldering mass— Too much of a chore.

I started in on cigars. Just the ordinary PX type—that's all we had. There would be a certain amount of mold creeping over the unsmoked

cigars, but it was easy to wipe that off, and then you could smoke. Just
try wiping mildew off pipe tobacco.

So I became The Cigar.

. . . Don't like to do anything half-heartedly, even if it's a wicked
and self-destructive avocation like smoking cigars.

At least I didn't bounce when I made that landing after my check
flight, even if I did land long. If I had bounced, then Red MacKinnon
would have been privileged to kick Peewee Wheeler in the rear. That
was a perquisite awarded to the flight-check officers if one of the students whom they were checking off did a primary-secondary-tertiary
bounce when he came in on that all-important flight.

According to tradition, the erring student's instructor, who was usually out by the stage house in the middle of the field, watching anxiously or in trepidation for the approach of his fledglings— After the
bad bouncy landing was duly assessed, then the cadet's regular instructor had to bend over, doubled up; and the flight-check officer applied
his boot to the other unfortunate's posterior.

Could be that Peewee Wheeler really deserved a kick, for I still consider him an utterly lousy instructor. But he didn't get one. Instructors
went to inordinate and unethical lengths to check what was supposed
to be your first real individual activity. (For the first time you were
on your own, and with a different man in the front seat.) A lot of the
teachers primed especially on landing procedure and let some of the
rest of it go. There was one resourceful soul who spotted a nicely
plowed field away down south, ten or twenty miles along the edge of
the desert. He was reputed to have taken his students down there one
by one, where they couldn't be observed by anyone from home; and he
made them shoot landings across the furrows. At least the earth was
soft, since it was newly turned. But anyone who could land one of
those light underpowered aircraft across furrows without bouncing,
was bound to come in on the hard level of March in fine style.

Some pretty bizarre occurrences were apt to mark the termination of
one phase of training and transition into the next. A fellow classmate,
Ivan L. Farman, still recounts plaintively an experience on his check
flight with a handsome lieutenant who put him through a hard course
of rolls, acrobatics and what-have-you. (Farman insists that when he
tried to snap roll to the left, the whole airplane went *swooosh;* and
that, further, when that same lieutenant-instructor tried the identical
snap roll to the left, the whole airplane went *swooosh* again.)

Anyway they were coming in for their landing on the check
flight. . . .

Procedure as follows: if circumstances, wind and engine noises permitted conversation between front and rear cockpits, well and good. But if there was too much noise, and no proper interchange might be conducted conversationally, a series of standard signals could be employed. For instance, if the instructor started jerking his thumb back over his shoulder, it meant that the student was to take over the controls, and immediately. But if the instructor didn't point back over his shoulder with his thumb, every student knew that it was as much as his career was worth (whatever it *was* worth) to touch any one of those controls.

So they were coming in for their landing, and hard appraising eyes watched from the stage house, and Cadet Farman's heart was a-thumping. He waited and waited for the signal informing him that he was to take over the controls, complete the approach, and land.

Nothing happened.

The instructor had been flying the plane during the previous few minutes. Here they were, coming in to the field and losing altitude, and losing more altitude. And Farman was wondering if that tail wasn't up in the air mighty far.

So the ground ascended to meet them, and still the instructor did nothing. At last, in utter desperation, not wishing to be a sitting duck or even a sitting dodo in a crack-up, Farman grabbed the control column and hauled back on that stick like crazy.

It was one of those featherbed landings, when you don't even know when you've touched the ground.

They taxied and parked. The handsome lieutenant got out slowly and looked with curiosity at his student.

"Do you always make a landing like that?" he inquired, as if he couldn't believe his senses.

With shuddering voice Cadet Farman answered, "No, *sir*. But I'm sorry, sir— You didn't tell me to take over, and we were getting down there on the deck, and I got scared, and I just grabbed for the controls—"

The instructor stood staring at him. He was more than staring, his eyes were starting out of his head. In a low steely voice he said, "For God's sake, don't tell anyone about this, ever. *I utterly forgot to signal you to take over those controls.*"

The handsome lieutenant-instructor's name was Nathan F. Twining. Third Chief of Staff of the USAF. Chairman of the JCS, 1957–1960.

Now we were finished with PT-3's, and half the class was scheduled to go into de Havillands and half into O-2's. Actually the designation was the O-2-H. This was just the last word in modern aircraft, we thought. The DH's would be phased out in the immediate future.

I didn't get the break everybody hoped for (we all wanted to go into the new stuff, naturally) and was gazetted to the DH contingent. But we were informed that halfway through the next four months of training we would switch with the O-2 boys, and they would go into DH's. It worked out that way, during our seventh and eighth months at March.

The O-2's were really beauties. We had admired them hungrily from a distance, with their sky-blue fuselages—as when we were dodos we gazed wistfully at the white fuselages and yellow wings of the PT-3's. The O-2's (both the H's we had at first, and the K's which came later) were built by Douglas. They had a Liberty engine and just about everything else which was wonderful: hydraulic shock-absorbers (first we had ever seen) and, wonder of wonders, an actual tail-wheel instead of a tail-skid. These latter were always smashing when you made a rough landing. How remarkable, we thought, it would be to land with a tail wheel instead of a skid. . . .

Now I had no more of Peewee Wheeler. I got Joe Dawson. He was a regular World War I ace type. A most excellent pilot . . . frankly I don't think that he had the technique or the skill which Wheeler had. But the point was: *he could tell you what you were doing wrong.* He could communicate, and what an enormous difference that made.

I realized that it would have been much better for me if, in the initial stage when saddled with Wheeler as an instructor, I had demanded to be switched to somebody else. There really wasn't supposed to be any odium attached to such a transaction if you resorted to it. But I was afraid that there would be, one way or another—people would say that I was a cry-baby. So I hadn't done it.

My error was brought home to me dramatically. In two weeks I learned more from Joe Dawson than I had all the rest of the time I'd been at March. I didn't have any real trouble from then on. Matter of fact, I was the first in our half-a-class to check off on the DH's. Then, during the last two months, I was the first to check off on the O-2's.

I'd like to say right now, with a remembered ache for long hours of training a young lifetime ago, that it didn't come easy. I really worked at it. Some of the boys would manage to sneak off and go on a joyride once in a while, instead of doing what they were told to do. Well, I'd wanted to have a joyride ever since that first two-dollar-and-a-half flight at Columbus; but I wasn't about to undertake it in this year of 1929. I didn't sneak off, I didn't joyride. If I was supposed to practice Eights then by God I practiced Eights. I told myself, night and morning, that I must do exactly what I was ordered to do.

The one thing that I wanted to do more than anything else was just to go up and take a ride in an airplane. Never did.

There's an old RAF term—"prang." That's what you do to an aircraft when you bust it up; you prang. There seems to be a remarkably significant sound in this word; it's representative of the onomatopoeia which our English teacher at South Side High used to explain to us and which we tried dutifully to figure out. *Prang.* Sounds like something busting up.

There is extant a shabby photo album which I put together back in those days. A lot of the boys had kodaks, and we traded snapshots back and forth. Generally speaking, I think my album is a pretty good visual record of what life was like at both March and Kelly. Many photos survive: different classes, informal groups, so on. Also there is a Chamber of Horrors devoted to smashed aircraft. Under each print I wrote merely the name of the guy who wrecked his plane. *Bordman's. Sullivan's. Wright's. Draper's.* And, inevitably, *Mine.*

Recently I came across the album and examined it, and felt the flow of memory.

. . . Here's that fellow—what was his name, Lieutenant Brown? One of our instructors out at March. He had a forced landing in a Los Angeles street. . . . That's Whitcomb, down at Kelly. He was killed in that fighter, just before we graduated. . . . Somebody made a sorry landing in this one. . . . Here's Sullivan. He tried to take off in that DH without advancing his spark, and never did get off the ground. He wound up in a ditch over on the far side of the field. . . .

Herb Tellman apparently ground looped or something; just washed out the landing gear; not much damage to that. . . . Yes, there's Bordman. That one burned up. He was in our upper class when he was killed. . . . Here's another one: 63 landed on top of 27; nobody killed in that one. . . . And that's Draper's. He was finished in that. . . . Here's just a busted prop. . . .

And here's *Mine.*

The field was divided into two parts, with a stage house (call it the instructors' HQ) sitting out in the middle. Everything over there in the southwest belonged to the dodos; and everything over on the other side was the advanced students. By this time I was in Advanced, flying the first Douglas observation airplane, the beautiful O-2.

Well, we were in formation, and we had just landed. I was flying in Number 3 position on the wing, and we were taxiing up to the center of the field to climb out, change students, and get another flight off the ground.

Primary students on the other side of the field were doing the same thing. We came taxiing up, and I was looking out on the left side, watching my leader taxiing on in. When you're in formation on the ground like that, your leader is really leading you. He's the one who doesn't run into anything, he must be the Indian guide. You merely follow in your proper position.

. . . Dry as a bone, and a desert wind; hot, scorchy, gritty; dust blowing all over everything. Visibility pretty bad; and the dust was in everybody's mouth and peppering against everybody's goggles. . . .

Here came a primary student in his trainer, rambling right across the line, onto our side of the field.

People waved and yelled warnings, over at the stage house, they told us later; but that didn't do any good. The dodo just kept plowing grandly ahead. Then he saw our formation.

Instead of giving his engine the gun and getting out of there—ground looping or whatever he had to do—he just leaped out of that airplane, left it sitting, and ran like a whitehead. That was how I taxied right into it. (Actually I did see it in the split second before I hit; but I couldn't stop in time, so my prop chewed up his wing.)

At this moment I can't recollect whatever became of that dodo— whether they washed him out automatically or not. Maybe somewhere across the lonely ridges down there south of Riverside (if the desert hasn't all been subdivided by this time) there is still a frightened dodo from 1929—trotting, gray-haired and exhausted, fleeing the scene of his crime.

3

IT WAS TIME to leave March and go down to Kelly.

They ran two primary schools. Not only the one out in California; but also a primary school at Brooks Field, adjacent to Kelly at San Antonio, Texas. There another gang of tyros had been undergoing the preliminaries of flight, simultaneously with our own struggles. Brooks differed from March in one way. It had the elite for their primary training: young U. S. Military Academy officers who had been commissioned in various branches of the Service on their graduation the previous summer, but who wanted to go into the Air Corps. They came from the Corps of Engineers, from Infantry, Cavalry, Field Artillery, Coast Artillery—any and all branches. They were united with each other in a common desire to fly, and united to us flying cadets by the same bond.

Simultaneously with our arrival at Kelly, the Brooks boys moved over there to join us in an advanced training program—second lieutenants, flying cadets and all. Here I met a lot of people with whom I was destined to work closely in the future. We became a part of each others' lives, and would continue through flak and through applause, and through weather, in the same fashion. We would own our enthusiasms, our rivalries, our affection, our jealousies and respect and resentment and ardor, up until the moment of the last enemy attack or the last crumple and burst of flame . . . up until the moment of Terminal Leave which comes to all.

At Kelly the new amalgamated class divided up. You went into either Pursuit, Observation, Attack or Bombardment.

Things were smooth from the start. I went into Pursuit, and the head of the Pursuit division was Joe Cannon. Immediately I drew an instructor named Rus Keeler, and he was really good—not only a superb pilot but a skilled teacher.

When I say that he was a skilled teacher I don't mean that he hovered over us every minute, trying to open up our skulls and drill some holes through which he could pump fresh fuel into our aching brains. As a matter of fact he made it difficult. I think he may have done so deliberately. So many things which we learned we had to discover for ourselves. (Actually that's one of the greatest systems of pedagogy in the world. Whatever the student learns for himself, *by* himself, and at his own instigation, is a hard-won trophy; he won't relinquish it easily.) Under Rus Keeler you had to be alert enough to pick things up for yourself as you went along. If you weren't ardent and alert you didn't belong in that class anyway.

Long afterward Rus gave me a compliment. He told me that in his teaching career he had only one other student that he thought to be a better student than I had been. Thank the Lord I didn't know his true opinion at the time. It would have scared me to death. I thought I was having just as much trouble as anybody else. Maybe more.

About a month after we went to work at Kelly there came some real excitement. Those of us who didn't have college degrees were compelled to take examinations, to see how good we were academically. All of us, if we completed successfully the advanced training course at Kelly, were slated to be Regular Army officers in the near future: flying cadets, as well as those West Pointers who already held their commissions as second lieutenants in some other branch. *If* we made the grade.

Remember, I didn't have any degree. I owned my Reserve commission from the ROTC, and then later my commission in the Ohio National Guard (from which technically I was still on leave) but I had never graduated academically. I was no bachelor of anything (except a bachelor in the true sense of the word, in that I wasn't married). Every student who already possessed a degree could be excused from these examinations, if he chose, by accepting an automatic grade of eighty per cent. Some of the boys wanted to rank higher than eighty per cent, and thought they could do so, so we degree-less customers had some real competition. We were confronted with rivals who had already been through the academic mill.

We had our choice of courses. I chose surveying. Already I tallied sufficient college credits to excuse me from taking more than one phase of the academic examination.

It was just my own blame fault that I didn't rank first, when all the papers were in. Because, after the examination was handed to me, the initial thing I did was to read it all through, thoroughly; and I discovered that I knew the answer to every question. There wasn't a thing in there that I didn't know. *Boy*, I said to myself, *I'm really going to max this—* (Slang: meant that I was going to do a hundred per cent.)

There were three problems to work out. The rest of the examination was just definitions, and writing answers to questions. Trouble with ambitious Me was I spent so much time writing in abundant detail on every question, to demonstrate how bright I was in this subject, that I hadn't finished the last problem when we came to the end of our allotted time. I had let my own enthusiasm run away with me. All I could do was to put down the formula; didn't have time to do the arithmetic. So, too bad— I got marked down on that.

Just the same, I received a grade which ranked me third in the class, and a lot of those other people had degrees. Actually it was important to rank as high on the list as you could.

When I think of cadet days I think chiefly of March rather than Kelly. The reason is obvious: I don't remember too much about Kelly because everything went so smoothly down there.

In Pursuit we got to fly everything that was standing around. We had one PT-9 and a couple of AT-11's. That one, I seem to remember, was a P-1 with a radial engine on it; then the rest of them were P-1's with Curtis engines. It wasn't a matter of checking off. They were all single-seaters . . . all had the same thing: a stabilizer, a stick, a rudder, a throttle, a spark control. That was it. You just got in and flew.

There wasn't any braking: you cut your throttle so you would slow down and stop. When you'd come in for a landing, you'd be on glide and you just sat there. Pull back on the stick, pull the nose up . . . finally you ran out of lift and settled on the ground. Keep holding your stick back to keep the tail down, and finally the aircraft stopped rolling.

We had our normal training in fighters: formation, night flying, cross-country. Then we used to go down and fly the airplanes of the Bomber people, the Attack people and the Observation people. The whole class kind of rotated around. Everybody flew everything that was on the field. Not much time, perhaps; but we all got a flight or two in them.

And the discipline, which had seemed like an affliction sometimes at March, was relaxed considerably at Kelly. We were becoming adult. We could go to town most weekends; sometimes we went, sometimes not. But we always came back for that magnificent Sunday morning breakfast in the cadet mess. If ever I am so unfortunate as to lose my appetite in my old age, all I'll have to do is think of that Sunday morning mess, and I'm positive that the appetite will return full force. I can see those platters of white and golden eggs yet, taste the ham and sausage, smell breakfast chops or minute steaks and hashed-brown potatoes . . . see the glint of jams and jellies. . . .

Way I remember it, I didn't have any weekend dates while I was in San Antonio; so I was still a novice where the girl stuff was concerned. Once in a while I went to a movie. . . .

I stuck pretty close to business (but without the worry felt constantly when we were at March, a worry that gnawed and plagued, and settled above like an overcast . . . dank gray childish worry of knowing that you weren't doing well, and realizing half-heartedly that you didn't have a good instructor, but being too afraid to do anything about it).

Here in Texas I had a wonderful instructor. I was proud, felt able and confident when I was flying—day or night.

As for night flying, we did get in quite a little, but it was kind of crude. The lights consisted merely of floodlights put down at the end of the field. When you came over to land, you had to land in the path that the floodlights put there. There were no radio aids or anything of that sort; so it was rather easy to become lost in the darkness. Of course we only ventured up at night when there was good ceiling and visibility; we had no weather flying, no instrument flying at all. We flew only during good weather; never would fly on top of clouds unless there were big breaks—very broken—so that we could be sure we weren't going to get caught up there.

Night work: you'd stay out in your sector, in sight of your field all the time. You'd fly around, and then when you got the proper light signal, winking that it was your turn to land, you'd come in and practice landing. But each had to stay in his proper sector when he was upstairs; they didn't want us running into each other.

To tell the truth, I've described about the only running-into-each-other which occurred during the cadet stage, in a couple of those accidents already mentioned. The *deliberate* running-into-each-other came after we had graduated and were regularly assigned to units in the Air Corps.

When I say deliberately running-into-each-other I mean just that. Flyers and buffs of this generation may be appalled; but that's what happened.

4

SATURDAY, October 12th, 1929, was a clear day, the bright clear kind of day that Texans brag about (with some justification).

They put on the usual aerial review and outside ceremonies.

Day before, we had lined up for our graduation picture: forty-seven

United States Army second lieutenants, sixty-nine flying cadets, and one non-commissioned officer from the Air Corps. (Guy named Waugh.) We were all on the same basis at last, for cadets and the enlisted man would receive commissions as Reserve officers in the Air Corps. And within a very short space of time we would join those second lieutenants in our class, by becoming officers of the Regular Army. But every graduate received his wings on the 12th.

There were a couple of grads who should have lined up with us, but weren't permitted to. One Emmett O'Donnell, Jr. (if the name Rosie O'Donnell needs any explanation to the public in this day and age then somebody else will have to undertake that little job) was still recovering from injuries received in an airplane accident. He had to go through the graduating motions with a later class.

Also a very popular youth named Woodley had his head cut off by a cadet captain, within hours of the final ceremony. This was a penalty for reckless flying. The cadet captain reported Woodley's violation of flying regulations; the ordinary school machinery then took over, with our commandant as final authority in the matter. Woodley was told to pack his bags and get the hell out of there. This was the night before graduation: a majority of the boys thought that our cadet captain might have had enough decency to look the other way. If there was a character in that class who hadn't ruptured regulations one time or another, either through carelessness or intent, then I don't know who he was. Woodley shook hands with everybody, said Goodbye, walked into the cadet captain's room and hung a beautiful shiner on him; then walked away into civilian life. Matter of fact, today (1965) Arthur G. Woodley isn't hurting too badly. No one should, if he's president and general manager of Pacific Northern Airlines. . . .

Well, the Air Corps Training Command band played, and Chaplain Burling gave both the Invocation and the Benediction, and Brigadier-General Frank P. Lahm, commander of the Air Corps Training Command, gave the introductory remarks. (We listened to him with veneration. The Wright brothers themselves had taught Lieutenant Lahm to fly, twenty years before.) Then came an address by Brigadier-General Samuel D. Rockenbach of the United States Army. General Rockenbach also presented us with our diplomas, and General Lahm gave us our Reserve commissions.

. . . Who stands forth now to present the wings so long desired? He is tall, dark-haired, just a bit slumped from the very tall man's habit of bending down to those of shorter stature. You look at his face, and suddenly you think of old stories about Osage Indians. It is Major Clarence L. Tinker. "Indian Tink" has been our Assistant Commandant; he's a great flyer and a great officer. Somehow the mere fact that he is the one who hands out the wings puts an extra shine on the gloss of those long-sought insignia.

The Battle of the Midway is far off. There will be a million airplane engines resounding in our ears before there comes the last growl of that plane bearing General Tinker to his final Rendezvous.

He has a lot of company out there—wherever that Place is. Many of his companions will come from this same graduating class, to whom he now presents their wings, with a quick smile and hearty hand-shake. But Nate Forrest is only a proud lieutenant on this day, glad to be commissioned in the Air Corps instead of the Cavalry. So is Bob Travis glad to be commissioned now in the Air Corps instead of the Field Artillery.

Flight after flight will join Indian Tink in the near future, and leave the rest of us to come lagging in when we are old and tired.

Alexander will have preceded Tinker by ten years: 1932 for him. Harold Brown . . . fighter smash at Selfridge. The other Brown, James, will die over in China in World War II. Caldwell . . . 1930—next year.

(Stuart McLennan is still around, in these 1960's, chipper as a man can be. Maybe you need to have a homemade face in order to be as gay as McLennan. Early in World War II he was heading for the Pacific in a B-26; in fact, practically the whole staff of a new group was jammed in there. The aircraft busted up at El Paso and McLennan was the only one who got out alive. He spent the rest of the war in hospitals: skin grafts, etc. His whole face was burned off, the one that God gave him. He has a new face, given him by the surgeons. Not much left in the way of fingers, either. An awful lot left in the way of guts.)

. . . Art Meehan will die in the South Pacific, and MacArthur in the Third Attack Group before the war. Mills: during the war. Also it will be during the war for Murtha, Air Officer for an invasion force—standing on the bridge of a ship when it's hit by a Japanese bomber.

Bob Travis will have old Fairfield-Suisun renamed for him.

This gets to be quite a necrology. Jesse Auton will finish up on the runway at Offutt while I'm commanding SAC out there. Dolan will be killed in Newfoundland. Durfee: 1946. Judd will end up in an airplane accident, and so will George Brinton McClellan (there's a name for history—like Nathan Bedford Forrest).

Mace will die by his own hand.

. . . More accidents, more flak, more fighters, more accidents. Massie, Meisenholder, Mitchell. Redetzke and Rawlins. Robert W. Goetz, youngest man in the class: 1935. Roger Ramey will live to retire after long service; and then die of a heart attack in decorous civilian fashion, but after a lot of time in the air.

Several other young lieutenants; the names elude me now. . . .

Actually the roster of graduates, be they second lieutenants or be they flying cadets (be they living or be they dead in this 1965 year) is something to conjure with. Through the level of later decades it begins to resemble pages from *Who's Who in the Air Force.*

You don't run up against names like these every day. William H. Tunner . . . Robert Whitney Burns . . . John K. Gerhart . . . Frederick L. Anderson . . . August W. Kissner . . . George W. Mundy . . . La-Verne G. Saunders. (Far ahead, far ahead is a thunder of engines unlike any of the engines we've heard here at Kelly. I'm in an airplane, and Blondie Saunders is vanished somewhere in India; and Al Kalberer and I look down and see that gash in the jungle, and we begin to guess where Blondie Saunders is.)

There are the little triplets, the three shortest men in our formation of flying cadets. That same Ivan Lonsdale Farman and Bobby Cork and William John Clinch, Jr., known to the rest of us as Half-inch Clinch. Habitually they all used to fly sitting up on three leather cushions, and pushed forward by three more at the back, because otherwise they couldn't reach the controls, not one of the three.

Then a DH landed, and suddenly there was just a big cloud of dust, and people at the stage house couldn't see anything but dust. Finally the dust drifted away and there was that DH upside down, and one of the three midget triplets (I don't recollect which one) hanging upside down, sustained by his safety belt.

Then he releases the belt and down he topples, smack on his head. Six big leather cushions come socking down on top of him, one after the other.

. . . Here's his instructor standing beside the upset plane, yelling: "Next time, jettison the cushions *first*. Then they won't fall on top of you."

Little recollections come swarming upon us now . . . these and many others. We will remember them long. Some folks will remember longer than others. And there will be certain things we can't forget, and some of those things won't happen for almost another third of a century.

. . . Thirty years later, when I was Vice Chief of Staff, it was decided that we surviving members of that Air Corps Advanced Flying School class of 12 October, 1929— We'd have a class reunion. Personally I saw to it that every member of that class, no matter where he was, who was still alive, got an invitation in no uncertain terms. So invitations went out to Sam Anderson, to A. V. P. Anderson, to Frank F. Everest, Jr., to Bryant L. Boatner, Bill Kennedy, Howard Bunker, everybody else.

And one invitation was addressed to a man named Alfred Lot Beatie.

Beatie had had hard luck. Not long after graduation he was broken to pieces in an airplane crash, and was thus forced into retirement. They gave him a disability pension: ninety dollars a month or somewhere in that ball park.

None of us, up ahead in 1959, had seen Alfred Lot Beatie for a very long time.

I wouldn't tell this now, except it was in the papers when it happened.

They found Beatie dead in bed, in a miserable flop-house hotel in San Francisco. Skid Row in Frisco is just about the same as any Skid Row on Earth, and populated by the same scrawny derelicts, the same red-eyed men who drift from doorway to doorway.

That was where Beatie died. He didn't have much in the way of possessions in the room with him; but he had that invitation. It lay spread on the dirty dresser. He must have been reading it shortly before he was found.

So he didn't get to the thirtieth reunion. He had that invitation . . . maybe he had hoped to come.

5

ORDERS WERE tacked on the bulletin-board, and sweet boy graduates crowded round to see about assignments. I squeezed in with the rest of them. My name wasn't even on the list.

There they all were: names, serial numbers, unit and base to which assigned. No LeMay in sight.

I high-tailed it into the orderly room to see what had happened, and no one knew why or what. It was really baffling. So they quizzed Washington.

We got the ungarbled word. Washington said that I couldn't be given a commission in the Air Force Reserve until I had resigned my commission in the Ohio National Guard. Nobody at Kelly knew that I was *in* the Ohio National Guard. What with one thing and another, I had pretty well forgotten it myself.

First I fired off a telegram to the Adjutant-General of Ohio, resigning my commission. Then I informed Washington that I had resigned and was a free agent, ready to take my place in the Air Corps Reserve. In a few days I received orders for Selfridge Field, Michigan. 27th Pursuit Squadron of the First Pursuit Group. But it was a little over three months before I got my commission in the Regular Army.

I had a few days leave, then reported at Selfridge.

Privately most of us newly bewinged Kelly graduates owned a pretty sharp opinion of ourselves. We would have opined if pressed—or even if not pressed very hard—that we were just about the hottest pilots who ever came out of flying school.

Then we landed up there in Michigan, rubbing elbows with the First Team. Far as they were concerned, we weren't even qualified to fly airplanes. We had harbored notions of being welcomed as fellow airmen, all part of the same noble glittering fraternity and— They had never heard of us. We were dust beneath their feet.

Our hearts sank when we learned that *no one could fly until the Operations Officer had taken him up in the old PT-3 and checked him out.* It was like March Field and Red MacKinnon all over again.

(Fortunately by this time I had learned to do a snap roll to the left.)

We newcomers were hurting badly, but there was no help for it. Apparently this was another form of Advanced Training over Advanced Training which we had to go through. Might as well be philosophical about it.

There were three squadrons: 17th, 27th, 94th. There weren't enough airplanes to supply every squadron. The normal fighter formation of that day called for twenty-five ships to a unit, in order to furnish an eighteen-ship formation. The only way we ever got an eighteen-ship formation into the air was by pooling the airplanes of all three squadrons.

A customary flying day went something like this:

First thing in the morning the pilots would meet in Base Operations office. Engineering officers of the three squadrons would make with the airplanes which were in commission, and put them up on the board. Then the Operations Officer would get together with those pilots who were present for duty, and they would draw up a flight. Sometimes the Group commander led the flight, sometimes one of the staff officers, sometimes one of the squadron commanders. They kept records of times, so everybody got training flights with the big formation. The work consisted mostly of climbing up as high as you could get, and then diving at the hangar line. This was the way we strove to make the Team: to be considered combat ready, and qualified to fly with the Big Boys.

After the main Group training flight of the morning we were released to our own squadrons. We'd go home, and in each case one of the older boys would take us out and put us through the ropes. That was when we realized that a gentle process of hazing was still current in our lives. (Hadn't been any hazing at Kelly, since we were the only class there.)

O.K. So one of the older boys would take us up to see whether we could fly or not. We'd get in formation, and the old boy would roll over and put us in a dive, and see if we could stay there. Some of them weren't above jiggling . . . flopping around in order to make it tough for you to remain in position. They'd jiggle a little bit, and more than a little bit. Of course, if you got to jiggling along with them, pretty soon you were out of formation. Couldn't possibly stay there. And then you caught the very devil.

"*What* a sorry pilot. . . ."

There was a way of dealing with this situation, however; and Bill Morgan, one of my classmates, was the fellow who found the way.

Actually I've forgotten who was leading us that day. But he was a feisty little bastard, and he kept slamming us through the ropes . . . trying to beat our swelled heads down a bit, *he* said.

Our dear little leader got to jiggling on the way down, and Bill Morgan got to flopping, and had to pull out of formation.

On this particular day Bill came to see me, after that flight, when we were in front of our lockers. He looked all around to see that no one else was there, and then leaned forward and whispered as seriously as anyone could whisper.

"You know, Curt— God damn it, this is the last time I'm going to pull out of formation. I may run *into* one of those guys. But I'm definitely not going to pull out of formation again."

The tone of his voice and the look in his eyes showed me that he meant business, and gave me a rather chilly feeling.

"Oh, relax, Bill. All they're doing is putting us through the wringer. You know that."

Bill says, "Yeah. But I don't like it. I'm going to stay *in* the next time —not pull out of formation, even if I have to hit him. Next time that son of a bitch jiggles me, I'm just going to get in that much closer."

Next day we had the same character leading, and he did the same thing. Sure enough, Bill ran into him. He got right in closer, and—bang —they hit their wings together. Actually they escaped severe structural damage; ran in and tapped wings, that was all.

Bill had been right. He didn't make an angel out of the other guy, but he made a Christian out of him. No more jiggling.

I mean, no more jiggling of Bill Morgan by that squirt who had tried to give him a rough time. But there was plenty of other jiggling; we all got a taste of it. I have a keen recollection about the first time I was hit, myself. We slid together endways and it jammed the ailerons in neutral. I couldn't move the stick, so it was a matter of using the rudder to keep level, and making a big flat turn, and getting lined up, and then going in to land, just using rudders and throttle. I had no aileron control but had elevator control. Got down all right.

Oh, we racked up quite a few collisions in the air . . . some in which they had to bail out, also. We used to fly those formations as tight as all hell, with wings overlapping. All in all I was hit several times. Of course it wouldn't be the same today. We were only traveling at a hundred and forty or a hundred and fifty mph.

We weren't upstairs every minute: we all had squadron jobs at the same time we were pilots. The Operations Officer was not necessarily a pilot in the outfit. He had a staff job, and that was his primary duty. But we pilots all had staff duties. I became Mess Officer (for the enlisted men's mess). Later I was assistant Operations Officer, and still later assistant Communications Officer, and had various other jobs. Before finally winding up at Selfridge in 1934 I had been Base Communications Officer for quite a while.

In summer we all went up, one squadron at a time, to Oscoda. That's just above Au Sable Point, north of Saginaw Bay. There we would disturb the peaceful waters of Lake Huron with our gunnery and bombing. That's all we did up there: working on that range, bombing and shooting. I did all right at this, and was on the Selfridge team which went to the national gunnery matches at Langley Field in Virginia.

(They called it a team, but actually it wasn't much of a match. A contingent from Selfridge went down, and some folks came up from Rockwell in California—that was the only other Pursuit squadron in existence then in the Continental U.S. Observation people came, Staff and Attack people came. All of the front gunnery people were there with various types of equipment. It was more of an individual competition than anything else. Still it wasn't competition in the regular sense of teams and trophies: we just went down there . . . everybody shot, and exchanged ideas . . . folks bombed, and exchanged ideas . . . that was the way.)

I had no precognition whatsoever about Langley. Didn't dream that I would be stationed there for a long period eventually, and in Bombardment of all things.

A recurrent duty in 1930 and 1931 was to go out and open up airports. You had to be qualified for cross-country in order to get in on that work. (Matter of fact, a certain amount of cross-country was mandatory after we arrived at Selfridge.) Little by little some of us were getting to be recognized as qualified to fly with the Big Boys.

Depression or no Depression, they were opening up airports all over the country. I don't know where the money came from, but certainly they were doing it . . . county seat towns, big towns, everywhere. Naturally the Air Corps snapped at the opportunity to advertise the Air Corps. We would do formation flying, put on a show, and then some individual acrobatics. If it was one of the large municipal airports which was being saluted, we sent enough airplanes to make up our eighteen-ship formation. Smaller airports, they would send perhaps a flight.

Sounds very busy and fly-boyish and it was. But don't forget: we had our ground jobs too.

In memory I was haunted by that astounding contrast between a meal at March and a meal at Kelly. It wouldn't take an overactive imagination to decide that my ideal would be the Kelly mess, forever and ever. But as Mess Officer at Selfridge I was in an entirely different situation.

. . . Was coming in as a greenhorn, newly commissioned, and the reception which we'd received from the flying personnel had been mighty deflating. So I wasn't going to start throwing my weight around in the direction of the creamed corn and the creamed chipped beef. I proceeded cautiously (as in the old Michigan forest joke about porcupines).

Didn't start instituting a lot of reforms. There was a skilled mess sergeant on hand, and he knew more about the business than I did, so we had a fairly good mess to begin with. Furthermore I'd never attended cooking school. But I could add and I could subtract.

First off I went in and inventoried all our supplies. Tried to keep my eye on the stuff that we drew; and lined up the mess accounts properly. We didn't eat too high but we ate moderately well. Certainly I didn't have anything to do with improving the quality of the food itself. But I think that the accounts made more sense when I left than when I came.

There isn't much that a second lieutenant can do about messes. A general can do a hell of a lot.

(It was a long way down the pike to the year when I would be tapped for SAC. When I traveled from Germany to head the Strategic Air Command I was a lieutenant-general. If there could be fur in SAC messes—and, by golly, there was, plenty of it—it started to fly.)

No fur flew in our little mess there in Michigan in 1930. It wasn't indicated. I was a Tenderfoot; and it's a toilsome journey, as all Boy Scouts know, from Tenderfoot to Eagle.

There was too much of a club aspect about the whole blame Air Corps in those days anyway. Take the summer of 1930. It was thirteen years since the first U. S. Regulars had landed in France; twelve years since they had resisted stubbornly along the Vesle and the Ourcq and the Marne; eleven years since whistles were blowing long and loud in New York harbor to welcome returning troopships. The memory of bursting shells and the stammer of machine guns was not too ugly even with most of those individuals who had been exposed to them in fact. To us younger people, war was a mass of theories in a textbook . . . and presiding over all of them, of course, a hoary legend.

Only thing which kept us more or less vigilant in the Air Corps was the inevitable attrition which occurred during training and during later air activity.

Not many ground soldiers or salt-water sailors are apt to be killed through the process of preliminary training or in operational-type exercises. Once in a while a fire breaks out in the magazine of a ship, or a welder's equipment starts a fire at a Navy yard. We read about this in the papers, just as we do about the short round or the long round which fell during live-fire Louisiana maneuvers, and killed some boys. It's bad when this happens. But it occurs much more frequently in the airplane business.

It was that persisting element of physical uncertainty and possible tragedy which kept us from becoming completely la-di-da country club people.

. . . There is no war in the offing, there hasn't been any war for a long time. Sure, we work, but nobody works very hard. There is no sense of urgency.

"You must immediately train, and develop a combat capability in the organizations."

. . . Nothing like that. Because we know that even if we do go to war, our organizations are not going to fight as such. You have that atmosphere where there's a little ground school and a little flying, and a little of this and a little of that, and you're not on your toes . . . you haven't even got any toes to be on. . . .

It wasn't until seven years later, when I got to Langley under Bob Olds, that it finally filtered through my thick skull what the Air Corps was really in business for.

There exists a certain song, well known to the people who wear wings, which remarks on this subject. Several old-time AC types—Madeline Smith (an officer's wife), Earl H. DeFord and Roland Birnn—are credited with coming up with the first edition of the ballad; but a lot of other people have hammered their hallmarks into it through the years. It's bawdy, and has other values. It is a case of airmen standing in front of a mirror and taking a good look at themselves; although sometimes that mirror is a trifle like the distorted glass in a fun-house at Coney Island.

> Come on and join the Air Corps—
> It's a great life, so they say.
> You lie around in the sack all night
> And you fly around all day. . . .

We weren't fully equipped squadrons there at Selfridge, and we were operating under the old Army principle: you never fight the outfits which you have in time of peace. You're actually just a holding operation, to develop new tactics, perhaps—new equipment, new training measures and aids. But when war comes—if it comes—you will need to form your outfits from the Reserves, and build them up. Then, eventually, you go out and fight.

There was absolutely no feeling of that exigency which, years later, we were at last successful in instilling in our various Air Force commands. *We may need to fight tomorrow, and we can fight tomorrow,*

and we will fight with the people we have and the equipment we have.
None of that feeling at all.

Certainly some dedicated souls were trying to increase their professional knowledge, and succeeded in doing so. But there wasn't the
prevailing overall sensation: *If there's a war, we fight with what we
have here. This is the unit which will go into combat, and it's ready to
go now.*

It would seem that, to feel justified in their own existence, our flyers
had to manufacture increased hazards. They did manufacture them.
This jiggling of wings and controls in order to give the newcomers a
hard time and make them desperate— Witness the Bill Morgan episode. That's exactly what I'm talking about.

> Just show them all how hot you are,
> And while they stand behind,
> Just you grow bold while the rest grow old,
> And you will never mind.

When the Army punished Billy Mitchell they were in effect trying
to punish the entire then-existent Air Service. When the Army sought
to force an iron gag into Billy Mitchell's mouth, they were trying to
gag all proponents of air power under their command. They had done
their best to break the man to bits. And historically this was very
recent. It was less than five years since Mitchell had cried his public
charges of "incompetency, criminal negligence, and almost treason-
able administration of the National defense" in his accusation against
the Departments of War and Navy.

(Fifteen more years elapsed, graven with bitter explosive lessons
learned in World War II, before the United States Senate voted William Mitchell his posthumous Congressional Medal of Honor.)

In 1930, and during successive seasons through which we would
have to skimp and save and Do Without, our Corps was treated like
the bereaved orphan in fairy tales. We had a pallet of straw in a cold
garret; and the cook threw us some scraps only after everyone else in
the household staff had been fed.

The evolvement of the Gentlemen's Flying and Country Club was
a most natural result. We snubbed everybody who wasn't in the air,
and even snubbed each other, as described above. Misguided, low-
budgeted, under-equipped, the personnel of that era may be forgiven
for their errors in judgment. Someone Away Up There didn't like them
and they knew it.

Matter of fact, we've been in that identical struggle ever since the
airplane was invented.

6

DURING my first year at Selfridge it became increasingly apparent that I should go back to school and make up that extra work. A mere fifteen credit hours stood between me and a Civil Engineering degree. Of course there was the matter of a thesis as well.

Most of the people surrounding me were people with degrees. I became certain that there might be embarrassments and disappointments in the future if I didn't have a more solid scholastic background. It was as if I stood with one foot on the ground and one foot stepping up into an airplane . . . there I was, caught in between, motionless.

The Army had a policy of sending officers back to school. But usually this was in order for them to receive advanced training and advanced degrees.

From time to time I would wage a new campaign to get sent to Ohio State. No dice. The day came, while we were on flying duty temporarily in the Washington area, when, with the blessing of my CO, I stood before the Chief of the Air Corps, and asked him about it. He shook his head and said No.

Along about this time I met a girl who made me acutely aware of my scholastic lacks, just by the complete assurance with which she accepted her own accomplishments. Her name was Helen Maitland, and her father was a corporation lawyer over in Cleveland. She said that her family had wanted her to be a doctor—and she wished to be one also, to start with. Later she changed her mind. She'd graduated from Western Reserve in pre-med, and then switched over and finished in nursing. After that she went to the University of Michigan and took up post-graduate study as a dental hygienist. For a young and lovely blue-eyed wench she had certainly been around the academic lot. I felt increasingly ashamed of the missing quarter's work which stood between me and my diploma—almost won a couple of years earlier, but never grasped completely.

One of my old classmates from Kelly was Herb Tellman, who was stationed also at Selfridge in the First Pursuit Group. So was another classmate whom I knew well: Louis Vaupre. Herb was engaged to a girl at the University of Michigan, and he got over there to see her every time he could make it. He kept hounding Louis and me, describing the glories of luscious Ann Arbor gals, and declaring that we were making a big mistake in not going around and beating the bushes to see what variety of dryads might come swaying forth.

It was in the spring of 1931 that he finally arranged a couple of blind dates for us: Helen Maitland and another girl. Neither Louis Vaupre nor I knew which girl we were going to have; nor did the girls know which of the heretofore unknown Air Corps officers they would be dating.

. . . Louis and I walked across the street to go in and claim our dinner partners. They lived in a dormitory called Mosher Hall. The ladies were on Alert (the Air Force Dictionary defines this as "a state of readiness against impending danger, or for going into action") and were peeking out through curtains upstairs. They studied us cagily.

Long afterward I learned that Helen spoke first, with decision. I was pretty chunky and—

Helen says, "I think I'll take the fat one."

Probably I would have been mad as hell if I'd known what she said, then. But when eventually I came into the knowledge—well, it didn't seem to make much difference.

Louis and I took our dates out to dinner and we had a lot of chitter-chatter together. But when Helen and I were alone in my car we could talk a little more seriously. I was attracted to her from the start. I liked her wild blue eyes—no Yonder about *them*—and her hair. (Don't know whether you'd call it dark blonde or light brown . . . somewhere in there. Kind of curly and wiry . . . seeming alive). She talked plenty, couldn't seem to stop. And it was all in a bubbling effusion which I found myself rather enjoying. She'd skip from one topic to another, like a dancer just hitting the high points. Often you couldn't get a word in edgewise.

But Helen inspired in me a desire to try to emulate her frankness of conversation, her honesty of recollection.

On the way home I found myself telling Helen about my ambition to go back and finish up that college work, and declared that I had been thwarted at every turn.

Also found myself telling a personal anecdote, one of my earliest.

. . . It was when we lived near Lithopolis, just before we left to go back to Columbus, and I was sent to a country school, although scarcely old enough to go. One teacher for all the classes: a little schoolhouse; neighborhood children all the way from hulking over-grown boys who were ready for high school, in size at least (but never would go); down through demure maidens of diminishing stairstep stature; down to tykes like myself. I decided that I didn't like the teacher and I didn't like any part of that school. Longer I stayed there the more I became convinced that this wasn't my cup of chalk and I wasn't going to drink very deeply of it. Next thing I knew, I was being disciplined for some infraction of rules, and I didn't like this either—considered it highly unfair—a brutal infraction of my rights. Told Teacher, "I'm going home." Teacher locked the door and put the key in her pocket. There was a window near; and I went over, raised the window, threw my books out, and started to go through the window head-first. That was one of the most tactless tactical projects I ever embarked on. There I was, head and arms through the window, and Teacher had me as if I were in antique 17th Century stocks. The window secured me nicely in position: my rear end was still in the school, subject to Teacher's whim. And it was quite a whim.

She had a big broad pair of hands. One of those she used to cement me more firmly into position, and the other she plied in the very best fashion. I got the merry hell whaled out of me.

"I yelled bloody murder," I told Helen Maitland. "But that didn't do any good either."

She laughed a little. Then she asked, "Curt, why are you telling me all this?"

"I don't know. Except that it seems now I am being punished for some sort of infant misdeed. See, in the first place they *wanted me* to go to school, and I didn't want to go. Now *I want* very much to go to school. The Army won't let me."

When she spoke it was with all seriousness. "Then it's up to you. You've got to use your best resources, whatever they are. Figure out a way. You might take your Commanding Officer into your confidence, if you haven't done so already. But there must be a way. And you figure it out."

This was damn good advice and I knew it the moment that it was uttered. I repaid Miss Helen Maitland by inviting her to the Military Ball, there at the University of Michigan. It was given by the ROTC types, but we genuine AC officers were welcome. I thought that Helen was a great gal; but I didn't have any more intention of seriously considering marriage, there in 1931, than I did of flying to the moon. In 1931 people had no intention whatsoever of flying to the moon. Odd but true.

In spare time I did a lot of pillow-pounding and investigating, and finally came up with a workable proposition to present to Major Brett, my CO.

Norton Field, down at Columbus (the place where I'd taken my first ride for two-and-a-half bucks, and where also a benevolent pilot had flown me on a half-hour's jaunt in 1928) was still in about the same stage that it was when I left college. There was one Regular officer on duty down there, and two or three sergeants. They in turn hired some civilian mechanics in order to take care of the half-dozen airplanes in their pool. Reserve officers of the area got their flying time in these planes.

I set my sights on Norton.

According to standing edict an officer could be sent on Detached Service for five months and twenty-nine days. Otherwise it had to be a permanent change of station . . . six months, and it was permanent. Five months and twenty-nine days was still Detached Service. It was necessary to pin these facts down thoroughly before making a move.

Ohio State functioned on the quarter system instead of having two semesters in the school year. School year consisted of three quarters; fourth quarter was a summer session. So, if I went down in the fall and remained for five months and twenty-nine days, I could fit in with two quarters of part-time work at the University. It would be necessary to report at school just a few days late and leave just a few days early. But I thought this might be arranged with the college authorities. If I reported for duty at Norton Field on the 1st of October, and remained for five months and twenty-nine days, that would bring it up to the end of March.

Major Brett coöperated in the plan, once I presented my whole project to him. He knew well enough, as every discerning commander in our destitute establishment knew, that the Reserve program could do with a little booster transfusion of fresh active blood from the Regular outfits whenever possible. The single Regular officer on duty at Norton would be grateful for some assistance; the Reserve training program would thus be expedited. (Sounds like a lot of Conscience Salve for getting LeMay back in college. Happened to be true, though.)

My primary function—*only* function, insofar as the Air Corps was concerned—was to serve at Norton. But what I did during off-duty time would be my own business. Anyone familiar with the Reserves knew that the bulk of work fell during weekends, when employed Reserve officers could break away from their civilian jobs and get in some flying time. (Still does.) Weekends had been pretty ghastly at Norton with only one Regular officer on the job.

The whole deal was set up just as I have described it here. The Air Corps was satisfied in having a slightly experienced pilot to assist Captain McConnell, in command at Norton. God knows I was delighted in my own right. And Ohio State was willing to admit me for the two quarters part-time work, even arriving a few days late and leaving a few days early.

. . . Went trotting over to the Theta Tau house, soon as I got squared away with the military. I didn't expect to find many of the old crowd around. But still there would be some boys who came in as lower classmen about the time I was finishing up, in 1928; and I knew a few of those.

Came face to face with a good friend—one from my own class—Cale Osborne. If you tried to seek out two physical opposites, perhaps to enter them in a competition of opposites, you couldn't have done better than to take Cale and me. He was small, slim and blond; so handsome that every woman turned to look at him; but with all his pretty appearance he was a man, and he was utterly unspoiled . . . a real salt-of-the-earth type.

Cale had never been especially active in the ROTC nor did he have any yearning toward a military career. Our only common interest was in engineering. Still we were always harmonious personally. I wondered what he was doing, still fooling around in school, and I soon learned. Although he had entered college the same year I did, he'd had a little more money at the time, and could take his freshman year complete, without working. After that he had to work part time and could carry only a limited schedule of studies.

In his sophomore year he started in a job with the State Highway Department. They had a few vacancies like that, where student engineers could do an ample job for the State and at the same time take a few classes; but it took about twice as long to graduate that way.

Meanwhile I had spent four years at Ohio State, one year as a flying cadet, and almost another two years in the Air Corps. If I did manage to finish up and get my degree in March, I would be well into my third year as a Regular Army officer.

Cale needed about the same amount of academic work which I needed; also he'd be required to present a thesis for graduation. He was fed up with the college routine—as who wouldn't be after seven years of messing around with it, at least part time. He'd tapered off, and wasn't even going to pick up the ball and run for his degree, until I came back and encountered him.

I said, "I'm going to finish up. That's the reason I wangled this job down at Norton. Why don't you come back to school and we'll finish up together? And—look—" It came over me for the first time in a happy rush that, for the moment, I was a man of substance . . . Cale had his job with the Highway Department. "What do you say? Let's get an apartment together, up in the university district. Then we'll be close to school."

Right lately I haven't examined any price indexes comparing the year 1931 against 1965. All I can say now is that ten bucks was a great big sawbuck of a bill in those days. Depression prices shivered at rock bottom. For example, I had a married friend who was then living in Columbus with his wife and baby. His mother-in-law sent occasional eggs and, once in a while, butter and scrapple from the country. Mike and Aline bought their milk by delivery from a local dairy, and made a great point of ordering certified milk for the baby. But everything else in the way of meats and staples, vegetables, fruit, etc.— He looked quite tragic as he said to me, "Aline and I have been figuring it out. No matter which one of us goes shopping—and we're both very careful shoppers—we can't get by for— Even leaving out the fresh things we get from the country, and the milk bill. Aside from all that, no matter how closely we watch, we can't get by on less than *one dollar per day* in groceries for the three of us." After a moment or two he brightened, and added, "Course, that does include soap and soap flakes. And we use a lot of that for the baby's clothes."

Dollars were big and round. I had close to two hundred and fifty of them coming in every month. A hundred and twenty-five dollars basic pay, fifty per cent flight pay, quarters allowance, ration allowance—the whole thing in gross was just about double my basic. Cale Osborne's job with the Highway Department was now sufficiently rewarding for him to enjoy Freedom from Care also.

I moved along those hilltop and hillside streets of the Ohio State campus and remembered how plagued I'd been when I was there before, obsessed with the thought of making every minute and every nickel count. I thought of occasions when there had been a few hours for relaxation but no money in the kit for it. There would be something good coming to town: a musical show, a famous actress or actor—

"You going, Curt?"

"No. Got to work."

Which wasn't always the truth. What I really meant on many occasions was, "I've got to conserve those quarters. Even the dimes."

. . . 1931 was a gorgeous autumn. The way I think of it now, it was all pink and yellow leaves, flaming oaks; and a smell of walnuts in the air . . . hazelbrush. Smoke seemed to dream through valleys of the Scioto and Olentangy rivers. Nice to go on picnics. It may have rained in that autumn and early winter—Lord knows it may have rained *a lot* —but I don't remember dark clouds or discomfort.

Cale and I had the world by the tail in more ways than one. We were in good health; we had work and we had ambition . . . we were bubbling with it.

And I owned a good car. For the first time in my life I seemed to know what it was like to be young and alive, to be intent, and yet at the same time not self-disciplined to the point of crucifixion.

Captain McConnell gave me plenty to do out at Norton, and was Oh-So-Glad that I had come. It was agreeable with him that I go to Ohio State in the mornings, just so long as I held up my proper end there at the field during the afternoons, and on weekends when work piled up. There was all the normal administrative ordeal of the detachment: keeping airplanes in shape, keeping supplies accounted for, so on. Then I did a lot of direct work with the Reserve officers, grading their papers for all sub-courses and the ground school.

Once in a while I would look out of the window and think of two boys who had come walking across that very turf on a long-ago Sunday. I could see them there, talking to the pilot beside his Waco three-seater. Then I'd close my eyes and remember the strange feeling which overwhelmed me when we were once off the ground and the horizon was tilting.

> Come on and get promoted
> As high as you desire.
> You're riding on the gravy train
> When you're an Army flyer. . . .

I could wear civilian clothes almost as minded. Usually I wore civilian clothes to school, then went back to the apartment and changed, and wore my uniform to work in the afternoon. Although there was no reason why interchange shouldn't happen, and often it did. Sometimes I'd have something to do in the morning, out at Norton: then I'd go to school in uniform. And on the other hand sometimes I'd be delayed up at college, and so go back to work in civilian clothes. It didn't matter. The Reserve officers were always ducking in and out both ways, too, as a matter of convenience.

Both Cale and I needed a thesis. An inspiration hit me like a ton of bricks. I told Cale: "I know just the thing. Do an aerial mosaic—" Which was mapping, of course; another engineering word—

"I'll fly the mosaic and get it laid down. Then you can write up the report on it—the whole process: how we go about doing it. Realize something? This is the first time it's ever been done in these parts."

It wasn't hard to sell this idea. Everybody involved was in favor of it —our college professor and all.

I flew over to Wright Field near Dayton and borrowed a camera: we possessed no aerial cameras in the Reserve unit at Norton. Don't know what the model number was. Doubtless it was a Fairchild: they made most of the cameras then as they do now. I'd say it was the standard vertical camera with about a twelve-inch focal length. Also I latched on to a magazine of film, and told the people over there what we were attempting. Encountered no problem except that I had to do the mosaic in conjunction with my other work. But that wasn't difficult —actually I was called upon for a good deal of flying. One of the Reserve officers who came out to Norton had been an observer when he was on active duty and had learned how to operate a camera. So I flew, he took the pictures.

The spool of film and the take-up spool were both in the magazine— eight-inch film, if I remember correctly. Fasten the magazine on top of the camera, fold the slide out, and you were in business. As you took a picture the film rolled to the next frame; then, when you were finished, you put the slide back on. Perhaps there was a hundred feet of film in the magazine; but we were able to do only about half the job with that first magazine.

I was faced with the task of taking that magazine back over to Wright— Had to get it developed; get another roll of film put in— The combination of problems was severe. Find time to fly to Dayton; return; get my Reserve Officer Observer some free time to coincide with the period when I had some free time also, and when an airplane was available. No wonder that it took an extra couple of months.

There was a funny pay-off on this. First things came first. I wasn't going to endanger my standing with the Air Corps in general or with my then commander, Captain McConnell, specifically—in slipping up in order to construct an aerial mosaic which was not demanded in any orders, and which would aid me only in winning my degree at Ohio State. I had a million other things to do. Result was, we took one roll of film in the autumn; and it was the middle of winter before we could get the other roll taken.

I remember the old prof looking at that thing when we presented it proudly. It was a rather peculiar mosaic: autumn foliage and leafless trees here, snow-covered landscape over there. But it was still the same terrain. For the purpose of securing an aerial map— Well, it served.

I was getting the best grades I'd ever received. Seemed like life in the Air Corps had taught me a thing or two about study and about the whole uncertain process of learning itself. My old buddy-buddy Professor Wall was still extant, but I didn't have to take any classes under him; so there was no point in going up and saying: "See? I'm not asleep *this* time."

Cale and I had assigned to us as our instructor for our particular project a prof named Sloane. He was a real character—short, baldish, with a regular Pat-or-Mike type of face—called by all and sundry, "Slicker" Sloane. We were in the post-graduate age group . . . even when seniors came close to graduation they were all calling Slicker Sloane by his nickname, instead of Sir.

Just the same, hail-fellow-well-met or not, Slicker Sloane was tough. You couldn't handle him—at least *we* couldn't, not with any means at our disposal, including originality, hard work, and a good thesis.

We presented our aerial mosaic and the accompanying report in triumph, and Slicker Sloane said that it was fine. We went through a brief period of mutual congratulation and living it up, because we had done so well with our thesis. Then came our grades.

Both Cale and I received B's on our project.

We were really burned up about this. We talked it over, and decided to wait on Slicker firsthand.

We arrived protesting. "*We* thought we were doing *pretty well.* Here we have something unique, something no student has ever done before! You've got a damn good map of Columbus!" Etc., etc. "So why did we only get a B on this?"

"Oh," says Slicker, as if surprised to find that that was what was worrying us. "I *never* give A's in thesis."

A matter of pride with him.

It wasn't a fatal disappointment. I didn't commit suicide and neither did Cale. (But he died young, only a few years later. I always think of him as being forever alive and young.)

We were in our twenties . . . and steaks and chops tasted good at dinner, especially if you ate that dinner in scented and fragile company. Snow crushed contentedly, crisply under our tires and under our feet. Winter flames of candles and the smell of pine trees put a sparkle in the air, and you looked up at icy winking stars at night, and thought great thoughts. When you drew in your breath you felt as if you ought to pound your chest. It was good, having a little real fun for the first time, and having a little leisure. A fireplace was a nice thing to sit before. And there were *girls around*.

I wasn't so stupid as to emphasize all this shemale stuff to Helen Maitland when she came down there from Cleveland. For she did come. I invited her and— She came.

I was flattered. Because, besides thinking that Helen was beautiful and liking her very much as a social companion, I'd stood a little in awe of her. She seemed more advanced as a person than I. She had been doing post-graduate work at Michigan when we met; but that was all finished now, and she was planning to work out in the civilian world rather than the scholastic one. She expected that soon she would be employed in Akron as a dental hygienist. We had written back and forth a little during the fall and on into the winter; not too often, but at least I knew where she was.

Actually she came to Columbus twice, when there were some interesting things going on. But there was nothing in any way serious between us—nothing said or written down. I didn't need to have any twinges of conscience. There was no reason why I shouldn't play the field as much as I wished, right there in Columbus.

. . . Thing was, I got all excited at the idea of Helen Maitland's coming down there, and wished that she would come more often . . . both that I had had enough sense to invite her more frequently, and that she had been able to come. But she wasn't eating her heart out over the vanished Lieutenant LeMay, not hardly. She was playing the field in her own more decorous way. She had lots of friends, both in Akron and back home in Cleveland where she went for holidays and vacations.

The day came when I must be evicted from this wintry little paradise which Columbus had become. I didn't dare overstay my time. More than five months and twenty-nine days, and I'd be in trouble. So would the people who had put me on Detached Service. But just as I had come in a couple of days late, so was I able to leave a little early. The head of the civil engineering department knew exactly what I was trying to do, and arrangements had been made in advance. They let me take my final exams early; but of course I couldn't stay for the Convocation and other exercises.

My diploma reached me in the mail, out there at Selfridge, just about the last day of March, or maybe even it was April Fools' Day. Nothing significant about that. I felt fine, I didn't feel foolish; and went back to routine flying activities and whatever ground jobs ensued, with renewed confidence and verve.

The rest of 1932 was in pattern much like the years which had preceded . . . so much gunnery at Oscoda, so much cross-country . . . again we'd be flying to some airport to put on a show . . . again we might be going down to Langley for a shooting demonstration. Everything went along at just about the same pace until another year had passed.

F.D.R. took office in March of 1933, close to a year after I graduated from Ohio State. With the first warmth of spring a new shadow was cast upon the lives of us AC types. It was called the CCC.

7

IN THE FUTURE it may be noted historically that President Roosevelt had a habit of calling on the Army to help out, whenever he dreamed up something new. The Air Mail event in 1934 was a fair sample.

So was the CCC.

There were—between April, 1933, and June, 1939—exactly 3,018,184 men and boys enrolled in the Civilian Conservation Corps. To ride herd on them during the first nine months there were assigned 2,044 officers from the Regular Army and 3,128 officers from the Reserves, together with a total of more than 4,000 enlisted men from the Regulars.

The Administration detached officers and enlisted men from the Army for CCC assignments right up through 1938. That was the first year that Naval and Marine officers and warrant officers of the Coast Guard were called for this work. It took the President a long time to get around to the Navy, despite his affection for that arm of the Service. There might have been a tacit awareness that CCC duty wasn't so sharp. We certainly didn't hanker after it in the Air Corps. But we had to go. They said, "Go and do it," and we went.

They were considerate enough to designate bachelor officers first; but eventually they ran out of bachelors and had to detail married officers to the task.

This was one of the many weapons which President Roosevelt devised to battle the Depression. (Nowadays they'd call it a War Against Poverty, and probably have Sargent Shriver in command.) To begin with, they enlisted flocks of kids in the late teens and early twenties, and sent them out into the byways of the Nation to build roads, bridges, facilities for State and National parks, dams, etc. They did grading, tree planting, fencing, all such chores.

The bulk of these young fellows were drawn from industrialized urban areas where the fangs of the Depression bit deepest. Soon the program was expanded to include World War I veterans, an age group far beyond that of the kids. It was mainly veterans who died in 1935 on the Florida Keys when Government workers were overwhelmed by a hurricane.

It wasn't in the cards to mix up the two aggregations. There'd be one camp of young boys, another camp of the older bonus-marcher types. This latter category posed a much more acute problem; you had a lot of professional indigents, boozers, so on. Poor Tommy Power got stuck with a bunch like that, up in New England.

Enrollees of the Civilian Conservation Corps were fed, clothed, housed by the Government. We Army officers were fortunate in that we didn't have to preside over the working hours of these characters: that was up to the regular CCC civilian staff. What we did do was manage the camp itself. We were glorified housekeepers.

Quite a come-down—to be pulled out of the sky, and sent off to a rustic site in a forest or among rolling farmlands, to look after the needs of the CCC boys. If there had been any possible way to beat this duty, we would have beaten it. Not a chance.

I was second in command of our camp, located near a small town called Brethren, Michigan. This was on the lower peninsula, well over two hundred miles northwest of Selfridge, close to Lake Michigan.

Our commander was a Regular Army officer, ground forces, pulled over there from Fort Sheridan, Illinois. I'd had that mess experience at Selfridge, so promptly I became Mess Officer in addition to other duties. As emphasized previously, I was always hell-bound to make a good mess. We were allowed the regular enlisted men's ration in funds; food wasn't fancy, but it was well-cooked and well-presented and there was plenty of it. Proud to report that we had no morale problems because of a lousy mess.

Reluctant as we were to enter upon it, I think that we all might have enjoyed the duty up there except for the way in which it was brought about. They started at the bottom of the roster; lowest-ranking officers went first. Lowest-ranking bachelors, naturally. It was typified as an undesirable detail right from the beginning. No one knew how long the duty was going to last. It might be years, we hazarded miserably.

We were away off there in the farmlands, away from our flying. And we were GI pilots, not a bunch of damn chaperones.

Our CCC contingent was composed of the real wild and the real woolly. They came from Hamtramck. That is a part of the greater Detroit complex. Funny name; but Colonel John Francis Hamtramck held

Revolutionary fame, and was the first American commander of the Detroit fort after the British troops surrendered it.

I shouldn't wish to insult the Hamtramck people and call their region a slum. But in this century the population is chiefly Polish, and those thick-necked boys who showed up to be supported by the Government and to be scrubbed pure in the great green bowl of Mother Nature, and to be administered by us clean-limbed Air Corps types— You wouldn't have mistaken them for a form of students from Groton.

I was in the first covey of officers listed for this stewardship. We assembled our boys at the Detroit depot, with the smoke of Hamtramck still in their hair and the soot still in their ears. We shepherded them all the way up country; then we had to set up tents and get the camp to functioning. We had to draw supplies from an Army quartermaster, and gather up clothes and equipment; had to get a mess organized, and everything else.

That was the bulk of our job: control them, feed them, get some sort of discipline into them . . . train them a little bit. At least so they could stand up in a rank and be counted, or so that they knew how to buck a chow-line. Then the Conservation Corps folks—often National Park personnel or State Park people—took over. They planned, plotted, platted —outlined the projects and set them up. They worked the boys.

At first, disciplinary problems were acute. Suppose one of these gravel-voiced young Polacks said, "Naw, I don't feel like getting up this morning. I don't want to go to work." Well, on the face of it you could throw him out of the CCC (in fact, people were thrown out if they made themselves too obnoxious). But it wasn't very acceptable to your superiors if the only cure you could offer was to kick the guy out, the first time he became a thorn in your side. Naturally if he were to commit a criminal act, civilian courts would take care of that; but we had no MP's, no military courts or anything of that kind. Our big task was one of leadership—persuasion, if you want to call it that. Good old-fashioned Moral 'Suasion.

Certainly not every lad among those two hundred and fifty or so with whom we started, was a juvenile delinquent. There were some real good leader types—boys who were natural-born sergeants or foremen—who had been properly trained and disciplined by their parents, and came from respectable homes. It was easy to pick the leaders out, and we did just that.

Main trouble, to begin with, was the kids getting into fights among themselves. I tried to cope with this, and finally got an athletic program going. It was a good way for them to work off a little steam. The moment they'd start to scrap, a yell would go up for the boxing-gloves. The contestants would be pulled apart, they'd get themselves nicely gloved, and the circle would form again. We'd let them go to it. After it was all over and the blood was being washed away from the cracked

lips, and the black eyes were being tended to, I'd try to point out to
them— "This actually didn't settle very much, did it?"

Gradually, through example, and through the simplest kind of
preaching—if you can call it that—we beat a little sense into their heads.
In a few weeks they were coming along in damn good shape, and
we were gratified.

. . . And glad, too, that we weren't numbered among those unfortunates such as Tommy Power, who soon drew the job of being Campfire
Guardian to an aggregation of World War I "heroes" who in many cases
had spent the lion's share of their military careers in the stockade. We
were a lot better off with our Hamtramck Poles.

Considered in these aspects, it was a somewhat enlivening duty;
but constantly we Air Corps officers felt cheated. We were being bilked
out of our flying time. Our careers demanded the perpetual application of the posterior to the pilot's seat, the hand to the throttle and the
stick, the feet to the rudders. We were part of a combat fighting unit,
or had been. It was more to our nature to be *in* a combat fighting unit,
rather than to be in the Boy Scout business or the YMCA, or feeling
like a counselor at Camp Minnehaha—blowing a whistle and saying,
"Now, all the Bucks over on this side, all the Stags over there. . . ."

I began to get some rather cute ideas about what could be done to
correct this situation—at least I thought they were pretty cute. But I
kept my own counsel—didn't talk to any of the other officers about this.
Seemed to me that it was essential that once again I instigate the bull-
by-the-horns procedure.

So, when at last everything seemed to be going smoothly, and especially when I had the mess functioning, I asked my commander for a
brief chunk of leave, and got it. Hopped in my car and aimed the radiator at Selfridge Field. I went up and bearded Major George H. Brett
in his office.

During the long motor trip I had had ample opportunity to plan just
how I was going to approach my subject. So all I did was to utter a
brief lamentation about how we people were stuck away up in the
woods, away from our flying, away from all airplanes, and having no
chance whatsoever to keep up with our acquired skills. Of course Brett
was well aware of our shrinkage in combat potential; he didn't need
any second lieutenants to point that out to him. But any commander
who is at all human is pleased when he finds a subordinate, however
lowly, reflecting his ideas.

I suggested that we were fast losing our skills up there in the dairy
patches, and pretty soon we might turn into the rankest of dodos.

Brett appraised me for a while. Then— "LeMay, if you can find a
place to keep an airplane up there— God damn it, you *take* an airplane
with you. My officers are going to *fly*."

No one would have needed more *carte blanche* than that. I chased myself back up into the country, and went prospecting for a good pasture. Found one. Went up and talked to the old farmer, and got him to agree that we could land an airplane in there. I then made a careful sketch of the field—a plat on which I put in the approaches and everything. Those were really copious sketches. I showed how far any obstacles were, on course from the fence-line; showed the elevation of adjacent objects such as trees, etc. My whole effort was to convince Major Brett that I had a usable field. In the end: no sweat. He was convinced, and I got my airplane. P-12.

These more-or-less-sub-rosa-air-planning activities had to be secondary to my main job in camp, which was that of Mess Officer. We had a ration allowance of twenty-seven-plus cents apiece, and we were to hell and gone up there. There were staples coming in: flour, beans, rice, other cereals and such; but no fresh meat or poultry. And we weren't equipped for extensive refrigeration. We had to build field iceboxes and dig a cellar for storage. The Army awarded us a mess sergeant and a supply sergeant. In addition I had one pretty good man who could really cook; he wasn't a Regular Army man, just a civilian employee; but he knew his stuff when it came to putting out the food. Then we culled through the boys themselves and named some of them to be cooks. Coming from a large industrial community, some were bound to have had restaurant background or experience in food handling.

Very soon, too, I got the nearby farmers coming in. They were fetching fresh vegetables; eggs; every now and then a pig or a couple of quarters of beef. But promptly I was compelled to stop my purchasing of local fresh meats . . . the stuff wasn't Government-inspected. Before long we got it set up so that our fresh meat could come in on the railroad. Still, every time a farmer would appear at the camp with a quantity of produce offered for sale, I'd buy something from him, whether we needed it urgently or not—just so he'd come back and bring the fresh things. We always purchased at local market prices. So, with all that fresh stuff in the summer, right off the farm— We didn't eat like kings, perhaps, but maybe like dukes.

We were in tents all the time I was there at the Brethren camp. Never did get out of the tents. In the meantime we were in the process of constructing permanent barracks; but I left before the barracks were finished.

Between the mess duties and the P-12 which had been placed on Detached Service from Selfridge, I was a right busy lieutenant.

Part of my flying activities were concerned not with girl-chasing (which is by legend the avocation of all airmen when they're not in the air) but with cow-chasing. If I wanted to take off from that pasture which I'd selected as home base, I had to chase the cows off the field first. Then, when I came back for a landing, often it was essential to do a little cow-buzzing in order to persuade the critters that they belonged over at the end of the field. Probably wasn't good for the milk, but— And after the airplane was landed, there arose the labor of fencing it off so that the cows couldn't come up and chew the cellulose off the wings. They just loved cellulose.

I have to smile now when I think of the fuel situation. Our CCC camp was away over on the west side of the lower peninsula, maybe three-quarters of the way up. So the routine would run like this: I'd fly from Selfridge, land, and— The only way I could keep flying was, next chance I got, fly the two hundred miles back to Selfridge in order to get gasoline. Just had about enough to get back there. It was one hour and twenty-five minutes regular flying time, to go back to the base where Government gasoline was available. Then I could fly around near Selfridge till I started looking at my watch. Then I'd land at the base, gas up, fly back to the Brethren region, and land. Next time I needed to fly— Back to Selfridge.

There were other officers working around, and it didn't take them long to discover that I had an airplane stashed away in our nice fertile countryside. I wasn't the only pilot in that particular neck of the woods. So they started coming over, practically with their tongues hanging out, dying to get in that aircraft. Since Major Brett hadn't suggested that it was actually my private plane, and since he had firmly declared that his *officers* were going to fly, I couldn't do any holding out on this. When I didn't have time off to get back in the air, I'd make the P-12 available to the other boys. They'd go through the same routine: flying down to Selfridge for gas, flying around in the Selfridge area, gassing up, then returning.

One joker didn't do that. There is always a squeaky piece somewhere in the machinery, and he was it. He went off on some little side excursion of his own, then returned to our cow-pasture and landed the P-12 with nigh-onto-empty gas tanks. Sweet boy. I should have liked to have caught up with him, but never managed to.

Probably the air did turn blue when I discovered that I had been stranded without gas. But blue air has never been used successfully as fuel for an airplane; so I had to come up with something better. I shall confess vaingloriously that it didn't take me too long. We had trucks up there for the CCC people to work with. Well, what I did was to put some truck gasoline in the belly tank of my aircraft. Our entire fuel capacity was one hundred gallons, if I remember correctly: fifty gallons in the main tank and fifty in the belly tank. That gave a radius of operation, if you started out with full tanks, of four hundred and fifty miles at least, safely. Still, it was a tight squeeze, and you didn't dare do any extra stooging around. That is just what that cuss had done.

(In 1933 you couldn't think of going to a civilian airport and buying gas to put in a military aircraft. There was no money for that sort of thing.)

As for octanage: we needed a higher octane rating assuredly. But I was fresh out of ethyl lead, and didn't know where any other magic elixirs could be purchased. It had to be good old run-of-the-mill truck gasoline or nothing.

When I say that that character who had flown the P-12 previously had left the plane sitting there with empty tanks, I don't mean that they were dust-dry—he hadn't come in with a dead stick. After careful investigation I believed that there was enough of the regular airplane fuel left in the main tank for takeoff, and even to climb to a little altitude. About then I would have used it up.

. . . Thought it would work or I wouldn't have taken off with that belly tank full of truck gas.

I followed my blueprint. Took off on the good fuel in the main tank, and climbed up; then I switched to the belly tank and burned truck gasoline for the rest of the trip. Oh, it belched black smoke and it coughed at first, but by reducing the spark a little bit, why— And not pulling high power— I was able to get down to Selfridge all right.

Must admit that this called for some burning of sparkplugs and getting the carbon cleaned out, after it was all over—with high-powered operation to tune the engine up again. But very quickly she was in good shape.

In late summer I got the break of my young life. Here came orders telling me to proceed to the Communications School down at Chanute Field in Illinois. I was to report back at Selfridge first, however. Matter of fact, I was the only one of our outfit who was being ordered to the Communications School, and of course I greeted the prospect with glee. I wanted to fly, and I wanted to study, and I was heartily sick of the summer camp business and the more-or-less stolen hours in the P-12 . . . going through that eternal routine of scooting back to Selfridge for gasoline before I could proceed with the real business of flying.

Flattered myself that I had run a good mess, though; and I wonder if the boys ate as well after I left as they had eaten before.

Then, one night, someone left a newspaper lying around, and I picked it up. It was a local paper from somewhere in that region— Grand Rapids, Muskegon or maybe Traverse City. And here, buried among columns of other news and advertisements, I saw a short squib which fairly put my hair on end. *The hangar which housed the Communications School at Chanute* had caught fire and burned down. . . .

Golly Moses. Well, I wasn't about to say anything about this. I was hoping that I could get loose from the CCC before, inevitably, my orders to the Communications School were rescinded.

I made it, just under the wire. The change of orders was lying on somebody's desk, I reckon; but on the required date, according to the original orders, I was on my way back to Selfridge, and reported there.

They told me, "Hey, your orders were cancelled."

"I wasn't apprised of that."

"Well now, Lieutenant, I guess you weren't. . . ."

The big point was that I was *off* CCC. Selfridge didn't have to send a replacement up there; he came from someplace else. I didn't know where he was coming from, and didn't care—just so I was emancipated from the Hamtramck boys and Farmer Hayseed's pasture, and the cows. As for the P-12, it had been left a-settin', with one of the other pilots taking over the responsibility. (*Not* the character who landed her nigh-onto-dry.)

Must have been at Selfridge maybe a week or ten days, and then another requirement came in. They were told to send somebody to the new Navigation School at Langley Field. Off I went.

8

The name of Harold Gatty will not be remembered commonly today. To the younger generation of readers that name may mean absolutely nothing. Thirty-odd years ago in aeronautical circles it was quite a name.

Gatty came from Tasmania. He had graduated from the Royal Australian Naval College; also he made later studies of navigation under one Lieutenant-Commander Weems of the United States Navy.

When Wiley Post flew his millionaire boss's airplane, the "Winnie Mae," around the world during the summer of 1931, Harold Gatty was his navigator. That was a real trail-blazing flight in many respects. They made it in 8 days, 15 hours and 51 minutes. A couple of years later, while we Air Corps types were up to our knees in the new green CCC, Wiley Post again took the "Winnie Mae" around the world. He went alone, with no Gatty to navigate, and he flew the same route, give or take a hundred miles of distance, in twenty-one hours less time than the previous trip. Observe that it was his second time over this course; also there were all of Gatty's navigational findings from the previous flight that now accrued to Post's advantage.

Harold Gatty was no longer a part of the slightly barnstorming atmosphere which always surrounded Wiley Post until his death in 1935. (Post was flying Will Rogers on a trip when they finished up in a crash in Alaska.) Gatty had been engaged by the United States Army Air Corps as a senior navigation research engineer. To begin with, he sharpened the skills of key officers who worked directly under the Chief; but before long they set up two schools for us younger fry. One was at Langley in Virginia, the other at Rockwell Field out on the California coast—near San Diego, on North Island. Later this field was transferred to the Navy, and still belongs to them.

As a commissioned ship's officer and at the same time a veteran navigator in the air, Gatty seemed a natural for his job with our Air Corps. He shuttled back and forth from Virginia to California. Technical lore which we absorbed from this man and from his system of teaching seems rather crude now, considered in the light of later knowledge, but truly it was advanced for the time.

There was little or no celestial navigation practiced in the Air Corps previously. In fact if Gatty hadn't had that experience at sea, he would have been floundering. He had figured out a way to adapt some of the shipboard methods to airplanes; that was the reason we were interested in his curriculum and came to profit from it. All the students were pilots. A navigator wasn't a three-headed monster in those days, as they grew to be called later; he was just an unidentified beast, unrecognized and unchronicled.

We had been using mainly pilotage, following the railroad tracks or highways. There had been very little dead reckoning: we only fell back on that when we had to. So now, in Gatty's classes and under the system devised by him, we entered a new world.

The tiny amount of dead reckoning studies which we had achieved previously occurred in the classroom. No formal schooling at all, where it was necessary to use dead reckoning over water.

No celestial at all. The Air Corps just didn't use celestial—there was no reason for it. Airplanes were of such short range that studies wouldn't have been justified. Up until this time the only system devised for celestial navigation was the venerable maritime method which sailors used. You shot the sun or shot a star at dusk or at dawn, so you could see the horizon in the sextant, and get the elevation. That gave you a line of position.

But in airplanes the mathematical method of computing the line of position after you got your altitude was extremely cumbersome. It might take you forty minutes to achieve a line of position. You had to take a number of shots, average them out, and then effect the solution.

Aboard ship that made very little difference. If it took you forty minutes to work out your position after the initial shot, you would have it set down pretty accurately on your chart and in your log, because of the slow speed of the vessel. But in an airplane, even at the speeds of those days, you were covering a lot of distance in forty minutes. Nice to know, *Where were we forty minutes ago?*—but a little nicer to know, *Where are we now? . . . Here.*

In previous years we possessed no aircraft which might be consid-

ered as really being long range. But in 1933 the B-10 was in the frying
pan and almost ready to be served up to us. According to reports, the
B-10 was going to be It for the time being. We had great faith in the
program. Everyone would have the latest Poop-from-the-Group, and
we used to sit around discussing the capabilities of an airplane which
none of us had yet seen.

As usual, whenever we got to really speeding on the slick ice of a
program, the Army Brass, represented by the ground-molded minds
in control, would be the old lady who comes out and throws ashes on
the slope where the kids are sliding. . . .

The Navy, of course, fought the whole idea of our flying over water.
More about that later.

Still, we had the B-10 coming, and we were going to have to learn
how to navigate over water and land masses alike. We were going to
have to get a fix on our position in a lot less than forty minutes, or there
was no use in flying the damn thing. Gatty was the most knowledgeable of his species alive, and owned more experience, especially over
water. He had developed some excellent short cuts through the thickets
of aerial navigation. These he tried to teach to us. Shades of Peewee
Wheeler again . . . Gatty wasn't a very good instructor.

There wasn't much known at that time to instruct *on*, anyway. But
he knew the bulk of it. And the students weren't numerous: there may
have been less than a dozen out at Rockwell on the West Coast, and
maybe a few more than that, there at Langley.

Another nice thing: in the process, all of us were getting some time
under the hood. God knows that was needed in the Air Corps, then
or any other time. Our Instrument Flight Course was either a by-
product or a natural outgrowth of our navigational training—I've never
been able to decide which.

As for the latter program: it was essential that we should get the
hydrographic office to realize our needs. Desperately we needed new
tables and short cuts, much quicker methods of calculating, speedier
machinery for solving the celestial triangle to get a line of position.
This was all in the mill at that period, but our needs and our demands
were far ahead of any mechanical assistance available. New approaches were being made constantly . . . then it would be discovered
that they were impractical, or could be more readily superseded by a
simpler process.

It seems weird now to look back and observe the great stark staring
fact: no one in this end of the business had really foreseen the long-
range aircraft. Nor, it would seem, had ventured even a guess at the
navigational problems which would ensue. . . . A weather officer on a
surface vessel, comfortably standing by the rail with his sextant in
hand, and shooting the planet Venus at sundown, was one thing. A
navigator in a 150 or 200 mph plane was quite another.

We didn't find any of the answers right off, but our friends kept on trying. I think now of our first celestial computer, known commonly as the Black Box. It was a gadget with counters on it, and cranks which you turned. All it did was solve mechanically the celestial triangle, instead of employing trigonometry and logarithmic tables. You first set in the time, in the form of the local hour angle. Then you set in the latitude, and the altitude of the heavenly body . . . when these all synchronized, you had your answer in longitude.

It was one of those situations where every time you recognize a problem you come up with a new puzzle.

The Navy threw a tantrum at the idea of our flying over water; but we were going to fly over water, and we did. Along the Virginia shoreline. We tried to do all of our navigation between lighthouses which were, of course, precisely located points. You could fly directly over one, and use your driftmeter and your compass, and then use double drifts to get the ground speed—things of that sort. In the short time we were at the school we were actively navigating, and were learning to evaluate our results.

Just as far-reaching as anything else, at least in my particular personal case, was the time under the hood, practicing blind flying. Not much had been done in this line before. There was a major over at the engineering section of Wright Field—man named Ocker—who had been doing a lot of blind work with banks and turns, maneuvers of that sort. The results had been fascinating.

Doubtless our new equipment came as a result of Ocker's initial experiments. The authorities decided to fix up two airplanes for blind instruction—one for the school at Langley and one for Rockwell. In each case it was an O-2 with the rear seat equipped for instrument flying. Very simple instruments installed there: just the bank and turn indicator, with a hood over the top.

As I say, there were only about a dozen students in each place, so we all got in a little time in these blind O-2's, during the two or three months we were down at Langley. It's not too astonishing to record that we were learning to fly straight and level, hold courses, get out of spins—all under the hood. I should say that the average was about twenty-five hours apiece of instrument training under these conditions. In my own case, I was told later that I had achieved more time under the hood than anyone else in the entire Air Corps. I think it was about twenty-seven hours. The program fascinated me. I hung around and pestered my instructors, and managed to rack up that extra time just because I was so hot-and-bothered about the whole thing.

A few of the earliest B-10's soon appeared at Langley, right there in 1933; but more advanced designs were on the way. These would be a great improvement over the first models. We hoped that the advanced B-10's would be delivered while we were still in Virginia, but hoped in vain. It was, after all, a very brief school course. I can't remember that any one of us got checked off in the B-10 while we were then at Langley.

To return to the actual navigational end, we had, besides Gatty, a couple of other people who were a little more knowledgeable than the norm. One, a man by the name of Tommy Thurlow (killed later in an airplane accident) was an accomplished mathematician, assigned to the laboratory at Wright. He came over and helped us as an instructor. So did Norris B. Harbold, a West Point graduate and a fellow classmate of mine at Kelly. He had all sorts of arithmetical accomplishments. He worked closely with Gatty, and I think that the Australian was able to communicate a lot of his ideas to Skippy Harbold, who in turn instructed the rest of us.

Have I said that Gatty couldn't communicate very well, himself, to the ordinary student mind . . . ?

Skippy Harbold could.

In a recent letter, Harbold reminisces concerning Thurlow: "He was a student in the first course at Rockwell; but an astronomy course at Stanford made him more knowledgeable than all others present; so he became an instructor in celestial. . . ."

Skippy points out that Tommy Thurlow was Howard Hughes' navigator on his flight around the world.

He discusses Gatty's methods and accomplishments, but is compelled by the facts to conclude rather gloomily: "Gatty always had about six irons in the fire at one time. Although he was the initial spark, he soon lost interest and went off to endeavors that offered greater return."

Greater return to Harold Gatty, it must be assumed. For nothing at that particular time could have benefited us more.

It would have been a fine thing for the immediate future of our long-range program if we'd had more planes and more instruments available for this type of training. As it was, there were only our couple-of-dozen graduates from those twin navigational schools who had achieved such advanced proficiency. Some of these were destined to be lost between the cracks, or mistakenly shuffled on to other assignments.

As for the bulk of us, scattered back among our various outfits again, I think it was prayed in Washington that we would spread the good news around whenever and wherever possible. In other words, our commanders trusted that little scraps of our advanced training would rub off on the personnel with whom we came in contact. That was the best the Air Corps could hope for at the time.

9

THROUGH 1932 and 1933 my romantic life grew increasingly dependent upon the presence of Miss Helen Maitland. I took every opportunity to see her; and there came abundant opportunities, as my sophistication in the Air Corps increased and as acquaintanceship developed with others of Helen's friends.

There had been and still was a great deal of running to and from Cleveland, if it could possibly be wangled whenever Helen was home for holidays. But she had gone down to Akron by this time, to take a big job (or so it seemed to us) as dental hygienist with the Firestone people.

It so happened that Akron was just about the right distance from Selfridge for those routine cross-country trips we Pursuit people were always making. Fact is, my commanding officers used to be amazed at how willing I was to go to Akron. Anybody else didn't want to go, LeMay was always eager to make the trip for them. Nice guy.

. . . Social excuses develop easily in the young. Our expediting of plans often resembled something out of a Sherlock Holmes detective story. One thing, however, I had realized in the back of my mind—without actually pinning it up on the wall and taking a good look at it. I knew it, yet refused to recognize it officially.

Helen Maitland was a terrific flirt.

And forever I had been schooled in—or at least had adhered to—the notion that coquettes couldn't be trusted. It was rumored (she may even have bragged about it) that she had accumulated three fraternity pins at one time, when she was only a sophomore at Western Reserve. And with each victim being serene in the knowledge that he was the One and Only! Also, I knew for a fact that before I became involved with this killer-diller she had worn two Theta Xi pins alternately, although one belonged to a masochist type who knew all about it, and still kept hanging unhappily around.

But there in 1933, were we engaged? By no means. Some of the younger LeMays were in high school and had to be provided for; it was necessary for me to send home a chunk of my pay each month.

Once again it was a case of, "It may be fine for most people, but not for me." Like a social career back in South High School, marriage was a luxury. It was diamonds and pearls on velvet in a jeweler's window. . . . Somehow most of my friends had managed to acquire a diamond or a pearl by this time. (Grim thought: in some cases a mere rhinestone.) But I just couldn't see myself investing in these gauds. So I sternly kept from thinking how nice it would be.

In October of 1933 I had just left the navigation school at Langley. Had a little leave coming, and went up to Cleveland. Helen, although employed regularly with Firestone those days, was taking a weekend off to go home for a few family delights with her folks, and I was invited to join them. I got along just great with the elder Maitland, Helen's father. I think her mother looked upon me with dark suspicion, because I was an impecunious youngster in the fly business; and in common sense the mother thought her daughter could do better than that.

On arriving in Cleveland, I was thunderstruck at being presented with the news of Helen's engagement. An engagement not to me, but to someone else. She seemed very smug about it. She told me that night, chattering with her usual colorful detail: the fiancé was a doctor, busy at some clinic down in Brazil now, but planning to meet her in Bermuda for a marriage ceremony there.

Secretly I was horrified, but still not too much surprised. Nevertheless I really felt sodden and sad. But I wasn't about to put up a great howl to Helen—wasn't about to get down on my knees and plead with her to demolish this engagement. If that was what she wanted, O.K., let her have it.

(The fact that simultaneously there was a Man Number Three lurking somewhere in the background, who also considered himself engaged to Miss Maitland, was something which didn't come out at that moment. I guess the reader knows by this time that eventually I became wedded to the Ohio State Flirt Champion.)

We have two versions in the family about subsequent occurrences of that weekend, just as most husbands and wives do. Helen's story goes that, on my departure, she asked me when I was coming back again. I said, "I won't come back until you get over this nonsense."

My memory runs differently. I say that she stood there in the hall doorway and asked, "Well, Curt, when are you coming back?"

"Not coming back."

"You're *not?*"

"Nope."

I declare that we didn't patch it up until she had gone through some lengthy Italian medieval plot about luring me down there for her sister's wedding, and getting me to substitute at the last minute as best man for her brother-in-law.

She says that's absurd. She says that I came running back in no time at all, and she very generously dissolved all her other engagements; and we agreed that very month to get married just as soon as possible. Doesn't matter really. Point is, we were married on June 9th, 1934. Undoubtedly we would have been married a lot sooner if suddenly the AC flyers hadn't had to go into the air mail business.

10

IN FEBRUARY, 1934, President Roosevelt cancelled the mail contracts which had been given to various airlines, and ordered the U. S. Army to take over the flying of the mail.

Whenever I hear the air mail episode mentioned, automatically one thing rises before my eyes very clearly. It is not, as might be believed, a graph or a breakdown or a summary of Army Air Corps mail operations.

Mileage of scheduled trips flown: 1,590,155 miles. Mail poundage flown: 777,389 pounds. Actual hours flown, carrying the mail: 14, 108:37 hours.

Correct. But that's not what I see. I see a stewpot on a plumber's burner.

. . . It is an evil March day down in the Carolinas. Wet snow drives from the northwest, then changes quickly from wet snow to a storm of sleet; then melts into rain, congeals into sleet once more. The ceiling is pulled away down over the field. Horizontal visibility is lousy. So the mail plane is sitting grimly in an open shed-like hangar. I am standing around just as grimly, looking across that field and cussing the weather.

I do not cuss the maintenance men. They have done everything that good mechanics could possibly do, to get my aircraft ready for this flight; and now they are having a meal, or are about to have one. Call it dinner, call it lunch (the word *brunch* had not offended our ears as yet). Call it a belated breakfast . . . it was food. It was important. It was stew.

Didn't cost much. I don't know where they dug up their stewpot, but they had bought a few vegetables and some chunks of soup-bone with not a lot of meat sticking to it. This was going to be mighty thin stew. And where were they cooking it? Over a plumber's flame at the corner of the hangar. That was the way the Air Corps people lived, the way they fed themselves.

Figure it out. President Roosevelt issued his order to Postmaster-General James A. Farley on the 9th of February, 1934. Major-General Benjamin D. Foulois, Chief of the Army Air Corps, was ordered to start flying the mail on Monday, February 19th. We had just ten days in which to set up shop.

. . . Air Corps was a skinny little entity in those days. We boasted exactly thirteen hundred and seventy-two Regular officers on active duty, in and outside of the Continental United States. Every domestic base drew from the same depot: Wright Field, near Dayton, Ohio. So just the logistic aspect of these activities—to get supplies spread out so that we could operate all through the countryside—was an overwhelming task.

Once again, to get back to that pot of stew on the plumber's burner—

There was no such thing as per diem paid under normal circumstances. About the only time we ever collected any subsistence expenses for a trip was when we went to the factory to pick up new airplanes. I think this was because there was money available in the procurement funds for errands of that sort. It was regarded as part of the cost of the aircraft itself. But never had any per diem, as such, been appropriated for other purposes and shelled out to us.

If we went on maneuvers or aerial demonstrations, necessarily we had our ground people along for maintenance purposes. Then the organizations had their own messes set up. And on a little trip which wasn't any part of a laid-on exercise, you just went and paid your own expenses.

No one in the Air Corps had ever run into a contingency like the air mail problem before. We were ordered quickly away from our bases, slashed into tiny detachments, and scattered all over the Nation. We were to set up new mail stations and fly new mail runs. No messes were established, no quarters provided: there just wasn't any money for such a program. Everybody was out on his own. If you were one of the few lucky stiffs who had a sizable bank account, well and good. You could write checks and get them cashed; and you ate steaks, and you slept on clean new sheets, and all the rest of it. But if you didn't have any money (most folks didn't) you got along as best you could.

The monthly wage of a private in those days was twenty-one bucks. We second lieutenants got that same old hundred-and-twenty-five a month, plus flying pay and allowances to practically double the amount. So it was the enlisted men who ran out of money first. They had so much less to start with.

They were eating homemade mulligan and they were sleeping on planks laid across saw-horses in cold hangars. Lucky to be out of the rain. And they were scrounging around for blankets.

A sergeant would come beaming in and tell how that nice old lady at the hot dog stand down on the corner—the one they all owed for hot dogs and hamburgers, until they were ashamed to ask for any more credit— That nice old lady had just given him a pillow!—she said she didn't need it, and she had found out he didn't have any pillow; so she said, what good was that thing doing, lying on her sofa? And she up and gave it to the sergeant. . . .

A wartime psychology ruled. The boys were out fighting and bleeding and dying; generous-hearted folks tried to do whatever they could for them. If one end of your run was at—say, Newark, New Jersey— and you had a second cousin living in Newark— Cousin Emily might have a spare bed. Lucky you.

If people on active duty in the Air Corps at that time had been polled as to their opinion of Congress, the Congressmen would have shuddered. It took that Congress until the 27th day of March to appropriate an excruciatingly generous five-dollar per day allowance for our living expenses. Meanwhile, it was hand-to-mouth.

First off I was ordered to Atlanta but I didn't stay there long. Another set of orders sent me right back up to Richmond. My mail run was from Richmond to Greensboro, North Carolina. On this run I flew mostly an O-2.

. . . Your aircraft would be there in front of the hangar on an old cracked concrete apron, and you'd wait for the mail to be sent out from the Post Office in a truck, all sacked up. There were special forms for registered mail, insured mail and so on; you had some paper work to do on that. There was a manifest also for the ordinary mail.

Then the crew would load it into the airplane. We'd stuff mail in, wherever we could get a sack in: in the small baggage compartment under the rear cockpit, under the cowling, everyplace else.

(Regret to state that some mail was lost, and lost for a long time, because it had slipped away up under the cowling, and people didn't find that little sack when they were unloading the stuff at the other end. They wouldn't find it, perhaps, until they started to do a regular inspection job on the aircraft.)

. . . Then, with all the sacks loaded, you'd taxi and take off, and lug the mail down to the end of your run.

We couldn't help wondering what was in those dirty drab sacks.

Dear Gladdy, Just got time for a few quick lines to tell you that I love you—

I am sending herewith a refill prescription order for the medication prescribed by me for Mrs. Ellis—

Sorry to have to inform you that your employment with this company will terminate on the last day of this month. Mr. Aaronson is reorganizing, and it has been decided that—

Honest to Pete, honey, I never did care for Jimmy! When I pretended that I was crazy about dancing with him I was only kidding—

Enclosed check for five thousand, six hundred and thirty-three dollars and seven cents in full settlement for—

We weren't wild romancers or would-be poets or novelists or anything like that. We were just young Air Corps types who had been ordered to perform a difficult drudgery and, in most cases, were doing the best we could.

But we were human. It would be impossible for any human being to be given suddenly this strange unprecedented assignment, and not get to speculating about the load he carried when he was up there alone with the engine and the wind.

When people who are old enough to remember that late winter and early spring of 1934 think about the Army flying the mail, they have a vague but shuddering recollection of vastly more casualties than actually were incurred.

This followed logically on the public hysteria attending every announcement of an airplane's meeting with disaster.

The press didn't discriminate too accurately in its evaluation of such accidents. Every Air Corps plane which crashed during that period was adjudged to be mixed up, one way or another, with the mail business.

It is readily forgotten by the bulk of civilians—or it might be a fact neglected from its very beginnings—that there is a normal attrition in any flying establishment. So many airplanes fly, so many people fly them, such-and-such a hazard prevails; the weather has deteriorated; this-or-that piece of mechanical equipment decides to malfunction— You're going to have accidents.

What we've always tried to do is to keep that percentage *down*. That's why we have immutable rules, definite procedures, endless inspections. (One whole team in the modern Air Force is known as Flying Safety.)

Sounds a little cold-blooded maybe. But every pilot is not at a peak of one hundred per cent efficiency one hundred per cent of the time. *There will be accidents.*

Also it must be remembered that many newspapers and radio stations of 1934 were apt to slant any and every story in order to discredit the Roosevelt Administration. Editorially it was emphasized that the President or the Postmaster-General or the Secretary of War or the Commander of the Army Air Corps— Someone was a deliberate butcher. Maybe the whole bunch.

Also publicity and promotion people for those commercial airlines, which had been relieved of their lucrative contracts, were not behindhand in recognizing the emotional value of Air Corps deaths. The airlines wanted to get the mail back, period.

A book called *The Airmail. Jennies to Jets*, which appeared as recently as 1951, exemplifies the attitude described above. Observe the following quotation:

"This terrible and needless slaughter continued through the end of February and into March. . . . Each day the stories in the newspapers were worse. Deaths, injuries, planes forced down, planes washed out."

The public bought the idea (and still retains it) that scores of Air

Corps pilots lost their lives in an heroic but absurd effort to emulate the superb performance of the commercial airlines.

Let us go probing into the files of the USAF Historical Division. We find that there were four deaths while actually flying the mail: Lowry, Sell, Weinecke, Wood. Three men died in flights incident to air mail activity, but prior to the beginning of operations: Grenier, White, Eastham. During the period of operations, three people were killed in training: Howard, Kerwin, Richardson. And a pilot named McDermott went to his death during an administrative flight associated with the air mail.

There seems to have been some discussion in 1934 as to whether an additional name should have been included—that of McAllister, a Reserve officer who died near Duncansville, Pennsylvania, on 5 April. But in a report to the Executive Officer, Military Intelligence Division, G-2, General Staff, the PRO of that same Military Intelligence Division "stated that this accident 'had no connection with the air mail.'"

There were many accidents, however, besides these. I was lucky and had none. But even as good a flyer as Pete Quesada got—shall we say, delayed—up in Pennsylvania, and had to walk away from it.

Despite all exaggerations and misconceptions, that wave of public concern had a valuable repercussive effect. I'll go into that later.

Our chief problem was in staying alive in a different way. Our chief problem was not to starve to death, and not to sleep out in the rain.

Naturally it would have been more convenient to use a hotel at either end of the run, if we could have afforded to do so. Most of us started out that way, but we ran out of cash. Then it was a case of furnished rooms, when and if we could get them. Or even of sleeping in hangars along with the ground crew.

My own situation down in Dixie, to start with, was fairly simple. They scheduled one flight each way, per day, and there were two of us on that route to do it. I worked opposite another second lieutenant; but I did more flying than he did because I had more experience. If there was an extra flight I usually made it. If something happened that both of us were caught at the same end of the line, I usually went down to the other end and took that extra flight.

It was SOP for one of us to be in Richmond and the other in Greensboro. We kept a room at each end of the line. Theoretically one of us was in each room each night. (Frequently on other runs, in other people's experience, there was not only one sleepy lieutenant to a rooming-house room: there might be two or even more, if bad weather had fouled everything up. There was also that business about sacking up at Cousin Emily's house in Newark; and sometimes being a guest in a house where you didn't even know the people.)

Americans rose in a kind of desperate hospitality. There were kindly citizens who took those poor homeless waifs in, and offered them every generosity. I remember from personal observation that many people —boarding-house keepers, or small restaurant owners, or grocers—extended credit far beyond their ordinary economic ability to offer it. Many doors were opened, and many hearts.

This was like a war exercise which had come on overnight: it demanded an enormous spread of supplies. So in effect it *was* a wartime exercise, insofar as the logistics people were concerned.

I was a GI pilot. I didn't get into any of the staff work, the planning for operations or supply. There were many hold-ups; but they weren't apparent to us boys out in the field. None of my flights was ever cancelled because the airplane wouldn't fly; nor do I remember my airplane ever quitting on me, due to bad maintenance. The maintenance people did a remarkable job. Consider this: if a mechanic needed a wrench of a certain type, there was no way for him to get it except to go to a hardware shop and buy it out of his own money.

Everyone turned out, just as if we were going into battle. Men worked days and nights to get things going.

As a matter of fact we overdid it: that's the reason we lost some people and wrecked a lot of airplanes. We were attempting to do more than we were capable of doing at that time, or had the equipment to do.

You might say that the first flyaway kit which later we devised so successfully for the Strategic Air Command— You might say that the first flyaway kit was used while we were spread around on the air mail. When we needed parts, we flew them around to the various little fields. Sometimes mail and parts were all mixed up together in the airplanes.

If you were to reëxamine newspapers of this period you could easily gather the idea that the Army's flying of the air mail was one enormous catastrophe—that the Army just couldn't do it. This is not exactly the case. We certainly weren't equipped to do it at the onset, but we were getting equipped very rapidly.

Congress began to wake up to the fact that we needed help and some money in this field, and with many a yawn and groan they began to get something done about it.

. . . I remember a shopworn clipping from the *New York Times*, date of March 23rd, 1934. This clipping was all fuzzed up from much handling, and we wished that the citizen who wrote that letter to the *Times* had signed his name (so that we could express our appreciation) instead of just signing Citizen.

"Can we assume," Citizen wrote, "that . . . the gods will awake us a year before the guns are loosed?"

Americans were learning to their astonishment and terror that the Army Air Corps had been starved to death. This was something which we were glad to have the public understand, even at long last.

(1) Erving LeMay and Arizona Carpenter—their wedding picture, 1905

(2) Curtis Emerson LeMay, 1907

(3) "I liked sitting on the donkey."

(4) Young LeMays at the Panama-Pacific International Exposition, 1915. "If you look close, you can see a couple of airplanes."

(5) "A Chamber of Horrors devoted to smashed aircraft . . . *Mine.*"

(6) Sworn into the Regular Army Air Corps, February 1, 1930, Selfridge Field—Second-Lieutenant LeMay, third from left

(7) A water-cooled Curtiss P-1

(8) LeMay in the cockpit of his P-1

(9) Bob Olds

(10) LeMay, 1931—"Arranged a couple of blind dates for us: Helen Maitland and another girl."

(11) CCC camp

(12) When the U.S. Army carried the U.S. Mail

(13) Airborne pony express—an 0-19 flies the mail over Elkhorn Ridge

(14) Half the country's entire Heavy Bombardment force en route non-stop to Buenos Aires, Argentina, February 20, 1938. Lead navigator was First-Lieutenant Curtis E. LeMay.

(15) The officers of the lead B-17 on the non-stop flight to Bogotá, Colombia, 1938—Aircraft Commander C. V. Haynes is standing to LeMay's left

(16) LeMay directs successful *Rex* intercept 776 miles out to sea—May 12, 1938. "1225 . . . Dead ahead was the Italian liner."

(17) Japanese strike photo of Wheeler Field—December 7, 1941

(18) LeMay, a father at last, holds seven-month-old Janie

(19) The commander of the 305th Bomb Group with Joe Preston

General Benny Foulois declared a King's-X of eight days, there in March. Some new patterns and policies were being worked out. This was to draw breath, and more or less reassemble ourselves after the first desperate encountering of the problem. So the Air Corps licked its wounds for a week, and then started in again on a somewhat curtailed scheme of operations.

In the meantime I was ordered up to Wright Field. They had started a new school, a Blind Landing School.

You must remember that at this time we didn't have much in the way of instruments in our airplanes. We were away behind. There was practically no instrument flying in the Air Corps then. You flew when you could see. If you couldn't see you didn't fly. I recall that once, long before the air mail incident, we came in to Uniontown, Pennsylvania, on our way to Washington or Langley. If we couldn't see to get over the mountains, we couldn't get over the mountains. *We sat at Uniontown for ten days.*

So in flying the mail we never flew on instruments. Weren't equipped for it, nor were we trained for it either. But you'll recall that I had gone to the navigation school, and chalked up those hours under the hood before the air mail thing started in. Guess it was natural for me to be picked as a candidate for the Blind Landing School.

Up there at Wright we trained on O-2's, then finished by getting checked off on the B-10. In this case it was to *fly* the B-10, as well as to be able to fly on instruments and make blind landings.

On graduation in May, we took a B-10 and went back to the air mail. I was ordered to Cleveland then, with that same B-10. It was a brand new airplane and everybody wanted to fly it. Somebody else grabbed it and made a flight to Chicago. So the B-10 was gone, and I had to make my own air mail flight to Chicago in an O-38. I got in one trip; then the mail job folded up on us.

A conference of airline operators had been called by Postmaster-General Farley on April 20th, and at that conference bids had been opened for reinstatement of civilian air mail routes. Most of the companies had been reorganized because of a restriction stemming from charges of venal conditions at the awarding of the original contracts. Through the technicality of reorganization, commercial airlines got back into the air mail pattern once more.

The very last mail flown by the Army was sent across the Continent in "new Curtis attack planes and Martin bombers." They made it all the way from San Francisco to Newark in fourteen hours and eight minutes. Pretty good, for the time and the conditions and the aircraft involved.

But we who had studied at the Blind Landing School were disappointed bitterly. We had learned that blind landing was a simple thing, though not foolproof by any means. You wound up by getting a glide path established after you started heading into the field, and you sat there waiting until you hit the ground. We had just really become operational, and now here we were with our war taken away from us.

So much, so very much, had been learned and learned the hard way. At first they'd tried to keep the bomber boys in bombers and the fighter boys in fighter aircraft. But before long we were flying anything that stood on the flight line: P-12's, O-2's, B-2's—the Keystone bombers—

Our crew chief system had been whetted up, clean and sharp. The crew chief was the chief mechanic on a particular airplane, and he had his bunch of assistants to help him. An old crew chief knew everything there was to know about that airplane, and the whole crew went along with it if it moved to a new station. Considering everything, we enjoyed the best maintenance in the world. Maybe these guys on the ground didn't have a lot of the tools and equipment they should have had, but they really *knew* what equipment they did have. They were devoted. *Dedicated* wouldn't be too strong a word.

As for attrition, the lives which were lost, the planes which were smashed— That was the result of people flying over their heads. They were trying to get that mail through when they didn't have the proper equipment or the proper training to fly the instrument weather that we were trying to fly. If ever the maintenance was down a little bit, it was down not because of lack of skill, but only lack of parts and equipment. Never were there enough tools furnished by the Government. That's why a sergeant went out and bought a wrench out of his own dough.

We were just getting able to do a good job of flying the mail, when they cancelled it and gave it back to the commercial folks.

But one thing had been dramatized ably, and it was valuable to us that the newspaper people played it up the way they did. Full attention was called to the fact that we had been pauperized: the Air Corps had not been getting anything like the money it needed, and that's the reason we were in such a beggarly condition. It focused attention, and made it possible for us to get a terrific boost. Congress was spurred into action by the revealing of our shortcomings. We had taken an enormous step forward.

Let's go back to this blind instrument business for a minute. Here we were, with brand new equipment on the B-10's to make those blind landings. The civilian airlines weren't even close to that in 1934. To be perfectly frank, they're not close to it yet.

We were actually making those blind landings, we were landing under the hood. We were doing it, and doing it damn well. The big commercial airplanes of today which carry the mail don't do that now.

Naturally we're talking about a different situation. The skies weren't full of airplanes, as they are in this year of 1965. We didn't have runways then on our wide fields, so you didn't have to be too precise about getting on a runway. You came in, and just sat there, and waited and waited, and then you came down and were rolling on the ground. With planes which landed in a comparatively short distance, with big fields— You could do a thing like that.

Within a couple of weeks, or maybe three at the most, back there in 1934, we of the Air Corps would have had a transcontinental airline which could have landed on instruments all the way across the Nation: the first all-weather airline.

If we'd been allowed to go a little bit further I think we would have learned more, and more quickly than we actually did. It would have benefited us when it came to World War II, now rumbling only a few years in the future. Of course it was asking a lot, and in the face of all that hysterical popular pressure, for the President not to give the mail back to the Indians quite so soon. We in the Air Corps would have been well availed by more extensive opportunity. Too bad President Roosevelt couldn't have seen that.

11

It was duly announced that Saturday, June 9th, was the fatal day on which Miss Helen Maitland and Lieutenant Curtis E. LeMay would be united in bonds of holy matrimony. The flap was on.

Never before had I realized that there was so much to the mere mechanical process of getting married. For complication, the air mail wasn't in it. Whenever I was in touch with Helen—which was as frequently as could be managed—I was notified concerning major crises which ensued about every two hours, and minor ones every five minutes.

I had my own worries, and decided to do something about that, too. It was this business about possibly being transferred to a new base. I'd seen that happen to a lot of people: it wasn't any fun for either of them, especially for the new bride.

The Army displayed diabolical efficiency in dealing with such matters. It was as if a witch-like Board sat in some haunted cavern, looked over the lists, and said, "Now, who's nicely settled down in some new quarters? Let's put *him* on the list for this far-distant assignment—and *immediately*."

Chances were, it seemed to me, that I might be ordered out very soon. As June arrived, I figured that I had been a Regular Army officer for four years and four months, and during all that time was home-based at Selfridge. There was my Detached Service down at Norton; there were the few months with the CCC, and recent months with the air mail; but those last two calamities were something not peculiar to my own situation in life—they were happening to everybody. So, to all intents and purposes, I could look for a change. The Air Corps wasn't notorious for having its personnel take root and grow into the soil.

A little more bull-by-the-horns, I thought, and watched my chance to make a trip to Washington. Once there I headed for the office of the Chief of Personnel, but fast. It was normal to do this: everybody who went through Washington was always scooting over there to take a look at their Efficiency Reports, and so on. It was a simple procedure to check with the Personnel people, to see if they had any plans for sending me overseas.

. . . I pointed out to them that I'd been up there in Michigan over four years, and naturally expected a transfer along about now.

The answer? "Relax, Lieutenant. Nothing in sight for you. Nothing whatever."

This made all the difference in the world, and I heaved a sigh of relief. Felt pretty smart, too. This was the way to handle such situations: go to the horse's mouth and find out. Take my friend Bryant Boatner—he had received orders that he was to depart for Hawaii in September; and he and his wife had barely three months in which to get ready for the move. . . .

But Helen and I could approach this business of furnishing our new home, with light hearts. There would be a lot of fixing up to do. . . .

At that time the officers' quarters at Selfridge had just been built, and the houses were really very nice. Of course you had to have some degree of rank in order to live on the Base. I was still only a second lieutenant. Matter of fact, almost *everybody* was a second lieutenant. We had two majors, a couple or three captains, a couple or three first lieutenants, and about ninety-five second lieutenants. At various times there was considerable jockeying around to get hold of these quarters, because most of us were of marriageable age. (I was one of the last to be married, of my contemporaries, except for those who never married at all.) But there was a set of quarters available, and I was entitled to them. . . . So O.K., Helen, let's see what's in the hope chest. (All the girls had hope chests in those days; but it took a lot more than their contents to furnish up a home.)

Ten days leave was coming. After considerable confabulation, we decided that I should take this leave with the wedding day in the middle—arrive in Cleveland a few days beforehand; and we'd depart a few days after. That would make it all easier from the social standpoint. We had no wish for a wedding trip, anyway—wanted to spend our time and money in fixing up our home. Once again: I had never known there was so much to the job.

Frantic letter from my bride-to-be. "You promised that you would go right over and measure those *windows* and send me the dimensions, and you haven't *done it*. Now, you get over there right *away*, because I've *got* to know how much *material. . . .*"

I thought the Moment of Truth would never arrive, but it did. We both said *I do* smack in the middle of one of the biggest fights we ever had. The subject was entirely hirsute. Helen announced that she was going to have her hair trimmed much shorter than the way she had been wearing it, and I didn't like this. Told her so, and told her not to cut her hair; if she did, I'd grow a mustache. Guess she thought I was bluffing, but I wasn't. She went ahead and cut off some of my very favorite hair from her head, so I grew the mustache. This was a mistake, and I realized it about as soon as anybody else, but I had to act tough for a while. Then I let Helen win out, and shaved off the mustache, and that was a great victory for the bride. . . . Good idea to let them have obvious victories every now and then. Helps the morale.

So we shook the rice out of our ears, and managed to make a sneakaway from celebrating friends, and honeymooned in a Cleveland hotel for a couple of days. Then we continued the honeymoon in new quarters at Selfridge . . . shot all our meager savings on curtains and bedspreads and furniture and rugs. Every time Helen hemmed a new piece of cretonne, I congratulated myself that I had gone to Washington, down to that Personnel office, and found out exactly how things stood.

We savored this rose-covered-cottage mood for about ten or eleven weeks. Then I was told that the adjutant wanted to see me. . . .

This was really in the Department of the Feeble Smile. I went home to give Helen the glad word.

"We are assigned," I told her, "to the Sixth Pursuit Squadron at Schofield Barracks, Wheeler Field, Hawaii."

"But you went down to Personnel— They told you, they *assured* you—"

"Yeah. I'm smart that way. Always go in advance and find out."

"But— Why, Boatner's going this month, and *he* had *his* orders away back in *June*, and— Curt, when must we leave?"

"Week from Tuesday."

"But why do we *have* to go to Hawaii? Are they suddenly expanding the Air Corps or—or something?"

"Nope. They plan ahead. They decide who they're going to move out to a place like that; and they get people all assigned and listed and notified; and then people get sick and can't go, or people die and can't go, and—"

No use standing there holding a wake on the subject. We quit yakking and started packing.

The biggest troop transport operated by the Army was the *Republic,* and that was ours. In regular procedure we were ordered to our port a couple of days before we were due to sail, to get through necessary red tape, have papers processed, etc. It was essential that we ship our household goods and personal possessions immediately on receipt of those devastating new orders. This household stuff had to get to New York before we did, in order to be loaded on the same vessel. Our car would go on the ship as well.

Interesting to observe how they ran the transport business in those days. (Maybe they still do.) In this instance of September, 1934, and in the case of the *Republic,* there was an unexpected delay. Something was wrong with the ship's machinery; it had to be rectified. She couldn't sail on the appointed date, and here was a whole horde of people waiting to travel on her.

For instance, us. We had reached New York at the required time and were staying at the St. George Hotel in Brooklyn. When it became evident that the sailing date must be set back, prospective passengers were ordered out to the Port of Embarkation *en masse.* There were a few quarters there, which were soon overflowing; but another transport lay in the harbor, the *St. Mihiel.* Promptly the *St. Mihiel* became a vast hotel or barracks to accommodate the troops who were rotating overseas with their families. Families always went along with the enlisted men, and most of the officers were accompanied by dependents. Additional expense loomed, the moment a sailing was delayed. The majority of those people just couldn't have made it—didn't have the extra cash to tide them over. This arranging of quarters and mess on another ship was just about the sharpest thing that could have been done.

On embarkation date everybody moved back aboard the *Republic,* and off we sailed.

At the Canal Zone, people who were ordered to Panamanian duty disembarked and were replaced by military personnel and dependents en route back to the United States from Panama. They boarded the *Republic* and were carried up to San Francisco, and disembarked there —at least, all who were destined for stations in the western part of the United States. Probably those headed for duty in the Middle West or along the Atlantic seaboard simply waited in Panama until there came a military transport bound for New York, and then sailed on that.

I was interested in all this deployment and re-deployment, and in studying out the reasons. (Just as always I'd been vitally interested in mess facilities.) Talked to some of the transportation officers. Discovered one—to me—very amazing thing: i.e., it would have been cheaper

to send us from Selfridge to New York, *and then all the way around
Cape Horn* and up through the Pacific to San Francisco— It would have
been cheaper to do this than to send us by rail from Michigan to the
West Coast.

That stuck in my mind.

Astonishing; but sometimes the cheapest thing is also the most com-
mon-sensible thing to do.

In Hawaii they didn't have enough quarters to go around, and there
I didn't have enough rank to achieve quarters on the Base. At least,
not at first. We had to find housing off the Base, and that turned into
a real hunt. Helen couldn't stand to even think of Selfridge. She remembered the minimums which had formed in her mind as a result of
that comfortable experience of two or three months. She needed so
much kitchen space, so many bedrooms, so on, so on; and nothing like
that existed on Oahu. What we finally settled for was a beach cottage
down on the north shore of the island. It looked like something out of
the old play *Rain* with Sadie Thompson and all, and a tropical down-
pour a-pouring. We had a living-room; one bedroom; tiny kitchen
opening right onto the beach. No hot water in the bath. Matter of fact,
the bath was a shower, with a floor made of wooden slats. You stood
on the slats, and the water went right through to the sand . . . we were
on the beach literally, if not figuratively.

Just as at Selfridge, I had a lot of jobs; everybody did. Forever there
were several chores demanding your attention simultaneously (man
gets mixed up now in his recollection, trying to recall where and when,
and just how many jobs he had at any given moment, and what they
were). One time or another, there at Wheeler, I appeared in the role
of Communications Officer, Assistant Operations Officer, Engineering
Officer, Mess Officer— There were a lot of other odds and ends too.
There just weren't enough people to fill the jobs; so an individual had
to double or triple or quadruple in brass, like oldtime musicians. Or
like an actor in a barnstorming company, he had to change hats repeatedly in the course of a day. There was never a full complement.
You had a group of pilots, and they all flew as air crew members; but
they had their ground assignments—and many—when they weren't flying. The same people who flew the airplanes, and fought the airplanes,
also administered and staffed the squadron.

Ours was a composite group. We had two Pursuit squadrons and an
Attack squadron, and what we called a Service squadron—really a
maintenance and housekeeping outfit which ran the Base. It was very
good to have your own maintenance. That knowledge came back to me
forcefully and profitably in a future time.

Next thing I knew, however, I was handed a schoolmaster's mortar-board on top of everything else. Navigational training of 1933 under the Gatty plan had come back to haunt me.

I discovered that my old friend John Egan was down at Luke, doing the same thing with the Bomber people which I was assigned to do at Wheeler. Let me explain that there were two John Egans: one was a fighter type up at Selfridge, an older man than I by several years. The John Waldron Egan to whom I'm referring was a tall blue-eyed calm-spoken character who graduated in our class at Kelly in 1929. Nowadays he was stationed at Luke Field on Ford Island, where Observation and Bomber folks were organized into another composite group.

Well, John and I got together and shook our heads over the whole business. He had been in the Gatty program also—went to the Rock-well school in California while I was at Langley. Each of us had in-gested the same course and we had arrived at a mutual verdict. We knew for a certainty that *no one there in Hawaii was going to learn any navigation in a program which allotted one hour per week* to this in-tricate and rewarding study. Actually all they were offering was what-ever navigational studies might be included, along with a variety of other subjects, as a part of the regular ground school course. Everyone took this. It was more of a review than anything else.

What the Air Corps would need in the foreseeable future, it seemed to John Egan and myself, was more and more men specifically trained for navigation—not those who had just dabbled in it. The thing to do, we agreed, was to go to our respective commanding officers and receive permission to approach the department commander of the air forces in the district. This was (then) Colonel Delos C. Emmons.

. . . A couple of very nervous but still determined second lieutenants waited respectfully in Colonel Emmons' anteroom, and sweated it out until we were called upon to present our case. We may have been frightened, true; but we were by no means uncertain in our approach. We had spent a lot of time figuring out just what we were going to say. It was good, both for us and for the immediate future of naviga-tional training, that Emmons was a forward-looking man. In no time at all we got the green light. Egan moved up from Luke and joined me at Wheeler, and we set up the curriculum.

It was a full-time school, and we had a dozen students assigned to us to start, on what we determined should be a three months' course. More than that, we had assigned also an amphibian: an OA-4. And soon we got a second (those were the old twin-engined types). Seems like the Navy didn't relish the idea of our tooling amphibians around—certainly that implied a program of use over water—but nevertheless the Air Corps owned a few of them in Hawaii. As for these special navigational school OA-4's, we flew the damn things to death.

I set up the class in two parts: one section would be flying, the other section in ground school. Then switch.

True, there had always been a navigation school of sorts in Hawaii; but it was mainly pilotage, with a little bit of dead reckoning, and schooling on the compass . . . some deviation . . . just plain simple pilotage and dead reckoning was practically all that had ever been taught.

Now we were going ahead with celestial. I need scarcely add that it was essential for the two ambitious instructors to keep well in advance of their students. We worked all day with our scholars; then we had to drive ourselves through the evening hours as insurance against questions which might come up the next day.

Poor Helen. Freshly arrived on Oahu, and so very recently married, she was still entertaining all sorts of romantic notions about tropical surf on the beach, and lover-like strollings in which we would wander forth in a kind of hibiscus-hued dusk to watch the moon come up beyond the cocoanuts. We wandered forth all right, but I needed to do homework just to keep ahead of that damn class. So it was necessary to take a position out there on the beach, and make celestial shots of the stars; then Helen would have to hold the flashlight while I made my calculations. It was pretty shattering to her previously treasured romantic concepts. She's still griping about that, more than thirty years later.

But John and I really got ahead of the game at school. Those amphibians made all the difference. It was a joy to see how zealous our students were, biting deeply into the problem of long-range navigation for the first time, and flying over water. As we had done on the Virginia coast near Langley, we tried to do our navigation between lighthouses—precisely located points. Same old driftmeter and compass routine.

Hard work or no hard work, John and I were happy as larks. We recalled how we had gone to our respective commanders in order eventually to get permission to see Colonel Emmons, and how in neither case was there too much interest; but we had pestered around and pestered around, until finally they let us go to the overall air commander. I don't know what Emmons' antecedent history had been—whether he was an old Signal Corps type or not. But he was a wise enough Air Corps officer to foresee that celestial navigation was an essential of the future. He wasn't afraid to give his O.K. for the formation of a class and a program which had never existed before—had never been countenanced, requested, or even dreamed of.

On top of everything else, Egan and I were drawing dividends from the experience too. For we still had personally a lot to learn about navigation; would have, for a long time to come.

Our students were from both Luke and Wheeler. There were

Bomber people and Pursuit people and Attack people in attendance, and we ran several classes through. To the best of my recollection, that would have been three classes in an overall period of nine months. Then we ran out of material and the school had a Fire Sale and closed down.

We were always getting short of personnel out there. Once I remember at Wheeler we were down to twenty-seven officers. Far as human resources were concerned, we just didn't have 'em. For that reason the deal was stopped—not because it was frowned upon by our commanders. Already it had become apparent that there was a realistic advantage to the whole thing, an accrual for the future. Some thirty or forty more career people were now equipped to wrestle firsthand with the problems of long-range navigation over water.

In normal operations at Wheeler you'd get up and fly around the island to the right, or fly around the island to the left, and that was it. There were safety reasons and policy reasons for our not going out to sea. Safety: folks didn't think that we could get back. Policy: the Navy raised hell.

But during school months I had taken this situation apart and examined it. Didn't see any reason why we couldn't conduct flights in an amphibian out to Bird Island. (That's also called Niihau; it's west and a little south of Kauai, about a hundred and fifty miles from Oahu.) But in those dark ages it was a very venturesome thing for a commander to approve.

I felt that the risk was only implied and not actual. "I'm positive, sir," I said to my CO, "that we can find the island."

He shook his head. "Look on the chart here. See what it says? *Position doubtful*. It hasn't been precisely surveyed in."

I had two choices . . . sit back and accept the verdict, and say, "Sorry I bothered you," thus yielding to the whole business about the island not being accurately placed on the chart.

Or I could stick my neck away out, which I did.

"Actually, sir, that doesn't make any difference. Because the island is fairly close. Under certain conditions of visibility we can see it when we've got a little altitude along the coastline here. We'll find the island; no trouble about that. And if we *don't* find it, we'll just turn around and come home after we've run a search problem. No danger whatsoever."

It struck me that already those of us juniors who had had the benefit of up-to-date navigational research and instruction were way ahead of our seniors who hadn't had it. There seemed to be some awe in his voice as he asked, "How are you going to get back?"

Nothing to do but to say merely: "Our navigation is precise enough for that."

In the end he was convinced, and gave his permission. Before long all the crews were going out to Niihau. It was a damn good demonstration in the art of building up confidence in students. We were shooting for a dead-reckoning area of about a quarter of a degree or, say, a quarter of a mile in-sixty-miles-away. Consistently we hit it. When the students found that they could do this again and again, they began to feel like celebrating Old Home Week.

We received no protest directly from the Navy at this time. That came later. It was the ancient sore subject again: the weed-grown question of surface vessels' vulnerability to air attack. They realized that an exercise such as ours, suggesting future long-range navigation by aircraft over water, would eventually point up that same vulnerability.

More tenacious than this, however, was the tradition that the ocean was the Navy's sphere of operation, and Army airplanes shouldn't be flying over it—they ought to fly over land.

About the same time we had new developments, coincidental with the arrival of a major named Clayton L. Bissell.

I relax into a lot of old-age musing now, trying to decide just what to say about Major Bissell. (A major-general when he retired.) He possessed a lot of energy and a lot of ideas, and was responsible for a much more realistic training program than we had had out there in Hawaii before. His job was that of Operations Officer for our composite Group. At one time he had been an aide to General Billy Mitchell. Such an association loomed importantly in any airman's career, at least when it came to taking a factual view of things.

Not long ago I sat with another oldtimer, and we both spoke of Bissell. Finally the other veteran summed it up, at least to his own satisfaction. He said, "You know, he did a lot of good; but he made everybody mad doing it." Thinking back on the whole deal now, you couldn't imagine Bissell's ever winning any popularity contests with his associates or subordinates. But there have been plenty of times in my own career when I wouldn't have won any such contests either. Fact is, I would have been in the Tail-End-Charley position.

. . . You mention the name of this officer, and immediately you'll hear the crackle of live ammunition and the thump of live bombs. He got hold of the ordnance; that was something no one else had ever done before. We ex-Selfridge folks of course had fired live ammunition . . . that was in the little training program where we flew to Oscoda each summer, where we could fire on the margin of Lake Huron. There was no place for us to shoot, anywhere in the Selfridge area. So we had the so-called matches down at Langley for those of us who could make the grade to get there, and that was that.

Very shortly our new Operations Officer at Wheeler had us bursting out with live stuff all over the place. I still remember the thrill in that moment when I dropped a live bomb. First time I'd ever had the opportunity. We'd all dropped practice bombs, yes. But a live bomb—

Major Bissell secured some realistic targets, too: some old salvaged boats. He needed the Navy's coöperation for this, and to his enormous credit be it said that he won that coöperation. Maybe the Navy didn't like it particularly, but they towed those lame old boats out for us, and we went to work with our bombs. And on the heels of our little scholarly sorties to Bird Island, Bissell instigated a whole series of interisland flying programs.

This might suggest some attrition of aircraft and personnel. There had been those original fears that we wouldn't be able to make it offshore, flying from island to island. Fact is, I don't recall that we ever dropped an airplane in the drink on an inter-island flight. Certainly we didn't tally any more accidents than we'd been absorbing in our normal buzzing around Oahu. Because, even though you were flying *over* the island, there were only about three or four places where you could land. If you weren't within gliding distance of one of those, you had to set a conked-out aircraft down in the water anyway.

Historically we must consider the plight of a lieutenant named Moe Spicer, who was honored by a visit from his fiancée. She came from the mainland, duly chaperoned, to take up quarters at the Royal Hawaiian Hotel during her visit. As all the world knows, the Royal Hawaiian is located directly on the Waikiki beach in a marvelous setting. Popular song and story have blended to build up a composite legend: the long wide beautiful beach, great Pacific combers rolling in, a whine of ukuleles and steel guitars in the background, and the rustle of hula girls in grass skirts . . . generally an ideal background for young lovers or even older ones.

Nothing would do except that Moe Spicer must naturally fly his P-12 offshore, parading along so his girl could see how well he flew. Something went wrong, his engine cut out, he made a forced landing. When he came down in the drink, it was right off the Royal Hawaiian Hotel. The weather being hot over there all of the time, our usual attire for flying was simply our under shorts, a light flying suit pulled on over the shorts. On this tragic day, Spicer had to take off his flying suit to swim ashore. Trouble was, his shorts had been torn in the process of getting out of the airplane.

When he smacked into the water opposite the beach, he drew a big crowd. Same crowd was on hand, fiancée and all, to witness his arrival as he crawled up on shore.

. . . Something pretty sorry about a man in torn pants, anyway.

Speaking of P-12's, those elderly Boeing biplanes went on serving indefinitely and hanging up an enviable record, year after year. The Boeing P-26 was on its way to us at this same time. They had already

set altitude and speed records, before ever I was assigned to duty in
Hawaii; and we pilots knew that we were about to go into the 26's.
There was a vivid excitement in viewing the capabilities of this low-
winged monoplane. (During our early warfare in the ETO during
World War II, it seemed that there was something reminiscent of the
P-26 in the elliptical plan of wings of the British Spitfire . . . fuselage
and nose were entirely dissimilar.)

The P-26 had a top speed of well over two hundred and twenty-five
miles per hour, and in the 1930's that was really speed. Some of our
old 26's survived to get into the World War II act; Philippine pilots
and the Chinese still had some of them, and they flew those against
the Japs.

As for the P-12's, a lot of them went to noble deaths when they were
used as radio-controlled targets for our own gunners.

In reviewing the difficulties which might have faced an objective
newcomer like Major Bissell, one has to take into account the peacetime garrison atmosphere which prevailed in those days.

And it appears now that I have left the LeMays domestically
stranded down there amid seashells all of this time. Twasn't so. There
were wails at first, of course, when we occupied that little shack. It's
SOP in our business for all of the curtains to be forever obsolete—they
won't fit the windows of the new house you move into. People in the
Services will smile grimly when they read this: happens to everybody
all the time. It's an expense which you run into, an agony and a chore.

But well before Egan and I were through conducting the navigational school, I had made first lieutenant. At last Helen and I possessed
enough rank to move into quarters on the Base. We had a big living
room; a *lanai* (kind of patio); and three bedrooms; dining room,
kitchen.

We had been our own bosses when we lived in that cottage on the
sand. I used to look back with doleful nostalgia to those evenings when
Helen held the flashlight (even though she hollered about it), and I
spent hours with sextant and notes.

Our navigational school was a thing of the past. The long chilly arm
of the Air Corps Country Club had extended, and there were new
ramifications. We were Showing the Flag, we were accepting the
White Man's Burden. Believe it or not, we dressed for dinner every
night. *Every* night. They couldn't tell us what to do down there in that
rattly beach shebang, but they sure as hell could tell us what to do,
once we were dwelling at Wheeler.

I began to feel a little rule-happy about all this. Maybe that's the
reason I got absolutely pie-eyed for the first time in my life. I don't

mean just in a slightly singing or slightly bellicose mood. We used to get that way in the pioneer times; if we didn't have to fly next day, that could happen. What I'm talking about is ossified, pickled, embalmed.

One of the problems inherent in possessing rank and owning the responsibility of command is that people don't think you're quite human. You can't get drunk even every now and then. (But there have never been too many teetotalers among the military, if we leave out Stonewall Jackson and—I suppose—Sir Galahad.)

If you drink too much and too often, then you're no good in your slot. You just can't exercise the responsibility and functions of command. Man has to watch his step, no matter how much he would like to tie one on, on some particular night. Otherwise he gets talked about, and unfavorable opinions are formed about him. They may be erroneous but they can be devastating.

. . . Like Grant's being in a bunk on one of the boats at Pittsburg Landing, when the battle of Shiloh began. Was he drunk, or wasn't he? Historians and biographers have argued about that ever since. . . . Same way with General Joe Hooker at Chancellorsville. Was he drunk; or was he stunned when a chunk of solid shot struck the column against which he was leaning, on the front porch of the old mansion? That's never been straightened out to a lot of people's satisfaction either.

I read about these episodes when I was in high school, and thought at the time that it would be dangerous for an Army man to so indulge himself, or even give the appearance that he was indulging himself.

Also in life I was compelled to observe what a too-careless tolerance of the habit of imbibing could do—not necessarily to a leader or a great military figure, but to just an ordinary man supposed to be holding a job and supporting his family. That could be bad, too.

Usually I've taken it pretty easy. In turn, comparative abstinence on many occasions has brought its own grist of gossip. I've heard that I owned ice-water in my veins. Have heard it told that I didn't know what it was to let go—that I had never been drunk in my life.

Sure as hell I was: twice at least. The most recent time was on that occasion in 1947 when the separate Air Force became a reality, when we had won our wearying fight to achieve autonomy. Helen drove us home that night.

The other time was when we were lieutenants, there in Hawaii.

Butch and Jeff Griswold invited the Morris (Nelly) Nelsons and us to dinner on Saturday night. Just as simple as that: it wasn't New Year's Eve or anybody's birthday or anniversary. Just a plain ordinary garden variety of dinner party.

This routine of the black tie and the evening gown wasn't so bad on the girls (fact, they liked to do this, just as most women do. And they could wear full-skirted cotton dresses, light-weight and comfortable and cool; it didn't cost a mint to keep up a wardrobe like that). We men, on the other hand, had to wear stiff collars and all. It was a real pain.

You must be dressed after six p.m., and that wasn't just if you were dining out, either. If you were sitting at home in your own quarters, you were still dressed after six. A man would usually put on the mess-jacket type of dinner coat; those were a lot more comfortable. Still, it was all a damn nuisance.

The night of the Griswolds' little dinner party, Helen and I were just about walking out of our quarters when the phone rang. It was Bissell, our demon Operations Officer.

"Get down here to the line right away. I need to talk to you about—"

I can't for the life of me recollect what it was that he wished to see me about. But I know—and knew at the time—that it was some dratted little thing which could easily have waited until the next day.

Well, I peeled off my dress-up clothes, put on my working clothes, dropped Helen at the Griswolds', and hit for the line. Was down there about two hours. On this weekend evening there was absolutely no necessity for my being on the job; the longer I thought about it the more I bridled, and the angrier I became, deep inside.

Finally got through with the allotted task. Went back to our quarters, changed into dinner clothes once more, and headed for Grizzy's.

Things had been happening over there. It was decided unanimously that they would wait dinner on me, and also decided unanimously that they must try out the Griswolds' new cocktail glasses. These were of the huge double old-fashioned type, the first we'd ever seen. It was a novelty, a profound social stunt to have them. Little sawed-off old-fashioned glasses: everybody knew those. But these whoppers— Each had the cubic capacity of a junior cocktail shaker.

First off Grizzy had served an experimental round to his wife, to the Nelsons, and Helen, not forgetting himself in the process. He had a reputation for making lethal drinks anyway. Butch Griswold's idea of a good old-fashioned was to put a couple of puny lumps of ice in the glass, with the attendant shot of angostura bitters on sugar, and a wee wad of fruit; then fill up the whole glass with straight bourbon.

This is what he had been doing to the others, during those hours while I was fighting and dying on the flight line, and changing clothes and getting back over there.

Lucille Nelson was pregnant at the time, and she couldn't drink too much; and Jeff Griswold was never much of a drinker anyway, or so all the other wives said. Privately I didn't think that Helen was much of a drinker, far as that goes; but she always tried valiantly to keep up with the leaders.

Well, I came in, mad as a hornet. Here were these others weaving around with monstrous glasses in their hands. I asked how many of those they had had. They argued the question back and forth, but finally agreed: there had been four rounds, at least for Helen and the boys.

I said, "O.K. Wanted to know just how much the rest of you have had. Line 'em up."

Grizzy went to work. He mixed four of the double old-fashioneds, big brimming glasses, and I drank them down one after another. Just about as silly a stunt as I ever pulled in my life. It was a wonder I didn't fall over dead. But I was young and not too bright, or at least not as bright as the young sometimes think they are.

Dinner, as may be imagined, was pretty disorganized. Here Jeff Griswold, a lovely hostess, had gone to every possible length to get together the most eatable dinner ever seen on a Saturday night at Wheeler. But people were drifting and fading all over the place. I remember Nelly Nelson: he went in the guest bathroom, and locked himself in there, and wouldn't yield space to anybody.

I sat down at table and started to eat the candles. My hostess took those away from me and brought some more conventional food; but I wasn't very much in the mood for dinner by that time anyway.

As for Helen: she tried unsuccessfully to storm that bathroom; but Nelly Nelson wasn't giving ground. So she couldn't get to the bathroom . . . Helen made it into the guest bedroom, and lay down on one of the beds, and didn't have the strength to get up again, and kept feeling sicker and sicker.

Finally she could hear the rest of us out in the yard. Nelson had emerged from the bathroom by that time, and he was there with Grizzy and me, and we were all trying to minister to each other. The prime idea seemed to be that Nelly should put his finger down his throat and thus start a chain of operations which would lead to self-relief. This he tried to do assiduously . . . only trouble was he had his arm around a post. It is difficult to put your finger down your throat when you've got your arm wrapped around a post.

Overhearing us didn't help Helen's equanimity very much. She lay moaning and repeating a kind of doggerel, according to Jeff Griswold . . . "Oh, I'm so ashamed, so ashamed. Oh, I'm so sick, so sick. . . ." Finally she couldn't talk any more about it. She just acted.

. . . Grizzy, as a scheming host, was least intoxicated. It was he who drove Helen and me to our quarters. Helen managed to get some of her clothes off, and lay down on the bed . . . she thinks she was out like a light for a while, and then she roused up. Goodness sake, where was her husband?

There was a light in the bathroom.

She called, "Curt. What are you doing in there?"

"Taking a bath."

Helen went to sleep again . . . awakened again. The bathroom light was still on, and there she was, alone in bed.

"Curt, *what are* you doing in the bathroom?"

"Taking a bath."

She finally managed to get on her feet, and came and took a look.

I don't know how long I'd been sitting there. I was in the tub; this was our good modern bathroom, as in all quarters up there at Wheeler —not the old slat place on the beach. I was in the tub, soaping myself all over. Helen said she never saw such a soaping job as I was doing. The thing was, I didn't have any water in the tub or any soap either. But I thought I was working up a real good lather.

Actually that wasn't the most wicked occurrence of the whole night. Helen says she still starts up sometimes, having nightmares. . . .

Well, Sunday morning I felt a lot better. Got up, ate a huge breakfast, and then fetched a well-stocked breakfast tray to my well-stacked bride. She protested, but I told her, "You'll feel much better if you eat a big breakfast." She didn't agree with me; in fact she scarcely agreed with herself all day. She was sick, hour after hour, and we were having guests in to dinner that night. . . .

The pay-off came the following (Monday) morning, when my convalescent Helen came face to face with the Griswolds in the PX. She poured out heartbroken apologies. "Oh, I'm so sorry, so dreadfully sorry for what *happened*. I don't know *how* I could ever have allowed myself to *get* in such a condition—"

They both clucked commiseratingly, and then Helen brightened a little. "Anyway, there was one good thing about it: I lost five pounds."

Grizzy said, "Yes, I know. We found it."

In those days the average tour of duty in Hawaii ran two or two-and-a-half years. You can call our tour minimum average, since we departed for Hawaii in September, 1934, and were back in the Zone of the Interior (mainland, United States) in time for Christmas, 1936.

And after our leave had been spent, when I first reported for my new job, I reported at a place and for a type of duty which I never would have thought possible a couple of years before.

There were a lot of reasons for this. Both at the time and long afterward, I tried to examine my motives and discover what the incentive was. Certain influences in work and in associations affected this choice; but I think most of the change came about through my own evaluation of the matter, and the conclusions drawn.

I (who had trained and worked industriously in the Pursuit business ever since our class went down to Kelly in the summer of 1929) requested a job in Bombardment, and got it.

Sometimes I have been asked if this was because of my recognizing an imminent Japanese threat in the Pacific as early as five years before Pearl Harbor. The answer is strictly Negative—at least from the echelon in which I was working at the time. War Lords of the Rising Sun might have been a general menace in some distant military future, but they were by way of being permanent bogeymen . . . something like the advance or recession of glaciers . . . something not quite of our own time.

Nor do I believe that my recent hard-working association with John Egan had much to do with it, either. Side by side we had toiled professionally, just because we were enthusiastic about navigation, and had both been exposed to the Gatty school. Neither one of us really knew much about celestial but we were willing to die a-trying. We were just one jump ahead of our students, all the time; had to study harder than they did, spend more time on homework than they did, and more time on practice—all in order that we might take a shot and say, "Look. Here it is."

But I don't recall that John ever sat down and offered any lectures on the vast importance of Bombardment over that of the fighter business. This was just something I figured out for myself, somewhere amid all that island-hopping . . . in that aiming of a sextant toward a star from a dark beach.

The fighter had evolved as a defensive weapon. How the hell were you going to win a war with it? It might have its innings in certain phases of warfare, just as the Attack people might have their innings. But who was it who'd go far beyond the enemy lines and attempt to destroy not only armies in the field, not only supplies and fuel dumps and tank concentrations up near the front; but would go deep into the enemy's homeland, and thus try to eliminate his basic potential to wage war? Bombers, nothing but bombers.

Truly I had worked very hard, had hunted up extra jobs for myself. I'd taken on a great deal of work through the years—work which was not scheduled originally and which I might have avoided had I been less ambitious. But I *was* ambitious. I wanted to be capable, not only in Pursuit but in other Air Corps activities as well. If I was going to learn something about the rest of the Air Corps, firsthand, by God I had to go and learn it.

Undoubtedly the navigational school had sharpened up my thinking along this line. At least it got me to speculating in terms of long-range flying and the defense of the Islands, or defense of the American continental shoreline. And, considering certain well-tested and unimpaired axioms, an even more capable defense by means of an offense waged from some other point on the Earth's surface. . . .

It was obvious that we needed longer and longer-ranged airplanes. Also obvious that historically we would get them, or else we'd not survive. Patently, also, the fighter aircraft was purely a tactical phase of warfare. If you desired a strategic role, you had to get into Bombardment. It would be *the* strong arm. Perhaps, in the end, the primary arm of the Air Force.

Therefore, when it came to filling out my preference card for a new assignment, I asked for the Second Bomb Group at Langley.

(I was getting a little restless and edgy in that duty out there, after I had made up my mind that I wanted to work in Bombers. One week they had some little exercise or maneuver; it wasn't much of a war, but I felt that we as a squadron were humiliated, and hadn't done very well in the job. A critique was held afterward; and the squadron commander asked me what I thought about the whole exercise. I was just too blame frank. As I recall still further, this crime was reflected in my Efficiency Report. Undoubtedly it's there, deep in the archives today. Anyone has an opportunity, and digs deep enough— He can find it, and read how I didn't think very much of the squadron's effort in that maneuver, and said so.)

Obviously it was known in Washington and at Langley Field that I'd been through that original navigation school, under Gatty. Also information concerning the Egan & LeMay Young Men's Navigational Seminary had trickled down the line.

You never knew how it was going to come out when you expressed a preference, any more than you would today. But you could request and you could hope. In this case I was a lucky duck.

Folks kept coming around and saying that they wanted to touch me, in the hope that some of the luck would rub off on them. This business of asking for something and *getting* it, and not being assigned to flying box-kites at Skull Dump, Nevada— We were more than ready and willing to say *Aloha* to the *lanais*, to the *leis* and the bays, and disappear into the comfortable hulk of our good friend the transport *Republic*.

Back in the States we took our leave over the Christmas and New Year's holidays; then drove down to Langley and reported for work.

BOOK III

GHQ Air Force

(1937 – 1941)

1

FIRST OFF they wanted me to go back to school-teaching. They seemed to think that I was a natural born prof.

But the B-17 was really emerging from the works and would be delivered soon. It had far greater range than the B-10, which was our first-line bombardment aircraft at the moment; so there was a growing need for pilots with an understanding of long-range navigation. Fact is, the moment I hit Langley, the Personnel Officer announced that it was all set up: I should start a navigation school for the Second Bomb Group.

Right then I discovered it was very fortunate that I knew John Egan would be coming that way in another three months. I didn't know whether I was selling John down the river or not; but I simply had to learn something about bombardment, and Egan was already up to his ears in such experience.

Here was one job I must dodge if I could possibly manage to do so.

. . . I can fairly hear the papers rustling now, as I stand in front of that desk, and feel Captain McCormick's eyes coming up to appraise me again.

"You've been running that navigation school over in Hawaii—"

"Well, I was one of the two in on it—"

"Pretty good school, we heard over here. You people did a good job."

"Thank you, sir."

"Lieutenant, we've got to start a school here at Langley. And you're going to run it for us."

I could hear my voice going on rapidly, "Oh, sir! No, no, no! Actually I'm not too good at that sort of thing. Believe it or not, I had to study harder than the students over there at Wheeler, to keep ahead of the game. It's all very interesting, of course; but the trouble is I come from Pursuit, you know, and I need to find out something about bombers, and get to flying a little bit, so I'll know what the score is.

"John Egan is a *much* better instructor than I am. And he's due here— Oh, it's only a month or so now. He's *infinitely better* qualified for this job than I. So why not let him run the school?—and let me get into—into finding out something about bombers—?"

The hesitation. Then the dry voice saying, "Well. O.K."

Never heard such a beautiful sound in my life.

They put me into the 49th Squadron, and initially gave me the job of Assistant Operations Officer. Somewhat later on I became Operations Officer.

Call them influences, call them associations. Whatever you term them, two keen and strengthening elements entered my life in this year. One was a machine, the other a man.

Consider the machine first. It was the Boeing Flying Fortress, the B-17—the first of our four-engined bombers and, in many ways, the greatest. To quote General Arnold: "It had only one predecessor of equal importance in air history. That was the first 'military aircraft' of the Wright brothers in which Lieutenant Tom Selfridge was killed in 1908."

This latter calamity befell at Fort Myer, Virginia (my home during final years of active duty). Early in 1908, the Army Signal Corps had signed a contract with Orville and Wilbur Wright. Far as I know, this must have been the first contract ever signed for a military aircraft any time, any place. The Signal Corps required an airplane which would carry a passenger (beside and) besides the pilot; it had to remain airborne for at least one hour, and fly at a speed of at least forty mph. In September whole throngs came out to Fort Myer to witness the flight tests which would precede acceptance by the Army. On the 17th of the month, after several successful demonstrations, Orville cracked up the first plane, killing Selfridge and seriously injuring himself. Wright was incapacitated for some months, but both he and his brother returned to their task with resolution, and soon produced an airplane whose performance exceeded their and the Army's fondest hopes.

. . . You'd think about that sometimes, if you lived so close to the scene of the original attempt, the original tragedy. When certain winds are blowing and certain runways are being used at the National Airport, planes seem to fly almost directly over the Fort Myer flagpole. The howl of jet engines cannot quite drown out the imagined throbbing of that other little four-cylinder forty-five hp machine of long ago.

Also the B-17 was attended with disaster in its earliest phases. As in the case of the Wright machine of 1908, a number of outstanding flights had been made; then came October 30th, 1935. Maintenance people didn't unlock the horizontal tail surfaces properly, and the first Fort went to flaming destruction on the field at Dayton. Wright Field, yet.

We heard about this in Hawaii at the time, but people didn't shake their heads too much. They regretted deeply the death of Major Hill, Air Corps test pilot, and the Boeing test pilot who was killed with him. But the previous performances of the B-17 had been so startlingly impressive that there was no danger of the program's being scrubbed.

Not in *that* year, anyway. A foolish and suicidal condemnation of the B-17 program and other advanced four-engined programs to follow, came a few years later.

Fate had it in store for me to go all the way with the 17. The first of these aircraft rubbed its tires on the runway at Langley in 1937. By June of that year we had seven of the Flying Fortresses squatting on their ramp. I fell in love with the 17 at first sight. The two-fan B-10's and B-18's just weren't in it. . . . Only six years later I would be leading an entire Air Division of Fortresses in combat over the continent of Europe. Not until 1944 would I need to relinquish the B-17, and transfer my attention to its larger newer sister, the Boeing B-29.

One of the people who flew with my Forts in the Eighth Air Force had something to say about them after the war. He wrote: "The smell of 17 . . . B-17 . . . and somehow different from the smell of any other plane."

Some people may consider this to be nonsense. It just so happens that I can't make myself believe that all airplanes smell alike, either.

My new boss, who came to command the Second Bomb Group shortly after I arrived, was Lieutenant-Colonel Robert Olds. I can't imagine any experience more demanding and more valuable to a young officer than a tour of duty serving under Bob Olds. In my own case he was the first man I'd ever come in contact with who really penetrated my thick skull with a sense of urgency in getting things done. Guess I've said a thousand times that I didn't know what it was all about, until I got to Langley and began work under Bob Olds.

The whole purpose of the Air Corps was to fly and fight in a war, and to be ready to fly and fight in that war at any given moment, if the war should come. That capability was what Olds required of his equipment and his people. Any individual or any ideal which worked toward an increased state of efficiency in his organization was welcomed. Anything which mitigated against that efficiency was not tolerated. Life was just as simple as that; and thus life was made inspiring.

Olds' professional standards were exalted. But he insisted that everybody in the outfit should embrace them also. Bit by bit he got us going on the proper track.

As related previously, after my successful evasion of a continuance of a schoolmaster's career, eventually I became Operations Officer of the 49th Squadron. A little later the Group Operations Officer was taken sick, and I was sent over there as acting Group Operations Officer.

This was a hell of an exacting job for a newcomer. If it hadn't been for Bob Olds, I might have made a mess of my career then and there.

My office was on the first floor of the hangar, and Olds' office was on the second floor. In order to reach his sanctum he had to pass by my door. One of the first things I discovered was that I had better be at work before the Boss came in. No lingering at home for that extra cup of coffee or that tag-end of gossip trilled forth by your bride.

So I managed to beat Colonel Olds down to that hangar every morning . . . I'm sitting at my desk. So he stops by, on the way to his own office, and proceeds to give me *three days' work*. I mean that literally.

He always had ideas, things that the group should be doing. Wonderful ideas, every one of them. He'd stand there telling me about what we *should be doing,* and in no time at all I'd be all fired up. He had that rare and wonderful talent, pure gold in any commander: the ability to transmit exuberance and enthusiasm for the work, and to keep a blaze hot in the hearts and minds of his subordinates.

Maybe it would take him five minutes to do that—dish out the three days' work. Result: I was behind all the time. Never did get caught up.

He didn't summon you down to the flight line on trivialities; he wasn't a needler, he was never pestiferous (though he could bawl the hell out of you if he thought it necessary). Bob Olds seemed constructed of a mass of jeweled machineries, all of them functioning. When he tossed a few of these items in your direction, you felt as if you were rushing around picking them up off the floor, and then trying to decide which had the highest priority. You'd never overtake, but you had to keep on going.

From him I absorbed a special wisdom then and there which accrued to my advantage in commanding SAC many years later. That was this notion of *keeping out of people's way after I had told them what I wanted to have done.*

I don't mean that Olds wasn't always around to see how you were doing. He was around, all right. And if you didn't make sufficient progress, he was aware of that too. He had means of divination unknown to the common mind. He knew everything that went on. Or, in the case of certain luckless officers, which *didn't* go on.

So many things to learn, things that just hadn't dawned on me before. . . .

For example, one morning he came in, face shining, eyes squinted in thought. "LeMay, what's the weather report for today?"

Not that I knew the first damn thing about it. Just hadn't gotten around to finding out what the weather was, *if* the weather was, even locally . . . let alone what was going on out West or any place else.

Then Olds would tell me off, and reveal what a slipshod person I was. "Aren't you the Operations Officer? Suppose you had to lay out an operation today, a mission to Wright Field. What's the weather out there? You'd have to know, wouldn't you?"

Needless to say, from then on I never showed up at my desk without having visited the Weather Room first, and having studied the weather picture as thoroughly as possible.

Glad to say that's standard throughout our commands in 1965.

"LeMay, how many airplanes have we got in commission today?"

. . . No use looking at the picture for yesterday, either. Yesterday wouldn't suffice. You couldn't tell: overnight a couple of airplanes might have decided to become hangar queens. You had to know how many were ready to go, and how many were having engines pulled, and all about it; and you had to have the answers when Colonel Olds asked you. No use in darting right off to find out, or trying to call up people and ask over the telephone. I started getting that dope in, bright and early, along with the weather.

On top of these demands of the job in squadron or group operations, there was my own flying to do. Time of my arrival at Langley, we were still equipped with B-10's. I had of course flown the B-10 at the Blind Landing school, during the air mail episode. But, hell's bells, that was nigh onto three years before. So I needed to be checked off all over again on the B-10.

We knew that the 17 was on the way. You couldn't approach any conversational group of Bombardment people in those days without hearing B-17 all over the place. But still we'd been laggardly in getting equipped with them; and in the meantime the B-10 was our instrument. Work to be done in that department.

The oncoming Fortresses would offer new concepts in training, new concepts of use of airplanes for strategic purposes. We were hazarding and speculating constantly. It must be remembered that this was long before we had made any lengthy over-the-ocean flights. We had never had a four-engined bomber before.

Even as great a mind as that of Major-General F. M. Andrews could be deluded into misconception concerning possible uses of the B-17 at that stage of the game. So too with us very very junior officers, far down the list in years or experience or in rank. I wish that it had been possible to make tape recordings of some of those early discussions. They would be interesting and often amusing reading if transcribed now.

At the same time we weren't all wrong or just plain silly. There were charts floating around offering performance data on the military airplanes which had already been flown. They revealed, considering all factors, an entirely different set of assumptions than might be assembled on a purely mathematical basis. It was considered that you might assume one engine failure out of each five hundred flights of a single-engined aircraft, no matter how expert the maintenance. Thus it was reckoned that a two-engined aircraft, capable of continuing flight on one engine, had two-hundred-and-forty-times the chance of continuing flight that a one-engined job did. By this same reckoning, the four-engined aircraft—which was indeed capable of continuing flight on two engines—had sixty-five-hundred-times the reliability that a one-engined aircraft owned.

Adhering to the same process of reasoning, the B-17 Flying Fortress would have twenty-seven times the reliability of the two-engined B-10's or B-18's.

I remember that in one report General Andrews made much of the fact that the B-17 "has five defensive gun positions, instead of three." (Note for the future: at the time General Andrews was killed in 1943, we were messing around with perhaps seven to nine defensive gun positions and ten to thirteen guns.)

Hap Arnold pointed out that Great Britain had gone in for four-engined transports and flying-boats, and that Russia was believed (1937) to "have large four-engined airplanes actually operating at the North Pole." You can well believe that this statement by the Acting Chief of the Air Corps provided a lot of material for bunk-flying sessions by the time it trickled down to us.

One way or another the four-engined airplane was It, and would be It for a long time to come.

At this time General Andrews, in a report to the Adjutant-General, made the following statements: "The situation of the United States is probably unique among the major world powers. We have friendly neighbors to the north and to the south of us, and vast oceans to the east and to the west. Our national policy is one of pure defense, and our natural sphere of influence in world affairs lies primarily within the Western Hemisphere. With these facts in mind, it is clear that any serious threat against our defensive jurisdiction must come across the water from overseas. For at least some years to come, foreign aggression can be brought to bear against us only by expeditions of hostile ground forces supported by aircraft carriers and other men of war, or *by air attacks launched from air bases previously seized and prepared in the Western Hemisphere.*"

The above italics are my own, in view of the modern situation wherein successive Administrations have permitted potential-enemy air bases to be established and maintained in Cuba.

General Andrews was not solitary in any misconception he may have owned concerning whether a B-17 was a reconnaissance aircraft, a defensive bomber, or an offensive bomber. Everybody was a little uncertain as to just what kind of four-engined bear we had by the tail. It took a lot of missions—*Utah*, Buenos Aires, Colombia, Rio, *Rex*—to find out.

We possessed in Andrews one of the great American pilots of all time, and one of the most aggressive. Well past his first youth when he joined the Air Corps, he carried into the skies some of the hell-for-leather sentiments of his old Cavalry days. Men who served under him will remember how Andrews insisted again and again on flying in thick soup—bad weather in which he wouldn't have allowed any of the rest of us to take off. He was what we called a Real Active Pilot. We didn't call him "Andy" but we knew that his intimates did; and somehow he looked the part.

Bob Olds was the same way about flying.

He and Andrews could do anything and everything which they might have to ask us to do, and they were respected for it. That's pretty good leadership in any league.

While I was out in Hawaii, the General Headquarters Air Force had come into existence. Initially this might have been regarded merely as a change in designation; but anyone entering Bombardment and coming to Langley would soon observe the enormous differences in the set-up. General Andrews was commanding the GHQ AF. This consisted of all combat units in the Air Corps: Pursuit, Attack, Bombardment.

Observation wasn't included, being assigned to the various divisions. It must be remembered also that there were still the Training Command and all our Service groups, with depots and support elements. Those were still assigned as before.

The purpose of the GHQ Air Force was to weld combat units into a single organization for operational purposes. As an inevitable result the combat units were soon manipulated on a more practical and streamlined basis, and continued thus through crucial maneuvers and experiments of the next several years.

In the Second Bomb Group we had a ready awareness, naturally, of challenges inherent in this modern organization. But we were still so excited about the oncoming B-17's that we couldn't think of much else. I'm positive that it was Bob Olds who went out to Seattle and picked up the first one (first B-17 delivered to the Army. The one which crashed in 1935 had not yet been turned over to us at the time of the accident). We got them one at a time. Seven were delivered by the first week of June, with thirteen in all scheduled for delivery by August.

To my grief I was not invited to go along to the West and fetch one of the Fortresses back to Langley. Remember, I was a comparatively low-ranking character, and we had a lot of rank at Langley. All of the first pilots of the original B-17's were at least captains, and mighty experienced captains. Some were of field grade or soon to be. Eventually a lot of us were checked off on those airplanes, and qualified to fly if necessary as first pilot; but the original assigned combat crews were all commanded by such people as Caleb V. Haynes and Harold

George, and oldtimers of that description—Vince Meloy, Neil Harding, A. Y. Smith, such folks.

(Probably seems peculiar to people who have solely a World War II background in the Army Air Force, to hear captains called "a lot of rank." They are thinking of an organization which puffed like a mushroom overnight, and oozed with majors or light-colonels who had been high school sophomores only a few years before. It wasn't like that in the old days. . . . I remember when a nineteen-year-old kid came in to see me in 1943, when I was commanding the 305th in England. I asked him what was on his mind. "Sir, I'm Lieutenant Blank from the 422nd Squadron, and I have Major Price's permission to speak to the CO. Sir, the major doesn't like me, and I guess Captain Aber doesn't like me either—" "How do you know?" "Sir, I'm always being passed over for promotion. Everybody else who came in with me has been promoted. They're all first lieutenants—everyone except me. And I haven't incurred any disciplinary action or anything. I've got just as much flying time and just as many missions as these other guys and—" I asked him, "How long have you been a second lieutenant?" He says, very much aggrieved, "Almost seven months." "Just wondered," I told him. "I was a second lieutenant for about six and a half years." He got out of my office pretty fast.)

C. V. Haynes I considered especially impressive although I never dreamed that I would soon be flying in his crew. He was a North Carolinian with an inimitable accent; he stood burly and heavy-set; must have weighed well over two hundred pounds. Those huge shoulders of his came in very handy when he was faced with the necessity for subduing a twelve- or twenty-ton bomber which had suddenly decided to become a bucking bronco. (During World War II, after service with our ferry command, C.V. went to North Africa and China. Eventually he retired as a major-general.)

Everything was different with the 17. Everything, or so they told me. It was an "aerodynamic revolution," they declared. Of course I knew practically nothing about bombers or bomber crews, and how they had been operating previously.

All the officers assigned to the outfit already were pilots. On the B-10 crews there wasn't even a navigator per se; we had a pilot, co-pilot, an enlisted man radio operator, and a bombardier (officer). They'd just pick out someone and say, "We'll have him be bombardier for the crew." Then this gentleman had to get busy and learn how to bomb.

We did have the Norden bombsight by that time. We knew so little about high altitude bombardment that it was a breeze for an experienced navigator to memorize just about all the information which had been accumulated concerning the bombsight and bombing. First-off he read up on the dope relating to the Norden; then he taught himself something about bomb tables. There was indeed a little math involved, but nothing much more than we had been exposed to previously. Then— We went out and practiced bombing. Nearly every day.

There were no simulators, although we did have one of those A-type trainers, the first model. This was an apparatus which would move across the hangar floor: a little tower about ten feet high. It looked something like a miniature model of those scaling towers which the Ancients used to shove by brute slave force against the walls of towns they besieged.

Bombardiers of World War II vintage will recall our improved trainer, the A-2. It had a chassis with rubber tires on the wheels and a chain drive at the rear; the bombsight was located at the front. There was a seat for the instructor, one for the student, one for the driver. Electricity propelled the machine, and the driver sat at a wheel simulating an airplane control. We started in by having a kind of little bug run across the floor, and tried to hit him with a plumb-bob. Later on, just as the performance and capabilities of the B-17 improved, so did bombardment procedures improve, and so did the technique of instruction improve along with them.

A paper bull's-eye was spread on a metal platform about a foot off the floor. The idea was to enter on the bomb run, make your adjustments just as you would in actuality, and then drop your bombs when you were at the proper point. The appropriate number of seconds after *Bombs Away* a plumb-bob dropped with a sharp tap on the target platform, and made a hole in whatever portion of the target your supposed bombs had struck.

It was again a little like our school in Hawaii: the instructors didn't know much more than the students. But gradually Instructor would let Student take over more and more of the operation, until Student was able to do his bomb run completely solo.

"Now, then. If we release a bomb in a climb, remember that it will climb with the airplane momentarily until it begins to assume its normal trajectory. . . ."

Far as actual flight training went for bombardiers, we had a program to which we adhered faithfully. So many hours of trainer work (as above); so many hours of different types of flying—bombing, navigation, visual daytime cross-country, night cross-country; and instrument-under-the-hood. Everything was coming along beautifully—at least it would have been, if we had had more money and more people and more airplanes. Never while I was with the Second Bomb Group did we enjoy our full complement of B-17's or even our full complement of bombers.

I'll say again that it took Olds' leadership to ignite the real spark and get us going. Forever there were new things to be learned . . . not only in this unpenetrated wilderness of bombardment, but in navigation.

We had a big old horizontal type compass. That was back by the navigator's position; and you could read and interpolate to perhaps— Say, pretty close to a quarter of a degree. But the little compass up on the instrument panel in front of the pilots: the smallest reading there was five degrees.

So you, as navigator, would be sitting back there confronted by your huge compass; and you would calculate the course out, measure the drift and apply the variation, deviation, etc., to the nearest quarter of a degree. And when the pilot asked you for a course, you gave it to him.

You said, "Steer thirty-one and three-quarters degrees."

Here's that baffled pilot glaring at his compass. "Thirty-one and three-quarters— For Christ's sake, how are you going to do *that?*"

Naturally he was suspicious of anything which he couldn't read. But I noticed that after you had been flying about five hours, perhaps over water or clouds or both, and the pilot didn't know where the hell he was— Well, when you asked for a quarter of a degree change to the right, *you got* a quarter of a degree change to the right. He had to guess; but with a desperate and still capable pilot his guesses were pretty good. Still, none of the lead pilots had much overall confidence in our navigational attainments, when based on such procedures. Those quarter-degree courses were just too much for 'em.

And when I say no one had confidence, I mean none of the aircraft commanders, including Bob Olds. Will tell more about that when we come up to the *Utah* incident.

No reason for waiting much longer for that one. It happened very early in the game: August, 1937. Our B-17's were spanking new—and very very few.

That early year or two at Langley, with Fortresses coming in, and our primary deployment of them in various directions— Those were excellent seasons professionally. It was the first time in my life that I was really shaken up enough to learn what we were in business for, and to get going.

You felt that you had a real purpose in existence. You wanted to dive right in and learn everything there was to learn.

Personally, however, for the LeMays, those were wretched times. I don't mean just because we had relinquished our easy-going island existence. When families who were lieutenants in those days get together after so many decades have passed, you should hear the gals carry on about how charming life was for them in Hawaii or the Philippines . . . and so very cheap, too!

Did I mention that most of us had little Korean girls out there in Hawaii for cooks, nursemaids, etc.? We had Etta Koo.

Helen says: "Etta was a perfectly marvelous cook. She couldn't cook at all, though, when I got her; I kept teaching and teaching, and each time that she would cook something, she would do better, for she was a natural born cook. She owned the real feel for good food and its preparation and flavoring. . . . She was a fat little rascal; schoolgirl; attended school every weekday. And her wage was ten dollars a month and keep. That was what we all paid these girls, and the girls were delighted with their wage. Etta would prepare breakfast, straighten up the house, make the beds, then take her lunch and go to school. Then she'd return at two p.m., and perhaps clean house or do the special bits of hand laundry. . . ."

Sounds like a homemaker's dream come true. So that was what we had in Hawaii. On the other hand, we weren't doing too badly at Langley when it came to quarters, help, and all that.

What I'm talking about was our intimate personal lives. We were so eager to have children. But Helen suffered frightful and dangerous experiences, trying to be a mother. She lost one baby when she was pretty far along. That would have been a little boy, our first. Then she lost another; had to undergo surgery, and of course that terminated that pregnancy. We knew that in any future pregnancy there was going to have to be a Caesarean section.

Each time these crises came up, I tried to be with my wife. Then, soon as the thing was over, and Helen out of danger, I'd throw myself into my work again.

Sometimes I'd be so emotionally upset that I feared for the successful completion of whatever job was at hand. Told myself that what I needed was self-discipline. You might be feeling pretty upset emotionally, but it didn't do any good to take the portions of that emotion which had spilled over, and mix them up with exacting elements of the task at hand.

This I had to learn the hard way.

2

THERE used to be, circulating through the Commands, a pamphlet entitled *Joint Action of the Army and Navy.*

Here is paragraph *4c:*

In order that the most effective coöperation may be attained, the following general principles will govern:

(1) Neither service will attempt to restrict in any way the means and weapons used by the other service in carrying out its functions.

(2) Neither service will attempt to restrict in any way the area of operations of the other service in carrying out its functions.

(3) Each service will lend the utmost assistance possible to the other service in carrying out its functions.

Viewed side by side with the actual practices which ensued during the 1937 joint exercises, this was just so much malarkey. It was well-intentioned—that's all you could say for it.

Previously my enthusiasm for the Boy Scout organization has been mentioned, since it contributed a value to my young years; but I doubt that the boy ever breathed who was able to live up to the nobility suggested in the twelve points of the Scout Law. No human being could ever be trustworthy, loyal and helpful, friendly, courteous, kind, obedient, cheerful and thrifty, brave, clean and reverent all at once and in the same breath.

We Air Corps folks were no angels. But I can't remember that we broke any rules or failed to live up to inspired adjuration at any time during joint maneuvers with the Navy. It was the Navy who sinned. There was so much evidence against them piled up at the time that no evidence was ever made public. The whole thing was too utterly damning.

I am talking about Joint Air Exercise No. 4, commonly referred to as the bombing of the battleship *Utah*.

Let us go now, in 1965, and peep into Record Group 18, Box 15, AAF Central Files (353.C). You will find, under date of August 19, 1937, a communication from the Headquarters of the First Air Wing, GHQ Air Force, sent to the Adjutant-General (through Commanding General GHQ Air Force). It says *Extracts;* and the only Extract which survives is a list of our aircraft employed in the exercise. Thirty-four B-10-B's, three B-18's, seven B-17's. That's from Bombardment. Reconnaissance offered three OA-4's, one OA-5, and one B-18. Cargo employed four C-33's in sustaining the exercise.

Otherwise we read: "The exercise was completed at noon 13 August 1937. A supplementary exercise took place 14 August 1937."

And that's every living *official* word which appears, available to a researcher, concerning the 12–13 August, 1937, bombing of the battleship *Utah*. It is as if the waxy hands of a long-dead commander (one who admired a sentimental illusion of the Navy better than he respected a practical defense of his Nation) reached out of the grave to lock a box, and to pantomime, "The record is here, the facts are here. But you shan't have 'em," and then to throw the key away.

Sounds as if the Navy was assuredly a Big Bad Wolf where the Army Air Corps was concerned, and the only one. By no means. The Army was a Big Bad Wolf as well.

The same type of intellect which presided over Billy Mitchell's fortunes, and skulked around to nullify whatever advances he had made, and to impugn his findings as well as his motives— That same intellect set the pattern for the Army's procedure in May, 1938.

"No military requirement exists for the procurement of experimental pressure cabin bombers in the fiscal year 1939 or the fiscal year 1940, of the size and type described (four-engine planes). The Chief of the Air Corps has been informed that the experimentation and development for the fiscal years 1939–40 will be restricted to that class of aviation designed for the close-in support of ground troops and for the production of that type of aircraft such as medium and light aircraft, pursuit and other light aircraft."

Or again, to put it even more bluntly:

"Experimentation and research will be confined to types of aircraft for the close support of ground troops."

You might say that insofar as obtaining any elasticity of mental attitude in the ground-controlled mind of the Army went, all our B-17 effort and experience of the 1930's—and those were fascinating and productive experiences—was poured down a hole. Like General Mitchell before him, Frank M. Andrews had the courage to beard the House Military Affairs Committee in its den on the Hill. He endorsed an Air Corps Reorganization Bill. This bill proposed that the Air Corps would have equal status with the rest of the Army, but a separate budget and a separate promotion list.

Result: Billy Mitchell history repeating itself again. Frank Andrews was transferred to Texas and busted all the way back to colonel. The Army practically dissolved the GHQ Air Force staff. They transferred Kenny, McNarney, Knerr and Follett Bradley all over the place. . . . Course, it wasn't very long before they had to get them all back again and, with the eventually-expanding Army Air Forces, in the long run these discerning men lost nothing in the way of rank or other emoluments.

Sometimes I have thought that General Andrews was singled out for such spiteful discipline because of being so long identified with that now-most-obsolescent of all the ground forces: the old horse Cavalry. He was commissioned in the Cavalry on graduating from West Point in 1906, and spent a dozen years of his life in that branch before he went into the Air Service. Did some of those mutton-heads regard him as a traitor? It's hard to say, but it's possible. All because he decided that the airplane might bring us to victory a little faster than the horse, and proceeded to devote the rest of his dedicated life to proving just that. . . .

These lines are written neither pettishly nor because I am now relieved of the responsibility of attempting to maintain my share of an inter-Service harmony. They stem rather from historical cognizance that the entrenched military hierarchy—military or naval, it matters not—has always disputed the power of a weapon which was not a part of their traditional arsenal.

In the case of air power, for the first time in recorded history a new element had become a factor. The new element must be mastered, and that mastery must in turn be extended into all plans or considerations for warfare.

About three years before Hitler launched his *Blitzkrieg* against Poland, an Army general, obviously a spokesman for the General Staff type of thinking, delivered himself of the following analysis of this subject at a committee hearing:

". . . An air force can remain in its peculiar element for only a short time; it must rise from and return to the element of one of the other two forces, and it cannot control any element, even its own, except temporarily, throughout a limited area. So an air force cannot obtain a decision against troops on the ground, nor occupy territory nor exercise control of the sea."

It should be observed readily that in our attempting to demonstrate that multi-engined bombers could seek out, discover and sink a battleship approaching our United States coast, we were faced not only with congenital resentment of the Naval Brass (all battle-wagon types at that time). We were faced with the jealousy and suspicion of the Army itself—the dirt-behind-their-ears-over-hill-over-dale people who envisioned future international conflict wherein flying artillery flew overhead and applied its fire power to the battlefield in an immediate tactical area, period.

No purpose in paying any more attention to the lichen-grown brains of that age. They were there, wet or dry, Navy or Army. In the case of the *Utah* they were wet, for the Blue Suits ran the show.

This was the first deployment of the B-17 beyond ordinary pursuits of operational training. This was the first exercise, real or sham, in which the Fortresses participated. They tried to send us to the job with our hands tied. If there were any restraints to be cast off, we had to cast them off ourselves. Nobody else was going to pull them loose for us.

. . . First we knew about the *Utah* exercise was when, on our bombing range, we were confronted with targets in the shape of battleships. That we proceeded to attack these targets with all the verve we possessed, would be a masterpiece of understatement. We really went to town on those. And the targets were immobile, they were there on land, they were fakes, they were sitting ducks. They were as useless, really, for our eventual purpose as the bull's-eye circles we put out on the desert immediately prior to combat action in World War II. We sent our bombardiers over targets like those—desert circles; then expected the same bombardiers to fly over a German factory metropolis complete with its industrial haze, and recognize a specific target in all that welter and confusion five miles beneath, and attack that target successfully.

On the phony battleship silhouettes we were using our ordinary practice bombs. These were filled with sand, with a small charge of black powder to show smoke where they struck the ground.

It was essential that we also have some practice over towed targets on the surface of the sea. Andrews and Olds and the rest at the top believed that we might work toward a successful attack on the *Utah* through these successive stages: (first) bombing the land targets; (second) bombing towed targets on the ocean surface; and moving (third) to the actual battleship mission.

But General Andrews, Colonel Olds and the rest were compelled to realize acutely that they were not receiving coöperation from the War Department. People in the GHQ Air Force became aware that their suggestions and recommendations were being reviewed by some other authority. We believed then (and those of us who are alive still believe) that someone in the War Department carried each of those communications directly over to the Navy, fast as they appeared on the desk, and yielded to the Navy's verdict in every case.

The idea seemed to be that an upstart GHQ Air Force should be slapped down by its wise elders, even if it were necessary to resort to such perfidious tactics. After all, wasn't this just a mere competition between various branches? Etc.

We B-17 people held no such belief. Far from considering that we were engaging in some sort of jolly Hare-and-Hounds, we thought seriously that the future of our Country might be at stake. A great deal of the Nation's effort in men and money was tied up in a surface-vessel program. If this was erroneous, in the broad conception of National defense, we wanted to make it apparent.

We believed this was the first step toward defending our Country in the future. The War Department didn't seem to feel the same way about it.

We headed our Fortresses for the West Coast early in August, and Bob Olds came along; he was going to fly the mission with us. C. V. Haynes would pilot the lead aircraft. I was selected to serve as lead navigator. Olds would be in our airplane.

The Navy had loaded the dice for this crap game, but still we were going to play with them. To begin with, they had specified the Pacific Ocean off the coast of California in August. Consistently over that area in August there is a heavy bank of fog. It's apt to run out over the water from three to five hundred miles. The Navy knew that, and Bob Olds knew it too. Nevertheless he said, "All right. We'll do it." It might be wondered why Olds would agree to such a preposterous limitation regarding a maneuver which was to prove or disprove the effectiveness of so important an attack. It was agree to that, or nothing. It *had* to be on the Navy's terms. Otherwise they would not participate.

Herewith a sample of the kind of concurrence offered us. I mentioned that we had been using the heavy sand-filled-powder-charged bombs on land targets. For attacking any surface vessels, however—including the eventual and primary *Utah*—we would be compelled to employ the Navy Mark VII water-filled bombs. These weighed no more than fifty pounds and were constructed of stove-pipe type metal . . . had a round nose and fins, conventionally enough. They would burst on impact, and thus were comparatively harmless where ships' decks, superstructure, etc., were concerned.

In advance, we needed desperately a quota of such ordnance in order to study the obvious differences in performance. Did we get them? Negative. The Navy people were so sorry, but they were experiencing "supply difficulties." General Emmons, commanding the First Wing out West, received some of the Mark VII's just a few days before the show was due to go on the road.

Blue Suits were to furnish the reconnaissance as well. The Navy was to locate the *Utah*, give us the information, and then we were supposed to go out and find the *Utah* and bomb it.

Years later I put together a description of this incident, with the assistance of a staff officer. The rules read:

"No surface or sub-surface vessels were to operate on the defending side [our side], except as rescue craft for airplanes which might be forced down. These surface vessels would not be permitted to report weather conditions. . . . The problem was limited to an area bounded between the parallels drawn westerly from San Francisco Bay on the north, San Pedro Bay on the south, and a line three hundred nautical miles off the coast; something over one hundred thousand square miles of sea area. The time set aside for the exercise was from noon, August 12, to noon, August 13. No bombs were to be dropped after dark on the 12th, or after 12 noon the 13th.

"The Navy reconnaissance planes would not be permitted to make any movement from their bases until noon, the first day. As soon as they located the *Utah*, they would radio to Navy headquarters, which would relay to us before our planes would take off. . . ."

In order to get as close as possible to the thing, we went up and landed at Oakland Airport, and sat by a telephone at the radio station. This station was supposed to receive from the Navy flying-boats the position of the *Utah*. . . . We were up there long before noon, sitting and waiting. Noon came; and the exercise was in progress officially; and nothing happened, and we sat there, and nothing happened, and we sat there.

It became apparent that if the ship was very far out at sea, we couldn't possibly reach it before dark, even were we to receive the position immediately.

General Emmons (same Emmons to whom I referred in Hawaii) was commanding the so-called Defending Forces. He estimated "that the *Utah* would enter the area at its extreme southwest corner, making a feint in the direction of San Francisco, and when night came, would head for San Pedro Bay, to attack [theoretically] the aircraft factories located in the Los Angeles area."

We, in the 17's, held little hope that the B-10's and B-18's might assume an important role in the defensive attack. They just didn't have the range to go wandering around searching for a battleship, especially since the Navy had delayed so long, either in discovering the *Utah's* position or else in reporting it.

Bob Olds and General Andrews sat there looking at each other, and they didn't need to say much: the looks were enough.

There was absolutely not a blessed thing for us to do except to take off right then and there, and head out to sea. If we hung around any longer on land, waiting for that delayed reconnaissance report, we'd never make it before dark. And we weren't allowed to bomb after dark.

Let me reëmphasize that no one had given us any position report— not even a guess, except for the theory promulgated by General Emmons.

We took off and went out to sea. The rest of that brief afternoon we cruised and hunted and hoped.

Shortly before dark we received a radio message from the Navy, giving us the alleged position of the *Utah*. Navy didn't expect that we would already be out there at sea, but we were. I plotted the position at once, and saw that it wasn't very far from where we were. Obviously they thought that we'd still be back on land, and we couldn't have made it out there before dark.

Speeding across the top of the persistent fog, we raced for the position. When we got there, C.V. threw our lead 17 down through the fog, and the other six Forts circled up above.

Our aircraft broke out of the fog about— Oh, I should say we had five to seven hundred feet ceiling underneath. Naturally we couldn't see very far. But there wasn't anything there, nothing to be seen, no *Utah*.

Because of the absence of extended visibility I made a square search problem. We didn't have long; darkness was coming. We ran the search problem and did the squares until it was dark, and found absolutely nothing. Our aircraft went back upstairs and we started home.

Bob Olds came back out of the cockpit. He looked down at me and said meaningly, "Are you sure you knew where that boat was supposed to be?"

I stared at him. "Yes, sir, I'm sure."

"How do you know that we were there?"

"Well, I'm going to take a celestial shot right now, and see how far off we are."

He waited while I took the celestial and made the calculations. . . . We weren't very far off: maybe two or three miles.

"How do you know *that's* right?"

"If it's right—" I held my pencil above the chart. "Here's where we are. Now, it takes so long to get to San Francisco— This is the dead reckoning position. Now, we're so far from San Francisco, and we're making such-and-such a speed; so we'll be at San Francisco at such-and-such a time."

Olds said something about, "Well, there's still tomorrow morning, before noon—" (when the exercise would terminate). Then he added clearly, "I want the *Utah*. You'd better find it for me."

He made it plain that not only the future fate of the B-17 but also the future of the GHQ AF might hinge upon our success or failure. He said, "You were selected to fly lead navigator because I thought you were the best in the Group." Then he went back into the cockpit and sat down in the co-pilot's seat.

I picked up my octant again and made new observations on the stars, and re-computed our position. I computed an Estimated Time of Arrival for San Francisco. I scribbled it on a piece of paper and went up and handed it to Colonel Olds. "This is it."

He didn't turn his head. "I hope you're right, Curt."

. . . I came back up into the cockpit about ten minutes before my ETA was due to expire. I stood there between the pilots' seats and watched the fog underneath. With all that weather we'd never see San Francisco; but I knew damn well that we could see lights burning up through the murk. The minutes passed, then slowly ahead a glow began to appear, a great golden smear in the fog. San Francisco.

Olds rolled up that little scrap of paper on which I'd written the ETA, and tossed the paper ball at me. "By God. You were right. Then why didn't we find the *Utah*?"

"Maybe they gave us the wrong position."

"Well, something wasn't right."

Bob Olds never questioned my navigation from that moment forth (except to get nervous about imagined islands and things).

Of course we couldn't let down at Oakland. We landed at Sacramento Municipal Airport (the Mather base at Sacramento was long since in existence, but it had neither runways of sufficient length nor other facilities to take care of the 17's, nor any runway lights). Bob hustled to the telephone and called our Post of Command. No news yet. We seemed to have flubbed, but didn't know why.

There was nothing to do now, at eleven p.m., but to get our airplanes in condition for renewing the search, first moment we could fly in the morning.

The Navy was supposed to maintain surveillance all night; but soon it was announced that they had lost contact with the *Utah* in the fog.

We checked carefully on the condition of our Forts. News was all to the good on this: nothing seriously wrong in any of the twenty-eight engines involved; and we could buy gas here from the municipal officials. By the small hours of the morning tired crews had the ships serviced. Then we all ate a kind of supper-breakfast of hot dogs, and lay down on the floor in the hangar, and passed out.

Next thing I knew Bob Olds was hauling on my foot, waking me not too gently. I blinked at him stupidly, but his first words brought me alive.

"I want to tell you," he said, "how right you were last night. The Navy now admits that they were one degree off in the position which they gave us. An unfortunate mistake, they said. One degree! They were sixty miles off. No wonder we couldn't find that son of a bitch!"

General Andrews arrived by car from San Francisco a few minutes later. He announced that fog was thick all over the coast, closing down most of the fields. It was doubtful that the Navy search planes could be airborne in time to serve effectively.

". . . To General Andrews the results of the first day's exercise were: Navy patrol planes located the target, but Army airplanes were unable to attack it before dark because of the time and space factors involved; the B-10-B's did not have sufficient radius of action to carry out the task as presented; Navy patrol planes were unable to maintain contact with the target throughout the night. About the only things the GHQ Air Force proved this first day were that we could navigate and that our initial conception of the difficulties due to time and space factors was essentially correct. All factors favored the *Utah*. Our failure would confirm that the surface ships were invulnerable to air power."

With all of which we agreed, except for that fact of "Naval patrol planes locating the target." Maybe they had; but either through carelessness or intention we had not been given the proper position. We were positive by that time that if the information had been correct we would have found the *Utah*.

. . . Waited and waited, and still no word. Telephone inquiry revealed that the Navy amphibians were reported to be still fogged in at their own bases. Maybe so. The innocent assumption by some people in Washington that Naval patrol planes would coöperate heartily with the Army Air Corps in attempting to find the *Utah* began to seem palpably absurd. But, as before it was the only war the Navy was willing to give Bob Olds, and he had to settle for it.

The exercise was due to end at twelve o'clock noon, and we hadn't been furnished with any position, erroneous or otherwise. So there was nothing to do but to go out to sea again, and hope to God that a position report would be relayed to us before too late.

We flew out to sea.

. . . Don't know how far offshore we were when finally we received a fix on the *Utah* from one of the Navy planes. We found out later that in order for them to discover the position of the *Utah*, relay the information to us, and then in order for us to fly out to sea and intercept the *Utah* after receiving that information— They would have had to take off at four forty-five in the morning. Weren't about to do that: fog, you see. They didn't take off until over an hour after that time. Obviously it was supposed by the "enemy" that we were still back there at Sacramento, waiting in futility and exasperation for the position report. That we didn't do just that was because of Bob Olds' enterprise and General Emmons' willingness to play along with him.

And of course General Andrews' willingness to lend a hand. He was flying out with us this day and he had only one comment as he climbed aboard our B-17. "Don't fly below one thousand feet," he said.

C. V. Haynes and the radio operator could cope with such instructions. They worked out a deal: if Haynes went below a thousand feet, the radio operator was going to fiddle with the altimeter, there in the back of the aircraft where General Andrews was sitting. It would take only a small adjustment for the altimeter to read well above a thousand feet when actually we were well below that altitude. We were desperate men, and one crew member was just as desperate as another. . . .

Well, we got that second message about the vessel. I plotted it, and we headed in that direction; I worked out the interception problem. Studying the time element, it was apparent that we couldn't get into that position before twelve o'clock, and that was when the exercise would terminate.

There was not one solitary thing in the world we could do but go down underneath that fog again and spread out; although we kept within sight of each other.

It was the greatest happenstance in the world that we ran over that damn vessel shortly before noon.

It wasn't *supposed* to be there. We had been handed an erroneous position for the second time. We were heading roughly south, and they had given us the wrong latitude by one degree. If they had erred in the longitude we would have missed them completely.

It might be charitable to assume that an incorrect position could have been relayed to us on the first occasion quite unwittingly; or maybe, say, half-wittingly. But twice in a row—

Haynes and Olds let go with a combined yell which would have done credit to a tribe of Comanches. The noise they made fairly blasted me away from my desk. I grabbed some binoculars and went diving through the hatch into the nose. Our bombardier, a lieutenant named Doug Kilpatrick, was staring disbelievingly through the Plexiglas. Then he fell across his bombsight.

". . . *Utah?* I'm going to bomb it, 'less you tell me not to!"

This was a Moment of Truth as well as a Moment of Uncertainty. All battleships looked alike to us; we weren't accustomed to observing them. We had been informed that the *Utah* would be flying the International Preparatory Flag. When we first heard this, we didn't know what the International Preparatory Flag was; but I got a book and looked it up. Blue with a yellow cross.

I kept sweeping those decks with my binoculars, trying to find that elusive flag . . . it must be the *Utah* which lay below us . . . through receivers clamped against my ears I could hear C. V. Haynes ordering the rest of the B-17's in for the kill . . . it *had* to be the *Utah*. And we were at the wrong position; it wasn't yet noon; we were in the clear to bomb; and according to the position given us by the Navy reconnaissance patrol, our quarry was in an area which we couldn't have reached before noon. All pretty puzzling.

I spotted the flag. The wind shook it out for me.

"O.K., Doug. That's it." Glanced at my watch: five minutes to twelve. Then I turned those binoculars down toward the vessel again.

On the air you could hear everybody yakking at once as other B-17's closed in excitedly. You could even hear B-10's talking about it. They were away back yonder, and no stroke of fortune could propel them rapidly to our position. (Matter of fact, some of them damn near made it. Got there at three minutes after twelve.)

In detail we had learned of elaborate precautions taken to insure the *Utah's* safety and that of her ship's company. Any object or area which could conceivably be injured by a fifty-pound practice bomb traveling at an estimated 180 mph had been secured with heavy planking. All personnel would be kept below during the period of attack. So on.

Well, those people sure as hell hadn't expected to be attacked. I can't believe that news of a falsification program of position reports could have permeated down through the ranks and invested the crew of the *Utah* with general lethargy and carelessness. But that's the situation they were in when we spotted them. Sailors were sunbathing—or fogbathing—all over the decks, sitting round in groups chatting. I found them like that with my binoculars when the ship came into correct focus.

Then, as they discovered our approach, you never saw such a rat-race. It was like scratching open an ant-hill with a stick, and seeing the disorganized insects all going every which way. Decks of the ship were just one mad welter of sailors diving for the hatches; and the first bombs were already sighing down toward them.

. . . They tell us now that no one was killed. There were rumors floating around, years ago . . . some of those rumors said that three or four personnel had been killed. One account which found its way into print says that a number of sailors were hurt. One was injured severely because he stuck his head out of a gun turret during the attack, and a water bomb hit the turret right next to his position.

I remember watching the first bomb which smashed into the deck. It sent splintered pieces of wood flying in every direction. I hadn't realized that wood could frag like that.

All in all we got three direct hits on the *Utah*, and so many near misses immediately around her that the sea seemed to fairly froth with tumbling bombs. All I could think of for a while was, *Thank God I saw that International Preparatory Flag!* Otherwise there would have been a horrid choice between possibly attacking the wrong vessel or, on the other hand, letting the *Utah* go safe and free at the very moment when we had her in our sights.

The big ship turned, or started to turn, soon as she spotted us. But there wasn't time enough for any fancy maneuvers. We clobbered her.

. . . Everybody closed up bomb-bay doors and awaited Bob Olds' orders. There didn't seem to be much point in going back to Sacramento. We pulled back above the clouds, and Bob says, "Can you get to March Field from here?" Meaning, of course, did we have sufficient gas?—and all that.

"We can make it."

Olds and C. V. Haynes were walking on clouds or at least sitting on them. You never saw anyone grin like General Andrews. He had forgotten all about his order—that thousand-foot-altitude-safety-margin business.

But I had something else on my mind. I put down a little row of figures and then another, and called Olds over to observe my calculations.

"Look," I said. "Remember I told you that the *Utah* was too far away, and we'd never make it by twelve o'clock?"

"Yeah. . . ."

"Well, we ran over it, as you've just observed. And they were sixty miles from where they were supposed to be. Know what they did? They gave us that old business of one degree off again."

"Are you sure?"

I said, "I'll prove it to you. Here we are now: we're headed for this cape." Point Arguello or Point Conception or one of those. "If I'm right, we'll cut this cape in two at such-and-such a time. Because *I think I know* what our position is now. And it's not the position which was given us by the Navy reconnaissance people. But if I'm wrong, we'll be off course by sixty miles."

Fog had thinned by the time we crossed the coast, and we had enough visibility. There was the cape. We hit her on the nose, and proceeded to March Field at Riverside.

Telephones and radio sets were really buzzing that night. The Navy was trying to give Olds a hard time. They said, "Sure. Of course you could hit us with those bombs, coming out of the fog at only five hundred feet. We didn't have a chance to maneuver. If we had seen you coming, we would have followed a course of evasive action, and you couldn't have hit us. The exercise doesn't prove a thing."

They picked the wrong man to say that to. Olds returned the fire quickly. "All right, God damn you! Get out from under those clouds. Get out where you can see us, and where we can see you. We'll bomb you from altitude, and see what happens."

He forced their hand. The weather people admitted that next day they had forecast a hole in the fog south of San Francisco and just offshore.

It was clear, as they prophesied. So we got our posse together and went up there, and this time— No trouble finding the ship. There was no search problem here: it was just a bombing exercise.

We made our runs from altitudes, and they maneuvered, they used their evasive action. We bombed that ship systematically, beginning at eight thousand feet, and went all the way up to the ceiling of the B-10 (about eighteen thousand). Our 17's and the three B-18's—the Second Bombardment Group's contribution to the effort— We were each loaded with fourteen of the so-called Mark VII bombs. The thirty-four B-10-B's which came down from Hamilton were each loaded with nine bombs.

Nothing can be found in the files relating to the search for the *Utah* and the first attack made upon that vessel. There does survive a lengthy account of the above exercise held on the 14th. In which, God knows, they had no opportunity to falsify their position, or any reason for doing so.

What amuses me especially now (well, amuse is scarcely the word. It still gets my back up) is a paragraph in Section V of that report. Paragraph 4, reading as follows: "The number of hits obtained on 14 August during the supplementary practice is shown graphically on the attached chart, and numerically in the attached tabulation. Three copies of photographs of bomb impacts are also attached." Comes the unhappy message from our researcher, in italics and parentheses: (*Attachments referred to are not with basic report*).

So those have gone a-wandering too.

Anyway, we got a higher percentage of deck hits than the Navy's own bombers had done from a lower altitude in 1936, when they attacked under target practice conditions. Actually our total of effective hits was 11.9 per cent.

It was General Emmons, when he met us on the flight line at March, who gave us a first inkling of the disappointment which would be ours. He had just heard from Washington.

There was to be absolutely no publicity on the exercise. That was an order.

And well obeyed. I can't remember that there appeared anything in the newspapers about it either—even opinions or speculations of outsiders.

Our own report still lies buried in the files some place, or else was permanently expunged therefrom. Because the Government still went on building battleships. It wasn't until World War II, when the British *Prince of Wales* and the *Repulse* were sunk off the Malay peninsula— Then people became convinced that airplanes could sink battleships and cruisers.

Generally speaking, as Hap Arnold said in his book, "The Navy raised hell like a country gentleman finding poachers on his property." That's no exaggeration. I recollect the day when our squadron was out stooging around just south of Bermuda, and we happened to run over the Atlantic fleet. Next day we received an order from Washington, instructing us to confine our flying to within one hundred miles of the U.S. shoreline. I don't know who they were covering up for. It's impossible, even after all these years, to understand such an order, or to divine the intellect which authored it. We weren't planning to drop any bombs on our blue-suited friends, not even water-filled ones.

When we turned off on our last bombing run, down there south of San Francisco on that August day, the *Utah* had just four years, three months and twenty-three days of life left to her.

Then she lay in a Pacific harbor, and maybe people were sunbathing on her decks, even on a December morning. Planes which filled the air above her were not marked like the planes of the Second Bomb Group, and they carried ordnance other than Mark VII stove-pipe water-filled bombs. There resounded fragmentation and flame and misery, and the *Utah* turned over and went down, stunned and dying.

3

The following news release was issued by the Department of State, 9 February, 1938:

FOR THE PRESS. The President-Elect of the Argentine Republic, Dr. Roberto M. Ortiz, will be inaugurated on February 20, 1938, at Buenos Aires. . . .

As a gesture of good will, and with a view to emphasizing still further the community of interests between our two republics, arrangements have been made for a flight of United States Army airplanes to Buenos Aires, in order to participate in the inauguration ceremonies. . . . It is planned that the planes will follow the west coast route in proceeding to and returning from Buenos Aires, with brief visits of courtesy at Lima, Peru, and Santiago, Chile.

Sounds like a very benevolent gesture, and of course in some ways it was. But that wasn't the primary purpose of the trip—to make the newly elected President of Argentina feel happy at his inauguration, and to parade our reassuring Big Brother silhouette before other Latin nations.

Probably the whole deal was dreamed up by General Andrews and some of his people (no doubt Bob Olds and Ira C. Eaker came into the planning, early in the game) as an essential part of our training program, and as a demonstration of what we could do in the way of long-range flying.

Our initial South American flight was made up of six airplanes. No. 10 was the flagship, commanded by Lieutenant-Colonel Olds. Major Vincent J. Meloy commanded the second aircraft, No. 51; and Neil Harding commanded 52. I was in the crew of No. 80, commanded by Major Caleb V. Haynes. Behind us Archie Smith had 82, and Major Harold L. George commanded 61.

I have just been examining a copy of the letter which Ira Eaker sent as a memorandum for the Chief of the Air Corps on 8 February, 1938. "Subject: Expenses for Special Flight." Gas and oil were to cost $19,570, and there was a planned expenditure of $250 for ethyl lead to be used in raising the octane rating of certain gasolines which we might encounter. There is an estimate for $500 to be expended in services and labor. . . .

"This is a rough estimate only, since it is impossible to foresee all the eventualities which may require local services and labor in the progress of this flight," wrote Colonel Eaker, with lucidity and honesty. The prize item is the per diem expenses of personnel. $2,400: this estimate being based on a crew of eight per airplane, a flight of six airplanes, ten days of operation, at five dollars per day. Imagine what a similar South American trip would cost nowadays. Of course if anything was ever unrealistic, it was that five dollars per day, even at the time.

Officially the trip was to begin in Miami; we all went down there from Langley to get ready for the big event. I recall that on a later South American trip we had quite a time in Miami—landing, servicing, adjusting equipment, looking after maintenance, and then going off to the Rod and Reel Club for dinner. But on this first occasion we were all pretty much on the q.v. I don't recall that any of us left the field at any time before takeoff.

We flew straight to Lima, Peru, in fourteen hours and thirty-five minutes, timed from takeoff to our appearance over the objective. Actual takeoff time to landing: fifteen hours and fifteen minutes. We had flown two thousand eight hundred and forty-four miles, and that included about a hundred and fifty miles spent in detouring around a storm at the Equator. From studying prevailing weather conditions of this season, I had rather expected that: the intertropical front which it is normal to encounter between Panama and Lima. That was a fairly rough ride. We got split up a little bit.

But what I was most excited about— I had the only gyro-stabilized drift sight in the whole aggregation. This came to me as a reward for all the extra time I'd spent in trying to turn the intricacies of navigation inside out.

They placed our aircraft in the middle of the flight, so that I could offer, over the radio, the drifts which I was getting. Everyone expected that with the new equipment my readings would be more accurate than those we were getting with the other type of drift sights. Turned out to be true.

There was some alarm in the fact that we had to change altitude and weave around the biggest of the thunderheads while we were going through that intertropical front. But actually we all came in to Lima without the slightest difficulty.

There is in existence, far back in Washington archives, an indignant letter from a gentleman at our Peruvian embassy. He was busily engaged, under date of 19 February, in bawling the hell out of the State Department for a general foul-up which he considered should be dragged directly to State's door.

"Solely as a matter of record I feel obligated to refer to the Department's telegram . . . in which the Embassy was advised . . ." etc.

One can sympathize with the distressed official when he studies the details of this communication. Those folks down there had been advised that each airplane would transmit on 6230 kilocycles, and "only after the lapse of many hours was it established that messages were being transmitted from the planes on 5692 kilocycles." They had been told that the navigational call letter would be GBB 10; but we were using the call letter RT 8.

In addition they'd been informed that our flight commander would notify the American Embassy at Lima of our Estimated Time of Arrival twenty-four hours in advance. Our flight commander had never been instructed to send this message. In fact, he didn't know quite whom to communicate with, and finally sent a notification to Pan-

American Grace Airways, Inc., giving his ETA. Pan-Am in turn notified our Embassy.

Still, there were a good many people out on the flight line when we
got there three or four hours later—including, no doubt, the unhappy
State Department minion with both hands full of his own hair. It was
quite a deal: impressive to young officers and enlisted men, most of
whom were at that moment setting foot on foreign soil for the first time
in their lives (leaving out a stray sortie or two to the Mexican border,
when we were kids in flight training at Kelly or at March.)

Here were glitter and shine, and a babble of Spanish . . . aide-de-
camp of the Peruvian president; the President of the Cabinet; Ministers of War, Navy, Aviation, Public Health, Justice. Here were the
mayor of Lima, the Commander General of Aviation; and many high-
ranking officers from the army and navy, to say nothing of newspaper
editors, prominent capitalists, all the rest of it. And the inevitable children dancing and darting in the background where other talkative
crowds were massed, and where the police locked their arms and held
throngs away from our aircraft.

Most of us had at least learned to mumble *muchas gracias;* we got
along very well with the populace. Actually our time on the ground at
Lima was occupied in preparing for the next leg of the flight. We had
to gas up, had to find out about the weather; both of these projects
took considerable management to accomplish. In between times the
good people of Lima were serving us a whale of a buffet—right out
there in the airport, all set up. They had everything you could think of
to eat, and there were bottles in profusion. But we airplane people
couldn't do any drinking—we were going to be flying all night. Grab a
few bites of cold chicken and roast pork and delicious seafood, eat an
olive, and that was it.

It's odd about a situation like this: part of your mind is busy reviewing the flying time just accumulated and trying to note where you went
wrong, if you did go wrong in any way, and resolving to correct those
procedures during the next portion of the flight. There at Limatambo
Airport I went over and over all the technical matters, reviewing the
flight from Miami. We had taken off at five-minute intervals and done
our own individual navigation—both for the purpose of training and
also to check each other out. And I had been in the middle of the column, to pass out my drift readings accumulated from the new equipment. We hadn't tried to stay in sight of one another; usually we
weren't in sight. But with that five-minute interval observed at takeoff,
and remaining in constant touch by radio throughout the flight, it was
no trick at all for us to get together as we approached the Peruvian
capital, and we went over Lima in formation. That had impressed our
Latin brothers intensely. In fact it may have impressed them more
than anything else about the trip.

We had quite a gassing problem . . . it seemed to take forever to get the stuff into the tanks. There was only one fuel truck on the field and it had a very slow rate of flow. We gassed some of the airplanes directly out of drums, using hand-pumps. Gasoline had been ordered from Pan American a week or two before, and it was fortunate that they were able to get it there for us.

Once we were full of fuel, our problems weren't over by a long shot. As a navigator who concluded that a navigator's first interest was to concentrate on navigation, I observed that the weather was getting bad. I forgot all about the tempting delicacies offered to us by the hospitable and engaging townspeople, male and female, of Lima. Fog was rolling in.

It must be remembered that there was no weather reporting down there in those days, such as we have now.

We grew resourceful. Started calling up the mines—shacks of the mines where there were telephones, at various levels up and down the sides of the Andes. We would ask the operator to go out and take a look at the stars—to see the stars if he could. "O.K.," he says. "Yes. I can see the stars." And he's at such-and-such an altitude.

If I am recalling correctly, we got clear up to the sixteen thousand foot level, and no one could see clouds. We decided we'd better take off before it got any worse.

You could call it an interesting process, there in early 1938, to start out from Lima for Buenos Aires at eleven p.m. in a high fog. Knowing that we were going to fly down the coast of South America west of the Andes, proceed through the pass opposite Santiago, Chile; and go over east above Argentina until we hit the capital. . . .

So we were a collection of rather ambitious young men. The Andes peaks in that area run tall. If you had been avidly studying books about South America, as some of us had, you'd have an inclination to look at the fog and the clouds and start ticking off the names of some Andean mountains, together with their respective altitudes . . . Huascarán: 22,051 feet . . . Chachani: 19,820 feet . . . Huandoy: 21,089 feet. . . .

We took off individually, made right turns, went out to sea as we climbed. (All except one airplane; I'll tell about that later.) Finally we broke loose from the weather but we were still between cloud strata. It was impossible to do any celestial navigation and, with that cloud layer underneath, it was impossible to see the ocean. There wasn't a thing in the world I could do except use dead reckoning.

I had one of those monthly wind charts which gave you a general average of the direction of the winds in whatever section of the world the chart was published for, in that particular month of the year. There was no assurance, naturally, that we'd be getting anything like the weather indicated in that wind chart at this given moment.

But I went to work and plotted out the average winds; then I plotted the anticipated positions for the next several hours. Gave these to the radio operator and said, "When you can see both the stars *and* the water, wake me up." I went to the back of the airplane, lay down on the floor, and was out like a light.

. . . Then it was cold high altitude daybreak, and we were in one piece, and we were still flying. I awakened, and went up front to C. V. Haynes.

C.V. was sitting there in his pilot's seat with a hydrographic chart of the area. Those were all we had: hydrographic charts which show the shoreline, depth of water, islands, things of that sort, with fair accuracy— But the land is just a blank— In addition we possessed a few National Geographic Society maps. The Army Air Corps hadn't gone into the tourist business as yet. It was puzzling to sort out the basic facts of position and altitude above lands or waters over which we were flying, and coördinate them with such primitive maps and charts.

I asked, "Major, where are we?"

"Well, we passed Arica ten minutes ago."

That was the place I had headed for on the coast of Chile, coming in from the sea. We had hit it right on the nose, and within a minute or two of the estimated time. Those averages for the wind charts worked out pretty damn well.

C.V. changed course after we passed our Arica checkpoint and he was heading south along the coast for Antofagasta, Santiago and all. After daylight the weather shone clear over the land: you could see those towering mountains lined up along the eastern horizon. But fog clung stubbornly above the actual coastline. Trouble was now: we didn't have any details on the National Geographic map; and on the hydrographic chart the land— Blank. Thus there was no way in which I could use pilotage as a navigational aid.

So what I did was to take a double drift, establish our ground speed, and then employ a dead reckoning position. It was quite a challenge, trying to recognize those different towns which we could see and which we passed over, going south. We flew all the way down until we were opposite the pass east of Santiago, and that was clearly identifiable.

I was just aching to get through that pass. When we reached the other side I could start using a detailed map borrowed from Pan-American Airways—not a mimeographed job, but photostated. That offered plenty of detail on Argentina. Also we would be more comfortable when those vast beautiful sharp solid rocky Andes lay behind us, and we had the *travesías* and *pampas* underneath. Wild bulls or no wild bulls.

We didn't know too much about anoxia and the demonstrated need for oxygen at medium altitudes. There just hadn't been enough flying at altitudes where oxygen is deemed necessary. You might think that we would have learned a good deal from the balloon people, but their trips were very short in duration. They went up, came down, and that was that. There had been very little sustained flight in any type of aircraft over many hours of time and at those critical altitudes.

Yes, we knew something about the basic human need for oxygen—or thought we did. Our first equipment was all of the constant flow type: that's where, when it's connected and turned on, there comes a perpetual stream through the subject's air-hose. In the first days which I can recall, we had bottles, and an oxygen hose going to the bottle . . . what we did was to get an old pipe-stem, stick it into the oxygen hose, and then you'd sit there with that pipe-stem in your mouth, sucking oxygen as you needed it. It had a reassuring effect. You could feel it flowing out, you knew that you were *getting* oxygen.

From time to time these rudely cobbled pieces of equipment would get ice all over them. I don't remember any experience when the bottle actually froze up, or the hose, so badly that no oxygen came through at all. But you would get ice on those. Also, once in a while, your pipe-stem would freeze to your lips; then when you pulled it loose you'd lose a little hide.

Well, we were all Brave and Bold, as young people frequently are, and we thought that we were pretty tough when it came to anoxia, altitudes, oxygen, all that business. We knew that we could go to very high altitudes for a short period of time. Matter of fact, I'd been at twenty-one thousand feet without any oxygen, several times, and suffered no apparent ill effects.

. . . Did have a rather guilty feeling one afternoon, however, while I was still in fighters. We had gone on a regular altitude exercise—one of those cases where each individual is supposed to climb to a certain altitude.

I climbed up, and I remember being at twenty-seven thousand feet; and the next thing I knew I was flying around at *seventeen* thousand, and trying to climb again.

Let me explain the simple and most obvious thing about altimeters. They run in a circle on the dial, ten thousand feet at a clip; then they start registering again. So you have to look very carefully to see whether you are at seven thousand, seventeen thousand, or twenty-seven thousand. In this case I began to blink when it dawned on me that I wasn't away up there at twenty-seven thousand any more. I had come down to seventeen thousand, and that lost ten thousand feet was a complete nothingness. I don't know how I got down there, when or where. Just found myself flying around. Furthermore I didn't know how much time had elapsed . . . wasn't paying much attention to the clock. And this dawned on me: I had drawn a complete blank wherein I was descending for ten thousand feet.

I thought, "Something wrong with this picture." I went on down and landed, you might say with my tail between my legs. . . .

Before the days of the pipe-stems, even, we had merely stuck the small green or gray tubes between our jaws, and turned the stuff on when we thought we needed it. It was a hit or miss system. We didn't know exactly when we *did* need it. A lot of queer things happened. I suppose also there were some fatal crashes not identified with anoxia at that stage of the game.

By the time we went to South America we had graduated. Actually the visible equipment was very much like that which will be remembered by thousands of flyers whose recollection goes back to World War II: big yellow oxygen bottles, hoses, masks. Naturally our masks hadn't reached the stage of improvement which we attained during World War II, although you couldn't call that perfection, either.

Point was, we didn't know how long we should be on oxygen in order to keep functioning with any degree of efficiency and dependability. We were just guessing. Certainly we had been to those altitudes, and many times, without oxygen, or with only an occasional whiff. What we didn't understand was the *cumulative* effect. And we didn't have enough oxygen in our airplane tanks to grant us the privilege of going on oxygen—say, at nine or ten thousand feet, and then staying there blissfully throughout the entire journey.

We were going to have to fly well over twenty-two hundred miles between Lima and Buenos Aires. If all personnel used oxygen in lavish or even seemingly necessary quantities, we would find ourselves eventually up amid some clouds and peaks with no oxygen, Ma. So we were cautious, we husbanded our supply. We were too cautious, as it began to turn out. But still we were just country boys beginning to learn a little about life amid the oxygen-pots if not the flesh-pots.

. . . C. V. Haynes had left his seat sometime after Antofagasta; the co-pilot took the controls; C.V. went back to stretch out in the waist and have a nap. I remained in the cockpit with the pilot. This was all very exciting now. We would continue down the coast toward Santiago, then change course to the left, and cut through the mountain pass. Once through that pass, with the Andes behind us, I could rely on my photostatic copies of the Pan-Am charts . . . was looking forward to that, most eagerly. I was damn sick of using dead reckoning, trying to estimate the average prevailing winds, so on.

We found the pass. C. V. Haynes was still slumbering back yonder in the waist.

We looked over the situation. The minimum altitude at which we could progress through that pass was seventeen thousand feet. Even then we had to do a good deal of weaving around.

Someone must have sent a psychic communication back to C.V., for he woke up. There he'd been, snoring away without any oxygen at seventeen thousand. Anoxia hit him, though none of us realized it at the moment.

For hours we had been traveling at an altitude of approximately twelve thousand feet, long before we climbed and bore to the east to penetrate that mountain pass. Once again: the cumulative effect on the individual of being deprived of an essential amount of oxygen for so many hours.

This was all new. We were pioneers, and at the moment C.V. was the biggest pioneer of all.

He looked at that altimeter (funny how these sevens crop up in the anecdotes, but so it was . . . with myself in fighters at twenty-seven, and again at seventeen thousand). And now here we were, at seventeen thousand feet, going through that pass. Poor dopey C.V. was reading the dial as *seven* thousand feet.

He began to scream. "Seven thousand feet! Seven thousand feet! We can't get through the pass! Look at that! Seven thousand feet. My God! We can't—"

We told him as patiently as possible, "Why, we know that, C.V. But take a look. Please—look at the altimeter. See? We're at *seventeen* thousand."

Eventually he got it into his alarmed brain that we were at a safe altitude—or shall we say, reasonably safe—for making our way through that narrow twisting avenue.

O.K.—anoxia went on and went on. This time it wasn't C.V. who was the sufferer: it was myself. Once through the pass I was delighted to use those Pan-Am charts so laboriously prepared and so painfully acquired. They weren't growing around on trees in those days. I spread them before me, and went to work.

Picked up a couple of checkpoints on the ground, and started in to check my ground speed. Boy, what a fabulous ground speed. It was out of all proportion to what we were actually doing. I began to think that there was something in the rarified South American air which made our four engines out-perform anything which had been built since the days of Icarus. I checked again, and gazed stupidly at the numerals. My brain felt feeble and empty, and sounds began to seem very far off. Engines hummed and whined, but they were far far away.

Anoxia, just as I said.

I took time out for a big dose of oxygen. I had been using kilometers instead of statute miles. No wonder I got a fantastic ground speed.

There were other peculiar things which happened on that flight, but I didn't know about them until a kind of informal panel session took place after we were ensconced in Buenos Aires. My old friend John Egan was a navigator on one of the other airplanes, and— As I say,

John and I would talk things over, and mention things to each other which we wouldn't say to anybody else.

He whispered mysteriously, "Did you notice anything funny about your navigation logs?"

"Just exactly what do you mean?"

"Well, I found where I had written a note in my navigation log, warning me to pay my dues in the duck club up at Aberdeen, Maryland. See, I had written a note to myself. Get this, now. I'd written it in my own navigation log. Reminding myself that I must pay my dues in that duck club—"

I studied John for a moment. I couldn't see much wrong with that picture. "O.K.," I said. "So what's funny about that?"

John sighed. "It so happens that I'm not even a *member* of any duck club."

Normally in those days there were eight crew members in a B-17. We hadn't yet acquired a ball turret or a tail turret. There were the pilot, co-pilot, navigator, bombardier, flight engineer; and the radio operator who was also a gunner; and two waist gunners.

Far as the big Browning machine guns went, I don't recall that we took them along on the trip to Buenos Aires, much as they might have pleasured our Latin neighbors. Didn't have too many guns at the start, anyway. When the first B-17's came in at Langley they were too huge to go in the hangars—had to sit outside. So, not wishing our defensive weapons to be exposed constantly to the weather, we kept them in the armament shop and just put them in the aircraft when the program called for it. Also, on a long trip like this, we needed to save weight.

But we did fetch along a few extra people. No ground echelons had been sent on in advance. Except for the dickering for gas, as noted previously, there wasn't much of a program set up for ground maintenance and refueling. We had employed the commercial facilities at Lima—slow-hose-on-the-truck, hand-pumps and all. We were going to land at a military field in Buenos Aires, where we would have some help from the Argentine Air Force. But, by and large, we must be self-sustaining.

We were off to a good start in that all the officer members of the crew also were engineers: gunnery officers, engineer officers, communications officers, so on. Normally we served in those capacities on the ground, back home, as well as doing our regular flying duties. So we had with us enough skills to see us through, *if* each aircraft could manage to carry an extra crew member or two. These folks were a form of insurance; they would help out on the maintenance when necessary.

Our extras along with us in No. 80 were Bob Williams and Lee

Tucker. On the flight between Lima and Santiago, they were roosting in the radio compartment, sharing a little oxygen between them.

. . . One of the anoxia characteristics, as we learned cruelly, is that some people begin to feel like God. You are divorced from ordinary procedures; certain laws of the land are applicable to other people perhaps, but not to you. You don't need this and you don't need that. You don't need to concern yourself with trivial things, the way ordinary mortals have to do.

I guess Bob Williams was showing some of these traits, up there in the radio room. At any rate he wasn't using oxygen, and he wasn't giving a damn about anything. He was serene and remote, dwelling between the worlds literally and figuratively.

Lee Tucker had been whiffing oxygen right along (just a little bit —he wasn't treating himself too generously). So Williams was away ahead of him when it came to anoxia.

Here was Williams, all serene, not hurting in any way, and Lee Tucker poked him.

Williams broke out of his half-asleep condition. "What is it?"

Tucker says, "Bob, give me that five bucks you borrowed from me, back in Lima."

Dutiful old Bob reaches in his pocket, hauls out his wallet, and extracts a five.

He handed this to Lee, and Lee accepted it happily, and put it away with his own thin bankroll.

Bob sat back and started thinking as well as he could. He began to get the idea that he ought to have a little oxygen too. He reached over, grabbed the mask away from Tucker, and after a few breaths his brain began to clear.

He sat staring at Lee Tucker. Then the whole thing dawned on him. "You so-and-so. I didn't *borrow* any five bucks from you back at Lima."

Thus we learned about the quantitative effect of flying at medium altitudes with no oxygen; or without an adequate supply, and without adequate exposure to it. The experience was cheap at the price.

I looked down at those *travesías* and *pampas* after the Andes were behind us (and after we didn't have to haunt ourselves any longer with the spectacle of a threatening mountain somewhere in those ranges—we couldn't remember exactly where—a peak named Aconcagua, which towered to a reported 22,860 feet). Observing that strange terrain, I recalled my going up to Washington with Bob Olds, to see what they had in the way of maps. Was there anything available in the War Department which might help us? I guess it was on that trip that we picked up those National Geographic maps.

Believe it or not, there was absolutely nothing in our Langley files concerning South America at all. Not a single chart. And at Langley Field were based all the long-range aircraft we possessed, belonging to the military establishment of the United States.

. . . 1938? Seems like 1849 in retrospect now. We were pioneers in covered wagons, though the Indians hadn't yet begun to come circling out of the clouds to shoot at us.

Our official log shows twelve hours and fifteen minutes from takeoff at Lima to our flight over our objective at Buenos Aires. Twelve hours and forty minutes, takeoff to landing. We logged two thousand two hundred and seventy-two miles. Come to think of it right now, and with a proper salute to those same covered-wagon days, it wasn't such damn bad time.

Our 17's usually indicated above a hundred and fifty miles an hour, which wasn't a great deal lower than the speed achieved in much later models of this same aircraft during World War II, at the peak of the B-17's performance. The speed of those bombers didn't change much. There wasn't too much change in the Forts from start to finish.

The first B-17's were not called B-17-A's; they were just B-17's, period. The next model, the B-17-B, came in at Langley in that same year of 1938; we used it first on the Brazilian mission which followed by many months our trip to the Argentine. This airplane had a very steep tail without dorsal fins. Jumping up several years to World War II, our first combat model, the B-17-E, had a dorsal-fin-type tail. Then you went on . . . there were other differences, too . . . flight modifications. Came the F's, and they had an astrodome in the nose which the E's didn't have; and then later in the war along came the G's with a chin-turret housing twin fifty-calibers up front. Still the speed didn't change too much. There was better ability in this direction and that; and of course better fire-power.

Main difference, in the case of the earliest models, was that they had hand-held guns. Later models had turrets, with the exception of the waist-guns and cheek-guns which were still hand-held. But later models had self-sealing tanks and other improvements.

There in the wilds of South America we did lose a B-17 for a while. That was Vince Meloy, in No. 51 from the 20th Bomb Squadron. They had had prop trouble before we got to Peru, and they worked hard to get the problem corrected while we were on the ground at Limatambo. They couldn't get her fixed in time, so they had to take off after we did.

Instead of going south along the coast, they climbed straight up and headed directly for Buenos Aires. Top of the Andes, staying up high. It seems rather casual, an understatement of fact and of prevailing uncertainty, to say in an easy breath that they got down there all right. Yes, they were all right—came in perhaps a couple of hours or so after the rest of us. In that season of the year thunderstorms build up forever in the afternoon, in that area. But, by ducking around, Meloy and his crew made it O.K.

In the "Conclusions and Recommendations" portion of a report submitted following a later South American flight in that same year, Major C. Y. Banfill recommends "that full-feathering propellers are urgently needed for large multi-motored aircraft." He couldn't have been more correct, but it was a while before we got them.

Talk about Argentinian hospitality. There was every kind of activity in the world. When it came to the inauguration of President Ortiz, part of us did a fly-over during the inaugural procession (you might say that we were *in* the parade) and the rest watched from reserved seats. There were official government parties a mile high; Argentine Air Force parties; private parties given by rich and patriotic citizens. Our own Embassy had some parties. We didn't get to spend much time in bed. They keep pretty late hours down there.

Far as that goes, when I look back on the whole trip, I realize that we never got much sleep while we were on the ground. Either we were perpetually busy with the airplanes themselves, or we were being welcomed around from here to there on these complex social maneuvers.

Same thing on the way back. With the excitement of the inauguration and all attendant ceremonies and festivities behind us, we did the eight hundred and ten miles between Buenos Aires and Santiago in five hours, takeoff to landing. We had been several days in Buenos Aires; now we were a day or so in Santiago, then back to Lima, and up to Panama.

We made the fifteen hundred and fifty-six miles from Lima to Albrook Field in eight hours and forty-five minutes, takeoff to overobjective; and then took the usual twenty-five minutes to complete our landings. There in Panama we halted to do a lot of work on the airplanes, and ended up with a routine inspection of each plane. Then back to Langley, direct from Panama, with no stop in Miami.

There were a lot of miles of wet water to be flown over before we got home, and there was a lot of navigating to be done; and there were precious minutes and hours of sleep to be grabbed whenever possible. But still I had time to do some thinking. I looked back on the whole experience and the ruling situation, and tried to decide how it affected me and my career.

Here I was, thirty-one years old, and I had been commissioned in the Air Corps something over eight years. And on this first mass flight, the first long-range flight of any bombers to South America, I had been the white-haired boy who was given the only gyro-stabilized drift-meter. I felt the responsibility, but I felt the pride too.

. . . Say a little less than eight and a half years, from the day we got our wings at Kelly, until now. Where would I be, in another eight years? I was a first lieutenant now, and had only been in grade for a couple of years or thereabouts. When I clocked up those magic eight years to come, would it be possible that I might have attained field grade? Might even be a lieutenant-colonel? I'd heard of things like that happening; but it did seem to entail considerable acceleration.

(Eight years later I was a major-general, and had been for two years.)

Ours was a rough tough threatening fighting world. The Civil War in Spain erupted with new violence.

During recent months the Japanese had bombed the hell out of Chinese cities, and were seizing this area and that. They had sunk the United States gunboat *Panay* and killed some of our personnel.

Hitler was ready-poised for the invasion of Austria.

Italy had withdrawn from the League of Nations. . . .

A man could guess that there might be considerable turbulence in those thunderheads which loomed.

But leaving out the implication of European or Asiatic or even—Lord forbid—world-wide warfare to come in the near future, what exactly had we accomplished on this flight? And what did it indicate for the future of our Air Corps or our Nation at large?

A lot of imponderables had presented themselves. But just about the first step in dealing with so-called imponderables is to recognize their existence.

We had demonstrated that a flight of heavy bombers could proceed across land and water masses to visit an objective successfully at even as great a distance as twenty-eight hundred miles—a fifteen-hour flight. Of course we had had to land then, and refuel.

But *if* we could fly for fifteen hours *without* refueling, we had proved that we could fly for seven-and-a-half hours, visit an objective, and come back to our base in another seven-and-a-half hours. And if we could carry good will, and evidence of aerial efficiency, and plenty of handshakes— If we could carry these commodities on a seven-and-a-half-hour flight and/or a fifteen-hour round trip— It meant that, with a reduced gas loading, we could carry bombs on a shorter round trip.

By no means were we threatening the Argentine Republic or the Republic of Chile or the Republic of Peru. What we had displayed was the capability inherent in our accomplishment. Certainly it meant basing aircraft outside the continental United States, if we wanted to fight wars abroad; but also we had proved that our new B-17's weren't just Flying Fortresses in name only. Say that we might be compelled by historical circumstance to ally ourselves with Great Britain in a war against Nazi Germany. Could we carry bombs from a British base and place them on a German target? Yes, we could.

(In those quaint old-fashioned days, Americans believed humbly in the Monroe Doctrine, in fact as well as in theory. If anyone had told us that the day would come, within a quarter of a century, when the United States would permit a European-Asiatic government, which had expressed and demonstrated nothing but hostility during recent years, to establish itself ninety miles from our soil and set up an essential military structure within a strife-torn local situation— It was like the San Francisco Exposition and the Panama Canal all over again. We would have jeered at such prophecy, and seen no logical reason for such a series of events ever occurring. Matter of fact, there wasn't any logical reason.)

Better than everything else, however, for our immediate program, was what we had shown to our own Army people. Forever our Brass belittled the airplane's competency just as they had back in the Billy Mitchell days. We had shown them something which we hoped they wouldn't forget very soon. We had performed the hands-across-the-sea gesture in a big way, and our gesture was well received.

In triumph we could now come back home and take some deep breaths, and not draw them from the oxygen tank. It was funny, though: no one had felt the strain of the flight much, while we were in the process of doing it. Even oxygen difficulties didn't seem to affect us in the long run. We all felt in excellent shape when we landed at Langley. But there is a sad sequel: some three days later every single one of us suffered a delayed reaction. We collapsed—literally collapsed.

Our adrenalin had ceased to function. We were no longer faced with the actual problems we had faced on that eleven-thousand-mile mission. We didn't have to square off and tackle them. It was a *fait accompli*: Over and Out. And we just died on the vine. Pretty sorry business.

It was rumored that many young men were regarded with suspicion by their wives. The wives were thinking of South America, and all the flowers, and guitar music, and the rustle of festive gowns—most of all, those wicked little *señoritas*. When our ladies saw us laid out in rows, as it were, there was a feeling of indignation. Wives, suspicious as all women have been since the dawn of Time, couldn't help entertaining notions of sloe-eyed beauties in Latin America.

Hell, they didn't need to worry. There wasn't anything like that going on. We were all kept too busy. Didn't have time.

4

In May of that same 1938 an entirely different deployment of the B-17 took place—one which demonstrated a capability inherent in this equipment, but not popularly admitted or even recognized before. This story belongs in a separate package. I'll try to wrap it up later on, and continue herewith with our south-of-the-Border adventures.

We were unaware whether our trip to the Argentine proved anything to the State Department or proved anything to the Brass of the United States Army. But it proved a lot to the Air Corps. Plans went right ahead for another such trip. This time to Colombia.

I hoped to goodness that I would be included. Thought that I would, too, because of the navigation angle: new driftmeter et al. . . . Correct: No. 80 was tapped, with C. V. Haynes in the pilot's seat again. We started setting up the complicated system of advance details: logistics, personnel—

On Sunday 24 July, a crowd estimated at more than fifty thousand people swarmed over a new military airfield, the Campa de Marte, which was being dedicated at Santa Ana, near Bogotá. A plane of the Colombian Air Force smashed into the throng at full speed.

Stories of the disaster were relayed to us at Langley. We had arranged to be applaudingly present at Bogotá for the inauguration of President-Elect Eduardo Santos, just as we had witnessed the inauguration of President Roberto Ortiz in Buenos Aires. But it seemed to us, that night, that the mere notion of airplanes would make Colombia sick at its national stomach.

On that fatal Sunday they were celebrating the one hundred and fifty-fifth anniversary of Simon Bolivar's birth. The pilot of the doomed aircraft had been stunting wildly, a mere ninety feet above the enraptured crowd. President-Elect Santos looked up disapprovingly and remarked to the War Minister that he didn't like such damn foolishness. War Minister agreed with him. Next moment the dare-devil Pilot Lieutenant Abadia was spreading himself and his plane all over the landscape and the people.

We feared that our Colombian trip would be cancelled (but it wasn't). More than sixty persons killed outright, many scores mutilated or crippled for life. You thought of propellers scrambling into a soft wall of women and children, you thought of gasoline spraying out. Then you didn't like to think about it further.

I recalled eager cheering spectators, the tiny tots being boosted up by their fathers. *Mira, niño! Mira!* They wanted the children to see our 17's. . . .

Mobs like that: we'd observed them four times. But at the moment who would wish to listen to our engines, or watch us come in for a landing?

In the night I had a dream; or it might be more correct to say I dreamed a memory. It was something which had happened, it was not imagined.

Out in Emeryville, long ago, we children were fascinated by the race track. Instead of having a fence, the great circle of barns provided a barricade, and the way we'd get to the race track was by climbing over the roofs of those barns. We loved playing there, and had our own races when nothing else was doing.

. . . We're all crawling up on the barn roof, and down goes my brother Lloyd, smack into a pile of broken bottles. Blood spurted high, it came in squirts. Lloyd was howling but he wasn't the only one: everybody was yelling.

. . . I fastened my hand around his palm and his wrist . . . froze a grip on there as tight as I could clamp it; and the next moment we were dragging Lloyd away from that barn and up the street.

. . . Nearest doctor's office was that of a woman doctor. Her place was right across the road from the firehouse; we knew that well, since one of our chief joys had been to watch the firemen. Up the street we wrestled our way; somebody had hold of Lloyd on the other side, and I still kept my brutal grip on his wrist, holding down that severed artery. Matter of fact, I think it probably saved his life; although he had a real struggle ahead. The woman doctor sewed it up. Lloyd got lockjaw. He had a close call, but she pulled him through.

I woke up mourning for those cut-to-pieces people down there in Colombia—people with whom I now had some affinity because I had seen Latin American folks at first hand. I knew what they looked like, how they sounded. Their tragedy could bring back, disturbing it deeply in my heart and mind, the memory of a crucial moment in childhood. Coupled with this (because I thought in my sleep of Emeryville) there must have been the awareness again of Lincoln Beachy and the stunt flights he flew before he died; and of that other flight in which he, too, drew blood from the women who stood applauding him.

It is sad that all people in the World cannot know all other people in the World. If they could it would simplify a lot of things. Man's affectionate sympathy ought to extend to all nationalities; but it doesn't. It just extends to the ones he knows, or feels that he understands—the ones which he can reconstruct personally in image when they're absent.

That's unless the man is a god. Not many gods around.

On our August, 1938, flight to Colombia, we were accompanied by an officer who came from the General Staff, Major Charles Y. Banfill. Also the Weather Officer from Langley came along—Lieutenant T. G. Wold. The rest of our few extras were Second Bomb Group personnel: human mechanical insurance, as on the trip to Buenos Aires.

Many of the folks in our three crews were veterans of that February mission. But this time Bob Olds didn't go, and Major Vince Meloy became flight commander. He flew plane No. 51 from the 20th Squadron. Plane No. 62 from the 96th Squadron was commanded by Major George; and old C. V. Haynes had our reliable No. 80 from the 49th. In our aircraft the only two enlisted men who had been with us on the Buenos Aires venture were Tech. Sgt. Adolph Cattarius and Corporal James F. Sands. Otherwise we had a new crew.

We arrived in Miami on August 3rd, and didn't depart until about 3 a.m. on the 5th. It took us eight-and-a-half hours to fly to Bogotá. We effected our rendezvous over Barranquilla about 9 a.m., and from then on maintained visual contact all the way to our objective, even though there were very strong headwinds. We landed within thirty minutes of the ETA which had been sent to the American Legation by cable the day before.

By this time, having landed previously at Lima, Buenos Aires, Santiago, Lima again—it was all beginning to seem pretty familiar. The immaculate uniforms, each so different from our own; shrill squawking of children on the outskirts of the crowd; the trample-trample as a squad of guards marched close, the slam as they grounded their weapons; formal greetings, smiles, handshakes, flowers; proffered food and drink. A well-known diplomat, Mr. Jefferson Caffery, had come down as Special Ambassador to attend the inauguration . . . lo and behold, where was our military attaché? Not present.

Can't tell you why he wasn't there or where he had gone. Don't even remember his name, although a lot of heated remarks were spewed forth about this matter at the time. It remained for one of the personnel of our traditional rival, the United States Navy, to take over in place of the vanished Army officer. This was Captain John C. Munn of the United States Marines. (Far as that goes, the Marines have never considered themselves as Navy either, although they used to be billed as part of the organization.) Captain Munn couldn't have done a better job.

Eventually in his own report to the Commanding Officer of the Second Bombardment Group, Major Meloy recommended "that a letter of commendation issue through War Department channels in the interest of Captain John C. Munn, USMC, Naval Attaché, who gave unsparingly of his time and efforts in order that many details relative to supply, billeting, social customs, diplomatic procedure, etc., were properly coördinated." Vince Meloy also recommended (I take it with a tongue in a rather sardonic cheek, when thinking of the absent Army officer) "that the arrival of any flight of this nature should . . . be afforded the services of a Military Attaché in order that the personnel may be cognizant of local conditions and customs."

The reports reek with implied censure of the absentee. Maybe he went Over the Hill—which would be the Andes in this case. Maybe he was shacked up somewhere closer at hand.

We can assume that his career was somewhat less than meteoric in the future.

The skillful hand of the gyrene, Captain Munn, manipulated a participation by our personnel in a memorial service for those killed in the July 24th catastrophe. Vince Meloy was credited with dreaming this one up. The entire membership of our flight was present, as arranged through our Legation.

There were a band and a detachment of cadets from the Colombian military school; the new President with his escort of dignitaries; Mr. Caffery. We offered a wreath to be deposited at the entrance of a receiving vault in the cemetery. Major Meloy spoke briefly, with a response following from President Santos. *El Presidente* could speak with feeling, where the recent disaster was concerned. That out-of-control aircraft had torn the steps off the reviewing platform on which the official party stood. That's coming close.

It was the first time most of us had ever stood in a Latin-type graveyard. We gazed at the extravagant statuary, the architecture of tombs, the labyrinth of crosses and Saints . . . casual introduction of carved stone and marble figures which weirdly suggest a convocation of angels shaking hands informally. We thought, "How different these people are from our folks at home," and then we saw faces in the crowd . . . witnessed the intensity and tears. Eventually we thought, "How very much alike we are, after all," and we considered our own dead. We were beginning to rack up quite a list of dead airmen by that time.

On the infinitely brighter side of the ledger we went to a *corrida*. (Had to pay our own way into the fight, I might add. We didn't own any contingent fund for the buying of wreaths or the purchasing of bullfight seats; so that all came out of the momentary per diem.)

When you read the enthusiastic description of that bullfight included in the report by our General Staff officer, you get one picture. If you abide by my memory you'll get quite another.

The report reads: "The party took seats unnoticed as a fight was in progress, but just prior to the last fight attention was focussed on the group and a tremendous ovation ensued. The Matador, taking his cue from the attitude of the crowd, dedicated the bull to the flight, causing a further demonstration. Local residents stated later that dedicating a bull to a foreign delegation was a hitherto unheard of event and the demonstration of the Bogotanos was also most unusual as they are celebrated . . . for an attitude of cool, aloof indifference to strangers."

Now let me speak with the voice of truth. That was just about the sorriest bullfight anyone ever saw. There had been a great deal of advertising. The critters were Spanish bulls; there was a big to-do about this. Well, if they were Spanish bulls of the most famous type, they were Miuras; and if they were of an almost equal quality, they might have come from one or two or three other traditional farms. I have a friend in Spain who among other activities owns a couple of bull-breeding ranches. Lots of people from the United States know Don Pedro Garandarias; he is very cordial to North Americans, very fond of them. But his bulls aren't bred at any eight or nine thousand feet altitude, and that's where Bogotá lies. (Actually I think the altitude of the airport is eighty-six hundred, and of course there are areas nearby higher than that.)

Spanish bulls or not, they were sea-level bulls. God pity a sea-level bull who is lugged up to Bogotá and then released in a bull ring which is circa nine thousand feet in altitude!

In every case the character would come out, do one fast circle around the ring, then flop. One turn around that ring, and he had had it. . . . Charge? The *toreros* couldn't get them to charge, no matter what they did.

At a glance it doesn't seem like much of a compliment to have such a sad-apple bullfight dedicated to you. But it was the thought behind the deed which we needed to consider. So we felt duly complimented, and grateful to the generosity of the Bogotá people. C. V. Haynes, our own aircraft commander, was right on the ball too. Moment after the dedication, he sent a piece of his own insignia down to the bullfighter. It gave the crowd another chance to yell *Olé.*

In one of these reports there appears that recommendation mentioned previously about full-feathering props. They were, as stated, needed urgently; but on this trip no really serious incident took place as a result of not having them. The way it was in those days: if you lost an engine it just windmilled . . . if you were lucky, it would seize and stand still. Ordinarily most of them would seize after a while. (Trouble is, it puts a big drag on your aircraft.) But that didn't happen to us. It could have happened to the aircraft in which Major Banfill was riding, because he included this *Urgently* in his report.

What I remember in particular is a lot of discussion we had about whether we should take off from Bogotá on high blower or low blower. Our engines in those days didn't have turbo-superchargers. We had instead two-stage engines. You needed to shift gears to get into high blower and—

Say you'd taken off at Langley and climbed to nine thousand feet. That was just about the altitude where normally you would shift from one blower to the other. But here we were ready for takeoff at approximately nine thousand feet. We had sense enough to keep our gas load down; we were only going to run over to Panama.

When you are running at high blower it takes more horsepower to turn the high blower than it does the low blower. Still, at the same time you're putting more air in, which *gives* you more horsepower. There we were, right at the cut-off point. We had a hell of a discussion: whether we would gain more horsepower out of using the high blower than we'd lose in running the damn thing. It was a pretty tricky subject, and no one was quite certain. There were opponents to the plan, and proponents for it.

"With gasoline load reduced to 1000 gallons, no difficulty was experienced on takeoff." So the high-blower-low-blower question was left behind us for the time being. I don't believe anyone ever thought that anything was proved on that particular flight.

We made some detours to avoid thunderstorms, and got into France Field, Panama, at 1 p.m. on the 9th of August.

Incidentally, our average speed from the time we left Bogotá until we passed over Colón, came out at 205 mph. That was good traveling in a B-17, for then or later. By this time also we had cut our interval on takeoff to two minutes instead of five.

Vince Meloy took off first, there at France Field when we were leaving for Miami two days later. His takeoff was at 0830 hours, and two minutes later he passed over the breakwater at Colón, on course to Miami. . . .

We had more storms and detours, and then about ten o'clock in the morning Meloy decided that we should assemble over Cienfuegos, Cuba, and he informed the rest of us to that effect. Major George's No. 62 and our No. 80 came up with Meloy over Cienfuegos as directed, and we departed that point at one o'clock in the afternoon.

It was on this return trip to the United States that Lieutenant Curtis E. LeMay covered himself with glory. Bob Olds had decided to come out and meet us, over Chapman Field. We would rendezvous with our commander, pass in formation over Miami, then land at Miami Municipal Field. Naturally it was necessary that Bob should be possessed of our ETA over Chapman, in order to effect the rendezvous smartly and efficiently. People would be watching; the press would be there, etc., etc.

Here we consider oxygen again. If anyone wishes to read the report in this modern time, he can learn that Major Banfill recommended that in the future "a specification for oxygen exact enough to insure proper quality is needed."

Actually I don't know whether the trouble was due to bad oxygen or whether I didn't get enough oxygen. Doubtless it wasn't as pure as it could have been, because always after using it you'd have a dry throat, and you would feel groggy when you were once more on the ground.

I've told about the bizarre things which happened on the trip to Buenos Aires. This time I really demonstrated in a big way.

Our Estimated Time of Arrival, our rendezvous with Colonel Olds . . . all very tricky and all very exacting. So I gave our ETA, and promptly that was radioed ahead. What had I done?

Added two and two and got five.

Literally. First time I ever did that in my life, and I hope the last. You can imagine what ensued. Even though I discovered the mistake later on, and it was rectified (by radio again) there ensued a few nasty remarks from the airplane commander and from Bob Olds himself. Not that I blame them.

Two plus two gives five. Pretty sad.

5

BAD ARITHMETIC wasn't the only thing that was happening, along with the anoxia. I made my first public address. Got invited over to the Propeller Club at Norfolk. Don't remember what I talked about, nor is there a copy of my speech extant.

I didn't like delivering a public address then any better than I like it now; although perhaps I have learned a few things about speechifying during the intervening two or three decades. As far as the many necessary addresses which a Chief of Staff must plan, prepare, and finally deliver— We'll take care of that later, when we have to encounter the disagreeable topic chronologically. Just let me say that at Norfolk I didn't disgrace myself and wasn't ridden out of town on a rail.

Come to think about it, I wasn't invited back, either.

Another experience befell, one more far-reaching and profound. That was the business of waking up one fine day and realizing that I was a father at last.

. . . Our way to parenthood was so fraught with difficulties, and Helen had been so brave about the whole thing.

We regarded the oncoming event with awe as well as with the usual excitement of young parents-to-be. My first knowledge of the facts came in August, 1938, when the B-17's returned to Langley after the flight to Colombia. We had some kind of conversation about a well-kept secret; and then Helen announced that she had a secret which was very well kept, too. From then on we both entertained the feeling that this was It; Fortune would favor us, this time we would really make the grade.

The way Helen's doctor interpreted the situation she was due for an eight months' pregnancy. One thing about a Caesarean birth: you can pick the day, even the hour. The date was February 8th. I made sure in advance that I shouldn't have to be flying on that particular Wednesday.

Helen was in such wonderful health and spirits as she approached the deadline (maybe we should call it the lifeline) that it did everybody's heart good. Her mother wanted to come to Virginia from Ohio, and hover around. "Nonsense, Mother," says Helen. "Wait until the baby and I come home from the hospital, and then we can have a fine visit." In those days they hospitalized mothers and infants a lot longer than they do now. Still, she was home pretty fast.

Here we had our daughter, Patricia Jane; she became Janie overnight. Fate decreed that she should be an only child, and we had to adjust ourselves to this future.

(With Janie it took quite a little adjusting. She was always asking why she couldn't have a little brother or sister. Folks who have been in the same situation will know how we felt about this. . . . Eventually Janie got bravely over the agony of the solitary child. We inherited temporarily a little boy, the son of friends, who had to live in our family quite a while. Janie discovered that her nose could get pretty much out of joint with a younger child around requiring and/or demanding attention. The Why-can't-I-have-a-little-brother? routine became obsolescent right then and there.)

Mrs. Maitland came on from Cleveland and that was all to the good. Our quarters were roomy and comfortable, and all the nursery equipment which Helen had gotten together was just fine; but suddenly we were the noisiest place on Officers' Row.

The poor baby howled her head off after every meal. Then she upchucked, just like Helen had done long before at the Griswolds'. It was one of those pyloric valve deals. Fortunately the ailment is not too common, but it can really scare the hell out of inexperienced parents; so it did in our case. Here was the baby, fundamentally healthy . . . she was so pretty, looking just like Helen from the start, and essentially such a good baby too. She never cried except when in real trouble like this.

She'd be hungry, and she'd want to eat, and she would eat. And then, the food couldn't proceed from her little stomach into the intestine in normal style, because of that balky pyloric valve. Up it would come. We had one hell of a time, to state it blandly.

But the surgeons fooled around and eventually hit upon the proper medication . . . the tiny valve was relaxed, and soon it got to functioning. Then we could sleep nights; nor would we be agonized, daytimes, by the child's yowls. She got her weight back, began to grow, began to laugh. . . .

There were a lot of wonderful years ahead, and maybe a greater happiness with my daughter than I ever deserved. She was a proper Army Air Corps Brat from the start. She took her duty along with us wherever we got it; sometimes the quarters were pretty rocky; sometimes they were mighty hard to find. Janie was a good soldier or airman then, and she always has been.

If we could have looked ahead into a long future and seen the day when she would wear her wedding dress, and the flashlights would be popping, and her husband would bend beside her, and they'd do the traditional cake-cutting with the blade— Sure. We would have been happy in contemplating such future joy. But it wouldn't have made any big difference in the beginning or along the way. We've always been profoundly happy with Janie. We've had a good time together and still do.

6

A detailed analysis of sunrise and sunset tables, trade winds, seasonal weather conditions, and the availability of suitable landing fields indicated conclusively the desirability of proceeding to Rio de Janeiro via the west coast of South America, and returning to Washington, D.C., via the east coast. In addition thereto, utilization of the aforementioned route afforded an excellent opportunity to secure available information from a standpoint of air operations on the important Natal sector, to include its local characteristics as well as lines of air communication thereto.

The above paragraph lacks nothing in candor, especially the last sentence. It appears under date of December 7, 1939, in a report which Bob Olds rendered on the subject, "Good Will Flight to Rio de Janeiro and Return."

Likely enough when this report was properly carpentered, examined, revised, and signed, the date December 7 was typed in its proper place on all copies without anyone's imagination exerting itself in the direction of future historical significance. December 7th, 1939, and December 7th, 1941, were still a hell of a long way apart.

But a lot of things had happened since we South American flight

Columbuses and Balboas first started whiffing our oxygen above the Andes. Major-General Henry H. Arnold was named Chief of the Air Corps during the previous year, and in 1939 a huge expansion of the organization began. President Roosevelt signed a bill authorizing an appropriation of $300,000,000 and 6,000 airplanes for the Air Corps. Reserve officers were recalled to active duty. During 1939 our strength increased to include more than 3,200 officers and 45,000 enlisted men. Sounds like a modest number today, but it seemed pretty big then.

War in Europe had begun ten weeks before we ever left Langley on our flight to Rio. Catastrophe had befallen Poland; but not much else happened in Europe, and practically nothing on the Western Front. Already we were hearing talk about the "phony war" in the press and on the radio. Russia didn't invade Finland until after we'd come back from South America.

Certainly there were many puzzling aspects to European developments at that time. But what our military leaders had to take cognizance of and predicate their future attitude on, was the fact that World War II *was* in progress. It loomed ahead of us like torn cumulus clouds which contained already a good deal of frontal activity.

If eventually we were going to have to fight, we expected to fight in the air above Europe before we fought in the air above the United States. If eventually we were going to have to fight in Europe, we had to get our equipment over there in an efficient manner.

There were two possible routes for transit by air. Nobody knew how far the Navy could go toward keeping mid-Atlantic surface routes open. We had to think in terms of proceeding by air. There were the North Atlantic route and the South Atlantic route. Any fifth-grade scholar might open his geography, take one look at the map, and recognize that much.

The bulge of South America and the bulge of Africa push themselves out into the ocean as if they are trying to meet . . . the Atlantic shrinks and narrows at that point. Say it's about the distance from Chicago to San Francisco. . . .

Our Brazilian flight plan showed that we would proceed to Rio by the west coast route: Panama to Lima, then across the Andes to Asunción, and thence to Rio de Janeiro. But we would return by way of Natal, and Natal is on the northeast tip of the South American bulge. To people in the airplane business, that spoke volumes.

There were several other aspects which made this venture unique and exciting. Seven B-17's were making up the flight; of these, three were the new B-17-B's. By this time we commanded a lot of rank for the venture as well. Major-General Delos C. Emmons was named as Flight Commander, with Bob Olds as Deputy. Major George was Exec. It was a wholesome satisfaction for me when I was tapped for the job of Operations Officer. Maybe I had been forgiven for my bad record in primary addition. Apparently two and two *did* make four in the end.

On the whole we accomplished the entire mission as planned. There were a few minor deviations. The field was soft at Asunción, and No. 81 went deep into the mud, damaging three propellers. Repairs were effected, and 81 got into Rio four days after the rest of us. . . . Then No. 90 had lost their navigational aids early in the game, while we were en route from Lima to Asunción. No. 90 was plagued all the way along. When they took off eventually from Asunción on the flight to Rio de Janeiro, they were still without their radio compass, and weather looked like instrument weather in the Rio area. They were ordered over to a place called Porto Alegre instead (there are at least four Porto Alegres in Brazil). But it cleared up enough by the 17th of November to allow No. 90 to join us at Rio. Also they had further trouble on the way back home. . . . Old 81 had engine trouble on the trip from Natal to Dutch Guiana, and got in there four hours late.

No use in going over the details of takeoff and landing, or inserting an actual log of the flight. In many ways it would be a re-hash of the trips to Buenos Aires and Bogotá.

But there appear a number of interesting paragraphs here and there, both in Bob Olds' report and in my own.

Said Olds, in his Section I, Paragraph 8: "The B-17 type of airplane met every requirement of this difficult project. Performance obtained with the B-17-B model was thoroughly satisfactory, and represented a distinct advance over its predecessor. As a military type of airplane, the four-engine bomber, in the unanimous opinion of operating crews, remains superior in its particular class of aviation."

As for myself, I was harping away on maps again. Being a navigator by nature, I would do just that. Here's my recommendation: "That the information section of the Office of the Chief of the Air Corps procure and maintain sufficient quantities of the best maps available to supply any organization that might be sent to South America in the future. Maps of the types needed for Air Navigation are not available commercially for this area. It is recommended that the following sources be contacted to procure these maps," and then I went on to suggest that they try to secure material from Pan American, Air France, and Pan-Grace; also from various South American Air Forces, and certain oil and mining companies which conducted air operations on that continent.

"Our knowledge," my report goes on to say, "of established airdromes, navigational aids and emergency fields is inadequate for extended operations in South America. It is recommended that our military attachés in South America be instructed to contact the sources mentioned in the preceding paragraph at frequent intervals to secure this information and keep it up to date."

Come to think of it, I guess that little recommendation is just about the first shot I managed to fire at the enemy in World War II. Everybody went to work promptly and the map business boomed.

Lest anyone think that my concern with charts was inordinate or at least disproportionate to the necessity, let me tell about the leg of our flight from Lima to Asunción. As in 1938, we went down the coast south of Lima as far as Antofagasta. But this time, since we were bound for Paraguay instead of the Argentine Republic, we cut directly across the Andes, heading for the Paraguay capital on a compass bearing of about 90 degrees.

. . . Clear enough on the west side of the Andes, but clouds were piled up against the highlands on the east. There was no pass: we had to go up on top, on oxygen. We climbed to twenty-five thousand, got on top of the clouds, and came over.

There we were, with only a large-scale map of South America, and no detailed map of Paraguay at all. So I used a plotting sheet which had the latitude and longitude plotted on it. We knew generally where the rivers ran—the Parana, the Paraguay, the Rio Verde. The thing to do, obviously, was to shake Asunción out of the landscape by using rivers. What we did was to head up river about twenty-five miles so when we hit the river, we could turn down. Everybody hit it all right except one— Don Olds (no relation to Bob). He was over on the wrong side of the stream and it took him a while to find out where he was, and come back.

But before that we had to get past those dratted mountains. There was not much detail on our large-scale map, and we didn't know exactly where the mountains ended. It was quite a decision as to when to come down, from our altitude. We were all up there at twenty-five thousand feet, and we *all* started to have prop trouble because the air was so cold. Props were running away—they wouldn't stay stabilized at the rpm we set. We didn't lose any engines, but you couldn't keep the damn props synchronized. They were all running away and most earnestly we wanted to get down.

Bob Olds called and said, "LeMay, how about it? Let's go down."

I said, "Nope. I'm not sure that we're clear of the mountains yet."

This decision on my part wasn't very popular, I guess, but there was nothing to do except to use that map, and figure out how far the mountains went. Even then I allowed a generous cushion of extra time.

Finally I said, "All right. We can go down." I don't know how it would have been if C. V. Haynes had been sitting in that left-hand seat of our aircraft. But I know how it was with Bob Olds in that seat: he was just raring to come down.

The other planes were ordered to continue up there on top, and down we came through nine layers of clouds. We had been guinea pigs, and we hadn't banged into any mountains. I guess we were just about the most relieved guinea pigs anybody ever saw.

We called up the rest of the Flight and told them: "O.K. You'll come down through nine layers, but you've got plenty of ceiling underneath."

We went on from there, just using a plotting-sheet and dead reckoning, and hit the river. . . .

When fooling around with clouds and mountains a detailed map is a very nice thing to have. We didn't have one . . . just felt our way.

Same thing was true when we left Asunción and were approaching Rio.

You're right there over the bay and the ocean; but you've got peaks within the actual environs of Rio de Janeiro which run seven hundred, eight hundred, a thousand meters in height. Even that picturesque Sugar Loaf, down there by the straits, is three hundred and ninety-five meters high. A meter is nearly three-and-a-third feet, so figure it out.

Major-General Emmons may have been nominally the commander of the flight; but Bob Olds (his Deputy, and veteran of our previous South American adventures) was running the show.

Imagine how Bob feels. The weather is stinko. He's worried. What is he worried about?—he's worried about losing airplanes, that's what. His and everybody else's.

He's yakking at me about every thirty seconds. "Where are we now? What's that island over there?"

"Where?"

"Over to the right."

"Tain't no island."

Olds, stubbornly: "Well, there *is* an island there. Look out— See it? Over *there—*"

Me, wearily: "I don't think that's an island. It looks just like low clouds. There aren't *supposed* to be any islands over there. . . ."

This sort of thing went on all the way up to Rio, and there we encountered the glories of Sugar Loaf and other picturesque little peaks. I remember distinctly the detail of getting into Rio. There was bad weather, so we went out to sea and—we, in the lead aircraft—let down over the water. Ceiling was just about four hundred feet. So may we say that the boys felt they should come down very very gingerly indeed. Well, we all got down through that stuff and clung low over the water, and went up the coast almost on the deck. . . .

You look at one of those tourist pictures of Rio, and Sugar Loaf is just the cutest thing around. We stayed clear of it. As our British friends would say, good job that we did. There's another little bump over at the side . . . there are cable cars in there, running across. Ceiling was low, weather misty, and we didn't even see those cables that the cars travel on. We all missed hitting them.

"Total distance flown: 10,939 nautical miles. Total time between points: 63 hours, 25 minutes. Average ground speed: 173 knots. Total gas consumed: 75,210 gallons. Total oil consumed: 626 gallons. . . ."

Might as well put my old report back in the file. I guess on the whole it was a good report; because it was accepted, and won a nod from the Boss. But it doesn't tell the whole story any more than any report ever tells the whole story, be it a report of a banquet or a battle.

For instance, Natal. Natal in that year didn't look much like it appears today. A long generation and a long war and long years of air development following have put their mark on the town. But in 1939 there wasn't much of a place for anyone to stay, let alone crews from our seven B-17's. Also we had guests—ten Brazilian Army officers were accompanying us to the United States for a technical look-see. We spilled over, out of the single and inadequate hotel, into a local hospital. You might say that the nuns waved the olive branch and we waved the sheaf of arrows. I remember how sweet the Sisters were to us, and how they scampered about to feed the whole flock.

However, a man might be pardoned, after this long lapse of time, if he went astray on a few points such as the accommodations arranged for us, etc. There were several trips to South America, as related, and a lot of stops here and there.

Far as per diem goes, it seems that in every report there is some sort of recommendation about "the Flight Commander should be provided with a contingent fund by the State or War Departments—" Probably the recommendation was about as close as we ever came to getting such a fund.

Sometimes we were led into barracks, sometimes hotels. In Bogotá we were guests of the Secretary of War in his private house. That was something.

On a certain trip we had a finance officer, and he was provided with Government money to pay per diem with. Out of this fund, literally peeling the banknotes off the roll, he paid our hotel bills and any incidental mess expenses. The idea was that when we returned to Langley, if there was any residue, we would then submit—each of us—a voucher for the trip, and draw our share.

Well, back at Langley we submitted our vouchers; and it turned out that we all owed money to the finance officer. Of course you couldn't live down there at an average rate of five dollars per day. We were all in the red.

Trouble was, our finance officer made a tactical error a couple of weeks later when he bought himself a new Buick. You should have seen his face when we accused him of knocking down on our per diem in order to acquire a fine new car. Of course he hadn't actually stolen any of our money. But for a while he was the most agonizingly defensive young man who ever sweat it out at the bar in the Officers' Club.

In those days Air France flew a weekly or bi-weekly service from Paris down to Dakar, then across the Atlantic to Brazil. So they had a homing beacon at Natal.

And Natal, approached not from the coast but from the interior of Brazil, could be a hard place to find. The country up that way is about like portions of Texas—very arid, and not much discernible in the way of landmarks. We were depending on the homing beacon at Natal: arrangements had been made in advance to have it turned on between certain hours.

We landed . . . everybody was down except Al Harvey: his airplane was quite late. We didn't know where on earth that 17 had gone to.

Next thing I knew, Bob Olds comes up and says, "LeMay, you're French."

I just stood and stared. I had never thought of myself as being French. Pop had a French name, but he was born in Ohio and—

Colonel Olds pursued the subject. "How is your French?"

"Not very good," I told him. "In fact, not good at all. In fact, I don't know a *word* of French." And I didn't.

Bob says, nevertheless, "You go down there to that radio shack, and see if you can convince that Frenchman to turn the homing beacon back on. I tried to convince him, and failed."

Seems like the Frenchman who managed the beacon for Air France had decided that all our 17's were happily landed; and he wasn't going to operate that beacon any more, because he had been told to turn it on only from such-and-such a time to such-and-such a time. There we were, in and landed; he had turned it off.

It occurred to me as I followed dutifully on the course set by Bob Olds, that the man might understand Brazilian—or rather, Portuguese —but the trouble was that I couldn't speak Portuguese either.

The important thing was to overcome whatever linguistic difficulties existed, and get that damn beacon working again, so Al Harvey could use it coming in.

I hustled to the shack and waved my hands at the Frenchman, and he waved and sputtered in return. I went over to the radio set and made motions of turning the thing on (at least I tried to make them. I wasn't checked out on that particular machine). I pointed out of the window to one of the airplanes, and then made more signs, pointing up in the air again.

"It is still up in the *air!* It is not *here!* It is not on the *ground!* It is up in the *air!*"

Well, by golly, I finally had him hypnotized into the belief that he *should* turn on the set. But—no, sir—he wasn't going to *turn it on*, because apparently he didn't have any authority to do so. He had to call up someone first and get the authority.

Over he went to the telephone. It was one of those old country-line types—the kind which hang up on the wall, with a little shelf below. He cranked up the phone, and then began to yell in French or Portuguese or Amazonian or Sanskrit or something. At one point during this voluble conversation, he put the receiver down on the shelf and he was screaming into the telephone *with both hands*.

We never did get the beacon turned on before Al Harvey came chugging in on his own.

I might be pardoned for suggesting in my report that the available navigation aids were damn unreliable and we had better not depend on them.

Natal to Paramaribo, Dutch Guiana; Paramaribo to Maricaibo, Venezuela; then back to Bolling Air Force Base. But on the way No. 90 had troubles again; this time it was bad gas obtained at Maricaibo. They had to land at Jacksonville, and their complement of visiting Brazilians were picked up by No. 70 and toted along to Washington.

We had blazed out a route which a lot of other 17's would fly in reverse, eventually. Very definitely we had performed a military job, with the welfare of the Air Corps in mind and the future welfare of our Country. But also we had done a good Good Neighbor job, and were commended for our efforts in that direction.

The Whiz Kid Liberal of today smirks cynically at our attempts at Good Brotherhood in the 1930's. We are, in his trifocal estimation, still "the Colossus of the North." We, he declares in spoken and written utterance, are responsible for the ugly economic plight of certain sister nations adjacent to the Equator.

In so doing I fear that he discounts those unruly and selfish dictatorships which have sprung from domestic cells and germs, consistently, through the whole Latin American record.

They didn't need any outside tillage or influences. They could grow by their lonesome.

Our efforts of the time may now appear bumbling or childish; but at least they were well-intentioned.

It is easy enough to sneer when we observe the historical situation from our sophisticated complicated height (or depth) of the middle 1960's. How internationally simple life was in those days!

To be frank, we all thought it was a lot more simple than it was. If we had indulged in further gestures, and more concretely, and had exerted ourselves to follow them up—economically, militarily and politically—I don't think that South and Central America would be constantly threatened with Communism the way they are today.

Could be wrong. I'm no State Department type.

7

A WHILE back I mentioned that an entirely different deployment of the B-17's occurred during the year of 1938.

The incident took place in May, midway between the flight to the Argentine Republic and the flight to Colombia.

The 1938 war games were the most extensive in which our Air Corps had as yet participated. We brought everybody into the act. People came from California and Texas and the rest of the suburbs. There was a full concentration of Army air power at fields all over the Northeast.

Enemy was the Black Force. (Black is bad.) We were the Blue Force, with Mexico and Canada standing by, strictly neutral. The Blacks were an amalgamation of bandits from Asia and Europe.

By mere coincidence it turned out that the war games were scheduled for a time when Roosevelt's huge naval construction bill was about to be submitted to a final vote of the Congress. Navy proponents believed that we would be utterly defenseless on the east coast of the United States without a big Atlantic fleet. Therefore, during this exercise, our main friendly Blue Fleet was supposedly operating in the Pacific. The sea forces in the Atlantic would be incapable of more than patrol duties.

Years ago one of my people, Colonel Heiman, wrote up a version of these maneuvers for one of the magazines. He said in part:

"The GHQ Force was ordered to concentrate in the New England area to counter a Black invasion force. The fleet of a European power would be escorting troop transports; and Intelligence indicated that the landing attempt would be made in the New England area."

Actually the Navy was committing no surface vessels to participation in the game. They were still smarting over the *Utah* incident of the previous year, and had no intention of being discovered and bombed, suffering theoretical destruction, as the *Utah* had been eradicated off California. To quote from the magazine article again: "As the ground rules for this maneuver were laid out, the desperate need for a powerful fleet in the Atlantic would be very obvious."

It could be and was possible, when laboring under a command

which leaned graphically toward a concept of preponderant naval power, to approach the whole working plan thus unrealistically. If Air Corps planes could discover and attack a battleship offshore in the Pacific, even when furnished with an erroneous description of the area in which the surface craft operated, they could seek out and attack vessels in the Atlantic. Or so it would seem that the Navy feared.

They reckoned without the crafty imagination of Ira Eaker, who was just as resourceful, in his current position as Chief of Information for the Air Corps, as he had been when flying in the *Question Mark* along with the rest of that historic crew.

Eaker decided that the range and capability of the B-17 could be brought strikingly to the public attention. A famous passenger liner was to be selected as a theoretical enemy vessel and was to be intercepted at sea. Anyone acquainted with our General Headquarters Air Force commander, Frank M. Andrews, would not exactly expect General Andrews to hurl cold water on such a plan.

"He was taking every opportunity to reiterate to the stubborn General Staff that long-range air power was the answer to an invading fleet of carriers, and only the B-17 had the range to do the job. . . . Andrews fully expected the General Staff to see the import of this plan, but there was no interference or restriction. As events turned out, both sides underestimated the other's intents and capabilities."

The Italian liner *Rex* got the nod. She would be in-bound on the 12th of May, perhaps 700 miles out east of New York harbor. In this particular exercise we had to consider the time element as well as the fuel element. Andrews and Eaker weren't about to discard any impact which this interception could have on the public consciousness.

From the start there burgeoned an ambitious but somewhat risky plan. It had been decided that a complement of newspaper reporters and radio broadcasters would be invited to come along in the three B-17's told off for the task. Major Vincent Meloy would be designated as commander of this reconnaissance and theoretical strike. He would be flying along in our old No. 80, with C. V. Haynes as pilot and in practical command of the aircraft. Since C.V. was to fly lead, that meant that I would be lead navigator for the project. Responsibilities and puzzles inherent in these glad tidings were enough to cool me all the way down to my toes.

"If there had been a U. S. Naval fleet in the Atlantic of course there couldn't have been a maneuver, since the battleships would have sunk the invaders long before the hostile fleet could have come close enough for the Air Corps to enter into the fray."

But there wasn't any U. S. Naval fleet in the Atlantic, and we knew it, and the judges knew it. The obligation now devolved upon a certain lucky first lieutenant, to lead those B-17's squarely to the *Rex*, out there in the wide wet ocean, no matter what the weather. His name was LeMay but at the moment it might have been DisMay.

Some of Ira Eaker's boys had gone around to call on Italian steamship company officials when this idea was dreamed up initially. The Italians agreed to coöperate, with alacrity. No doubt they had visions of profitable publicity as a result of radio broadcasts and news stories which would ensue—granted that the proposed rendezvous was kept. The name *Rex* would appear in a thousand headlines and—the steamship people hoped—hordes of tourists would come elbowing aboard on future voyages.

For the period of the maneuvers our 49th Bombardment Squadron moved up to the municipal airport at Harrisburg, Pennsylvania. However, since Harrisburg was a long way from New York City, it was planned that the three Forts to be engaged in this search would move over to Mitchel Field on Long Island, the night before the exercise took place. Thus reporters and radio people could come out to Mitchel in the early morning and board the airplanes there. Besides our No. 80, Captain Cornelius Cousland was flying No. 81, and Captain A. Y. Smith, one of our South American veterans, was flying in No. 82. Our crew in No. 80 would be hosts to the NBC representatives—two radio technicians and an announcer. Newspaper reporters would travel on the other planes.

Major George Goddard, the Air Corps' ace photographer, would come along to shoot pictures of this history-making interception. With awe we heard that Hanson Baldwin, the *New York Times* expert on naval and military matters, was to be a passenger. Just one more good reason why I didn't want to be caught with my sextant down. I began to see rain-squalls and storm fronts under the bed. Didn't have to imagine them, either. They were coming. They were *there*.

May 11th was a Wednesday. When we got over to Mitchel along in the middle of the afternoon, there arrived a radiogram from the *Rex*. They had sent their noontime position. I seized on that radio message as eagerly as if I were going to win a fortune in the ship's pool when mileage numbers were posted. Of course I had been studying every available chart for days. If the *Rex* proceeded at normal speed along the regular route from Gibraltar to New York, she might be about six hundred miles or a little more off Sandy Hook by the following noon. That was when we were supposed to intercept her.

At Mitchel we haunted the Weather people. We were supposed to receive another position report from the *Rex* that evening, to guide us further in our calculations, and I had my charts all set up ready to go. But the picture grew darker increasingly. We would be finding the *Rex*—if we did find her—away south of Nova Scotia: latitude 40-odd North, longitude 60-odd West. For that area, Weather kept coming up with ominous forecasts of low ceilings, increased precipitation, etc.

To this day I don't know why the *Rex* didn't send us their position report that night, but we never received it. Maybe electrical conditions knocked out the radio message.

Some of the rest of the people may have slept; I couldn't sleep. With the first paleness of daylight I heard a gusty rain slapping at the windows of my transient quarters. I got up, chilly and dejected, and took a look. It resembled some of that good old Air Mail Weather. I dressed and tried to eat, but— Bah. The rest were in the same condition.

We went out to Old Eighty. Just to make the situation completely adorable, I found that the window beside my position was leaking, and water had splashed all over my charts.

We heard then that General Andrews would be greeting the newspaper and radio folks up at his headquarters in a few minutes, which information didn't exactly exhilarate our mood. If I should desire nowadays to become a complete masochist, and deliberately torture myself with a vision of the most gruesome morning on which any airman should choose not to be alive, I would select that morning and that ramp at Mitchel.

. . . Torrents driving down as if actually trying to scrub the grease off the concrete, clouds scudding and lowering above the white-capped Atlantic so close at hand and stretching far beyond the horizon. Wave-troughs, winds and—above all—the clouds. Low, storm-driven, opaque.

It was an errand of courtesy for us to go up to HQ and meet our guests and passengers. It was said, too, that the Old Man wanted to talk to us. So I took along my computer and some rolled-up charts. Good thing I did.

The civilian reporters and radio personnel were assembled. We shook hands, then the pilots began handing out the usual instructions. Passengers were fitted with chutes, and apprised of emergency procedures. I heard the word *ditching* and looked out of the window again. Worse than ever.

The other two navigators and I didn't hang around there long, however. We wanted to go over to Weather, and also we were in a tizzy about that *Rex* position. By this time, certainly, the latest position report should have been relayed to us. The steamship company had promised faithfully to send it over at least by midnight.

No report whatsoever. One sergeant had been calling the steamship office perpetually, and nobody answered, not even a janitor. It was around eight o'clock in the morning now. I started thinking about a broadcast to be made from our airplane when we met up with an object exactly eight hundred and seventy-nine feet and nine inches long, out there in bad weather on the stormy Atlantic *that very noon*. My stomach turned over.

Weather report as follows: a cold front was barricading our entire route. There would be all sorts of turbulence. Heavy precipitation was forecast. Ahead of this front there was also intense shower activity. Ceilings would be down to nothing in the area where it was hoped we could find the steamship.

Next thing I knew, C. V. Haynes was standing beside me. I asked him what time he planned to take off.

He glanced at his wrist-watch. "Something like twenty-nine minutes from now. Eight-thirty, to be exact."

All the hopelessness which I felt was reflected in Haynes' own face, as in a sad gray mirror. "Curt, can you figure out— If the *Rex* is on her normal course, do you have an idea about what time we'll encounter her? We've *got* to know."

I leaned over the counter and went to work. Dully I was aware that General Andrews also had come into the room, and his face didn't seem any gladder than ours. Several of the staff began crowding around the general and talking in hushed sepulchral tones . . . I went on with my calculations. Not that I hadn't been doing them mentally ever since I was out of bed that morning.

Before long I had an answer for C.V.

"I make it twelve-twenty-five," I told him. "That's provided she's on course."

C.V. said, "O.K. Repeat: we'll take off at eight-thirty."

General Andrews said a few words to all of us, in the soft unhurried voice in which he always spoke formally. Briefly he emphasized the importance of this mission. The *Utah* report had been buried behind bars and in the dungeons of secrecy. Thus it was all the more urgent that we make apparent to the American people the capabilities of our aircraft, and let them consider what might occur were the *Rex* a hostile vessel discovered out there.

General Andrews knew damn well what the lead navigator was in for on this trip. He looked directly at me as he concluded his brief address.

"Good luck."

I wanted to go somewhere and hide, I wanted to run home to Mother.

But— O.K. Time's a-wasting. Let's navigate. Let's fly.

And this was May. Strangely as we splashed back across that gray ramp toward the big yellow-cowled 17's, Herrick's words came to spook me. I don't go around quoting poetry to myself or to anyone else . . . *well, hardly ever*. But if you have had certain lines trepanned into your skull during a required course in Literature, you'll never be quite rid of them.

> Get up, get up for shame, the blooming morn
> Upon her wings presents the god unshorn.
> See how Aurora throws her fair
> Fresh-quilted colors through the air.

Aurora was really muddying up that landscape. Sure enough, when I squeezed up to my little navigator's table, several new leaks had developed around the windows. Charts which I'd left there were soggier than ever.

"So we never got that last position report, C.V."

"Sure as hell didn't."

"So what do we do?" I asked.

"Take off right now."

One by one the twelve engines on the three Forts came thunderingly alive. C.V. started to taxi, then slowed down. I didn't know what was happening, but some kind of excitement was going on out there in the rain. Next thing our hatch was opened, and eventually a wet scrap of paper made its way into my hands.

Our laggardly Italian friends had finally come through with the latest coördinates of the *Rex*. And the best sprinter at Operations had caught up with us, with not a second to spare.

C.V. poured on the coal. Next minute we were bucking aloft through the murk, and I was hanging on to my desk with one hand and trying to jot down figures with the other.

Immediately I saw that the *Rex* wasn't nearly as close in as we had expected her to be. So, by the time I'd plotted the position of the boat and worked out the problem of when we were going to get there, there wasn't much margin remaining.

. . . C. V. Haynes had asked for an ETA in that area, and I had given it to him. He'd said, "We've *got* to know." And I had said twelve-twenty-five and now an awful suspicion was plaguing me. I had a hunch why Haynes had demanded that I give him an ETA at that particular moment. Nobody had said anything, but I could guess.

We passed over Sandy Hook at 0845, then the storms claimed us. Most of the time we couldn't even see the water, and turbulence was heaving us all over the sky.

Frequently I have been asked about the altitude on which we were proceeding on this trip, and people rather blink when I give them the honest answer: "All the way from six hundred to six thousand feet." I have been in a great deal of turbulence through some thirteen thousand hours of military flying. I doubt that we ever flew in worse turbulence than on that 12th of May.

Weightlessness was a real problem. Every now and then we were sucked down toward the ocean by gigantic drafts, and all my navigational equipment would be suspended in the air. The result was that I was busier than a bird-dog, trying to navigate while the pieces of my equipment kept wandering around in space.

Good thing that Haynes had a massive pair of shoulders, and powerful arms. It was as if a giant clung to the other end of that control column and kept trying to wrench it away from C.V. I don't know how many thunderstorms were around; maybe a dozen. We kept turning and twisting, trying to avoid the worst turbulence in these, and were changing altitude constantly. Didn't dare lose complete contact with the water, for I had to measure our drift—hoping eventually for an opportunity to keep our ground speed accurate by taking double drifts and making necessary allowances for the change in altitude.

Matter of fact, I could do those drift readings with fair frequency by trying hard. Also got to do a double drift once, when we were in a patch of clear weather long enough for C. V. Haynes to fly it. Then I calculated the headwind, which was infinitely more intense than in the forecast given us by Weather. Our ground speed was at least ten knots slower than predicted.

Previously I had laid out a cushion of time during which it might be possible to bisect the *Rex's* course ahead of the vessel, then turn back and fly the reciprocal of the course. That was a welcome safety factor —included, naturally, in my estimate given to C.V. back at Mitchel. But now everything was working against us. We were traveling just too damn slow.

Vince Meloy made his way up out of the waist where he had been reassuring a very apprehensive radio crew. He was hanging on to anything which could be hung on to. He shouted in my direction—at first I didn't know what he was yelling—perhaps he was telling me that the radio people were airsick, as who shouldn't be?

But his next words came screeching remotely into my ears. Sounded like: "NBC will broadcast at twelve-twenty-five."

I groped for a hand-hold and lurched closer to Meloy. He shouted again. My worst fears were realized.

"Do you mean they're going to broadcast at that time?"

"R-Roger," he said. "There'll be millions of listeners."

"But at twelve-twenty-five—" I was gasping for breath. "Why does it have to be at twelve-twenty-five?"

"That was your estimate. You said we'd encounter the *Rex* at that time."

I asked, "And suppose we don't?"

He looked as thoughtful as a man can look when he is trying to keep his feet from poking holes in the floor and trying to keep his head from splitting open against the roof.

"We'll fake it," he said.

"Fake it, hell! With a bunch of radio reporters aboard?"

Meloy says, "Well, either we find the *Rex* or we don't." He made his precarious return to the radio room.

I crept over to C. V. Haynes' seat, and hung there while I tried to yell in his ear and explain the exact situation. I told him about our ground speed: at least ten knots slower than prophesied. I explained about not having any margin of time in which to fly the reciprocal of the course, if we cut the *Rex's* path ahead of the ship. Wasn't there any way of delaying that broadcast? . . . No, it appeared that there was not. These things had to be set up in advance. That was the reason Haynes had asked me for an estimate while we were still on the ground at Mitchel.

Glad he didn't tell me what it was all about, at the time. They really would have had to carry me aboard that aircraft.

We plunged into another line squall. Our pilot was fighting wheel and column while he tried to listen to me.

"You're the navigator, Curt," was the best I could get out of him.

I tottered back to my own position, and picked up a pencil; shook the charts, tried to blow the water off. I went to work once more. That was my only refuge.

The cockpit area darkened. I looked out to see what in—

We had a great big dusky wall looming ahead of us. That was the cold front. Above the growl of the four engines, above all the banging and crashing and clanking, and distant quacking of radio voices . . . yes, C.V. was telling Smith and Cousland, in 82 and 81 respectively, to move out on his wing, in order to penetrate the front individually. We were out of sight of one another, but we had been in constant radio contact.

Boom. We went into that Maytime cold front like a bullet going into a back-stop on the target range, no matter how hard C.V. sought to retard our speed.

> . . . Come, we'll abroad; and let's obey
> The proclamation made for May:
> And sin no more, as we have done, by staying;
> But, my Corinna, come, let's go a-Maying.

It took us about ten minutes to get through the front. Haynes might as well have been rolling all over the mat with Strangler Lewis. But he won, Ma. We felt like slapping him on the shoulders to indicate that fall was his.

We came out into bright sunshine. C.V. called in the other airplanes. Soon as they had rejoined us, I asked him to fly another series of turns. Again and again I checked: there seemed to be nothing wrong with my results. There was no longer any safety margin, but the present course should bring us into a perfect interception of the liner. *If* I was correct in my calculations.

It had all been dead reckoning; there were no cities or rivers or any other landmarks underneath—only thousands of square miles of agitated water.

I thought about what Meloy had said . . . *either we find it or we don't.*

We were now flying the three Forts in a thirty-mile-broad search band. Still, thirty miles was a narrow little ribbon when extended against those tossing empty masses of gray swells and torn spume.

. . . Looked at my watch. 1221. Sunlight vanished, again we were in the clutch of a squall; the rain beat like leaden pellets against the windows.

1223. Columns of murky clouds split, staggered aside; we were coming out of this later squall, we could even see the ocean. 1225. . . .

Dead ahead was the Italian liner: a toy beauty, neat and proud and compact. We could even see the fat bands of red-white-and-green encircling her thick modern funnels. Yes, this was the *Rex*. We didn't have to come close enough to read the golden name emblazoned on her bows, in order to know that.

It was all a movie. It was happening to someone else, it wasn't real, wasn't happening to us.

Now we were down there joining her, at mast level. Hundreds of passengers swarmed the decks, wrapped in raincoats and scarves, waving madly up at us.

Back in the radio compartment Vince Meloy had already achieved contact with the *Rex's* captain. The captain's invitation came sputtering over the air. "It will be so nice if you gentlemen will please come down for lunch!"

Meloy sighed. Like the rest of us, he had done nothing but nibble on a scrap of Hershey bar since getting up that morning.

"I thank you, Captain Cavallini, from the bottom of my heart. But here is one *antipasto* and one *pasta* which we must forego. To say nothing of the bottle of Chianti!"

While all this was going on, I gazed out and down and over at the *Rex* phlegmatically. I still couldn't quite believe that she was there, but she was. Somewhere back behind all this I was also aware foggily that Major Goddard must be shooting his pictures. And the broadcast must be going on, on quite another wave length: the one originating in the waist of our airplane.

I tried to envision all those millions of listeners, clear back across the continent, listening amiably and contentedly to that broadcast.

"Pa."

"What say?"

"You ought to come here and listen to the radio."

"What's going on?"

"Oh, the announcer's in a great big Army airplane, and they're just flown away out in the Atlantic Ocean, and they met an Eye-talian boat, and he's telling about it."

"My, my."

Actually we had a worse time weatherwise going back than we had coming out. The cold front had moved to a position where we had to punch it going back. It was getting later in the afternoon, when thunderstorms always build up in intensity. We didn't have enough gas to fly around those storms; they were all up and down the coast; just had to go smack through the middle. When we hit that stuff it was rougher than hell.

. . . The artificial horizon went blooey just as quick as snapping your fingers. That was the last we saw of *that*. The rate-of-climb indicator was jiggling so badly you couldn't see a damn thing. The bank-and-turn indicator was hitting the peg on both sides. I remember watching our air speed: it would run down to about 80 miles an hour, then up to about 240. Old No. 80 banged and trembled as if she were coming apart at the seams.

J. B. Montgomery had been co-pilot on the way out. After the interception of the *Rex* he retreated to the rear, and Meloy came up and sat in the co-pilot's seat. Then all this flopping started in. I'll say it again at the risk of wearying the reader: this was positively *twice* as bad as going out.

Montgomery appeared—staggering, crawling, flapping, swaying—and there I was, hanging onto my navigator's seat like grim death. Monty went past me. I suppose he had some thought of taking over and letting Meloy go back into the waist instead. But he took one look, saw those instruments, and he turned absolutely green. Next thing I knew he had disappeared back yonder again. There were some very very unhappy NBC people back there, too, no matter how successful their broadcast.

At times on that return to land we began to wonder whether we'd really make it. It was that close.

After we landed at Mitchel, Cousland beckoned me over to take a look at his aircraft. He had been some miles away from us when they got into hail, and it was big hail too. All the leading edges of the wings, and the nose of the airplane, were pebbled and pitted. Looked like a gang of blacksmiths had been beating on them with ball-peen hammers.

The *New York Times* said: "The performance of the giant Boeings in intercepting the Italian liner Rex 610 miles off Sandy Hook was the feature of the first day of mimic war. . . . It was an imaginary and bloodless conflict, but one from which valuable lessons about the aerial defense of the United States will be drawn, and one which already has furnished . . . a striking example of the mobility and range of modern aviation."

Time magazine took note of the maneuver and devoted two pages to the story. The name of the lead navigator appeared as Lieutenant Curtis Selby, but I knew it was LeMay all the time.

It would be difficult to exaggerate the elation of General Andrews at our successful accomplishment of the *Rex* interception. The next few days of the war games were conducted with a lot of dash and imagination. One hundred and eighty-seven combat planes had been assembled on airfields in the Northeast, and all of these got into the act. On paper we sank nearly half of the enemy's carriers. The Black Fleet was really ripped apart, and there was little modesty exemplified among the GHQ flyers.

It remained for General Andrews to soothe a troubled military climate with one of his gentle little statements:

"I notice from some press reports that there is a tendency to indicate that the Army GHQ Air Force is planning to fight a war by itself. I would like to correct that impression. . . . We must realize that in common with the mobilization of the Air Force in this area, the ground arms of the Army would also be assembling, prepared to take the major role in repelling the actual landing forces . . . I want to ask that you do not accuse us of trying to win a war alone."

Obviously this was in answer to Army General Staff pressure. But another pressure force was at work, and its effect was to restrict our simulated combat and patrol operations to within one hundred miles of the shore. (Did not apply to South American Good Will Suburban Delivery Co. activities.)

This was the Bermuda incident all over again.

Interesting little follow-up on this, later—years later, in fact. When Tooey Spaatz became Chief of Staff he had reason to seek out a copy of that restrictive order, the one keeping us within one hundred miles of land.

His people came up empty-handed.

"But where is the copy of that order? I remember it, at the time it was received. . . ."

"Sorry, sir. We've searched every file for that year. Can't find it any place."

It had been removed from the Army files. I won't attempt to guess *who* snuck it out of there. But I think I know *why*.

BOOK IV

AAF: War Against Germany

(1941 – 1944)

Late in 1940 and early in 1941 the expansion of the Air Corps was no longer an entity hoped for, begged for, but not yet bought. It was no longer a vague dream suspended in the future. It was urgently alive and all around us, confusing, demanding and—soon—terrifying. A lightning-speed growth, even if required desperately, can be a mixed blessing for those who must manipulate it.

(On 20 June, 1941, the Army Air Forces came into existence with Major-General Hap Arnold in command. The old Air Corps ceased to exist on that date, but American public and press refused to be convinced. Still refuse, in 1965. All through World War II it was, "Our grandson is in the Air *Corps*." "Local Young Man Enlists in Air *Corps*." So on. We achieved autonomy in 1947, and got loose from the Army, and became the United States Air *Force*. Didn't make a particle of difference to Grandma, Grandpa and the *Judith Junction Weekly Herald*. "Our grandson is in the Army Air *Corps*." "Local Young Man Enlists in Air *Corps*." So on.)

No longer were there any limitations on the number of aircraft which we might maintain. Also sales of modern combat planes to the anti-Axis allies were in full swing.

Soon the Second Bomb Group was divided into three groups. One went to MacDill, one to Puerto Rico, one stayed at Langley. It was like splitting kindlings when you were a kid: first there was a split in two, and then maybe each of those pieces was split in three. That was the way it went: you found yourself in a group, then suddenly you were in one of two groups; then they were split again.

Along about February or March of '41, with new organizations mushrooming in every damp dawn, I found myself a squadron commander in the 34th Bomb Group. I had made captain in late January of 1940; now I was, only thirteen or fourteen months later, a temporary major. But the stuff was hitting the fan all over the place. I didn't have time to meditate on what seemed a miraculously rapid promotion. It was happening to everybody.

They were starting to build up Westover Air Base. That's the installation near Springfield, Massachusetts, which was for years the jumping-off place for transport planes which cross the Atlantic. Westover is quite a plant in modern times, but this was less than a year before Pearl Harbor. No barracks . . . all the men quartered in hangars. . . .

We went to Massachusetts, and Helen found a house. Or maybe

Janie found it; I don't know, I was too busy to turn around and look when we moved in. I installed our stuff at the base; it didn't take long —we only had a few airplanes, and our equipment seemed to have come out of the tool-shed at the Poor Farm. Next thing I knew, I was relieved as squadron commander and made group Operations Officer. This was because of long experience racked up in B-17's.

One afternoon the telephone rang. It was C. V. Haynes, former commander of the 49th Squadron. You could never mistake him for anyone else when he was on the phone; the voice always came through then, though his North Carolina pronunciations were so extreme that lots of people couldn't understand him well in ordinary conversation.

C.V. says, "Want you to meet me in Montreal."

"What for?"

"Can't tell you that. I've got a job to do, and I think you may have a new job also."

"Where and when?"

C.V. says, "Get on a commercial airliner and come on up to Montreal tonight. I want you to meet me here tomorrow morning at nine."

"But *where?*"

It seemed that he replied, "At Farrell." I thought, "What Farrell does he mean? Hotel Farrell? Is there a suburb or an airport in Montreal called Farrell?"

He said, "Oh, come on, you'll find it." He spelled it out. *A-T-F-E-R-O.*

On this one I was a real dope. Later we were told that the name originated in a division of the Canadian Pacific Railroad; they were then busily engaged in ferrying airplanes from Canada to Britain. That was part of Canadian Pacific's wartime job. But it was a code name, and I still think it's funny that I didn't recognize it as such: AT for Atlantic, FER for ferry, O for Organization. It operated under the aegis of the British Ministry of Aircraft Production.

The Canucks had been hiring barnstormers and ex-airline pilots by the bushel. They would engage almost anyone who was willing to go up to Canada and apply—anyone who knew how to fly an airplane at all, and was willing to try to fly one across the Atlantic. I couldn't quite bring myself to believe that C. V. Haynes was recommending a resignation from the U. S. Army for both of us, and a subsequent pledging of ourselves to a well-paid job in this racket. But when Haynes said go or come, the idea was to go or come.

I told my CO that something was cooking—I didn't know what. "But C. V. Haynes said to me, 'Orders will come.' So I'm calling you up, as he told me to do."

Our group commander didn't hesitate. "If Colonel Haynes told you to meet him up there, you'd better do it. I'll find somebody to do your work. Go ahead and take off."

Dressed in civilian clothes, I got on a small airliner (I think it was

Northeast) and started for Montreal. We ran into a wicked storm and landed someplace up in northern Vermont—maybe St. Albans. There wasn't anything to do but leave the airplane. The airline provided a taxicab to run me up to Montreal. That's not very far above the border, only takes an hour or two. When we were stopped at the border station, I got out of the cab and drew a couple of the Canadian customs people or immigration officers off to one side.

"Where on earth is this ATFERO place? I'm supposed to go there, but don't know where it is."

One of the officials responded quickly in his clipped Canadian accent, "Really, I don't know anything about it. But— This is what you want—" He handed over a mimeographed sheet which showed all the Royal Canadian Air Force recruiting stations. He knew well enough what and where ATFERO was, but undoubtedly had received instructions not to talk about it, especially to people coming from the United States side of the line. Obviously he thought that I was coming up there to get into the fly business. In a way I was. But not the RCAF, as he believed.

It was late at night when we reached Montreal. I managed to grab a few hours' sleep in the first hotel I could find. In the early morning I went to the U. S. Consulate; was there when they opened up. I identified myself to the consul. He knew all about ATFERO and sent me over to the right place.

. . . Here was C. V. Haynes, big as life, along with some more Air Corps types whom I knew right well.

C.V. briefed us on his plan. "We Yanks are going to start our own airline across the North Atlantic. The Canadians and British have demonstrated that the traffic is clogging up already. We've got to get passengers back and forth, especially *forth,* more quickly than they've been doing."

The trick, as he related it to us, dealt with new B-24's which were just starting to come off the production line. We would take the 24 and load the bomb-bay with passengers—British and American Brass, diplomats, technicians, journalists—instead of GP bombs.

To begin with, I might add, some people had big plans for the B-15 getting into the act. But when we studied that particular aircraft in relation to the North Atlantic route we began to shake our heads. C.V. especially was shaking his. The 15 wouldn't fly high enough to get above that soup, and on the North Atlantic route you're bound to be in the stuff much of the time at cruising altitudes. You'd be icing up and everything else. The B-24, with its enormously increased fuel capacity, greater speed and range and altitude capability, was more to the point.

Eventually we had it squared away to use our lone B-15 to haul passengers up as far as Gander Lake, and then switch our cargo of humans into a B-24 for the long jump across the Atlantic.

Bob Olds had been ordered to the job of founding our ferry command (superseded later by the Air Transport Command). First off, Olds wanted to get together some of the experienced long-range people from the Second Bomb Group. He gave C. V. Haynes the chore of discovering what our Canadian cousins were doing in the ferry direction.

C.V. had looked into their communications, learned what routes they were flying, what frequencies they were using, where their weather forecasting was coming from: all about the operation. In the future we could assume that we would be using some of the same matériel and proceeding along the same lines. We would be employing identical weather procedures and (if possible) dispatching procedures.

That's why we people were all suddenly plucked off our regular jobs and put on this Detached Service.

Even though we weren't technically a belligerent as yet, the United States was getting more and more into the war effort. We were shipping Government people to Europe all the time. High-ranking Britishers and Americans alike were to be crowded into those waists and bomb-bays. (I remember taking Lady Halifax over on my first trip— wife of the British Ambassador. Necessarily there was some kind of flap about getting a special Ladies' Room set up for Her Ladyship, back in the waist somewhere. But I don't recall that she instigated the procedure, or ever made any demand for special consideration because of her sex or rank.)

Domestically also there would be necessarily a new system in the acceptance and delivery of airplanes from factories to Army Air Force units. Previously—as in 1937, when we picked up our first few B-17's— the outfit which was going to get the airplane would send a pilot and crew out to the factory, and they'd fly the plane back to their outfit in the field. But those had been driblets before, insofar as new equipment was concerned. Now there was an increasing stream . . . soon there would be a mighty flow of bombers and fighters to supply the vast number of groups which were being penciled in on paper, and which would eventually be actual flesh and blood at scores of new bases. It was essential to establish a more businesslike way of getting the planes to the people. A ferry organization was the answer.

The first North Atlantic Ferry Command is a story in itself. The man who was running this at the start was a comparatively young fellow named Bennett. He was a civilian, working for the Canadian Pacific Railroad. But shortly thereafter the RAF took the whole system over; Bennett, as boss of this operation, found himself in the Royal Air Force as a pilot officer. A pilot officer is identical with our rank of second lieutenant. I must say, when I saw Bennett in his RAF uniform for the first time, and with that thin single stripe on his sleeve, he was mumbling a little about his lowly status.

The next time I saw him was when I was in England, commanding a lot of B-17's over there, and our insignificant pilot officer had become Air Commodore Donald Clifford Tydall Bennett.

He had left the ferry business and gone into Bomber Command. (An air commodore is opposite our own rank of brigadier-general.) Here was this mild-mannered slim little character, very very British, (even though an Australian by birth, I think), quiet-voiced, carrying his handkerchief in his sleeve—

He and his crew had been shot down over Norway, and they made their way across Norway in the dead of winter. Not so easy to do, at that season. I seem to recall that they had to do quite a little fighting, in order to make it out of Norway; but at last· they got into Sweden and, ultimately, back to England.

Bennett commanded the Pathfinder force for RAF Bomber Command. That was a pretty good outfit. Donald Clifford Tydall Bennett was a pretty good man.

We all left Montreal; repaired to our home bases or offices to get rid of any tasks or duties which might suffer from a lack of performance while we were ferrying. Then we gathered out at Wright Field in Ohio. There were C.V. and Montgomery, Rothrock, C. J. Cochrane: a great many of the old bunch from Langley. We were about to check off on a brand new airplane again.

There was just one aircraft available. I think the fellow who had flown it there from the factory was the first one to take us off the ground in the 24. We all went up together, and watched while he made a landing. Then C.V. sat in the pilot's seat and made a couple of landings (normally he wouldn't let anybody else fly the airplane if he was in it; but this time he had to give up on that, if we were all going to fly the North Atlantic route). Everybody got to make a landing . . . I got to make one. By this time Caleb Haynes was kind of twitchy. He says, "That's enough. We're all right."

So I'd made one landing in a B-24. Next time I saw one of the so-called Liberators, I had been ordered to fly it across the Atlantic Ocean.

C.V. was going to take the first one across; J. B. Montgomery was assigned to him as navigator. It seems funny now: he came around whispering to me, "Is Montgomery all right? Can he really navigate?"

I told C.V., "Monty is topnotch. You'll never have any trouble with him. Just fly the course he lays out for you."

Laying out that course up there in the sub-Arctic is a rather complicated procedure. First thing that happens when you take off— By the time you've added all the variation—which is about thirty degrees up there—and the wind drift and things of that sort— The lines of force that run around our globe, run in screwy positions in different places. By the time you've taken that into consideration, and added the deviation of the compass (because the structure of the airplane itself affects the needle of the compass) and your drift all together, you come out with a reading which amounts to maybe forty-five degrees off.

So Monty set the course, and C.V. says, "No, that's the wrong course."

Montgomery had a big argument with him on this, and Haynes was the original Doubting Thomas although his name is Caleb. "That'll take us to *Spain*. We want to go to Prestwick, *Scot*land!"

Monty just had to be patient and shake his head. "That's the right course." Only at long last did he convince the reluctant C.V.

They really had a horrid time on the initial crossing. Weather unbelievable, etc. On Haynes' return trip, I was to come up to meet him at Gander in a B-15 with a load of passengers ready to transfer to the B-24. I went chugging up there, and the weather was stinko. Thus Haynes had been delayed on his return flight. When he approached Gander the weather was so ugly there that he couldn't even try to get in. He went on, landed at Montreal and—subsequently, after refueling and servicing the aircraft—carried his passengers on down to Washington, where most of them were headed anyway.

I had to twiddle my thumbs at Gander for three or four days until Haynes got the B-24 back up there. For amusement I could listen to the wails of my passengers, each of whom had some blood-sweat-and-tears reason for needing to be in England at two o'clock last Tuesday. No one was about to attempt that North Atlantic crossing in a B-15 with a full load—least of all me. But finally C.V. came a-chugging, and I could prepare to start my first trans-Atlantic trip.

Passengers were all off somewhere inside a building, away from the weather, and I walked around that B-24 sitting there on the flight line, and looked at it. Seemed to me I ought to land it at least *once* more before taking off for Europe. The more I thought about this the more it seemed like a good idea. Finally I climbed in; we cranked it up, and I circled the field, and landed. I said, "Let's gas it up."

. . . All the way over, through fog and sleet and slambang drafts, there was a vague secret portion of my brain which wondered constantly if any other pilots had ever taken loaded airplanes across oceans with as little previous time in them as we.

And again I thought, "Good thing our poor passengers back there in the waist and bomb-bay don't know about this."

Trouble was, they did know it. Those things have a way of getting

(20) Henry MacDonald in the mud at Chelveston, 1942

) Kantor was there too

(22)

Colonel Curtis. E. Le May from Bruce Bairnsfather

s mud pretty good mate, but this 'ere's new to me.
they imports it, special for aerodromes.

(20) Two Forts collide in fog over England while forming for first mission.

(24) Fighter escort joining up overhead

(25) LeMay's "combat box" under fire

(26) Five seconds to drop point

(27) LeMay with Possum Hansel

(28) "Elveden Hall has been described in a guidebook as 'one of the most surprising sights in Suffolk.' You can say that again."

(29) Ear-marked for Bremen

(30) At the waist gunners' station

(31) Straight and level over target, disregarding the flak bursts virtually at their wing-tips

(32) Sometimes it was almost thick enough to walk on

(33) Strike photo, Regensburg, August 17, 1945

(34) The Beresford painting of Regensburg bombers crossing the Alps (note the hole in the canvas below nose of next to last plane)

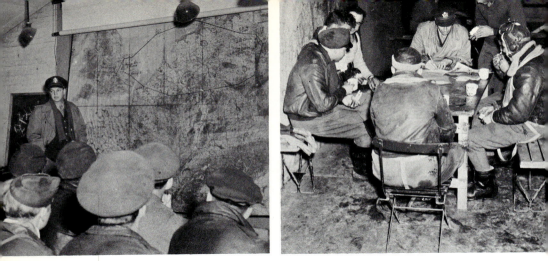

(35) Briefing for Berlin

(36) De-briefing

(37) Results of a direct flak hit

around. After we had landed in Scotland I talked with Put Mundy about this. He was a fellow classmate from Kelly, George W. Mundy (Put retired as lieutenant-general a couple of years ago, having finished off at the head of the Alaskan Command).

There at Prestwick I uttered a few feeble words about how much time I had had in that B-24. Mundy seemed to think that everybody was aware of it. He said, "Oh, that didn't bother us *at all*. We had all the confidence in the world in *you*."

Figuratively speaking, we were all feeling our way on this job. I rather shudder to announce now that often we were literally feeling our way too.

Nobody knew much about flying the North Atlantic, and above all else loomed the question of ice. Whenever we started to pick up ice, even a little bit, we tried to get the bombers above it. Regularly we were at about six or eight thousand feet, a non-oxygen altitude; but we couldn't go too high, no matter what the conditions, because we had no oxygen for our passengers. There was oxygen available at the crew positions, but none in the bomb-bay. Sometimes we had to go pretty high, but we tried not to stay there too long. I don't recall that we ever had any fatalities or even severe physical effects among our passengers for lack of oxygen.

As for fronts: even in the better class of weather conditions you usually had about three fronts to go through in those latitudes. Most of the time, when you weren't actually punching a front, you were between layers. Sometimes it was broken above, so that you could do a little celestial navigation.

The lovely part about this career was the complete absence of traffic control. There just couldn't *be* any traffic control. It must be remembered that a great percentage of the traffic, Canadian and British, consisted of brand new airplanes which were being ferried over to England for their use. Sometimes there would be as many as thirty or forty planes ganged up on the ground back in Newfoundland, waiting for halfway decent weather in order to get across. Then, when the weather seemed to be breaking right, they would all take off at five-minute intervals and head for Prestwick, Scotland.

We on the passenger ferry, on the other hand, were flying both ways across the Atlantic. These combat aircraft were coming one way only. But there were so many of them.

Once, when I took off from Prestwick to head back for Gander, the weather was perfectly clear to begin with. But about three hundred miles off the coast we hit some bad stuff. You could see it, it looked like Ringlings' big top being pulled up by cables, a vast canvas of clouds arising. We were flying right toward it; had to; no way around. Just as I was about to sock into the clouds, an airplane popped out, coming right toward me. Suddenly I realized that there were about thirty-five more planes back in that front somewhere. Gave a rather disquieting feeling, to say the least.

There were no special altitudes assigned, no even-numbered altitude flying one way, odd-numbered altitude flying the other way, or anything like that. No restriction whatsoever: every pilot chose his own altitude. Thus when we went into a front we went in absolutely blind.

I suppose we would have had a hard time arranging to hit somebody *on purpose*. Mathematical chances were against our doing it, but still there was nothing in our outlined procedure to prevent it.

We old ferry types look back on those days now, and wonder why the surface of the North Atlantic was not fairly crawling with dismembered airplanes, crews and passengers. Wish I had some figures on this, but it would be extremely difficult to assemble them. Actually the ratio of success was very high. The bulk of the airplanes got safely over to Britain and so did most of the people.

It is amusing to recall how those planes started out on their enterprising flight. Particularly I think of the process of ferrying the Lockheeds. Those were the old Hudson bombers which we built for the RAF in the United States—the ones with the partially retractable undercarriage and twin tail unit. In order to maintain the letter of our supposed neutrality, we Americans would fly them up to the border and land them on the south side. Then the Maple Leaf boys would get out a cable and fasten it to an airplane, and tow the Lockheed across by means of a tractor. Sometimes they were even pushed and pulled across the line by hand.

Everything was cockeyed just then.

2

ALONG ABOUT the 1st of September, C. V. Haynes and C. J. Cochrane and I got together in a B-24 set aside for a very special purpose. At Washington we picked up General Brett and a party of his people, and went down to Natal in Brazil. We were surveying a route across the South Atlantic and across Africa. The plan was to assemble fighters at some place on the west coast of Africa and, flying them across the wastes in between, get them into the Middle East. So from Natal we zipped right across to Freetown in the Sierra Leone.

In the North Atlantic we'd already learned a lot about flying the ocean, and were really becoming proficient in our knowledge of icing conditions, our knowledge of salt-water navigation, and allied mysteries. I gravitated between regular duty as a pilot and special assignments in the role of navigator, as on General Brett's survey trip to Africa.

(First two or three flights that I made across the Atlantic as pilot, I had a new man—his name was Kester—for navigator. Like all hard-line old navigators I was suspicious. I remember Kester said that he had just taken his first celestial fix. I said, "One moment," and got my co-pilot to take over flying the 24. Then I went back to the dome and took a celestial fix of my own, and did my computations. Compared notes with Kester. We were *two miles apart* at the time we projected our dead-reckoning course forward. Well, that made a Christian out of me, far as Kester was concerned. I didn't bother him any more. . . . But the Japs did, later on, I'm sorry to say. Kester was trying to fly a load of people out of Java—in that same airplane, seems like—and the enemy clobbered him. No self-sealing tanks in those first B-24's. Sitting duck.)

I used to watch General Brett and his party when they boarded the aircraft or when they got off; or we'd see them sitting together at one of the tropical stations where we were halted. I'd smile to myself and think back to the CCC days. It was not much over eight years since I'd gone down to try to explain to Major Brett our sorry airplane-less state, up there among the cow-pastures of Michigan. And to hear him say with ardor: "My officers are going to *fly.*" Wondered if he remembered that occasion. Certainly I did.

(Incidentally, our modern General Bernard Schriever, famed in the missile business, is George H. Brett's son-in-law.)

At no time during the African and Near East survey trip did we have any trouble with the enemy. In flight we stayed well away from territory where the Germans might be encountered. Sierra Leone, to begin with, was under control of the British. Then we went down the coast and landed at Kano, in Nigeria. Next time it was El Fasher, out in the Egyptian Sudan. Then we went north down the Nile, by way of Khartoum, to Cairo.

We'd had President Roosevelt's Four Freedoms speech back in the previous January. The Marines had occupied Iceland on July 7th. The Atlantic Charter was signed by Roosevelt and Churchill on the British battleship *Prince of Wales*, off the coast of Newfoundland, 14 August. We were a great deal more in the way of being allies of the British after that Atlantic Charter declaration than we had been previously, when we people first went to Canada for the ferry stuff.

Here in Egypt in the early autumn of 1941, we crew members had two weeks to kill while General Brett and the officers he'd brought with him disappeared into the north. There wasn't much for us to do, except look out for our airplane; so we sneaked a ride to the grass airdromes —forward airdromes in the desert near the front lines. We flew out there with some friendly Raf types who were perfectly willing to give us a lift. We thought it might be valuable to us as military men if we could see exactly what was going on; but all we managed to do was talk to some of the pilots and operations people, and examine a few shot-up planes. I remember one of them still had blood spattered around in it—the blood of wounded personnel. This impressed the hell out of us: the first blood we'd seen in the war. *Looks kind of like sticky paint. But it isn't. It's the blood of people.*

So we hung around with the British; and also met some Free American types who were carrying on along with the British. And some newspaper men draped around. We picked up a lot of firsthand stories about the war, and picked up something else much more devastating. We became fellow sufferers in the eternal epidemic of Gyppy-tummy. That sort of diarrhea can be plain sheer hell, but you couldn't strike much sympathy from those stony hearts. The British paid no attention whatsoever to the stuff. "What? Oh, Gyppy-tummy. We all have it, you know."

There was a scale in my room at Shepheard's Hotel, and I kept checking. Lost fifteen pounds in five days.

One of the war correspondents was thoughtful enough to give me some pills. They were made in France, but he had picked them up in Turkey, and he said they would cork us up enough so that we could fly home to the U.S.A. I took those and they did help, so I shared them with the others. As for the British: we tried them and their surgeons, and all they'd do was to give you a bottle of bismuth and paregoric. Might as well have been cambric tea.

Fairly oozing with our misery we made it back across the Atlantic, the moment General Brett gave us the high sign. We delivered passengers, got rid of the B-24, tore loose from that job, and everybody staggered away toward home.

I got up there at Westover and barely made a crawl into the house to die. I definitely *wanted* to die. Helen meets me at the door and says, "Why, you look wonderful. What have you been doing? You look perfectly *grand.*" I suppose it was probably that desert sun. Here I had lost over fifteen pounds, and edged along to my quarters like a wounded cockroach— Didn't know whether I'd make it into bed, or just die there on the floor in the hallway— And Helen says I look wonderful.

It behooved me to really do something about this stubborn dysentery because I was supposed to plunge into 34th Bomb Group activities again, and wanted to help get our program rolling. One of the suggested panaceas was a combination of brewers' yeast and milk—which is, for my dough, one of the most God-awful concoctions ever put together by man. I demonstrated extraordinary heroism in getting that foul stuff down my throat. Also I fed heartily on sulfaquanidine, one of the new drugs just coming out. Our flight surgeon insisted that I try it. Well, I guess the Army did give me one bottle for free, at the hospital, but I ate those up right quick. At the rate of sixteen per day, as recommended. From then on I had to buy my own, and the damn pills cost thirty-five cents apiece. That was five dollars and sixty cents a day. Wondered how long it would be before Helen and I were bankrupt, and Janie had to go out in the cold and sell matches or shoestrings.

Hate to admit that the brewers' yeast and milk may have helped. Between these medicaments I was finally over the Gyppy in another three months.

3

GENERAL KROGSTAD commanded either the Wing to which we belonged at the moment, or else he was one of the Staff Officers at Army Air Forces HQ. Can't say for a certainty, since he held both of those jobs at one time or another, and we were in a demoralized condition because of the rapid expansion of the air arm.

But he came up to Westover that autumn and really let his hair down when he talked to us underlings. It made a profound impression on me. Krogstad was convinced that the United States would be entering the war, and soon. He was no prophet and he gave no target date for our participation in hostilities; just said "soon." Thinking over my experiences of the past several months, and what we had seen in Great Britain and seen in Egypt— General Krogstad had it nailed down.

So I was flying in the soup again . . . Operations Officer of the 34th Bomb Group . . . really started to worry. What did we have? Nothing. Scarcely any airplanes to train with. All the equipment of our old Second Bomb Group had been divided up forty-ways-for-Sunday. New groups were sprouting in every direction; but where did we get the airplanes? We didn't have a training program, didn't have any range to bomb on, didn't have anything, period. Soon it would be necessary for us to go off to fight. What the hell were we going to fight with?

Night after night, going wearily to bed, I'd turn to soul-searching instead of sleep. What does an Operations Officer *do*, I'd ask myself, trying to get a training program laid out under such conditions?

To begin with, I wasn't well trained enough myself to do a hundred-per-cent-effective job in that particular slot. I had a pale feeling of inadequacy. Wasn't getting much help there in the 34th, and didn't know where to turn to *get* help.

Thought of the childhood Boy Scout days when we had to make a fire without matches. It took an insufferably long time to get a smudge going from that set of rubbing-sticks. You'd hold the spindle in place, and press down with the bow-drill, and operate that bow until your young arm was ready to drop off; and then peek down to see if there was any fire in the hot wood-dust which was ground out at the bottom of the spindle. Took so long to get a coal in the middle of that stuff . . . coal big enough to blow on, to burst into flame. . . .

When Pearl Harbor came a-crashing on a memorable Sunday afternoon, our main response was a feeling of complete unreality. It was something like finding the *Rex* in 1938: going through a lot of clouds and turbulence, and then breaking out, and there she was, right in our path.

Sure—there wasn't anything very pretty in the spectacle of our sailors and soldiers lying burned or drowned out there in Hawaii; but at least we did have some sense of relief. Now we knew where we were going. We were going to war.

With *what?* Gad.

The West Coast dwelt in a vast state of jitters over the possibility— nay, probability, it was considered—of immediate Japanese invasion. Result of this, our 34th Bomb Group was ordered to Pendleton, Oregon.

Hadn't any more than landed there when I received orders telling me to go back to Wright Field and report in to the Engineering Section for an accelerated service test on the B-24. An obvious result of those hours I had piled up during the previous summer and early autumn, pushing a new B-24 back and forth across the Atlantic. B-24 pilots were a scarce article.

Back I went to Ohio and reported at Wright to participate in the service test. We had only two airplanes, as I remember, but we certainly flew the hell out of them.

Guess I couldn't be blamed for thinking that nothing was ever solid or permanent in my military life any more. Just to review the domestic situation was bad enough: (a) we had been there at Westover in Massachusetts; then (b) we were ordered to Pendleton. So I packed up, sent Helen and Janie and the furniture to Cleveland; and I went to Oregon. Just landed at Pendleton when (c) they had that telegram waiting for me to go to Wright (couldn't blame the Army Air Forces too much for that one. Remember, we had taken the first B-24's right off the line and put them directly into the business of flying the ocean. There had never been any opportunity for normal service tests, and those were essential).

So I got Helen on the telephone and told her I was coming back to Ohio, headed for Dayton. Didn't know how long I would be there; maybe she could come down? Next thing, we were in Dayton and Fairborn, wandering all over, trying to find a place where we could dwell. I thought I'd be there for a month at least. It had seemed awfully exciting when Helen first appeared with Janie in tow. But we never dreamed it would be so difficult to find any place to live. The area was really jumping in those days. Airmen and other Army personnel converging from every possible direction, all headed for Wright and Patterson, and wanting to be close to their jobs, and needing a place where the wife could cook some supper, and where there would be room for a high-chair and baby-carriage . . . too much to hope for a yard for the children to play in.

(Any crape-hangers who ever doubted the fiber of young American women previously, and sold them short on the rare old-fashioned feminine virtues, should have had their eyes opened up, in any opportunity to observe those Service wives close-hand. They were camp followers. Damn resourceful ones.)

We played into a chunk of luck. Ran into an old friend from Langley, Doug Kilpatrick. (Remember—he was bombardier on the *Utah* deal.) He was already stationed at Wright; and they invited us over for dinner, and next thing they were offering to put us up. We stayed with the Kilpatricks a couple of nights until we found a place of our own. Kilpatrick's kids came down with the chicken-pox and next thing of course Janie came down with the chicken-pox. I'd had the disease when I was a child; so had Helen; so I wasn't worried about catching the itchy little spots and taking them back to the outfit. Never did.

The furnished rooms which we found were in Yellow Springs, away over east of Wright, where Antioch College is. So I flew the B-24's around the block on this service test for about a month.

Next thing, I was bundling Helen and Janie off to Cleveland (d) and I headed back to Pendleton. They were trying to get a new group shaken down out there, and one of my Kelly classmates, old Zipper Koon (Ralph E.) was the group commander. . . . But I wasn't there for long. Next thing (e) was a brand new job under Chip Overacker, at Wendover, Utah. Colonel Charles B. Overacker, Jr., had the 306th Bomb Group down there. I was named to be his Exec. No. 2.

Wendover was a beaut. Eventually they developed a big modern plant; but you should have seen it in the first days of 1942. Everybody took one look, and the general opinion was that Wendover might be the Alamogoogoo of the new Army Air Forces.

Will have to digress here for a moment and explain about Alamogoogoo. That was old Air Corps slang for Alamogordo, New Mexico. Nowadays the White Sands establishment is there, out in the sticks, just adjacent to Alamogordo which lies far south of Albuquerque. Effete personnel of these 1960's, with their long exposure to everything from air conditioning to deep freezes to electric tooth-brushes, don't have any idea what it was like to be at a lonely desert installation in the long long ago. Alamogordo wasn't even granted the dignity of its own name: it was spoken of by the other designation, and with a shudder into the bargain.

It was notorious as the one Army field where the chaplain ever deserted. Fact. (So they say.) They were getting an awful lot of desertions, and finally someone sent in a new trouble-shooting chaplain to try to straighten the boys out, remind them of their duty to God, Mother, Yale, etc. Well, the chaplain didn't like Alamogoogoo any better than anyone else had liked it, and in no time at all *he* went Over the Hill. Never been seen or heard from since.

May be a mere legend. But a lot of us oldtimers, who remember what the desert bases were like, still get the shivers when anyone says that fatal name.

. . . Looked like Wendover, Utah, was going to be a bad word for all of us. It's out there on the west side of what is known as the Great Salt Lake Desert, smack on the Bonneville salt flats where all that fancy high speed automobile activity has taken place through the years. Good place to land and take off; that was about all you could say for it. In fact you just *looked,* and you wanted to take off right away.

There was a rudimentary runway, but no hangars, no barracks. Everybody was in tents at the start. No adjacent civilian residential areas; hell, maybe Salt Lake City was as close as anything, and that was a hundred and thirty miles away. We straddled the State line. There was a fantastic establishment right on that State line. It was a combination filling-station-gambling-casino-restaurant-bus-stop-and-small-hotel. They called it the State Line Hotel, because half of it was in Utah and half in Nevada. How original can you get.

A few of us managed to rent rooms in the hotel, and I sent for Helen, and out she came—Janie and all. The three of us shacked up in one room while we were there. Might add that Janie took over the hotel—lock, stock and barrel—including chef and hotel clerk. The kitchen people especially tried to spoil the hell out of her. *Ugh,* no: she didn't want her orange juice in the mornings . . . *ugh,* no egg or oatmeal or anything like that. Helen went investigating around and discovered that the help were stuffing our infant with Cokes and cakes and candy every time she rolled her eyes at these items, which was constantly. Promptly a one-woman earthquake shook the premises, and Miss Janie became a reformed character (for the moment).

But I only had the folks there about a month before being ordered elsewhere.

In the meantime, back at the ranch, here was this 306th Bomb Group being put together. Once more it was the Boy Scouts attempting to build a fire without matches, or the put-upon Israelites in the Bible trying to make bricks without straw.

A whole mess of recruits would come in at one time: untrained, not properly officered . . . there'd be a mob arriving, and perhaps they'd have a corporal in command, some frantic character who'd just gotten out of Sheppard Field or was shaken loose from some technical training plan.

What a sorry lot of personnel. Hadn't been paid, didn't have any clothes—half their baggage gone one way and half the other. That was really a mess, trying to get them sorted out. Very few of them had any records along with them. It had been only a few months since they were lolling on the home farm tractor seat. What do I mean, months? Weeks, in many cases.

. . . Weeks since they'd been stacking groceries in cartons at the A & P; weeks since they'd been running job-presses in the back room of a printing establishment, or slinging the chocolate malts at Walgreen's. It was a case of going down the line and picking out the most intelligent-looking guys. "O.K., you're a sergeant. . . . You're a corporal. . . ." And getting a little organization in there, and getting them paid, and trying to dig up some clothes. And here we were, with no airplanes or equipment yet, trying to requisition for the equipment we *hoped* to get. Trying to build the tar-paper shacks we were supposed to move into. . . .

Everything seemed ephemeral. There was no time-honored tradition. No framework had been set up. It seemed like this whole enterprise would evaporate, diffuse into space any moment. Or worse than that: descend into a dragged-out incompetent future, wherein the group never became effective, never had any equipment, was unable to achieve any training, and never got on combat status; wherein the 306th Bomb Group was a drag on the military economy, and a blight on everyone's spirits, including the spirits of its own personnel.

This was long before the war itself gave birth to the now time-honored jest about *Me got no mamma, no papa, no Uncle Sam, no flight pay, no PX.* But that was the way we felt. Enlisted personnel considered that they had been weighed in the balance and found wanting; they had been sent out to the salt flats permanently, just because the Army wanted to get rid of them and couldn't contrive any less painful way. We people in the echelons of command had much the same idea. Where had we sinned along the line? Must have sinned somewhere. Otherwise we wouldn't have been given a job like this, nor under such conditions.

In my own case it was the recollection of a minor family tragedy which saved me from complete self-abnegation. One miserable evening, when the cold sandy salty wind had been blowing all day, and nothing went right, the people had fouled up on their jobs, and I was positive that I had fouled up on mine— I came back to the State Line Hotel, and Helen was surprised to hear me burst suddenly into laughter—real laughter, not the bitter or hysterical kind. She spoke her amazement.

I said, "Well, I've just thought of something."

"What can that be?"

"I thought of Uncle Oscar."

"Uncle Oscar?"

She hadn't heard much about him. He was my father's eldest brother, and during our childhood, while we of the Erving LeMay family squatted at the trout hatchery in Montana, Uncle Oscar was a big shot down in Emeryville, California. At least that was the impression I gained. He seemed to be capable, and very well entrenched economically, and he was most persuasive with my father, his baby brother. Damned if I know what Uncle Oscar was doing at the time. But he had a good job, or said that he did, and there was a job for my father, too. It was to this insistence that Pop yielded when we made the move from Montana to Emeryville, and came trekking all the way down there from the Montana mountains.

Lord knows what route we followed. But there were no interstate bus lines in those days, nor were there adequate roads for automobile travel even if we had been the proud possessors of an automobile. You went on the train or else you walked.

First we had the long trip in a wagon to a railroad, and then— We must have gone to Salt Lake City, and thence by rail to California. Seemed to take forever. I remember tired people in a big smoky station; and the back of my head hurt where it had rested against that wooden bench, and my foot had gone to sleep. Mom looked awfully tired . . . Velma had her head against her on one side, and Mom was holding the baby with the other arm. I remember an old man who climbed aboard our day coach at one stop . . . he wore a long kind of duster, and he rang a big bell which he carried in his hand. He sold sandwiches—or that was what *he* called them—and coffee packed in middle-sized medicine bottles. The coffee was whitish; it had condensed milk and sugar already in it; there wasn't any choice. But we children weren't allowed to drink any of the coffee. It was hard to chew the dry sandwiches. . . .

Well, I went on about this to Helen until I had her practically weeping in the aisles. Then I said, "But that wasn't the worst part. Worst was when we got to Emeryville, and there was no Uncle Oscar in sight. He wasn't anywhere around."

"What do you mean? I thought he was established there."

. . . Well, he had been. But something happened in Uncle Oscar's life; and while we were struggling down that tortuous route from the Nez Perce lakes to the environs of San Francisco, Uncle Oscar changed his plans and decamped. He had enlisted in the Army and was already shipped out to the Philippines when we hit town. He was the one who'd sung the siren song to Pop; and Pop made the move; and now Oscar was gone. No house, no job, no anything else.

I wish we had had that expression then about *No Uncle Sam, no PX, etc.* It would have come in handy.

"That's the real old LeMay acumen, you see. Seems to be working again in this generation, same way."

"Oh, hush."

"Well, Pop was forced to it: his back was to the wall. So he went and got a job in a cannery, and found a great big tenement-type building for us to move into. Maybe I can do the same."

"Hush. Aren't you going to take me down to dinner? Janie says they've got hamburger and onions tonight."

That sounded all right. But I was still smiling inside as we went down to eat in the crowded lunchroom. I was thinking of the incident of Uncle Oscar. Somehow it helped.

4

In May I was ordered back across those same barren salt flats to take command of the 305th Bomb Group at Salt Lake City. This organization was a twin of the 306th: constituted 28 Jan 1942, activated 1 Mar 1942. Captain John deRussy is listed as the first commander, in those days when the 305th was more of a series of typewritten sheets than anything else. Warren Higgins and Fay Upthegrove also got into the initial picture, and I think it was Ernest H. Lawson, a lieutenant-colonel like myself, who preceded me. (He would return to the 305th at a much later date, and die in combat on a mission over Hamburg.)

Might be interesting to examine the historical picture at this point and see what our needs were prophesied to be, and what strength eventually would be attained. Back about 1940, when everything looked bad in Europe, President Roosevelt asked for an estimate "of overall production requirements . . . to defeat our potential enemies." Far as the Air Corps was concerned, four officers were named to make a forecast of our needs: an estimate of the strength which it would be necessary for us to achieve, in order to win a victory. The veterans Harold George and Ken Walker were named to this panel, along with Larry Kuter and H. S. Hansell, Jr. from the younger echelon.

Here is their prog on what the Army Air Corps would need, in order to defeat our enemies:

2,200,000 men.

63,467 airplanes.

239 combat groups; along with 108 separate squadrons not formed in groups.

Here's what we actually ended up with, as of 1945:

2,400,000 men.

80,000 aircraft.

243 combat groups.

That's how close those people came to hitting it on the nose. Pretty close.

In addition to the fantastic accuracy of this forecast, they had estimated that our full-strength air offensive against Germany could not be developed before April, 1944.

In fact we had been able to mount, and could continue to mount, such a severe offensive against Germany that by June of 1944 the Normandy landings were made possible. Normandy landings could not have been accomplished in 1943. Our Maximum Effort over-two-thousand-planes-bomber-missions were an event of the winter of 1944–45.

Considering all the murk and confusion of an earlier year, the prophecy of that panel of four officers seems astounding.

With human beings as they are, and economics and politics and raw resources and transportation and employment as they are also, it is a wonder that we got any airplanes at all into the act in Europe in 1942.

Seemed like some very earnest people up in Arnold's office might say, "Now, this month, as part of our program, we must establish so many new groups." And they had the program all laid out: how fast the people were going to come into the Service, how rapidly they could be run into the technical schools and given a quick course . . . a rate of flow would be established . . . when enough men emerged from the technical schools, they could be formed into an outfit.

Of course what actually happened was that the timing was utterly confused. Outfits would be already formed, but there wouldn't be the people to channel into them. At long last I'll admit they got the system pretty well refined; and toward the end of the war they were grinding these outfits through like sausages from a machine. But in the early days it was distinctly a hit-or-miss proposition.

Naturally the ideal thing would have been to schedule a Group with a mere cadre of experienced people; then have all the rest of the personnel, emerging from schools, hit the outfit at the proper time; thus the organization could be formed and equipped in strength. You'd start your training as a Group, and train perhaps three months as a Group; then off you went to the wars.

That didn't happen to most commanders, not in 1942. It didn't happen to me when I was given command of the 305th. I didn't get my people in time, and I wasn't given sufficient airplanes to train them on anyway.

My immediate predecessor had been ordered up to Second Air Force HQ (that was our training command in those days, and eventually would profit from the contribution of Robert S. Olds). He had departed by the time I got to Salt Lake City. Ship without a sail, etc.

Big thing was to try to get the training program under way immediately. We had three B-17-E's to do it with.

Temporary Expediency. Everything was a temporary expediency. I thought that I should never wish to hear those words again . . . I heard them and heard them and heard them to death, through the years which followed.

Right off there was a troubled and frightening aspect to the Pacific situation. The Japs were moving steadily eastward: that's how the Battle of the Midway came about. I'd only been at Salt Lake a few weeks when orders came for me to take my 305th Group, such as it was, and proceed immediately to Spokane, Washington.

Temporary Expediency once more. If the Japanese weren't stopped out there in the Pacific somewhere, chances were they would attempt to invade our West Coast. We long-range bombardment groups would dispute them in their approach.

Our raggle-taggle-gypsy crowd traipsed up to Spokane, and there I found myself commanding a composite assemblage of B-24's along with the B-17's. Since none of the groups in the Western areas was at full strength, there was no sense in sending any more paper organizations to Spokane. They sent crews and airplanes instead. They filled up my command with Liberators as well as Forts. But these were only on loan . . . *Temporary Expediency.* As soon as (and if) any threat of invasion was lifted, all these other airplanes and crews would return to the units from which they came.

A few kind friends took time out to tell me that I should feel flattered at being elected chairman of the Japanese Reception Committee in the North Pacific States. Couldn't find time to feel flattered or even pleased.

What did we have, what could we do?

First thing I looked for, when we got to Spokane: did we have bombs? Did we have bomb-racks? Could we get the airplanes loaded? Did we have the proper bomb tables? All that sort of stuff. What about our fuel? What about our maintenance? What about ammunition and guns for air-to-air defense? For ground-to-air defense? What were the quarters like? What about the food? In a situation like that you had to think of everything. But principally I let the housekeeping go, and stuck to my airplanes if not to my guns.

We had one big thing to concern us here: we would bomb the enemy fleet if it approached. We tried to get set up for that purpose.

A lot of the crews were short some people when they came in, and we had to get those crews filled up. And don't forget: we had two types of airplanes. That made all the difference in the world when you faced the demands on maintenance, loading operations, etc. . . .

Check equipment in each plane. Make sure that they brought all their shackles along for the various types of bombs. (Those are the gadgets by which bombs hang in the bomb-bay, and which release them at the flick of a switch. You need different shackles when you're dealing with 250-lb. General Purpose bombs, 500-lb. General Purpose, 1,000-lb. GP's, etc.)

It might have been well if we could have flown some patrols as part of our training exercise, but No Soap. At least not out over water. We did fly a few practice bomb runs over land, and practiced on crew coördination. Everything was primed toward this one possible operation; it was the only thing I could think of at the moment. There was absolutely no thought of our being part of a big training program. We were to be poised to go out and strike, the moment the Jap fleet came within range. That was our whole purpose in being at Spokane.

Then the Battle of the Midway exploded, the invasion threat was dispelled. Fast as news spread around the landscape, orders began to come clicking in. The borrowed, the temporarily-assigned crews were directed to take their equipment and go back home and rejoin their parent outfits.

As for the 305th, we were to fly at once to Muroc Dry Lake, California (that's Edwards Air Force Base today. Quite a different place in 1965). At Muroc we would proceed with and/or complete our training program.

Thank God. Once more I was commanding solely B-17's.

Didn't have enough of them—usually only about three ready to go—but we surely used what we had. The feeling of inadequacy which had plagued me earlier, when I was with the 306th at Wendover, returned once more. The realization that I had just made bird colonel didn't help much.

But at least I had *my own* whip cracking about my own ears and ankles. This was *my* outfit. This was what *I was going to take to the war and fight with.*

Oh, I felt the vague resentment any commander feels when he looks at his people and his equipment, and realizes that personnel are coming into his organization who have never been trained for the jobs they must hold—that airplanes may or may not be ferried to him out of the skies, long after they have been needed desperately in the program. Still, *this is what I am going to take to war.* Made up my mind that I was going to do everything I could to get in all the practice and all the training which could be humanly accumulated, before we went to fight.

So I had three airplanes. We flew 'em every minute they were capable of being flown, day and night. Everybody worked—

We had four squadrons on paper: 364th, 365th, 366th and 422nd. We

had them, as I say; but they weren't full. We just didn't get the people
. . . they were still at school . . . drifting in from time to time.

Some of our navigators were assigned to us only two weeks before
we went overseas. Some of our gunners we received only a few *days*
before we went overseas. Remember also: new outfits were being
formed almost every hour, and as fast as those new units came into
being, it was necessary to redistribute airplanes. Production of aircraft
was nowhere close to matching the nominal formation of new bomb
groups.

We might have five, six or seven airplanes; then some fine morning
we'd wake up and find that we had only three. The others were gone
to a new outfit once more.

I would say that the bulk of the time we were at Muroc we trained
on three airplanes. Seldom more. Far as training went, our pilots were
coming directly from basic trainers right into B-17's. They knew nothing about formation flying. We merely prayed to get 'em off the ground,
and get 'em down again.

You'd go to bed at night and think: *How could anybody ever have
the gall to bring a rabble like this into battle?*

And then you'd say to yourself: *You, too. How will you stand up?
You've never been shot at, you don't know how you'll feel. Maybe you
know more about the business of being a pilot; maybe you know more
about navigation and bombardment, and even gunnery, than your men.
But what do you know about how it feels to be in combat? Will you
stand up? Will you have the nerve to ask them to stand up to it?*

Things like that you'd keep thinking. Then you'd be too exhausted,
and go to sleep.

It was in those days that I won my vulgar nickname: Iron Ass. Newspapers and magazines would try to soften it up through the years; they
called me Iron Pants, for fear of offending some delicate old-maid-type
readers. This was my natural reward for working everybody as hard
as I did, all personnel included.

Helen was stashed away over in Santa Monica by this time, not too
far from Muroc, and other married people had their wives stuck
around here and there nearby. Our pretty camp followers had done
their best to come following the camp; but by God there was to be no
going to town at night. You just couldn't have people making love at
night, or listening to a baby's wails, or listening to domestic difficulties,
or making love again— You couldn't have that and expect them to do
a proper job of work the next day.

As for the droves of unmarried personnel: like most youngsters of
their kind they were hell-bent on comparing the intimate statistics of
the last blonde against the intimate statistics of the new brunette, perhaps with a view to later comparison with a future redhead.

I set up a schedule: every other weekend off. That was It: that was for all personnel including myself.

It hadn't dawned on a lot of these characters that somebody was going to be shooting at them before long. They would rather have gone to town every night and then try to goof off as much as possible the next day. They took a dim view of this program I had laid out and was adhering to strictly.

. . . I wasn't real, I wasn't human. I was a machine. When I went to the bathroom, it wasn't in the ordinary human process. If I defecated, I defecated nuts and bolts. I was made of metal throughout. Iron Ass LeMay.

(In spite of all the hard work we were still a sorry outfit when we left Muroc to go overseas. Most of our navigators had never navigated over water. Most of our gunners had never fired at a flying target from an airplane.)

When we came to Muroc there were exactly three of us in the Group who had ever flown a B-17. Those were Johnny deRussy and Joe Preston and myself. . . . You'll hear those names deRussy and Preston again and again. There are also a couple of other names which you'll hear—the names of two men who made all the difference to the 305th. Both had been enlisted men formerly, one in the Army, the other in the Marines. The names? Fulkrod and Cohen.

I'll go on record and say that if it hadn't been for Ben Fulkrod the 305th would never have become the 305th which now ranks importantly in the history of strategic bombardment in World War II.

Joe Preston (retired, 1964, with the rank of major-general) said in a recent letter, "My first contact with Ben was in December, 1941, when ferrying a new B-17 from the Boeing plant at Seattle down to Sacramento. The co-pilot, Ben Fulkrod and myself circled Portland at seventeen thousand feet, trying to make those 'new fancy superchargers' work." Joe continues dryly, "We finally eliminated ice in the engines, and continued to fly."

Fulkrod had been a tech sergeant, an old line chief. When the Army Air Forces roared into expansion he was promptly commissioned as a lieutenant. Promoted later, naturally. He was a practical engineering officer to the point of genius. Heaven smiled on me and on the Group when I got hold of Fulkrod.

Then gradually I was able to get my hands on a few other people who knew something. For instance, our Ralph Cohen was a great armament officer—really great. I'd never seen him before either. He came from the Marines; how he got into the Army Air Forces I have no idea. But there he was, commissioned in a brown suit. Or green and pink (more up-to-date).

He said that his mother was French, his father an American Jew. After the Marine occupation of Nicaragua, Cohen was one of those soldiers-of-fortune who stayed down there and accepted a commission with the Nicaraguans. His job was to police up the country, clean out bandits, so on. Professional doves-of-peace might have frowned upon his methods sometimes; but professional doves-of-peace don't have much reason to be in the gunnery business anyway. Come rain, come sleet, come flak, come shortages, Cohen was really tops in armament. Not necessarily because his methods were predicated on tropical experience. Fact is, I recall his musing . . . "God damn it. The best way to lead those people down there in Nicaragua was to trail along behind 'em with a Tom-gun. . . ."

At Muroc airplanes were in short supply, sagacious human beings in short supply. But bit by bit we managed to sieve out a few enlisted men who were more adroit than the bulk, and we began to find more and more officers who knew something about airplanes or bombsights —rather than having their entire sum of human knowledge amount to the ability to go around collecting nickels from peanut machines in Wauwatosa, Wisconsin, or the ability to do a little modest embalming at a funeral home in Nutley, New Jersey.

Actually we were trying to reverse the course of military experience: *we had to build our original cadre while trying to build the entire outfit*. That was, shall we say, kind of difficult. But gradually we discovered better people among those coming in, and we began to find a little equipment too. We never did receive all of our matériel which we were supposed to have. But we had stuff that we *weren't* supposed to have.

We could thank Ben Fulkrod for that. As time drew near for us to depart for the European theater, Ben began to assemble his logistic gadgets; these would be shipped out when the ground echelon went overseas. After we reached England nothing whatsoever was furnished to us. The only matériel we had was what we'd fetched along. Good supply people and good engineering people naturally scrounged whenever and wherever they could; but the most ambitious genius in the lot would never have been able to come up with the resources we had, after the 305th was settled at Chelveston.

Believe it or not, over there in the Eighth Air Force Bomber Command, we had the only set of reamers to ream wing bushings. And we had a lot of bushing stock and such little items which we weren't supposed to have. Fulkrod again. This stuff was invaluable. Everybody was short of parts and short of machinery. As for bushing material and articles of that nature— Fulkrod would turn the parts out on his lathe, he'd make them for other groups.

Word got around that we had all of our airplanes in commission, when parts weren't supposed to be available. So here would come everybody from the other groups, sniffing around after Fulkrod. They needed that stuff desperately. In the first place, we started giving it to 'em. But they fairly pauperized us. It got to the point inevitably where we couldn't give any parts to any other group, unless they came up with some raw stock to make new parts out of.

. . . I'm away over there in England, way ahead of my story. But let me say before I forget, that with Fulkrod's set of wing reamers we were *changing wings on our airplanes*.

Nine months before, it would have been impossible for the Air Force to attempt anything like that, even at home. They would have let a contract to Boeing for the job. Also, more praises on Fulkrod's head, he was doing it with a gang of ex-filling-station-employees, or farmers who had been cutting silage the year before. And they were all doing a remarkable job.

Well. They'd turned out to be remarkable guys.

In September, when our ground echelon left Muroc for the ETO, we people in the air echelon were definitely orphans. We couldn't keep flying without maintenance personnel. We hoped to make the thing dovetail where England was concerned: i.e., we would arrive in Britain, going by air, shortly after our ground people and ground equipment got there by surface craft.

No use getting rusty in the meantime; I wanted to keep our crews flying as much as possible. We arranged to move over to Tucson, Arizona, and we became visiting guests for a couple of weeks. The ferry people brought us a few more new 17's, so we were able to get in substantial flying by using the maintenance facilities of the outfit stationed there at Tucson. Then we moved on to Syracuse, New York, where we were to pick up the rest of the B-17's which we would fly overseas. From Syracuse we would proceed to Gander, Newfoundland; thence to Prestwick, Scotland; thence to whatever station was designated in England.

We reached Syracuse early in October. An unseasonable cold front came wafting down from Canada; and, newly arrived from the southwestern desert as we were, it knocked us flat. Everybody was shivering and sneezing.

In my case it settled in my back. I had the most gosh-awful ache all night, and couldn't sleep much. Next day I went down to the hospital and they burned away at my back with a heat lamp.

Next morning, when I woke up, it had settled in the back of my neck. Should have stayed in bed, I suppose, but I couldn't see it that way. There was too much stuff on my desk; too many people to quiz; the flight line was a madhouse. We all might have colds, but we damn well had to get ready to fly overseas. So I worked slavishly all morning; then, at lunch time—un-hungry indeed, but trying to keep up my strength—I took a drink of coffee. That whole mouthful of coffee sloshed right out on the front of my shirt.

I went to the adjacent latrine to get some cold water and sponge off the stain; and after I'd looked in the mirror I realized that something was radically wrong with my face and mouth.

Went down to the hospital, and the flight surgeon took one look. "You've got Bell's palsy."

That really scared me to death—just the way he said it. Finally I got up my nerve and managed to comment, "It sounds perfectly horrible. What in the *hell* is Bell's palsy?"

The flight surgeon gave me an extensive lecture on the subject. He had just come from a clinic which specialized in various types of paralysis, and he could elucidate profoundly. He explained that Dr. Charles Bell had identified this paralysis to begin with. The muscles of one side of the face only, were involved; in my case the right side.

Obviously in a wearied physical condition when I acquired the cold, I was easy prey to a virus. Such an infection had claimed those nerves which run through the skull structure in front of the ear. That's where the facial nerve emerges. In Bell's palsy the nerve is strangled by inflammation and swelling—it is squeezed to death in that narrow passageway. If the swelling goes down, you're going to be O.K. again. If it doesn't go down, you've got troubles.

. . . He seemed to be a most sophisticated flight surgeon where this particular topic was concerned, but that wasn't doing me much good. He talked about Landry's palsy and Erb's palsy (an arm was affected in this latter case). He even told about drunks who had become paralyzed because they passed out in one position, and didn't move, and thus exerted too much pressure on the nerves in a particular spot.

. . . Recently I came across a syndicated article by Dr. T. R. Van Dellen, in which he also had considerable to say about this complaint. He drew a fearful picture of how the victim's eyelids couldn't be closed completely, and lips sagged in grotesque fashion, and saliva dribbled out of the mouth. The unfortunate critter was unable to whistle or sneer—or snarl, I guess—or spit straight after brushing his teeth.

Thus the popular medical columnist gave an accurate description of my case as it occurred a generation ago. Not that I wanted to *sneer*, or that I had any particular reason for spitting straight at the moment. Still, it was disheartening to look in the mirror and see what a mess my face had become; and it was disconcerting not to have any control over the right side of my mouth.

"Well, give me the ungarbled word," I demanded. "Are you going to do anything about it, or *can* you do anything about it? What's the treatment? Will I be all right eventually, or not?"

Our flight surgeon shrugged. "Most people get all right. Although, on the other hand, this condition may not improve."

That was a great help. "Describe the treatment."

"Sir, we kept history files, at the clinic. As I told you, these complaints were our specialty there. We treated the last four hundred and ninety-five cases with electric shock. A certain number we treated with heat, a certain other number with massage. And there were various other forms of therapy."

He rattled off the whole list, then added wryly, "As nearly as we could discern, the cases which we *didn't treat at all* came through just as well as those which were treated."

I told him, "You've named my treatment. Goodbye."

In a way I was rather glad that this decision had been made for me. I needed to work about twenty hours a day in order to get the 305th across the ocean in as effective condition as it was humanly possible to tailor such a group—under-trained as we were, inexperienced and ill-equipped.

Surgeon yelled after me, "One thing. Be sure to keep the right side of your face warm, and stay out of drafts."

We were in the airplane business, and we were going to England! "O.K.," I said again. "Goodbye."

He came running out on the step to call, "Here's a good idea. You stand in front of a mirror every day for at least one hour, and practice trying to move your facial muscles—"

Where the hell did he think I was going to find that hour? Extra hours weren't growing on trees just then, whether we were at Syracuse or anywhere else.

There wasn't a thing I could do except let it go, and that's just what I did. Ignored it completely. After about a year they told me that if the muscles of my face were going to function properly again, they would have done so by that time. I would say that it was practically all back by the end of the year; but it's never come back completely. I have about a ninety-five per cent recovery, except in the expression of the face: that is set and can never be altered. Also my right eye always waters first, whenever I get into a wind. The right side of my upper lip is immobile: it doesn't smile when the rest of the mouth smiles, and has helped to promote the legend that I never smile.

Of course anyone who knows about the ailment can take one look and say, "Aha. Bell's palsy."

It all gave rise to a rather heroic fairy tale. Story goes as follows: there I was, flying, sitting in the left-hand seat, and the Plexiglas in front of me blew out or got shot out or something. Anyhow there was a minus-50° F. draft directed against the right side of my face. But brave LeMay never faltered—he just sat there letting his face freeze and letting his face freeze, and it has never thawed out since.

There are different versions, but that one comes back to me now and then.

All I can say is that, if the circumstance had occurred as related, and there was anyone else in the airplane who was capable of flying it, I would have been seventeen kinds of a damn fool to sit there steadily and get Bell's palsy. At least we could have taken turns.

I repeat: what I had was a virus infection of the nerve, and I recovered a lot better than certain people. Some of my friends have been afflicted also. Larry Kuter had the same thing when we were out on Guam. Matter of fact, when he showed up on Guam he was suffering from it (General Kuter was on my staff in those days). The way things worked out, he did the exact opposite of what I did. He absorbed every treatment in the book. Not just one treatment, he took them all—electric shock, massage, heat therapy—the works. Larry didn't make as good a recovery as I did.

Then, not too long ago, Butch Blanchard was over in England, and he accumulated a fine case of Bell's palsy. I don't think that his recovery is as good as mine, yet.

Next time I see General Blanchard, however, I'd better tell him that there are happy by-products. It gives people a chance, on studying your photograph in the newspapers or magazines, to say, "Is he really as vicious as he looks?"

Reminds me now of a story which Tooey Spaatz is fond of telling on himself. I might as well give it here, to relieve the somewhat dreary saga of our inadequate preparation for combat.

During World War II there was a portrait painter in Washington who cut a great swath there. Result was that he painted most of the prominent figures in the Administration and among the military as well. One of the portraits was of General Spaatz.

A round-up of this portraiture was shown at a local gallery while Spaatz and a lot of the others were overseas. It was to be quite a ceremony . . . Mrs. Roosevelt would be present to open the exhibit, etc.

The general's wife, Ruth, received her invitation. Only one of her three daughters was around to accompany her—the youngest, nicknamed Boopsie. Boopsie Spaatz was a bobby-soxer most reluctant to visit any art exhibit at the moment. Through threats or cajolery Ruth managed to drag the gal along. Once arrived at the exhibit, Mrs. Spaatz had to go over and make her manners to Mrs. Roosevelt and the painter, but Boopsie would not accompany her. Instead the kid planted herself right next to her father's portrait and refused to move. Ruth Spaatz said that she was considerably annoyed with her daughter, but there wasn't anything she could do about it. So she made her polite tour of the exhibit and then came back, collared the youngun, and marched her out to the street.

"For heaven's *sake*," Ruth demanded, "why on earth just *stand* there? Why didn't you go around and see the whole exhibit?"

"Didn't want to. Just wanted to stay there, and hear what people had to say about Popsie's portrait."

To tell the truth, Ruth herself thought that the portrait looked a little grim. "Well, what was the verdict?"

"Oh," says Boopsie, "it was about the usual thing, both for the men and the women. Almost without exception the women would say, 'Well, he *is* good-looking . . . in a peculiar sort of way.' Without exception the men said, 'Christ! What a mean-looking old son of a bitch!' "

At Syracuse we were destined to receive the balance of our full complement: thirty-five B-17's. We couldn't start right off to Europe with them, however, because we had been ordered to perform a modification. There was something or other which had to be done to the ball-turret guns; and a few other things.

Of course it would be necessary also to check out each new aircraft, see that all the planes were flying properly, all the equipment sound and functioning. In addition to these chores I wanted to get in an overwater navigation leg, in practice, for our pilots. And by golly we managed that.

The way work piled up, you'd forget all about Bell's palsy or any other kind of palsy. You wouldn't be able to do anything except to push out your spiritual arms like a swimmer doing the breaststroke, and try to shove the work aside as you progressed.

For instance, winter equipment: underwear and outer clothing for the men. We didn't have a stitch of it. Every man wore what he'd been wearing at Tucson and, as demonstrated by all the coughing and sneezing and hacking which was going on, this wasn't a very good deal.

Before long I learned of a quartermaster depot not far from Syracuse, and I went over there, thinking determined thoughts about galoshes, woollen drawers, jackets, gloves. Just as we didn't have a shred of winter equipment, so I didn't possess a shred of authority to go and get this stuff, either. I didn't even have a blank requisition form. Just went in there and beat on the desk and cried, "By God, we're going overseas! We need *underwear*. Anything you've got, let me have it. Any overshoes—anything like that—" Guess I must have looked pretty cold, what with the palsy and all, because those quartermasters' hearts really melted; and quartermasters' hearts are notorious for being made of dry ice. They let me have at least a minimal amount of duds, and we threw the stuff in a couple of trucks and took it home. Big celebration. We weren't going to freeze our personal equipment off, not quite yet.

In the middle of this, Fred Anderson came by, sandy eyebrows and all. That's the Frederick Lewis Anderson (Major-General, Ret.) who graduated in our class at Kelly. He was from the Academy, and previously had held a commission in the Cavalry. He held one of the few DFC's ever awarded in peacetime before World War II. (Parenthetically, let me say that there were no less than five Andersons in our Kelly class. The two Edward Andersons; Fred; Sam; and old A. V. P. Anderson, Jr. But we've had other General Andersons in the Air establishment. Take Orvil—)

Let's get back to Syracuse, and Fred's descending on us there. He had been doing a terrific job ever since 1940, when he ran the first bombardier instructors' school; that was the foundation for a greatly enlarged program which followed later. Then he went to Washington and became Deputy Director of Bombardment; and in 1941 was one of those sent over to England to observe firsthand the tactics and methods employed by the RAF. Actually, with the North Atlantic route closed because of ice, Fred was down in Brazil on his way back from Europe when he heard about Pearl Harbor. His job, at the time he came to Syracuse, was in Hap Arnold's office. Couldn't get much closer to the heart of things than that.

When he spoke I listened, and when he kept on speaking I began to shiver.

He announced that the Pacific people, especially General Kenney, were screaming for additional bomb groups. It had been pointed out to Arnold that another group must be sent to the Pacific immediately.

Fred said, "You're almost ready to go. They're thinking of sending *you*."

I walked up and down the floor to get control of myself before I could speak. "Fred, they can't do this to us! Let's see: how much time has it been? We were at Tucson ten days or two weeks and— Donald Fargo has taken my ground echelon. They've been gone three weeks. Probably in Europe this minute."

Fred said, "I know it doesn't make good sense. But they're yelling their heads off for a heavy bomb group out there in the Pacific. At the moment you're more ready to go than anyone else."

"Look, Fred, all our baggage is in England. You should see the maintenance equipment which was sent over there! Our ground crews are there, the people we've been working with. This will be one screwed-up mess if they try to send us to the Pacific. Nobody will be pleased except the Japs."

"Couldn't agree with you more," says Fred. "But this is what they're talking about."

I begged, "For God's sake, stall them as much as you can, will you?"

"Will do."

The moment he was gone I got the boys together: deRussy, Preston,

Fulkrod, Cohen, everybody. I told them, "Our orders are to proceed to Prestwick the moment we're ready to go. We came here to get our airplanes, and we've got most of them now. We were ordered to perform those modifications, and we've got most of the modifications performed. Unless we get the hell out of here—and fast—proceeding on our original orders— Unless we get out of here before new orders overtake us, we're going to be damn unhappy. We'll find ourselves grinding away toward the Pacific without any ground crews ahead, without any equipment, without any personal belongings—"

There were certainly some grim faces in the circle.

Someone recalled that we had only two airplanes still coming, and those would probably be in, next morning.

I said, "O.K., there's one thing we can do: button up, and button up damn fast. Everybody get to work on those airplanes. Work on each airplane until it's ready to go, then go on to the next one. Let's shake the flu germs of Syracuse off our feet but quick. Before they change those orders."

I remember how wonderfully reassuring old Cohen's voice sounded. "We'll be ready."

. . . He was ready, so was everybody else. We got out of Syracuse so fast it would make your head swim. Next thing the flight echelon of the poor Eager-Beaver green-as-a-gourd 305th Bomb Group knew, they were all in the air headed for Gander.

I was worried to death about hoisting our outfit across the pond . . . couldn't help recalling certain difficulties involved when we were busy with the ferry command. We used to say, "Well, after the first football game you can have it." Nobody wanted to fly that ice. And here it was late October.

Far as consciences were concerned, mine was clear enough. I wanted to take my Group into a theater of operation, ready for combat, in the most effective condition in which I could bring them. We had been programmed to go to Europe on the completion of our training. Everything had been set up; it was planned that we should arrive in England to mesh with the arrival of our ground echelon. They had left Muroc, gone to the East Coast, gone with the convoy. They were in England already, waiting for us. We hoped.

But Fred Anderson's warning still made us sympathetic to any elopers who flee in the night, with Daddy and Big Brothers coming fast behind. Or a poor lonesome cowboy who risks a minute to pause up there on the ridge and listen for hoof-beats of the posse.

We made our getaway complete: thirty-five airplanes loaded to the hilt with stuff and people and more stuff. Took off for Gander, and got there in one piece. Or rather, thirty-five well-ordered pieces.

Now I would have the pleasure of leading my Group over to Prestwick, along the route and through those same air spaces which I had traversed time after time, only about fifteen months before.

I suppose any commander worth his salt has always felt proud when he took his people off to war. And I was humanly proud; and also inordinately delighted that we had managed to squeeze out of that hare-brained scheme to send us to the Pacific Theater minus ground echelon, group maintenance, baggage, et cetera. But once again there was a lot of time to think, when flying over the ocean. I tried to consider the *Utah* and the *Rex,* and the South American trips, and how all those ventures had come to satisfactory fulfillment . . . tried to think of the ferry once more, and of that journey to Africa and back with General Brett.

It didn't add up the same way now. The situation wasn't the same.

Our propellers ripped into the North Atlantic fog, the late autumnal murk where we watched anxiously for ice, and saw moisture purling and dancing along edges of the windows when we looked up and out. But most of the time our eyes were on our instruments, just as the engineer's eyes were on his dials.

Some musician type who used to fly in the 17's once said that the engines sang a steady song . . . over two octaves in the lower register . . . A-E-A-E. I think that's what he said; but I'm no musician. Whatever little tune the four engines of my aircraft were champing out, there were also unpleasant lyrics to go with it.

. . . *Rmmmmm.*

. . . *Crews are not coördinated.*

. . . *Pilots came right from basic trainers to B-17's.*

. . . *Rmmmmm.*

. . . *Navigators . . . we got a lot of 'em just two weeks before we started overseas.*

. . . *Most of the gunners haven't fired. No range. No gunnery school.*

. . . *Bombardiers haven't had much practice.*

. . . *Rmmmmm.*

. . . *And no formation flying. We've never had enough airplanes to fly formation. We'll have to fly our first formation in England.*

. . . *Rmmmmm.*

One time I had heard one of our characters make a crack and say something about LeMay's Irregulars. I didn't turn my head, pretended that I hadn't heard. But I had heard, and it hurt. And it was true, and it hurt all the more because it was true.

The fact that there were a lot of other Irregulars around didn't help any either. But we were about as irregular as they came.

We started out with our thirty-five airplanes and crews, and landed in Prestwick with thirty-three. Besides that, one of the thirty-three was a substitute: the original B-17 had been damaged at Gander. That airdrome had three runways at the time, but they were enormously wide. One of our pilots tried to take off *across* the runway instead of down the length of it. It's hard to believe; but even a more experienced pilot might have been misled on an unfamiliar field like this one . . . the runways were so unholy wide. So of course he ran off the edge, and bunged up the 17 a bit. Not too badly: they finally brought another plane up and gave it to him while they fixed the one he had damaged, and he trailed us over to Scotland.

On the way there many of us were having propeller trouble. The props were really running away. One of our 17's lost a prop a couple of hours after takeoff, so he turned around. Weather had deteriorated seriously at Gander: no chance of getting in there. Our pilot with the lost propeller went to Nova Scotia, and the weather was still bad; but finally he could let down underneath the stuff. He found the coastline but had to land in the water. Ben Fulkrod was a passenger on this 17. They ditched at the shore and did one marvelous job of ditching. When the aircraft came to rest, the tail was hanging out over the beach. The crew took the precious bombsight out, walked out on the fuselage to the tail, and jumped off on dry sand. Pretty good going, when you consider all the circumstances involved. I didn't react too wretchedly when I heard the details on this incident.

Another of our Forts lost two props instead of one; but he was well across the ocean by that time, so he came on to Scotland. They were just barely able to maintain altitude. Matter of fact, they had to throw out everything they could lay their hands on: baggage, machinery, guns, everything. They finally staggered to the ground in Scotland on some other field, not Prestwick. Later we had to gather up that airplane, get it repaired, and get it down to England.

Considering the rattle-trap state our outfit was in, we'd done remarkably well in journeying across.

And those crews had demonstrated plenty of resource. We began to think, "Might be that we could do some good in this war, after all."

5

A NOTABLE experience at Prestwick was our running into Frank Armstrong, who, as I remember, was on his way back to the States to do some job or other. Eager and aggressive by nature, Armstrong had been proud to be selected as one of the half-dozen who came over to England with Ira C. Eaker early in 1942 to set up our Eighth Bomber Command. (All there was to the Eighth Air Force, at the start.)

Armstrong served as Eaker's Operations Officer to begin with; later he took command of the 97th Bomb Group, which had been brought into the theater by Cousland (remember? One of the *Rex* interception pilots).

The point was that Frank had been in combat. I don't recall exactly how many missions he had flown; someone said three; maybe it was more than that. But he led the first B-17 assault against German-occupied Europe. This occurred on the previous August 17th, when a dozen of our Forts attacked the marshaling yards at Rouen. Those first missions were very skimpy. It wasn't until the attack on Lille in October that the Eighth AF was able to put a hundred planes over a target.

We looked across the room and saw Frank standing there with those same flat little curls plastered all over his head. And he had been in *combat*. He had been *shot at*. Maybe he would tell us about it, and maybe some of his recently-acquired erudition would rub off on us. We felt almost that we should bow from the waist when we shook his hand.

Let me say that, although he had already commanded a group, Frank's experience in bombardment was (October, 1942) limited. He had spent his young career as an Attack pilot, much of the time down at Galveston, Texas. And they were starting to phase out Attack. Acquaintance with German tactics had taught the British and our people a different concept. The Army Air Forces cannibalized Attack, and took their people away, thrusting them into fighters in some cases and into bombers for the rest. Attack airplanes as such were disappearing from the scene.

The whole proposition of Attack was designed primarily to support ground troops, and it was going to be a long while before we had any ground forces operational in Europe. The thing to do, obviously, was to concentrate on bombers first, then the fighters. Attack normally would have fulfilled some of the functions which were filled in later by the various Tactical commands and even the Ninth Air Force as a whole. (IX TAC, XIX TAC and XXIX TAC eventually were part of the Ninth, under the command of General Vandenberg. But that was much later in the war.)

Light bombers, such as B-26's and B-25's, had been designed originally for low altitude bombardment work. The fallacy of this belief was proven in an early mission over Holland, when a medium bomber outfit suffered a one-hundred-per-cent loss. Not a single plane came home that day; the Germans shot them down with ease from their flak towers. After that, medium bombers were shoved upstairs, and they began to get somewhere.

Tactical Air Forces eventually were equipped with light attack bombers, such as the A-20 and A-26; but they had fighters as well which could be used in normal pursuit procedure, and on which they could also hang bombs for direct support of the ground forces.

It gave some of us experienced B-17 and former B-10 types a queer feeling to see in the flesh an Attack man made almost overnight into a Bombardment commander. But it was happening everywhere. There were very few of our old Second Bomb Group toggle-knobbers around. Fred Anderson hadn't yet come to take over the Bomber Command. Possum Hansell was there by that time; and Larry Kuter had come earlier, if I'm not mistaken; but a lot of our Langley folks had gone to the Pacific. Zipper Koon and such. Don't forget: also many of them had necessarily gone into the Second Air Force, now embarked on a program of combat training. Some of them did get groups for a while, and then were pulled back and boosted up on the staff. It was hoped that this would help the program to speed ahead.

But here before our eyes was Armstrong, an actual veteran of actual bombardment missions, and—

"Here's somebody who's been *shot at!*" Once again. We grabbed him but fast. He was the original straw in the clutch of the original drowning men. I got all my pilots together, and fortunately Frank had some time: a little time, not very much.

I said, "Please. Don't leave yet. You've got to talk to us *here.*"

We began firing questions, and he very courteously stayed until the last moment when he had to hurry to his airplane.

What did we get out of this?

(A) *The flak is really terrific.*

(B) *If you fly straight and level for as much as ten seconds, the enemy are bound to shoot you down.*

He honestly believed this, as the result of his missions. Far as the rest of us were concerned at that moment, it was Gospel. Colonel Armstrong had been shot at. We hadn't been. Colonel Armstrong was a veteran. We weren't.

Underneath all the horrid little realizations that we had just heard the word of God, a few stubborn questions crawled around in my mind. But I couldn't shape them up quite yet. I thought that I must do some detective work in the near future. Meanwhile I was handed my orders by the people who received us, and learned that we were to proceed at once to a station called Grafton-Underwood. Our ground echelon was already there, yelling for us.

The RAF briefed us on how to get down there. It was rumored that we wouldn't be very long at Grafton-Underwood, not more than a few weeks at the most. G-U wasn't a good operational field, but had to serve as a fill-in for the moment. Eventually we would proceed to a newly-enlarged base next to the village of Higham Ferrers, in Northants near the Bedfordshire border. There had been some Raf types there to begin with; but now a large colony of Irishmen, old-sod coolie types (or should we say O'Coolie types?) were extending runways and generally building up the station.

It would be renamed as Chelveston, after an elderly estate and Norman family of the region: originally Cheauveston or something similar.

Thus we were installed temporarily at Grafton-Underwood, which did duty as an emergency-ward reception center. We wouldn't be there long, and we knew it, and we were glad of it, because the runways were all wrong. And the fog was awful, and everybody moaned and wailed, "So this is England?" The pilot sat in the 17, and the tower says to him, "Can you see the runway lights?" and he says, "S——t. I can't even see my co-pilot."

Before we were ordered to fly our first mission, I went around making a nuisance of myself, hunting for photographs of bomb damage. Couldn't find much.

I kept thinking about this business of, "If you fly straight level for as much as ten seconds, you'll get knocked down." Not just Armstrong's opinion. He had plenty of folks in deep accord with him.

. . . Other people believed that, and they had been flying missions, and I hadn't. They had seen flak and fighters, and I hadn't, and they ought to know. I was still suspicious. The only point in flying a bomber in this war, and crewing it up and bombing it up and gassing it up and arming it, and spending all the money and all the effort—and all the lives— Only point in proceeding on such an operation was to drop bombs where they would do the most harm to the enemy. I wondered whether we were doing just that.

There were strike photos extant but they weren't available for every mission which had been flown. So there was nothing to do but plot whatever strike photos they had, regardless (or, as Rosie O'Donnell likes to say, *irregardamnless*). Then you could look over the post-strike reconnaissance photographs as well. That way you'd get all the information which it was possible to receive, and you laid it out and tallied up, and you stared.

I sat and couldn't believe my eyes, and couldn't believe the sum of the evidence; but here it was.

These people didn't know where half their bombs fell. And most of the bombs didn't hit the target anyway.

So they just weren't hitting the targets. So the bombing was stinko.

It was SOP to use evasive action over the targets. Everybody was doing it. And everybody was throwing bombs every which way.

I knew well enough that even J. B. Montgomery or Doug Kilpatrick, a couple of the real old hot-shot bombardiers, couldn't hit a target with a ten-second bomb run. Purely impossible. If *they* couldn't do it with years of practice behind them (and they were the best that we'd had in peacetime) how were these young kids of ours going to do it?

Couldn't be done. It meant that if we were going to get some bombs on those targets, we had to go straight in, and for a lot longer than ten seconds.

Let me explain that, the way we were set up in Bombardment in those days, we flew to an Initial Point somewhere near the target area. Then—and only then—did we turn and make our run to the AP or Aiming Point (target itself). The Initial Point varied, but usually it was far enough away to allow us to make a turn— Swing the whole formation around and get leveled out pretty well. The IP might be all the way from fifteen to thirty miles away from the AP.

I kept mulling this over, all the time we were getting set at Grafton-Underwood and shaping up to fly our first mission. Of course there were a million other things confronting me as well. But hot and bitter, burning in my mind all the time, was the thought: "What are we going to do about the bombing?"

Always in the end there was only one answer to be found. It was apparent that we would have to go straight in on the target. It was also apparent that we would have to fly a much longer bomb run. There just weren't any two ways about it. You couldn't swing evasively all over the sky without throwing your bombs all over the lot too.

Next big problem which loomed, was: "So we'll have all our airplanes shot down. That's really too much attrition in any war. No equipment or personnel left for the next mission." If we could believe what other people told us, we'd all get pulverized by the enemy ground-to-air fire. No percentage in that.

I prayed there must be an answer lurking around somewhere, but I hadn't found it yet.

I didn't say anything to anyone else about this straight-and-level idea—the notion of dispensing utterly with evasive action. It wasn't the right time yet to mention such a revolutionary concept.

What we did have to do was to get together some semblance of a workable formation. I told everybody, "We're going to fly formation, the first day the weather lets us fly."

. . . You never saw such a lousy assemblage of B-17's in your life. I made one severe mistake on that first one: I flew in the pilot's seat in the lead aircraft, and that was no good. I couldn't see what went on. In fact the handling of the B-17's was so utterly weird and impossible that I immediately canceled out the type of formation which I had planned on using, and started to get together something which I thought they *could* fly. This would call for a lot of modification. I still thought that there was just one way to do it right.

There must be a master formation, a combination of formations, which would present a maximum opportunity for perfect bombing results, and still constitute itself as an aggregation in which the maximum defensive effort could be maintained. In other words, destructive firepower of our 50-caliber machine guns, firing from their different positions on the planes, and from those airplanes' different positions in the formation, would constitute an effective deterrent against enemy fighter attack.

A sad part of this all was that there was nobody to talk things over with. Consistently you were on your own. You were weighted with the woes of the Ages in order to become effectively operational.

. . . Couldn't waste time in going down and hanging around Pinetree (code name for Bomber Command HQ at High Wycombe). Some weeks later they had a commanders' meeting down there, and I went to that; and then there was one other time, while I still bossed the 305th: Winston Churchill came out to have dinner with Fred Anderson, and very generously brought along a few British DFC's for some of us.

They used to tell a very pleasant story about High Wycombe. The impressive castle-like structure, which afforded both quarters and HQ office space for Eighth Bomber Command, had been an exclusive girls' school before the war. And they're back in the same occupation today. . . . But that night when Americans first moved in, the dark hours came alive with buzzing electric bells, whirring and clamoring all over the place. It was discovered that little cards had been left, neatly fastened to the walls in chambers once sacred to the virginal slumbering of schoolgirls: *Please ring bell twice, should it become necessary to summon Mistress.*

We could have rung a million bells, there toward the end of 1942, and no one would have come to any commander at his lonely Group —no mistresses, no Ladies' Aid, no Colonels' and Generals' Aid Society, nobody.

A little later on, after we got things organized, we set up a system whereby new outfits coming in could get Golden Words of Advice from those who were already on the scene. For instance, when Archie Old brought his outfit in, I was assigned to him as Papa; we were right next door. We tried to help him along and get him started with some on-the-job training, and we tried to be as wise as possible, with whatever wisdom our feeble battered brains could exude.

The night after our first attempt at formation flying, when at last I went to bed, I sat up suddenly and said, "Top turret. That's where I belong." Then I got up again, and studied a chart and some rough notes I had made. Immediately I could see a properly effective formation taking shape.

I think that it was two or three days later that the weather was again clear enough for us to fly, and this time we really socked it in. Someone else flew my aircraft. I climbed up into the top turret, plugged in the radio extension, and personally placed each pilot in that formation. I could see them and talk to them, all at once. If I couldn't see them properly, I'd climb around to some other window or hatch and take a look; then talk to them again. This was the evolution of the Lead-High-Low, the wedge-shaped combat box which finally was adopted. Later on it was used by everybody in the Eighth Air Force throughout the war. But, as I say, actually it was a modification of my original plan.

We had discovered something which it wasn't too hideously difficult for non-veteran pilots to manage in their positioning and spacing and speed, and in their maintaining position. Once in a while some muttonhead wouldn't be on the ball, and we would have mid-air collisions. I saw some, and heard about others; but in any war there's bound to be some character who lets his wits go wool-gathering. The foundation was sound and firm; it was good for bombardment and good for defensive purposes; these were what we wanted. It took a little whittling and twisting and application of the wrench and the screwdriver here and there, but mainly the pattern which we flew all along came into being on that second attempt while the 305th was still at Grafton-Underwood.

Don't get the idea that our new formation was perfect on the second try. It wasn't. Nor on the third, nor on the fourth. People roved around for this reason or that, people broke formation. But generally speaking we maintained in the 305th a hell of a tight and effective formation, and later we had plenty of opportunities to observe that the Jerry fighters picked viciously on those groups who let their people straggle. It was easier for the Germans to get a kill that way. Almost without exception they attacked (first) wandering cripples; (second) sloppy formations.

. . . Reminiscently I consider our first St. Nazaire mission. The pilot right behind me, leading the second element, was too far back after we left the target. I saw him in that position and gave him hell for it. He said, "Well, maybe I was further back than I should have been; but I would have been *hit* if I was up there where you wanted me to be. Because that flak was right on your tail all the way through." I told him, "Doesn't make any difference. You get up there next time. You can't tell exactly where the flak is bursting, anyway. You concern yourself with staying in formation, and let someone else worry about the flak."

We worked and planned by threes, as always with airplanes, and the formation which we devised was an eighteen-ship or twenty-one-ship formation.

(Just occurred to me that perhaps some readers should be informed of the fact that when you say, "We had thirty-five B-17's in a group in those days," it doesn't mean that, when you went out and flew, you put thirty-five B-17's over the target. Not by any means. A certain number of planes are always undergoing modifications, or repairs due to battle damage. There may be a mission already ordered for tomorrow, and one for the next day. No CO is going to fly the same crews day after day, unless he's more crazy or more desperate than most of us were . . . except in very dark run-down moments of the war. People have to rest, and, believe it or not, bomber crews even have to have some recreation.)

Constantly I kept telling myself that I must not demand too much from these pilots at the start. They had come to B-17's directly from BT-8's. They had never flown multi-engined airplanes before they came to the 305th . . . didn't I mention that there were three of us in the Group who had ever flown 17's earlier: John deRussy, Joe Preston and myself? One of us personally checked off every pilot who was sent to us in the summer and fall of 1942. You can imagine how much flying time they'd had in Forts . . . actually there was a little formation flying at the schools, in the BT-8's; but none at all in four-engine airplanes.

Doubtless the first formation we attempted was too demanding: it required more skill and experience than they possessed. But that second try, when I talked them into position— They could fly that one all right. We didn't try to go any further. We just concentrated on trying to maintain a decent frame and shape. On the whole we did maintain it. With a little judicious fire at long range, we got along pretty well.

Larry Kuter commanded our Wing at the time. A more-or-less official history, *The Army Air Forces in World War II*, says: "General Kuter set about to weld the squadrons and groups into the largest practicable combat units. . . . Thus a formation composed of eighteen to twenty-one bombers, known as a combat box, became the standard minimum combat unit, and it was stacked in such a way as to uncover as many of the top and bottom turrets as possible in order to bring the maximum fire to bear on the critical forward hemisphere. It was considered the smallest unit feasible for defensive purposes and the largest that could be handled readily on the bombing run."

Before that time every commander had been going his own gait. Certainly I experienced some satisfaction when finally our 305th formula was adopted and practiced throughout the Eighth Bomber Command; but personal gratification seemed childish when one considered the dividends in accuracy, in airplanes, and in lives.

The next time our Group flew, we went on a diversion over France. Diversionary operations are as old as warfare itself—soldiers didn't have to wait for airplanes to be invented. Annals of ancient campaigns, all the way from Persians up to the Goths, are full of tales about diversions.

For the benefit of those readers who might be somewhat unsophisticated militarily, let me say that the use of this word *diversion* suggests no reference to USO entertainers. Diversionary action to which we refer consists of flights and counter-flights or marches and counter-marches which may lead an enemy to believe that you plan to attack some area other than the point which you do intend to attack. It's part of the gentle art of fooling the enemy, or attempting to. The British used to call it "fogging the Jerries." In our own Civil War, at Second Manassas, the Southerners stirred up a prodigious dust on a hard-baked Virginia road. They even had their horses dragging pieces of brush back and forth, in order to raise a huge dust-cloud. A Northern general, Fitz-John Porter, saw the dust-cloud above the trees, and felt certain that Rebels were advancing in force on that road. He altered his attitude and his plans because of this, to the eventual blasting of his career. Those few Rebs employed in stirring the dust were engaged in a diversionary action.

Thus constantly in World War II groups would fly over certain targets which weren't to be attacked at all. It was trusted that this would confuse the German defensive systems—to have airplanes going off in one direction, and the main body of the attack centering upon a quite different target.

On the whole I have never been able to believe, viewing results at the time and while engaged in operations, and talking later with German Air Force personnel— I have never been able to believe that these diversions did any particular good. The GAF had been fighting a long war before we ever got over there, and they had had a hell of a lot of experience. They weren't very often caught off base. Unhappily for us, enemy fighters usually appeared where they were least desired, to gnaw and bite at main flocks of bombers; and usually their ground artillery concentrations (flak batteries) were on the ball as well.

Nevertheless, far as the 305th was concerned, our first two missions were both diversions. We didn't carry any bombs; but neither did we encounter any enemy fighters. I seem to recall that we observed a small amount of flak in crossing the coastline.

I used the opportunity to advantage in strengthening our formations by constant study and shifting. Again I rode with my head in the top turret, positioning the pilots, talking them up or talking them down or talking them ahead, as the case might be.

Our boys grumbled a little about this. They couldn't see the sense of my being such a stickler for formation. What they wanted to do was to bomb and fight. So did I. We got to do that on our third mission.

Again I tried to sleep and couldn't, and I imagined that I heard little voices gossiping about it. Little voices saying, "You made a grand nuisance of yourself. You went prying around for bomb results that weren't there. You sent the Group Bombardier up to Wing, and up to Bomber Command, to see what was going on. You found that they didn't have any statistics on half the bombs they had loaded. Strike photos didn't show them. Nobody knew where they fell."

The voices said, "They've all been bombing in turns during this evasive action. They've been slinging bombs clear out of the picture . . . don't know where half of them fell. It must be perfectly apparent that if you're going to get bombs on the target, you've got to do something about this evasive action."

Voices said, "You'll always get back to the same thing. It's got to be straight in, and it's got to be for a lot more than ten seconds."

Then I had an inspiration, and I climbed out of bed, closed the windows, pulled the blackout curtains into place, turned on a light, and went prying into my foot locker. Suddenly I'd remembered that there was an old artillery manual in there, left over from ROTC days at Ohio State. Why the hell I ever put that in the locker I'll never know. I don't think it was even a conscious act, it was more or less automatic: in packing my clothes I'd thrown that artillery manual in along with them. So I got the book out, and felt triumphant already. I sat up in bed, pulled the light around to a better position, and reached for a notebook and pencils.

"I'm going to figure this; see what it is. . . ."

In our artillery school days I had been trained on the French 75-millimeter gun—the common artillery arm used by American troops in World War I. Believe me, we had had that 75 business drilled into us. Lieutenant Chester Horn had been with the 75's, and he knew what 75-millimeter firepower was all about. I remember being thrilled by an anecdote of the Great War: about a Minnesota brigade, big Swedes and Nordskis from the wheat farms and lakes and forests up there, who fired those mobile cannon with such assembly-line precision that the Germans could scarcely believe what was happening. Those Scandahoovians, stripped to the waist, would be lined up back from the breech of the gun, and they would pass shells along with lightning speed. Every time the breech came back on recoil, the breech-block rotated and opened; empty shell flipped out, new shell was slipped in as the gun went forward. Then the round would be fired and another shell would be waiting to be hurled in on recoil. It was said that those gunners melted down a lot of guns.

The pay-off came when German artillerymen were captured and

marched back as prisoners. One and all they were begging, "Please let us see those seventy-five-millimeter machine guns you've got."

So I did know a little about the workings of the 75: facts that had been hammered into us by our instructor. (Funny, it's so much easier to remember the things you learned when you were very young, than the things you learn however soundly and importantly, later on.)

The enemy's ground defenses, far as we were concerned, consisted mainly of 88-millimeter guns, larger than the 75's. But it was easy to make allowance for this, and work out a fire procedure for the German flak batteries.

My challenge, as now set up, was the construction of a precision fire problem on a target the size of a B-17 sitting away over there on an imaginary hillside, twenty-five thousand feet away. Of course that was translated into 8,333.3 yards. Then I could go ahead mathematically.

It was odd, doing this in the middle of the night, sitting in bed with my sweater pulled around my shoulders against the clammy November chill. But I was too excited to freeze, even if I hadn't had the sweater. There were all those wild statements which had been made. *If you flew for ten seconds in a straight line, you got shot down.* Well, hell's bells, they weren't shooting everybody down. Of course everybody wasn't flying in a straight line, either.

In the back of my mind, while the pencil added and multiplied, I kept thinking, "You've been here only a short period of time, and you haven't had much experience flying in Europe, and no true combat experience yet. But you've got to imagine what the actual situation will be. You've got to figure out their precision fire." And then again: "Even though they are shooting at you, down there on the ground, they've got to lift a lot of rounds upstairs to get a hit on a target our size. They can only fire so many rounds in the time you're in their field of fire. Seems to me that the dispersion that they've got, with normal shell-fire . . . normal scattering, lack of accuracy, if that's what you want to call it, for that range. . . ."

Three hundred and seventy-two rounds. That was the way the answer came out.

I'd computed how fast they could fire over a target, how many guns they had—all according to guesses based on what our Intelligence reports showed. It didn't look too bad. Of course I wasn't figuring on the identical cannon which the enemy was using; but it was roughly in the same category. Had the same sort of performance.

It was maybe fifteen years since I'd done this sort of calculating. But I was confident that everything had come out all right, that I had the correct results.

Three hundred and seventy-two rounds, in order to hit a B-17 flying dead level, straight in. That was a lot of rounds, even for those busy

batteries. I concluded that we could take this . . . thought it was worth
a try. . . .

Was.

Before I went back to sleep again, I proceeded (in recollection) to
rebuild a car. Maybe *build* would be a better word, because our raw
material came from a lot of sources.

My friend Bob Kalb was in on the deal, and we were at his home in
Bradford, Pennsylvania. That's in the direction of the upper Allegheny
River, just below the New York State line. It was the summer of 1927,
between my junior and senior years. Bob was a Theta Tau fraternity
brother, and we had gone to ROTC camp together. After camp was
over I went home with him and found a temporary job in a little factory at Bradford.

. . . All the fire sirens in town were wailing, and everybody was
running . . . inevitable mobs forming toward the scene, on foot and on
wheels. The fire was in a garage, and it burned up a lot of cars. After
the blaze had been quenched and ruins were cooled a little, Bob and
I went wandering down there to look things over. We found a Ford
sitting off in one corner—a little extension off the main garage. Ford
touring car . . . oh, it might have been three years old, a Model-T.
Certainly it was years younger than my own old faithful 1918 type.

The wheels had been burned off. The rest of the car was just lying
there in ashes, with the top charred off and upholstery scorched out.
But we made bold to step on the starter, and the engine turned over.
That meant it hadn't been too hot, after all, because the battery still
had a charge in it. Here was a workable engine, and there was a good
chassis on the thing. I figured that we could make a deal, and did, with
the insurance company. Bought the thing as it sat.

On my old 1918 job I had a touring body too; but by that time the
top was gone and practically everything else. So down we went to the
local junkyard, and found a coupe body which wasn't in too bad shape.
We needed wiring for our new car, because most of the wiring was
burnt out of it: lights and all that. So I made a trade to the junk dealer:
my car, less the wheels, for the coupe body, a new steering-wheel, and
some wiring and lights. We shook hands on that one. Then Bob and I
made a little procession back down to that junkyard, me driving my
old wreck, and Bob driving the Kalb family machine. Left my old car
there, minus the wheels, put the wheels in the Kalb car, and drove up
to the ruined garage. Put the wheels on the burned-up job, and then
towed it behind the Kalb car again down to the junkyard, and parked
it right beside the coupe. Pulled the burned body off the old car. Seems
to me nowadays, thinking of the incident, that the body and fenders

came off separately . . . guess we just left the old fenders on. Paint
was burned off of 'em: I remember that. So we dumped the body, put
the coupe body on; we wired the thing, and put on a new steering
gear from some junked car—that steering gear which was part of the
bargain with the dealer.

We didn't have time to paint it. We put this job together (the deal
started on Friday) and we worked all day Saturday, and Sunday morning until we were ready to start for Ohio. Had to be back at Columbus
by Monday.

There are a great many mountains and curves and steep grades
twisting between Bradford, Pennsylvania, and Columbus, Ohio. Every
time we swerved round one of those curves or crawled up or down a
long slope I had an enormous feeling of satisfaction. The fire had occurred on Thursday night. Friday, Bob Kalb and I poked in the ashes,
and I made the deals; first, with the insurance company and/or garage
people; second, with the junk dealer. Then, with Bob's excellent help,
we had put all the elements together: my old car; burned wreck; coupe
at the junkyard, extra steering-wheel and wiring— Everything had
been stirred up and mixed together and bolted up, and here was this
car. All it needed was a new coat of paint, which I promptly gave it,
after we got back to Ohio.

Obviously it was my working out of that problem with the aid of the
old artillery manual that had stirred this recollection of ROTC camp,
college senior year, and the building of the car in between. I needed
sleep desperately; nevertheless, I lay for a while and wondered if this
memory might be some sort of portent or augury. If so, it must be
favorable.

Certainly we commanders were compelled to build our bomb groups
of assorted materials right then; and some of the material might even
be said to come from the junkyard, and some of it might be designated
as tired veteran or retread material; certainly a lot of it was reclaimed.
But if you could patiently—but rapidly, nevertheless—rewire the thing
and grease it and oil it and get it on the road, you might eventually
have an instrument which would offer sound performance. Even the
coat of paint wasn't too necessary.

And yet, and yet— It would help to keep the weather out.

6

OUR GROUP got into combat for the first time on November 23rd. In
that way I celebrated my thirty-sixth birthday with real live fire-
crackers, although eight days late.

We started out with twenty airplanes. But our ground crews weren't
really rolling yet, mechanically speaking. We had four abortions due

to mechanical failure, and two because the bombs were hung up. Thus thirty per cent of the 305th's planes aborted, which would look like a very unenviable record. Well, that was about par for the Eighth Air Force golf course at that stage of the game.

On this same day, aiming for this same target, our good neighbors the 306th Bomb Group (still operating under the command of Chip Overacker, as they had been ever since they left Wendover, and soon to snuggle up to us across the Thurleigh hedge after we moved to Chelveston)— They could only get up eight airplanes at takeoff. Of those, fifty per cent came home because of mechanical failure, and one was lost to enemy action before they ever reached the target. So 62.5 per cent of their effectives didn't bomb at all. As for the 91st BG (they would be neighbors also, at Kimbolton. We'd all be part of the same master traffic pattern)— They started out with ten airplanes, had mechanical failure on four, personnel failure on one, and the Jerries chalked up five more. So exactly 100 per cent of the 91st didn't bomb the target that fine November day.

The Eighth Air Force of late '42 was a far cry from the Eighth Air Force of six or twelve or twenty-four months later.

Everybody in our Group knew what I planned to do, and they were really howling. Say, at the *worst* howling; and at the best regarding me with raised eyebrows. To begin with, I'd talked with the squadron commanders, with C. J. Malec, our Group Bombardier, and the staff; then eventually shot the whole thing to everybody else, in Briefing before we flew.

Didn't blame them at all for their reaction; it was just about what I'd expected. In fact, I'd reacted a little that way to *my own* idea, to begin with. It seemed a brash thing to decide; especially to have such decision made by a guy who had never been over a target. To say that our people were a little leery about this fine scheme of mine is to put it mildly.

. . . Lots of tall tales have grown out of this incident, the way they're bound to do. For instance, I've heard on occasion that some joker stood up, after I had asked if there were any more questions, and said, "Yes, sir. I have a question." "What is it?" "Sir, shall we go to the stockade *now*, or wait for the MP's to take us?" Meaning that one grand insurrection was about to begin.

Which is a lot of bull. It didn't happen at Grafton-Underwood; never happened in any similar situation later on at Chelveston; it didn't happen over at Elveden Hall, after I took the Third Air Division; didn't happen in China or India, nor on Guam. Actually I've heard, though, that it *did* happen on Guam, when I ordered the unprecedented low-level B-29 attack against Japan, March 9th–10th, 1945. It's still a lot of bull. Maybe someone wished that he *could* say that, or wanted to, or something; but I was there on all the occasions mentioned, and such a thing was never spoken to my face or within my hearing.

I told my outfit that I was going straight in, and that I thought we could get away with it, and that I would be flying the lead aircraft. I told them we were going to put some bombs on that target—in this, the fifth attack made by Eighth Bomber Command against St. Nazaire.

Told 'em that anyone in his right mind knew you couldn't shoot a qualifying score by zigging around every ten seconds. It was just impossible. Might as well not go. Might as well have remained at Muroc or Syracuse; and they—the personnel involved—might as well have stayed in that old A & P store or Amoco station back home.

"If we're going to St. Nazaire we're going to get some bombs on that target, by God. And this is the only way I can see to do it. Fly a straight course and get in there."

An intimate friend informs me that I told him subsequently that I fully expected to be shot down that day. Maybe so, but I don't recall saying or thinking that. Could be that it's just all too long ago. Seems to me now that I didn't think much about that phase of it: I was too concerned about this revolutionary rabbit I was pulling out of the hat. Course, I wasn't in the same position as the average commander. I'd never been over a target before, and I was trying a thing like this!

. . . Kept telling myself, just the way I told the men, that it was going to be a lot better to fly straight instead of zigging. We'd get through the area where they could shoot at us more rapidly, and the enemy would necessarily fire fewer rounds. All in all, we'd have a better chance of getting off with whole hides—people and airplanes alike.

Kept saying to myself: "Is this a good bet?"

And answering: "Looks like. According to the best—but limited—calculations I could make."

"Is this good plain common *sense?*"

Answer: "Yep. Maybe not very *common*. But this is what we're going to do."

So folks were a little worried and a little touchy, and I couldn't hold it against them.

I remember now distinctly: it was seven minutes from the time we saw the target until the bombs fell off the shackles. Quite a long seven minutes for everybody concerned.

Doubtless I was enjoying the normal reactions of any human being who flies his first bombardment mission over a well-defended enemy target. Actually I don't remember any more reaction out of that first mission than the tenth or the last: they were all pretty much the same. Your tough period comes to you the moment you know you're going on a mission, and it lasts until you push that throttle forward. After that you're too busy to sustain much reaction about fear or anything of that sort. I mean, *if* you are a *commander*, responsible to your superior officers and your Nation, and God Almighty, for the people whom you're commanding.

(Except that I was a kind of dumb-bunny commander right then, flying in the left-hand seat of that lead aircraft. I should have been in another position, where I could see what went on, and see it a lot better than I was able to when flying as lead pilot.)

If ever I did make the statement that I expected to be shot down that day, there was a good deal of horse sense about it from the German point of view. Commonly the batteries would start tracking the *lead aircraft* in the *first element* of the *first lead combat box*. It is normal for enemy fighters or enemy ack-ack gunners to try to knock down the leader of a formation. This pays off handsome dividends: it busts up the formation. The airplanes have to get back together in makeshift style when they've lost their leader. Obviously it is an enormous advantage to split them up. The defensive firepower of the formation is confused for a time, and probably impaired throughout the mission.

O.K. So we're over St. Nazaire, and it's seven minutes from the time we see the target until the bombs go sinking down.

Next thing I know I'm talking to my bombardier. "How did you do? How was the run?"

"It was a good run, and we got bombs on the target."

"You sure of that?"

He said, "Yes, I am sure of it. It was a good run. But I could have done a little better if it hadn't been for those clouds: they kind of got in the way."

There wasn't a speck of cloud over the target in that hour. The clouds he was talking about were flak-bursts.

Just shows what complete tenderfeet we all were. This boy was looking down through the bombsight, and he saw those big black clouds drifting by . . . no wonder it bothered him.

Not one aircraft from the 305th was shot down by enemy flak batteries over St. Nazaire on 23 November, 1942, when we made the longest, straightest bomb run which had ever been made by B-17's over the continent of Europe.

We lost two Forts, both to enemy fighters.

As for the fighter problem, let me quote again from *The Army Air Forces in World War II*. (Matter of fact, we'll be sampling this history on other occasions, and to simplify matters I'll refer to the history hereafter as *AAFWW II*).

"Though many types of attack were tried, tail attacks predominated. This had been the accepted angle of attack against bombers. . . . Beginning with the St. Nazaire mission of 23 November, the Germans changed their tactics abruptly. Oberleutnant Egon Mayer, who commanded the attacking fighters that day, is credited with developing the head-on attack . . . he ordered a frontal attack, leading one element

personally. The tactic worked well, for it caught the American bombers in their most vulnerable spot. At that time some B-17's had one .30-
cal. hand-held gun, firing through one of four eyelets just off center,
and some mounted two .50-cal. side nose guns. [Often called cheek
guns.] In either case, a blind spot was left in front which neither the
upper turret nor the ball turret could reach."

That sums up the situation pretty well. They really came on a col-
lision course, and it was obvious that "the only disadvantage to the
head-on attack from the enemy point of view was that it made necessary a high degree of skill and training on the part of the fighter pilots,
in order to make effective use of the short time allowed by the very
rapid rate of closure."

The Group had now suffered its first losses, but they weren't due to
our straight and level dedication. Those gunners down there on the
ground hadn't yet fired that 372nd round, it appeared. Guess I would
have been jubilant about this, if I hadn't been too tired to feel jubilant,
the way one is always so plain aching weary after a mission.

Some people whose combat experience was confined to the Pacific
areas might wonder what all the yakking is about. There were plenty
of times, out *there*, when no evasive action was used over targets.
That went back to the Battle of the Midway and subsequent operations over certain targets in other portions of the Pacific.

It was a different theater and a different experience. They didn't
have flak in the amount that we had flak batteries over occupied Europe. They didn't have a fraction of the flak which we encountered
over Germany, especially around Berlin or the Ruhr. Europe was just
a different deal.

Reminds me of a song. People in the air have always exhibited a
remarkable propensity for dwelling on the grim as well as the titillat-
ing features of their existence.

> I don't want to fly a tour
> Over Berlin or the Ruhr.
> Flak always makes me put my lunch. . . .

So we got back home to Grafton-Underwood, which wasn't to be
our home very much longer, and there was that grayish-looking coffee
in the Interrogation room, which made me think of the coffee the old
man offered for sale aboard our California railroad train of ancient
times—the coffee that I didn't get to drink any *of*— But I took it now,
and deviled Spam sandwiches; we ate those while we described the
mission to our Interrogation people. I moved around soon, and heard
the questioning of this crew and that crew by our Intelligence officers.
After listening to what they had to say, I still couldn't see any reason
for having done the thing any differently than the way we'd done it.

Messerschmitts and Focke-Wulfs had put a lot of holes in our airplanes, and we were shy two crews, and we didn't like that. (Maybe I can tell you later how a commander feels about these losses. Just at the moment there was a kind of blankness and numbness when I thought of those Forts.)

I told myself, "Be concerned with the bombing. Stick to that. What actually matters is the destruction achieved—if any. It matters less whether someone is shot down, yourself included. And remember: fighters got those two B-17's, *not* flak. . . . Shoot you down if you stay straight and level as much as ten seconds? Nuts. We flew straight and level for four hundred and twenty seconds, after we first saw that target and came in on the bomb run. Not one of us was knocked down by ground batteries."

I was in a complete lather to learn the bombing results, both of our 305th and of other groups attacking that same target. Now our folks at least had some decent strike photos. If you're zigging and zagging all over the damn cow pasture you're bombing in the turns. You can't get good pictures of your strikes and those soft gray-colored little lichens which bloom suddenly all over the ground: the bomb-bursts. You're throwing bombs one way and shooting pictures another. On the straight-and-level deal we could really take pictures.

The whole thing was evaluated by General Kuter. The 305th got more than twice the number of bombs on that target that day, which any other group put down.

Now I knew just how we were going to bomb.

Certainly we'd try to kill off as many fighters as possible in our un-covered and un-fighter-defended state (no P-38's or P-47's available). We'd just pray that the Jerry fighters didn't gradually carve us down to size (or below size) before we could get replacements both in men and machines.

I wrote my letters to the families of the crews which had gone down. That meant twenty letters. And then, finally, I went to bed.

. . . No. Twenty-one letters. I wrote to Helen. I wrote to Helen nearly every day while I was gone to the war. Sometimes not much, sometimes it was just a scratch and a scribble. But I wrote to her most every day. It made me able to tell my wife, when next I saw her, that she didn't have a kick coming.

7

ONE REASON why we had a hard time building to proper stature in the Eighth was the fact that Operation TORCH, down in the Mediterranean and in North Africa, was soaking up a lot of strength. TORCH had priority right then. We didn't. A group might just get settled and operationally-minded in England; next thing, the cry would go out, "More strength needed for TORCH!" and away they would travel from the cold windy English Channel down to the cold windy Mediterranean. (Yes, they do have a nice day in winter down in the Med sometimes; but don't get that portion of the world's watery surface confused with Tahiti.)

Not knowing much about TORCH or the emergent Twelfth Air Force in North Africa, our men spoke of the Med operation as "Junior," as if Junior were a spoiled little brother. "Damn it to hell, Junior gets everything."

They sang a sinful parody on an old Sunday School song.

> Dropping, dropping, dropping, dropping—
> Hear the pennies fall.
> Every one for Junior—
> The big pig gets them all.

The 301st had been at Chelveston, now they were sent to Africa. We moved to their vacated Northants-Bedfordshire border station. It would be the 305th's home until they went off strategic bombardment, 25 April, 1945.

At first it seemed merely that we were exchanging one brand of mud for another.

Maybe the length and disposition of the runways had it all over the situation we had left behind us at Grafton-Underwood. Maybe the mud was a little browner; but it seemed just as deep or maybe even deeper, and it stuck to everything just as tight or maybe even tighter.

A good way to reconstruct the conditions under which we lived and worked that winter might be to lease one of our modern indoor ice-skating rinks, or an outdoor one like the installation at Rockefeller Plaza in New York City; and instead of using regular ice, employ a gentle mixture of okra gumbo soup and the plasticine which children use for modeling clay. Recipe: chill until the mixture hovers around the edge of freezing; then go out and try to walk through it, try to fly airplanes off it, or land them there. Try to set up working docks alongside infinitesimal islands of concrete or tarmac. Should you fall over the edge, down you go.

. . . If any person went wrong in his taxi procedure, and deviated the slightest from a carefully-prepared course, down he went. Mud was everywhere. We didn't love it. We didn't think Chelveston was so hot.

Years ago Tommy Thompson, who used to run the photo lab, gave me a candid snapshot in which Henry MacDonald, one of our young pilots, has stepped by mistake into a slough at the edge of the road. (MacDonald went on to become a colonel and to command the 305th at the end of the war and also—I believe—during their photographic tour in Germany, 1945–46.) . . . He has gone in deep with one foot. He stands with the other great muddy boot waving in the air; he's doubled over half backwards, just about to lose his balance, and his face scowls, and you can imagine what he is saying.

This happened to all of us all the time. The mud was atmosphere: you breathed it even if you didn't want to, it was under your nails, it was in grooves of your hands. We took off in it, flew in it, often had to abort because of it. On takeoff the mud would be splashing and whirling over the Plexiglas; it was sticky, and wouldn't drain after the airplane had climbed aloft. The guck interfered so severely with visibility that no one could see anything. You couldn't bomb, you had to come home. It would have been like trying to sight a target from inside a blown-up football.

Groaning and messing and muttering around through this sea of misery at our Base, were the most dreadful crew of Irish laborers anyone ever saw.

AAFWW II says: "Construction had lagged, almost inevitably, but it did not prevent the use of airdromes on schedule. American and British personnel joined hands to rush the installation of communications facilities, always of the greatest importance to operations. Other work might be completed after the field had been occupied by the Americans."

So that's what the Irish laborers were doing: putting final extension on the runways, and fabricating the last of the brick-and-mortar and lath-and-plaster buildings, or shoving final sections of Quonset huts together. Let me be the first to deny that I have reputation as a Black-and-Tan. Ordinarily I don't go around shooting down Irishmen in cold blood; and some of my best friends are Irish, etc., etc. But this bunch of lugs—

Makes me think of one of Bruce Bairnsfather's cartoons (Bruce became our 305th artist-in-residence for many months). The cartoon shows a couple of Tommies riding along in some Land Rover or jeep-type machine, and passing a North Irish cottage where an old man is raving on a bench in front of the door. This gaffer is really having a fit—yelling all by himself, and waving his fists in the air, and fairly beating his head against the cottage wall. One soldier says to the other: "What's he so mad about? Hitler?" And the other says: "No. Cromwell."

Obviously we had some of that old man's descendants, helping to put the war machine together at Chelveston. We were delighted when at last they finished up and were herded away.

Our Services of Supply ETO commander Major-General John C. H. Lee and his loyal yeomen were getting coal to us. Food too. But coal had to be rationed, and the food was rather limited in variety.

We boasted heat in our offices around the clock—Operations, Intelligence, all such places. The clubs were warm and the mess-halls were warm. Where we had to cut down on the coal was in quarters; but our belief was that people didn't spend too much time there anyway, and when they were at their quarters they were usually in bed.

Any cozy comfort in the barracks came from stolen coal. When this was complained about, we had to go to the length of putting a constant guard of sentries on the coal dump. There was a big fence around the pile too; but always some coal lumps were bound to be sliding almost under the fence. There was a regular coal-stealing routine, fully laid out, SOP for squadrons who lived in that direction.

The 422nd squadron in particular had to pass the coal pile when they went from the offices out to their home site—even from the mess-hall, if I recall precisely. In a single barracks no officer worthy of the approbation of Congress was supposed to ever come home without at least one piece of stolen coal in his pocket. They would halt beside the guarded fence, and wait until Mr. Sentry was looking the other way, then grab a piece of coal and put it in a pocket. Then, on reaching the barracks, the coal would be treasured chunk by chunk in a bucket for common use. There was only enough fuel each evening to keep a single fire in a single stove. If certain rooms were more comfortable than others, they got the nod from the fire-maker more often; and everybody would gang up in that room to shoot the breeze at night.

We did try to keep hot water in the showers all the time; but our ablutions, as such sanitary installations are called, were in most cases so blame far away from the place where people lived that it was a major project to take a bath.

The reason for curtailment of coal and food was that such a high percentage of available British manpower was in the Armed Services, not in mines or out in the fields. Also an extra heavy supply of coal was required for the enormous demands of industrial activity. Rationing was in effect; but actually it was an organized attempt to cut down consumption so there *wouldn't be a shortage*. Same way with food rationing. No one actually went hungry in Britain, though the choice of foods was strictly limited. You could get pretty tired of Brussels sprouts, but you always had something to eat.

In the case of us Americans, as month after month went by we were building up a good cache of our own supplies. Originally we had been provisioned by the British, almost completely; but we started getting in our own meats and staples before too long. As for the fresh stuff— greengrocers' items—most of it still came out of the British economy up until the end of the war. Even when our own supply system had been fully developed. Carrots, onions, cabbage, so on.

That winter we weren't truly in too much misery, but we thought we were suffering horribly. Trouble was, we weren't accustomed to the dampness of the climate: that chill which turned you clammy through and through. Most of our men had never conceived of a winter where it rained all the time between fogs. They didn't realize that England can be one huge mud hole, the moment you get off the pavement. We had some paved roads, but they were extremely narrow: designed for the English automobile. When we got our two-and-a-half-ton trucks over there, there just wasn't enough room to pass. So vehicles would get off the road, and then bring mud back on the road; and pretty soon you couldn't tell where the road ended and the mud began. It was all a bog.

One of our busy little tries was a Mud Control Program. We drove stakes all along there, to keep people on the pavement, so they wouldn't pull the mud out of the fields and heap it up on the pavement again. If drivers wanted to pass or meet, they'd have to back up and coöperate with each other.

Had any of us commanded a seasoned veteran organization, where people knew their jobs and were accustomed to working with one another on top of that, there might have been a different story to tell. But, however earnest and devoted they might be, some of the folks in responsible positions were carrying on with the military efficiency of Campfire Girls.

They were all so new, so inexperienced; there was just too much to do and too much to learn. You wanted to go berserk, like Bairnsfather's old Irishman, and beat your head against a wall. These people just weren't getting around to doing anything right.

To begin with, practically no one was using a proper form of field orders. (These were orders for the missions.) A real conglomeration of stuff filtered down to you at the group level. They put anything and everything in, whenever they thought of it, and omitted when they didn't think about it.

There was no Communications paragraph in the orders. "Oh, yeah, we'll use *this* frequency," and then they'd put down the frequency. You had to hunt for it; it was liable to be any place instead of in Paragraph 3 where it belonged. You wanted to lose your temper; it would have been a relief; but also it wouldn't have done any good.

The thing to do was to go to the Operations folks and say, "Look. Here's the way you write a field order." Give 'em the form and a sample outline. "Send down the dope like this, and it will be a lot easier on everyone."

Most of those key people didn't know any better than to do just what they'd been doing. Sophisticated men, for instance—old Second Bomb Group relics—were scattered to the four winds. And many were back home in the ZI, scrambling to train more outfits so they could be sent overseas.

. . . Thus initially, by the same token, there were inadequate mission reports of missions flown. I take quite a little pride in the fact that I started to get mission reports together. Finally I sent a copy up to our Wing; after a few of them got up there, they decided everybody ought to do this. But still you can't find the complete dope on those earliest missions—any dope that's written up in a fashion to be of historical value. Larry Kuter took command of the First Wing in October, but it took him a while to get them all to keeping adequate records. . . . We started having commanders' meetings. I retain an uncomfortable recollection of Kuter's singling me out, when the 305th's derelictions in the Intelligence area came to his attention. That was not nice, to have him point the finger, literally and figuratively. I remember coming back to my own Group and giving them hell, because of these very omissions and weaknesses.

But the point is that *these faults had become apparent through my complete reports.* Otherwise the Wing commander wouldn't have known a thing about it.

On the credit side of the ledger, let me say that the 305th had more airplanes in commission than anybody else. It was a pleasure to pat Ben Fulkrod on the shoulder for that one.

You go browsing through the files today, and maybe you want to find some specific information about an early mission: how many bombs were dropped, how many were on the target, and so forth. But if the report shows so many bombs on the target, that report may have been made up at the time: so many bombs dropped—and the pilot *said* they hit the target; but the strike photos hadn't been processed yet—"so *that* may be changed later on."

Could be that you'd find statistics some place else, or could be that you'd never find them at all. Or statistics might even have been manufactured by some wise-aleck as *Special Information For the Commander For His Commanders' Meeting.* Then, like as not, the man threw it over his shoulder after he had finished with it.

Targets mounted up: Lille, Rouen, Romilly, Lille again, Lorient. We were gaining experience and we were having experiences too—not all of them good.

Painted on the dark skin of our airplanes, little rows of swastikas began to grow. These represented enemy fighter planes destroyed by our gunners. The sum was quite impressive, when you looked at B-17 after B-17 and saw what had been awarded in all faith by Intelligence after Interrogation.

We were living in a fool's paradise, far as that stuff was concerned. Eventual disclosures, coming years later, after a careful re-examination and evaluation of GAF records, would reveal the fact that our claims, even when whittled down and seriously weighed in the balance and found wanting, and carved down again by our own people— They were simply all wrong.

We destroyed a mere fraction of the German planes claimed and awarded.

Take the Romilly mission of 20 December, 1942. Seventy-two heavy bombers from the Eighth Air Force attacked the target, losing six of their number, but achieving only minor damage on the German airfield there. There was a lot of shooting. *AAFWW II* says: "Interrogation of crews returning from Romilly indicated that seven enemy planes had been seen to crash, that eighteen broke up in mid-air, and that twenty-seven more went down in flames. Total claims originally registered included fifty-three destroyed, thirteen probably destroyed and eight damaged. These claims seemed to be excessive in view of the number of aircraft—estimated at not over 120—which could have intercepted."

Excessive is the word.

"An Air Ministry analysis set probable figures for the Romilly action at a much lower level. Keeping in mind the heavy fire-power of the U.S. force, the fact that this force had been under attack by fighters for nearly two hours, and that the visual evidence of planes destroyed —even allowing for duplication in claims—pointed to heavy enemy losses, this report suggested thirty enemy fighters destroyed and fifteen to twenty damaged as a not unreasonable estimate."

There follows later the most deflating remark of all: "German records suggest instead that the Americans shot down only two planes and damaged a third."

Not for one moment will I minimize the effectiveness of defensive fire by the best gunners of my own group or of other groups, once the gunners had learned how to shoot. We couldn't have done the bombing we achieved eventually with unarmed Forts. That much is for sure. But it was inevitable that many of our claims would be made up, you might say, in septuplicate. One gunner on one Fort says that he got in a burst as that FW swept alongside him, and he saw it disintegrate in mid-air; but he says that was shortly *before they approached* the target. Another gunner, in another airplane over at the side and above or below the one making the first report, says that a fighter attacked him from a high or a low nine o'clock, and that he chewed into the fighter; and the Jerry's wing came off, and the canopy flew loose, and the Jerry bailed out, chute and all, and so on and so on. But he says this was two minutes *after they left* the target. So of course that sounds to the Intelligence people like a different aircraft. But maybe it was the same one all along.

War is just one living and dying mass of confusion and delusion and stupidity and brilliance and ineptitude and hysteria and heroism anyway.

At the same time that German airplane was disintegrating or whatever it did do, and being tallied up by those two pilots in our lead squadron, let us say that people in the high squadron just behind them observed these things happening and were confident that the airplane or airplanes they saw breaking up were the ones (or the one) which had just attacked *them* from an entirely different altitude and point of the compass; and maybe a guy says it was five minutes *before* Time over Target, and some other warrior says it was five minutes *after*.

There you are: four enemy aircraft reported as shot down. And it was only one.

We were losing planes and crews right along, as testified, and we weren't getting replacements. Not yet. It wasn't a case of cutting ourselves down to size, when we realized that incompetence and over-confidence are no virtue in any man's war. It was the war itself, and the Jerries, who were cutting us down to size.

There are things which you can't put out of your mind, and which you would have no reason for putting out of your mind if you could put them out. I mean the way the cold wind blew around a dispersal point, and how wintry the thin brown grass looked; and there might be two or three metal bolts which had dropped in that shabby grass next to the concrete. You'd stand and look down at them, and shake your head over the carelessness; at the same time you'd think, "I wonder, if I come back to this same hardstand tomorrow, will the bolts be here? I wonder if I will *be* here to come back to this same hardstand tomorrow, or next week or next month, as the case may be?" And you'd know that if someone hadn't picked them up the bolts would still be lying forgotten, exactly the same way; and they wouldn't be caring about the day or the Group, or who had gone down or who had lived to come back, or how the bombing went. They wouldn't care because they were inanimate. You'd hate them then because they were inanimate. Still, they were bolts, and you had to depend on them when you needed them.

I remember the little square church steeple sticking up out of a cluster of trees, and I remember the back gate off the Base, where boys went walking or riding their bicycles, if the weather let them, to go down to the village of Rushden and seek drinks or seek babes . . . remember how the hedgerows looked, all along edges of the site, and the long spreading wet cold fields. An occasional Land Girl was out there doing something or other, trying to trundle a wheelbarrow through the muck; and some of the irrepressible boys naturally would have their eyes on that Land Girl, or others like her, no matter how ungirlishly brawny and sweaty they looked. The guys would be over there at the fences and the hedgerows whenever they got a chance, trying to strike up conversation. A lot of them struck up more than conversation.

I remember a lane, where it turned off from the Bedford road to come up to the main gate of Chelveston. There was a haystack there, and times after I left the Group and went to my new job in the Third Division, or before that, over at Thurleigh— When I had occasion to come back to Chelveston the haystack was always there, same size, same old place.

And down that road a little further there was an inn. Our community used to tell quite a literary-historical tale about that inn. They said that maybe eighty-five or ninety years before our time, there had been a guest at the inn: a poet named FitzGerald. He had settled down in that house for a year or two, or a season or two, or a summer or two— no one seemed to know exactly which. They said that FitzGerald did a lot of work there. Must have, the way some of our people were always quoting him.

Few in the echelons of command had much time to waste in hanging around picturesque old inns; but I guess most of us got down to this Blue Goose or Purple Lark or whatever it was called, one time or another. I didn't know much about the Rubáiyát, and I certainly never could remember how to spell Omar Khayyám. We had a character on the staff who must have known the thing by heart, and he and a few others were always going around spewing out those verses . . . being especially thrilled, they said, at the thought that the famous literary interpreter had done his immortal work so close to what later became our runways and our air space, there at Chelveston or at nearby Thurleigh.

The staff officer who was most expert shouted the other voices down. He said that he knew a lot about FitzGerald's life, and he didn't believe the guy had ever left his comfortable home away over east in Suffolk, and moved over here to our Bedford-Northampton region, in order to achieve his alleged translations. He says, "So what? Edward FitzGerald may have been a pansy; Lord knows he didn't get married until he was forty-five, and that didn't last long— But he wasn't a plain damn fool. He had a splendid house in Woodbridge—a nice garden— and he had his library; and why the hell is he going to come over here to Chelveston to write Omar Khayyám? It must have been F. Scott Fitzgerald, twenty years ago!"

Somebody else would say, "Yeah, but Edward FitzGerald was separated from his wife, just about the time he was working on Omar. Maybe *that's* when he was here."

I didn't know any of the background, so I couldn't participate in the squabble. All I remember is that some of the verses they used to quote were certainly appropriate for a region of bomber bases, where people were dying on every mission.

> And, as the Cock crew, those who stood before
> The Tavern shouted—"Open then the door!
> You know how little while we have to stay,
> And, once departed, may return no more."

There was a girl in South High, back in Columbus of the long ago, who used to like to recite Omar too, and she was always blinking her eyes when she did it. She rather got me off the whole idea. She was always talking about that book of verses, and the jug, and Thou, and batting her eyes again; and I didn't know what she was talking about and cared less.

(I'm told that there was a girl like that in just about every high school, every place. Probably so.)

But, with fresh casualties sharpening everything up, I rather pricked my ears when people joined in these FitzGerald-Omar discussions about the little inn down the road. I thought that business about the rose and the buried Caesar was really something, and also "the loveliest and the best," and all the other preoccupation with death. Made me wish that I hadn't let some sophomore in a middy-blouse scare me away from Omar; and I liked it when our expert would recite,

> Ah, make the most of what we yet may spend,
> Before we too into the dust descend. . . .

We were right busy with our new muddy war, so there wasn't much time to be spent in speculation on the great poet-translator, or whatever work he put out, or where he did it. I was a lot more interested in bomb tables.

8

AS TO BOMBARDMENT, we weren't batting any .400. True—our formations improved steadily. Our pilots were getting the message through their heads about the tight formation and the straight-and-level; they took increasing pride in their accomplishment along this line, and so did I.

But the bombing didn't satisfy me at all. It wasn't enough to look back on an old feat like the 23 November attack on those sub pens at St. Nazaire. Might have been fine at the time, but damn poor comfort a couple of months later. You kept thinking about Napoleon saying to his general, "Yes. But what did you do the *next* day?"

The more I chewed this over in my mind, the more I became convinced that our bombardiers weren't hitting targets properly because they *didn't have a chance* to hit targets.

Let's do a little breakdown on the life of Lieutenant Norden, a bombardier of that time and place.

Put yourself in his position. He comes into the Briefing room at four o'clock in the morning, and he's just been hauled out of bed, or hauled himself out. He's sleepy and groggy and homesick, and he's thinking that this is a hell of a war.

Then they pull the curtains apart (for Security reasons there was no unveiling until Briefing began) and there is a big map on the wall, with a string of red yarn going from our Base all the way over to an Initial Point somewhere on the continent of Europe; and then breaking away from that IP in another direction, and leading to the Aiming Point. So that path of red yarn shows our bombardier that he's going somewhere, and this is the first time he's ever seen the damn place on a map. Maybe the first time he's ever *heard* of it.

We will call the target Gutville or Gutburg or Guthaven; and it may be important as a communications center or as a marshaling yard junction, or as a sub base or a synthetic rubber plant or God knows what. Anyhow, it's a strategic target, and our Lieutenant Norden knows nothing about that city, nothing whatsoever.

Following regular Briefing we give the bombardiers and navigators a Specialized Briefing, hoping to make them recognize the target. We get out some pictures of the place—or at least one—and it's been blown up for a slide. And that's put on the screen. Or maybe there's just a drawing of the target. So our Bold Bombardier Norden examines these pictures also. And that's all the target study he's had.

That's what I mean when I say, "The trouble was, the bombardiers *never had a chance.*"

All their practice had been against a pretty little circle out in the desert where you couldn't possibly miss . . . nice clear desert weather. But here in Europe, when approaching the AP at Gutville or Gutburg or Guthaven, there are bad weather and bad clouds and bad troubles, troubles, troubles . . . houses or factories or warehouses crowded around, and an industrial haze to boot. Bad going.

"O.K., Joe. You fly. You're going to lead the next mission." Then he sees the map on the wall, and the yarn, and he looks at the queer little picture or the drawing, and he really begins to sweat it out. How's he going to pick up that target, anyway, through the haze and the guck and the broken clouds?

And, if our navigation wasn't too good, as often it was *not*, instead of the target's appearing out in front where it was supposed to be, it would be away over to the right or away over to the left. They'd have to make a quick sharp turn, in order to get in on it.

The more I thought about the situation the more I realized that we had been just plain silly. . . . So we're going to Gutville, are we? The bombardier gets out his target folder and tries desperately to do some study before he climbs into that airplane.

Like trying to cram for a semester examination in maybe five minutes.

I worked this over with Preston and deRussy and everybody else whom I could trust and who understood the situation thoroughly. I didn't want them to just say, Yes, yes, yes. If there was a vital objection to my plan, I wanted to know about it. I told them: "We've got to have people who know their target areas as well as they know their own backyards. Then, when the guy comes up on that target, he won't be caught short. He'll *know*. Even though he can't see it, he'll see other check points around there which he can recognize. If he sees that curve on the waterfront and those docks, he knows just how far the actual Aiming Point is, over there to the right. If he sees those big round gas-tanks, or those long machine-shops right there next to the Y of the railroad, he knows what lies to the north and south, to the east and the west. He *knows* the target."

I said, "This is what we've got to make possible."

There weren't any serious objections. They all believed, and were willing to coöperate.

. . . We didn't call them Lead Crews then, but we did later. I got a bunch of crews together, and divided up the areas in which we might conceivably attack. We assembled target folders for each crew, folders containing as many pictures of specific targets as we could get our hands on. We found that there were some pretty good reconnaissance photos floating around; we catalogued these, had them blown up, and our crews started studying them.

The rest is obvious. When that target was flashed on the screen at Briefing, it wasn't a surprise to at least one or two of those bombardier-navigator teams. They had soaked it up, they knew it well. They were the people who led the mission that day.

Gradually this developed into a real Lead Crew School proposition.

But it was discovered that it took a particular type of person to accept such training. There were those individuals who wanted to rush right through, and get their missions over, and go home. They had no thought of a military career; they wanted to skip through the war game—and hope that they didn't get tagged—and then skip right back to the States again. They weren't ideal material for our Lead Crews. Lead Crew folks were going to have to stay overseas longer; they would fly some of the tougher missions; that much was certain.

Strangely enough a lot of our Lead Crew bombardiers hadn't been particularly hot when it came to getting bombs down, out on the bombing range. There may have been numerous individuals around who could actually operate a Norden bombsight more skillfully than they. But when it came to putting explosives down on Guthaven, by God they put the explosives down on Guthaven. Only because of one thing: they *knew* the target and the area immediately surrounding.

This was where the program started, right there in the 305th at Chelveston. Let me anticipate my story by saying that later, when I took over the Third Air Division, of course I started the same system over there—the first time I'd had a whole Air Division to work with. In no time at all we were achieving better results, over there in the Third, than were the air crews of other divisions.

Orvil Anderson had shown up as A-3 (Operations Officer) for Fred Anderson, down at High Wycombe. I trust that in his retirement Orvil will not be insulted when I say that he was a textbook type who could really add and subtract and add again. He could put things together. It soon became apparent to him that the Third Division was the real Annie Oakley or Deadeye Dick among air divisions. Therefore we always led the tough missions—the ones where Bomber Command wanted to be sure that we knocked the targets out. Hell's bells—the leaders took the big brunt in any attack—

(Up go the howls! Many bombardment veterans are now going to declare that I am mistaken: that the so-called Purple Heart Corner— low rear element of low squadron—took the rap. Yes, often they did; *but not in the primary resistance of ground-to-air fire and air-to-air attack when we were approaching a target.* Then the flak batteries united in trying to knock down the leaders, in a manner previously described and for a reason previously explained. Also the vicious and effective frontal assault by enemy fighters accounted for the bulk of our losses ascribed to air-to-air attack. But, once they had run through our formation head-on, there was not sufficient opportunity for surviving ME's or FW's to rush around in front of us again and reassemble for a second identical onset. It was *then* that, hanging behind our combat boxes, they would pounce down to give the Purple Heart Corner its unenviable reputation. Also cripples who had fallen out of their original slots might be tagging pathetically along in that area, if they could possibly do so; and the GAF would lick its chops and come to second table.)

When you laid out a mission you could almost calculate exactly what the losses were going to *be*, and *where* they were going to occur. I knew that this was happening to me; but a lot of the time I was just too groggy and sleepy and tired, I guess, to complain about the situation and do something about it. Vaguely I knew that I was losing more Lead Crews than I was producing, and that our Division would be bound to go downhill as a result. Finally I woke up, and put a big input of crews into the Lead Crew training program. That's the kind of thing that happens to you, though: you've got to be on top all the time, or you're going to be in trouble. Nobody's going to bail you out, either.

Long years afterward we brought the target study procedure to its ultimate in the Strategic Air Command. We had our enemy targets lined up. Still have. Those SAC people know exactly which targets they are bound to attack, when and if somebody hits the switch on them. And, just as in the long ago at Chelveston, when our sleepy young amateurs began to learn about the German air base at Gutville or the sub pen at Guthaven, so our pros in SAC, a generation later, know their specified targets. Know them like they know their own backyards. Probably better (since necessarily SAC claims so much of a man's time away from family life).

I don't want anyone to get the idea that I'm blaming Orvil Anderson for what happened insofar as the Third Air Division was concerned. He had a job to do. He was told to get those targets destroyed; and, as Operations Officer of Eighth Bomber Command, he wanted to destroy them as efficiently as possible. All I wished at the time was that Orvil had *told* me what he was going to do, and had not preserved that delicate element of surprise. Maybe I should have figured it all out myself, in advance, or at least sooner than I did. But I wasn't bright enough right then.

A field order would come down, telling me what I was going to do, and so we'd get it plotted on the map; and you could stand there and look at it and see exactly which outfits were going to be hit the hardest. Usually it was *us*.

When I complained about this, Orvil was very sympathetic. But he was going to get those targets, and he figured that he could depend on the Lead Crews of the Third Air Division to usher the rest of our bombers in there. Thus I had to redouble every effort in training the Leads.

We had a little dip there in 1943 or early 1944. But we were going back up by the summer of 1944, when I left England to go out to the B-29's.

Previously there had always existed the benign assumption that any crew in the Command could fly to any target in the world, and bomb it; and it would be bombed, and stay bombed. Why not? Anybody could go out on the California or Arizona desert, in picture-postcard weather when you could see for a hundred miles— Anybody could bomb a friendly distinct white circle, there on the ground. No smog, no industrial haze, no seven-tenths cloud. The area wasn't built up. No floundering mass of rail lines, canals, bridges, factories, docks, civilian residential areas, hospitals, oil-tanks, prisoner-of-war concentrations— No mangled puzzle of things to be attacked and things to be missed at all hazards.

So you got lost. You weren't on course, you didn't know your way around. You couldn't *understand* where you were. And so you got lost again.

That is exactly where the skill in picking up routes came in. If you could find your IP, with a river running right into the target, and a road beside the railroad running into the target— You could get on that, and ride as if you were on an escalator. You'd run down the river; the target *had* to show.

And if you enjoyed enough time, you could get your bombsight leveled, you could get your drift killed, you could get your rate practically killed, before you ever got to the target. Or, maybe even better: you could do this before your turn at the IP. . . . You know what the wind velocity is, and you know what your drift is going to be when you turn on it. So you turn on the proper heading; you don't drift off, even if there's no river or road or canal or railroad to follow. . . .

All this could be developed in Lead Crews by sheer concentrated study in advance. Not only was the bombardier on the ball: the navigator was on the ball and he took you to the right place at the right time. The crew was set, coördinated.

That is what got more bombs on the targets for us, and got so many people killed, first in the 305th, later in the Third Division. Knowledgeable personnel out there leading a pack who were (at least at the moment) just as courageous and just as hard-working and just as dedicated and just as patriotic and just as admirable in every way as the Lead boys. Yet they weren't so *knowledgeable* about the targets. So they didn't lead. The Lead boys led.

You can get killed that way.

A lot of them did get killed.

At no time during the war in Europe did we observe any such speedy one-hundred-per-cent eradication of targets as was witnessed Way Back When, in the old Second Bomb Group days.

. . . We possessed two ranges on which we could do live bombing, there in Virginia: one on Plum Tree Island, the other over at Fort Eustis on the James River. Everything is marshy there: low and flat and weedy and soggy. Great place for ducks. But the only way to put a target out on the Eustis range was to build a sort of raft with a superstructure on it—say, a raft about twenty feet square. With a pyramid erected on that, it could be seen from a distance.

Bob Olds gave our Bob Travis the job of fabricating those rafts and pyramids, and hauling them out on the range. That was quite a chore; not to get them built, that was easy enough; but to drag them through marshes to the proper positions. So they had to be constructed in sections, and then assembled out there. Three of 'em. And the way Bob Olds always was, he wanted them built *yesterday*.

It took Travis several days to get those things nailed up, and then they had to be pulled through weeds and water, and located and assembled.

The other Bob (our boss, Bob Olds) would be harping away on this every morning. "Where are the targets? Where are my targets, out on the Eustis range?"

Finally a night came when Bob Travis was able to tell me wearily that he had concluded his own contribution to Operation Target: the damn things were in position. So, as Operations Officer, I scheduled an early morning mission.

Of course all our regular bombardiers had been officers, all along. By and large they had better educational backgrounds than the enlisted men—better skill in mathematics (it would be assumed) to permit them to cope both with bombsight and bomb tables. But now we were running an experiment. We were attempting to discover whether it would be possible to take people without such educational background, and teach them how to use the tables and the sight, right from scratch.

Thus we had a brace of young GI recruits on the string: two privates. They were really freshmen—either fresh off the farm or fresh from the Good Humor cart or the Socony hose.

Doug Kilpatrick was Papa and slave driver, both in one. But if those boys were clay in his hands, they were very promising clay. We had been using them for bombing with practice bombs. And by golly they were pretty good.

Probably it was about six o'clock in the evening when Travis told me that the targets were installed on the Eustis marsh. Promptly I set up a mission for seven a.m. next day, before the office was open; and I set it up with our two GI recruits as bombardiers. And I set it up with live ammunition.

I've forgotten who the pilots were. Anyhow, away they went after sunrise, flying over the range to seek the new little pyramids.

They got direct hits on all three of those targets and blew them to smithereens.

Be it remembered, however, that the salt water soon seeped in to camouflage any wreckage. There were no bomb craters apparent, or anything like that.

Now let old Bob Olds enter the picture. He gets up in due course, goes out and flies; he's going to make sure, by God, that Bob Travis has set those targets up on the rafts, as ordered. So Colonel Olds flies, and then he flies some more; and he works out his own little search problem; and he flies some more, searching in vain.

By the time he lands he's really in a towering temper.

"You find Lieutenant Travis for me!"

That was all he wanted. Then he would take Travis' hide off and nail it up on the wall of his office.

In due course of time, maybe it was about ten a.m., Travis showed up.

"*Where in hell* are my targets?"

Travis says, "Out there in the weeds. I finally got 'em out late yesterday. It was quite a job to—"

"The hell they're out there in the weeds! I just flew all over the God damn place, and they're not there!"

"But, Colonel, maybe the visibility wasn't—"

"The visibility was damn good, that's what it was! I've been all over that place, I've combed it from one end to the other. There are no targets *there*. By God, *you get them out there today!* I've told you this for several days—" etc., etc., etc.

Poor Bob Travis. It took a little time for them to get straightened out on this.

First: the fact that I had set up the mission with live ammunition yet. Second: Doug Kilpatrick had some exceptionally competent raw-recruit enlisted men protégés who had already gone a-bombing in the dawn and had demolished rafts, pyramids and all the adjacent mud.

Too bad we didn't have some strike photos of that operation.

Incidentally, one of those boy bombardiers was commissioned as an officer after World War II began. His name was Sarnosky. He won the Congressional Medal in the South Pacific. It was a posthumous award.

9

. . . Sorry things to get cleaned up, rough things to get ironed smooth. There could never be perfection but there could be a greater efficiency. We tried hard to attain it.

Nasty results may follow sometimes when people try to act just too cute.

Once the French coast had been crossed on the return trip, usually the pursuing enemy fighters turned back. Almost always they turned back, too, when little dots of friendly Spitfires appeared on the cloudy horizon, come to meet our 17's and escort them home. A lot of the gunners, anticipating an early shower and shave and a liberty run in a truck to Rushden or Bedford—or maybe, save the day, a real forty-eight-hour pass to London— They had a pleasant little habit of stripping their machine guns for cleaning, while still being carried homeward in the airplanes. Such practice wasn't confined to the enlisted men either. Numerous responsible bombardiers and navigators who should have known better were doing the same stunt.

Result was that some homecoming crews got lacerated by Jerry fighters, who seemed to come into the attack with diabolical awareness of the disassembled state of those machine guns.

You'd think crews or individuals—at least, individuals in *combat* crews—would have better sense than was demonstrated. Really it didn't take much of a stretch of imagination to envision a few Messerschmitts skulking off there in the cumulus somewhere, and biding their time until they could pounce upon some carefree smarties who thought they were almost home.

We had to pass a law that if anyone field-stripped his gun before he had landed at the Base, he was rushed to the guillotine but quick. Well, maybe be-heading wasn't the penalty . . . I guess it was de-striping.

. . . Then there was the dope who'd leave the guns on his ball turret pointing straight down instead of cranking the turret around to the proper position, with guns horizontal instead of vertical. And all the other dreamers in other airplanes who just didn't happen to see what was going on, and thus didn't talk to the ship whereon the guns were vertical, and warn them. Result: damndest display of pyrotechnics when the steel of those big .50's hit the flint of the runway.

Cohen couldn't do anything about the ruined guns, but maybe Fulkrod could do something about the turret.

. . . And there was a jittery gunner who called me on the intercom, soon after we'd taken off on a mission. "Ball turret to Pilot," he cried in alarm. "My guns are not functioning. Repeat: my guns are *not functioning!*" I told him, "You're going to look pretty silly when those 109's start coming in." Well, he got his guns fixed right quick.

The longer you live, the less you cease to be amazed at constant demonstrations of the human mind gone a-Maying.

Right at home there were attacks which might be expected, however remotely. For instance, intruders. They never did hit us, although we were alerted on several occasions. Away over on the North Sea coast or down by the Channel, some of the bases—mainly British, throughout the war—suffered frequent daylight fropping by ME-110's or JU's. Also there was the matter of regular Luftwaffe air raids—bombing attacks either by day or by night (mostly the latter). We didn't have any anti-aircraft guns, there were none in the neighborhood. So we did what we could: mounted 50-caliber machine guns on the back ends of jeeps, and had them standing around to shoot at possible intruders or pursuing fighters when the boys took off or when they came back.

As for air raids: all the shelters and bunkers we had were filled up mostly with mud and water. No matter how hard you worked or pumped or cleaned, they stayed full of mud and water. We were on our own to do what we could. There was a Base Defense Plan worked out in conjunction with the British Home Guard. Every once in a while they'd simulate an attack on our field, and we'd have to repel them. It wasn't beyond the realm of possibility that there might be commando raids carried out by German forces landing on the coast, and attempting to hamstring or negate the air bases. But at Chelveston we were pretty far inland for anything like that.

Still we had been directed to prepare that Base Defense Plan, and we had one. How good it was, I don't know. Certainly we didn't get any weapons' training; there was no place to receive weapons' training. We had a few small arms given to us for the proper purpose, but I fear that they were used mostly to shoot Lord So-and-so's pheasants, there in the neighborhood. The enraged gentry waited on me on several occasions, and I really had to talk my way out of it. Palpably they considered that the Tower and the Axe would be too good for my offending personnel who'd shot those precious birds.

Had to do something about this. Finally I gathered up all the ammunition—got it all back. Ammunition was contraband from then on. When a man went on guard he was issued so many rounds, and by God he had better turn that many rounds in, too.

So I don't know how good we would have been if we had ever undergone an attack. Probably not very.

When our young men gave up Paramount-theater-ushering or dragline-operation or whatever it was that they were doing, and came to grips with life in the raw, under the shadow of the Army Air Forces, we were too busy teaching them something about their jobs—or at least teaching them what to *expect* in those jobs—to be able to make them versed in soldierly attributes. People who were alive in that day and age will remember clearly how the Air Forces had a reputation for sloppy uniforms, slatternly salutes, and general shoddiness when it came to military behavior and appearance. There was a good deal of justification in that belief, too. It had been imperative that we devote our energies and time, and the newcomers' time, to teaching them something about their business with the airplanes—whether it was to operate in some capacity with those flying crews, or to keep an airplane alive and whole and well-fed on the ground. Performances of that type were vital to our phase of the war effort; and a kind of Rock-ettes' precision at drill was not.

Too bad we couldn't have had both. I've never been quite able to shake off the idea that a smart-looking soldier is apt to be a better soldier than an untidy-looking one.

The mere fact that nowadays an Air Force Academy cadet can sa-lute with fantastic mechanical precision doesn't make him any worse as a cadet, either.

Once in a while at the 305th we had a ceremony. Flyers were to be given Air Medals or DFC's or sometimes even better gongs than those, which they had jolly well earned. It was believed that we would all profit if a real occasion were made of the deal; so dutifully we tried to make a real occasion.

(In months to follow, the Group had a band. That was in the days of Fargo or Del Wilson, when folks had just a little more time to find a little fun in life. 305th veterans still declare that the whole world should have seen their band and heard it. Actually they played a lot better than they marched. Never could keep in step; and they gave forth a real joyous noise when they came booming and banging onto the strip of sodden earth which did duty as parade ground and reviewing stand all in one. They could play *Dixie* and *Stars and Stripes Forever* and *Off We Go Into the Wild Blue Yonder* like all possessed. It was the kind of situation where three clarinets would still be tootling on, when they came to the end of the tune. . . . Don't get the idea that they were a *real* band, like the noted Marine Band or the Air Force Band of today. These were riveters, gunners, cooks, medical orderlies—all united by a common background in high school orchestras or Podunk Silver Cornet bands, and a common love for percussion and brass.)

Every now and then some of our staff officers would turn utterly horrified at what was going on in this well of sloppiness. There were a number of dedicated souls present to whom the raunchy attitude of so many personnel was complete anathema. Thus they'd promote grim reminders and increased enforcement of orders and regulations. A lot of those had to appear over my signature.

There is a classic anecdote which still drifts around among ex-305th personnel, wherein I signed a directive and it went up on bulletin boards all over the Base, and most especially in the Officers' Club. "Subject: Military Etiquette. (1) There has been a noticeable falling off in the observance of formalities here at the Base—" The idea was that henceforth all enlisted men would salute all officers, and all of-ficers of company grade would salute all officers of field grade, and so on, whenever and wherever they met.

As punishment, maybe the commissioned personnel might be re-stricted to the Base for a couple of days. Lord knows it happened. Usually they really had it coming.

Anyway, the story goes that after one particularly dire citation of
crimes and penalties of this nature, everybody expected that I would
next appear on the scene in the manner of a drillmaster of the Royal
Horse Guards. Men swore that they stood for hours in front of their
mirrors, just practicing that snappy salute. A whole bunch of them
then are supposed to have been spread out along the road in front of
the Club, when here comes the CO, which is me, in the back seat of a
staff car—a CO with a whole bunch of papers in his lap, and a big pipe
stuck in his mouth. It is claimed that they handed me salutes all the
way from the Club out to the gate: stiff, sharp salutes which cut like a
knife. They claim that I acknowledged them by a somewhat feeble
wave of my left hand, and with my pipe still in my mouth, and my
eyes glued to those flimsies or whatever it was that I was studying.

I don't remember this incident, and regard it as fiction and calumny.
Nevertheless, I admit to having been more interested in bombardment
and maintenance and loading and fuses and ammunition and targets,
right then and there, than I was in saluting.

In war the main idea is to get the bombs on the targets.

A good salute is nice, too.

Often when a commander looks back on the people who served under him in intrinsic relationship, when he was living one particular
portion of his life at one particular moment— It's odd. Often the commander doesn't remember the good boys nearly so well as he remem-
bers the bad.

I recall one character we had: a little guy, with all the little man's
assertiveness. He was Lee C. Gordon. Inevitably he was called Shorty.
He could fit in a ball turret nicely.

As I recollect, he was with the Group all along, but don't recall that
he ever flew in my crew. Maybe he was a tech-sergeant by the time
we reached Europe; but we didn't have to wait any time at all until
it was necessary to bust him back to private. Forever he was in trouble
—not serious trouble, but still trouble.

Normally I would leave disciplinary matters of this nature to squadron commanders; but Shorty was a very special case. He was always
being brought up to me, and recurrently we found ourselves busting
Shorty back to private again.

As related elsewhere, I lost nearly half my crews before we started
getting any replacements. We made up crews of anybody and everybody. We went around scratching the bottoms of barrels and bins. We
took people out of offices. Bombardiers assumed navigators' chores. As
for gunners, if anyone wanted to go and shoot, we'd walk him once

through the armory shop, and he was a gunner. That went for cooks, medical orderlies, Supply people, truck drivers, anybody, everybody.

It was like one of those fine British movies wherein a suicide detachment from the Lancers or the Buffs is attacked by about five zillion Fuzzy-Wuzzies, and the guy who was considered only fit to scrub the latrine buckets before— He up and wins the VC.

We kept waiting for our own heroes to show up. (N.B. In due course of time, they did. But they weren't from the honey-bucket detail.)

Shorty Gordon had been trained and was experienced in the air and we needed him for crew duty. As I say, his sins were as scarlet, but never quite deserving of capital punishment. He would overstay his leave, sass some officer, take a swing at an MP, or not be at the proper place at the proper time— Generally he wasn't, shall we say, in a high state of discipline. He resented being bossed. In combat he was O.K. Back on the Base: No, no, no.

But we needed Shorty. So the way we'd work it was, when time came for a mission, we would make him a buck sergeant, send him on the mission; then take his stripes away from him when he came home. We did that a lot of times. What we were trying to do, of course, was to protect him and get better treatment for him, if the airplane happened to be shot down. In that case Shorty would be a non-com, and get somewhat more preferential prisoner-of-war treatment than he would have received as a private. Also, of course, all the rest of the gunners on the combat crews were non-commissioned officers. The skill requires it, no matter which position is flown. I felt that it was highly unfair to send Shorty into battle as a buck private.

Well, the Group took off to attack Bremen on February 26th. I think Joe Preston led that one, and I stayed home. Our Group Bombardier, C. J. Malec, observed that the entire area of the Primary was covered up, so it was decided to try for the Secondary Target, at Wilhelmshaven. Cloud conditions weren't very good there, either, and the bombing wasn't exactly out of this world. But what happened was that, wandering around North Germany in this fashion, about yay dozen GAF fighters had been alerted. They came in for the attack, and kept attacking.

Shorty Gordon was occupying the ball turret in an aircraft piloted by one Lieutenant Stallman. In addition to the fighter attacks, this B-17 suffered severely from heavy flak bursts. Shorty Gordon got his face and head cut; he was trying to cope with that blood when the message came over the intercom, telling the crew to bail out. Shorty opened up the turret and away he went.

He said afterward that the flak was bursting unpleasantly close, and like an idiot he had pulled his rip cord the moment he got out of the airplane. Should have fallen free for a while: they were up there around twenty-two or twenty-five thousand. And, sloppy character that he was, he hadn't adjusted his chute harness properly. When that thing popped open above him, he got a jolt that might have torn a taller man in two. It knocked off his boots and shoes and gloves, and he had a nice freezing time of it until he landed on the German waterfront, and was quickly picked up by the Jerries.

Our friend Shorty, it turns out, was as much trouble to the Germans as he was to me. He escaped five times from prison-camps. Captured four times, the fifth time he made it. Wish I could remember all the details of each escape; but Shorty did pay me the honor of coming over to call, next year when he made it safely back to England, and I was commanding the Third Division at Elveden Hall. (When finally he got out of Germany he went through France, down through Spain, by that escape route. Aided along the way, naturally, by the Underground.)

Certainly I was surprised when they informed me that Sergeant Gordon was at the gate, come to pay his respects and say Hello. He was just about to go home, but I was somewhat touched by this friendly gesture from a man whom I'd personally knocked loose from his stripes so many times. He wasn't in my command any longer, so I couldn't have busted him even if I'd wanted to. When I say he was going home, I mean really home—back to the States. That was our normal policy for escapees. They were taken out of combat and sent back to the States, no matter how many or how few missions they had flown. I guess there may have been exceptions to this rule, but not many.

One thing especially sticks in my mind about Shorty's experiences with the Germans. Every prisoner was court-martialed by his captors if he was caught trying to escape; and I suppose Shorty wouldn't have been happy otherwise; he was always being put in the jug when he was with the 305th, so he must have felt right at home.

He noted this, he said: the better the escape, the less the punishment. If he made a real sorry attempt at escape, they really smacked him around. If it had been a good attempt, one that almost succeeded, he got off very lightly. Twice he did it the stupid way, he said, and was recaptured promptly; on other occasions he got quite a way farther. On one of his trips he got clear to the Swiss border. He was nicely dressed up in *Lederhosen* and wore a cute little Bavarian hat with a chamois beard on it. He was on a stolen bicycle, complete with rucksack, for all the world like any young German soldier who had bravely earned a generous leave by fighting *für den Führer und das Vaterland*. He came pedaling up to the Swiss border and decided that the best thing to do would be to wait and try to slip across at night. There was a haystack over in a field, so Shorty got off his bicycle, wheeled it over to the haystack, and flopped down to wait for dark.

German guards at the border had been covering that road with their field-glasses, and they witnessed the whole thing; went over to investigate, and nailed Shorty.

I believe it was on the successful escape that he got a painter's bucket and brush, along with overalls and cap, and he proceeded to paint a white line down the middle of the road—inside the prison camp, up to the guards' shack, and right out of the gate and down the road.

Could be that Shorty's in one of those anthologies of great escapes.

Also I keep thinking of another escape story. This was something which befell one of our Operations staff types, named Mayo. When we first got to England I had laid down the law about no combat missions for Operations staff people until we were all settled down and had the outfit really rolling. Then, with mounting losses and no replacements flying in, the opportunity came sooner than might have been expected.

I believe that the target that day was St. Nazaire (Lord Almighty, how many times did we go to St. Nazaire?) and Mayo was going on his first mission. He bunked with Harold Fox, an Intelligence officer who later became our PRO.

Bang, down goes the 17 that Mayo's in.

Next time Foxy came into the room they had shared, he saw a letter lying on the dresser with his name on it. Mayo had left it for him, in case he got shot down. People were always doing that. Sometimes they'd write special letters to their wives or sweethearts, and leave them to be forwarded; and often they would write to their companions there in the Group, telling them what to do with various possessions. Most guys knew there wasn't any use in sending a lot of clothes and uniforms back home, to be sobbed over and saved in an attic full of moth-balls; so they'd give 'em away.

"George wears my size shoes. Give my shoes to him. Give my flying jackets to Tony."

Like the old Western song about the cowboy who got killed because a horse on him did fall.

> Oh Bill, you take my saddle, and Joe you take my bed.
> And Fred, you take my pistol, after I am dead. . . .

In the case of Mayo, there was a postscript. "Oh yes, Foxy. That bottle of gin in my top dresser drawer: you can have that."

By golly, it isn't more than ten days or two weeks from the time that crew got shot down until Mayo is back. We're notified from London.

"Send someone to identify him."

That was the way it had to be, of course, to keep the Germans from infiltrating us with spies posing as Eighth AF personnel.

Everybody will recall that there was a regular escape route running through the Pyrénées and across Spain; one exit was through Gibraltar and another through Portugal. I don't know which way Mayo had come, but the Spanish had had him in jail for a few days, and he was really a sight. Spanish authorities had shaved his head, the way they do with all prisoners. Actually it would have taken his roommate to recognize him. So Foxy rides up to London to the rescue, and the first thing Mayo says is, "You son of a bitch. I suppose you've drunk up my gin." He had, too.

That's a story with a happy ending, just as Shorty Gordon's was. All of the stories didn't have such happy endings.

. . . There were so many letters, as related, left around on people's bedside tables or chests in their rooms. Very often those had to be sent, mailed intact, the way they were. There wasn't any business about going up to London to identify the repatriated soul, because that soul just wasn't ever going to be repatriated.

One of our 422nd Squadron people wrote a letter home, telling about the death of a lieutenant named Truesdell, called True for short. True was a former Raf type who had come in as a replacement—after we began to *get* replacements—and somebody wrote a letter about his death. The letter has survived a generation of vicissitudes, since it was written in 1943; but the writer thereof has very kindly allowed me to use it here. I quote the letter now, because it tells how we felt about the war.

". . . Well, one of the fellows was going through the drawers of the old battered bureau in Truesdell's room, and he found six pounds there: English pounds Sterling, all folded up. Truesdell had left instructions about what he wanted done with that six pounds. He wanted the boys of the squadron to go over to the club and have drinks on him.

"So they waited until Major Price got back (he is the squadron commander, and was on leave) and then everybody went over to the club and had drinks. Some took beer and some took whiskey. Rum and coke, too: that's about the most popular drink here. And a few just had coke, because there are some fellows who don't drink liquor because they have promised their mothers that they won't, or maybe just because they don't like liquor. It doesn't matter, either way; whether you drink or whether you don't—that's your own business.

"It was pretty nice of True to leave that six pounds (twenty-four U.S. dollars) in his bureau drawer. Everybody had several drinks, because six pounds will buy a lot. Cokes or rums: both are cheap at our Base. Life is a little cheap over here, too, these days. But there was nothing cheap about Truesdell. Everybody feels that war is pretty expensive when it keeps demanding nice guys like True, and doesn't give any of them back in change.

"That is the way we buy Liberty today. Liberty is expensive; sometimes it costs more than six pounds Sterling.

"Everybody was glad to have a drink on First Lieutenant Floyd H. Truesdell, age twenty-four, of Anchorage, Alaska. That was what he wanted them to do with his six pounds."

10

IN EVERY FIELD of activity there are men who want to make changes, and who are balked and discouraged in the process. And sometimes blocked. But they keep trying.

I saw a lot of things which I wanted changed, and I tried to change them. Often I bit off more than I could chew. But I never abandoned any of my projects; we went forward whenever it was possible to do so.

One thing I didn't get done, and couldn't get done while I was in Europe—

Take a look at our set-up. When I moved into Chelveston there was what was called a Service Group there. They operated the heavy shop equipment and heavy maintenance equipment—all the housekeeping stuff. So the Service Group was supposed to do second-line maintenance for me.

Our Combat Group was charged with responsibility for the normal inspections (first-line maintenance). But, you see, the Service Group was not under my command. It was under another commander; and the chain ran down, not through Bomber Command, but through the Service Command. So, if I turned an airplane over to the Service Group for repair— Far as I was concerned, that airplane was gone. The Service Group could work on it at their own damn leisure. When the Service Group commander declared the plane to be ready, he'd give it back to me.

The point was, he'd never give it back to me. This sorry situation haunted me days and nights.

Those people weren't combat troops and naturally didn't feel like combat troops. They were service troops and they felt like service troops. They didn't belong in the fight, according to their attitude. It was the old idea of fortress soldiers and assault soldiers. You could tell which was which in an instant, just by looking at them. I dreamed of the day when we could have everybody on the Base assigned to one commander.

Never got the situation corrected in England. After I went out to India, with a wide-reaching command of my own—and later in the Marianas—we did fix it. Eventually this system prevailed in the entire organization of all the commands, and it's there in the operation of SAC today.

Our traditional fault—the one against which I coped hopelessly in earlier days of the Eighth Air Force—went all the way back to Langley Field. There they had the usual Base commander and Group commander. The Base commander wanted to mow the grass; the Group commander wanted to fly his airplanes. . . . Answer? They mowed the grass.

Because why? Because the Base commander made out the efficiency report on the Group commander. He got rated on whether his grass was cut or not, or whether his buildings were painted. By gad, that's what he was going to do: mow grass.

In the years which have gone by, many people have examined my policy, and have said: "Why wasn't this done long before? Obviously, on the face of it, it makes sense. So what happened? Who held it up?"

Well, you're apt to get so tied up in administrative processes, in peacetime, that you forget exactly what you're in business for. The emphasis is on something else—not on a ruckus which doesn't exist. But when you get out there and start fighting, it is the people who are actually *fighting* who see these things and realize that they are necessary. Then they've still got to prod and slug and struggle, all the way up through the normal bureaucracy which every military organization owns.

What kind of sacred cow were they guarding? The Service commander. He says, "*I* am supposed to fix these planes. *I* have the responsibility. *I* know how to do it." Would have been fine if we'd got the airplanes back when we needed them. We didn't.

The fault was never really licked in England. I knew this was the way to do it, but had to bide my time. I needed more command and more rank; then I could impose the correct system myself, within *my* organization, and let the value of it be demonstrated therein.

Some critics may have blamed Uncle Ira Eaker or Fred Anderson for the then-existing state of things. Not I. In a war every boss has more to do than he can possibly get done. Some things people get done, some things they don't. This was one of the things that didn't get done. Well, they won the war, even though they didn't get this done. So?

Let me illustrate the difference dramatically:

In England, right there in the middle of an industrial empire, they were able to get about thirty hours a month, combat time, out of their airplanes. I put my new system into effect in the Marianas, away to hell and gone out there in the Pacific, away from supplies. Soon we were flying a hundred and twenty hours a month on our airplanes. Four times as much as in England. That's the difference between the two systems. And also—take note—this was with the B-29, an aircraft much more demanding than the B-17.

We had endless contention in 1942–43 about who was to do what. I finally wound up by not giving much of my stuff to the Service Com-

mand, because if we gave them an airplane— They dwelt in a different
world. They were on a different schedule, and they had a different
sense of the urgency which ruled. When would we get that airplane
back? A year from Next-Tuesday-at-Two.

If we could possibly do the work ourselves we did it ourselves. We
did a lot of things ourselves that other Groups couldn't do—solely because of Ben Fulkrod and the magnificent assortment of equipment
he'd lugged along—those fantastic wing reamers, for instance—and
which he well knew how to use. I've mentioned this before. It was as
if Ben enjoyed a real precognitive experience, and knew exactly what
we were going to run up against.

Originally each squadron had its own maintenance set-up, its own
sheet-metal section, its own electrical section, etc. But in combat we
discovered that one squadron would be shot up and swamped with demands in the sheet-metal area, and another squadron might assay
scarcely any damage at all. One outfit would be staying up all night;
the other would be enjoying plenty of sack time. Why should the
364th Squadron get more sleep than the 366th? It wasn't fair; worse
than that, it wasn't practical. You'd have some of your people exhausted and in an appalling situation for airplanes to fly; and another
outfit preening themselves—in good shape, ready to go, undamaged.

It was the unevenness of the whole proposition which mitigated
against us. Finally we established one community sheet-metal shop
where we could throw everybody on those needy airplanes, no matter
which squadron they belonged to. This was a real pooling of effort at
its best, and above all a pooling of skill; for there just wasn't enough
skill to go around. Never is. Skill is a thin varnish . . . you have to use
great care in spreading it, and covering the whole surface if you can.

I had abandoned the traditional crew chief concept. Good enough in
the old days, but not for now. Long before, we had a crew . . . and the
crew chief had an electrician, a sheet-metal man, so on. It worked fine
in those leisurely days when there was plenty of time to train people,
and when those few people we had were all remarkably expert in their
several fields. It didn't work in the Eighth. Greenhorns to the right of
us, greenhorns to the left. When we pooled what talent we *did have*
we got along better.

Bruce Bairnsfather came to Chelveston. We made him welcome, and
in no time at all he was a component part of our Group.

Readers whose memories go back to World War I will react to the
name of Bairnsfather. It would not be accurate to say that he was the
Bill Mauldin of World War I because he was a lot more than that. He
went out to France with the earliest British Expeditionary force; but

before long was delighting both the soldiers and people back home with cartooned adventures of a fat, bald, heavily-mustached character known as Old Bill, the real Cockney soldier to end Cockney soldiers. Old Bill had a pal named Alf who went everywhere with him.

Doubtless the most famous single cartoon relating to the British Army in that war was the one where Bill and Alf are crouched down in a shell-hole with all sorts of German ordnance bursting merrily around them. It would seem that Alf has just said in Cockney, "This is a 'ell of a 'ole." And Bill retorts, "Well, if you knows a better 'ole, go to it."

Old Bill swept the whole United Kingdom, the whole British Empire, and later gratified the Americans as well. There was a play in London, a most successful play—*The Better 'Ole*. Old Bill was something like Mickey Mouse or Donald Duck: he didn't truly exist, yet he was a real personality to the whole public.

So we had his creator with us—a mild-mannered, soft-spoken man of moderate physical stature, and a good companion. He had been doing a stint as war correspondent in North Ireland before he appeared at Chelveston, and we were treated to many rewarding anecdotes about that experience.

He painted all over the place. He painted the noses of airplanes, he painted walls. Our Public Relations Officer, Harold Fox, had a little coop of an office, and Bruce decorated the wall with an unforgettable shelf. In this case he worked in the style of William Harnett, who drew everything in exaggerated three-dimensional quality. Paintings of fruit in a bowl, and so on. The fruit is so perfect, so round and real—it doesn't look like a painting of fruit, it looks like a bowl of fruit. My wife says that the French call that sort of thing *trompe l'oeil:* fool-the-eye.

That's the way Bruce Bairnsfather did his shelf. It had some books on it; I've forgotten the titles, but they were suggestive of various ramifications of a PRO's life. Then he put a few other things on the shelf. There was a bottle of Vat 69 and a carton of Luckies, and some loose packages of cigarettes lying around. Also one cigarette on the edge of the shelf, lighted; it was burning down close to the shelf, and the ash was just about to fall off. Strangers would come into that office, and they'd take one look, and either start to grab the bottle of Vat 69 and take a swig, or rush to the rescue of the burning cigarette— You had to be up on top of the thing before you realized that it was all a trick of painting.

The best feat which Bruce performed in the *trompe l'oeil* line was a decoration he put on the wall of our Officers' Club. That was down at the lower end of the long room, quite some distance from the bar. Bruce painted a big mural (this was after I left Chelveston to take a new command, but the story belongs here nevertheless).

The artist went to town with a life-sized job which showed an Army

Air Force GI standing on the deck of a ship coming into New York harbor. I got to see that picture eventually. . . . Course, the GI has his back to the room. He's at the rail, looking out at the skyline . . . big bottle of booze sticking out of one of his hip-pockets. There he is, safely returned from the war in one piece.

But even Bruce Bairnsfather didn't realize quite how far he was carrying his fool-the-eye routine.

. . . I won't say just who the general was. He was a man of importance, very serious by nature, and he wanted everything to go just right and according to the book. He dedicated himself to seeing that it went that way. Probably it was a good idea that he wasn't around in 1942, because things weren't going according to the book, and he would have been pretty badly disturbed.

Anyway, he came up to Chelveston for an official visit and look-see; and when duty was done he repaired to the Officers' Club, along with the current commander of the 305th (won't say who he was, either) and a few of the select and elect. They were all standing there at the bar, and it was along toward sunset, cloudy and rainy outside, and only a few lights turned on, and not many people around.

The general looked down the room critically. Other people were attempting to keep up a conversation, but he seemed to have something on his mind.

He spoke, sharply and to the point. "Sergeant!"

The bartender, who was the only sergeant around, came quickly to see what the distinguished visitor wanted. "Yes, sir?"

General What's-his-name gestured with his glass. "I don't like to see this sort of thing, Sergeant."

"Excuse me, sir. I don't quite get—"

"I mean *that* sort of thing," said the general firmly, gesturing with his glass again. "I mean that enlisted man down there at the end of the room. He shouldn't be standing there like that. Furthermore, he's not in Class A uniform, and I like to see only Class A in a club. But this is an *officers'* club; he doesn't belong here. Go down and tell him to go over to his own club where he belongs!"

. . . In due course of time our distinguished general had to walk the length of the room and see for himself just what was a-doing. It has been recorded that he was somewhat embarrassed and annoyed about the whole episode.

Bairnsfather became particularly friendly with one of our pilots, a lieutenant named Whitson, and he painted his Old Bill on Whitson's airplane. (There were a lot of gay pictures on the Forts, and some not so gay. And some which caused at least one visiting Congressman to raise shocked eyebrows when he went around and looked at our B-17's. He demanded that those obscene names and caricatures be covered up, so they wouldn't offend the Germans.)

On 15 May the B-17 named *Old Bill* headed for Wilhelmshaven along with the rest of the 305th; but that was a disastrous day. Weather all wrong . . . complete overcast in the target area. One of our squadrons had to jettison their bombs in the North Sea. Some of the others did better, and got hits on Heligoland.

To return to *Old Bill*. They were badly chewed over: first by a 190, and then more 190's, and finally a two-engine Messerschmitt, or so it was reported. Net result was that Whitson and his co-pilot Holt were both badly wounded, and Venable the navigator was killed, and Barrall the bombardier was also wounded. Flight engineer was wounded, ball-turret gunner wounded, and I think some others in the crew. They came back with *Old Bill's* nose shot clean off, and the dural metal thoroughly sieved. They did manage to get home, terminating the mission with a ground loop because they had no brakes or flaps—couldn't control the landing speed.

Old Bill sat in front of the hangars for a long time, an object of terror for green crews who invariably were marched over to get a good look at it.

Barrall, bombardier on *Old Bill,* and who managed to repel a Messerschmitt attack after he was wounded, was killed later while training for night missions wherein a half-dozen airplanes from the 422nd Squadron were usually sent to fly along with the RAF and drop leaflets. No one enjoyed those missions. You had to club our people over the head in order to get them to drop leaflets instead of bombs.

They were up on a night training mission and collided head-on with a British Beaufighter. Maybe Floyd Truesdell was the pilot on that one. Seem to recall that only the two waist-gunners got out, and one of those had his face busted open and his front teeth knocked out because he didn't have his chute properly secured; when his chute opened, the buckle flew up and struck him in the face.

A year or so before I left my job as Chief of Staff, Whitson came through Washington with his wife and two children, and dropped in for a chat. He told me that he still has that section of the airplane: the piece of the nose with Old Bill painted on it. He managed to get it back home, shell-holes and all.

A few of our folks dropped in to call on Bruce Bairnsfather at his home in Surrey after the war. Bruce died in 1959. I'll always remember him for his cool devastating remarks about certain professional military experts who were writing in the papers and magazines. I can hear his mild dry voice saying, "These professional military experts!—who explain out of the wealth of their erudition that it is much more difficult for an enemy force to land upon a beach which *is* defended, than one which is *not*."

There were other—more personal—strings reaching back into the past, and one of those extended right to Bob Olds. I know it irked the hell out of him to have to remain in the States as an organizer and training director. Let no one doubt that he would have made a terrific commander in the field. But also he owned a loyalty which dictated that he accept without question the orders which held him in the ZI.

He'd got the Ferry Command organized and operating, and then in May of 1942 he went into the training profession in a big way. Nor was there another soul in the Army Air Forces better qualified to do *that*. Thus he commanded the Second Air Force, and produced the expansive number of crews which had to be constructed from scratch, starting as the 305th had started: on a little piece of paper. That was the way Bob spent his last months on active duty: manufacturing new groups, getting them trained, getting them overseas.

We corresponded constantly, from the time I first traveled to England until Olds went to the hospital. I wrote him a lot of letters in longhand. He asked me to do this: there was no profit in our going through channels in the prescribed fashion. There he was, at Fort George Wright, Washington; and here I was, out in the field, or often over the Continent among flak bursts. I could tell him what we needed and what we wanted; and he could figure out ways of getting us what we needed and wanted. So I'd sit down and pour out a little piece of my soul to him in longhand, and mail the letter; and almost immediately Bob Olds could shape up the idea and put it right into the program. It was an excellent method for short-cutting a lot of channels.

Might not have been approved by some people. We didn't care. It was all an aid and an advance in getting the job done.

Suddenly in February of '43 Major-General Olds sent me a brief note saying that he was being released from duty in order to enter the Station Hospital at Tucson. Previously he had not bragged of bounding health and energy; he'd just gone on carrying the work-load of five normal men. Bob Olds died at the Desert Sanatorium, out there in Arizona, 28 April, 1943. His ailment was an extremely uncommon form of heart disease, with many complications. It was a form of myocarditis known as Libman-Sacks disease.

Some of us mourners had the feeling that it was appropriate in that it took a very rare complaint to kill a very rare individual. (He was only in his forty-seventh year; that seems youthful to me now in 1965, when I'm about to enter my sixtieth year.) General B. K. Yount had summed it up when he said, a couple of years before Olds died: "An officer of superior initiative, imagination, and enthusiasm, who gets things done. He is untiring in his devotion to duty."

Good epitaph for one of our real Greats.

11

OUR MORALE got down to a pretty low ebb late in the winter; but things turned for the better before spring. As I've said, we were getting no replacements, either in men or crews, and even when they started to appear they were mighty slow trickling in. The North Atlantic just wasn't being flown; and back home the crews weren't being turned out as fast as we needed them. Nor were the airplanes whisking themselves merrily off the assembly lines. There occurred some pleasant little strikes to slow down production.

It would start with a coal miners' strike, and that would be reflected in the metal industry in no time at all; and without metals the airplanes just couldn't be built. Our crews flew, and watched their friends burning up over German targets because our military policy was dedicated to high-altitude precision bombing in daytime; and here we were operating without proper fighter cover. Then the crews who survived would hear that they *might* have had fighter cover on that mission—there were a lot of P-47's over at this station or that station— But there had been no sense in sending fighters along on the mission, because they could only patrol about as far as the real need began, and then they'd have to come back. Too short-ranged.

We were asking for extra tanks of all capacities: seventy-five gallons on up. We couldn't get 'em. The British would undertake to make them for us, and then their production would bog down. "Why can't we get them from *home?*" the crews would ask. "Then the fighters could go along and cover us. And Smith—" or O'Brien or Olson or Ovransky— "wouldn't have burned up yesterday."

Maybe about the same time Mom would write a letter, or maybe it would be Sister Sue, and say, "We keep pitying you poor boys over there; and wish we could do something about these dreadful strikes at home."

All in all it added up to the fact that if John L. Lewis had come to Chelveston on a tour of inspection, as was occasionally hinted at, our crews would have loved to invite him to fly along on a mission, and then they would have dropped him through the bomb-bay. There was a lot of argument about this. Some of the boys said he couldn't be dropped from a bomb-bay because he was too big to go through. But there were few defensive remarks emanating from the Lewis corner.

Last year our President gave the very elderly John L. Lewis America's highest award to civilians: the Medal of Freedom. Maybe that seemed odd to those who could look back on distant years when the Medal of Freedom went only to people who had been shall we say somewhat shot-at. But History performs upside-downs and back-flips and snap-rolls to the left as well as to the right. I hung our Legion of

Merit on the Japanese Air Chief of Staff during my own tenure as Chief of Staff, USAF; and a few months before I retired from the Service there was quite a flap in the international press because the Japanese had awarded me the First Class of the Order of the Rising Sun.

. . . Not many particularly capable prophets around, either, then or now.

One thing is sure: no one in his right mind in the Eighth AF would have hung anything except a shiner on John L. Lewis, back there in early 1943. Nor were any Americans about to decorate high-ranking Japanese officers (any more than the Japanese would have been eager to decorate *me*, after the fire-bomb raid on Tokyo in 1945).

To get back to our morale problems: morale sagged along in late January and early February. Then all of a sudden everybody bounced back to normal or even higher than normal, and started working hard.

It took me a little while to figure out what had happened; but finally we were able to understand.

All the combat crews had been sitting around, figuring out what their chances were. And the chances weren't very good. They got their statistics together, crudely but with terrible effect, and discovered that we were averaging an eight-per-cent loss on each mission. The tour of duty (then) was twenty-five. Taking it from there, a four-per-cent loss would still leave any theoretical crew completely shot down —or shot up—with the completion of their specified twenty-five missions. If there were a two-per-cent loss on every mission, a crew at the start would have a fifty-fifty chance of finishing up their tour and going home. Beyond that, the ratio declined speedily and abruptly. Thus a twelve-mission tour, if we'd ever had anything like that, would have burned up just about a hundred per cent of our effectives in men and planes.

In the end everybody was going to be shot down.

This kind of talk wasn't lamenting on into the still watches of the days or nights solely at Chelveston. It was all over. Every commander in the Eighth was reporting the same thing. Someone sat down there at Widewing, General Eaker's headquarters, and told him that it was on the graph: the last B-17 would take off for its last mission early in March.

General Eaker said, "O.K. I'll be on it."

This impressed those who heard it, although that wasn't what Ira Eaker had in mind especially. There could be no upsurge, no new invigoration throughout our Bomber Command, until it happened *within the Command*. That was the way it did happen.

The psychology went like this: "Well, we're going to get killed anyway. What the hell's the use of worrying about it?"

People shook themselves as if they'd been a little tired or groggy, and were appropriately ashamed; and then they got up and said,

"Let's get cracking. It might as well be this mission as the next mission. So— What the hell?" Thus it didn't make any difference any more. Everybody stopped worrying and everybody got back in the act.

(Later on, in my too-slow-moving fashion, I got this related to the question of so-called combat fatigue.)

Strangely enough, just about that same time we began to get a few replacements. The ones who had been coming in before—a very few airplanes and crews had been making it up from Marrakech— They had gone to other outfits whose commanders were worse off than I was. Matter of fact, I lost nearly half my people during that dismal season. Then replacements started dribbling in.

Crews came intact but initially we didn't use these new crews; we broke them up, and put people in vacancies where they were needed. There had been individuals lost out of our original crews—people who were wounded and still on the road to recovery, but needing their slots filled. So the first thing we did was to build up the crews we had, and then take personnel who were left over and fit them in with somebody else: give them a job with the Operations Officer or something of that sort. We tried to get them some crew training and some gunnery training, so that they'd have half a chance when they began to fly missions.

Somewhere the other day I saw a snapshot (taken probably by Tommy Thompson) showing me presenting the Distinguished Flying Cross to a tall young navigator named Webb. If I'm not too severely mistaken, I remember why he got that one. He was flying in a crew coming up from Africa, in his regular role as navigator. The pilot and co-pilot started congratulating themselves because they had finally reached England. There seemed to be nice friendly airfields down below, and the radio was crackling with welcome messages, and the colors-of-the-day were being fired, right within their sight. It looked like Old Home Week and God bless you, Yank; glad you're here, old chap.

The pilot was preparing to go down and land. Webb told him not to. "It ain't England," says Webb. "Not on my charts it ain't."

. . . Well then, how about all this? Landing directions being offered, and flares shooting out the colors-of-the-day? And, sure enough, you could even see another B-17 down there. . . .

"Tain't England," says old Webb in his best Texas accents.

Anyone can take a look at the map and see how this happened. There is the Brittany peninsula and the Normandy peninsula and there's southwestern England up above. If a very green and heedless navigator and a very green and heedless pilot agreed on something like this— The Germans were successful in their effort more times than we Yanks enjoyed. That was the way they acquired, intact, new B-17's, with—worse—all our standard equipment in them. Some of those lunkhead crews landed, thinking they were in England, yielding to the welcoming hails of the Jerries. They didn't know where they really were until enemy soldiers started poking machine-pistols in their faces. It was quite an act. The Germans were always trying something like that throughout the war. Got away with a lot of it, too.

But in this particular case the navigator won out. He pried a reluctant agreement out of the pilot that they'd keep flying a little while longer and see what happened. So they kept on flying, and a lot more wet water appeared, and then finally England loomed up ahead: Scilly Islands or some such landfall.

I can't remember the exact details at the moment. But it does seem to me that it was Webb's own aircraft commander who recommended him for the DFC. Well, I heard that Webb made it through his whole tour all right, and was glad of that, just as I was glad when I heard that any of my people finished up in one piece.

I was gone away from Chelveston by that time. There was another job ahead, then another.

Missions kept stacking up . . . old and new targets. There were Lorient, Wilhelmshaven, Hamm, Emden. There were Antwerp and Bremen and Méaulte, and that Renault plant at Paris. Nor can anyone connected therewith forget Kiel or Rouen or Vegesack, or another of those trips to Amiens.

I don't want to give the impression that I flew all those missions. Certainly I did not. You couldn't run a bomb group and fly every mission; you'd be out on your feet on the third day, and not responsible for any decisions. But I flew whenever it seemed that my actual presence and physical direction and command of the mission—simultaneously with the activity of others—would result in a benefit to the Group at large, and to the whole effort of Eighth Bomber Command.

It got so that if the chore looked routine, with no especial challenges about it, I'd stay home and work on one of the many things I had to do; and let Johnny or Joe or Fargo or Tom or Jerry lead that one. Then, maybe next time, there would be a development known to the entire staff, or sometimes known only to myself, which would cause me to go along and see what actually happened . . . something new in the way of enemy defenses, enemy fighter tactics, enemy ground-to-air bombardment, something new somewhere. Then I'd go.

So we went to the shipyards, the U-boat pens or bases; went to railroad marshaling yards and GAF air bases and vital factories. (Incidentally, our ordnance couldn't do much in those days against thick concrete submarine pens. We did hamper the submarine effort in the destruction of adjacent and essential structures: parts, repair, barracks, operations, all that sort of stuff . . . the ordnance depots where the actual torpedoes were, the routes that brought them up to the docks and the pens. You don't actually need to destroy a submarine in order to at least *postpone* its effectiveness. Same thing applies if you get the submarine's fuel, the submarine's personnel, or the submarine's armament. It takes them awhile to recoup.)

So I remember England and the targets, and the airplanes, just as others will always remember them . . . big wall-maps with the yarn or the wrinkled ribbon stretched tight. I remember the Eighth Air Force patch on just about every shoulder: a figure 8 with a star in the bottom loop and wings attached. Looked like it was just taking off for somewhere. . . .

I remember the wind blowing up through open bomb-bays; and I remember times when something went wrong and the bomb-bay doors wouldn't close, and then there'd be a drag and an impediment to speed and operation; and sometimes that impediment was fatal.

I remember B-17's with the top blades of their propellers sticking out like mules' ears. I remember wide shapeless leather jackets of the enlisted men, with curly wool oozing out around the collars. I remember the time hacks at Briefing . . . time ticks . . . voice calling off the numbers, then a faint universal *click* as all the people shoved their watch-stems into place.

It was my first combat command. It was the small unit, the group unit. I knew the four squadrons. I could never know any other four squadrons as well as I knew those four, because, when I had more rank and more command and more responsibility, I would be bound to lose out on the proportionate intimacies. I went on to command air wings and air divisions, and then to command even larger assemblages in the field. And finally to command all of SAC; and eventually to my job as Chief of Staff of the United States Air Force.

But the 305th— It was my 305th, our 305th.

You never get over anything like that. It was The Group.

Probably many other commanders felt the same way about their groups. Probably Frank Armstrong felt that way, and Archie Old. Maybe the commander over at Kimbolton felt that way, and the one at Molesworth.

The thing would be with you forever; it would always be your memory and your pride.

So I remember the loose looping swing and roll-over of the enemy fighters as they attacked. I can still see the solid GI green of the 50-caliber ammunition boxes we used for benches, bedside tables, stepladders, stair-steps . . . used for just about everything. There were those crews who began to appear as replacements: the ones coming up from Marrakech, with their names traced out in both English and Arabic on little patches sewn on their leather flying jackets. And I remember silhouette posters of fighter aircraft—stuck up in blank spaces all over the Base, to confront our men constantly with the difference between an FW and a P-47, a Messerschmitt and a Spitfire. And I remember the blue salted-peanut cans we used for ash trays, used for dogs' feeding dishes, for soap bowls . . . used for just about everything.

I remember the dogs too.

And low dollies trundling up from the bomb-dump with their weighty cargoes . . . and all the cranes and chains and cables. And most of all, all the effort and strength of the men . . . muscles stretched or muscles knotted . . . a grunt and shove as that most important freight was eased up into position in the bomb-bay and hung upon the shackles.

12

ONE DAY a subordinate said, slowly and seriously, "Boss, I don't think you're long for—" and then he stopped.

I filled it in for him. "Long for this world?"

He smiled. "No, sir. I was going to say— Long for the 305th."

It turned out that he was correct in this, and soon I sat regarding the situation with mixed emotions. I held a flimsy piece of paper in my hand, looking again and again at the formal notification which had come in over the wire.

I was to relinquish my command of the 305th Bomb Group (H) and assume command of the 102nd Provisional Combat Wing. Neither General Eaker nor Fred Anderson had offered any advance hint about this; but I suppose they'd had the change in mind for quite some time.

Various forms of reorganization were going on. At this stage of the game—late May to early July, 1943—there was a vagueness extant when one considered the future of any organizational structure. Our flow of replacements was broadening and speeding and strengthening. One of these days the Eighth Air Force, which had started as a general store on a country road, was going to be about as big as Macy's or Marshall Field's. Just as we expanded our business tolerance and capacity and activity, so would we go through a lot of shuffling and designating and redesignating. It happens in the growth of any organization.

At this moment we were forming the Combat Wings. Such a Wing was purely a tactical organization: it had no administration or support or anything like that. It was a fighting organization; it existed in that manner solely for the purpose of fighting, which made sense.

My promotion in command would result also in a promotion in rank. I wasn't too much concerned with that, although it would be nice to have a star instead of an eagle. What concerned me more intently was the fact that I would be amputated from the 305th. That hurt.

On the bright side of the ledger I could face the fact that with a larger and more important command I would be a few steps nearer the possibility of putting into practical effect some of the changes long since dreamed up, and which I felt would result in a more successful prosecution of the war effort.

Very recently, in going through my papers, I discovered a letter which I sent to Helen in 1943. It was a transcribed typewritten copy: the original letter—addressed by one of our men to his next-of-kin— had been in longhand. On reading it I was so impressed that I had a copy made for Helen, then I wrote on the bottom.

"This letter was left by one of my boys shot down over Lorient. I am constantly amazed at the heights these kids rise to, when the big test comes. I sometimes wonder what I have ever done to deserve the command of an outfit like this. You have always complained about my not being sentimental enough. I think sometimes I'm too soft to properly fight a war. After raising these kids from pups and leading them against the best pursuit and anti-aircraft defenses in the world, and having them come through the way they have, it hurts like hell to lose them."

It's very odd about the effectiveness of a group. How the luck is running, who's commanding, whether replacements are coming in, whether essential equipment is being supplied— Weather, the vulnerability or impregnability of targets, who's commanding once more, weather again—

Maintenance, housing, food, degree of losses, weather again, command again—

Let's take a mythical outfit and call it the Forty-ninth Bomb Group (there wasn't any Forty-ninth Bombardment Group in the Army Air Forces in World War II). So they were famous or notorious or to be pitied as "the Bloody Forty-ninth." They had very heavy losses.

Here's how I feel about the Forty-ninth. A lot of their hard luck couldn't necessarily be due to sloppiness, bad flying, weak formation, anything definite. A lot of it could have been just who the Luftwaffe happened to gang up on. I could go back now and run over all these things and a lot more, and become an excellent Monday morning quarterback.

Who knows what percentage of praise or blame may be placed upon leadership? How much is charged to skill, how much to coincidence? What is the contribution of gallantry itself, in any battle? In the case of the Bloody Forty-ninth (and Lord knows that could go for a lot of groups in the Eighth at that time) it was a combination of all such things. No one factor could be responsible solely. It might have been a combination of coincidence which put German fighters at the wrong place at the wrong time—at the time the Forty-ninth Bomb Group wasn't flying a good formation. So they got hit . . . lost a lot of their people. This got them off to a bad start. Then they received replacements who were even less skilled. So they never did recover from it. They were a hard-luck organization from start to finish; and yet it can't all be blamed on luck itself.

Some people call it poor leadership, poor this, poor that. Again I say it was a combination of circumstances. Doubtless it could have happened to any outfit we had over there. Once the combination of weak flying or weak leadership or weak something busted out all over them, they started going downhill. They never went up.

You can't tell a thing about it in advance. Sometimes you can't even tell when reviewing the circumstance through the telescopic lens of Time, looking back from that Monday morning a whole generation in the future.

Take the 305th. At one time we incurred far more than our share of battle damage and far more than our share of losses, simply because a proficiency had been developed which put us on the spot, and in a position to incur those damages. Later on, by the same token, we did a real job on a great many targets, and incurred fewer losses proportionately than other groups. Could have been due to superior flying, superior morale, superior leadership in the squadrons— You name it, and it will still be guesswork.

Then historically we crash suddenly against the 14th of October, 1943, and Second Schweinfurt. And the 305th putting up eighteen airplanes for this mission, and having three abortions; yet fifteen airplanes go on to the Continent.

How many come home? Two.

The 305th on that date lost thirteen out of fifteen. I think this may have been the highest percentage of loss sustained by any Heavy Bombardment Group, at any time, in any theater, during World War II. If not, the 305th was runner-up.

Yet, when it comes to searching around for the peg on which to hang the garment of blame, you can't even find it. You'll put that jacket up against the wall, and it will fall down because you can't find any place to hang it.

There were so *damn* many things to do over there in order to get going. The commanders were on their own, all too early in the game. They were hard put to secure bombs and supplies and field orders. We hadn't gotten around to being organized well enough to know what was happening, and to be able to see who was getting into trouble. And then— To get a staff together to help them. Or additional people. Or a change of commanders. Not time to do anything before the axe-blade fell, and somebody's head was lopped off; or maybe a lot of heads were lopped off.

Time was short, people were green.

Later we became set up to receive new Groups properly; and have them advised, and baby them along and keep them under proper supervision so they could get into combat efficiently and avoid the pitfalls which had plagued the pioneers who came before them.

But that was all in 1944, or maybe in very latest '43.

Let's take another outfit—one which was under my command after I went over to the Third Division. This time we'll call it the Thirty-second Bomb Group (there didn't exist any Thirty-second Bomb Group in the war, either). So I saw the best outfit I had go from best to worst in only ten days. It just deteriorated.

Let's take the commander of that Thirty-second Bomb Group (H). We'll call him Colonel Turret. Colonel Turret was a capable commander and more than capable; and I needed somebody to command one of my combat wings. So I pulled him out of his group and gave him a wing. What happened? The group went downhill. When I say downhill, I mean to the bottom of the swamps—the slums. Real city dump.

First there was the loss of their old commander . . . new one coming in. Difficult target . . . lot of bad fighter attacks coming on several missions in a row . . . key people shot down . . . old personnel looking with loathing on the new replacements. This thing jimmed up, that thing jammed up. . . .

We have to go back to the metaphor of the football team. Today they play over their heads, and they lick the State University team, avowed champions of a league which the little school doesn't even belong in. But the very next week that winning team goes to pieces. A high school aggregation whips them.

In my new job as chief of that Provisional Combat Wing, I hadn't moved very far away—just across the hedge, over to Thurleigh. But I was only there for a couple of weeks. Then they sent me to command the old Fourth Combat Wing, which very soon was redesignated as the nucleus of the Third Air Division. (Officially the redesignation of certain Combat Wings as Air Divisions wouldn't become effective until September, but people started using the terminology well in advance.) I had to go far afield geographically. I moved all the way over to East Anglia on the North Sea coast. Found my new headquarters established in a weird and wonderful place.

The village of Elveden has its elderly roots in the soil of Suffolk, away up in the northwest corner of Suffolk, very close to the Norfolk border. That area is known as the Brecklands. A breck is a large field in that region (whereas over in Northumberland a breck is a portion of a field which is cultivated by itself). My main concern with these brecklands was not etymological. I was more interested in how the groups which I would command were set up, and what their facilities were like.

(All the time I served as Chief of Staff I kept a picture of Elveden Hall hanging in my office suite at the Pentagon. Maybe I was moved subconsciously to do this; but I do know that there was a conscious element involved. I wanted, as Chief of Staff of the Air Force, to remind myself constantly of the day when I went over to Elveden Hall: a very frightened colonel, wondering what variety of bears he was holding by their assorted tails.)

I reviewed my situation and found it about as comfortable as a barbwire fence. God Almighty. I had so little experience. I had commanded a squadron for only a short period of time—certainly not long enough to learn anything much. Next thing I knew, I had a group, and I was still engaged in learning the Commerce and Industry there when I got fired upstairs. In fact I really hadn't learned it well, yet. Hadn't been able to get going on the things I wanted to try out.

Next thing, they threw a Division at me. That was a major-general's job, and I knew damn well I wasn't qualified. I was still only a colonel, and there were a lot of people in that outfit who had seniority beyond my own.

Example: I ran right up against the second squadron commander I had ever had over me. Here he was, a group commander in *my* new Division. His name was Aaron Kessler. I was trying to cover up a bad case of jitters inside; then all of a sudden Kessler comes to me and says, "Don't worry about this, Curt. You've been in combat, you've had the experience; I haven't. I just got over here, and I'll be thankful for anything you can do to help me with my Group. Let's get to work, and forget that I ever was your squadron commander."

His attitude was appreciated deeply by the nervous new boss of the Third Air Division. Naturally it was in the works for me to have a star, but I didn't make brigadier-general until September.

I try now to think of a comparable situation . . . maybe we can manufacture one. Let's say that there is an ardent young high school physics student. That's all the physics he's ever had: high school. Then they heave him into a nuclear physics laboratory and say, "Get to work in nuclear physics." Might be about the same reaction. Indubitably there'd be the same uncertainty, the doubting of oneself.

Looking back, I'm grateful for the beautiful yet bizarre quality of my physical surroundings at Elveden. There was always something to take my mind off complicated worries when that aching mind needed a change.

Even bare statistics about the place are fascinating—at least they were to me, with my limited midwestern United States and Army background. First off, I had never realized that so many nationalities could be intermingled in the history of a single structure. The story starts off with one Arnold Joost Van Keppel, who followed the Prince of Orange back to England from the Netherlands. As a reward for his friendship with and support of the King, he was named to be Duke of Albemarle. His grandson became a famous admiral in the navy, and finally ended up as Viscount Keppel of Elveden. He lies there in the churchyard; but his descendants sold the estate, since they had another place in Norfolk. They sold it to a Mr. Newton, from whose family it was purchased for the Maharajah Dhuleep Singh about a hundred years ago. In 1943 it belonged to the Earl of Iveagh, current representative of the Guinness Stout family of Ireland.

Dutch, Indian, Irish: all these were bound up there together with the native East Anglian tradition.

Actually it was the Maharajah who remodeled the place into the form which it shows today. There is the Indian Hall, all "made of richly veined marble, with twenty-eight columns and three big galleries and remarkable doors covered with beaten copper strangely ornamented."

So the hall eventually went out of the hands of the Maharajah and his family, and was bought by the first Earl of Iveagh in 1894. Let me quote from a little paper which was prepared some years ago in order to describe Elveden Hall and its history to the general public. The paper is based chiefly on the Suffolk volume in that series of English travel books done about each county in turn by the well-known writer Arthur Mee. *The King's England,* the series is called. Or used to be. Maybe it's *The Queen's* now.

The paper goes on to say, in speaking of the Earl of Iveagh: "Here he established a hunting lodge for sports loving people. The house, however, was not large enough for his requirements so he added the Marble Hall with a handsome south doorway and a majestic north portico on great columns, west wing, and servants' quarters. The most striking feature is the immense copper dome built above this wonderful hall. He built the stables block, the water tower and the cottages adjacent thereto. . . . For four years one hundred and fifty men were working here, and today this great house with its many treasures has something of the splendour of an Eastern temple, and is one of the most surprising sights in Suffolk." You can say that again.

At Chelveston the CO's quarters were built the same as the other structures: just a hut, flimsy and shacklike. Our HQ offices and other workaday chambers were built of the same stuff. It was primitive, it was raw, it was in the field. Most bomber stations were alike and looked alike. Now I found myself with a copper dome over my head

and God knows how much "richly veined marble" staring me in the
face. Guess I would have been bewildered, if I'd had time to be, but
there just wasn't time.

First day when I entered Elveden Hall I could not foretell that a
future day would come when a stained-glass memorial window would
be installed in the nearby church, dedicated to our men who died in
the Third Air Division of the Eighth Air Force. That day came . . .
the window is handsome. As in the case of most war memorials, something happens inside your chest and behind your eyes when you read
the inscription.

A great many of those men died under my command. Many of them
died on the mission to Regensburg, August 17th, 1943. I led that mission.

13

REGENSBURG was the day when the GAF threw everything against us
which they could possibly throw. They had more FW's and more ME-
109's on the job than most of us had ever seen before. They brought in
JU-88's, and the also-twin-engined ME-110's. They had Heinkels and
Dorniers, God knows what all. They were using every type of ammunition they could scrounge . . . they were heaving experimental rockets
at us: air-to-air stuff.

Down there at Regensburg—the primary target for my Third Air
Division—there were some German test pilots who for this reason or
that reason were not active in combat duty. But even they got into the
act on August 17th. Those test pilots were really sampling out Messerschmitts the hard way. They were right good. Unhappily for us, the
rest of the Luftwaffe were right good too. We lost ourselves twenty-
four bombers before nightfall, from my division.

This operation grew out of an original plan, code-named JUGGLER,
in which a long-range attack was to be projected simultaneously
against Regensburg and Wiener Neustadt. Army Air Force units from
England and from the Mediterranean were to combine in the assault,
which would put a double burden on German defenses and render
them less effective—it was hoped.

B-24's in the Mediterranean area had been tapped also for Operation
TIDALWAVE—the bombing of the Ploesti oil refineries in Rumania.
The first Ploesti attack came on 1 August. *AAFWW II* says, "JUG-
GLER was then set for 7 August. But weather conditions over north-
western Europe interfered with the projected assault by the Eighth
[Air Force] against Regensburg. After several postponements the idea
of a coördinated attack was abandoned, and the decision made to allow
either force to stage its mission as soon as conditions proved favorable."

Regensburg and Wiener Neustadt boasted the bulk of the Messer-schmitt production.

Weather conditions began to improve as the end of the second week of August approached. Our 15th Air Force friends went to Wiener Neustadt on Friday, August 13th.

So the combined Wiener Neustadt-Regensburg attack never oc-curred. There was to be instead a combined Schweinfurt-Regensburg mission. Our First Air Division of the Eighth AF would go to Schwein-furt, and we in the Third would hit Regensburg.

I didn't have anything to do with dreaming up this operation. The first I ever knew about it was when General Eaker came out to Elveden Hall and told the story. Since he wanted me to lead this mission, it seemed essential that I go down to North Africa and arrange for the trip. We had to know where we were going to land and what the fa-cilities would be.

Sounds odd to be bringing Africa into the scheme of things. Here's how and why:

This operation was the outgrowth of a search by those intellectual souls in Plans and Intelligence to find an easy way of winning the war in Europe. That's just about like searching for the Fountain of Youth —there *is* no such thing; never was. But they were trying to find it, and they hit on bearings. The idea was that if we could knock out ball-bear-ing production, that would automatically cut industry out of the future picture. The German war machine would grind to a halt.

Schweinfurt had the bulk of the antifriction-bearing production right there in that one spot. So the Eighth Air Force should hit Schweinfurt. But it was a very deep journey, farther than we had ever ventured before on a bombing mission. And whoever went to Schweinfurt would have to have mighty good weather to get in there. Also it was felt that if they went in that deep, they would take a real heavy beating. Per-fectly correct.

So they worked up a scheme for attacking Regensburg and Schwein-furt on the same day. And Regensburg was even farther away—clear down on the Danube River.

If one air division went in first—say, perhaps ten minutes ahead of the other—and took the burden of the fight launched against them by defending German aircraft while *going in*— The other air division could come in behind them, relatively free from attack, as they went to their target; and they would have to fight on the way *out*.

Because why? Because the air division which had preceded them would not turn round and fly out of Germany, back across enemy ter-ritory or enemy-occupied territory, to England. They would simply continue down to the Allied-held areas in North Africa. Later, after re-fueling and bombing up, they would have a chance to attack some other target while they were returning to England.

It was the old shuttle idea again: same thing they were working on, in plans, with the Russians. We were going to attack East German targets, and then go on to Russia. Bomb up there, gas up again, and attack German targets once more during the return trip to England. (Actually several of those missions were flown. They didn't work out well, for a variety of reasons. Anyway, in the overall picture, the rapid advance of Russian armies up through the Balkans did away with the necessity for any air operations of that sort.)

North Africa was an entirely different proposition. It was one thing to know that you'd have a Russian air base awaiting you at the end of the trip; and quite another thing to know that you'd have a United States Army Air Force base, run by our people, waiting for you down there in Tunisia.

I left Rus Wilson in command of the Third Division, and headed for Tunis. The safe and easy way to journey to Africa—if indeed anything was safe and easy in those days—was to fly down across the Bay of Biscay, keep out of Spain and Portugal, go clear around the lower end of the Iberian peninsula, and land at Marrakech. Then I flew up to Tunis to see Larry Norstad. He was chief of staff for Tooey Spaatz, at that time commanding the 15th Air Force.

I told Norstad what I was down there for, gave him the whole story, and asked for his recommendation on a field where we should land. I planned to use all (then) seven groups of my division in the attack. That would mean that we'd have somewhere around a hundred and thirty-or-forty B-17's dispatched on the mission—our part of it, the Regensburg part. There would be even more airplanes in the other prong of the assault when the First Air Division attacked Schweinfurt.

Some of my Forts would be bound to go down over the target, or before, or after. But still, if we didn't get completely crucified, there were a whale of a lot of 17's to be welcomed to Africa, to be gassed up and bombed up, and have their crews fed and housed and taken care of. To say nothing of physical maintenance. There would be battle damage. There would be, undoubtedly, some damage which might be repaired right on the spot, without much delay. If other airplanes came in too badly chewed-up to be repaired immediately, we'd simply leave them behind.

Larry Norstad said, "Telergma is your field. It's both a depot and a combat field. There you'll have supplies, extra mechanics—everything you need. That's the place to land. You can get well serviced there. All the parts you need, all the maintenance people and support."

Telergma was not too far from Tunis . . . oh, I don't know . . . fifty or seventy miles. Think it was about forty miles in from the coast, and not too far from Constantine. Everything looked right and sounded right. We were all set.

I said to Norstad, "Fine. We'll run this according to Bomber Command instructions, the very first day we get the proper weather. God knows when that will be."

I left Norstad, and went out to see my old friend Hamp Atkinson and his bomber folks. Spent the night there, then flew back to England next day.

On the way home I mulled the situation over. From what I had learned of European Continental weather and English weather during the past eight months or so, I wondered just when we would get that amazing day with perfect visibility at home and perfect visibility over the target.

It boiled down to this: we would be unlikely to attack Regensburg and Schweinfurt when there was sorry weather down thataway, and clear weather in England. We'd be much more apt to start off under lousy circumstances of our own, but with the target areas progged for good bombardment conditions.

I put my crews on bad weather practice. They trained hard on this. When ceiling and horizontal visibility were O.K. then I'd make our pilots take off on instruments—get the seat down, and take off completely on instruments. Over in the right-hand seat the co-pilot would be ready to operate visually. If something went wrong, he could take over, and that would save the airplane and crew. But in the meantime, our pilot was training for an instrument takeoff in case he had to do that when the big day came.

(We held to this procedure all through the rest of the war; and I clung to the same policy later in the SAC years. Nothing can be worse than a pilot trying to take off on instruments when he hasn't had sufficient time or experience doing just that thing. There is no substitute for time on the job. No substitute, ever, for experience.)

It was a month or more from the date I'd been down to Africa before we got the green light for our Big One. Our weather was really something in England that morning. The air was like dark gray jellied madrilene, if there could be any such thing. It was so foggy that we had to lead the airplanes out with flashlights and lanterns, in order to get them onto the runway.

In those days the procedure on assembly was as follows: airplanes took off individually, made the standard turn; they picked up their own flights; then their own group. Then they went over to the Splasher Beacon to pick up a couple of other groups, and thus get the combat wings together. Finally the whole division was put together: seven groups, in our case. But with so many airplanes flying around— If visibility was rotten you were apt to get lost. That happened; the inevitable happened.

Every now and then there was that grim moment when you broke out of the overcast . . . there you were on top of it, in brilliant sunlight, and just ahead or maybe off to one side there'd be a couple of black columns of smoke puffing right through the clouds. A couple of Forts had plowed into each other. It was something you didn't like to see. Very few people ever got out of mid-air collisions.

. . . The talk about Casey Jones didn't do much good, either. Someone would be yakking, "'Here's two locomotives that are going to bump.' Hell. Those were two locomotives what *did* bump!"

If you were a pilot or a crew member you just hoped that that wouldn't happen to your airplane. If you were a commander you lay awake nights, trying to figure out ways and means to keep those bubbly black smoke columns from ever being born.

An old song resounded in the back of your mind.

> We loop in the purple twilight,
> We spin in the silver dawn,
> With the smoke coming up before us
> To show where our friends have gone.

One time, when I was slapping my old beat-up brain around, I got the idea of putting that same smoke idea to account. What about trailing some smoke candles, when the soup was thick? We'd have a lot of smoke issuing from the lead airplane, and that way everybody could identify it; pilots would recognize their leaders.

So we got a bunch of smoke candles and built a hopper right next to the waist gun. The idea was to light the candles and throw 'em in there. We thought one candle might do it. . . . Nope. Didn't give enough smoke. . . . Finally we had to burn about eight all at once, and even that wasn't perfect. Still wasn't as much smoke as I wanted, but it helped.

On this fateful Tuesday, August 17th, we in the Third Division got together all right, delayed a bit by weather. Possibly we were ten or fifteen minutes behind the original schedule. We wondered what was happening to our friends over in the First. Had we known the truth, we would have thought that we should have stood in bed. The First Division just wasn't getting off the ground.

Let me try to clarify the plan of battle once more. I was going in first with my division, and we would fly right straight through and hit Regensburg, and go on out through the Alps, down to the Med and to Africa. Ten minutes behind us, the (elder and vastly more numerous) First Air Division, commanded by General Bob Williams, was to proceed on their attack against Schweinfurt. (That wasn't as deep a penetration as ours, not by over a hundred miles.) They'd hit Schweinfurt, then turn around and fly back to England.

In our division we'd have the benefit of fighter support as far as the range of the fighters would permit them to go, inland over the Continent. Then, as Williams came out, they would pick him up, and cover him on the way out.

I flew in the first aircraft of the 96th Bomb Group. In all we dispatched a hundred and forty-six airplanes to strike Regensburg, and a hundred and twenty-seven of these succeeded in attacking the primary target. But I'm getting ahead of myself.

Here we were, up in the air, all assembled, and there were no fighters around, and there wasn't any First Division airborne. Old Fred Anderson down there at Pinetree was in severe trouble. He had to decide whether to scrub the whole mission, or send me in alone. So he said Go. We went.

Actually what he was doing was holding up the Schweinfurt people for three and a half hours. Their weather was stinko, as ours had been.

Folks tried to look on the bright side: (a) the weather was due to improve; couldn't get any worse; and (b) they would have the benefit of fresh fighter cover. The fighter boys could finish escorting us, and have time to return to England, land, refuel, and get airborne once more to offer their best possible protection to the First Division. (Still weren't enough belly-tanks in Fighter Command; there were only a few around. And their range couldn't be extended without belly-tanks.)

Now here's what seems apparent to me about that mission:

If the First Division had been concentrating on the same sort of bad-weather-instrument-take-off procedure which we had been developing for a solid month, they might have been able to get off the ground as we in the Third did. A few minutes late, perhaps; but still part of the originally-planned show.

And we couldn't horse around about this—return to our bases, sit on the ground, take off once more—even if weather permitted. We had to land in Africa before dark. It's a long long way to Africa from England. I was faced with the unhappy notion that we might drop at least three or four 17's down there in the Mediterranean—just because they were out of gas.

Yep. We did.

The history books will tell you that eighteen squadrons of Thunderbolts (P-47's) and sixteen squadrons of Spitfires were assigned to provide cover for our bombers on that day. And I will tell you that I led that mission, and not one damn Jug (P-47) or one damn Spit did I see.

Our fighter escort had black crosses on their wings.

I lost twenty-four out of my hundred and twenty-seven planes which attacked the target at Regensburg. Hours later the First Division lost thirty-six bombers, but they had one hundred and eighty-three planes in the battle. That made a total of sixty which went down that day. The previous high had been suffered when we went to Bremen, 13 June: the Eighth Air Force lost twenty-six.

Four or five of my crews managed to limp over to Switzerland and they got down more or less safely there. The rest, in the B-17's which had become casualties, were either Prisoners of War or they were dead.

A friend wrote me a descriptive letter, a while after that mission.

He said, "That's what I still can't get out of my mind. There were two different 17's which went *whuff*. That was it: just *whuff*, and they were gone. We saw debris flying around from one and saw absolutely nothing from the other. The plane and its entire crew and bomb load and everything else, seemed to disappear as if some old-fashioned magician had waved a wand.

"There were Forts falling out of formation with bad fires. Then we'd try to count the chutes, and then our attention would be directed somewhere else and we couldn't count any more chutes. We'd look again, and the airplanes were gone, and also the people with chutes. There were more fighters coming in, with the leading edges of their wings all fiery. . . .

"And there was that one airman going down, doubled up, just turning over and over. He went right through the formation, and nobody seemed to hit him, and he didn't seem to collide with any of the airplanes. He just fell fast and furious, over and over, no chute, no nothing. I wondered who he was. Did he come out of a Fort named *Lewd Lucy* or one named *Wayfaring Stranger* or the *Nebraska Cornball?* I had friends flying in crews of Forts like that, and maybe he was one of my friends. But his own mother wouldn't have known him then, and certainly she wouldn't have known him after he hit the ground.

"As we got on the target it appeared that the flak was as nothing to the flak over the Ruhr or over a lot of other targets—Kassel, for instance. Keroway took off his mask to shake some water out of the hose, and he leaned across to me before he put it on again, and he said, 'I was down there once on a tour with a bunch of students. They've got awful good beer. Will you have light or dark?' I told him I'd have both.

"Regensburg was the Ratisbon of that Robert Browning thing we had to learn in school. Think back now, to a certain very good play, *Life With Father,* in which a red-headed boy recited this poem on stage. And when he said *the boy fell dead* by gosh the little boy who was reciting fell down as if dead.

"Funny that the same town could be both Regensburg and Ratisbon; but it all depends upon where you went to school, I guess—whether you were born under a tricolor or under German eagles.

> You looked twice ere you saw his breast
> Was all but shot in two. . . .

"You're wounded!" "Nay," his soldier's pride
    Touched to the quick, he said:
"I'm killed, Sire!" And his chief beside,
    Smiling, the boy fell dead.

"You know, that night after we landed down there in Africa, I kept hearing those words over and over. *Smiling, the boy fell dead.* Then I'd see that hunched-up figure, upsy-daisy, over and over, coming down through the formation. I guess he fell dead all right, there on a little mound near Ratisbon."

We got punched all over the ring that day, and sometimes it looked as if we were going to be knocked through the ropes, but we weren't.

AAFWW II says: "Despite the ferocity of the air battle, which extended all the way to the targets, the bombers did an extremely good job. This was especially true at Regensburg, where they blanketed the entire area with high explosives and incendiary bombs, damaging every important building in the plant and destroying a number of finished single-engined fighters on the field."

I still keep some of those strike photos and the later reconnaissance-evaluation photos in my personal file. Pockmarks of bombs stud the whole area. Workshops, boiler house, hangar, the testing range, offices —everything was hit. That Messerschmitt plant was completely out of action—briefly.

What we did not realize (where we underestimated in *particular*) was the recovery capability of the Jerries in the Messerschmitt business. To be utterly frank, this was true in all our bombing of Germany. The recovery capability was infinitely better than we had imagined it to be.

On August 17th we really thought that we had turned the trick, and that perhaps no Messerschmitts would ever be manufactured down there on the ground again. We couldn't envision how resourceful or determined the Germans really were. Oh, they didn't have all the damage repaired—not even after months. But they stretched tarpaulins to keep the snow out, and they cleaned up the debris. All in all, I think they were pretty well back in production in three months.

The overall dispersal of industry had just begun; but this particular plant was indeed repaired. It had to be hit again later on.

. . . So my cripples went stumbling off to Switzerland; and my pilots whose gas had been expended went down to their wet ditchings in the Mediterranean. The rest of us flew to North Africa. We saw our last enemy fighter about the time we were heading into the Brenner Pass; then no more fighters. Just a lot of worry about gas, and worry about their ditchings in the case of the unfortunates who had to try to get out and walk on the water.

I was comforting myself all the time with Norstad's assurances. *Telergma is your field. . . . There you'll have supplies . . . everything you need. That's the place to land. You can get well serviced there. . . .*

Sounded real nice when he was saying those words. But later, on August 17th—

Let me show you how things are apt to happen in wartime. They had had to move their damn depot because of a change in the North African war condition. Norstad and that bunch down there had promptly forgotten that I ever existed. The war moved on, and they moved with it.

No one had told me one word about this. Here I was, coming in with my whole division, minus losses. And where the hell were we going to get bombs, and where were we going to get gas, and how were we going to get the maintenance?

Somebody had dropped the ball. No touchdown.

There were a few people on the field still, of course. They hustled around to get some more over to help us; and we helped ourselves. It meant sleeping under the wings of our airplanes, or in them. But everybody got to work to fix their crates up. What we couldn't repair we abandoned. Let some of that bunch down there go to work on them later and shove 'em over into their second- or third-line maintenance, or wherever they needed, to make the airplanes serviceable. We had a lot of new planes coming into England for our crews by that time, so we'd not be too hampered for lack of B-17's.

My guess now would be that we left about twenty airplanes down there, and came back with around eighty flyable 17's out of the one hundred and twenty-seven which had proceeded on the Regensburg attack.

Eventually after several days we were ready to bomb once again. Let me say, too, that there had been some pretty surprised crews, when eventually they found themselves down there on the Dark Continent. Before we left our bases in England, crews were told only to pack their toothbrushes and a change of underwear. From there on they had to get the well-known poop from the group and, as is also well-known, that can be rather inaccurate. But you couldn't keep good men down—not for long. They were up to their usual antics, but wholly ready for combat.

. . . There was a North African donkey who came to England to shack up with the Third Air Division. Those characters had brought the donkey along with them together with a million other souvenirs. It was rumored, too, back in England, that they had fetched a little Arab boy for a mascot. I don't think that was correct. At least I never saw the little Arab boy or heard any more about him.

Parenthetically, the reader must never underestimate the intricacies of the American airman's imagination, or his willingness to carry out the dictates of that imagination. They used to have a story in the Ninth Air Force in France: true one, I guess.

It was the old expression about, "How did you do with your bombing today?"

"Oh, boy, we dropped everything on them but the kitchen stove!"

It was one of those bromides like "shooting fish in a barrel" or "the flak was so thick you could walk on it." *We dropped everything but the kitchen stove.*

Folks were always saying that, and by golly one of those crews got sick and tired of hearing it. So what did they do? They discovered an old kitchen stove in some battle-blasted French farmhouse; they up and hauled that stove over to their base on a jeep. Put it aboard their B-26 (probably wasn't a very heavy stove anyway). They attacked the enemy positions they'd been told to attack that day; then, while the bomb-bay doors were still held open, a couple of those characters mauled that kitchen stove over to the open bomb-bay and tossed it down through. They were said to be very proud of this. The first crew in history who actually dropped *the kitchen stove.*

I had gone into the Regensburg thing with a perfectly open mind. I was willing to accept the advantages—in fact, eager to accept them —if any could be demonstrated.

AAFWW II says: "Colonel Curtis E. LeMay . . . reported unfavorably on the experiment. As he pointed out, it was difficult to operate heavy bombers without their ground crews, especially if maintenance and base facilities were insufficient, as in Africa, where the changing nature of operations demanded that the supplies and equipment be constantly moved. Moreover, landing away from their bases put an additional strain on combat crews and affected their efficiency adversely."

They are quoting me correctly. This shuttle deal just wasn't going to prosper us, and that's all there was to it.

. . . You'd feel like the guy in that movie—Alec Guinness or whoever it was—who had two wives in different towns and countries, and went back and forth in his boat. You've got one home here and one home over there, and a wife in each place. You've got to keep both of 'em interested and interesting, too, or you're going to be in trouble. Too big a job for most men. Too complex a job for people in bombardment. How confident are you going to feel in having two different ground crews operating on the same airplane a couple of thousand miles apart?

So First Regensburg became history, just as other names and other targets and other days had become history; and it looked like that history-making was going to go on for a mighty long time.

People who were burned up in the air or on the ground, were burned up; and people buried by the Germans when there was anything left to bury, were buried; and people who were alive were carted off to Stalag Luft-something-or-other. The ones who drowned in the ocean were drowned, and the ones who were picked up by Air-Sea Rescue were picked up. The crews who were in Switzerland sat and ate Swiss chocolate, far as I know. And the crews who were left B-17-less because of battle damage which could not be quickly repaired at Telergma—they went home by transport. The rest of us attacked the Bordeaux/Merignac airfield on Tuesday, August 24th, just one week after Regensburg. Then we came home too (minus three more airplanes) and went to work on other targets.

When we were going south through the Brenner Pass, headed for Africa after being kicked around over Regensburg, someone snapped a picture from one of the hatches. They photographed the low squadron of our group which led the mission. The surviving B-17's kept in their studied formation—gaps all filled, the square (Third Division) and the C (96th) showing up proudly on every vertical stabilizer. Alps were towering and snowy and icy across the background.

. . . About the time we became actively engaged in World War II, I remember seeing the movie *Mrs. Miniver* which was produced by Sidney Franklin. They had a lot of scenes about Dunkirk, and troops being rescued and conveyed over to England áfter that fropping they had taken in Flanders and on the beach itself. There was an unforgettable scene in which the Guards appear—one battalion of them, or its remains—and they are formed up and marshaled into ranks by a real old-line sergeant-major with the big mustache and all. Then they march off the dock just as if they were parading down Whitehall in London. The scene was directed with skill and understanding by William Wyler, and would not fail to quicken the heart of any military man who witnessed it.

I think that was the way the Third Air Division looked when they went on to Africa through the Brenner Pass. They flew a good formation no matter what had happened.

In England was a well-known artist named Frank Beresford. He had spent a lot of his younger life in Holland, and he painted in the old Dutch reds and other colors—that style. I guess he spent one year of the war down at Eighth Fighter Command. Then he decided to come up to the bombardment people. He was with us at Elveden Hall, recording our activities the way Bruce Bairnsfather had done at Chelveston. Except that Bruce was a cartoonist as well as a good painter in other media. I don't think Beresford ever plastered any figures on the noses of our Fortresses.

After we returned from the shuttle-bombing mission to Africa, Beresford happened to get a look at that snapshot which had been taken out of the left waist-gun window. Somehow he was deeply affected by it. He'd spent time down there in the Alps, too, and was familiar with the light and topography.

Using the little photo of our low squadron as a guide, he painted a large oil of the same scene. It turned out to be a beauty. I liked it, and told him so. At the time he wasn't interested in selling any original paintings he had done—just reproductions of them were available. I think somebody made some prints of this B-17 picture and they were sold at the PX. But the artist wanted to keep his collection intact—did so deliberately. And thank the Lord he did, because afterward the entire Frank Beresford collection was purchased and donated to the United States Air Force. We have the whole set: everything which he finished to his satisfaction and determined to include.

But long before all this happened, Beresford left our B-17 picture stored up in London some place. Don't know why he sent it to London, but he did. Along came the buzz-bomb activity. Blooey. A buzz-bomb hits the building, and a piece of its fragmentation goes right through the Beresford painting and makes a good-sized hole in it.

I guess the artist thought that his choice oil was ruined for all practical purposes, and there was nothing to do but to repaint the whole job. This is what he did. He made another picture exactly like the first, but minus the hole. (If the Japanese had been doing the job, they would have faithfully put in the hole too.)

I was lucky enough to inherit painting Number One—hole and all. Beresford inscribed and presented it. I was tickled pink, and am still tickled pink every time I look at it. There has been plenty of opportunity. I had it in the Pentagon for a while; and always it hung in our quarters, both at SAC and at Fort Myer. The wartime varnish which Beresford used was of an inferior grade; couldn't get proper ingredients during the war, so this varnish has turned a little yellow. The snow-covered Alps look yellowish, and the gleam of the metal skins of the B-17's is yellowish as well. Honestly the painting appears to be hundreds of years old.

You might know how our art people would react when they saw the hole. At the time I let them hang my precious painting in the Pentagon, they wanted to repair the hole right away. I had to tell them Nothing Doing. "Hell, no, that would ruin the painting as far as I'm concerned. Leave the hole there! Beresford circled it in charcoal, and made notes of what had happened."

So the picture remains one of our choicest possessions. It will always hang on the wall of our home, now, in retirement. I mean it will hang on the wall as long as Helen and I are around to see it.

Next to the triangle-G of the 305th, I have an especial fondness for the square-C of the 96th.

14

AUTUMN brought its own problems; some of them new, some of them perennial, all demanding.

People who were present for duty in the Eighth Air Force at that time will not be apt to forget the 6th of September, when the largest attack yet projected was despatched. Four hundred and seven bombers went out that day.

Primary targets were the aircraft factories and antifriction-bearing factories in the Stuttgart area. That was a real hurly-burly. The weather went bad, covered up most of the targets; and B-17's were compelled to bomb Targets of Opportunity. We had forty-five Forts in the minus bracket that day. Not so bad as Schweinfurt-Regensburg, but nothing to brag about at Pinetree or back in Washington.

Strange thing is that the very next day we had a hundred and five airplanes attacking Brussels industrial aviation areas, and fifty-eight attacking a rocket site at Watten, and twenty-two bombers attacking another airfield and a convoy. This adds up to a hundred and eighty-five airplanes bombing hither and yon, and they received excellent fighter support. Result: not a single bomber lost. In fact, no bomber had an encounter that day with any enemy aircraft. The fighters kept them away.

It demonstrated what we could do when we had *enough* fighters and when they had *enough range* to give us the kind of support we needed. Would have taken only a few Schweinfurts and Regensburgs to really put us in the garbage can for good. Speaking of that, it was the 14th of October before the Eighth Air Force returned to Schweinfurt; they marshaled that day two hundred and twenty-nine planes, and lost sixty. That was when the 305th dropped their thirteen out of fifteen.

(By that time, of course, they weren't any longer under my command. Matter of fact, I didn't know too many of the people involved— just a few. Most of my old boys had either finished up and were off on other jobs somewhere, or else they were dead.)

We endured our weather problems and our replacement problems and our bad bombing problems; and we had all that fuss and fury about trying to work radar into the business in a big way. Those first attempts seem pitiful now; but I guess it runs like that in any enterprise. Observe the old photographs . . . Henry Ford looks kind of queer, sitting up in that high-wheeled buggy thing. It doesn't much resemble the streamlined low-and-sleek critters which float off the assembly lines up at Dearborn nowadays. And radar today is a bit different from the radar of late 1943.

In November they made me into a Bond Show Bill, along with some others. General Eaker felt that Americans back home, both in and out of the Service, would benefit from a few honest statements uttered by people who had come straight from the scene of action. He felt also that, at least in this case, the emissaries should be commanders or experts in their various fields.

He picked Hub Zemke from Fighters, Nye from the Mediums, myself from Bomber Command. Also he sent along a very fine A-2 British type. His name was Robinson; besides his experience in the RAF he was a member of Parliament, and as such would be listened to.

I hated to leave my division. On the other hand here was a chance to find the answers to a few questions: the sort of questions which might be answered only by General Arnold and his staff. And I would get to see Helen and Janie briefly— Well, it was an order.

The transportation folks planned at first that we should go by way of Prestwick and Gander. As emphasized previously, nobody liked to fly that northern route in the winter. For a couple of years they closed up the North Atlantic completely. During the previous winter and up until it was really warm in the spring, our meager flow of replacements had come to us by way of the middle Atlantic—Ascension Island, Marrakech, then up to England. But this was earliest winter—only halfway cold, you could call it—so we believed that the northern course might still be quickest and easiest.

At Prestwick we discovered that the ferry route had been closed. In fact, local weather deteriorated so badly after we arrived that they closed the fields there. No one was flying anywhere. We chafed, not wishing to waste time. It might take nearly a week to fly the southern trip, but that looked like a necessity.

Then old John C. H. Lee, commander of Services of Supply, came to the rescue.

"Why don't you take the QE (Queen Elizabeth)? She's sailing tonight. You'll get to New York in four and a half days."

They hustled us up from Prestwick to Greenock in a couple of fast cars, and there we boarded the QE. General Lee's prediction had been a shade on the optimistic side: actually it took us five days. But then we were back home, and proceeded immediately to Washington from New York. Had to get the schedules of our lecture tour lined up.

Once this was done, we each were allowed a couple of days leave. Helen had met me in Washington so that we could spend as much time together as possible. Now, with the tour all lined up, Helen flew with me to Cleveland.

Janie had grown into the biggest almost-five-year-old girl I'd ever seen. Snapshots sent along from time to time had never told the true story, just as they never tell the true story to any father. She looked to me as if she was about ready for college. I didn't know what to do, with such a grown-up character on my hands.

She knew what she was going to do with me. She was going to put me out in the cold.

Sounds funny, but that's exactly what she did. November can be as chilly in northern Ohio as in the England I'd just left, so I had been luxuriating in the comfort of central heating.

So I'm home with my daughter for the first evening, and she says, "Let's go out on the porch."

"Certainly not. It's miserable out there."

"Daddy, I want you to go out on the porch with me. I want to sit in the porch swing."

"Good *night*, Janie! Let's stay inside. It's real nice in here."

"Nope. Out on the porch—"

Nothing else would satisfy her. I insisted that we put our coats on— I don't think *she* would even have bothered with that—and we marched out on the porch and stood around or sat in the porch swing for an hour.

I didn't have an idea what was in the child's mind. It didn't dawn on me until I talked to Helen afterward.

There were all those people walking up and down the street . . . it was late, dusk was falling . . . and folks were coming home from work, and youngsters trotting from belated classes at school.

Janie wanted the neighbors to *see* me. Some of the kids had told her they didn't believe that she had a father, and she wanted to prove that they were wrong.

Must have been the warmth of her affection which kept me from catching cold.

The itinerary for the lecture tour was concentrated in order for us speakers to appear before the greatest possible number of auditors. We were to talk both to personnel in the Army Air Forces and to civilian workers in key airplane factories.

A few portions from a speech prepared especially for one of these latter audiences are included in this chapter. At that stage of the game I was certainly more qualified for bombardment than I was for speech-writing. Sy Bartlett put the thing together for me. Without this assistance I should probably have done badly—especially in comparison with Robinson, who had a silver tongue.

The excerpts presented herewith do not pretend to expound my personal language and thought as they occur. But the incident is related graphically. I cannot help but believe that it had some effect on those masses of workers who stood in the great echoing sheds where our bombers and fighters were coming into being.

Assuredly we needed their support and coöperation, and every one of us speakers felt that we were operating in a good cause. As can be understood, the other speeches—the ones made by Zemke and Nye and Robinson—were more or less along the same lines.

In one way it seems strange that workers back in the United States had to be bopped in the face with such accounts, in order for them to offer a whole-souled devotion to the job which they were doing, in providing the mechanical equipment with which we warred. But there was that calculable difference between the initiated and the uninitiated—the person at the Front and the person at home—the soldier and the civilian.

"The list of targets battered is long and impressive, and Hitler knows that he must stop our bombings or his war supplies will be choked off at the source. That is why he has concentrated the bulk of his fighter planes on the Western front; why he has strengthened his antiaircraft defenses; why he has his experts working feverishly on new defensive tactics. But our men are going through and they will continue to go through. . . .

"I should like to suggest here that it might be a good idea to drop the word 'raid' from all references to aerial combat activities. The word 'raid,' it seems to me, is usually associated with a sudden thrust into enemy territory by a small force whose intention is more to harass the enemy than to destroy him; to make a nuisance of themselves and to cause temporary annoyance.

"Our so-called 'raids' are much more than that; they are full-scale battles, fought in the thin air, miles above the land. They are battles just as surely as Guadalcanal was a battle; as the North African campaign was a battle; as the struggles for Italy and Russia are battles. In each of our attacks there is a definite, invaluable objective, and powerful forces are employed on each side to conquer and defend. . . .

"Let me tell you the story of John Morgan and his crew. It will give you an idea of the hell-in-the-heavens our men go through in order to drop their bombs. I'm going to tell it to you without pretty phrases; it's not a pretty story. I'll leave out some of the names, for reasons you'll understand, I'm sure.

"John Morgan, a flight officer from New York City, was co-pilot on a Fortress assigned to participate in the attack on Hanover July 26. The plane was on its way into the enemy coast when Focke-Wulfs pounced on it, sending their 20-millimeter shells crashing into the ship. Wave after wave of FW's came in, and American gunners fought desperately to stave them off as the Fortress droned on toward the target.

"Shells tore the Fortress, ripped the oxygen lines, and put all the guns out of action except the ball turret gun. Still the Fortress droned on, while the FW's attacked from the rear.

"During the fight the navigator, Lieutenant Keith J. Koske of Milwaukee, felt a terrific explosion overhead. The ship rocked.

"A second later the top turret gunner fell through the hatch and slumped to the floor at the rear of the navigator's compartment. When Koske got to him, the gunner was lying in a pool of blood. His left arm had been blown off at the shoulder. Koske tried to inject morphine to ease the pain, but the needle was bent, and he couldn't. He tried to apply a tourniquet, but he couldn't do that; the gunner's arm was off too close to the shoulder to permit it.

"Koske knew the man would die without prompt medical attention. There was only one thing left to do.

"Koske opened the escape hatch, adjusted the gunner's parachute, and placed the ripcord firmly in the wounded man's hand. But the gunner became excited and pulled the ripcord. The chute opened in the updraft, but Koske managed to gather it together and tuck it under the gunner's right arm. Then he got the man into a crouched position with his legs through the hatch, made certain his good arm was holding the chute folds together, and toppled the gunner into space. The parachute opened and the gunner floated downward into enemy territory.

"Koske knew that the only chance the man had of surviving was the possibility he would be found quickly and given medical attention.

"While this grim drama was going on, the Fortress was under constant attack. But the ship went on, straight for the target, and dropped its bombs.

"Two hours later, when the enemy fighters finally gave up the struggle, and the Fort was headed for home, Koske went up to check with the pilot. He found him—half-dead in his seat, a mass of blood, with the back of his head shot away.

"He had been wounded two hours before, during the height of the attack. A 20-millimeter shell had entered the right side of the pilot's compartment, crossed in front of Morgan, the co-pilot, and hit the pilot in the head.

"Koske found Morgan flying the plane with one hand, holding the dying pilot off the controls with the other.

"The plane couldn't be landed from the co-pilot's seat because the Plexiglas on that side was shattered and Morgan couldn't see out sufficiently. The pilot had to be moved. Morgan and Koske struggled thirty minutes, getting the pilot out of his seat and into the navigator's compartment, where the bombardier held him from slipping out the open hatch. Morgan was operating the controls with one hand and helping Koske handle the pilot with the other.

"They couldn't get assistance because the oxygen lines were shattered. Most of the crew members were unconscious, with badly frozen hands and feet.

"I hope you grasp the picture. Morgan had kept the ship in formation when he could barely see out of the shattered glass-enclosed cabin. He had to fly while holding the bloody, dying pilot off the controls and instruments. He flew like a homing pigeon to the target in spite of the fact that he had every right and reason to turn back or bail out, and have his crew do the same.

"Alone and unaided, he handled the giant Fortress for two hours, although the plane had practically no guns with which to fight off the incessant attacks. He . . . got the plane back to the English coast, and landed it safely on an emergency field."

It might be appropriate to add here that Lieutenant John C. Morgan was awarded the Congressional Medal of Honor.

We were in the States for about a month. We went around to as many of the training bases as could be included in the set-up. We would go to a base, and sometimes talk two or three times, each of us, to various groups. They tried to grind everybody through; but they had a lot of trainees, and this called for some duplication or triplication of effort on our part.

On the side, in my brief relations with the Training Command (no Bob Olds around there any more, worse luck) I did everything I could to step up gunnery proficiency. People were quizzing me, and once again I had to tell them what we really needed and how we weren't getting it. My efforts may have helped for the future.

I do know this: when I got back to Elveden Hall I was just as worried about our condition in gunnery as I had been before.

I cannot over-emphasize how bad our defensive fire had been, to begin with. It was one of the many important things neglected in the old Langley days. Down there we didn't have a very good range, and— Oh, surely, we did some shooting; but what it boiled down to is that we knew nothing much about what we were doing.

Even the B-10's had had some flexible guns, but there was never any scientific approach to the problem. When we really got our teeth into it, we discovered that everybody was leading the wrong way. People whom we stuck in gun positions in those airplanes of the early days didn't have a single idea of what they were up against, or how to cope with the difficulties which would be bound to ensue. Furthermore they didn't get much practice. All they received was ground school work: how to take a machine gun apart, how to adjust the head space and oil-buffer setting. We tried to make them efficient enough to perform a field strip in three minutes or whatever the time goal might be at that particular stage of the game; and even then our results were poor.

And you could never convince a freshman gunner that *just a little bit* of oil on the guns wasn't good for them.

Oil on guns? Certainly!

Every youthful ex-cowpoke or ex-magazine-peddler who suddenly found himself trying to figure out the difference between a stud-bolt and a firing-pin extension *knew* that oil was just the thing for guns. Oil had been invented solely to heal and soothe and improve and accelerate any movable metallic portion of anything. A guy had always put oil on his old Daisy air rifle or his own .22, hadn't he? He put oil on his little brother's tricycle; he put oil on his sister's roller skates; and even over at Grandma's house where they had that old clock on the mantel with its clicking-swinging pendulum— They kept a ball of oily cotton in a corner of the clock-case, so the air would be impregnated with oil, so the clock would continue unwinding and striking with ease.

You fetch a hard-set preconceived opinion like that (or like those, because practically everyone had the same opinion) into high altitude defensive fire problems, and you've really got some suicides on your hands.

The veterans learned bitterly that if their guns had any oil on them at all, as soon as they got up to altitudes the guns would freeze. They'd be as useless in fending off enemy fighters as a broomstick or a vacuum cleaner.

You might think that because people had had the experience and knew what they were talking about, and passed their acquired wisdom on to the greenhorns, the same problems would never recur again. If you think that, you haven't studied the human race. Few folks ever learn anything from previous experience of elders, whether elders in years or elders in familiarity with a given task or problem. If this were not true the race would go ahead a lot faster.

No generation ever halts to turn around and examine the vast lore acquired by their predecessors who marched along the same route; and then to adjust a future plan (or a present crisis) accordingly. Instead they criticize the previous generations for making severe errors—such obvious errors, in the light of modern technocracy and modern emancipated philosophy! Then they turn around and make a whole new set of mistakes, all by their lonesome.

We couldn't convince a man that he shouldn't oil his guns—not until he got up there and found those yellow-nosed Jerries with the leading edges of their wings looking raw and bright, and 20-millimeter shells playing knock-knock with the Plexiglas and metal of his bomber.

If he survived, the next time he washed the movable parts of his machine gun in gasoline. Then he had a better chance of surviving on into the future. . . . In 1942, as I have reiterated, we were a pretty sorry lot. We had to learn in combat. Many people didn't last long enough to learn much.

If you're going to fight successfully you've got to develop ground rules and cling to them with a grip of iron. Later we had to make a new set of ground rules for the B-29's in the Pacific, just the way it was imperative to do with smaller slower-speed aircraft in the ETO.

For instance, in the Eighth Air Force one of our ground rules was that we would go over a target at a hundred and fifty-five miles per hour indicated airspeed; and when we left the target we throttled back to a hundred and fifty mph . . . that was just the point where an airplane which had lost an engine could stay in the formation. But if he'd lost more than one engine, or if he had suffered other structural damage which caused him to slow down and fall out, it was just too bad.

Positively we could not endanger the other planes just to accommodate that one.

If he couldn't stay in formation, he fell out; he had to do one or the other. Another airplane would fill in his slot, according to further rule; and there was the poor cripple off leading a solitary life. More often than not he wasn't able to lead it very long. He got picked on, if there were any enemy fighters around. It's a lot easier for a fighter to knock down a wounded airplane than a healthy one.

Going back to gunnery, I had complained plenty to Bob Olds when he was alive; and he did his best to rearrange things in the ZI so that future replacements would be coming over a little better equipped for the fray. But it took a long time for any results to become apparent. However, they were setting up more and more gunnery schools back in the States.

Eventually it was decided to order the commander of each of those schools over to England for a look-see. I guess there were half a dozen or more who came. Old Dan Jenkins and Del Spivey—I've forgotten the others— But they were lugged over to our theater, to see what it was all about.

We concluded that we should send them on some missions and let them see firsthand; then they'd have more incentive and more awareness when they got back to their schools again. Trouble was, the first mission we sent them on, half of them got shot down. Both Spivey and Jenkins were shot down. I will say that one good thing came out of *that*. It made a hell of a big impression on the theorists back home who had been reluctant to alter their gunnery training to fit our needs.

(When it is stated that these gunnery-school types were shot down, I don't mean that they were necessarily killed. Del Spivey is now a major-general, retired, and he's superintendent of Culver.)

In due time and by such demonstrations of our vulnerability, the people who had the power to provide us with proper equipment came to the conclusion that we must receive better turrets and better sights. It would be necessary to take the guesswork out of shooting. Computers were the answer.

(Right here let me mention something about the modern sort of computers, a generation later. When I was Chief of Staff there was a tendency among certain journalists to present me as about one step removed from Horatius-at-the-bridge or the old Scots warrior, Gillies MacBean, who held the breach with his busy red claymore. Since I persisted in furthering a mixture of weapons systems, including manned bombers, instead of demanding an overbalanced reliance on untested missiles, I must still be a rapt believer in the military importance of the crossbow and the mace. . . . Some reporter asked me for my opinion on computers. I told him that certainly I had nothing against computers—we employed a lot of them in the Air Force. "But," I said, "I never yet found one who was willing to die for his Country.")

If you worked the computing sight the way it was supposed to be worked, you were going to hit the target.

Thus by the time the B-29's came along, we had such a system, and it was functioning. Poor gunnery in the Orient was never the dreadful bugaboo which had confronted every commander in the European war, especially in the early days. On the other hand, the Japs were never able to mount a proportionate and effective fighter resistance against the 29's, as were the Germans against the 24's and the 17's. Our big foe in the Pacific war, besides the Japanese, was just the Globe itself: the distances, the water, the weather, the mountains, the ever-acute logistic menace.

I recollect a big hassle we had over our mercury-vapor bombsight. This sight had a bubble system in it, in which you had to level the gyro. The whole thing was gyro controlled; thus you needed to set your gyro properly by leveling those bubbles. And, in order to level your sight, you had to be flying straight and even, with no accelerations. Your speed, your altitude, your position—all must be maintained accurately. When you got leveled under those conditions, the gyro would keep the sight admirably accurate for the immediate future. If you made too many turns in the aircraft, it might wander off; but on the whole it would be fairly close.

Some of these merc-vapes came over with us and to us, early in the Eighth AF days, but only a few. Doubtless those first ones were mainly experimental. . . . Out on the desert ranges in the ZI, new bombardiers were bombing, and sage old officers were checking on them, and checking on their results. The eventual verdict was—out *there*—that you could bomb much more effectively with the regular Norden bombsight than you could with the mercury-vapor gadget.

They didn't understand that when you are approaching a target and being resisted—sometimes by everything the enemy can throw at you, from the ground or from the air itself: everything in the way of bullets, bursting shells, lobbed rockets, flak fragmentation, you name it—

When you're flying under those conditions you're not flying straight-and-level every second. Your speed is jumping up and down, and there's vibration and drafts, and sometimes demanded changes of position. Thus the so-called experimental mercury-vapor sight gave us infinitely better results in combat.

How to convince the people back home? Bet I wrote at least a dozen letters. I kept hounding them: "*Everybody* is hollering for those mercury-vapor sights." And the Great Minds at Wright said in reply, "You don't know what you're talking about. That thing is not as accurate as the one we are giving you *now*."

Would have been nice if we could have taken them along on a mission or two, also, and let them see for themselves.

Couldn't.

15

If I were to recount in detail the operations of the Third Air Division during the first half of the year 1944, we would need the something-like-5,000 pages which make up six volumes of *The Army Air Forces in World War II*. I can't tell it all in this book, nor will I ever be able to tell it in any other book.

My great hope has been that through a considered choice of material and facts available, we have given the reader an impression of what bombardment in the ETO, and especially in the Eighth Air Force, was like during the years 1942–44. Readers would be worn down by repetition if we proceeded to offer the particulars of each and every mission; and each and every change of command, change of equipment, change of tactics, so on. There's just too much to tell.

The big change in January of 1944, when the United States Strategic and Tactical Air Forces came into being, with Tooey Spaatz at the head; and Fred Anderson moved over to become Tooey's Deputy for Operations; and Doolittle coming up from the Mediterranean to the Eighth; and Ira Eaker going down to the Mediterranean—

There's the Big Week in late February, when more than 3,300 bombers from the Eighth AF attacked the heart of the German aircraft industry during a span of six days, and suffered only a little more than a four-per-cent loss. There are initial attacks on Berlin itself; there are the drops of supplies to the Maquis and other Resistance forces, both in France and in other countries. . . . Endless attacks on German rocket sites . . . missions flown in direct support of the invasion before D-Day. The struggle to isolate the battle area. The bombing of beaches in advance of the landings. There was a lot of strain and misery and danger, with heartbreak included, and often the bitterness of complete frustration in the end.

So— It was experience.

All that time I was doing my best to learn how to be a commander. I kept reviewing my past and trying to determine where I had been correct and where I had been mistaken. Tried not to make the same mistakes twice. Didn't like to see *that* in anyone who worked for me, and had no wish to be guilty myself.

The rest of my duty in the ETO must be summed up quickly. Even so, I fear that the ETO part is disproportionate to the whole length of this book. It's my own fault if this is true, because the tale includes the 305th. And, as I've said before and will probably say through the rest of my life, *that* somehow was the concentration of my career as an airman. I was close to the people with whom I worked, and I could fly along with them and share their perils. We felt the intimacy of proven human devotion while doing our job together. . . . Well, we've been all over that. Call it the Big Week of my life if you want to.

In June 1944, I was ordered to go to Asia and take command of our B-29's. The folks in Washington said that an experienced combat type was urgently needed for the job, and that was the reason they sent for me. There would be much to learn, all over again. New theater, new equipment, new personnel, an entirely new set of problems.

I had made major-general 3 March, 1944.

Command is a pretty lonesome job. There are multiple decisions which you have to make entirely by yourself. You can't lean on anybody else. And a good commander, once he issues an order, must receive complete compliance. An indecisive commander cannot achieve instant compliance. Or one who is unable to make up his own mind and tries to lean on his subordinates will never achieve instant compliance either.

He cannot afford to be ambiguous.

Ever since I was a boy and read about Gettysburg, I've thought that ambiguity was the reason for Lee's losing the battle. Lee said: "Gen-

eral Ewell was instructed to carry the hill occupied by the enemy, if
he found it practicable. . . ." I call that leaning on a subordinate,
most definitely. Ewell didn't find the attack practicable; so he didn't
attack that late afternoon or early evening. During the night the Fed-
erals became heavily reinforced, and were never driven from their
ridges, but instead repelled every Confederate attack poised against
them.

Lee left it up to Ewell to make a decision which I feel that great
general should have made himself. And Lee was a great general. Figure it out if you can.

. . . Always pretty much of a lonesome job.

They have a tradition in the Navy: the captain of the ship never
eats his meals with his officers. It would seem that this peculiar custom
stems from the fact that everyone at sea is dependent on the captain's
decision. It is a deliberate effort to set him off to one side, in order to
be assured of respect and instant compliance. We've never carried
things to such extremes in the Air Force or in the Army. Still, I think
there's something to be said in support of the idea.

My personal philosophy is that the best outfits are those wherein a
procedure is developed whereby every man who has an idea on a particular subject may bring it forward at the time of the discussion, without the slightest criticism or hesitation. He argues for his point of view
when you're discussing exactly how you're going to proceed. He
shouldn't hang back because his idea may appear radical, or because
the bulk of the crowd may not agree with it.

Everyone steps forward and expresses an idea.

Once the decision is *made,* however—

"This is the way we're going to do it."

Bang. Everybody complies. If a man doesn't comply, his official
head should roll. He may have thought originally that we should all
zig instead of zag. After hearing every argument, after listening carefully to all testimony relating to the subject, the commander has decided on zag. Everybody had better zag.

A sagacious leader can develop this system very simply. But if he
doesn't develop it, and if he doesn't get the advice he should get before
going in— And if he doesn't listen to all the advice— He won't profit a
mite. The whole outfit will go to hell in a handbasket, and so will that
particular operation. Everything dies on the vine.

And, if that commander has ignored the advice of others without
saying *why,* the entire effort will disintegrate too. Morale will shrivel;
the general loses the respect of his subordinates.

It would be easier if every problem in warfare was clearly cut, but
every problem isn't. There are always so many different ways of doing
a thing. War is an art, not a science.

There are numerous complex ways of solving some problems, just as there are numerous complex ways of winning a football game. But, in advance, who is to say which is the right way? And you never get a chance to fight the battle over again.

The point is: when you have a difference of opinion, and it's all going to be a close call, *somebody* has to call it. And you have to call the decision in such a way that those who were on one side are not resentful of those who were on the other side in the matter, simply because you called it *their* way.

Some people may think that an ultra-efficient computing machine can reason this all out. I don't agree with them. I regret to state that that was one of our principal difficulties in the Department of Defense when I was on duty as Chief of Staff of the Air Force.

I trust that I have stated the essential problem, the overall problem, the human problem confronting a commander. Civilians don't understand. You can talk about this to a civilian; he will turn and look at you and say, "Well, you know, I've heard that that man was a very unpopular commander."

You'll say, "The guy did the job, whatever it was. Didn't he?"

"Yes. But I heard that a lot of people didn't like him."

Trouble was, perhaps, he made everybody work hard. Most people don't like to work hard.

. . . And you, as commander, don't really have to like your people personally because they are doing a good job. If they do the job, everybody respects them for that. But you still don't have to enjoy them personally. You must separate your personal feeling about an individual from your judgment as a commander. In that way only can you produce a good outfit.

Once again: command has always been a well or a peak of loneliness. Oh yes, you can own friends among the people with whom you're laboring. But there has to be no doubt who is boss and who isn't.

You find yourself encountering considerable tragedy, as well, in overcoming a natural grief concerning casualties among the people whom you've led. You possess a natural inborn repugnance against killing people; yet you know you're going to have to do it. It's rough. It used to be particularly vile when I realized that I'd lost someone, and felt that I shouldn't have lost him. That's when it really comes home to you. I lost them because I made a mistake or somebody else made a mistake.

Actually this is the basic reason why I started those critiques following the missions. We began that in the 305th; nobody else had done it, over there in England. But I instituted a critique after each mission, to try to find out exactly what we'd done wrong. It worked. We carried out that idea in SAC later on. In every SAC outfit which was loaned to the Far East Air Force during the Korean War, they held thorough post-mission discussions. By that time it was just old hat in those well-trained SAC crews.

You must wring the greatest possible benefit out of every lesson.

And you must train yourself grimly to adopt a philosophical attitude with regard to those losses. If you're going to fight you're going to have some people killed. But if you have done everything humanly possible to prepare for that mission and plan it properly, and you have observed that it was properly executed, and you have attained the results which you wished to attain— Then you can think, and feel in your heart, "The losses were paid for."

I think every man who has had to nerve himself into the grim responsibility of leading other men in combat will agree to this:

You have to pay a price in warfare, and part of the price is human life.

Same way in getting ready for a war, as the Air Force must do every waking moment (many in the Air Force are awake and flying every moment). You're bound to have an accident rate of some kind, forever. It's only when your accident rate gets too high that you begin to wonder, "What the hell is wrong with *me?*"

So, while you don't like to see people killed, if you're going to fight you're going to have those losses. And, if you keep flying under simulated combat conditions and in every sort of weather, you're going to have losses. But if you've done the best you can in the way of preparation, planning, and execution, then you feel that if those people who were sacrificed came up in front of your desk and looked you in the eye, you could look *them* in the eye and say, "I think it was a good operation."

If you can't imagine yourself doing that, then you ought to start worrying.

While it tortured me to lose people in the ETO and in the Pacific war, I think that in most cases I would be willing to meet them, and I would say, "Well, you were properly expended, Gus. It was part of the price."

Can't tell. I might meet them eventually.

16

IN LATE-MIDDLE JUNE, just after I had been ordered to the Pacific, I went over and had a quick look at the ground activity on the Normandy peninsula. Except for being on the receiving end of bombing raids and enemy intruder attacks, this was the only phase of ground conflict which I witnessed firsthand during the war.

At that time our troops had gouged their way across the peninsula to the Bay of Biscay, and thus isolated the city of Cherbourg, which they planned to polish off in a separate operation later on, in order to secure the harbor for our purposes. There was just a holding operation toward the south and east; and on the other side of the area our lines were perhaps four miles from the city of Cherbourg.

Everybody and his dog would be asking me, once I got out to the Pacific, just how things were going in Europe and what was happening. There would be a lot of speculation about the landings in France, and the fact that we had been bottled up in that area much longer than the optimists believed possible. The Pacific people could learn plenty of facts from daily reports which were handed around, but there was nothing like an eyewitness account. I recalled clearly how we had hung on the words of Frank Armstrong when we first landed in Great Britain: a man who had been actually engaged in air combat. By the same token, it seemed that the statement of a man who had witnessed even a brief moment of fighting on the ground, would be more important than that of a man who hadn't.

I called up Bill Kepner, who had our Eighth Fighter Command, and told him that I wanted to go over to the beach if he'd loan me a plane in order to make the flight. We knew that the engineers had scraped out some temporary fighter fields over there, as soon as our troops landed. They had thrown down pier steel planking over the areas they'd hacked out; there were at least two strips in that region; and it should not be difficult to fly over there, land, and have a look around.

Kepner laughed over the phone. He had been planning to do exactly the same thing. "I'll go with you, Curt."

I got to his headquarters, and we went down and climbed into a couple of P-47's and headed for France. To a long-ago Pursuit type like myself, there was a lot of fun in flying this Jug, after so many missions in B-17's, or flying the ocean in 24's. But we stuck seriously to our plan, and landed on one of the new strips. First time I'd ever set foot on the soil of France.

We hunted up the Operations tent for the area, and their A-2 gave us a briefing on where the front lines were, and all that sort of thing. This was rather important if we were to escape capture, since there were enemies thronging on both sides of the cleaned-out area.

Next thing another Army Air Force type appeared on the scene: Brigadier-General James W. McCauley. He'd been with the Eighth earlier in the war; now he was commanding a fighter wing for Pete Quesada's Ninth Tactical Air Force. IX TAC's job, then as later, was to work in close support of the ground troops, using both fighters and fighter-bombers for the task.

McCauley had been concentrating on the demands of his own job conscientiously, and had found no free time to go exploring around. But Kepner's arrival, and mine, made him determined to aid and abet our prowling. "Come on. Crawl in my combat car."

We headed down the main highway.

We didn't see any war. Every once in a while we'd pass some dog-face ensconced in a ditch, sound asleep. The general's aide would jump out of the car and go over and wake up the soldier, ask him what he was doing there, what his unit was, so on. Always he wouldn't know a damn thing except that the umpty-umpth Field Artillery had a command post down thataway in the woods. . . .

Bill and I did feel kind of naked—there hadn't been any time or opportunity for us to equip ourselves with helmets like the ground people; we just wore our ordinary military caps. Nor had anyone thought to hand us any .45's. We felt like a couple of extremely unarmed and defenseless civilians. Course, the dogfaces looked at us as if they shared that opinion.

Once in a while a truck would go by, headed one way or the other. One was returning from the front, loaded with bodies they were toting back to bury.

Bill Kepner really shone; he knew what this was all about. He had been a doughboy in World War I—in the infantry, or maybe it was in the Marines. He showed the marks too: had a lot of scars around his face from machine gun fire. He was our real infantry expert, because of his soldiering proclivities of the half-forgotten past. "How far shall we go, Bill?" "Oh, let's just go up to the next rise." We'd get up on the rise, and there'd be nothing. "Well, let's go up to the *next* rise." We'd get up there, and suddenly find ourselves out in front of a mine detail who were searching for mines along the road. We would have much preferred to have been *behind* them.

Finally we reached a little group of farmhouses with half a dozen recently killed Germans lying around. But I didn't get to gaze at them very long: the intrepid Kepner was headed for the wars. "O.K., let's go up on the *next* rise."

Well, we drove up there, and just as we came out on the hilltop we also came to a screeching halt. The road ahead of us was gone. It looked as if a 500-pound bomb had hit dead center in the road. There was nothing there except a big crater. We all got out and stared, and when we discovered an object in the ditch on the other side of that crater we stared even more.

That object was a brand new Opel sedan, one of the most beautiful cars ever built in Europe. We went stepping around the bomb crater cautiously but quickly, and McCauley says, "Hot damn! I want this one. I'm sick and tired of riding in this combat car. Let's drag the Opel out of the ditch, and take it with us."

This was a lot of fun for Bill and myself too, because neither of us had ever seen a new Opel sitting innocently like a waif on a battlefield. We would reap none of the happy harvest, not if we'd found three Opels; there was no way we could carry them home with us. But Mc-

Cauley had made us more than welcome to the Continent of Europe, and we wanted to help him liberate the sedan.

We all started to go over it carefully to see if it was booby-trapped; looked like it might be, just resting there so prettily. About that time an engineer captain and maybe ten of his troops came creeping out of the woods.

The captain called to us. "That car's O.K. We just pushed it off the road about an hour ago. Not booby-trapped or anything. But the battery's dead." Somebody had left the key in the switch, turned on. It was the engineer captain's opinion that the car had been there since the night before, although he wasn't present when the shell came down.

Knowing that the Opel was clean, we could look it over a little more intimately. It had been the car of some high-ranking surgeon: there was a doctor's case of instruments in there. No sign of any blood. Looked like the driver had escaped intact, but had then fled the road and maybe left the key turned on, on purpose, so that Americans would find a car with a dead battery when inevitably they found it.

Point of having a combat car is that it's equipped for all sorts of emergencies. We hooked a winch onto the Opel and started to pull it across the bomb crater by its bumper, while the engineer officer and his men helped out—

Next moment there was a terrific noise, and some filthy character had thrown dirt all over us. At least that's what I thought. I was pretty slow on the uptake. Everybody else was in the ditch before I ever got there.

A German shell had come down and landed in the field right beside us.

I think I can offer adequate explanation for my tardiness in seeking cover. Bill Kepner had been shot at on the ground before: witness the First World War. Lord knows McCauley had been shot at, ever since the first days of June when he came in with the invasion. I had been shot at on many occasions as well; but always when I was away up in the air. I must have thought subconsciously that that was the only time people did try to kill you, with their shells or machine guns or 20-millimeter cannon. You got four or five miles up in the air over an enemy target, and you expected them to cut loose at you. But not when you were engaged in the pleasantly boyish task of trying to haul a handsome automobile across a great big hole in the ground.

But I wasn't standing there thinking all these thoughts in the above chronology. I was in that ditch along with the dogfaces and the other two generals. Shells kept coming all along that road, and we really shoved our faces into the soil of Normandy, and it didn't smell like blossoms either.

There were two sounds in between the bursts of high explosives: one was that engineer cussing his head off because the Jerries were tearing up his road again, and he would have to fix it. The other sound was the giggling of the GI's, who for some mysterious reason found something awfully funny in the idea that they were lying in the ditch with a brigadier-general and two major-generals.

Guess the shelling kept up about ten minutes; it seemed a lot longer. At first we thought that our gang had been spotted by some distant enemy observers, and they were taking this opportunity to kill off—or try to kill off—the commander of Eighth Fighter Command and the boss of the Third Bombardment Division, to say nothing of Brigadier-General McCauley of IX TAC.

Guess not, however. We figured out that this was merely map-fire. The Jerries were throwing that stuff around in order to interdict the roads and make it tough for American transport to move.

We came to the unanimous conclusion that that was as close to the front lines as we cared to go at the moment, and devoted ourselves to completing the task on which we were embarked. The little Opel hadn't been scratched by the shooting. But our driver was understandably nervous, and he jerked on that cable fastened to the Opel with such force that the bumper snapped off . . . had to be tied on again. Finally we got the car out of the ditch, across the vast shell crater, and onto the road on our side.

I remember studying the speedometer: the thing only had a few kilometers on it. Hadn't been driven from Germany at all; must have been shipped there by rail or air to the unknown surgeon.

So we got the combat car turned around and the winch-cable wound up; we hooked onto the Opel and started towing it down the road. After towing it three or four miles we got it started, and McCauley's aide drove it back to his headquarters.

But not before our little caravan had lost its way and gone barging almost into the southeast front lines. We ran into a reserve company who headed us in the right direction, much to our relief. You could get killed that way, prowling around back roads which sometimes belonged to us but sometimes belonged to the enemy. Pete Quesada had a jeep shot out from under him when he went a-wandering once too often.

After the war I ran into McCauley, and he said he drove that Opel throughout the rest of the European fighting, whenever he had a chance to be on the ground, and it was really a beaut.

Only one other thing stands out distinctly in recollection of that day: the sight of three or four German officers marching out of the woods with their hands up in the air, and a couple of GI's poking them along with carbines. That picture hangs in my mind along with the dead Germans, of course, and the taste of the Norman soil, and the deafening concussion of shells.

So that was it: an airman's-eye-view of the war on the ground.

On the whole I felt disappointed; I'd expected to see more in the way of actual fighting. All I got to see: a few dead Germans, a few captured Germans, a few shells exploding without causing any fatalities; and, in the middle of it all, a brand new Opel sedan waiting to be liberated. But I wasn't stupid enough to believe that I had really been in the war that day—the grim war of the French hedgerows, where casualties were thick as apples in every orchard.

BOOK V

AAF: War Against Japan

(1944 – 1945)

1

No one ever felt it essential to explain exactly what this switching me to Asia was all about. At the moment I knew very little relating to the 20th Air Force, or what the setup was. I knew practically nothing about the B-29. I'd heard rumors.

Ira Eaker announced, "You're going to India and China. B-29's." From then on it was a question of the mechanics of change of command, there in the Third Bombardment Division (Pat Partridge took over); and getting back to the United States, and getting checked off on the 29, and getting out to India.

Bit by bit along the line I absorbed the grim facts.

Our B-29 idea came to birth in those days when it appeared that England would go down to defeat, and there'd be no place left to us in the European portion of the Globe where we might base our planes for future sorties against the Axis powers. Thus a much longer ranged bomber than any we then possessed would be essential to our waging a victorious war. (No point in waging any other kind.)

The conception and gestation had occurred long before that, back in the Nineteen-thirties. It all stemmed from the B-17; and growing awareness of a necessity for an aircraft with increased capabilities for huge bomb loads, for heavy loads of fuel, for expanded range. I shouldn't wish to undertake any detailed history of the B-29 at this time or any other time: too many complications in the story.

But let it be said that, in the autumn of 1942, while I was still struggling and the 305th was still struggling, out there on the desert, to try to make ourselves into a halfway decent outfit, the first XB-29 had its initial test flight. It was flown by the great pilot Eddie T. Allen. Then, in February, 1943, Eddie Allen took off in another XB-29 along with a retinue of valuable people from the test flight section of Boeing. *Kaput.* Engine caught fire, wing caught fire . . . Eddie tried to come in for a landing . . . high tension wires. They pranged into a packing plant near the Boeing field.

B-29's had as many bugs as the entomological department of the Smithsonian Institution. Fast as they got the bugs licked, new ones crawled out from under the cowling.

Through all this we must realize that General Arnold—earnest dreamer and schemer for the whole B-29 program—had a dozen battles on his hands. He was fighting with the Joint Chiefs for resources; he was struggling to get an organizational setup for air power in that war; he had to rassle against the Army and the Navy every minute. Remember, this was years before we in the Air Force achieved our autonomy. Meanwhile a gang of dedicated souls were rushing to get the B-29 built and into production. They knew we'd need it, feared we might even need it before it was ready.

We did.

There were conflicts for material, for labor allocation. As the first-finished airplanes began to emerge from the assembly line, Arnold was hammering away to set up a Strategic Air Force to operate directly under the JCS rather than under the various theater commanders. He did manage to get that done. That was how the 20th Air Force came into being.

K. B. Wolfe was and is a man with a splendid record in the development and procurement business. Most of his important service, I think, had been at Wright Field. Thus he was selected to be the officer heading the B-29 program. He was charged with developing and procuring that airplane, and he fathered the thing all along. His reward was to be given the first 29 outfit which went to India. He wanted to get into combat, as any responsible commander wishes to prove himself in combat. Probably at the time he seemed the logical person to send. Trouble was, again, his main experience was not out in the field, but in development.

And the B-29 wasn't ready for combat, not by any means. People sat around a table and said, "Let K. B. Wolfe take it out there. He'll be able to do it."

What this commander, and any subsequent commander, was faced with was an utterly impossible situation. The scheme of operations had been dreamed up like something out of *The Wizard of Oz*. Fields had been built and were still being built, up around Chengtu in China, to accommodate our huge new bombers. From these strips the 20th Bomber Command was to attack Japan. But ports and railroads of China were in Japanese hands, and there was only one way to get fuel and ordnance up to Chengtu for any operation against the Japanese.

Haul the stuff by air over the hump of the highest mountains in the world.

I've never been able to shake off the idea that General Arnold himself never believed that this would work.

It didn't work. No one could have made it work. It was founded on an utterly absurd logistic basis. Nevertheless, our entire Nation howled like a pack of wolves for an attack on the Japanese homeland. The high command yielded. The instrument wasn't ready, the people weren't ready, nothing was ready. Folks were given an impossible task to perform. They tried to be good soldiers and do their duty.

The whole thing was stacked against them. Under these trying conditions I think that they did one whale of a job with what they had.

Well, I had had my brief experience in sticking my nose into the Battle of Normandy and helping to liberate a real snazzy Opel. I said goodbye to Elveden Hall. That was around the first of July. I flew back home and reported at Washington. Then I went up to Cleveland for three or four days with Helen and Janie. When they sent an airplane to tote me out to Grand Island, Nebraska, I kidnaped Helen and Janie and took them along. I was due to be in Grand Island for about a month.

People in Washington had wished me to proceed immediately to India to take over the tiny B-29 war that was being waged from there. But I said No Soap. "If I'm going to have command of a bunch of airplanes that are strange to me, I'm going to fly that airplane first."

Reluctantly . . . "O.K. We'll set up a special course for you at the B-29 school."

Out there on the summer prairies of Nebraska and in the air above, it was possible to review the somber story. If you ever saw a buggy airplane, this was it. I heard the bitter tale of how the first groups had flown out to India by way of Marrakech, Cairo and Karachi. They got across the Atlantic all right, but lost their first plane at Marrakech. The crew got out but the 29 burned. Practically everybody had trouble on every leg of that flight to India; and two more of the planes were lost at Karachi. One vanished into the ocean, no one knew why.

It seemed that the numerals 3 and 5 would again be most important in my life. The engine of the B-29 was designated as the Wright R-3350. This equipment should never have been destined to power operational aircraft without a long period of trial and investigation, and trial again. But it was so ordered.

Those engines overheated, cylinder heads often blew out the moment an engine started turning over, ignition was faulty, oil leaked excessively, fuel transfer systems gave endless trouble. There were scores of other defects, either readily apparent or—worse—appearing insidiously when an aircraft was actually at work and at altitude.

This situation existed at the start, in 1943. They didn't have a lot of these things fixed in 1944 or even, God help us, by 1945.

Early this year (1965) Possum Hansell sent me a copy of a letter which he had written to Major James M. Boyle, assistant professor of history at the U. S. Air Force Academy. General Hansell said, in part: "The engines of the B-29 had developed a very mean tendency to swallow valves and catch fire. The magnesium crank cases burned with a fury that defied all efforts to put them out. In addition, gun sighting blisters were either blowing out at high altitude or frosting up so badly that it was impossible to see through them. But we couldn't wait to fix them."

I should hazard a guess that more airplanes caught fire or went down over the Himalayas for unexplained causes, than went to such fate from causes which were known and recognized. As for myself, working and learning there beside the Platte River in the summer of 1944, some brand new bugs showed up right beneath my own feet and fingers.

So I checked off, and it was time to go sample the wars again, but out of a far different kettle than any I'd ever tasted before. I kissed my wife and daughter goodbye and shipped them back to Ohio.

The plan was for a B-29 to be taken out of modification, and I would fly it to India. I waited around some days for this; the damn thing was never ready. I was in a hurry to take over my new command, and it appeared that some other people were in a hurry to have me do so. Finally I wound up by getting on a C-54 and going to Karachi—in fact, all the way to Kharagpur—in that. Got there on the 29th of August. Call the numerologists again.

K. B. Wolfe had relinquished command early in July, and my old classmate Blondie Saunders was holding down the fort temporarily. Blondie was due to go back to the States and get a new wing of 29's and fetch them out to Asia. He stayed around for a fortnight or so, to help me get my feet on the ground.

Kharagpur was like nothing I'd ever seen before. The place is about ninety miles west of Calcutta, and the British and the Indians had built all the bases in that area. Typical Indian style: *basha* huts, with thatched straw roofs and so on. Our HQ was just outside the actual town of Kharagpur, and some distance away from the airfield. Headquarters had been an old prison at one time; there was a big wall all around the place, with buildings both inside and outside, but mainly inside. I lived in what was supposed to be the warden's house, outside the walls, with a few staff officers. Most of our personnel lived in *basha* huts scattered through the area.

The first few nights I went to bed with my ears buzzing from what I had heard, and my eyes aching from what I had seen, both in actuality and on paper. I don't know how long the runways of those fields in our area had been originally, but at least they had been extended and were all operational at this time. Same way up in the Chengtu area in China. There the strips had been built by coolie labor: thousands of families, from tots to creaking old grandsires, lugging those round water-worn stones from along the dry beds of the rivers, pounding them up, rolling them into place. It was like depending on a gang of ants, the construction people related. But still the ants got the job done.

Of course we were hauling all of our own supplies up there. Everything had to be flown in—every single item. So it meant *seven flights* with a B-29, off-loading gasoline—just putting on enough gas to get back—to build up a reserve of *enough gas for that B-29 to fly a mission against Japan.*

And our equipment had never been through the necessary shakedown period. It was as if no one thought that a shake-down period was essential. So we overheated, the cylinders blew, the engines failed. Airplanes were going down over the Hump all the time, or they were busting up on the strips in India and China alike.

I'd lie there on my cot, after finally getting to bed late in the muggy night, and try to battle the thing out. There must be some way of getting a course of realistic training into these people . . . and making them aware of the faults and weaknesses of their airplanes; and how to cope with those difficulties when they reared their ugly heads, before the whole plane and crew were smashed or fried.

. . . Get some people from Wright Field immediately, I thought. We need modifications on the cowl flaps and engines. We'll ship Eric Nelson and some people like that out from Wright.

. . . On-the-job training. We've got to do *that*. These folks have been thinking in terms of night individual attacks on industrial areas. They've done practically nothing in the way of formation flying. So we've got to get in some formation flying—do some daylight station stuff if we can— Knock out some station targets.

. . . Let's see: where can we find some Japs to practice on, someone within our range? Away down below, in Burma, there must be a few Japs . . . some of those ports down there. Maybe we could even go as far as Singapore.

. . . But the defenses are not too much in those areas; we wouldn't have to worry about defenses very much.

I'd ponder the urgency for realistic training again, and then find my brain foolishly stuffed with some anecdote told by folks who had been up in China . . . the coolies had wheelbarrows to wheel their stones in, and those wheelbarrows made the most gosh-awful noise, screaming and howling until people were going nuts. So the Americans oiled up the axles, and then the Chinese went on strike and were brokenhearted, and didn't want to wheel any more rocks. They claimed that the squeaky axles of the wheelbarrows— The screech which was emitted when the wheel turned was the very thing that kept demons away from the poor coolies. With a well-oiled axle there wasn't any screech; and the demons would surely prevail.

There'd be that kind of nonsense running around in your mind.

Then you'd get back to the fact that we had the buggiest damn airplane that ever came down the pike.

Blondie Saunders was a powerful vigorous guy, blessed by his parents with the name of LaVerne G. (but the boys in his life soon corrected that). He'd graduated from West Point with Fred Anderson and Boatner and Hank Everest and that bunch. So of course he wasn't in our early class out at March; he had the same training at Brooks, and we met first during the Kelly episode of our careers.

It was good to see an old friend like Blondie. Also I found there in India one Major Alfred F. Kalberer, who had demonstrated for several years those values which seasoned old commercial pilots could offer to the Army Air Forces. Kal had been busy in the Mediterranean during both the early and later phases. I think he'd ended up his service in that theater as A-3 for Pat Timberlake. Now he was down here in the CBI; and his encyclopedic knowledge of weather, terrain and nationals of the various countries—all gained through thousands of hours as a KLM pilot—was to help us enormously.

I appreciated it when Blondie Saunders offered to hang on awhile and help me run up the engines. Though he was really surplus around there, and due to go back to the States. . . . Think I mentioned before that there were several fields in the region of Kharagpur. They were designated as Chakulia, Dudhkundi, Charra and a couple of others. . . . I can't remember which field it was that Blondie Saunders took off from, late on Monday, September 18th. He had been up at that base to have dinner and say goodbye to some boys who had worked for him. He took off in a B-25.

Somebody woke me up about midnight. It was only about a twenty- or thirty-minute flight from Rudyard or Kipling, or whatever that place was called. Only a twenty- or thirty-minute flight; and Blondie had taken off after dinner, about ten-thirty, and had never arrived back at Kharagpur. There wasn't a thing we could do at night . . . jungle all around, up there. But I laid on a search with every plane we had available, to begin next morning the moment it was light enough. They were to make a thorough grid search—really comb the place to see what had happened to that unfortunate Mitchell bomber which Blondie Saunders had flown away in.

The more I thought about it, the more convinced I became that he must have cracked up right close to that northern field. He'd made no radio check-in, for one thing; and that he would have done if he'd been long in flight. No record from the moment of takeoff. Just silence.

I said to Kalberer, "Let's get a B-25 of our own and crank it up." So we went out and flew before daylight, and when it got light enough to see, we were right over the field where Blondie had taken off.

Sure enough. Out there about three miles off the end of the runway was a big gouge, a real rough gash, cut right through the jungle. We went down and flew very low, practically brushing the trees as we examined the wreckage. It was a real mess.

I said, "I don't think there's any use of our ever going in there." I spoke to the tower and called off the grid search; and told them the exact location of the wreckage. Then we flew back to the road, and gave the ground-searching parties a compass course on which to proceed in order to penetrate the jungle and bring out the bodies before the wild critters ate 'em up.

I said, "Let's go home."

Kalberer says, "Nope. Let's get down there on the ground, and go in. There just might be somebody alive. We just *might* be able to render a little bit of assistance."

So we landed, and started down the road, and went into the jungle with a hand compass. Following that compass through the underbrush, we hit the big splintered gouge and followed that down to the squashed airplane. There was old Blondie, still inhabiting that wreckage, big as life. Did he give us hell for taking so long to get there. One of the engines was crushed down on his busted leg.

The crew chief was still walking around, completely blundering, out on his feet. He had a hole in his head— I'll bet you could have put your fist in there. Why he was still alive nobody knew . . . incoherent, naturally, but talking still. . . . Crew chief died the next day. . . . Radio operator was alive, but all pinned down: his leg was broken too.

Well, the other searchers arrived, and we hoisted the engine off Blondie and hauled him out of there. A flight surgeon was along; he shook his head. He was very much worried about Blondie's leg, because it was a compound fracture, and had had the engine squeezing it, down around the ankle . . . grease and guck all over the place. . . .

Blondie said he didn't want his leg amputated, and I guess he would have fought anyone who tried to do it right then. They struggled to save his leg, but he very nearly died. In fact everyone decided that Blondie *was* going to die. We scurried around to find a grave site for him. The regular graveyard in our neighborhood was entirely under water, though this was the end of the monsoon season. But we didn't want to grub down and try to excavate under all that water, in order to make a submerged hole to bury Blondie in. We'd have had to tie him down or he would have floated away.

So we scouted, and picked out a real nice place to plant Blondie, up on a little hill. Well, he didn't die and he didn't die; they finally shipped him back to the States. But the leg wasn't doing as well as people could have wished; even though Blondie was still alive and more than alive—able to cuss about it all. Finally they had to take his leg off.

I last saw Blondie out at the Air Academy, when we had our thirty-fifth reunion of the Kelly class. That was last year—October, 1964. He was going full strength, strong as an ox. I haven't picked out any burial sites for him lately.

2

AAFWW II says, Volume Five, page 115: "LeMay . . . had been slated for a B-29 job earlier, but had stayed on in Washington to work on the long-heralded reorganization of the command."

Not so. I'd stayed on in the United States, out at Grand Island, Nebraska, to try to learn the correct way to fly a 29, if there was any such way.

I was yearning to put into effect some of the new procedures instigated in the ETO—not infallible, perhaps, but infinitely more realistic than the routines adhered to earlier.

Our Air Force HQ was in Washington; had to be; for that reason General Arnold dreamed it up. There in the 20th we had B-29's flying over the central Pacific, the southwest Pacific, and the China theater. In effect and in actuality we were flying over Nimitz's command, over MacArthur's command, over Stilwell's command. We couldn't assign our aircraft around to the theater commanders—it was absolutely essential to have a centralized command. So that's how the 20th Air Force differed from everything else in the AAF. It was General Arnold's dream of a Strategic Air Force come true. He sat in Washington and commanded the 20th as an executive agent for the Joint Chiefs of Staff. We were the only Air Force which did operate directly under the JCS. However, we were under General Stilwell, commander of the China-Burma-India Theater, for administration and supply—the latter obviously *most* important.

I wanted to get my Lead Crew school thing going out here, the way we'd practiced it successfully in England. My people didn't let any grass grow under their feet on that one. I wanted to change the maintenance setup (as described in Eighth Air Force accounts). I wanted to change the formation. They had been flying a four-ship diamond formation. I was going to use my combat box or know the reason why. And I wanted to fly missions, as I'd always done in the ETO.

There was a real rub on this: people upstairs were yipping shrilly at the idea, and they had yipped before I ever went over to India. Actually I was compelled to scratch and claw to get myself out to Grand Island, in order to qualify as Aircraft Commander of a B-29. Some of those misguided souls in Washington had the notion that a commanding officer didn't need to be qualified as an Aircraft Commander. He had a lot of *those* folks under him: lieutenants, captains, majors—whatever they were. *His* job was to proceed in his own echelon and on his own exalted level.

But, in asserting themselves in this direction, they bumped up against my hardshell old Chelveston attitude. And they weren't about to persuade me out of it. If I wanted to improve top-turret gunners' efficiency, then I went into the top turret, etc.

I told them this, but they weren't much impressed, not having been along on the job. So I tried to be as diplomatic as possible, after they said, "No combat for you."

"Look here. I've got to— I've got to fly a mission. I should fly missions regularly; but right now I must fly at least one, at the start. I won't know what's going on until I do."

At last, sourly, they said, "O.K. *One.*"

There may have been a reason for their really sticky attitude. They knew about Manhattan District, and I didn't. Never heard of it. I can't recollect that I'd ever really speculated much about splitting the atom . . . nuclear fission was a phase of science which we never embraced in old Slicker Sloane's classes at Ohio State. And there were people back there on the flowery shores of the Potomac who knew everything there was to know about the eventual deployment and employment of atomic weapons in WW II—or thought they did. They knew how far we had gone with the thing, from day to day and week to week. They knew how they planned to deliver the weapon—at least how they planned right *then.*

Well, it looked as if I'd be commanding the B-29's, and the B-29's had to figure in the picture if the first atomic bomb used in warfare was to be delivered against Japan rather than against a German target. I would be commanding when that time came, it seemed; and they didn't want to lose their boss beforehand. So— I hadn't been briefed, didn't know a particle about the whole business. Thus I would have had nothing profitable to reveal to the Japs if I went down and became a prisoner of war and had to submit to—shall we say—rigorous questioning.

It was palpably unwise to permit anyone with knowledge of this epoch-making new weapon to venture over enemy territory. But, in the early autumn of 1944, I didn't own a crumb of information. I had not one pale little notion of what we'd be dropping, come next August.

Anyway, they were willing to let me fly a mission, so I wanted to get going.

I looked at the target list, at the missions we had coming up, and picked out Anshan in Manchuria. That's where the big coke ovens were, and coke was a staff-of-life to Japanese industry. Already we had made one attack on that target, not too successfully. Anshan still had a high priority, therefore, on the lists.

But the main reason I chose it was that the Japs were alleged to have their best fighters up there. If I was going to learn anything about repelling the enemy fighter attack I ought to be along when and where the 29's were up against a well-mounted and well-disciplined attack, not a raunchy ineffective one. Our Intelligence learned a few facts about those Anshan fighter people. They had a new in-line engine fighter: liquid-cooled job. Their outfit was practically intact; they had never been really shot up. Definitely these were the best which we might encounter in any venture made into Jap-held territory or against Japan itself.

Therefore I'd been in the CBI about ten days before I flew my first mission, going up to Advance (Chengtu) across the Himalayas; and getting a hundred and fifteen B-29's up there on the Chengtu strips, all told. And taking off for the attack on September 8th— Guess we started out with about a hundred and eight.

When we approached the Anshan area we discovered that those fighters were there all right; and they were up and airborne too, in proper position for an interception. "Now we'll see what they can do." But they must have misjudged the speed of the B-29's; they turned the wrong way. Hell, they never mounted a decent attack. I think only one airplane got in close enough to fire.

As for the 29 in which I was crowded in the cockpit, observing, we got hit by flak. This was when we were right over the target at about 25,000 feet. First off the radio operator squawked that he was hit. And also Central Fire Control: he affirmed that he was hit too.

Well, I was still waiting for those fighters to approach, and I had to observe their tactics. That's why we were there. I talked to the wounded men on our intercom—Radio and CFC. I said, "Hope you're not too badly hit. Wait until the fighters have come in. Then I'll crawl back there and help you."

The fighter attack didn't develop, so I picked up the nearest First Aid pouch and started back to help Radio. He was back there in his hole, and by this time he had taken off his flak-vest.

(How well I remember the first flak-vest I ever saw in the ETO. There was a lot of doubt on the part of many crew members about wearing that heavy stuff: they felt that those dangling plates impeded their movements, and made it difficult to function when they were on oxygen at high altitudes. Many of the boys wouldn't wear the vests at all, but preferred to sit on them. If they could scrounge two or three extra ones from this source or that, they would make armor out of the whole bunch and then sit on the pile. Idea seemed to be that the batteries were shooting from the ground; and if a shell came in, it would come directly up through the airplane. It is quite unlike any other manner of submitting to enemy fire . . . when you're up there, the batteries are shooting at *your own rear end*. . . . Everyone always said in bunk-flying sessions, "There's just one place where I don't want to be wounded." No one ever seemed to tumble to the idea that a flak burst which occurred *above* or *alongside* the aircraft could send a chunk of white-hot metal sizzling to emasculate you, just as simply as would ensue if the shell came from underneath. . . . Well, it didn't happen too often; but it happened. I remember one of our 305th boys, Marvin Sirus, who was a prisoner of war and an amputee, telling about a fellow he was with, in POW camp. The other boy had been wounded in that nightmarish manner. He grew fatter and fatter and more lethargic and more lethargic. When they were exchanged and repatriated —a lot of the amputees and other personnel who had been seriously wounded—they came by way of Sweden, back to the United States, on the *Gripsholm*. Marvin said that the airman who had been emasculated lay in his bunk and cried; and then he'd jump up and break a glass or a mirror, and try to cut his own wrists. The other fellows took to guarding him every minute; so he didn't get to take the Big Trip until he was back home. Then he took it. . . . Could have happened to anybody. When a man goes a-risking in a war, it isn't only his life that he risks.)

Radio Operator was kind of crouched down, back there in that hole where he worked, and he had a most peculiar look on his face. He was examining his flak-vest, and also examining the fragment of shell which had hit him. It was a slice of flak three and a half or four inches long, and the vest had stopped it cold. All he'd felt was a big sock on the back. So of course he thought he was murdered.

O.K. There was still Central Fire Control to consider. I crawled back through the tunnel, not knowing what I'd find in the waist. I looked to see if CFC had fallen out of his perch. Hadn't: he was still sitting up there by his sights, under the dome. But he too had a sheepish look on his face. There are two spade-grips which work those sights; they are fashioned just like the original grips on the old Brownings. CFC swings the sight by these handles. Wherever goes the sight, there also revolve the exterior guns, in several positions aboard the aircraft. They are connected with that gunsight by remote control.

So a piece of flak had hit one of the spade-grips and just stung the hell out of CFC's hands. As the fragment glanced off it barely hit a knuckle: you could see a little white spot there on the skin of his finger, and the hide wasn't even broken. So that was *his* wound. Course, I was just as glad that I didn't have to put on any tourniquets or stick in any needles, or dust on any sulfa.

Thing was: the flak burst had put some holes in us, and we began to wonder how long our pressurization would stand up. Well, it stood up all it needed to, throughout the rest of the mission and the flight back to Chengtu.

A piece of flak has no built-in homing device. It goes wherever the explosion happens to send it. Those superficial wounds or almost-wounds incurred by our crew members might just as easily have been a hand lopped off or a skull broken in two.

After we got on the ground it was funny. It wasn't funny up there in the air at the time.

3

A RECENT WRITER in *Air Force* refers to the campaign flown by 20th Bomber Command by way of India and the Chengtu Valley as "a comparatively minor effort." The historian is correct. About four missions a month was the best we could do out of China, and sometimes we didn't even manage that. It was all due to the bad logistics, wherein our greatest share of flying effort had to be expended in bringing gas up to those Chengtu strips.

Present-day and future critics must accept the fact that there can be no sustained and intensive effort by any bombers who have to feed their own fuel to themselves.

Preliminary efforts had been scattered and mostly ineffectual: a little work against the Japs down in Burma, and one flight into Java against an oil target—things like that. But when it came to bombing Japan, it was bombing Japan from Chengtu or no place. So gasoline had to be hauled over the Himalayas.

Let me look at some of the dates. . . . 26 September we went to Anshan again. All in all, I think we got almost double the sorties in September which had been flown during the couple of months which preceded. I thought that was pretty good at the time, and still do, *under the circumstances*. But my new maintenance system was beginning to pay off a little bit.

On 14 October the B-29's flew to Formosa for the first time. And again, ten days later, they attacked aircraft factories there. We had made a concentrated effort to get a little ahead of the game on gas at Chengtu, so we were able to run another mission the next day. That was against Japan itself: aircraft assembly installations on Kyushu.

In those days I was trying to teach my crews to bomb in formation, as we had done with the 17's in Europe: put a pattern of bombs down. These weren't green crews by any means. They'd been bombing individually at night, but had absolutely no formation training in bombing. So I set up a training schedule to produce formation patterns. And what was the use of wasting bombs on any isolated range? Just as I surmised the first night or two after I got on the job, we could hunt up some Jap-held targets which might be attacked directly from India. That is, if we extended our range.

To do this it was necessary to push a lot of training in the use of fuel. That's something which we called "cruise control." In order to go to a target near the limit of one's range, it is essential that there be the soundest possible management of fuel. An inexperienced or heedless pilot pulls full throttle at the wrong altitude, and he's going to run out of coal before he gets home.

This meant that everybody had to work pretty hard. They did work hard. I've heard that some of them are still griping about it, and refusing to nominate me as their candidate in any WW II popularity contest.

We didn't have all the gas in the world, but at least we had more readily available in India than at Chengtu. We were only a commuter's distance from Calcutta, so a pipeline had been built all the way out to Kharagpur and beyond. It ran west to Chakulia, with a short branch going off to Dudhkundi; and the longest branch went to Piardoba, about forty miles north of our HQ. Charra was our only Very Heavy Bomber base in India which wasn't tied into the pipeline.

On 3 November, 20th Bomber Command attacked Rangoon; and 5 November they went to Singapore and hit the naval base there. That was the longest one yet: a target nearly two thousand miles away. Secondary was a group of oil refineries on Sumatra. Our crews had a rough time that day because of typhoons in the area. Also there were some busy little Jap fighters around. . . . November 11th the primary target was those assembly plants at Omura on Kyushu again; secondary targets in Shanghai and Nanking.

It didn't mean too much as yet. The B-29's hadn't made much of a splash in the war.

Just about this time the first Superfort units sent out from the ZI to the Marianas were beginning to arrive there. Possum Hansell tells a bitter story about this. He had asked that the units be flown to Saipan in squadron formation, in order to profit by the experience. His request was denied on the grounds that *the B-29 didn't have enough range to fly from Sacramento to Hawaii in formation*. Sacramento to Hawaii is a distance of twenty-four hundred miles. On any proposed mission in the future, from Saipan to a Japanese target, those same 29's would have to fly a round trip of nearly thirty-two hundred miles. Complete with a heavy bomb load, complete with enemy air-to-air and ground-to-air opposition. And "with no weather, communications or electronic navigation devices; and very restricted base facilities!"

In that letter to Major Boyle, previously quoted, General Hansell said: "I arrived on Saipan . . . early in October, to find that one of the bases could not be used at all by B-29's, and the other had *one* runway, 7000 feet long (5000 feet paved), a taxiway at one end only, about forty hardstands, and no other facilities whatever except for a bomb dump and a vehicle park with gasoline truck-trailers. Ground crews put up borrowed tents in what was certainly the most disorderly military encampment of the war. . . ."

So everybody had their troubles—the new 21st Bomber Command in the Marianas as well as our elder 20th Bomber Command in India. Our troubles down there were many and varied . . . troubles of the Himalayas in between, and then the troubles of China beyond.

Fate didn't even afford us complete coöperation when it came to using our advance bases around Chengtu: Pengshan, Hsinching and the others. When those pilots were being checked off in Salina, Kansas, or wherever, no one had told them that they might have to take off or land while some characters were trying to kill demons in front of them.

That is the literal truth. Every now and then some peasants would creep up and lie in waiting along the edge of the runway. They were very clever at eluding sentries; they'd lie there like rocks and never move. Then a B-29 would come a-roaring, either on takeoff or on landing, and promptly those same Chinese would go scuttling across the runway right in front of the aircraft.

You see, like the wheelbarrow operators, these people were always being pursued by vicious demons. Every vicious demon stayed immediately behind every unhappy Chinaman. But B-29's, in landing or takeoff procedure, were made to order for the purpose. You ran across in front of the 29; your demon started to high-tail it after you. And you got across, but the demon behind you got clobbered. Of course if you didn't figure out the situation properly, and if your timing was off, it was you who got hit; while the demon skidded to a halt and ran away safely, and could live on into the future to attach himself to some other unfortunate Chinese.

At this period there were three governments in China, scattered and spread over various areas. If you could have taken a large map and tinted it with different colored inks, the effect would have been indescribable. Say we put down red for the Communists under Mao Tse-tung, and blue for the Nationalists under Chiang Kai-shek. Then, for Japanese-occupied areas (where either Jap military leaders or puppets chosen from the ranks of the Chinese did the governing) we'd use yellow. Then try to paint the colors accurately in the regions where they belonged. The result might have resembled an old-fashioned crazy quilt, Chinese vintage. Or some of the modern abstract paintings.

I'd always been much interested in the story of how Mao conducted his famous Long March, 1934–35, fighting his way from the coast through at least twelve provinces, until finally he fetched up at Yenan, away up in the northwest. The actual campaign progressed over more than six thousand miles. So, as of 1944, Mao Tse-tung still controlled enormous areas in the north, northwest, and some in the east. Chiang had his own domains, ruled from the Nationalist capital at Chungking. The Japanese invaders held almost all the ports. In fact at one time I think the Japs held them all. As well as the large cities, highways and railroads.

Generally speaking, the Nationalist forces under Chiang and the Communists under Mao were both resistant to the Japanese. But, as Americans, our alliance in fact and theory was with Chiang Kai-shek and his Kuomintang armies, at Chungking or anywhere else.

Thus the posture of Mao was a kind of unsolved riddle. Would he persist in adopting the Russian Soviet attitude, or could he be persuaded into something like coöperation? There were also problems of illiteracy and ignorance on the part of the Chinese in rural and frontier areas. Most of those had never seen an American or even heard of one.

We knew that on our missions a certain percentage of B-29's were bound to sustain battle damage which would bring them to earth long before they reached Advance in the Chengtu Valley.

(In due time some of them actually did go down in Russian territory, and there ensued a weird series of events . . . the crews were treated more like prisoners than allies. They were shunted off and guarded in what amounted to jails. Their B-29's, if more or less intact, disappeared completely. We couldn't learn anything about our crews; didn't know whether they were dead or alive . . . the implacable infuriating silence of those Soviets ensued. Then, suddenly out of a clear sky, we'd hear that the boys were all right; they were being sent across the border. "Come down and get them." I think they kept one crew up there over a year.)

We had received every consideration from the Nationalist Chinese. But we could not help but wonder what would happen in Mao Tsetung's Communist areas. Those were *terra incognita* as far as we were concerned. We just didn't know how Mao would react. All I knew was that I wanted to get our crews out—and the 29's too, if it could be managed. So I sent an officer from our Communications section right up to Mao's headquarters. Sent him up in a Gooney Bird (C-47) with all the radio equipment which would be needed; and we asked Mao if he and his followers would help in getting our people out of there when they went down. He agreed to assist. That was something of a triumph for our side, because actually we were with Chiang. And, to the Communist mind, we were aiding and abetting Chiang in his opposition to their cause.

But these negotiations went through, and we secured the promise. Promptly I sent another C-47 up there, completely loaded with medi-

cal supplies. I knew that Mao had been cut off from the rest of the
world for about nine years. I should not pretend that this was all sweet-
ness and light on my part, and that I was making so free with our U.S.
taxpayers' sulfanilamide that I needed to furnish it to any Communists,
Chinese or otherwise. But I wanted to be *damn sure that there were
medical supplies in those areas when my own people came in,* busted
up or wounded. Naturally all we could do was subsidize the Chinese
Communists, medically and surgically speaking. Nor did I leave out
of the picture the fact that it would be bound to react favorably on our
people when Mao Tse-tung found himself possessed of those supplies.
He knew who'd given them to him.

The report came through, and it was all that we could have hoped.
Chinese Communist surgeons were actually in tears after that C-47
arrived and they began to offload the most important and valuable
freight which had ever landed there. The word went around; doctors
and medical orderlies came running in from far and near. They stayed
up the entire night, looking over the material we had sent, and Oh-ing
and Ah-ing over the contents of each case or crate. Some of them
hadn't even heard of the sulfa drugs; they were so new, and had come
into being since those Chinese doctors received their training on the
outside.

Our own medical personnel hastened to send up full instructions on
all the new stuff. We didn't want our charity to boomerang on us. . . .
Next thing it's announced that Mao Tse-tung has sent me a present: a
samurai sword, captured from the Japanese. Wouldn't be surprised if
Mao had taken it himself in hand-to-hand combat. He has a good reputation as a scrapper.

There were also some beautiful woodcuts made by artists at Yenan,
and a few other little odds and ends.

I reciprocated by sending Mao a fine pair of binoculars, and we had
some letters back and forth as well.

From then on everything was smooth as silk in our mutual relations.
He had his own radio system set up, with radio contact here and there
among his own people; and we had our own private station at Yenan.

One of our 29's would go down, and where was it? Next thing we
did was to report this to Mao. We'd lost somebody . . . didn't know
just where. . . . Fast as Mao got any report on the matter, he'd relay
it to me.

We were able to keep track of a lot of our crews this way. I remember one bunch: the 29 went down on the south shore of the Yellow
Sea. It was in a region more or less controlled by Mao's people, but
right next to the Japs. Next thing you knew there was a pitched battle
going, over that airplane and crews. As I remember it, the Communists
rescued all the crew except one man who fell into the hands of the
Japanese.

Then they fought another pitched battle over the airplane. Sometimes the information was a little garbled. We received a report that Communists were tearing engines out of the aircraft. I said, "Well, tell 'em to throw the engines away. What we want is our *crew*." So later we got reports on the crew. They were still walking when I left Assam and the Chengtu and went to the Marianas, in January of '45.

It was a long way home for those boys: four thousand miles across northern China and then down into friendly territory. Throughout that period I would receive reports, relayed along the line to those Old Faithfuls up there with our radio. Sometimes actually a report came in *every day*, just letting us know about the progress of our airmen. Their escort varied from ten to three thousand Chinese Communists. Sounds odd, but Mao's folks made very good sense about the whole thing. When it was just a case of going across country they would have merely enough Chinese along with our crew to guide them and care for them. But, in other areas, they might have to cross a railroad or a main highway which naturally was held by the Japanese. So they'd assemble enough people, in force, to take care of any Jap patrols which they might encounter.

. . . Sometimes elsewhere our crews had landed on or made their way to fields where we could actually fly in and pick them up. But in this particular region we didn't have any fields and we didn't know much about the topography either. Nothing to do but let our boys walk. And they walked, and in the end they got along fine. . . . You had people coming out of there sometimes on sturdy little Mongolian ponies, and wearing Chinese Communist uniforms, and with their pockets filled with Chinese Communist money. They were having a ball.

General Mao offered to build airdromes for us up in the north. He told me, "I can construct any number you wish." I replied that frankly we couldn't supply the ones we already had, down there in Chengtu.

But I thought it over, and then made a suggestion to Mao: it might be helpful if he improved the bad landing field already in existence there at his capital. We had to come in and land every now and then, to keep our radio detachment up to snuff. We had to haul in gasoline and other supplies to run his generators and radio. . . .

No sooner said than done. Everyone toiled to improve that field. There was one very high-ranking official who, according to accurate information which reached us later, made it a point to appear one day out of each week, and work on the field, hauling and pounding rocks just as hard as the next fellow. His name was Mao Tse-tung.

4

AROUND the first of the year I was suddenly ordered to Guam to meet Larry Norstad, who had become Hap Arnold's chief of staff for the 20th Air Force.

I didn't have an inkling what this was all about. All we'd heard was that the new B-29's over there in the Marianas didn't seem to have been earning any Merit Badges. At least their performance wasn't satisfying Hap Arnold.

The folks who gave me my orders wanted me to fly all around Robin Hood's barn in order to journey from Kharagpur to Guam. If any reader has a globe handy, he can take a look at it and see what was meant. A great deal of Jap-occupied territory lay in between.

I didn't see why we couldn't get there easily, flying across south of Formosa and right on to Guam. *My God,* they screamed. *Enemy territory!* But as yet I didn't know about The Bomb; so finally I was allowed to go by the route I'd selected, over enemy territory. Got out there without any difficulty, and sat down to talk with Norstad.

I was informed that they wanted me to taper off the 20th Bomber Command activities in India and China immediately, and instead come over to Guam and command the 21st Bomber Command. Operation MATTERHORN, code name for what we had been engaged in, would be phased out. Someone had finally tumbled to the fact that there was no profit in trying to supply the Chengtu Valley with gasoline for attacks on Japan.

General Arnold, fully committed to the B-29 program all along, had crawled out on a dozen limbs about a thousand times, in order to achieve physical resources and sufficient funds to build those airplanes and get them into combat. . . . So he finds they're not doing too well. He has to keep juggling missions and plans and people until the B-29's *do* do well. General Arnold was absolutely determined to get results out of this weapons system.

Here's another great big bear for you. Come and grab it by the tail.

Norstad told me, "We'll select a new commander for the 20th Bomber Command; and he'll stay in India, but only temporarily. The operations will be slowed. They can keep on with their system of on-the-job combat training against those lower targets; but they'll have to stop busting their ass to get supplies up to China. Get it set up for them to continue with your Lead Crew school system, and everything else you've got working, out there. But take it easy. They must husband their resources in crews and airplanes, because you can use them more effectively when you get them up here to the Marianas."

He said, "Just as fast as we have new fields open, the 20th Bomber

Command will be redeployed up here, and everything will be under the 21st, and under you."

Next thing was to decide who should take over my old job. Very quickly we picked on Roger Ramey for this.

. . . Kelly Field . . . Saturday, October 12th, 1929, was a clear day, the bright clear kind of day that Texans brag about. . . . Who stands forth now to present the wings so long desired? . . .

Those boy graduates were still getting around. Brigadier-General Roger M. Ramey had already had Fifth Bomber Command, and during his last stint he was chief of staff for Possum Hansell. Possum was going back to the States to Training Command. General Arnold had asked him to stay on in the Marianas as my Vice Commander; but Possum said Nothing Doing.

In that 1965 letter to Major Boyle, he spoke with complete frankness. "I declined. Not because of any friction with General LeMay. . . . But I knew him well enough to know that he didn't need any 'assistant commander' and I knew myself well enough to know that I would not be content to stay completely in the background. It is not a good thing to leave an ex-commander in the same outfit that he has commanded." True words.

So Roger Ramey cleared the base and packed his duds, and we cranked up the airplane and flew right back to India. I spent a few days with him there before I pulled out—doing the Blondie Saunders act all over again, helping him to get orientated.

Before departing on January 18th we had been able to run two or three rather exciting shows. I am thinking especially of the Formosa mission on January 14th, when for the first time we confined the operation to B-29's which had been fully modified. No use in dropping any extra ones because of the old bugs, especially now that the Chengtu Valley would be phased out.

A couple of days later the final mission from Chengtu was run against Shinchiku, and we had good weather and did a real good job on that one. Then the 20th Bomber Command said goodbye to the Chengtu Valley, and no tears were shed then—or ever will be shed, I reckon.

Incidentally it has been pointed out by postwar armchair critics that the selection of MATTERHORN as a code name for an operation which depended on flying all gas and supplies—and, eventually, all combat equipment—across tall snow-covered mountains— Some people have said that the Combined Planning Staff, or whoever was responsible for the designation, might as well have called our D-Day landings in France by the code name of NORMANDY. . . . Sure. The Matterhorn is in the Alps and not the Himalayas; but the theory has been advanced that it wouldn't have taken an excessively smart Japanese to figure out the whole thing.

5

IN SPEAKING about the construction on Guam, *AAFWW II* says: "The first troops and supplies for the depot were not unloaded until 9 November, at a time when construction work on warehouses, offices, and quarters had scarcely started. Seabee and aviation engineer troops were busy on airdome, harbor, road, and other high-priority projects. . . ."

So they're talking about early November, and I got to Guam on the 19th of January.

I've never been a master hand in the spy business; but I did get hold of a bootleg copy of the construction priority list on that island. Fact is, I sent it directly to General Arnold in Washington. That was really something.

It was *on the fifth page* of the priority list that we got anything to fight with.

The Navy had been hard at work otherwise. They had built tennis courts for the Island Commander; they had built fleet recreation centers, Marine rehabilitation centers, dockage facilities for inter-island surface craft, and every other damn thing in the world except subscribing to the original purpose in the occupation of those islands. The islands were attacked and taken and held because we needed them for air bases to strike against Japan. All along, that was the way it went. Guam, Tinian, Saipan, Iwo Jima, Okinawa— Thousands and thousands of young Americans died on those islands, in order to give us a base of operations against the Japanese homeland. And here people were, piddling around with all this other stuff, and not giving us anything to fly from or fight with.

When Tommy Power arrived to start operating at Guam, he came in on schedule. The only thing they'd built for him was a coral airstrip down through the jungle. He and his airmen slept on that, the first night they arrived. Next morning they had to tackle the jungle with pocketknives: no other equipment. That was the only manner in which they could clear away the brush and make space to set up their tents.

There was one huge basic fault inherent in the whole plan of organization out there. Admiral Nimitz was the theater commander; and first Possum Hansell, and now LeMay, commanded the B-29's. We were directly under General Hap Arnold, commanding the 20th Air Force as executive agent for the JCS. Nimitz had no operational control over the 29's. Thus he was awarded no credit for anything they accomplished, nor did he receive any censure for any failures which might come about. He had to give us his life's blood in logistics, in supply and support and so on. Quite naturally we didn't have things done for us.

And it was a great pity, from Arnold's standpoint. Because he and his folks in Washington had made a terrific effort and done a terrific job to get this thing set up. General Arnold did this so we would have a command in the Pacific where we were free to fly over anybody's theater, to do an overall job. Naturally Admiral Nimitz wanted everything he could get his hands on; General MacArthur wanted everything he could get his hands on; and General Stilwell wasn't behindhand in wanting everything as well. And we were flying over all three of their theaters. We simply *had* to have central coördination on this deal. But, on the other side of the coin, there was no way of insuring that we would receive proper logistic support in any sensible construction program.

At least in the Marianas we wouldn't be up against the tragic situation which had stifled us in the 20th Bomber Command. There every ounce of supplies—gas, bombs, the works—was shipped to the port of Calcutta. I think the bulk of it came across the Pacific from the United States; although some of the stuff may have come around through the South Atlantic. But we were a long way out, we were at the end of the line. And then we had that miserable business of lugging everything from the Assam Valley in India up to the Chengtu Valley in China: seven trips in order to fly one mission of an airplane. If we were going to put a hundred B-29's over a target, fetching them from India and gassing up and bombing up, and taking off from Chengtu, it meant the equivalent of seven hundred round trips across that hump of the Himalayas. Thus, in the Marianas, we were some thousands of miles nearer our source of supply. And we had—or were supposed to have—everything coming in by ship, everything we needed. And we wouldn't have to fly across the highest mountain range in the world.

However, may I point out that we were operating on a strictly utilitarian basis, especially in the days of our arrival. I wasn't really able to match the Navy, socially. Suppose I should have been very embarrassed about this, but actually I wasn't. I had been a poor relation plenty of times before.

First moment we landed on Guam, I received a nice invitation to dinner from the Theater Commander. I dragged my best uniform out of the B-4 bag, there in my tent, and hung it up so the clothing wouldn't be too wrinkled. But I did feel a little raunchy when I arrived at my host's for dinner, and found everyone in such immaculate turnouts. It was quite a place. The Theater Commander had built himself a splendid house, way up on the very highest peak of the island. That was Living. They had the usual retinue of Filipino boys, and they were immaculate too, those messboys; and here were cocktails and highballs and hors d'oeuvres such as you might find at an embassy in

Washington. We sat down to a gorgeous dinner: soup, fish course, then the roast and vegetables and salad, and a perfectly swell dessert, and demitasses, and brandy and cigars. It was great, and I appreciated it very much.

Next invitation was from the Island Commander. He had built a house on the second highest peak on the island. Didn't have quite so many Filipino messboys, and I think the dinner was one course less. But there was still plenty to drink, and wonderful cigars and after-dinner coffee, and mints and nuts. And it was still Living with a capital L.

Invitation Number Three: commander of the Submarine Force. His house turned out to be the Vanderbilt yacht, now bravely commissioned in the United States Navy. Our host was perfectly charming, and the Filipino messboys looked like something out of the Ritz or off the royal suite of the *Titanic*. Cocktails, hors d'oeuvres, roast beef. You name it, we had it.

About this time it looked like old LeMay was getting so involved socially that he'd have his back broken by obligations unless he started paying them off pretty quick. So I invited everybody down to my place. It was still the same tent, because we didn't have any quarters yet. Neither did we have the kind of quartermaster stores which were available to the Navy. I did promote a bottle of liquor, but I had to wheedle that out of some Neptune type. As for the rest, we took especial pains to serve up the best flight-rations available. That's what we were living on: canned stuff. I'll give the web-footed guests credit, and report that they stood up like real men throughout it all. Didn't complain, told stories, were right good company. They ate the canned rations because they were pretty hungry, and had been working hard. I don't remember exactly what was being built that week. Maybe a roller-skating rink.

The more I consider it in my old age, it seems that the Navy folks might not ever have eaten such rations before. Maybe they were a complete novelty. As such, the Navy found our food exciting.

And eventually they came up with the facilities we needed. And they built fine quarters for us, and we were right glad.

6

THE IMMEDIATE thing I was faced with there on Guam was a real training job once more. They had been going up to Japan at twenty-five and thirty thousand feet, high as they could get. Over in the ETO we hadn't known anything about jet streams, but now for the first time we ran into that ferocious jet stream of the Pacific. High winds, sometimes at two hundred mph. You could go on forever, trying to get up to a target in such a wind. And if you went cross-wind, your bomb-sight wouldn't take care of the drift you had. If you came in down-wind, you didn't have time to get a proper run on the target. This was really a tough proposition to lick.

In addition to that, of course, even during the best weather months over the Japanese area, there might be seven days per month when you could do any visual bombing. And what weatherman, professional or amateur, hankered after the job of determining *which* seven days of the month those visual days were going to be?

If we had had any weather coöperation from the Russians in Siberia, it might have helped some; but they gave us almost no assistance whatsoever. We received meager quantities of information from time to time, offered most grudgingly, but we could never depend on it. Of course we had put some weather stations of our own up there in deeper China. (Same time I was making the deal with Mao to get my people out of there. I did that completely on my own: furnished the gasoline out of my own ration, and sent it up to run the generators and stuff, and keep them supplied.) That helped in the end. But there is no way in which any weather personnel—however experienced, discerning, hard-working and/or devoted—can make good bombing weather out of bad bombing weather.

With those overheating engines, it began to seem that this high alti-tude stuff was strictly for the birds. The airplanes had been breaking down. There are something like 55,000 different parts in a B-29; and frequently it seemed that maybe 50,000 of them were all going wrong at once. I feel that the majority of our losses were due more to our own mechanical problems than they were to the Japanese defense system.

Main thing to do, it seemed, was to get them down in altitude. Then we'd get a lot more hours' service out of each engine. And, since the bombing had been stinko most of the time, to teach the crews to put patterns on the target.

This consideration makes me think now of a bet which I lost—one bet which I was very glad to lose. Going back to India for a moment, it will be remembered that we started a concentrated bombing practice over there. They weren't doing much good, early in the game. But later on they got so that they could really bomb just as well as people ever bombed in Europe. And in this case with more effect on the en-emy; because, naturally, there was a bigger load in the formation. The B-17 could carry three tons. The B-29 could carry seven or ten or more, depending on the range.

The first time they really got a pattern down out of the formation was on a cement plant in lower Burma somewhere. It was the only cement plant in the area. The Japs were building concrete roads and whatnot, so I thought it would be a good target to practice on. (The boys used to have some grim things to say about losses incurred in our "practice milk-runs." Bomber crews usually had a lot of grim things to say, anyway.)

Can't remember exactly what their load was on this target; but the thing was sufficiently close to enable us to devote part of our normal gasoline tonnage to bombs instead. When the smog cleared away there was absolutely nothing left of that cement plant. Our people had done a perfect job.

All right, now for the bet. After elements of the former 20th Bomber Command came up to Tinian in the Marianas, their first mission against a daylight target was a steel plant in the southern part of Japan. Butch Blanchard's outfit was going on the trip (that's the present General William H. Blanchard, Vice Chief of Staff, USAF). Well, they hadn't been flying daylight against Japan, and they were at a new home base, so on. I felt justified in betting five bucks against Butch that his group wouldn't do a very good job on that Japanese target.

They went up there, and they put down a perfect pattern on that steel mill. Afterward he showed me the telltale photographs, and I reached in my pocket and got out five bucks.

"Sign here," says Butch, making like it was a short snorter. He took the bill and had it framed.

Long years afterward (just a while back) somebody stole that five-dollar bill while Butch was working in the Pentagon. Too bad. But it was still the most profitable five bucks I ever invested.

When I spoke of seven days a month for bombing visually in Japan, that was a complete max. The average might have been three or four days a month. This was all we could hope for, based on past records. But it was necessary to forecast from Guam, with the very meager information available, which day was going to be *the visual day*. It was enough to make Weather and Operations and Planning and everybody else— Enough to make them want to take their dolls and go home.

We tried tinkering with the Russians' codes, and we did break their codes down every now and then, and salvaged whatever weather information they were sparking back and forth to each other. But when they changed codes, which they did with diabolical frequency, we had no help from that source. Had to start code-busting all over again. Once in a while also they went through the motions of assisting us with information, as I've said; but it was never adequate. They were reluctant and suspicious by nature.

I'd been doing a lot better in the academic department than I'd done with Bombardment. By this time we had the wing commanders convinced that I knew what I was talking about. The Lead Crew school routine was going full blast. Same old business all over again, as in

India and in the ETO before that: *get people educated as to what they should be doing.* At least I did know something about personnel available for various jobs, so I started casting around and reeling them in—people who, in my opinion, really knew their stuff. Here came old-timers like Augie Kissner and J. B. Montgomery. The eminent Professor J. J. Preston of the old 305th ran our Lead Crew school. By the last of January, I think, we had things pretty well organized. At least we knew where we were *going* to go.

But another month of indifferent operations went by, and when I summed it all up, I realized that we had not accomplished very much during those six or seven weeks. We were still going in too high, still running into those big jet stream winds upstairs. Weather was almost always bad.

I sat up nights, fine-tooth-combing all the pictures we had of every target which we had attacked or scouted. I examined Intelligence reports as well.

Did actually very much in the way of low-altitude flak exist up there in Japan? I just couldn't find it.

There was food for thought in this.

Far as radar was concerned, we were getting sets in our B-29's by this time. But no one knew much about radar. Over in Europe, the year before and the year before that, we had been fiddling around with the stuff but not doing well at all.

Most of the radar operators were ex-gunners: low men on the totem pole. The idea about a gunner was that he couldn't absorb enough training to become a radio operator or an engineer; so, frankly, many of the gunners weren't very good, and their training was pretty sorry as well. I mean after they got into the radar business. Their training consisted of (about): "This is a radar set. This is the way you turn it on."

I got Doc Gould, a capable scientific type, assigned to my headquarters out there, and sent him up to Saipan. I told Doc, "Look. You go up there and pick out a couple of the stupidest radar operators they have, and Lord knows that's pretty stupid. You go up and fly with them and see—" We went over and examined a chart. "—And see if they can fly over this spit of land sticking out on the northern side of the island. That's a real good land-water contrast. Go see if they can do that."

So Doc went up and spent several days with the Saipan people. When he came back he was really sick. He hadn't realized how inefficient those operators were, and how weak their training had been. How little, all in all, they knew about their equipment. . . .

And you can't blame this on the unfortunate radar people as a group. The first radar operators whom we received had been chosen from the body of gunners. They were unable to absorb much technical training. There hadn't been much time to devote to them.

I was aware of this. So was Doc Gould.

He said with reluctance, "I guess maybe they can do it. But they sure need a lot of training."

Well, I could see that we were going to add radar to our curriculum where schools were concerned, and do some on-the-job activity. If they could actually fly over a good land-water contrast, miserable as they were, there would be some point in stepping up the training.

In the other departments we had been seeking out some Japs to bomb: places not too far away, which we could handle. We'd gone down to Truk and up to Iwo Jima and similar spots, but that was about all the practice we'd had. For the radar people I needed another sort of target.

Thus eventually we based their first mission on the land-water contrast principle.

Old Doc Gould's words kept recurring to me. "Yes, they can fly over that teat of land, if the set's working. If the set's not working, they're not going to get it working. It's either in or out. But—if it's *in*, they'll be able to get there."

I said O.K., and kept thinking about it. And went back to studying the flak situation once more.

The Japanese just didn't seem to have those 20- and 40-millimeter guns. That's the type of defense which must be used against bombers coming in to attack at a low or medium altitude. Up at twenty-five or thirty thousand feet they have to shoot at you with 80- or 90-millimeter stuff, or they're never going to knock you down.

The Germans defended their principal targets with both types of guns. If you'd tried going in over a German target at five or seven thousand feet with heavy bombers, they would have murdered you. But 88-millimeter guns, *if you come in low,* are impotent. You're moving too fast. They cannot coördinate their fire in order to make it effective from a standpoint of defense.

I talked to a very few of the boys about this, and studied their reactions. Some of them thought that it would be O.K. to revolutionize our whole process and go over Japanese targets at low altitudes. Others said, "God. That would be slaughter," and they were fully convinced that it would be.

Also there was the assumption that we might surprise the Japs on a mission or two at low altitude, but certainly they would rectify the mistake immediately. If we did anything along this line, we'd have to do it quickly. Then we'd be forced back up to altitudes again.

And I could never be certain just how good my Intelligence really was. We had pictures; we couldn't find any low-altitude defense; but that didn't mean that it wasn't there.

My reasoning told me that I was heading toward a correct decision . . . still I couldn't substantiate it to myself, right up and down the line, with ironclad information. It got down to this:

We had, on the credit side of the ledger, (a) our photographic interpretation of targets where we'd taken pictures, and (b) other intelligence from the usual espionage sources, etc. It added up to practically no light flak defending the Japanese targets.

On the debit side: just one item. Great big one: (a) how the hell were we going to prove one hundred per cent that the light flak *wasn't* there?

General Arnold needed results. Larry Norstad had made that very plain. In effect he had said: "You go ahead and get results with the B-29. If you don't get results, you'll be fired. If you don't get results, also, there'll never be any Strategic Air Forces of the Pacific—after the battle is finally won in Europe, and those ETO forces can be deployed here. If you don't get results it will mean eventually a mass amphibious invasion of Japan, to cost probably half a million more American lives."

7

. . . Must have had the idea in the back of my brain when I talked to Norstad. I kept toying with it. I said to Norstad, "You know General Arnold. I don't know him. Does he ever go for a gamble? What do you think?"

. . . Let's see: we could load with E-46 clusters. Drop them to explode at about two thousand feet, say, or twenty-five hundred. Then each of those would release thirty-eight of the M-69 incendiary bombs. . . . Wouldn't have to employ all the same type of incendiaries, of course. Could use both napalm and phosphorus. Those napalm M-47's.

. . . They say that ninety per cent of the structures in Tokyo are built of wood. That's what Intelligence tells us, and what the guidebooks and the *National Geographic* and things like that— They all say the same. Very flimsy construction.

. . . *General Bush, sir. I'd be perfectly satisfied just to enlist, in order to get up on the priority list. Because I'm determined to go to flying school.*

. . . Bringing those 29's all the way down from thirty thousand to about nine or even five thousand. A lot of people will tell me that flesh and blood can't stand it. Maybe they'll be right: maybe flesh and blood *can't.*

. . . Norstad didn't have an idea what I was thinking about. But he did opine that he thought General Arnold was all for going in and getting the war won. Certainly Larry didn't say enough to convince me that I'd get off scot free if I made a mistake. But I did gain the impression that being a little unorthodox was all right with Hap Arnold.

. . . So this is what you call being a little unorthodox? What are you—British? Elveden Hall gone to your head? Want to be president of the Department of Understatement? O.K. You're elected.

. . . I think it was Velma—maybe it was Lloyd—who had that toy village. Well, maybe some other kid in the neighborhood really owned it. But it was one of those villages that you set up . . . the houses come all flat, but they're hinged at the corners; and then you spread 'em out and shove the roof down, with the eaves going up through slots and so on; and thus your house sits like a strawberry box. Well, I remember they had the village all set up out in the backyard. And some mean kid says, "Let's see if we can burn it down." So he set fire to the first house. And, brother, they all went.

. . . Just which Medium outfit was it? I know it was over in England, and it was Mediums. Yep. The 322nd, along in May of '43. I think they had one abortion. But the rest of the group went on to Holland and attacked at low altitude. Not one B-26 came home that day. So that's what happens at low altitudes.

. . . Always?

. . . The mother writes you a letter, and she says: "Dear General. This is the anniversary of my son Nicky being killed over Tokyo. You killed him, General. I just want to remind you of it. I'm going to send you a letter each year on the same date, the anniversary of his death, to remind you."

. . . All right, by God. If I do it I won't say a thing to General Arnold in advance. Why should I? He's on the hook, in order to get some results out of the B-29's. But if I set up *this* deal, and Arnold O.K.'s it beforehand, then he would have to assume some of the responsibility. And if I don't tell him, and it's all a failure, and I don't produce any results, then he can fire me. And he can put another commander in here, and still have a chance to make something out of the 29's. This is sound, this is practical, this is the way I'll do it: not say *one word* to General Arnold.

. . . No bomb-bay tanks either. Nothing but bombs in those bomb-bays. We won't need all that extra gas if we're not going to altitudes.

. . . How do I get that way, saying *we? I* can't go on this mission if we run it. A man came and talked to me, and I know something about a Firecracker. So I can't go. No use asking, no use trying to pry loose the permission. It won't work. I know about the Firecracker now, and no other one of my people does know about it. . . . Tommy Power is all in favor of this low-level incendiary attack. If we run it, I'll let him lead.

. . . Just because a few people are for it, that doesn't mean that *everybody* is for it. And if we go to hell in a handbasket, *nobody* will be for it. When you dream up something successful, everybody else thought of it first. You dream up something disastrous, and nobody wants a part of it. They knew all along that it wouldn't work.

. . . At least we could say forget the weather. We've proved that even the stupidest radar operators can get us over that land-water contrast up there at Tokyo. If we send some veterans in ahead, they're bound to get on the target, and they're bound to start the fires. If we really get a conflagration going, the ones that come in later can see the glow. They can drop on that.

. . . *LeMay, what's the weather report for today? LeMay, how many airplanes have we got in commission today?*

. . . And there's another way we can save weight. Take out all the defensive armament. Repeat: remove all defensive armament from every B-29. Every gun goes out, all the ammunition goes out. No guns, no ammunition. At least our folks won't be shooting at each other.

. . . So if we go in low—at night, singly, not in formation—I think we'll surprise the Japs. At least for a short period of time; but certainly they will adjust to our new tactics before long. But if this first attack is successful, we'll run another, right quick. Say twenty-four hours afterward. Two days at the most. And then maybe another.

. . . "Dear General Burnside. This is the anniversary of the death of my son Sam, whom you killed at Fredericksburg. Dear General Hancock. Twenty years ago today, you killed my son Benjy at Chancellorsville. I just want you to remember this. I will send you a letter every year."

. . . Not only take out the guns and the ammunition. Take out all the gunners too. Less weight, and fewer people jeopardized. But I think we'd better leave the tail gunners in, for observation purposes.

. . . Let's see. Say we use an intervalometer setting of fifty feet. I reckon one aircraft could burn up about sixteen acres of territory.

. . . Plenty of strategic targets right in that primary area I'm considering. All the people living around that Hattori factory where they make shell fuses. That's the way they disperse their industry: little kids helping out, working all day, little bits of kids. I wonder if they still wear kimonas, like the girls used to do in Columbus in those Epworth League entertainments, when they pretended to be Geisha girls, with knitting needles and their grandmother's old combs stuck in their hair.

. . . Well, the new maintenance setup worked. And the Lead Crew school worked. And the critiques after the missions worked. And the combat box worked; and the straight-and-level bomb run worked. But that doesn't mean that everything I decide to do is going to work. You can't disregard the law of averages. Or can you? One of these fine days

I'm going to dream up something that doesn't work, and this just might be the time.

. . . *LeMay, I want the* Utah. *You'd better find it for me.*

> They taught me how to fly,
> And they sent me here to die.
> I've got a bellyful of war. . . .
>
> Come on and get promoted
> As high as you desire.
> You're riding on the gravy train,
> When you're an Army flyer.
> But just about the time you are
> A general, you will find
> Your wings fall off, and your engine quits,
> And you will never mind.

. . . We don't *think* that their night fighters amount to anything. We don't think that their *night fighters* amount to anything. We don't think that their night fighters amount to *anything.* And we could be wrong as hell.

. . . If we try this, I want to try it with at least three hundred airplanes. Let's see: take the 73rd. I guess Rosie O'Donnell can put up at least a hundred and fifty, over there on Saipan. The 313th . . . I guess Skippy Davies ought to be able to put up at least a hundred; maybe more. The 314th, here on Guam, they're green as gourds. And they're not up to strength. I guess maybe Tommy could put up fifty.

. . . Need at least three hundred over that target to do the kind of job that should be done. I wish to God we could send five hundred B-29's instead.

. . . We can have some graphs drawn: indicate the experience which each crew has. That would help a lot in determining their gas loadings. Green crews always burn a lot more gas. An experienced crew can get the full range with a full bomb load. But an inexperienced crew always uses more gas.

. . . Yes, and I had one grand chore convincing the crews that they ought to come down (from twenty-eight or thirty thousand feet) to twenty or twenty-three, for daylight stuff. I finally got that done, but we still haven't achieved any special results. Now I'm speculating on telling them that they've got to come down to five or seven thousand feet. And no gunners, and no guns.

. . . *Why all the eagerness to enlist in one of my batteries, son?*

. . . With at least three hundred planes we can get a good concentration. So that'll be our first mission—with all those sorry radar operators as well as the capable ones. Just go up and fly over that wad of land in

Tokyo Bay, turn on the heading we give them, continue so many seconds, and pull the string.

. . . "Dear General Washington. Dear General Knox. Dear General Gates. Dear General Greene. This is the anniversary of the day you killed my son Eben, my son Jeremiah, my son Watson, my son John. You killed him at Princeton, at Monmouth, at Saratoga, at Germantown."

. . . How many times have we just died on the vine, right here on these islands? We assembled the airplanes, assembled the bombs, the gasoline, the supplies, the people. We got the crew set—everything ready, to go out and run the mission. Then what would we do? Sit on our butts and wait for the weather.

. . . So what am I trying to do now? Trying to get us to be *independent of weather*. And when we get ready we'll *go*.

. . . Intelligence says that every one of those factories is surrounded by a hundred-foot firebreak. But if we really got rolling with incendiaries, and had a wind to help us with the flames, firebreaks wouldn't make any difference.

. . . Ninety per cent of the structures made of wood. By golly, I believe that Intelligence report said ninety-*five!* And what do they call that other kind of cardboard stuff they use? *Shoji.* That's it.

. . . I remember running those missions for Chennault out of the Chengtu. He was always pestering me to do things for him. I ran that mission against Nanking, and the one against Hankow. Incendiary attacks: warehouse and supply installations at Nanking, and docks and storage facilities at Hankow. Everything was fouled up there, beginning with Chennault's last minute request for a change in our Time over Target . . . people dropped in the wrong sequence, smoke obscured the primary areas, so on. But that was an *incendiary* attack, and everything which was hit burned like crazy. And I think there was a vast similarity to the *type of construction* in Japan.

. . . That's over three thousand miles. And no gas in the bomb-bays. Let's see: I think we could average out at about six tons of incendiaries per airplane.

. . . *You concern yourself with staying in formation, and let someone else worry about the flak.* Well, I'm worrying about it now.

"Dear General Marshal Ney. This is the anniversary of the day you managed to kill off my son François. . . . Dear General Pompey. This is the anniversary of the day you slew my son Junius. Dear General. . . ."

. . . R-Roger. How many types do we employ? We use the E-46 clusters, but we don't load entirely with that stuff. We've got to use some other types as well. Also mix in some high explosive bombs, especially in the 314th if I have Tommy lead. Those HE's will make the Japs stay under cover, and not come rushing out to extinguish the first fires.

. . . Each type of weapon has some good points as well as some bad points; but if I now had my choice, and had available an overwhelming quantity of any type of fire bomb which could be employed, I wouldn't stick to one particular type. No. Of course magnesium makes the hottest fire, and it'll get things going where probably the napalm might not. But the napalm will splatter farther, cover a greater area. We've got to mix it up. We're not only going to run against those inflammable wooden structures. We're going to run against masonry too. That's where the magnesium comes handy.

. . . No matter how you slice it, you're going to kill an awful lot of civilians. Thousands and thousands. But, if you don't destroy the Japanese industry, we're going to have to invade Japan. And how many Americans will be killed in an invasion of Japan? Five hundred thousand seems to be the lowest estimate. Some say a million.

. . . We're at war with Japan. We were attacked by Japan. Do you want to kill Japanese, or would you rather have Americans killed?

. . . *I hope you're right, Curt.*

. . . Crank her up. Let's go.

8

Drafts from the Tokyo fires bounced our airplanes into the sky like ping-pong balls. A B-29 coming in after the flames were really on the tear would get caught in one of those searing updrafts. The bombers were staggered all the way from five to nine thousand feet, to begin with. But when fires sent them soaring, they got knocked up to twelve and fifteen thousand feet.

According to the Tokyo fire chief, the situation was out of control within thirty minutes. It was like an explosive forest fire in dry pine woods. The racing flames engulfed ninety-five fire engines and killed one hundred and twenty-five firemen.

Well, I told about it in the first chapter of this book . . . burning up nearly sixteen square miles of the world's largest city. I walked the floor down there on Guam all night long. Tommy Power (following my instructions) after he'd dropped his own bombs, flew back and forth over the scene, making pictures. He went up to twelve and even twenty thousand feet to examine the situation. He'd brought along some cartographic types who could sketch accurately; and unless I'm severely mistaken he made a lot of sketches himself. He reported to our HQ by radio, and told of the inferno. But—point is—I wouldn't know what our losses were until all the surviving planes were back on Tinian, Saipan, Guam.

. . . There were some photographs too, snapped in the glare of the flames, but of course they didn't compare with the candid record of next day, when reconnaissance planes flew over Tokyo. Fact is, fires were so intense that they didn't linger in the burning. The blaze was practically out by noon of March 10th. Then some very clear recco photographs could be taken. These I sent along promptly to General Arnold.

If it hadn't been for that big river curving through the metropolitan area, a lot more of the city would have gone. About one fourth of all the buildings in Tokyo went up in smoke that night anyway. More than two hundred and sixty-seven thousand buildings.

I quoted General Power . . . that line about casualties, and Nagasaki and Hiroshima, away back at the beginning of this book. No use repeating it now.

Contrary to supposition and cartoons and editorials of our enemies, I do not beam and gloat where human casualties are concerned.

I'll just quote *AAFWW II,* Volume V, page 617, and let it go at that. "The physical destruction and loss of life at Tokyo exceeded that at Rome . . . or that of any of the great conflagrations of the western world— London, 1666 . . . Moscow, 1812 . . . Chicago, 1871 . . . San Francisco, 1906. . . . Only Japan itself, with the earthquake and fire of 1923 at Tokyo and Yokohama, had suffered so terrible a disaster. *No other air attack of the war, either in Japan or Europe, was so destructive of life and property."*

The italics are my own.

General Arnold wired me. "Congratulations. This mission shows your crews have got the guts for anything." It was a nice telegram but I couldn't sit around preening myself on that. I wanted to get going, just as fast as was humanly possible. And my idea of what was humanly possible sometimes did not coincide with the opinions of others.

I saw that if we were to achieve the maximum effect in this attack, a second assault against an enemy target should come immediately after the first. It would be possible, I thought, to knock out all of Japan's major industrial cities during the next ten nights.

. . . Fourteen planes only, lost out of three hundred and twenty-five which started the mission. Not much like Regensburg.

I told my wing commanders that I hoped they'd be able to start for Nagoya on the evening of March 10th. They just couldn't make it. However they got three hundred and thirteen B-29's off the ground during the afternoon of March 11th, and went to Nagoya. That was Japan's third largest city . . . to the Japanese aircraft industry what Seattle is to Boeing.

This time we tried to step up the intervalometer settings to one hundred feet. It seemed to me that perhaps we had been concentrating our detonations at Tokyo more tightly than we actually needed to, and by scattering bombs more widely we could achieve the same results, but over a larger area.

Nagoya showed how wrong I was. We needed that close setting. Had it figured out right, from the start. But our bombing wasn't up to the Tokyo standard anyway. Tommy Power's people got right on the target, but the others were a little too short. Still there was a lot of blaze.

In one breath someone was telling me about the tail gunners who had been posted for observation in the gunless tails of 29's which left Tokyo a day or two before. They could see that red glow when they were gone a hundred and fifty miles away from the target. And in the next breath someone would be reporting about Nagoya, and telling how they had word from the Navy that a submarine had surfaced a hundred and fifty miles offshore from Nagoya, and the submarine reported that its visibility was cut to one mile by thick wood smoke.

We were putting some guns and gunners back in the airplanes again. Word might have gotten around to the Jap fighters about our lack of defensive equipment; and I didn't want any massacre to ensue on subsequent missions.

Osaka was Target Number Three. We still managed to get three hundred and one B-29's airborne on March 13th.

AAFWW II again: "The planes carried the same 6-ton bomb load, but the low wing was given 50-caliber ammunition for lower forward and aft turrets as well as for the tail guns. When the force of 274 planes that got over Osaka found an eight-tenths cloud cover, it had to resort to radar bombing. This proved an advantage rather than a handicap. Unable to sow their bombs by sighting visually on pathfinder fires, bombardiers were forced to drop after a controlled run, releasing on an offset aiming point. With this technique, the B-29's achieved a thicker and more uniform pattern than had been possible with the impressionistic methods used at Nagoya.

"The results showed conclusively that the Tokyo raid had not been a fluke."

Kobe was Number Four. We hit that on the night of March 16th. It's right across the bay from Osaka. And on the 19th of March we went back to Nagoya again . . . two hundred and ninety B-29's put down eighteen or nineteen hundred tons of explosives and incendiaries.

Then we ran out of bombs. Literally.

Let's go back and consult Major Boyle for the final time, and hear what he was to say in his *Air Force* article:

"The ten-day fire blitz of March was a turning point. The morale of the Japanese people began a steady decline, never to rise again. Industries suddenly ceased to exist, or operated at greatly reduced rates. The panic-stricken people began an exodus from the major cities. The rate of absenteeism in the war industries recorded an alarming rise. The population of Tokyo dropped from over five million on January 1, 1945, to two and one-third million on August 1."

All my logic, my reasoning, had told me that this would come about. But it still remained to be *proved*, until the operations had actually taken place. We could have been surprised; but thank God we weren't.

In any case it was my decision and my order which sent the B-29's to the task in the manner described. I was glad that I had not consulted General Arnold. I'd talked to subordinates, and some had gone along with me in the notion, and others had disapproved, sincerely and almost heartbrokenly. But again— *My* decision and *my* order. There has to be a commander.

Going up into the future again, one day in the summer of 1964 I had what you might call a turn. In old-fashioned slang: *it gave me a turn.*

The thing which set it off was a United Press story, front page in the newspapers. It ran like this, with a Tokyo dateline: "U.S. Air Force planes began bombing an inferno of burning oil refineries at Niigata with extinguishing chemicals Wednesday, to try to prevent further devastation from the worst earthquake to hit Japan since the 1923 cataclysm. Fires raged uncontrolled through three oil refineries in Japan's largest petroleum center, 160 miles across Honshu Island from Tokyo. Authorities said the fires would not burn themselves out for days, unless the flames were extinguished. . . ."

But the headlines which accompanied the story were the thing that really made me blink. U.S. PLANES BOMBING FIERCE JAPAN FIRES.

You could think to yourself, "What a whale of a difference nineteen years makes."

Well, in 1945, I didn't like the idea of running out of bombs; but it wasn't my fault, as I'll explain pretty soon. But I did think, with all that successful campaign, that a man might have the right to some sort of mild celebration.

I decided to celebrate. I would go to the Navy PX.

Back in the section dealing with cadet days, I told about learning to smoke cigars on Guam. This was the time. Pipe tobacco had gotten more mildewed and more mildewed, so a cigar was usually growing out of my mouth. All we had at our PX were just the ordinary PX types. Everyone will know what I mean: Muriels, Roi-Tans, Phillies, White Owls, so on. They're good enough cigars (I'll still smoke one

gladly if I don't happen to have anything around that I like better).
But in those days—

There hadn't been any Castro and there hadn't been any Cuban
Revolution, and the folks down there who made the juicy Partagas
and Belindas and Upmanns and Ramon Allones— They were still on
the job, still rolling wrappers around the filler in those pungent old
factory rooms with the guy sitting up on a high stool, reading aloud
news or mysteries or romance as the case might be, to all the workers.

And the Navy had *Havana cigars*. Every now and then you could
persuade a Jack Tar friend to go down there for you, maybe, if your
persuasive powers were operating. Trouble was, we were supposed
to use our own PX, not the Navy one. But I craved a celebration, and
I was going to celebrate with Havanas or know the reason why.

The idea was to go into that PX and stand around and look sort of
hopeless and starved and woebegone. Then, if you were lucky, the
good-natured web-footed Post Exchange officer might take pity on you
and let you have a box of Havanas.

By golly, I got my Havanas this trip.

. . . Same way with whiskey. Those unfortunate salt-sprayed characters were down to a bottle of whiskey a week and two cans of beer
a day. That was their ration. We, in the Army Air Forces, didn't have
any liquor ration. We used to listen to some of the blue-suited boys
complaining bitterly about that one bottle of whiskey a week. It just
broke our hearts to hear them.

9

ONE TIME I had a friend, another veteran who was by way of being a
musician in his spare time—when he had any spare time, which wasn't
often. He was fond of stringed instruments, and in boyhood had been
instructed in this skill: could play the violin and viola. I remember
something he said, after he'd returned from a particularly baffling and
demanding tour of duty. He spoke more or less in the following
manner:

"You know, the young human soul is like a gut or wire string on an
instrument. It's always pretty well tightened up. As any string grows
tauter, so does the note which it gives forth rise higher in the scale. I'd
say that the difference between being in combat and not being in
combat is just about a full octave. You wind up a string too tightly and
it's going to snap. If it's really defective, with a severe flaw in it, the
string will snap the moment you begin to twist the peg. . . . Good
strings have tolerance. They can be tightened and tautened until the
note goes higher and higher. And there are some superior strings
which won't break, no matter how long you twist. Those are rarities."

While I was still in Europe, a couple of first-lieutenant medico types—typical head-shrinkers—had shown up at my command. I asked them why they'd come. They said that they were down there to investigate combat fatigue.

"Investigate what?"

"Well, maybe you haven't observed any, sir, in your outfit. But certainly it's started showing up in some other outfits around in the various commands. Or at least some people think it's *going* to show up."

"What did you say you call it?"

"*Combat* fatigue."

"What's that?"

They said, "It depends on a man's mental attitude. In fact, combat fatigue *is* a certain attitude. It's a mental and/or physical breakdown, caused by shock, protracted strain, danger, fear, and all that sort of thing."

One of them added, "Frankly, we don't think much of the whole idea. We can't believe that there is such a constant pressure in this air combat routine as to cause any breakdowns of the sort described by believers."

All I got out of this was that he thought we didn't have a rough time in combat. So I made a hospitable suggestion. "If you want to look into this matter, I think the best way I can suggest is for you both to fly on some missions. We'll be happy to open our command here to the opportunity for—investigation or experimentation or whatever you want to call it. You people go get checked out on flight equipment, oxygen and so on; and then we'll send you on the next mission."

So they went. Matter of fact, our folks got really shot up that day. But these were pretty good boys. They not only went back to the few rudiments of gunnery in which they had once been instructed, and clung tightly to their machine guns; but they took care of the wounded as well. Indeed, they probably saved one man's life. Lucky for him that I took a notion to send them on that mission. . . .

In this manner they got the point early in the game. They were no longer inimical to the notion of combat fatigue.

Trouble was, the moment we found out about this mysterious ailment we started having it in droves. Very interesting point.

Eventually I proved to my own satisfaction, however, something which I had understood in rudimentary fashion, back in the days when the 305th went downhill and then went up again. That was when, as related, people decided that the attrition was too severe in a twenty-five mission tour. Everybody would get shot down, and the last B-17 would take off from Britain in early March; and Ira Eaker, by his own testimony, would be on it. So morale went up.

If there's no escape, you don't experience combat fatigue.

You may get the soul scared out of you and the life shot out of you —or pretty well shot out—but you won't be suffering from combat fatigue, so-called.

Take one ordinary mission, or any demanding and dangerous flight. You're frightened beforehand, perhaps . . . you're worried about whether you will deliver what you should deliver; whether you will exercise your command in proper fashion; whether you'll be able to live up to the job, generally speaking.

But once you're *committed,* once you go chugging down that runway, once you're off to the races—you're not scared. You're busy, you're doing your job. No chance to be scared. If you're going to be knocked down, or if you're going to burn up from a hit in the gas tank— O.K. So that's going to be. There's not one thing you can do about it.

Take the record down at Malta, in the Mediterranean. Malta suffered a frightful beating during the war. From the very start it was the nearest to the southern Axis positions—nearest by a cool thousand miles—of any base in British hands. The RAF and the Fleet Air Arm of the Royal Navy defended the island with resolution. Gasoline had to be brought in by submarine—gas and ammunition and a lot of other matériel, when the siege was at its worst. You can guess what the food situation was like.

Day after day, week after week, for three solid years the population of Malta was bombed and fropped and shelled. Civilian casualties came to more than 4,800.

And nobody ever reported any combat fatigue.

Ceremonial history was made in 1942. Never throughout the record of the British Empire or the British Commonwealth had any *portion* of those nations been honored by the award of a decoration. But King George gave the George Cross to the island and people of Malta.

And there *was* no combat fatigue.

Because there existed absolutely no escape from the threat, no avenue of retreat was open. Suppose a man did break down, and they flung him in the hospital? It was just as bad to be in the hospital as it was out on the airstrip.

The medicos tried to find a cure for the ailment; they never did find one. We in Command and in Operations evolved some procedures all by ourselves. Sometimes one approach was employed, sometimes another. Usually they worked pretty well. Different types of people required different treatment.

First, let's take the average boy as he appeared in the war. He's a young man from a respectable home. He was a moderately successful student, and maybe he worked after school, and maybe he went to church or temple, or maybe he didn't. He had his share of boyish pranks and sins. He had his share of stringency and going without, let us hope; and maybe we can also trust that he had his little nibbles at luxury now and then. He's a good boy, not an exceptional boy: just an average recruit, or—save the mark—an average second-lieutenant. He has a sense of responsibility, normal and natural fears and apprehensions, a normal amount of courage, the normal ratio of patriotism and all that.

Oh yes, he used to scrap a little when he was a kid, or if somebody picked on his sister, or somebody was brutal to a cat. Yes, he'd fight then. He's not by nature a slugger, and certainly not by nature a killer. Far as fighting in a war goes, he'd a lot rather goof off at touch football or bouncing a big rubber ball on the beach. He doesn't want to be killed; nor is he particularly anxious to kill any other mortal.

I guess everybody knew a lot of boys like that. Surely there were a lot of 'em around.

. . . But he doesn't agree with Hitler's ideology, and he doesn't like what the Germans were trying to do to the world; or what the Japs did to us at Pearl Harbor even while their envoys smirked, and talked about peace, in Washington. Fundamentally he's been brought up on a code which despises treachery and genocide and the rest of the enemy's methods and purposes. He thinks somebody ought to do something about it. And he grins and says maybe he's a sucker, but he thinks he's one of the ones who ought to do something.

So he's there. He's in that airplane; he's in that seat, or he's hanging behind that gun, or he's cramped in the ball-turret, or he's got the headphones clamped on in the radio room.

. . . Always we had those others too, who could go *beyond* what is expected ordinarily of the average individual. I'm not talking about people like that. They are a mystery—a great and valuable mystery which God gives to us sometimes in warfare. There's no use going into what motivates people like that: the Roger Youngs, the people who offer their all, and then all their More Than All. So we won't discuss them.

We're talking about the man who, if he survived, is probably living in a brand new city housing development today, or in a ranch house out along some newly paved highway. He's fussing at his own teen-agers for doing some slipshod things which he used to do himself. He's helping his wife shop at the supermarket, if he has time; and maybe once in a while he's shooting a duck or catching a fish, or even hitting a golf or tennis ball. Just the ordinary good guy American.

At the other end of the spectrum we had the No-Good sons of bitches. Yep, and we have these in civilian life today: really No-Good types. But they show up a little sharper and are observable more readily in wartime. Witness the twisting of the pegs and the taut strings which our musician-air-commander was talking about.

So we speak now of the louse, the rat, the bum, the yellow so-and-so. He has no pride, no sense of responsibility. He whines, cringes, snarls, bites back. He's selfish. He steals in his soul, if not in fact.

Combat fatigue can be produced or induced in either of the types of people cited above; but they react to different stimuli. As for this stinko character: he's just scairt. And he can suffer shock that way. The other man, the ordinary Joe, is fearful too; but that doesn't induce any shock. He just keeps going on and on, to a point where his soul, his heart, his mind, his spirit— They all still say Go. But the body rebels.

Last year one of our old Eighth Air Force vets, Beirne Lay, who has done things in pictures and on television, and who with Sy Bartlett wrote *Twelve O'Clock High*— Beirne put together a pilot film for a proposed TV program, and he was kind enough to send me a print of the film. I ran it one night, there in the living room of our quarters. There was a scene in that picture which suggests what I'm talking about.

. . . An air officer is in a state of shock. He is emotionally upset because of what has been said and done with regard to previous operations. So now he's going to fly this crucial mission, and attempt a new policy of bombardment.

He tries to crawl up through the hatch. His mind and his heart say Go, again; but the body just hangs there. He has an awful time getting up through that hatch. The body is fighting back at him all the way. He's a good boy, a brave boy; but still that old devil body says No.

A very real situation. And, unfortunately, common.

. . . Far as the No-Good S.O.B. is concerned: his commander or his immediate superior can't do anything about it, because the character *himself* is not trying to do anything about it.

You can do something about the Average Guy. We actually discovered that you could predict when an attack of this nature was coming on. Every man has a tolerance and a limit. It varies. But we learned something of exceeding interest, the more we studied the matter.

If a man was about a half or three-quarters of the way through his tour of missions, he was very tired. He had been worked over by the flak and the fighters, by the weather . . . all the hazards, urgencies, risks, heartbreaks.

Then, say, this airman (or officer, as the case may be) has a couple of bad missions in a row. Or maybe he loses a couple of particularly close friends. He might even see them burn up over Vegesack or Berlin or Tokyo; or he might watch them plunge to an unsuccessful ditching, halfway down to Iwo Jima. Perhaps he's had his own crew shot up, and lost half of them. Something of that sort.

Get a few things like that in a row, and then watch out. Indeed we had some people who could take all this and more, and go on and finish their missions without batting an eye, seemingly. But with most of the others— Their tolerance was a little lower, and they began to worry.

Oh, they'd go, all right. But you ran into funny things. For instance, on the ground these folks might be in a perpetual cold sweat—couldn't eat, couldn't keep anything on their stomachs. Some of them would have dizzy spells. Others would be tensed up to the point where they'd want to fight their best friends. They'd get in a slugging match at the club, simply because they imagined somebody had slandered the movie actress whom they adored from afar. Any motive as silly as that. Or maybe somebody said the chow was pretty good that night, and this other guy, he thought it was lousy.

Biff, bang, bang. Call the Officer of the Day.

"So you say your father voted for Willkie, instead of Roosevelt, hah?"

"Yeah! Want to make something out of it?"

Biff, bang, biff. "Try to break it up, guys, before they bust each other in two!"

War nerves, combat nerves, combat fatigue. But—

Once these men got into the airplane, all this nonsense vanished. They were just as good as they ever had been.

We witnessed various forms of combat fatigue. We learned that if you kept your eye on these people, you could see the disease coming on. You didn't have to be a flight surgeon in order to identify the symptoms.

I got so that I could tell when an attack was imminent. Often it would be one of my best people who was involved.

The solution:

"Say, Fuzz, the Supply is in a hell of a mess. That stupid Supply officer we did have—you know, the one we got rid of— He just screwed things up from top to bottom. Somebody's got to straighten it out. Well, you're elected. I'm taking you off combat. Get down there and fix the Supply. Then, when you've got it all fixed up, we'll talk about getting you back into the combat act."

So old Fuzz hits the ceiling. He says, "I've done twenty-three missions! I've only got two more to go. I want to finish up with my crew! You can't do this to me. You can't do this to my *crew!* They're depending on me to see them all the way *through!*" Etc.

So I say, "You heard me. You're *off combat*. Get the Supply job done. If you get it done well— Just as I said: we'll talk about your finishing up your missions. But, by God, if you don't get it done, we ain't *ever* going to talk about it. So get your ass down there to Supply and go to work."

Fuzz goes down to Supply. He grumbles, he complains, he cusses me out to everybody else. What a raw deal I gave him!

But he's off *combat* . . . his mind is relieved. Pretty soon he starts sleeping again, nights. He still cusses me out. But of course he does his Supply job, despite all the resentment which he feels, because intrinsically he's an honest and levelheaded and devoted citizen. Although still squawking about the raw deal.

In a couple of months he's all right again. I stick him back in the cockpit of an airplane or up on that flight engineer's pedestal or in the nose, or wherever else he belongs, and he sails on through his missions like a million dollars.

That was a method I used to employ, but there were others. And most were based on the same theory: that if there's no escape, you don't have any combat fatigue. If you can get home . . . O.K. Fine business.

Oh, how I remember. (Some characters would do anything in order to get home.) I'm talking about the lower orders now.

There was one group commander we had— When an enlisted man flopped on *him*, that commander would really give him the business. "You're yellow! You think you're going to get out of here and get home and pull a big hero act, don't you? Well, you're not. You're going to go down there to the latrines, and you're going to scrub out those latrines for the rest of this war, so your betters won't have to do it, and will be free to fight. Get out of here!"

And people used to say that *I* was rough on enlisted men.

Well, I guess they said I was rough on everybody.

Let me cite another type of the Good Joe who reaches his tolerance limit and collapses, and the treatment which we gave. This one I have in mind was an extremely able man, either a major or a lieutenant-colonel. He commanded a squadron. This happened when I headed up the Third Air Division, so the war had been going on for quite a while.

Our man (we'll make up a name, and call him Tracer) had a couple or three rough experiences in a row, and each time he lost part of his crew. It had him worried, more than a little bit.

He went along with me on the Regensburg deal. As you will remember, we got quite a working over on that one. Then, on the way home from Africa, we bombed the Merignac airfield near Bordeaux.

Our guy Tracer was leading the last element. By this time the Third Division—those of us who had actually figured in the Regensburg attack—had been carved down from a hundred and twenty-seven to only eighty-odd. On the whole, the surprise effect on the enemy was greater than we'd believed possible. There wasn't any interference as we approached the target; that is, on the part of enemy fighters. They were literally knocked off their feet. Of course the fact that some other big operations were taking place that day was of great assistance. Certain elements of the Eighth Air Force were attacking Villacoublay again, and also hitting at scattered airfields in France.

. . . Just a few enemy fighters in the Bordeaux area. They didn't manage to close until after we went out to sea. There was just a pass or two, and that was it.

Pass or two though it was, they got our friend Tracer. He ran fresh out of engines before he reached the British coast. I think he was about twenty miles off Land's End when he ditched. Maybe it was an hour before dark. We who landed safely in England promptly alerted the Air-Sea Rescue; but they couldn't find him on the ocean, in dinghies . . . darkness had spread solid and thick. It was morning before the Air-Sea Rescue people located Tracer and his crew; and by that time they had lost a man or two again.

This really pushed him over the line. He flopped on us. It bothered me terribly, because of his superb record until this series of wicked events took place.

I talked to him, and the surgeons talked to him, and then I compared notes with the other interrogators. This whole situation was now apparent. Tracer was not worried about *himself*. He had not gone yellow; he was perfectly willing to see himself expended in the war. But he simply couldn't bring himself to the point of taking another crew into combat, and then losing some of them. It had happened too often.

Actually it took me quite a while to figure out what to do. I had to consider the case from every angle; and then I decided on something which seemed to be an innovation . . . at least I'd never heard of anyone trying this before. Not any commander in our theater or anywhere else.

Tracer and I talked it over.

"So that's the way you feel? You've quit cold on us because you say you're not going to take another crew into action. Not ever again. . . ."

"Do you blame me, sir?"

"Have you ever checked off on the P-47?"

"Of course."

"How would you like to do a little work in fighters?"

"Fine!"

As long as he felt that way about it, I got old Hub Zemke on the phone, and told him my problem.

Hub says, "Send him down here to me. I'll personally get him into combat."

Tracer went. He did fine. Matter of fact, one day he and Hub became separated from the rest of their force, and they were jumped by an unholy number of Germans, and our friend Tracer shot down four enemy aircraft before he himself was shot down.

I never saw him afterward. But I recall that he was taken prisoner

and survived the war, and finally came back to the States safe and
sound.

Actually, I've forgotten his real name, and wouldn't think of men-
tioning it anyway. But I hope to be excused if I say that, for a moment
at least, I felt a little bit like King Solomon.

In these instances, I have cited the case of a good man who reached
the breaking point, and one cure for it; and of another good man who
was *past* the breaking point, and another good cure for it.

We may need to concern ourselves only briefly with the other
critter: the No-Good. There's no cure for No-Goodedness.

Take a bombardier who shows up as a replacement in the outfit:
he's assigned to a crew, and he goes through whatever crew training
we're able to give them in the short time and with the short opportunities which remain.

Comes the day when he's to fly on a mission. Well, that day he's sick.
Can't go.

Comes the next mission. Our bombardier is sick also, next time. Can't
go.

The boys are somewhat suspicious. A little inquiring is done, here
and there. And they find out that when Lieutenant Tom Toggle was
ordered overseas the first time, he was sick and had to drop out of his
crew and had to be replaced. He couldn't go *then,* either.

They came to me with this information. I said, "O.K. Order the slob
to go on a mission. If he doesn't go we'll court-martial him."

So he was ordered to go on a mission, and he wouldn't go. I said,
"Court-martial him." They did.

During the investigation by the court, it turned out that Lieutenant
T.T. said, "Sure. I was ordered to go on that mission. But my Aircraft
Commander told me not to go. He said he didn't feel that I was well
enough. So I didn't have to go."

Point is, his Aircraft Commander and the entire crew *had gone down*
on that mission. There was no way we could prove that the Aircraft
Commander *hadn't* said exactly what Tom Toggle insisted that he'd
said.

Start all over again. . . .

We had to consider this fact too: maybe the missing crew commander had recognized that Toggle was a yellow twerp and he preferred *not* to have him along. Maybe Toggle had come whining
around— "I'm sick again." And the A/C said, "All right, you bastard,
we don't want you anyway. We don't want you to fly with us. Beat
it!"

You see, it could have happened, but— No matter how you sliced it, the crew wasn't there to testify.

O.K. Order him to go on the next mission.

So we ordered him on the next one. Word came up that the flight surgeon had excused him—said he wasn't physically capable of flying a mission. And, by gravy, by that time he wasn't. He had worked himself into such a state of confusion and dismay and terror that he wasn't physically capable of flying. So nobody wanted him. There was one thing to do: pack up the so-and-so and send him home. That's what we did.

If he'd stayed, and we'd dragged him into the nose of a 29, there's no telling what might have happened. It wouldn't have been good, it could have been bad. He might even have got somebody else killed. We were glad to be rid of him.

There were some like that. Some like that at Chelveston . . . some in the Third . . . some when we were based in India and flying out of the Chengtu . . . some after we got to the Marianas. Not too many. There were some.

One thing which was sorely missed out in the Pacific was any contact with a benevolent civilian population, scissored out of the same bolt of goods as our boys. I refer to the English people and the English girls.

In England there was some attempt at hand-picking the shemales who appeared at our parties, but this came to naught in most cases. And I don't intend to become involved in any discussion as to whether the Wrens were better-looking than the Ats, or whether the Waafs were less commendable in appearance than either of the other Services, or perhaps more commendable.

And what about civilians? Our boys used to run their trucks down into Rushden, and pull up beside a corner and watch the girls coming past and say, "Hey, girls, do you want to come to a party?" So the girls would come. They'd have a whole truck full of them; and they'd get back to the Base, and some of the Women's Voluntary Service types had already sent in a lot of babes from the Forces. There certainly would be more than enough girls to go around.

I've been back in England many times since World War II, and no one yet has pulled out any of my hair; and I'm not going to give them a chance to do that in the future. I shall not discuss the comparative merits of civilian and military female personnel during the late unpleasantness over there.

All I shall do is relate an anecdote.

This happened when I was commanding the Third. There began to

travel a lot of rumors about gals . . . stories about certain bombardment groups who would be stood down (that's temporarily relieved
from active operational duty). And they'd have a dance on *Saturday*
night, and could be some of the gals didn't get home till *next*
Wednesday.

Maybe the remark which will terminate this anecdote is apocryphal,
maybe not. I'm informed that the story has been told about me. It was
said to have occurred at the 305th, at Chelveston.

Nothing could be further from the fact. I say that it happened with
Archie Old and his 96th BG.

I called up Archie and said, "Archie, I'm getting a lot of rumors
around here that there's a little too much going on at those Saturday
night dances of yours. And, shall we say, thereafter? Complaints have
been coming in from mothers and from officers of the British Services.
Here's what I hear: I hear that some of those girls don't get home until
the Wednesday after the Saturday when the party was held. I suggest
that you get to fixing up this situtation before I have to come down
there and fix it up myself."

So Archie summoned the boys together and proceeded to fix things
in his own way.

"This is one hell of a note! I'm ashamed of *all* of you. By God, this
business has got to *stop!* The next time we have a dance on Saturday
night, every one of those babes is going to be off this base by *Monday
morning.* Or else!"

10

MAKE NO mistake about it, there can be forms of fatigue other than
combat fatigue.

There was the weariness which overwhelmed ground crews and
ordnance people when they stuffed those clusters into the front bomb-
bay and the rear bomb-bay of every B-29 involved. It is brutal work,
to bomb up an airplane. But five Maximum Effort missions in ten
days— Everybody got in the act during our concentrated campaign:
the series of incendiary attacks which we were able to make before
(as I prophesied to the Navy) we used up all our bombs.

The effectiveness on the Japanese war machine and on the Japanese
population was intensified because of the rapidity with which each
assault followed the previous one.

I had given my ground personnel a back-breaking job; but they rose
so magnificently to the occasion that I was ready to salute the people
who toiled there at the bases just as readily as I saluted the crews who
flew the airplanes.

Far as that's concerned, the combat crews never had it so good.

We lost exactly 0.9 per cent of all those who participated in the March fire attacks.

So the bombs had to be brought from the bomb dump and loaded into the airplanes, hung on the shackles. That meant blood, sweat and tears. Sometimes it even meant serious injury or death. There were accidents: accidents in traffic, accidents right between those open bomb-bay doors. Equipment could slip and break, men could strain themselves too much, something could fall. Sometimes something did.

But their zeal was so magnificent it gave you goose-pimples. If morale had sagged before, when we were trying to attack along old orthodox lines and not getting any visible results, it now went up like a skyrocket. We had copies of those pictures of burned-out Tokyo, stuck up around on bulletin boards—recco photos which showed all the blackness and destruction. I think that if any individual had shown a lackadaisical response to this, the other folks would have dunked him in the Pacific Ocean.

Maybe I'd better relate a story which Tommy Power came down to HQ and told me. Tommy said that we were scheduled for a night mission—one of those incendiaries—and on this it was necessary to take off about four o'clock in the afternoon. About three-thirty a maintenance officer came stomping in and shouldered his way over to General Power's desk. The maintenance guy was dressed just the way everybody else dressed when working on those airplanes: he had on a pair of shorts and a hat, and GI shoes. He wasn't exactly ready for a hero's ticker-tape parade up Broadway; but he was ready for work, and he had been ready for work, and he had been working and was still working. He was filthy dirty, smeared with grease and grime . . . hadn't shaved for days . . . red-eyed, practically hysterical. He started beating his fist on Tommy's desk.

"General, you've got to do something about this!"

"What's your problem?"

"Well, I've got old Number—"

(Call his airplane anything you want to. Call it 7931.)

He said, "I've got Number 7931 ready to go on this mission. And Joe Blow [whoever he was; he meant the Operations Officer] won't take it! He said we're too *late*. Well, maybe we were late, but we had troubles. And now 7931 is ready to *go*. The rest of them haven't taken off yet. By God, it's *got* to go, General! We worked three days and nights straight on that airplane, to get her ready. Three days straight," he screamed. "I tell you she's *got* to go!"

There was only one thing to say. "O.K. She's going to go."

We hustled around and got a crew together. That aircraft took off forty minutes late; but by God it *went*. The maintenance officer stood there breathing heavily, watching her take off. . . .

So it wasn't the crews, air or ground, who broke down. They were higher than a kite, raring to go. It was only the people who worked in offices, people maybe in the topographic squadron who prepared target materials and other stuff of that sort. What you might call white-collar personnel. They dropped off like flies. Those were the ones I had to send home.

As for this hundred and twenty hours a month (per airplane) business, it turned out that we flew ourselves and incendiary-bombed ourselves and maintained ourselves right out of logistic support.

Nimitz's people didn't think we could do it.

Again I look at the record . . . in England, in the Third Division, for one short span we got up to about a sixty-hour rate. But only for a short period of time; and no other command had ever done this. The average was about thirty hours per month.

I had my new maintenance system going with the B-29's—and it had worked out increasingly well—in India, as far as in-commission airplanes were concerned. And after taking command at Guam I could see that indeed we would do a hundred and twenty hours a month on the planes . . . maybe eighty hours a month on each combat crew, eventually. It meant that very soon our stockpile of bombs would be exhausted, unless the stuff started coming in right away.

We put in our request to Nimitz's office, and they just laughed at us. "Nobody ever did this before. You can't do it."

I said, "Well, we're going to do it. And if you don't give us the supplies we need, we'll just sit here and go fishing."

It's all history now. On the return to Nagoya, 19 March, we put down every M-47 and M-69 and M-76 we had left. Exactly eighteen hundred and fifty-eight *tons* of scalding chemicals.

We couldn't mount another incendiary attack for almost four weeks. Folks hadn't believed us and folks hadn't supplied us. Oh, we had some iron bombs that we used; we flew some missions in between; but we couldn't do another hour of incendiary work. No ammunition for the job.

It was that rain and reign of flame which demoralized Japanese industry, and shattered the military heart, and whipped the populace into a state where they could—and would—accept the idea of surrender. Fire, not high explosives, did this. And we possessed no more fire with which to speed the capitulation.

Apparently the Nimitz crowd thought that we were uttering an empty boast when we told them we'd be out of incendiaries shortly.

A man often thinks, in a first flash of resentment— When he knows he is right, and when other people (who for the moment have their hands on the switch) stare him down in owlish disdain— He often thinks, or is inclined to think if he will so indulge himself: "The day is coming when I can say, 'I told you so.'"

Frequently I felt that way out there in the Marianas; and frequently I felt that way years later when I was Chief of Staff at the Pentagon. . . . But I found it a small satisfaction indeed. Anyone would be happier to have the job done right from the start, with every coöperation afforded.

I told you so is the hopeless little flutter of an exasperated childish voice, and it does no good to say the words or even evince the attitude.

The enemy's air-to-air resistance was weakening steadily. During that first big show over Tokyo, night of March 9–10, only forty attacks by Japanese planes were chronicled, and not one B-29 was shot down by a fighter.

If we'd had more fire to pour over the enemy industry we would have poured it. But we didn't have it, though it had been requested well in advance.

Suppose that you are interviewing me now. Suppose that you ask, "If you had had the incendiary bombs in your stockpile, the ones you asked for and didn't get, would you have flown more incendiary missions against Japanese targets, just as fast as you could mount them?"

"Yes."

"Do you think those attacks would have been as effective as the first series which occurred in March?"

"Yes. Probably even more so. The destruction and demoralization in Japan was being rapidly accelerated. Had increased like cube root."

"Do you think that by relying solely on incendiary attack, you could have knocked Japan out of the war, thus precluding any invasion of the Japanese homeland until after the collapse came?"

"Yes. I think it could have happened."

"Then it would have been possible to force Japan out of the war, and thus end the conflict, without actually employing atomic weapons?"

"It might have been possible."

I don't want to be a Monday morning quarterback. Never did. I'll say again: *I think it might have been possible.*

When those new fire-bombs started to come streaming in around the middle of April, we didn't have any bomb dumps. We didn't have any bomb dumps because we hadn't had any bombs. Actually, when the Navy got to stirring their stumps they did an excellent job of getting that stuff out there to us.

Still, we had flown our last fire attack on March 19th, and were not able to fly another one until April 13th.

It was necessary in the beginning to bypass the whole bomb dump idea altogether. We were short of manpower for uncrating and hauling and everything else. What we did was take the bombs right from the ships to the airplanes.

Those Seabees were terrific. They worked like supermen. They'd get up at four o'clock in the morning and dig in for two or three hours, helping us with the bombs, and then they'd go on to their regular jobs. There were some Marines . . . they worked like dogs. Anybody we could get our hands on was hauling bombs for us. Majors and lieutenant-commanders were handling those crates, if they were big enough and strong enough . . . able-bodied seamen and lieutenant-colonels and privates from the rear rank, all rolling out of bed in the middle of the night when they learned that another shipload of stuff had just come in.

Again they thought of those pictures of the embers of Japan, the black stuff hanging around on bulletin boards. I guess intermingled with that was the thought, "How soon can we go home?" Volunteers always think that in a war, and mainly ours was a volunteer or a drafted force, as we all know. You can't blame them for thinking that. You can thank them for working like demons, which is what they did.

Our failure to possess the incendiaries essential to the task came about because of a difference of opinion between people in Administrative control and people in Operations. In short, a difference of opinion between Admiral Nimitz, who was supposed to supply us, and myself, who was carrying out the campaign.

But something far different and in a way more serious and baffling occurred shortly thereafter.

For the Okinawa invasion, Operational control of the entire B-29 force was switched directly into the hands of Admiral Nimitz.

. . . An amphibious operation is a most difficult military maneuver, and everybody has to turn out in order to get the troops on the shore.

Obviously this switch in control of the B-29 force was decided in a huddle of the JCS. We in 21st Bomber Command were willing to do our share. But we trusted that there would be no demand for extended withdrawal of the 29's from our strategic attack on the whole of Japan. It had been demonstrated to all and sundry that our incendiary campaign was a howling success.

The task which we were handed for the Okinawa invasion was tactical: we were to keep the Japanese Air Force off the invasion's back. Our immediate mission was to knock out the airdromes on Kyushu. We did this in a hurry.

. . . Wondering what the *Encyclopaedia Britannica* had to say about

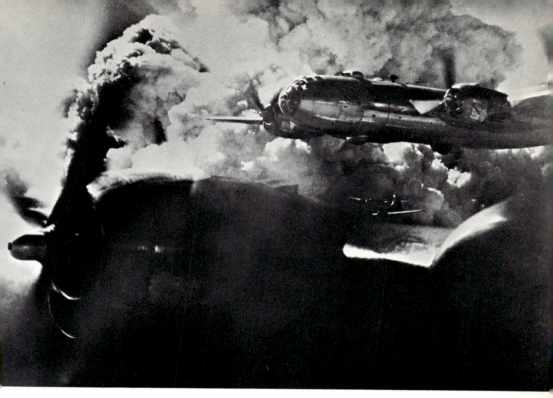

(38) Heading for Japan

(39) Intelligence reported that ninety per cent of the structures in the world's largest city were made of wood...The Tokyo fire chief reported that the situation was out of control within thirty minutes

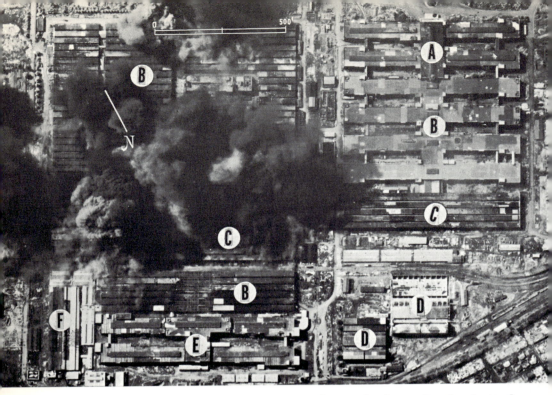

(40) The Musashino aircraft engine plant in Tokyo under heavy low-level attack, April 7, 1945: A—administrative headquarters, B—machine shops, C—engine assembly, D—test cells, E—offices, shops, F—probably foundry

(41) Musashino—after

(42) Yokohama—May 29, 1945

(43) Over Osaka with No. 3 losing oil

(44) Guam never looked so good!

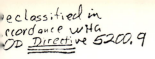

NONE   TELECON

7 Aug 45

CARL SPAATZ, GEN USA

FROM: COMGEN USASTAF   070722Z

TO   :   COMGEN USASTAF REAR

NBR :   1467

(PERSONAL TO NORSTAD FROM SPAATZ)

HAVE HAD OPPORTUNITY TO CHECK UP ON BAKER TWO NINE OPERATIONS

AND BELIEVE THIS IS THE BEST ORGANIZED AND MOST TECHNICALLY

AND TACTICALLY PROFICIENT MILITARY ORGANIZATION THAT THE WORLD

HAS SEEN TO DATE.

DISTRIBUTION: C/G
                  Dep CG

(45)

(46) After B-29 flight from Yokohama to Washington, September 19, 1945—LeMay, O'Donnell, Arnold, Giles

(47) Pinpointing Ground Zero on model of Bikini— McKee, LeMay, Partridge

(48) Taking off for Berlin—Airlift, 1948

(49) Loading flour for Berlin, 1948

(50) B-47

(51) Generals Eaker, LeMay, Spaatz

(52) "Probably I scrubbed half-a-dozen hunting trips for every one I got to take."

(53) On her eleventh birthday, Janie gets a dance with her father—February 8, 195

(54) LeMay leaning on his Cad-Allard

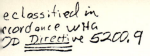

NONE   TELECON

7 Aug 45
                                    CARL SPAATZ, GEN USA

FROM: COMGEN USASTAF   O7072Z Z

TO :   COMGEN USASTAF REAR

NBR :   1467

(PERSONAL TO NORSTAD FROM SPAATZ)

HAVE HAD OPPORTUNITY TO CHECK UP ON BAKER TWO NINE OPERATIONS

AND BELIEVE THIS IS THE BEST ORGANIZED AND MOST TECHNICALLY

AND TACTICALLY PROFICIENT MILITARY ORGANIZATION THAT THE WORLD

HAS SEEN TO DATE.

DISTRIBUTION: C/G
               Dep CG

(45)

(46) After B-29 flight from Yokohama to Washington, September 19, 1945—LeMay, O'Donnell, Arnold, Giles

(47) Pinpointing Ground Zero on model of Bikini—McKee, LeMay, Partridge

(48) Taking off for Berlin—Airlift, 1948

(49) Loading flour for Berlin, 1948

(50) B-47

(51) Generals Eaker, LeMay, Spaatz

(52) "Probably I scrubbed half-a-dozen hunting trips for every one I got to take."

(53) On her eleventh birthday, Janie gets a dance with her father—February 8, 1951

(54) LeMay leaning on his Cad-Allard

that Okinawa campaign, I picked up Volume 23 of the 1960 edition, and found an account on page 793-F, designated as "The Ryukyus; Okinawa." The account was written by R. R. Sh., listed as a "Former Historian, Office of the Chief of Military History, U. S. Department of the Army."

According to this former historian it would seem that the B-29's weren't in the act at all, to begin with.

". . . The seizure of positions in the Ryukyus was to have been the last step in the Pacific war prior to actual invasion of the Japanese home islands. From bases there, pre-assault aerial bombardment of Japan could be intensified; the invasion forces could be provided with direct land-based air support; and the islands could be used as staging and supply bases.

"Okinawa, largest island in the Ryukyus, lies only 350 mi. S. of Kyushu Island, where the initial invasion of the Japanese home islands was to have taken place. . . ."

There follows a paragraph giving the composition of the U.S. 10th Army; then the account continues:

"Following extensive aerial and naval bombardment by the U.S. 5th fleet, landings in the Ryukyus began on March 26th, 1945. . . ."

Several paragraphs farther on, the former historian remarks that "the Allied air units, both carrier- and land-based, destroyed about 7,800 Japanese aircraft in the Ryukyus or Japan and sank 16 Japanese ships."

This reader was very glad to hear at last that there were some land-based aircraft in on the deal.

Actually I don't know how it would be possible to decide what particular destruction (insofar as Jap airfields were concerned) might be attributed to the 5th Fleet and how much to our team, except by comparing tonnages of bombs which they delivered. I'll compare them pretty soon.

We started bombing a few days before the invasion, at our assigned time, and we had a very good streak of weather. We flattened every airdrome we could find up Kyushu way. We not only had the facilities destroyed, but the runways were turned into rubble, the fields were solidly cratered. It would be impossible to make those fields less effective than they already were.

So I went down to see Admiral Nimitz, and told him, "We've finished now. There's not another thing we can do for you. May we go back to hitting our strategic targets? We'll do a lot more good there."

And Admiral Nimitz was most appreciative. "Yes, LeMay, you've done a very fine job. *Very* good. I guess it's about time you go back on your own type of operation. But let me check with Sherman—" (Admiral Sherman, his Operations Officer).

Sherman's idea was for the B-29's to keep dropping bombs in order to ward off *kamikaze* attacks. I didn't quite see how our Very Heavy

Bombers might ever become an instrument which would nullify the threat of suicide sorties. Whenever we beat up a field enough, they'd take whatever airplanes weren't destroyed—or those that they'd put together, wired up, ready to go—and take them down the road half a mile or a mile, and hide them in the bushes. Then the Japs would bring out one or two airplanes a day and, with a bunch of coolies working with baskets, they'd fill up enough of our cratered holes to take off on the grass. Remember, this was a suicidal airplane; it wasn't coming back anyway.

It was impossible for us to do anything from the air to stop *that*. There wasn't anything to bomb. But we were ordered to go over and keep dropping more bombs on those beat-up airdromes. We'd already expended the total of our delayed-action fuses. All we were doing at last was plowing the fields.

. . . This is all iron bombs. We didn't have any incendiaries as yet, to take the place of that ordnance we'd requested but never received. We used the iron bombs: High Explosive, General Purpose. Just about every size, I guess, beginning with 100-pounders. We employed a few 1000-pounders on the airfield facilities; but mostly it was 500's for the cratering deal.

I went back to Admiral Nimitz again, and then eventually got the same old reply from Admiral Sherman. *Continue*.

I complained all the way up to General Arnold. The Navy sent a hint in return, declaring that if we didn't stay on the job, they would pull off Okinawa and leave our doughboys there.

All in all, the Navy must have lost thirty-five or forty ships, mostly of the little picket ship types. Of course there were many larger vessels which were hit but not sunk by the *kamikazes* in their suicide dives.

Day after day we had to go out and bomb Target Nothing.

Admiral Nimitz released us from support of the Okinawa campaign on May 11th, and spoke kind words of thanks. Personally I don't know why we should have received much in the way of thanks. The B-29 was not a tactical bomber and never pretended to be. No matter how we socked away at those airdromes, we could not reduce the *kamikaze* threat to zero. In some proportion it was always there.

We had managed to squeeze in a couple of incendiary attacks, beginning on the 13th of April, when we were in the chips ammunition-wise once more. Then we put down the most fire bombs to date: over twenty-one hundred tons on Tokyo. We clobbered the arsenal section, and burned up over eleven square miles of new territory.

Two days later we hit Tokyo again, and also Kawasaki and Yokohama. We couldn't do any more of this for a while; had to go back to work in support of the Okinawa operation. But in the meantime our force was increasing. Roger Ramey had brought up the 58th Wing from the CBI; they were now ensconced on Tinian, and were part of our team by the time Admiral Nimitz allowed us to return to our primary strategic task.

In a communication to Larry Norstad—not then released to the public, naturally—in late April I had said:

"I am influenced by the conviction that the present stage of development of the air war against Japan presents the AAF for the first time with the opportunity of proving the power of the strategic air arm. I consider that for the first time strategic air bombardment faces a situation in which *its strength is proportionate to the magnitude of its task*. I feel that the destruction of Japan's ability to wage war lies within the capability of this command, provided its maximum capacity is exerted unstintingly during the next six months, which is considered to be the critical period. Though naturally reluctant to drive my force at an exorbitant rate, I believe that the opportunity now at hand warrants extraordinary measures on the part of all sharing it."

Once again, the above italics are my own. I cannot overemphasize how sincerely I believed this.

My dream began to come true on Monday, May 14th, when our people went up to get the Mitsubishi engine factory and electrical works in the north end of Nagoya. We had four hundred and seventy-two Superforts over that target, and put down twenty-five hundred tons of bombs. This was a daylight attack, and we lost exactly one airplane, each, to fighters and to flak.

Wednesday night we went back to Nagoya with a mixed load. We had used only the M-69's on the Mitsubishi works; but we used both M-47's and M-50's on the aircraft factories and other specified industrial targets at Nagoya. There was a lot of heavy masonry mixed up in these target areas, and we needed magnesium.

We plastered the as-yet-unburned areas of Tokyo with nearly nine thousand tons of incendiaries on the 23rd and 25th of May. We went socking ahead on other targets, including Yokohama. Then, nearing the end of the month, we were able to make use of our fighters as escorts. If these P-51's could do the job it was hoped they would do, we might have comparative freedom from enemy air-to-air interference whenever we decided to attack by day. It took a long time for the Japanese fighter resistance to diminish, however. They were numerous, determined, and deadly as all hell. In the meantime our people flew and fought and built up the blazes both by day and night in most of the larger Japanese cities. Osaka again, Kobe again, Osaka once more. . . .

June 1st I sent a daylight force of over five hundred B-29's to Osaka. Certain important targets lay scattered here and there amid the blackened neighborhoods, and could not be eradicated except by precision attack. We had to get those.

Heretofore I have neglected to mention that by this time we had a considerable force of P-51's (Mustangs) based on Iwo Jima, whose prime purpose was to escort the daylight B-29 missions. It's seven hundred miles over water from Iwo to Japan, and another nice seven hundred back to Iwo.

The fighters lacked the navigational equipment for this feat. Accordingly we assigned some Superforts to fly the same route to Japan, do the navigation for the Mustangs, meet them on the coast, and navigate them back to Iwo Jima once more. Such conduct was essential because there was always at least one weather front lying in the way—sometimes more. Frequently you could fly over the front, or ooze between the cloud strata; but there were occasions when you had to bang right through the thing.

Our P-51's tried to avoid clouds for any but very brief periods, due to the danger of drifting away from the formation. Necessarily we employed standard procedures for punching fronts when in formation—an SOP technique which minimized the possibility of mid-air collisions.

On this June 1st Osaka mission, the leader of the P-51's chose to try to punch the front. It was thicker than he thought, and also alive with excessive turbulence. As a result his formation became so dispersed that many of them were unable to regain their position on the other side of the front. There were tragic losses at sea. Twenty-seven P-51's never returned to their Iwo home. Rough day.

Just the same, despite a rugged Japanese defense, we managed to burn up more than four thousand factories in Osaka.

Our fighters never had any gas to spare. They were given a point and time to meet the B-29 navigational plane on the Japanese coast. If they couldn't make the rendezvous promptly— Too bad.

The story goes that one P-51 pilot was having such a merry time raising merry hell with Japanese locomotives that he arrived at the rendezvous five minutes late. No formation there, no B-29 navigational plane. This was real T.S. and no mistake.

Well, he started out for Iwo Jima on his own, yelling bloody murder for help on the radio. A B-29 happened to hear him, and the navigator took over. He got, from the poor little lamb who had lost his way, all pertinent information about his departure point, altitude, air speed, and course. He plotted the fighter's position . . . he was away off course, and headed for a lonely moist death at sea. So the navigator gave the Mustang pilot a new heading, and a time to let down through the clouds. The pilot followed instructions doggedly, and when he dropped down out of the clouds, there was Iwo. Good day for him.

I've been told that the B-29 guy and the fighter pilot never did meet, but some letters were exchanged. Must have been interesting letters.

. . . Before we had completed the first phase of our urban area program, about the middle of June, we had destroyed in Tokyo 56.3 square miles; in Nagoya, 12.4; Kobe, 8.8; Osaka, 15.6; Yokohama, 8.9; Kawasaki, 3.6. A total of 105.6 square miles.

Says *AAFWW II:* "The six most important industrial cities in Japan had been ruined."

At first the Navy Intelligence people were running the leaflet show. They had the usual old propaganda stuff. I looked these over and said, "Do we have to drop *these?* Let's cook up some of our own, and do a little good." So we got together on this, deciding what we should say, and found out what the lead time was to get them printed back in Hawaii and returned to us in quantity.

. . . We had, I think, ten towns on the list. Just got through reëxamining one of the original leaflets. It is printed in red and black Japanese script, without any pictures on the reverse, where it says merely: "Civilians! Evacuate at once!"

On the obverse:

"These leaflets are being dropped to notify you that your city has been listed for destruction by our powerful air force. The bombing will begin within 72 hours.

"This advance notice will give your military authorities ample time to take necessary defensive measures to protect you from our inevitable attack. Watch and see how powerless they are to protect you.

"We give the military clique this notification of our plans because we know there is nothing they can do to stop our overwhelming power and our iron determination. We want you to see how powerless the military is to protect you.

"Systematic destruction of city after city will continue as long as you blindly follow your military leaders whose blunders have placed you on the very brink of oblivion. It is your responsibility to overthrow the military government now and save what is left of your beautiful country.

"In the meanwhile, we urge all civilians to evacuate at once."

At first they thought we were bluffing, apparently. (That was more or less natural: one of the big things in warfare is, sometimes, to try to bluff your enemy.) There wasn't any mass exodus until we knocked the hell out of the first three towns on the list. Then the rest were practically depopulated in nothing flat.

Actually we had worried about our own situation in the announced series of attacks. With all this advance warning they might move a lot of antiaircraft guns in there. But what they did do was to bring in a gang of fire engines. J. B. Montgomery went in after the surrender and worked on a strategic bombing survey; he explored the charcoal ruins of those towns. He found fire engines lined up about a hundred feet apart, all up and down the streets, and they were burned up along with everything else.

I received an order from General Arnold directing me to support Admiral Halsey in his run up the Empire. The Navy was going to start, down at Nagoya . . . run in during the night; then launch planes off their carriers and let the planes go a-bombing; then come back out, run up the coast, go in the next night a little farther up. With these hit-and-run tactics they would flog a destructive path along the shoreline.

Never did we receive any direct word or explanation from Admiral Halsey about this. He literally *never said a word* to me. So I was waiting for him to tell me what to do, since General Arnold had ordered us to support this particular campaign. Finally I got a message from the Navy referring to this plan which, supposedly, we already knew.

What Admiral Halsey wished was to be supported by our bombing with a Maximum Effort on all airdromes in the regions he was going to attack.

The purpose of his campaign was to bomb shipping and harbors.

At this time, late in the war, it was actually safer to fly a combat mission over Japan in a B-29 than it was to fly a B-29 training mission back in the United States. Truth. The fatality rate in the training program was higher than the rate in combat.

I don't believe that, under such circumstances, Admiral Halsey would have received much opposition from Japanese air attack. But he must have decided that the land-based airplanes might render enough opposition to spoil his assault, which was of course a *pre-invasion* activity.

We knew from Intelligence sources (I should judge that the Navy knew also) that the Japs had pretty well decided just when the invasion was coming, and where. We intercepted a message or two . . . we knew that they G-2'd it properly. And we knew that most of their airplanes were off the fields, down the roads, hidden in weeds and bushes. But with the gas tanks full of gas, so they could be employed as *kamikazes* when the invasion came.

We knew this. Admiral Halsey must have known it. But still we had to do Maximum Effort to assist him.

Our strength was increasing enormously as new units flew in to join us. The 315th Wing was the last to arrive, commanded by that old Eighth AF warhorse, Frank Armstrong. Oil targets became the specialty of the 315th. They were the only B-29 wing equipped with the so-called Eagle radar (AN/APQ-7) instead of conventional radar instruments which had been developed originally to serve as navigational aids. The Eagle had been designed especially for bombardment, and the 315th had trained especially for night missions.

This added up to putting them on oil refineries, oil storage facilities, and even synthetic plants. They took care of those targets very nicely. By the end of the war the destruction was so severe as to render such targets mainly inoperable. Twelve hundred sorties flown; nine thousand tons of HE bombs dropped; and four airplanes lost. Quite a record.

Actually, in a single Maximum Effort mission at the end, we must have been dropping somewhere between six and eight thousand tons. If Admiral Halsey had a good day and ran three missions on that day, he might get three hundred tons of bombs off all the carriers of this—the world's mightiest fleet. In fact they averaged less than two hundred tons per day on that little soirée up there along the coast.

It didn't seem to make very good sense to me. I sent a message to Admiral Halsey saying, "Well, this performance doesn't jibe with the strategic plan. How's about our supporting you by bombing strategic targets in the areas involved?" I didn't hear a thing from Halsey; but he had gone right upstairs on this. Promptly I received a message from General Arnold. It said tersely: "Support Halsey in any way he asks."

We thought we knew what occurred. Admiral King had arisen in a meeting of the JCS, and accused General Arnold of not wishing to coöperate with the Navy. Hap Arnold had sworn that he would coöperate.

At least I wasn't back under the Theater Commander, and could still run my command according to my own judgment. That was what I was hired to do. I communicated with Admiral Halsey: "O.K. If the weather is suitable, I will bomb those airdromes in the vicinity which you intend to strike. But if we can't do precision bombing, we'll have to bomb by radar. We cannot bomb *tactical* targets by radar. If the weather compels me to resort to radar, I'll hit the targets that I *can* hit: *strategic* targets."

The weather was lousy, far as visual attacks went. We never did get to fly that Maximum Effort mission on the tactical targets which the Navy desired us to strike. But we put down thousands and thousands of tons on strategic targets where they would do some good.

In final analysis it turned out that we did make a great contribution to Naval *publicity*. I refer to the destructive bombardment of Hamamatsu. That's a town down there southeast of Nagoya on the coast—easy to identify, between a river and a bay. In population it had been originally about the size of modern Fort Wayne or Nashville or Hartford.

Month after month, Hamamatsu was Hometown for the B-29's. If anyone went into that area and experienced trouble— Say a pilot had an engine out, or some other mechanical problem which made it impossible for him to proceed to his primary target— In any case like this our people were instructed to dump their loads on Hamamatsu. And Hamamatsu absorbed an awful lot of bombs, because there were an awful lot of abortions in those B-29's.

I can't tell you exactly what tonnage Hamamatsu had been awarded. Neither could anyone else. The place was really beaten to a pulp. We didn't even give our crews credit for a sortie if they bombed Hamamatsu. It was the garbage-can target to end 'em.

. . . And after we got down to the smaller industrial towns for incendiary attacks, one day we put a group on Hamamatsu to clean up what was left. You couldn't say that *anything* was left after that.

I'm anticipating now: I think this occurred during Admiral Halsey's second run up the Empire. They were going to go in close and use their guns. I saw the plan: somebody gave it to me to read. They were going to shell Hamamatsu with battleship guns.

So I got hold of George McGee, my Navy liaison officer (1965: Ambassador to Bonn). "Look here. They're going to go in and shell Hamamatsu. Didn't you ever send any pictures of that town to the Navy?"

George says, "Heavens, yes. We always send our pictures right down to Nimitz's office."

"Well, you'd better take another batch of photos, and go down there and tell them not to waste their ammunition. No use in shelling poor old Hamamatsu. It's already destroyed."

So back comes George eventually, and says, "They're going to shell Hamamatsu. Plans can't be changed."

. . . I was too busy from then on to pay much attention to the fleet bombardment episode. After returning to the States, when the war had ended, I saw a report on this campaign. On the cover of the report was a huge picture of Hamamatsu. Destroyed! And you looked through that report, and it told how many shells the Navy had fired. They had fired them by radar, at night. Yep, they had every shell—just where it landed—plotted out in the middle of town. And here were the pictures of the town, showing it completely smeared.

Not one damn word appeared to say anything about the tonnage which had been put down on Hamamatsu previously. Believe it or not, some of that nonsense got out to the public, and appeared in popular magazines.

. . . I guess it's just human nature. For a long time the United States Navy was our first line of defense, and they received the lion's share of the budget in peacetime. They got accustomed traditionally to being the most important Service. And to see anyone with new weapons and new ideas take over and effectively pursue what had once been *their* task— It was resented. Perfectly natural, I reckon.

Before World War II there had been the *Utah* incident, the *Rex* incident. Even long before that, there had been Billy Mitchell, successfully bombing those old German vessels after World War I, and finding himself pilloried because he had insisted and finally demonstrated that battleships could be sunk by airplanes.

Officially the Navy didn't seem to get it through their heads, until the British lost two of their most important vessels off Singapore. Then it really came home to them.

You may remember, in the Battle of the Midway, that the Japs were defeated; they were on the run back to Truk. The United States Navy chased them, and could have followed them in and completely destroyed the Japs there. But they were fearful of getting under the influence of land-based Jap air-power in the Marshall Islands. The moment our naval vessels got up where they could be hit by land-based airplanes, they turned around and left the area. Thus they were tacitly admitting their vulnerability to the attack of land-based aircraft.

But it had taken a long time.

11

IF YOU HAVE a bomber command out in the field, and are a major-general accordingly— And if a scholarly field grade Army engineer officer comes and talks to your people, and presents credentials which indicate that he is on a mission of extreme importance, and that he has highly classified information to present to the commanding general— If you are the commanding general you may be pardoned for thinking that something big is in the wind.

I had never heard of the Manhattan District Project before. I didn't know that any nuclear bombs were in the works. My job had always been to get as many conventional bombs on enemy targets as it was possible to put there. Nothing more than that.

This officer's job was to appear at Guam and tell me about things; and then go on up to Tinian and get the pits built, and the equipment. All facilities constructed, so that we could employ our new ordnance. He didn't give me any TNT equivalents. I didn't know much about this whole thing and didn't ask about it, because it was so hot. Didn't wish to have any more information than it was necessary for me to have.

But I knew that the bomb was coming out there, and I knew that it was going to be our job to drop it. And I was told that it was a nuclear weapon. That didn't make too much of an impression: my college physics course was a long way behind. Generally speaking, I could understand what the Army man was talking about. We had a very powerful weapon. But it was late in the war, and I was busy. Rapidly we were wiping out Japanese industry with incendiaries—when we could get them in sufficient quantity.

So Colonel Manhattan District went on up to Tinian to get the place set up. Let me say this: it was one of the best-kept military secrets of the war.

The President and his Interim Committee had approved the use of these bombs, and 21st Bomber Command's responsibility was to see that they were used with the utmost competence. To begin with, we had to have a fresh target—at least a target whereon no great destructive capacity had yet been exerted. None of the burned-up towns would do. Tokyo wouldn't do. There would be no possible way to measure the new bomb's effectiveness against a landscape of cinders.

As early as the first week of July we received orders not to direct any attacks against Kyoto, Hiroshima, Kokura or Niigata. Later on they removed Kyoto from this list, and substituted Nagasaki. Kyoto was the ancient capital of Japan. Just as in the European war: if you'd have had a choice between Heidelberg and Mannheim, you would have razed Mannheim.

The essential annihilative capacity of the new weapon (or weapons, rather; two distinct types of atomic bombs were already in existence; and one was used against Hiroshima and the other against Nagasaki) was not known in exactitude. They didn't shoot that one off down there in the desert until the 16th of July. Until that date everything had been theoretical. Even after the eventual detonation, we *supposed* that it would knock the hell out of a town. Nobody knew exactly what it would do. The bomb had never been used in warfare.

If you judge from all the articles and editorials which have been written in the past twenty years, and all the prayers which have been prayed, and all the mourning and preaching that has been going on, you would judge that we crossed some kind of moral boundary with the use of these weapons. The assumption seems to be that it is much more wicked to kill people with a nuclear bomb, than to kill people by busting their heads with rocks. St. Stephen, in the Bible, was stoned to death—just as prostitutes had been stoned, before Christ came along and was kind to Mary Magdalene.

There are a select group of writers, clergymen, savants, and self-appointed philosophers, and a not-so-select group of youthful or agèd beatniks, who are ready to support any antimilitary demonstration in any clime or country, at any time of the day or night. These mooncalves would have you convinced that a big bang is far wickeder than a little bang. I suppose they believe also that a machine gun is a hundred times wickeder than a bow and arrow. I've been shot at with machine guns . . . haven't, to my knowledge, ever been shot at with a bow and arrow. If I'd been killed, I don't suppose it would have made much difference to me which weapon was used.

Actually we, in the bombardment business, were not at all concerned about this. That doesn't mean that we were more bloodthirsty than other folks. We just weren't bothered about the morality of the question. If we could shorten the war we wanted to shorten it.

Most of us in the Army Air Forces had been convinced for a long time that it would be possible to defeat the Japanese without invading their home islands. We needed to establish bases within reasonable range; then we could bomb and burn them until they quit. That was our theory, and history has proved that we were right. The ground-gripping Army, and the Navy, didn't agree. They discounted the whole idea.

They were getting set for that invasion. Americans were going to have to land on Kyushu and operate against millions of well-trained men. Adequate demonstration of how the cornered Japanese would and could fight, had been offered every time the U.S. forces made a landing in that war. The number of American casualties which would be incurred by an actual invasion of the islands of Kyushu and Honshu was well up in the imaginative brackets and then some.

Therefore, when informed that we were about to be given a piece of ordnance which would far surpass in accomplishment any bomb ever dropped before by any nation, we all said *Swell*. I think we would have won the war anyway, merely by sticking to our incendiary tactics. But we were given the bombs and told to go ahead and drop them.

If a nuclear weapon shortened the war by only a week, probably it saved more lives than were taken by that single glare of heat and radiation. Matter of fact, one time I was asked this same question in Japan, at a press conference. And that was the answer I gave. The Japanese reaction was all to the good. They believed along with me that it was a question of military expediency and not a moral issue.

I don't mean to imply that, in 1945, there were any editorials in the Japanese press saying what a nice guy I was. As far back as March and April the Tokyo broadcasters had declared me to be a "bloodthirsty maniac" and "wanton killer." One of the Japanese broadcasters spoke as follows:

"Beneath a photograph of unkempt and scowling Gen. LeMay, a leading Tokyo journal called the attention of its readers to his blood-thirsty career. The article said that, only a lieutenant in the United States Air Forces in 1938, he was promoted to major-general and was placed in command of the United States heavy bombers attacking Germany. It said it was none other than LeMay who reduced Hamburg to ashes."

. . . Guess that would be news to the RAF.

Also another commentator complained bitterly, because I had not held to the same pattern of tactics all along. "The enemy planes are closing over our heads with changing tactics. In the types of bombs too, the enemy is challenging us with new weapons we failed to anticipate. Consequently, when we expected the enemy would use only oil bombs, he suddenly raids us with large phosphorous and electronic incendiaries."

So the Japanese press and commentators were somewhat disturbed by our attacks, you can say, long before we ever brought the first atomic bomb over their mainland and kicked it loose.

Actually I think it's more immoral to use *less* force than necessary, than it is to use *more*. If you use less force, you kill off more of humanity in the long run, because you are merely protracting the struggle.

We have had the same situation all over again, both in Korea and in Viet Nam. I suggested informally, when the Korean flap started in 1950, that we go up north immediately with incendiaries and delete four or five of the largest towns: Wonsan, Pyongyang and so on.

The answer from Washington: "No, no, that's too utterly horrible! You'd kill a lot of noncombatants!"

Thus we went along, allowing ourselves to be cajoled into conducting a war under wraps, because the alternative was unacceptable morally. And what happened? We burned down just about every city in North Korea and South Korea *both*, including Pusan. That one was an accident. But we nearly burned all of it down just the same.

And during the three years of warfare we killed off over a million civilian Koreans and drove several million more from their homes, with the inevitable additional tragedies bound to ensue. The military casualties on both sides totaled nearly three and one-half million.

Over fifty-four thousand dead Americans. . . .

To expunge a few people to stop a war right at the start is unacceptable. Or a few hundred people, or a few thousand. Or—go all out on it—a few hundred thousand. But over a long period of time, wearily killing them off and killing them off, killing millions under the most horrible circumstances— That is acceptable. Mankind keeps on doing it.

Even the crews who freighted the ordnance up to Hiroshima and Nagasaki, and dumped it, didn't know just what they really had. Nobody was sure about the destructive capacity, not even the scientists. When that first bomb went off, and there was a gigantic flare, a burst brighter than the sun, a mushroom-shaped cloud of smoke— They were understandably bowled over by what they witnessed.

That's when a few individuals began to lie awake nights, debating in their own minds the ethical responsibility involved. . . . We had some men over in Europe who went loco just from dropping ordinary bombs, or helping to drop them. It gets back to the old situation concerning combat fatigue.

The pros who carry nuclear arms today feel exactly the same moral responsibility they might feel in carrying a carbine or a 250-pound GP bomb. Or (I suppose there are pros among the Jivaros in South America, but maybe *they're* not yet armed with nuclear weapons) a poisoned blow-gun dart.

There were absolutely no psychological repercussions in the attitude of our SAC personnel after they became equipped with these weapons. I never observed any reluctance among my subordinates to embrace a program which entailed the employment of nuclear ordnance.

I can see no more reason for a delegation of Japanese maidens who were injured in Hiroshima or Nagasaki coming over here to protest against weapons, than I can for a throng of German civilians to demonstrate in front of the White House; or survivors of the attacks on Plymouth, London or Coventry to go over and stage a sit-down at the residence of the Chancellor of West Germany.

Certainly the feeling must be very much the same throughout all armies. From a practical standpoint of the soldiers out in the field it doesn't make any difference how you slay an enemy. Everybody worries about their own losses . . . seeing their friends killed, so on. As I've told before, I used to be tormented in losing my airmen . . . how many were shot down today? What could we have done instead? Was the prize worth the *price*? What could I have done which might have saved an extra crew or two . . . ?

But to worry about the *morality* of what we were doing— Nuts. A soldier has to fight. We fought. If we accomplished the job in any given battle without exterminating too many of our own folks, we considered that we'd had a pretty good day.

I can recognize no more depravity in dropping a nuclear weapon than in having a V-2 rocket equipped with an orthodox warhead, and shooting it vaguely in the general direction of London, as the Germans did. No difference whatsoever.

In fact, I think the preponderance of justice is on the side with a skillful weapon attacking a specific target. It must be remembered that we did not start the bombing in these wars. The Japs and the Germans did a lot of bombing before we ever got into the act.

. . . So some young kids who don't know any better go out and demonstrate against the military; and a lot of old fools who ought to know better, inveigh against the military, et cetera. They are worried to death about our dropping nuclear bombs.

In SAC our bombardiers aren't worried about it.

We were going after military targets. No point in slaughtering civilians for the mere sake of slaughter. Of course there is a pretty thin veneer in Japan, but the veneer was there. It was their system of dispersal of industry. All you had to do was visit one of those targets after we'd roasted it, and see the ruins of a multitude of tiny houses, with a drill press sticking up through the wreckage of every home. The entire population got into the act and worked to make those airplanes or munitions of war . . . men, women, children. We knew we were going to kill a lot of women and kids when we burned that town. Had to be done.

Oh, there was considerable dispersal of German industry, but never to the extent of the Japanese system. In Japan they were set up like this: they'd have a factory; and then the families, in their homes throughout the area, would manufacture small parts. You might call it a home-folks assembly line deal. The Suzuki clan would manufacture Bolt 64; the Harunobu family next door might be making Nut 64; or 65 or 63, or all the gaskets in between. Those would be manufactured right in the same neighborhood. Then Mr. Kitagawa from the factory would scoot around with his cart and pick up the parts in proper order.

I'll never forget Yokohama. That was what impressed me: drill presses. There they were, like a forest of scorched trees and stumps, growing up throughout that residential area. Flimsy construction all gone . . . everything burned down, or up, and drill presses standing like skeletons.

The whole purpose of strategic warfare is to destroy the enemy's potential to wage war. And this was the enemy's potential. It had to be erased. If we didn't obliterate it, we would dwell subservient to it. Just as simple as that.

. . . Did someone just say the word *co-existence?*

There's nothing new about this massacre of civilian populations. In ancient times, when an army laid siege to a city, everybody was in the fight. And when that city had fallen, and was sacked, just as often as not every single soul was murdered.

I think now of that elderly wheeze about the stupid man who was not basically cruel—he was just well-meaning. The guy who cut off the dog's tail an inch at a time so that it wouldn't hurt so much.

In May the 509th Composite Group had become a part of our 21st Bomber Command, and had moved in on the island of Tinian. That was where special pits, mentioned before, had been prepared, along with other necessary facilities for the general care and feeding of atomic bombs.

The 509th Composite Group started in back in Utah, at Wendover (the old 306th hangout of 1942). From the beginning they were trained for this particular type of mission. Their B-29's had nothing in the way of gun turrets except for the twin 50's in the tail. Training was entirely different from that which fell to any other B-29 outfit. There was no formation flying. Any B-29 which dropped an atomic bomb of that vintage had to get away from the target mighty fast. Endlessly the 509th's pilots practiced those sharp diving turns which would be essential to take them to comparative safety. They'd have less than one minute during which they might escape the effect of the blast.

No one knew how many bombs it would be necessary to manufacture, and explode over Japanese cities, in order to bring the military clique to their knees—or, more literally, to the surrender table. Some people in the JCS, I've heard, thought as many as five bombs might be required. At any rate a supply of blue ribbon pilots, bombardiers and navigators were poured into the hopper of this program. There would be other airplanes accompanying the plane which actually carried the bomb, in order to photograph the explosion and all subsequent developments . . . measure radiation, shock waves . . . physical residue.

Paul Tibbets commanded the 509th. He was the pilot who flew the *Enola Gay* to Hiroshima on August 6th. If I remember correctly, he was only a light colonel at the time.

Let's affirm once more that this atomic business went from start to finish in perfect security—a magnificently kept secret. I had been told what it was about, yet still I didn't actually knew what the bomb would do. Nobody else knew either. They fired off that one down in the desert, and that was the only atomic explosion which had ever taken place. Nor could those few of us now let into the secret take much time to sit around and speculate on what was going to happen. We had too much work to do.

In the 509th, each man knew his own job; yet he didn't know anything about The Bomb. They were aware only that it was large in size, and required special training for the people who would handle it.

After this group came to Tinian, sharing some facilities with the 313th Wing (Skippy Davies' people), they were provided with an unusual bomb, very nearly the same size which the atomic bombs would assume. But these contained no uranium or plutonium or any other fissionable material. Nothing but good old-fashioned TNT.

Necessarily the crews needed practice with these. They had done a lot of training, beginning in the ZI, and then over water down around Cuba. But actually they hadn't dropped live bombs on any targets until they came to Tinian. We sent them to Japan to put down a few of the oversized TNT bombs. They made a huge hole, and knocked down a lot of buildings, and that was it; they had no relation to what was coming up.

These were regarded as practice bombs. I don't suppose the unfortunate people who connected with them down there on the ground thought they were practice bombs; but that's what we called 'em.

In bunk-flying sessions also, these TNT jobs were pretty well confused with the mines with which the 313th Wing was decorating the Japanese waters. This activity was an extremely important part of 21st Bomber Command, and had far-reaching results.

AAFWW II says: "The 313th Wing got into the game late, operating with mines for only four and one-half months and at a period when the enemy's merchant fleet had contracted in size and in scope of its activities. During that short period mines planted by the wing were more destructive than any other weapon, accounting for about half of the total tonnage disposed of. . . . In the early weeks of the campaign, mining operations carried a top secret classification, and LeMay was concerned lest the absence of any public recognition hurt the morale of B-29 crews engaged in mining—an unsatisfactory type of operations at best since the crewman never sees the result of his strike."

We had all of Skippy's wing at work for a while; then after the mine fields had been sowed, we retained one group on the job, the 505th, just keeping the fields filled to a point of major effectiveness. That they did so was the unanimous testimony of everybody concerned. The British said that our B-29 mining was "very much like a dream come true." Even Admiral Nimitz sent several messages of congratulation on this subject, in the final one of which he actually used the words "phenomenal results." The postwar testimony of Japanese experts underlines the prevailing opinion: that the mines which were parachuted down into the water from those B-29's had an enormous share in choking off the Japanese supply routes at sea.

By the time the nuclear strikes were launched against Hiroshima and Nagasaki, we were running out of major targets. We were still mining, and we were still hitting secondary Japanese cities and burning them up. Any secondary Japanese city worth its salt was a true industrial complex and, as such, contributed its proportion to the Japanese potential.

We were going into the railroad business too, knocking off transportation.

The war was long washed up over in Europe, and now we were about to inaugurate the Strategic Air Forces of the Pacific. This was the beginning of the end. In fact it was very near the *ending* of the end.

On July 20th Tooey Spaatz landed at Guam with the nucleus of a staff. The plan was for him to be commander of the Strategic Air Forces of the Pacific. He would have under him all the B-29's in the 20th Air Force. My job: Chief of Staff, under Tooey. Nate Twining was to command the 20th. Jimmy Doolittle would have the Eighth Air Force, based in the Philippines and on Okinawa, composed of the airplanes which had been bombing in Europe: 17's and 24's. Sir Hugh Lloyd came out, representing the British effort. If enough fields could be built for them to work from, the RAF would join us in the act.

General Spaatz told me all this, informing me just who was going to fit into each slot. Actually I wondered if these vast plans would ever come to fruition. I didn't think that there would be any military necessity for them. I told Tooey that I thought this all came a little bit late.

"I don't think, General, that they'll get fields built for these people before the war is over."

Seemed like it would be a good plan to show General Spaatz just what he was going to be commanding out there, so I took him around and let him look at the various outfits. He went down to Headquarters and was briefed on what we were doing then, what we had done, and what our plans were.

His telegram to Larry Norstad is reproduced among the illustrations in this book.

HAVE HAD OPPORTUNITY TO CHECK UP ON BAKER TWO NINE [B-29] OPERATIONS AND BELIEVE THIS IS THE BEST ORGANIZED AND MOST TECHNICALLY AND TACTICALLY PROFICIENT MILITARY ORGANIZATION THAT THE WORLD HAS SEEN TO DATE.

Uranium, plutonium; "Little Boy, Fat Man": the world knows those weapons now, every school child knows. No use describing the mushroom-shaped column, the unbelievable light, and weird color of the flash and resulting clouds . . . unearthly debris and steaming destruction and massive death. It's an old and familiar story now, from Bikini on.

These bombs brought into the world not only their own speed and extent of desolation. They brought a strange pervading fear which does not seem to have affected mankind previously, from any other source. This unmitigated terror has no justice, no basis in fact. Nothing new about death, nothing new about deaths caused militarily. We scorched and boiled and baked to death more people in Tokyo on that night of March 9–10 than went up in vapor at Hiroshima and Nagasaki combined.

(Odd about Kokura: that city had been saved for Number Two; and it was saved unto itself because of clouds. When Major Sweeney's plane went in to drop the second and more proficient "Fat Man" type of atom bomb, he found the target area badly obscured. He made three runs over the target, and it was still obscured. So they went to

Nagasaki, the Secondary, and it was clear enough by the time they got there to make a visual release. The thousands and thousands of people who were saved at Kokura must have gone trotting about their business, totally unaware. The ones at Nagasaki, who would have been totally unaware if the bomb had been dropped on its original destination—Kokura— They weren't trotting on any business any more.)

In postwar years I listened to a lecturer whose views very much reflected my own.

". . . Personally, I should just as soon have my grandchildren blown into Kingdom Come by some new-fangled bomb or missile, as to have their little heads hacked off by the blunt sword of Tamerlane or Genghis Khan. Examine the old records and translate them into your own idiom. *And we did take that city, and there were an hundred thousand people, and all of these we put to the sword.* We must not forget that there were ugly pyramids of skulls on the Asiatic plains long before Hiroshima or Nagasaki. *And then we destroyed their city, and left not one stone upon another.* Let us not forget how the site of the vanished, eradicated Carthage was sown to salt so that nothing would grow there. . . . Radiation, perhaps?"

General Twining is quoted by history: "I am convinced that the surrender would have occurred within a short time period even if the atomic bomb had never been used."

And my own view is stated as well: "I think it was anticlimactic in that the verdict was already rendered."

Certainly I did not and do not decry the use of the bomb. Anything which will achieve the desired results should be employed. If those bombs shortened the war only by days, they rendered an inestimable service, and so did the men who were responsible for their construction and delivery. There was no transgression, no venturing into a field illicit and immoral, as has so often been charged. Soldiers were ordered to do a job. They did it.

Hiroshima brought no instantaneous prostration of the Japanese military; nevertheless it was a startlingly rapid disintegration. Meanwhile we were still piling on the incendiaries. Our B-29's went to Yawata on August 8th, and burned up 21 per cent of the town, and on the same day some other 29's went to Fukuyama and burned up 73.3 per cent. Still there wasn't any gasp and collapse when the second nuclear bomb went down above Nagasaki on August 9th. We kept on flying. Went to Kumagaya on August 14th . . . 45 per cent of that town. Flew our final mission the same day against Isezaki, where we burned up 17 per cent of that target. Then the crews came home to the Marianas and were told that Japan had capitulated.

Arrangements were made by radio between General MacArthur and the Japanese authorities to send a peace delegation down to Manila in a white-painted airplane. Our people gave the Japs the route to travel and all similar instruction. They flew dutifully to Manila, where complete arrangements were made for the surrender. This would take place on September 2nd, aboard the battleship *Missouri* in Tokyo Harbor, off Yokohama.

It was arranged for our own personnel to land on an airfield south of Yokohama. The Japanese were to furnish quarters and transportation facilities. On landing up there, we observed that the enemy had complied faithfully in every detail, insofar as he was able. But the equipment was poor.

They gave us the best they had. And the automobiles would scarcely run . . . many malfunctioned . . . inoperable cars were off along the side of the road, all the way into town. We kept looking for Yokohama. It seemed that we journeyed through the outskirts for a very long time; but finally we came to the city itself. There were only a couple of streets left along the waterfront where any masonry construction was still standing. The rest of Yokohama was gone. That's why it had taken us so long to go through the outskirts. There just weren't any inskirts. And at the beginning of the war that had been a city of 866,200 (about as many as there are in the State of Rhode Island today). It had turned into an unpopulated wilderness.

There were a few Japanese waiters around to serve us . . . no one else. The inhabitants had either fled or else had died in the ruins.

Automatically—and forever this will be true in my mind—mention of the desolate shreds of Yokohama brings to memory the thought of a great American who is no longer with us. I refer to General Stilwell, the famous "Vinegar Joe."

In 1944, when I first went out to the CBI, I tried to make the usual courtesy call on Stilwell, who was then Theater Commander. But he was away. So I never set eyes on him until he appeared in the Chengtu Valley while I happened to be up there running a mission. After we got the mission off, I had dinner with Stilwell, and we spent practically the whole night in conversation. Again and again I tried to explain what our AAF intentions and ambitions were in the strategic field.

Without much success. He was a combat efficiency expert, but it seemed that I could never make him understand how we wanted to bomb, and why.

. . . After the surrender in Tokyo Bay was complete, and I had returned briefly to Guam, Stilwell flew over there. He said, "I came especially to see you. Here's the reason why—"

He had been present at the surrender ceremonies; we'd barely seen each other there, and certainly there was no time for a talk. Now he appeared, to say, "For the first time I appreciate what you were trying to tell me last year in the Chengtu Valley."

He said, "When I was a very young officer, I went to Yokohama as a language student. I know what Yokohama was like: I was completely familiar with the place. On September 2nd I saw what you B-29 people had done to Yokohama. Indeed it was the same thing you'd done to all the strategic cities of Japan. You had done what you set out to do. I recognize now the terrible military virtues of strategic bombardment."

It was the measure of the man that he should make a trip to Guam just to tell me this.

. . . There was the *Missouri* lying off Yokohama in Tokyo Bay. We had a very short boat ride over from what was left of the city docks. . . . I remember especially how General MacArthur looked when he sat at the table; and I remember the emaciated shape of ex-prisoner General Wainwright of Corregidor fame, towering behind him.

Wish I could recall exactly what went through my mind while standing on that open deck of the *Missouri*. I did think of the young men who died to bring about this moment of triumph and, as always, wondered just where I'd gone wrong in losing as many as we did. Seemed to me that if I had done a better job we might have saved a few more crews.

Our ears were filled with the roar of four hundred and sixty-two B-29's flying overhead. They came from every wing, every group, every squadron.

. . . Well, it was over and done, and whoever was down was down, and whoever was living was living.

Like many other folks, probably, I stood there and felt pretty tired.

BOOK VI

AAF and USAF: Immediate Postwar

(1945 – 1948)

A FEW WEEKS after hostilities were terminated we received orders from Washington to make a nonstop flight of three B-29's from Japan to Washington. Offhand I would guess that this flight was dreamed up to demonstrate and dramatize—and, eventually, publicize—the long-range capability of the 29 to the American people and to the world at large.

Barney Giles was to fly the lead airplane, and Rosie O'Donnell and I would fly the other two. Lieutenant-General Giles had commanded the Central Pacific Air Forces, with B-24's and a lot of defensive fighters. But he operated directly under Admiral Nimitz, while I operated under the JCS (except for that one period during the Okinawa campaign). Later on Barney became deputy commander of the entire 20th Air Force.

We got together and talked the thing over; we examined photographs and charts. The only field which might accommodate the B-29's was Mizutani, up on the northern Japanese island of Hokkaido. It's where the Jap Naval Academy was located. Trouble was, we didn't have any troops in there as yet, and wouldn't have until about three months after the surrender. There was nobody of whom we could make inquiry concerning the runways—all those essential hard and fast details as to whether our Very Heavy Bombers might be accommodated.

Nothing to do but send an emissary to find out. I picked on Butch Blanchard for this. The war's end, of course, had come so speedily and unexpectedly that our forces were caught flat-footed. They were hard put to send enough personnel into Japan just to get the surrender taken care of.

I told Butch to take along a liaison-type radio; to land on the field at Hokkaido, look the whole deal over, and decide whether in his estimation we could lift fully-loaded B-29's off of there. Judging from the photographs, we thought we could; but no one knew anything about the runway pavements. It was up to Butch to examine that base and make the all-important decision about pavement: whether it would crack and crumble under our weight, or whether we could use the field.

Can't remember exactly what Butch's comments were, when he found that he had been tapped for this very interesting little job of exploration; nor do I recall what his parting words were. He went up there in a B-17, alone except for his small crew. There had been persistent rumors about certain remote Japanese outfits who might refuse to accept the surrender, and fight to the last ditch—hold out fanatically until they themselves were faced with surrender; and then they'd probably commit hara-kiri. I guess Butch thought he'd be greeted either with a very sharp Japanese knife, or a shower of rose-petals and goldfish—he didn't know which.

Fortunately for us all, and especially for William H. Blanchard, the Japanese units at Hokkaido had got the ungarbled word from the Emperor. Butch landed, and they coöperated with him in his examination of the field.

"Affirmative," he radioed. "Come on up with your 29's."

Iwo Jima was the closest station where we could gas up. Rosie and Barney and I picked out our three airplanes and flew them to Iwo. We gassed up and landed, heavy as we could, on the field at Hokkaido. Besides that we had a couple of C-54's bringing drum gasoline in, in order for us to top off completely and be ready for the long flight to Washington.

That night we slept in a barracks with three thousand polite Japanese sailors surrounding us. No sweat. As it happened, I got some of my few pieces of loot out of the war at that time.

We each did want a pistol, and we told the commander of the Japanese base that we did. Very kindly he presented us with pistols. I brought mine home and gave it to Pop. Also we were awarded some Japanese naval blankets. And I already had that fine *samurai* sword from Mao Tse-tung. (I doubt that our crews did very badly at that Jap base, either. Airmen are usually pretty adept at picking up some attractive souvenirs.)

Souvenirs or no, on September 18th–19th we made it back to the United States but not to Washington. Some readers may remember the newspaper accounts at the time. The press made a big fuss about this, even with our going a little short at Chicago.

We were all flying together. By that, I mean we were within radio contact, each doing our own navigation. Normally the wind at that season is supposed to prevail from the west, and there shouldn't be any trouble at all in proceeding nonstop from Japan to Washington in the type of aircraft we had. Matter of fact, a month or so after we made the flight, Frank Armstrong came in nonstop from Japan; and he landed in Washington with enough gasoline left to go on down to Puerto Rico. In our case, however, we had adverse winds all the way. Unusual for middle September.

After we got into the Chicago area, we were informed that the weather situation in Washington was marginal. I thought I had enough gas to make it . . . we discussed the matter . . . both Rosie and Barney said definitely they didn't have enough fuel left to go on and complete the planned trip at its proper destination. They said they were going into Chicago to gas up.

I went on awhile, then received another Washington report. This time the weather was *really* marginal, and that didn't seem to make very good sense, with the small reserve of gas I'd have. I turned around and went back, and we all gassed at Chicago before we flew on to Washington.

Immediately we were handed a chore: go up to some big shindig which they were having in New York three days later. We went, dutifully enough, and then we each had about a week's leave. Our job in the Pacific was done.

That leave felt and tasted pretty good.

Back on the job again, we reported to Washington and sat down with Tooey Spaatz to talk about what we were going to do. We had a lot of discussion back and forth. Somebody must go out to Wright and take active command of Research and Development there, and somebody must do the staff job for R & D in Washington.

It was decided that I'd be the one to go to Wright Field, and O'Donnell would stay on the staff. I remember his bitching about *that*. He was going to have to buy a house; and all I'd have to do was to breeze out there to Ohio and move into a nice set of quarters.

Helen felt fine about the Ohio deal: it was our old stamping ground —our mutual native State—and why shouldn't we like to be in Ohio? Furthermore, I wasn't very keen on the idea of staff work. Told myself that I was a *field* commander. . . .

In the end it reminded me a little of the time when Helen and I moved happily into our honeymoon quarters at Selfridge, and then were told promptly about a new assignment to Hawaii. Worked out the same way in 1945, except it didn't take so long. I had been at Wright only a few days when I was informed that I was going to be Deputy Chief of Air Staff for Research and Development. They were going to fire off an elaborate program. That would be my job, down there in the Pentagon. And Rosie was coming out to Wright.

So I was the one who had to squeeze into Washington and hunt for the house, and buy it; while Rosie moved contentedly into quarters in Ohio. I don't think I was out there more than ten days, all in all. Every now and then I had to return, naturally. But until I was selected to command the United States Air Forces in Europe, the following year, I did that staff job.

We found a home in Arlington, and I went to work in the Big House.

There was plenty to do right then, and there was going to be a great deal more to do. I had to get organized, and plan for the budget, and try to get some money into the account.

Also we started Project Paper Clip.

. . . Must admit that in certain moments I worried about this peg-in-the-hole business. There had been only one other suggestion made concerning my new duties, and that came from General Eaker. He had wanted me to be A-4 of the whole Army Air Forces, and work into that sort of job as soon as we received the autonomy which we were fighting for. We were confident that we'd have a separate Air Force, and before too long. Eaker was convinced that in any case we'd need some combat people on the staff. That's the reason Fred Anderson went into Personnel, etc. But in the end I was ticketed for R & D anyway.

I certainly hadn't been screeching with enthusiasm about my new duties, but it didn't take me long to become mighty interested. It was strictly a management job. I didn't know much about Research and Development . . . I'd had my little bit of engineering education. So they gathered in a lot of folks who *did* know something about the whole program: Bim Wilson and such. And we went to work.

Thus I was never in the front ranks during the battle for autonomy. We had our own problems. Once in a while, when we stopped to draw breath, the rest of us folks could applaud from the sidelines.

Before the war, the budget for R & D was at an all-time low. I recall using this as an example in some testimony before a certain Congressional committee, pointing out how the annual budget for the propeller division out at Wright Field wouldn't buy one set of B-29 propellers— the budget for a *year,* mind you. That's how we came to be about ten years behind the Germans. (Surely we were at least a decade behind them: in advanced aerodynamics, in missilery. And we had to catch up, no two ways about it.)

Let me emphasize that during the war there had been little research done—I guess we're safe in saying *none*—except in relation to observations which might stem from combat experience. And prior to the war, we'd had practically nothing in the way of a program. We'd been just engineering, building what we had into mass production during the war.

A lot of catching up to do.

As I look back now, from a strictly selfish and personal standpoint, this was one of the most valuable things which could have happened to me at the time. Oh, I'll grant that forever I have felt ill-equipped for whatever command I was assigned to. I always thought I didn't know enough about the work; needed to know a lot more. I don't think

I would have done half as well in SAC, for instance, if I hadn't had this R & D experience first.

We had to study the whole situation thoroughly, with emphasis on what the Germans had done during the war and previously. When Hitler came into power in 1933, the Germans fired up an enormous research and development program. It paid off. They built a military machine, the most impressive that the world had ever seen.

But after Hitler overran Poland and France and the Lowlands in such a comparatively short period of time, and nullified all threat from Scandinavia, he cut off his intensive program. He built himself into a real gap, right then and there.

England didn't collapse as the Nazis expected; and we Americans got into the war. It looked like it was going to be a long-term affair, so Hitler had to blast off his whole program again.

It's impossible to estimate what trouble, what actual suffering and lives and wealth were saved to us by this delay. If Hitler had been able to get his buzz-bomb program working in the field— Get the V-1's flying, and the V-2's a little earlier than they did, there might have been an entirely different story to tell.

Also those air-to-air rockets used against our bombers: the ones they were shooting at us at the last of the war. If they'd had an improved guidance system (actually I mean if they'd had *any* guidance system. They didn't have any at all) our destruction of German strategic targets could not have been carried out as effectively as it was.

Despite all this, in this field of weaponry we were still far behind the Germans when the war was over.

A few intelligent deeds had been done, and that was what Project Paper Clip was all about. The moment enemy resistance collapsed in Europe we overran some of the research centers, and started gathering up papers and files—and the scientists—and trying to get them back to the States. Unlike the Russians, we didn't bring anyone over here who didn't want to come. It was all a matter of convincing them that they would be happy in the United States, and have a better future career over here than over there. And we had to guarantee to all of them that we would take good care of their families in Germany.

But the only way we could get them into this country was as Prisoners of War. It so happened that an effective majority of our scientists didn't want them around. Not so unbelievable as it seems. Frankly, I think that many of our scientists were frightened by their own deficiencies. They didn't welcome any German competition. Nevertheless, we did get quantities of them over here. I even found one batch behind barbed wire.

. . . You can't get anything out of scientists that way. You can take a man and stand over him with a club, and say, "Dig a ditch," and you can make him dig the ditch. But you can't stand over scientists and make them do something they don't want to do. It just doesn't work out.

Well, that was a crying need in my new job: rescue those able and intelligent Jerries from behind the barbed wire, and get them going in our various military projects, and feed them into American industry, so on. Mind you, they weren't in any disciplinary camps. No, they were Prisoners of *War*. So of course they had to be put in jail. Somebody's bright idea.

It may come as a shock and surprise to some readers to learn that Werner Von Braun was one of these people, and also his old teacher and boss, General Dornberger. Think of that, and it really makes you sit up and take notice. Wonder where we'd be today, if we'd let those people languish in the pen.

Very soon it became apparent to me that the first thing we needed was facilities. We didn't have the tools which were essential to the job. Made you think of the old Churchillian statement about Lend-Lease: "Give us the tools and we will finish the job." What sort of tools? We needed everything—everything from wind tunnels to laboratories to test facilities. We couldn't start on the Atlas missile—our first important one—without having some workbenches. That's where we concentrated the bulk of the money we could scrape up.

I've had to smile—maybe sourly—a lot of times during the years in Washington a generation later, when I plugged for the RS-70 and the mixed weapons system, and when I read remarks by pundits in a few newspapers and magazines which typified me as an enemy of all missiles. Hell's bells!—that's when we got our first missile program lined up, there in 1946, right after the war, when I had R & D. We studied the idea of the satellite, and received our scientific advisory board report. They said, "Yes, it is definitely possible to put a satellite into orbit." The bill was fantastic, however. We didn't have the cash, and couldn't get it from any source. It was only many years later, after we were further along with our missile program and got the boosters and so on, that it became feasible to orbit anything.

(In April, 1963, there appeared in *The Airpower Historian* an article by Thomas F. Dixon of NASA. In a summation he wrote: "Of importance to us today is the fundamental and continuing contributions to rocketry made by the A-4 rocket [German V-2] and its designers and developers. For it was from this program, and all the knowledge of it brought to this country after the war, that U.S. engineers and designers acquired the basic concepts for the development of larger rocket engines for the future. The Redstone engine, the Thor and Jupiter engines, the Navaho engine, the engines for the Saturn, for the Advanced

Saturn, and for all their stages, all grew out of the basic knowledge that was pioneered in the A-4 rocket. When F-1 engines with 1,500,000 pounds of thrust and J-2 engines with 200,000 pounds of thrust boost American astronauts to a landing on the moon, they will have done so in part because the concepts for the German A-4 rocket have done their job once more.")

You may understand now why Von Braun was an important element in our program, as also was Major-General or Doctor Walter Dornberger. (Call him whichever you want to; both titles apply.) Dornberger had been the commander at Peenemunde. Incidentally, both he and Von Braun were present in Peenemunde at the time the RAF made their famous attack in 1943. They were two who escaped. . . . Good thing that we got them over here, and ground into the act. I don't think we could even have considered the Atlas program without having people like that.

Once again: our crying need was for facilities. It was at this time that we laid down the Arnold Research and Development Center, at Tullahoma. We had a real hassle on that one. It was either going to be down there in Tennessee, or it would be built up in the Columbia River valley. Our overwhelming requirement was for power to run those enormous tunnels. You need unbelievable amounts of power for things like that. We people on the job considered that there was more potential force available in the Columbia River valley than there was down in Tennessee; and that was the way we recommended it.

But there are political considerations in choices like this. We lost out, and the thing was built in Tennessee. Matter of fact, it hasn't worked out too badly. Thus far we haven't had any shortage of electricity; but the project does use a frightening percentage of power at peak times. We would have preferred, originally, the Columbia River site; and I still think it would be better if the thing were there today. Better—where any problem of power in the future is concerned.

My main concentration, during the two years that I was with R & D, was on that particular project. Got really embroiled in it . . . which explains again why I had little part in the fuss about establishing a separate Air Force.

But I got in some licks in a new role, as a witness before committees. Had never done anything like that before. Every major commander in the field ought to have a siege on the staff. It's of untold benefit to recognize the problems which people run into in Washington, in getting programs for any of the Services going. Just how they are laid out; how you get the money; and the problems and headaches which plague you in trying to build up your own particular Service, for five to seven years *in advance*. If you've been there and know the workings of a staff in the Pentagon and with the Congress, it's valuable later on, when you're back in the field. You understand problems which you wouldn't have understood before. You are not so frustrated when you don't get action speedily.

Experience, experience. Again I affirm it: no substitute for experience.

Hand in hand with this demand marched the other problems. We had to cobble together a better organization than existed previously, for the purpose of examining the various recommendations and deciding what to concentrate on and where to spend our money. I did manage to improve the previously existing setup. We put together a weapons board, for instance, composed of both operational people and R & D people; and we included also scientists involved in adjacent undertakings. These folks were charged with the task of coming up with recommendations for whatever weapons system we needed. The Atlas program came out of this; so did the Navaho program. Even the B-52, which would not come to fruition for many years, emerged from this scheme. The B-52, as initially proposed, was a propeller job—not a jet. I doubt that the public realizes all the mutations which ensue, and how the whole program concerning any new airplane has been in the works for years.

When you observe that a modern plane has been taken out from under wraps, and has flown a much-publicized test flight or two, you can bet your bottom dollar that it all started Way Back When.

So we kicked off our very modest missile program. We knew that the rocket engine was here to stay, and that opened the gateway into Space.

I think back to that perpetual query: "Look. Could we put up a little satellite?" I remember how we asked our scientific advisory board for a study on this subject; and I remember how much money they said it would cost. That was when we began to fall by the wayside, as far as satellites were concerned. At that time everyone in Washington screamed that it wasn't worth the money. Then, after the Russians came along with their Sputniks, the Army said they could have done it sooner by using their Jupiter program. Correct. And we could have done it sooner, if we'd gone to work right then in 1946.

But this all happened during that sublime period when a lot of busy-bodies were busily engaged in pulling apart the very muscles and bones of our Armed Forces.

It was on July 26th, 1947, that President Truman signed the National Security Act. This was the bill which separated the Air Force from the Army and gave us our autonomy.

Actually the new regime went into effect on September 18th of that year, a fortnight before I was ordered over to Germany to take command of the United States Air Forces in Europe (USAFE). I think the AAF were at their lowest ebb just about a month before the President signed that bill. We went down to about 303,000 men. That's pretty rapid demobilization, when one considers that we had numbered around 2,400,000 in 1944. But in the middle of 1947 we actually possessed only thirty-eight combat groups—on paper, that is—and, according to the best information available, only eleven of those groups could be considered operationally effective.

General Carl A. Spaatz went in as the first Chief of Staff of the USAF, and I was posted for my new assignment almost immediately. I had become deeply immersed in the R & D business; but could never forget that essentially I still considered myself a field commander. Still I was grateful for the opportunities which had come my way to observe how things were done in Washington. Such awareness would be invaluable through the rest of my career.

There was a selfish reason for appreciation of the new command also. It would mean promotion: the slot called for three stars. Helen pinned on that little third star for me on the first day of October. We were en route to our new post soon afterward.

2

ON THE WAY to Germany I brooded a little about diplomacy . . . how would I get on with the civilians? (I got on mighty well with Mao Tse-tung, back in China, but this was *post*-war, and civilians were something else again.)

It turned out that I had very little to do in the way of diplomatic chores. I was stationed at Wiesbaden, one of the German state capitals. Dr. James R. Newman (formerly Colonel Newman) was the state governor then—our American man on the scene—so I had little to worry about in that direction. French and Belgians and a lot of other people were moving in and out of Wiesbaden constantly, so there was considerable contact with foreigners. But in my case and at my level it was with the military almost solely. When General Clay took over he was as much in the diplomatic business as he was in the military. It still meant that I didn't have to worry about being a square peg, etc.

Everyone coming cold into Germany during that period shuddered at the trance-like conditions. The war had been over for more than two years, but the Germans were still in a state of utter shock. They looked like zombies, like the walking dead. They went unheeding and aloof across the streets. An automobile would be coming . . . they didn't care, didn't look, didn't even turn their heads when the screech of brakes exploded behind them. There was an eternal nothingness about the place: nothing happening, no work going on; nothing much to eat at home. People sat and stared. A little girl would be crouched on the steps of a half-ruined house, or maybe two or three little girls; and one of them might be holding a toy, but she wouldn't be paying any attention to it; neither would the others. When you passed, their eyes followed you, but blankly, blankly. There was no response, no enlivening humanity in any countenance. The place was bewitched. You thought of a story you heard as a child . . . thought of the palace with everyone asleep, and brambles growing up outside, and a great pervading silence in halls and chambers.

Americans (somewhat bewildered by the state of things) approached the whole deal much more cautiously than did the French. The French clutched their zone in a heavy mailed hand. You could see why, after you were around there awhile. Right from the military governor on down, every Frenchman whom I met in Germany while I was there—military or civilian—had been a prisoner of the Germans in some way or other. He had either been a soldier who was grabbed and was placed in a military prison camp; or he'd been in a concentration camp; or had been in a forced labor battalion or something. Every damn one of them. . . . Did they have their zone under control! No German automobiles running around in *their* zone. If you saw an automobile on the road, it was French, or possibly one of ours which had wandered down there.

Left to their own devices, and operating out of their own country and in conquered territories, the Germans have never been very good at Winning Friends. I think we see the Germans at their best when they are mingled with other nationalities, as in the United States. They make an excellent alloy when metal is being mixed. Raw German silver or German lead is rather hard to take.

One of the first things that we had to do was to clean up all the ammunition dumps glowering and towering on every side. Army and Army Air Force supplies: whole square miles of them. This kind of waste happens at the conclusion of every war, I guess, or at least every war won by a Democracy.

From a high of two and a half million our Army Air Forces had gone down like mercury on the Great Plains when a norther hits. Everybody was concerned with getting Freddy Fuss home for Christmas and with getting Frank Fidget back into civilian clothes. We had shut up the nursery and gone away, leaving our dolls all over the floor. Didn't even have enough people over there to destroy the old ammunition.

The idea was that when outfits went home, they couldn't go home until they had turned their equipment in. The idea was to box everything up and send it to the depot. A lot of readers won't believe this, but we opened up sealed boxes which actually contained the contents of wastebaskets. Just trash. Soldiers had poured every variety of junk into the boxes in order to get them closed up, so they could go home.

Everything from pencils to toilet paper to pistol ammunition. You never knew what you'd find. The stuff was improperly marked . . . you didn't know whether you were going to open up a carton of dried orchids or a can of worms. Or maybe, like the alarmed police in detective stories . . . *that trunk smells suspiciously,* said the baggage agent. That happened too, for all I know.

Literally square miles of this clutter. We had to make lists of everything we could use; then serviceable goods were turned back into the Supply system so they could be employed again. Stuff that wasn't employable for our purposes, but had been useful for the war— We destroyed that. The in-between matériel, which we couldn't expend but which the German or French industries and economies could turn to account: we passed it off into such channels. It was a prodigious task. You had to get the entire stock properly classified, and do one of three things: (a) destroy it; (b) get it into civilian channels; or (c) get it back into our own Supply channels.

Far as that destruction went— Huh. Very much against the grain. We'd think back . . . actually it was only a matter of three or four years since we had been down on our knees, crying for just such equipment. Now look what was happening to it.

Brand new treasures . . . say there'd be specific calibrated tools . . . wealth that we would have given our eyeteeth for, in late '42 or early '43. *But this is war stuff; it's only usable along with bomb fuses; and bomb fuses are only usable along with bombs; and bombs are usable only in a war. So—* Hit it with a hammer, or run a tractor over it, or whatever you have to do, and throw it in the junk pile with the other refuse.

It is axiomatic, I guess. For the first two years after a war, you're in a destructive phase. This applied back in the United States just as well. Take our old gunnery school down there at Buckingham, in Florida, or any old school anywhere else . . . again, they were running tractors over brand new equipment. When you thought about it or witnessed it, you'd feel as if you had scratched your fingernail over rusty tin. You know how that feels: makes your nerves constrict and squeeze.

Miserable business.

If ever there was a conquered nation which didn't writhe in financial trouble— Guess there never was.

One of the first briefings I received was on the financial situation, and it really was a honey. Spurious currency oozing out of every crack, black markets a mile high. On the black market cigarettes were selling for twelve to fifteen hundred marks a carton; and that was the old *Reichsmark,* to all appearances the same folding money which had circulated during the Hitler years. It might have been worth something to its possessors then. It wasn't, two years after the war ended.

The Russians had come in and set up printing presses and printed marks like crazy. There were mountains of this phony wealth floating around. When you took that into consideration, along with the normal inflation which was bound to result, you realized why the bottom had gone out of everything.

You could tote a bushel of that trash down to the store and not be able to buy anything with it; and there was practically nothing to be had in the stores anyway. Take the carton of cigarettes on the black market again, as an example. That was the ruling price—twelve to fifteen hundred. The mark was supposed to be worth approximately twenty-five cents. So that carton of cigarettes was going at anywhere from three hundred to three hundred and seventy-five dollars.

It was a state of affairs which couldn't continue much longer. It didn't.

The German authorities themselves started manufacturing the miracle. But, since we were on the scene and in control, it is reasonable to assert that we were in on the act, and that everything was done with our approval.

They set up a new currency. It amounted practically to a moratorium. Everybody started from scratch. They were allowed to bring in the old marks for exchange, but only to the amount of approximately twenty-five dollars. They did this twice, at different periods; the whole exchange amounted to approximately fifty dollars per individual. They'd change the old money for the new, up to that amount, but then it stopped.

They had decided to scrub out the unreliable currency: wash it all off the slate. If you had more than the prescribed amount which you wanted to turn in, you had to produce evidence to show how you'd earned it. You must go before the government officials and prove just how you had acquired all those marks. If they turned out to be legitimate earnings— If you'd been conducting an honest business or profession which would stand up to investigation, then you were investigated. In rare instances eventually the government might allow the exchange to proceed at some lesser rate than one to one . . . a much lesser rate. . . .

And, if you couldn't prove how you had acquired all these barrels of soggy-looking cash, then you couldn't turn the currency in at all.

It amounted to each citizen starting with fifty bucks. It was the best thing which could have happened. A fantastic series of events took place, soon as this exchange was consummated.

I described the dead-pan faces, the gray blankness of the people themselves. There was the same kind of blankness in the stores. Shop and office windows seemed just as empty and dust-covered as those human visages. Most of the stores were for sale. There was practically no construction or reconstruction going on.

The moment that money was changed— Bang. Things began to appear from hiding places; they'd be offered for sale in the markets. Everybody began to work. Why wouldn't you work? You could get paid for it, now, *in currency that amounted to something.*

Out came the shovels and the picks, out came the barrows and carts. There was a gleam of acquisition in men's eyes. They repaired their sagging bicycles; they climbed astride those bicycles and went pedaling off at dawn so they could work all day.

The German black market barons were no longer barons. A lot of those were compelled to hoist an honest monkey-wrench or an honest maul or an honest scythe. Hammering and plowing and sawing and planting, and the scrubbing away and the clearing away, made a noise all over the landscape. Zombies forgot their zombie-hood; they started to give orders, or take them.

An incredible endeavor began there in 1948 and continued through new and promising years.

From that time up until the present, I've had opportunities to get back into Germany at least once a year, sometimes oftener. Each time I have been astonished at the progress. Even when I left USAFE after a year's duty—despite the fact that people seemed to be revivified and ambitious once more—I still thought it would take the Germans a hundred years just to dig out of their debris. But they had new cities set up on the old bombed-out sites within five or six years from the time they began.

Not everything they did was for the best. If war's destruction got rid of a lot of ancient ugliness, as well as wiping out a lot of ancient beauty, the builders demonstrated the usual lack of taste which we show and which other nations show in their embracing of the modern. There are some gosh-awful Hollywood-type-alleged-American-Californian buildings and store fronts adorning the German streets today. In observing them you receive the same kind of shock that you get when you watch some dusky half-clad native in another corner of the world, lugging along a box of Coca-Cola bottles.

The Germans lost a certain identity, a certain originality and national flavor, when they performed the new building. But the roofs don't leak; there is heat in winter.

Helen hadn't dwelt with me under the copper dome and amid the "richly veined marble" of Elveden Hall. She had lived with me in some decent quarters at Selfridge and Wheeler and Langley; and we'd lived in our shack on the beach at Hawaii; and we had lived in that State

Line Hotel on the salt flats of Utah. We'd had our little house in Arlington, and all sorts of queer quarters here and there: anything down to a hall bedroom.

It may be believed that the Henkell house in Wiesbaden was quite a surprise to my bride. To me too.

The family name had nothing to do with the *Heinkel* who gave his name to those early Jerry bombers. This was the champagne family. One of their daughters was married to Von Ribbentrop. It was a dainty little cottage consisting of one hundred and two rooms, and I'm not sure how many cubbyholes and closets besides; and I guess no dungeons. Never got around the whole shooting-match; never had time. It was almost as much a museum in its former condition as it was a residence. Bradley's troops had descended on it in the first place, when we invaded Germany in 1945, and I should like to have seen the mansion originally. Folks talked enthusiastically of the *objets d'art*—rugs, statuary, paintings, everything else.

I regret to state in all honesty that, in 1945, when those doughfeet left the house, they considered that the next place where they might squat would perhaps have nothing in it. So they backed up their trucks and took anything they wanted along. This was the great policy of so-called liberation. It went on all over Germany. Seems rather shocking now to consider it, and it even seemed a little shocking to certain people at the time. My guess is that conditions would have been worse in the United States if the situation had been reversed, and the Nazis had moved in on Georgetown and Quaker Heights.

. . . Old Joe Cannon came along, following the infantry and whoever else had been there. When he saw how the place had been stripped he put up quite a squawk. He got a lot of the Henkell property back, but some of it never did show up. General Cannon lived there with his staff right up to the end of the war, and when he departed Idwal Edwards took over. His staff lived there also. Then, after the war, they started bringing in their families. Dependents moved into the Henkell mansion; the rest of the staff kind of drifted away.

(I'll jump ahead a year right now, and relate that when I left Europe to come home and command SAC, Joe Cannon went back over to Germany to follow me in USAFE. He moved back into the Henkell house, right into the same room where he had ended the war.)

My wife is the real family historian when it comes to the Henkell mansion, and she has furnished me with a lot of details which I didn't know or had forgotten. . . . Besides being General Bradley's headquarters, Goering had been there earlier; the place was said to have served as the supreme Luftwaffe HQ.

There were still a number of officers dwelling there when we arrived late in '47. But Helen was adamant: she said that they must move. Her contention was that you can't mix up family life with club life and with a gang of bachelors who might want to give parties night after night. She was embattled; she had a young daughter to whom she was determined to offer as normal a childhood as was possible under the rather peculiar circumstances which ruled us.

She told the boys frankly, "The general is going to be tired when he gets home at night. He's not going to want to have parties every night, and of course it would be your prerogative to have them if you lived here. One or another of you would want a party of some sort almost every night. Isn't that true?" They admitted it, and they moved out gracefully.

When Helen puts her foot down, she really puts her foot down. She knew from experience also that it would complicate the domestic setup. She said, "There's just one kitchen in this whole establishment. When men run the household, as a rule there is never much care taken of anything. If you have a conscientious and honest cook, you have an honest mess. If you don't have, well— Everything will go out of the back door—it doesn't matter what nationality the servants are."

I'd better let Helen take over for a while. The domestic arrangements in Wiesbaden were somewhat bizarre.

She says, "So we moved in: Curt, Janie, myself, Janie's governess, the cook. Oh, he was an excellent cook: very honest and very loyal. We had a lock on the kitchen; he had one key to the kitchen, I had another key to the kitchen. Between us we ran the household. I hired and fired until I'd assembled eighteen good servants. That was the least you could run the house with, because by that time official visits were piling up. There were large numbers of staff people coming in all the time, and Curt would have to entertain them. As well as our own, there would be Chiefs of Staff from other countries, and they all stayed at our house. There was no place else for them to stay—no proper accommodations available in the town of Wiesbaden at that time. We had three chauffeurs on the run constantly, and we kept up thirteen guest suites. Not rooms, mind you, but *suites*. Kept them all made up, and they were occupied most of the time. We had to use all our own money: we were not permitted to live off the German economy—could buy scarcely any food off the German economy."

Let me interrupt at this point with the grim observation that, if the Germans had conquered us, they probably would have been living off the American economy first, and the Americans would have had to be content with what was left.

Helen says, "We had almost no fresh vegetables except potatoes and cabbages. Our frozen meat came through Frankfurt, so the Air Force was Tail-End-Charley on the meat situation too: other branches of the Occupation Forces latched onto the meat first. I think I practically owned Montgomery Ward and Sears, Roebuck before the year was out. I did all my commissary shopping with the one sergeant who was stationed in the house. We could draw a lot of bulk rations—dried beans, rice, dried peas, dehydrated potatoes, dehydrated bananas. But fruit— We had to depend on friends for that. If people came through Spain or Portugal or from southern Italy, for instance, or up from North Africa, they would always fetch fruit along if they had room in their planes. Some of them were even able to carry it from the States. Of course Air Force personnel knew just what our situation was, and they were eager to help—buy and bring fruit, and let us pay them for it. Our milk, eggs, cheese and other dairy products came from Denmark. But practically nothing in the way of canned goods was available in the commissary. . . . Write another order. Hurrah for S. S. Pierce!

"Not only that: there were the servants to be considered. I'd send back to the States for shoes, bicycle tires, children's and men's and women's clothing. We wanted to keep our people looking a little better than rag-pickers, and at that time the Germans were able to purchase for themselves exactly one pair of shoes per year: shoes with wooden soles, and uppers made of leather or synthetic leather. One pair of those things each year; and one pair of shoes with *leather* soles every two years. Otherwise they would have to buy shoes through the black market, and that was too expensive for most of them.

"We had everybody's family problems as well as our own. A crisis every day. What sort of crises? Well, for instance (the women will be interested in this)— One of our downstairs maids had a baby by the local policeman, who was already married; and her own family still had three children of their own—little children. The whole outfit—eight or ten altogether—lived in two rooms. It is a miracle of understatement to say that they couldn't really afford this other baby.

"Our little maid—let's call her Gerta—had very special problems. After the baby was born, Gerta had difficulty with her breasts and couldn't nurse the child. That meant that I shopped for baby food, mixed up formulas, got hold of orange juice by hook or crook. It was my responsibility. Gerta belonged to *us*. She was the American Woman's Burden."

I can't help recalling, when I witness Helen reviewing our local situation at Wiesbaden, that the United States made its own contribution to illegitimacy abroad, both during and following World War II and also back in World War I.

When we arrived at Wiesbaden we met up with a handsome servant, a man in his late twenties, who bowed deeply and greeted us in perfect English: "Good morning, sir and madam. I am so happy that you have arrived safely. I am glad to serve you. I am an American bastard."

That really set us back on our haunches. Let's call the guy Helmut
. . . we finally got the true story out of him, after Helen had explained
that he must never never go around greeting people with the news
that he was an American bastard. He was the post-World War I il-
legitimate son of a German girl; his father was an American. I don't
know how many languages he spoke, but plenty. And we were told
that he was always listening at doors. . . .

We had other perplexities of our own, right then, and they weren't
all concerned with worry about the international situation on my part,
or by the calamitous domestic predicament on Helen's.

(She was watching the LeMay fortune ooze away but fast, and I
don't mean just our ration allowance. Besides my entire salary it cost
us three thousand dollars of our own saved-up money that year, to try
to keep the place up and entertain those guests we had to entertain.
The Pentagon made some adjusted financial allowances about the time
I left Europe for home, but those weren't retroactive. Maybe some
people have gotten rich in the Air Force or the old Air Corps or the
Army Air Forces. But if they did, they did it by stumbling over pirate
gold, or stubbing their toes on the ground in Texas and starting an oil
well by mistake.)

Also we suffered a family disgrace. I have described the black market and its evils. Well—

It started with Janie's appetite for sweets, and with PX prices. Apples were two-bits apiece, so were oranges. Naturally the GI's were
looking for something cheaper. Janie also had been visiting the PX
and, just as in the case of the old days out at Wendover, she was eating too damn much of that sweet stuff. Candy and ice cream all over
the place.

We cracked down on her. "Janie, you're not *supposed* to spend all
your money on candy and ice cream—"

"It's *my* money, and I ought to be allowed to do what I please—"

Helen said, "I warn you! If you persist in squandering your allowance on candy and ice cream, we'll simply have to take your allowance
away from you."

Janie persisted, and so the allowance was canceled out. Like most
kids, she had a big appetite. When she found she couldn't go to the
PX because she was penniless, she'd scoot out to the kitchen. As Helen
has related, we received fruit pretty consistently through the tender
offices of friends lugging it in when they landed in Germany. Most
times there was an apple available for Miss Janie, and always the prov-
ender for one type of sandwich or another. Then there was the cook,
who was crazy about Janie, and he was forever baking delightful
messes of tasty little German cookies . . . all sorts of cookies, because
at last raw materials were available, and he loved making those
batches. Being a pal of Janie's, Cook was generous with the cookies.

What happened with all this? Doggonedest black market you ever saw. It busted wide open, and should go down as the Great LeMay Scandal of the Occupation.

Janie was grabbing apples out there in the kitchen, or she was concealing cookies which the admiring domestic supplied to her; or she would make sandwiches of the Dagwood variety. Know what she was doing with this stuff? Selling it to the guards out at the gate, selling it to the AP's. They were getting nice homemade sandwiches for a nickel a throw. Apples at the same price; mess of cookies for a nickel—

Helen said she was going to skin that youngun alive. I thought a firing squad more appropriate. It was a pretty gloomy business for the commander of the United States Air Forces in Europe to find his own daughter a confirmed black market criminal at the age of eight. Try *that* over on your Soap Opera.

We told Janie, "All right. Go out and give all those nickels back to the guards. We know that you were planning to spend that money on ice cream and candy. So go and give it back to 'em."

And she was perfectly furious. "Why should I give my nickels back to that AP out there? He's already *eaten* everything up! It's *my money!*"

I said wearily, "I don't care. You heard me. Give it back."

I don't think she's forgiven me yet.

3

The Soviets had been their usual sweet selves all along. Before turning over respective sectors of Berlin to the British, French and Americans, they had denuded the region of every shred of mechanical equipment which might be employed conceivably in any future dispensation. This meant not only removing machinery from factories, unscrewing motors and dynamos from the floors, or hauling off all the rolling stock on the railroads. It meant that the Russians actually removed the *rails*. Meant that they cut loose and rolled up electrical lines and telephone cables, above ground or below ground, and carted those away. Real thorough job. Probably they would have taken the very nails out of the woodwork if there had been time to pull 'em.

Thus the Soviets played their traditional role in bringing about that apathy and inertia which we encountered in the indigenous population.

They had badgered and heckled and elbowed and provoked; but in the year 1948 the "hot wind from the east" was really beginning to blow. The Communists intensified their obstructive tactics as the new *deutsche mark* was fed into the West German financial system. They thought with good reason that the sound money would have an adverse effect on currency in East Germany. When they clamped down on all surface traffic and transportation, we in the Occupation needed suddenly to consider something beyond the demolition or housekeeping duties which had concerned us during previous months. It looked like we might have to fight at any moment, and we weren't self-assured about what we had to fight with.

Officially we were instructed as to no change in our mission. But let me say that I got the word loud and clear.

At a cursory glance it looked like USAFE would be stupid to get mixed up in anything bigger than a cat-fight at a pet show. We had one Fighter group, and some transports, and some radar people, and that was about the story. I had to shake things up right quick, and I kept working day and night to shake them. I was happy in considering that we had Curly Edwinson commanding the Fighter folks. It didn't take *him* long to get his outfit on a business-like basis and ready to go. Also we got the transports poised, in just about nothing flat.

But take a look at the stupid situation, far as our supply lines were concerned. Our principal supplies arrived from America at the port of Bremerhaven. That was away out in front of our troops, or at least in front of and above the bulk of them—away up there at the mouth of the Weser River. The situation was a logical outgrowth of the God-bless - our-buddy-buddy-Russians-we-sure-can-trust-them-forever - and - ever philosophy which flowered away back in the Roosevelt Administration. All the Russians had to do was to whiz forward and they could cut our supply lines before they even made contact with our troops. Furthermore, we had nothing much with which to hold. A couple of divisions including the Constabulary—that was all, in our zone. The British had some people and some stuff up in their zone, not very many and not very much. Things looked mighty sour to me.

I asked for some B-29's to be flown over from the U.S. to England in a hurry; so promptly we had those, safe at British bases, ready to roll. And Edwinson's fighters were all set to take off.

Lieutenant-General Arthur G. Trudeau was in command of the Constabulary. (He just retired about three years ago, as I recall. Think his last job was with Research and Development for the Army staff.) Well, since General Clay was thinking in terms of moving troops up the *Autobahn,* Trudeau prepared to carry out that operation. He had his column all put together. In advance planning, it was decided that Trudeau must make up his mind, once he got going, as to what was just token opposition and what was real opposition. If it turned out that we had a fight on our hands, the Army would have their communications going through regular channels; and I would have my own communications setup along with them too, with my folks there and ready, to get communications direct to the Air arm. I would have the B-29's flown into radar dead-spots, right up close. I would have Curly's fighters moved to auxiliary fields, also as close as they could get to the proposed front.

So, if word came, either through the Army or through us, that the scrap was on, we would launch immediately against all the enemy airfields. Naturally we knew where they were; and we had observed that the Russian fighters were lined up in a nice smooth line on the aprons at every place. If it had happened, I think we would have cleaned them up pretty well, in no time at all.

We were prepared to do this; but of course nobody hit the switch in Washington.

I was still preoccupied with considering, however, the fight which might develop a little later on. Since we were to enjoy a breathing spell at the moment, I was determined to really get things in shape. I gave considerable thought to this problem; but let me say that the thinking process had to be very much accelerated. We didn't know just how long our King's-X was going to last.

First off I got together with the Chief of Staff of the French Air Force and the Chief of Staff of the Belgians, and talked the situation over with them. I told them that I wished to have some fields well in the rear of our troops, back in Belgium and France, all stocked up. Ammunition, gas, food, bombs, mechanical equipment: every type and condition of supplies which we might need. I told them that I wanted this to be a joint proposition—guarded, maintained and administered by some of my people and some of theirs.

If I could have taken time out to smile wryly at myself in the mirror (as that surgeon urged me to do long ago, back in Syracuse, when he recommended that I practice facial exercises) I surely would have smiled wryly. Here I was—the same character who had palpitated, in flying to take command of USAFE, with the dread that he might be called upon to engage in matters of international diplomacy. What the hell was I doing now? I was breaking other nations' laws into bits.

You couldn't *have* any foreign troops stationed in France in peacetime. Nothing was more illegal to the French mind or the French code. Same thing for Belgium.

I talked to our Army quartermaster and the Ordnance officers. We decided to load up a bunch of trains right away and start shuttling them around in France and Belgium. We had not only to elude enemy observation (there was plenty of that: their espionage system was plugged in all over the landscape). We had to fool the civilian populations—our late allies, the French and the Belgians—because of the extralegality of the whole procedure.

No one could possibly envy any researcher who might be charged with the task of running down even one of those ammunition trains during its travels. We zigzagged our trains from hell to breakfast. We wanted to lose them, and we did. We wanted to get them back in a far different area from the one in which we'd lost them. Then no one might possibly discern just where our stuff was going.

This turned out to be a masterpiece of a deliberate exercise in fouled-up transportation. That happens inadvertently, far too often; but this was on purpose. They would send a train to one town, and it would sit on a siding for a while; and then they would gather it up on another train, and take it some place else and let it sit there . . . another bill of lading would be made out . . . and then another, in another location; then another. Whole train-loads could be lost in the shuffle this way, and that was what we wanted.

Our transportation experts worked with maps and schedules and timetables by remote control. Actually we didn't have any troops accompanying the trains. But we got troops across the borders as soon as it was essential to meet the ammunition and other supplies at depots and bases where the matériel could be stored and made ready. And we sent our people in, in civilian clothes.

What this amounted to, in effect, was that we had our own private little NATO buzzing along, there in West Germany and France and Belgium, before the North Atlantic Treaty Organization ever existed.

It had been a source of satisfaction to me, to consider that I may have had some hand in the instigation of NATO. When I came back to the ZI, before I started work at SAC, first thing I did was to go in and report to Under-Secretary Robert M. Lovett and run over the entire situation. I briefed him on what the problems were currently, in Europe, and told him exactly what we had done when the heat was on. I pointed out that we must have some sort of international organization over there, if we were going to hold out against the Russians. We couldn't continue any longer, laboring under a system wherein it was illegal to have any of our troops in France and Belgium or at other bases scattered around. There had to be a better arrangement than that.

I was pretty emphatic about the whole thing, I guess, because it was a matter of recent and vital concern.

Well, not too long after that, NATO did come into being. But we had our own pocket-sized one, first, as far as the Air Force was concerned.

Nothing much was made of these preparations at the time, by the enemy or by their sympathizers. It might seem that the French Communists would have yelled a big yell. Fact is, they didn't know a thing about it. We had been thoroughly successful in our efforts to elude scrutiny and a correct definition of what we were about. I had informed General Clay what I was doing; I don't know whether he told anybody else or not. And, down at the grassroots level, our airmen were in civilian clothes. And the French helped us, and the Belgians helped us; and our people were kept out of sight as much as possible.

Too bad, really, that Curly Edwinson couldn't get rolling against the Russians just then. He would have had a ball. They would have been doing their level best to shoot him. For a very good reason.

For one whose wartime responsibility was that of a Bomber commander, I have a pretty soft spot in my heart for the Fighter types. Maybe that's because of the old P-12's and P-26's, and Selfridge and Wheeler and all the rest of it. . . .

Let me tell about Curly. He first won fame as a football player, out around Kansas somewhere—University of Kansas, maybe. Then he came into the Army Air Forces, and during World War II he was commanding a fighter outfit over in Italy. He got himself into a peck of trouble. He was sent out across the Adriatic to attack a German column beyond the Balkan coast. The reconnaissance report identified that enemy column as passing through such-and-such a valley. Well, with clouds and weather and whatnot, our friend Curly was either in the correct valley given him by the recco people, or he was not . . . either they were wrong or Curly was wrong. It's never been decided exactly who made the error.

He and his fighter boys saw this column of troops: there it was, just as briefed, and they went down and worked that column over mighty well. Then some Yaks showed up: not Messerschmitts (which they often used to be mistaken for) but real old Russian Yaks. By this time Curly began to think that maybe he was in the soup; so he talked to his pilots and told them to disengage; but the Yaks weren't having any of this disengagement stuff. I think that Curly lost one airplane, and they shot down three or four of the Russians before they ever did break off the fighting.

The point is that it was a Russian column which Curly had attacked, not a German one. Both had the same sort of grayish uniforms . . . those Balkan valleys are narrow and numerous, and one column looked a good deal like another column. When you're fighting a real loaded-gun war from the cockpit of an American aircraft, there isn't much opportunity to say to the guy on the ground, "Is your name Fritz, or is it Ivan?"

Well, when Curly had brought his boys home across the sea to their Italian base, all hell broke loose. Among other things, in lambasting that gray column in the hills, Curly had killed a lieutenant-general of the Russians. And, Lord sakes, he had even taken automatic pictures of this assassination.

The Russians were taking a very dim view of the whole deal. So our folks jumped in and screamed, "We were set upon by your Yaks! Your Yaks came in and attacked us!"

"All right," say the Russians, "we'll fix that. We will shoot the Yak squadron commander."

So they shot the squadron commander.

Then they said to the Americans, "Now. See what we have done? We have shot our Yak squadron commander. Now, you shoot your fighter plane squadron commander."

Lord sakes again. They had to smuggle Curly out of Italy in a hurry, in order to keep from shooting him.

As I say, the Russians might have liked to try, themselves, in 1948. The chance didn't come.

4

The Berlin trouble flared during the last week of June; it had been smoldering for months previously. During one period of eleven days in early April, when the Soviets demanded the right to search and investigate all military shipments by rail, we flew small quantities of food and other critical supplies into Berlin; something like three hundred tons. But, beginning about April 12th or 13th, we were able to use surface transportation once more, and the temporary airlift was discontinued.

It was renewed on the 22nd of June. From then on the Lift just grew, in time-honored Topsy fashion.

So I had only been on the job for six or seven months when there came that all-important telephone call from General Lucius B. Clay . . . could we haul some coal up to Berlin?

"Sure. We can haul anything. How much coal do you want us to haul?"

"All you can haul."

We sat down to examine the transport situation. We had only two transport outfits over there—I think the 60th and 61st TC Groups—and a few miscellaneous administrative airplanes. It was a pretty modest start. I never dreamed how consequential this could become, and certainly never dreamed—then—how serious General Clay was about the whole thing. He kept increasing his requests, and eventually it dawned on me what he was talking about. He was going to buckle down and support the city of Berlin entirely by activity in the air. Not being in the airplane business, obviously Clay himself never realized that when he talked in tonnages of such prodigious amount, it was far beyond our capacity to operate.

I told him, "We'll have to get some help from home."

Immediately I sent back for a bunch of transports to be flown over from the United States, and we put them to work. By that time I was able to form an organization. We started in with Joe Smith heading the job—he was our headquarters commander there at Wiesbaden. I told him to get going. . . . The stuff from the States came in piecemeal, a bit here, a bit there. Joe Smith took it over and ran it.

Then, when it looked like we were going into a long-term aspect— that we were really going to have to haul gigantic tonnages in a max effort—we were compelled to build an even larger and more defined organization.

That was when we yelled for Bill Tunner to come over and take the chore. He was the transportation expert to end transportation experts. He had run those ferries over the Hump in the CBI and he had headed Ferry Command for a while . . . it was rather like appointing John Ringling to get the circus on the road. Eventually General Vandenburg was prevailed upon to send Tunner to Europe. But it must have been a month or so after we actually started to fly the Lift, before Bill got over there.

I remember flying a load of coal myself, up to Berlin, around the first part of July. I didn't deliver Clay's initial coal; but in those early days I had to make several runs to see how things were going. Nobody regarded the enterprise very soberly at first. They kidded about it, called it LeMay's Coal and Feed Company. Big joke.

In his wildest surmises no one imagined that before the job was over and done, the Lift would carry two million, two hundred and twenty-three thousand tons of fuel and food and other supplies into Berlin. You can have some fun with statistics, and break that down roughly into something like five pounds *per day* for every Berliner, including babies in arms.

Let's say it in pounds. 4,446,000,000 pounds of food. That's quite a lot of pounds.

You'd think that we might have been driven to drink by the Russians constantly buzzing our airplanes. Actually they didn't bother very much. Once they discovered that we were firmly intentioned, and going to haul that stuff up there regardless, they let us pretty much alone.

We worked out a lot of special procedures. For instance, one time when I went up there with a load, I observed that the crews had to get out and go into the Operations office, as is normal at any field, to fill out their flight plans for the return trip back to Frankfurt. Regulations, of course. Everything has to be done according to regulations. In such a case, when things don't make sense, it is essential to get the regulations changed.

This didn't make sense. I observed that those crews were losing half an hour, fiddling around in that Operations office and filling out those plans. I called in my people and said, "Let's get smart. We'll have an Operations officer *out here on the line*, with the necessary clearance, and he will give that clearance to the pilot *right here*. Somebody else will bring some coffee out, so the crew can have a little coffee and a Nabisco or something, while they're filling out that clearance. This will all occur during those same five minutes while the Germans are unloading the flour and the coal. And then the plane can get the hell out of here, back to Frankfurt for another load. Our people will only have to be on the ground ten or fifteen minutes at the most."

It was necessary to cut corners if we really were going to deliver that coal and food. We didn't have enough people over in our European command to take on a job like this. To be brutally frank, we didn't have enough people in the Air Force, in 1948, to spare for a sudden bustling trip to Germany to discharge these new and horrific responsibilities.

There was one thing to do. Hire Germans.

We got old Luftwaffe characters, German mechanics who used to be in the GAF, and put them to work on our airplanes. Four or five years before they had been keeping the 109's and the 190's and the JU-88's in trim. Now— I won't say that we made Christians out of them, but we did make good C-54 and C-74 mechanics out of some of them. Considering all the circumstances, they did a whee of a job.

Our bilingual people could hear the Jerries talking.

"My old grandmother, she lives here in Berlin. So cold she was in wartime! Now she worries that we have no coal this winter—"

"*Ja*. And my wife said, 'Without flour we have no bread. The children—they cannot have bread.' So—"

"I am glad to work for the Americans. This is the only way food can come to Berlin."

"And medicines. If my little girl should grow sick, there might be no medicine. I am glad—"

They really made a big thing out of it. Had little competitions between individuals, between gangs and units. When one of those air loads of coal or other supplies hit the ground, it would astonish the life out of you to see how quickly those Germans got the sacks out of the airplane; and how soon they helped to get the airplane airborne again. Pretty soon we were running planes every five minutes. When weather got bad we'd have to drop down a little in our operations; but we kept arranging for better navigation aids and traffic procedures in the corridors. Also we opened up several new fields.

Don't forget that the RAF also operated a lift, and had done so previously . . . at the time of the April trouble and again in June they flew a lot of stuff to Berlin. But necessarily their contribution was in smaller quantity. The British didn't possess any air transport units comparable to ours—there on the Continent of Europe, at the time the total blockade of Berlin came into being. Immediately thereafter we coördinated our plans, and both the RAF and the British Civil Aircraft folks brought over a lot of transports from England, to assist and coöperate.

For a while we held only to the goal of a minimum daily tonnage. We would supply forty-five hundred tons per day: this by the combined efforts of the RAF and the Americans. But we had been in operation only about three and a half months when I issued an order to deliver *the maximum tonnage possible* which might be consistent with the combined resources of equipment and personnel available.

Air Marshal Sir Arthur P. M. Saunders put his name to this pronouncement along with me, in an order wherein Bill Tunner became commander of the Combined Airlift Task Force. Air Commodore J. W. F. Merer was made deputy commander; he was located up at Buckeburg. Tunner was situated down at Wiesbaden.

. . . The duty was rough on our people (not so much on the British; they were just a hop-skip-and-jump away from home). But thousands of USAF personnel had to be pulled in from other jobs elsewhere around the world, and nobody knew how long the doggone business was going to last. Generally it was believed that this emergency would be of fairly short duration. But if these fellows went in and prayed for an explanation and a prog as to how long their new duty might last, nobody could tell them a damn thing because nobody knew a damn thing.

Usually, at the start, the TDY (temporary duty) tours were set up for forty-five days. Next thing, they'd be extended to ninety days. Next thing, six months. It wasn't fair, they had no warning of this. It wasn't like SAC (in later years) because they weren't geared for it. All sorts of painful and dangerous personal problems arose in the officers' and airmen's family lives, sufficient to unsettle them in their jobs. It was something like fighting a war, except in wartime we couldn't send people home to bury their dead or consult on family crises.

At least that was one thing which we could do in 1948. We did a lot of it.

There were two-and-a-half American runways at Tempelhof airdrome. Used to be only grass and sod when the Jerries were running things. They employed the place for light aircraft during the war. Then we came along and put down steel mats on a rubber base. Good enough at first; but once the Lift had begun, our weighty transports really knocked hell out of those cobbled-together runways.

It got so bad that we had to keep a gang of laborers on the run with asphalt, mats, shovels, wheelbarrows and all. Down one of the transport planes would come slamming . . . loose material scattered wildly . . . out the workmen came a-skipping: they poured, pounded, beat the mats down into place . . . then they went scrambling back to get out of the way of the next C-54. They didn't want to kill any demons, either. Just tried to keep the runways in working condition.

Tempelhof was right in town. Crowded apartment buildings all around. Obviously Tempelhof could not be enlarged to meet our needs. There was another airport named Gatow, but because of local conditions there could be no further expansion in this case either. The Russians held the other airfields which originally had hemmed Berlin.

However, our engineers examined an area in the French sector: place called Tegel. The surrounding terrain here was comparatively unobstructed. A transport plane could get in, flying at a low altitude, with reasonable safety. There were good rail lines and highways adjacent: all together it would be a fine place for the Lift to land. Trouble was, there weren't any runways. During the war Tegel had been sacred to the training of antiaircraft units and such.

. . . Resorting to ordinary Stateside specifications, you'd think in terms of a concrete foundation, what is called a base course, at least two feet thick. The engineers scouted all over Berlin, but there wasn't any cement to be had; nor could they unearth any heavy equipment for use in building the runway. Our Lift was too busy toting coal and cereals and fats and the dehydrated eggs and potatoes, to take on any cement-lugging job.

What you had to do was sit down and think in terms of the Chinese families toiling on those 1944 runways in the Chengtu Valley. . . .

Let me add that it wasn't solely the fact that we couldn't spare the time or the cargo space to fly raw cement to Berlin, which mitigated against the project. Essential construction equipment was so huge and bulky that even our largest C-74 transport couldn't carry it.

An ingenious idea was born in somebody's brain. Cut the equipment into chunks (down at Rhein-Main) with blowtorches; lug the chunks up to Berlin via C-74; weld them back together.

It worked.

. . . Simple enough, too, to consider putting down a two-foot minimum foundation under a *perfectly flat* runway. But while the terrain at Tegel could be considered and accepted as advantageous to our Lift economy, that didn't mean that the whole thing was like a billiard table. Sometimes there had to be five feet of minimum foundation, in order to bridge lower spots and even the runway off. And we didn't have those millions and millions of pounds of water-rounded stones which had been available beside the Chinese rivers.

Thereupon ensued one of the greatest ironies of our time.

What was used for the foundation, the ballast on which to lay runways of crushed stone penetrated with asphalt binding?

Bricks, pieces of brick, brick rubble, brick dust.
Where did all this stuff come from?
From the scraps of Berlin; the city we had bombed to pieces.

The German people themselves were historically responsible for the Nazi hierarchy and the Nazi war machine. No little band of hand-picked zealots alone could have wrought such a fantastic massacre. It had to be done with people. It was done with and by the German people.

We can look back and salute a comparative handful of clear-minded and courageous Teutonic humans who were tortured out of existence by the *Schutzstaffel* or who decayed in concentration camps. But they were a distinct minority. The bulk of the German population was behind Hitler, or pretended to be. The bulk of the population applauded him, sustained him or (in the less evil instances) stood idly by, or turned their backs on the whole thing.

During my active duty in Germany and through subsequent years I became better and better acquainted with many individuals whom I had opposed directly during the war. I should not wish to have it pointed out to me by some Whiz Kid, at this late stage of the game, that World War II was a colossal mistake, an international misunderstanding for which the United States was proportionately responsible. World War II was nothing of the kind. It was an event wherein the military giants of those several Axis states decided that they could get away with an incredible land grab, a nation grab, a super-Napoleonic concept of defacement of a world-sized map. They did this with the enthusiasm of their nationals behind them. In minor dissension may have sounded the voices of a few ardent patriots and heroic philosophers; but those were not the majority. An horrific chorus shouted, *"Duce!"* or *"Banzai!"* or *"Heil Hitler!"* Eventually, because of the sacrifices offered and endured by our men and by the entire populations of Allied countries, the enemy went down to defeat. Enemy cities were pulverized or fried to a crisp. It was something they asked for and something they got.

(In reverse fashion, if we keep listening to the gospel of apology and equivocation which all too many politicians and savants are preaching today in the United States, we will be asking for the same thing. And in time may achieve it.)

I have met and grown to respect and have enjoyed socially certain men who—mutual anecdote convinced us—were literally firing at me or at my command when we attacked the cities of their nations. This has happened with both Germans and Japanese. Soldiers can associate tolerantly on the personal plane. A lot of our American airmen found

that they got on screamingly well with some of the ex-Luftwaffe vets:
they had something of the same sort of bitter humor. During my tenure
as Chief of Staff I entertained as a guest in our quarters a German
friend who'd survived a dozen parachute escapes and literally hundreds of aerial combats, when he was flying with the GAF. I recognized this man's skills, and respected him for possessing and demon-
strating them. But I did not find anything admirable in the record of
the s.o.b.'s whom he had served, and I don't ever expect to.

There is no sense in concentrating on the protraction of wartime
alignments and international feuds. Partners change and sides change.
I see nothing essentially treacherous in this; it's just a way history has
of remaking itself. Different blankets and quilts, but the same old bed.

Mainly there writhes a perpetual struggle between those who would
control through dictatorships, and those who abominate dictatorships
. . . those who would control through the machinery of the State, and
those who prefer to have the conscience of the individual do the governing. From century to century it breaks down that way. It was that
way in Egypt, that way in Rome. Hasn't changed yet.

One of our former 305th people told me about an experience he had
down at Heidelberg some years back. He had gone over there to attend a conference at EUCOM headquarters, and one night found himself with a little free time on his hands. In civilian clothes he strolled
the quaint old streets of that almost-completely-unbombed city, and
he ate *Kassler Rippchen* at the Red Ox. In general, he partook of whatever tourist joys were around. Late that evening he wandered into one
of the little *Weinsteube* joints on a side street. There was good zither
music; and our friend sat with his tall glass of Rhine wine. He acknowledged the friendly smiles and bowing of adjacent German couples.
Presently he was invited to join one group. He liked sitting with them
because they spoke good English, and were patient with his high
school German. Everybody told stories and had a right good time. One
of the men was an *Afrika Korps* type, another had been a Messerschmitt pilot. But nobody was trying to fight the war over at that moment. They could all understand one another as human beings.

Presently the proprietor, who had been listening to the conversation at this table, brought over his guest book and asked our American
visitor if he would sign it. The guest book was a huge volume, all
frayed and coming apart: an album about the size of an old-fashioned
family Bible. Our American started leafing through the pages, and in
the front part were a lot of wartime slogans, remarks, cartoons. Luftwaffe boys, on leave, had come to that wine cellar to enjoy themselves
during the war years.

Many of the cartoons showed American airplanes going down in
flames, and German airplanes flying away unscathed.

"By God," said the American, "it wasn't always like that! Where's the page where I'm supposed to sign? Can I draw a picture too?"

Sure he could draw a picture, and the Germans crowded around to watch him. He wasn't any graduate cartoonist, but his offering was recognizable. He had just seen, back there among earlier pages, the death of a B-17, rendered faithfully down to the markings on the vertical stabilizer. Those markings consisted of a triangle with the letter G in it. That triangle meant our old First Bombardment Division of the Eighth Air Force, and G meant the 305th Bomb Group.

So— The visitor drew, with equal clarity, a B-17 with those same markings, flying level and unhurt, and tracers were spewing out from every machine gun on that Fort, and you ought to have seen the FW's and ME's exploding in mid-air or burning as they went down.

Net result: a riot, an international incident? Nay. The Germans were all in stitches. They kept pointing and correcting and saying that he had drawn the dihedral wrong on that Messerschmitt, or had too narrow a nose on that Focke-Wulf.

Goes to show that population groups don't truly desire to hate each other. Hatred exists, however. It comes under the impact of war as a natural reaction. But it is the aggressors who really father wartime hatred.

Unfortunately we have a record of aggression in the past; take our war with Mexico, or many of our campaigns against the Indians. But World War I was not a war of aggression on the part of the United States, and neither was World War II.

We should be filled with rejoicing that we were on the winning team in those wars. But there seems to be a growing tendency to apologize for this too.

They were still building runways at Tegel when I left Germany late in 1948 to return home and take command of SAC.

We had offered German volunteers a wage of 9.60 marks plus a hot meal for eight hours' work. They came swarming: three full shifts, daytime and dark, around the clock. It was that hot meal, probably, which really did the trick. Everybody turned out: men, women, and children of acceptable size. Statistics show that seventeen thousand civilians built the Tegel airfield.

These were a defeated people. No one except a masochist wishes to be defeated. And these were poor people, and I rather think that the majority of people don't prefer being poor. They had been present, they had been part of the show when Berlin was knocked about their ears. They'd heard the sirens, and had been deafened by the impact of the bombs we dropped. They'd suffered the sort of hurt which comes only when noncombatant friends and relatives are destroyed in a war. I don't know how much bitterness was in their hearts as they toiled with those chunks of brick . . . maybe a lot. Although, in accordance with the usual proportions in any population—any time, any place—a lot of them must have been so insensitive as to feel nothing inside them. They just went and did. Their bodies demanded that hot meal, and they got it; and they were glad for the one and one-fifth marks per hour.

Say you were a family of five. You were an ex-soldier husband, wife, and three teen-age children. You went to work, making little stones out of big ones, crushing rock, hiking the rubble about. Altogether you were earning five nourishing meals per day, and you were earning forty-eight marks for the family coffer. Forty-eight marks wouldn't ex- actly put the family on millionaires' row, but it could buy a lot of things when you went to market.

In the past I think there may have lived certain conquerors who would have compelled these people to work without any hot meal, and without any 9.60 marks per employee. Just with whips biting into their backs, just with the urging kicks from brassbound shoes. I think that if the Nazis had won the war that's the way they would have operated. Another reason why I'm glad we defeated the Nazis.

Hollow-cheeked young-middle-aged men with beard stubble show- ing, and the sagging boots they had acquired in the *Afrika Korps* still encasing their feet . . . the *Frau* in her mended velvet suit, because that's the only thing she had left to wear (it was hidden carefully while the Ruskies were pulling open all the bureau drawers and rip- ping into all the closets). Maybe one of the kids wore shorts too small and tight for him; and maybe that sixteen-year-old girl wore overall pants and a jacket of British battle dress. They were really something, when it came to costuming; just what you'd expect from a beaten and impoverished people. But you ought to have seen them work. It made you glad that our Nation had partaken in its substance of the inflow of German blood which came to us—without which we would not possess our respectable hard-working colonies of rural Germans in Ohio and Pennsylvania and elsewhere. Without which the name of an Eisenhower or a Spaatz would never have shown up on our rosters.

The Soviets got in a lot of right good licks, from the standpoint of propaganda, during these phases. Over at Tempelhof, for instance. In that dark foggy weather we needed desperately to have additional runway lights. They had to be installed on high fixtures, and a lot of those fixtures were erected necessarily in a cemetery. We asked the city fathers of Berlin about this. They said, "Go ahead and get the lights in. They're vital to the undertaking. And if a few graves have to be moved, why, a few graves will have to be moved."

The moving job was carried out with dignity and reverence; but the Russians or their stooges among the German population were busy snapping pictures. They really went to town on that one.

"Just take a look! See how the wicked Americans are desecrating the ancient graves. This is what happens in the American Zone. And just see what they did to the little chapel in the graveyard. *Ja*—they have taken off the high beautiful roof—wilfully, wantonly!"

The fact that this job was done also with German approval, and with a new lower roof which we built for the edifice, designed by a qualified German architect— That didn't mean a thing.

Well, we got our emplacements in, and put up the towers with lights on them. And the big old C-54's could come grumbling in over the tops of the apartment buildings and over the sleeping dead, and rub their wheels safely on the runway at Tempelhof.

Before the Combined Airlift Task Force was phased out of existence in 1949, we had two hundred and twenty-five C-54's in the act. That's about one C-54 for every ten thousand people in Berlin. Those old jobs could carry twenty tons—more if overloaded. I seem to recollect that the British, operating both under the aegis of the Royal Air Force and under British Civil Aviation, had about a hundred or a hundred and twenty-five airplanes employed as well. Some of these were of small capacity, like the Haltons, and could carry only about six tons apiece. I don't think there was (employed in that operation) any British plane with a capacity of more than eleven or twelve tons of freight. Thus our 54's were the backbone of the enterprise.

Those—and our people. Soon as it was possible to set up a simulated approach to Berlin, we did it, out in Montana. There we trained crews especially for the Lift job. Most of them were used in Europe. As for those who weren't— In the Air Force no amount of extra training ever comes amiss.

The CATF continued operations in ever-increasing tempo until the Soviets knuckled under, in the summer of 1949, and opened up the rail and motor routes once more.

Can't recollect that I ever read any accurate breakdown on our casualties and attrition of aircraft during the whole show. As in the case of the air mail of 1934, this would be rather difficult to come by. There might be a tendency on the part of overenthusiastic statisticians to associate every aircraft accident, in Western Europe during that period, with the Combined Airlift Task Force. And every training accident back in the ZI as well.

There were mighty few accidents. This was a job for pros; and most of the folks on the job were pros.

Everyone connected with the task will recall one thing, with pride.

The strict food rationing by which Berliners existed was *relaxed*—the amount of the ration was actually *increased*—during those thirteen months of CATF's chief activity. That's how good the men were about getting those twenty-four tons of powdered milk and those hundred-and-eighty tons of dehydrated potatoes and those eighty-five tons of sugar—and all the other stuff—up there every damn day.

A military man, whose duty it is to fight wars when they need to be fought, and—in a period of so-called cold war—to strengthen and sharpen the machinery which will actually *prevent* the cold war from turning hot— Such a man cannot meditate on the process of death. Nor can he mope around about the deaths he has caused personally, by deed; or impersonally, in the act of command.

Early in his career he has to adjust to the realization that death is the ultimate in warfare; and the more deaths suffered by the enemy, the sooner the victory, generally speaking. We are atavistic in this world today, obviously descended from headhunters. The Hungarians do not stand free because the Reds brought in their tanks. The Congo runs blood-colored because adjacent free citizens are armed with Tom-guns and spears and bush-knives, and enjoy using them. What the late President Kennedy termed "peacefully emergent nations" seem to be emerging amid screams, riots, volleys and war dances.

In conflicts of this century the civilian mass has become blended with the industrial—the military, the target mass. This is increasingly true because of immense population areas surrounding strategic communities. It would be very nice if all target values could be as divorced from the civilian whole as were our old-fashioned bull's-eye circles, out on the California or Arizona desert. Unfortunately this hasn't been the case. New York City hangs heavy on the bough for picking in an imaginable future, as did London and Tokyo in World War II. They also were pretty ripe fruit.

So was Berlin.

A lot of us folks who worked hard on the Lift found a kind of tonic in the enterprise. We had knocked the place down; had battered it, burned it, slain or mutilated many of the inhabitants. Now we were doing just the opposite. We were feeding and healing.

. . . You drop a load of bombs and, if you're cursed with any imagination at all, you have at least one quick horrid glimpse of a child lying in bed with a whole ton of masonry tumbling down on top of him; or a three-year-old girl wailing for *Mutter . . . Mutter . . .* because she has been burned. Then you have to turn away from the picture if you intend to retain your sanity. And also if you intend to keep on doing the work your Nation expects of you.

And we in the Eighth Air Force had put down twenty-six thousand tons of high explosives on the city of Berlin.

So the Lift was a pretty satisfying proposition. I'd rather leave off contemplating the cripples we used to see around there—and some of those were children— Rather envision a whole troop of hungry Germans, kids and all, crowded around a table, eating the bread and milk and meat which we'd fetched up to them; and saying, *"Das ist gut!"* and beaming while they ate. So would anyone else in his right mind.

When you see some USAF type wearing a red-white-and-black ribbon with a miniature metal cargo aircraft affixed to it, you can now recognize what that one stands for. I'm honored to have it in my own private dish of fruit salad.

BOOK VII

USAF: SAC

(1948 – 1957)

A LITTLE LESS than a year after the USAF achieved its autonomy, Tooey Spaatz retired as Chief of Staff. He was succeeded by General Hoyt S. Vandenberg. Promptly General Van came over to Europe to see what was going on; he wanted to keep in close touch with developments there, as Tooey had done. Although he was the new boss, I didn't know him well. He had taken command of the Ninth Air Force just about the time I left Europe for the CBI in 1944.

I guided General Van around and showed him what we were doing, and told him why we'd done it. A lot of this stuff was beyond our mission; we were supposedly there merely as an occupational force; but I guess the new Chief liked what he saw. I had done my best to whip our United States Air Forces in Europe into first-class shape, and right quick, because this might be needed.

General Vandenberg said frankly that he was impressed with what we'd done with what we *had*, over there in Europe. So, in the early autumn of 1948, they hauled me out by the ears, and I was en route for the States with a new assignment.

I was to head the Strategic Air Command, succeeding General George C. Kenney. Nothing was said about the fact that I must build the whole thing up to make it effective and ready to go. They said merely that SAC was in my lap now.

The situation with USAFE was still pretty touchy at that time. General Van supplanted me with Joe Cannon, and he was basically a Tactical man, and knew his stuff in that direction. Joe took over, while I suppose the Russians stood and glowered, and I came back to Andrews Air Force Base just outside Washington.

I have been credited with the decision to move the HQ of the Strategic Air Command from Andrews out to Offutt. This is not correct. The decision was made before I ever arrived from Europe.

This occurred right at the time when the Air Force had gone to utter hell. This was in the days when, if you went into Flight Equipment Supply and needed to draw some equipment along about Saturday morning, you found some raunchy civilian in charge, sleeping on the counter. And, when you waked him up, he said that it would be impossible for you to draw any equipment before Monday: the sergeant had gone into town for the weekend with the keys to the lockers in his pocket. . . .

I should go on record and say this flatly: we didn't have one crew, *not one crew* in the entire command who could do a professional job. No one of the outfits was up to strength—neither in airplanes nor in people nor anything else.

The first B-36 had been delivered the previous June. That whole business was a mess too.

I never even unpacked. We were moving, immediately after I took command, from Andrews Air Force Base, near Washington, out to Offutt Air Force Base, on the edge of Omaha, Nebraska. That's the old Fort Crook. It started out as a cavalry post in the days of Indian campaigns.

. . . According to a magazine account, I got out of my airplane and started to walk to my car, and a gang of reporters ran alongside. I was smoking a cigar and concentrating on something or other, and didn't want to be bothered. One of the reporters came up beaming, and said, "General. Don't you think this will be a great thing for Omaha?"

And I am reported to have responded, "It doesn't mean a damn thing to Omaha, and it doesn't mean a damn thing to me."

The incident didn't happen exactly that way. But what I should have said—or perhaps meant to say, and was unable to say— The vague idea was romping around in my mind that SAC didn't amount to a damn at the moment, and Omaha couldn't be proud of it until SAC did amount to a damn. Nor was I very politic in my utterances in those days . . . I mean politic in the Oxford Dictionary sense of the word, which offers *prudent* as a synonym. I had a great deal to learn about public utterances, or any utterances which might be transcribed and eventually broadcast to the public. Helen had always tried to help me on this, but I'm afraid that she hadn't made too much impression.

"Curt, you oughtn't to *say* that."

At SAC, Al Kalberer helped a lot. I mentioned him before. We met when I went out to the CBI . . . the Blondie Saunders episode. Soon after taking command of SAC, I made Kal my Public Information Officer. He worked hard at whittling me down to size, or whatever metaphor you want to use. At least he taught me to put a little padding on the blunt mallet.

Nevertheless, leaving all this out, I can't envision a commander who wouldn't have been appalled by what he found in such a situation. If we had to go to war we would need to rebuild the organization completely before we'd be ready to fight.

By no means is this a direct or an implied criticism of any individuals then in command. What was going on might be termed OPERATION MILITARY SHUCK-OFF, and everybody had his shoulder to the wheel on that one.

In 1945 we had possessed the largest and best trained and most experienced and most effective Army and Navy in our history. In 1948 we were going around explaining to the world that we really didn't mean it; we were so sorry; and our bazookas had all been taken out to the city dump, and our airplanes had been smashed into junk. And Gus had gone back to the diner, and George had gone back to the real estate office, and Ronnie had gone back into the bank. And please forget that we ever tried to be soldiers, sailors or airmen.

It was the prevailing psychology of the year. The maintenance of a puissant force was regarded as a national aberration. You couldn't have a loaded shotgun behind the door and God in your heart; neither in one and the same moment, nor in the same year or same lifetime.

At the moment the whole idea in SAC seemed to be to cross-train everybody. Every bombardier was going to be a navigator, and every navigator was going to be a pilot, and every pilot was going to be a navigator and a bombardier, and I don't know what all.

In theory this is very fine. But you want to do your cross-training *after* you become really professionally qualified in your primary chore. If you can't do your primary chore and do it well, there's no use in trying to do your secondary chore. This was part of the torn-apart Air Force idea. We were all supposed to be demobilized, and I guess demoralized as well. But, since the Russians had started chomping around, people in Washington were getting a little disturbed; they really started to worry. They were perfectly willing to let me get some people back into SAC who knew their business.

There hadn't been enough Right People in the outfits or on the staff. I started gathering the old boys in, fast as I could. Take Tommy Power (my Deputy Commander in SAC for years, and later Commander of SAC, 1957–64). He was being sent to England as an air attaché, for God's sake. Matter of fact, he had already bought all of his stiff shirts, demanded by protocol, to go to England. Well, I got him snaked out of that, and started grabbing here and there, getting people who knew their business. I wasn't going to have Billy-the-Kid going into the front office or running a beauty shop when he should have been down on the flight line.

I said, "Let's take one group and get it ready to go. When we've got it ready, we'll go to work on the next one."

We started with the 509th. That was the outfit which dropped the atomic bombs on Japan. Bill Irvine had it in 1948. It was in better shape than any of the others. So it was more to the point to get the 509th up to snuff: wouldn't require such a repair job.

I got old J. B. Montgomery, made him Operations Officer; got hold of Cam Sweeney for Plans; resurrected Augie Kissner from somewhere or other. He became my Chief of Staff as soon as he finished his tour in Europe.

There wasn't much to Offutt except a big bomber plant and a cock-eyed runway ending in a steep bank—just about as silly a runway as you could imagine. (That was where my classmate Jesse Auton busted up eventually.) There had been an old grass field there, back around in the Fort Crook days; then, during the war, the bomber plant was constructed, and those folks improved the field somewhat. At first they built B-26's, and later the farmed-out B-29's. They never did much with the Army part of the place.

We moved our offices—the entire HQ—into the bomber plant. There may have been frightful construction problems facing us there at Offutt (I won't even pretend to say anything now about the *housing* problems at Offutt or throughout SAC as a whole)— Far as the ordinary SAC bases were concerned, they were the same old bases where they'd been training people during the war. Really a mess: flimsy barracks, tar-paper shacks. SAC didn't even have its pro rata share of the perma-nent bases in the Air Force—they had all belonged to some other command. It was a battle right from the start, just to get a place to live in and a place to work in.

First thing I did was to explore Headquarters and see what they had in the way of equipment and personnel and information. This was at Andrews, before I even went on to Offutt. I received briefings. . . .

Let's say we have some old fighter type who is in Operations. Try to get some dope out of him. . . .

"How's your bombing?"

"Oh, good. *Real* good."

"How's your radar bombing?"

"Good! Excellent. We were hitting fifteen hundred feet."

This sounds provocative but I start checking up. I find out nobody's flying at altitude any more. *Never* on oxygen. That's too much *work*. They're cruising around at about fifteen thousand feet all the time . . . the bombing they're doing, this superb, this excellent bombing, is by radar at sonar reflectors anchored out in the water someplace.

There's not a single realistic mission being flown. Practically noth-ing in the way of training. Sorry shape? You can say that again.

My immediate job was in convincing them that they *were* sorry. This was my first appalling realization at Andrews, and my first job when I reached Offutt.

Soon as I had J. B. Montgomery back there, buckled into his harness, I said, "Let's lay out a problem. Have 'em attack Wright. The whole damn command. By radar."

(All of SAC, shall we say—the total command—wasn't very big at the time.)

So we ran that Maximum Effort mission against Wright Field at Day-ton, Ohio. Oh, I'll admit the weather was bad. There were a lot of thun-derstorms in the area; that certainly was a factor. But on top of this, our crews were not accustomed to flying at altitude. Neither were the airplanes, far as that goes. Most of the pressurization wouldn't work, and the oxygen wouldn't work. Nobody seemed to know what life was like upstairs.

You might call that just about the darkest night in American military aviation history. Not one airplane finished that mission as briefed. *Not one.*

In 1964 we tried to get hold of some definite details to put in this book, and I discovered that those *details* of that mission against Dayton, Ohio, or Wright Field or whatever you want to call it, are still Classified.

There was a pretty violent reaction to the whole business. This really shook up our people, when they realized what sad shape they were in.

Could I handle the situation?

Didn't know. I was going to try.

Not once, during any switch of command, during any advancement in responsibility, have I ever considered that I was completely equipped for the new job at hand. Always I felt not fully qualified: needed more training, more information than I owned, more experience, more *wisdom.*

Forever there was so much to learn.

During those first baffling days at Offutt, I said once to Helen, "Wish I could handle any situation in the world. Like Fred Anderson."

"Like Fred—? Why, he's retired—"

"Course he is. But don't you remember what Liz said about him?"

Helen said I'd never told her the story. I declared that I had. Well, anyway, I'll tell it now. We go back to the 305th for this one.

While he was heading Eighth Bomber Command, Fred Anderson dropped in at Chelveston in time to eat an early breakfast, and to observe in detail how that day's mission was laid on. I've forgotten exactly what the target was. I know it was a fairly long mission for that stage of the game, the way the 17's were situated as to fuel and fighter cover.

The more General Anderson thought about that mission, the more he felt that he should be flying along. They hadn't nailed him down to the deck yet—that happened a little later on. And, since he had flown a number of missions when he was commanding the old Fourth Wing, he felt that he had every right to go on this one too.

He was down at the flight line, standing near a fully equipped and fully manned B-17, when he made his decision to go. Everybody else had their flying equipment handy or else were already wearing it. Not so General Anderson. He hadn't brought any such stuff along, since he and his aide came in a small aircraft at low altitude. Any questions concerning the general's oxygen mask, parachute, etc., had to be settled immediately, because engines were beginning to turn over in the leading aircraft.

Like the Three Bears, we had three sizes of Demand-Type oxygen masks in those days: one for a fat face, one for a thin face, one in between. Someone went racing up to the nearest supply hut, grabbed some masks, got a chute—chest-pack or peanut-pack—and harness and boots and all, and came speeding back to that dispersal point where Anderson waited.

The general wore pinks, and he did have the regular officers' insignia on his cap; but he was wearing one of those wrinkled poplin field jackets with no insignia of rank apparent.

Officers scuttled . . . one was hooking the harness around General Anderson's thighs and over his shoulders; another was checking to see that there weren't any twisted wires on the chute under its flap; another was trying oxygen masks over the general's face for size. It was quite a tangle.

Suddenly a voice exclaimed: "Mae West! The general hasn't got any Mae West!" and folks danced helplessly. Since the 305th was going to fly over a lot of wet water in the North Sea that day, it was required that General Anderson wear a Mae West, like all personnel. There wasn't time to go up to a supply room again, not even the nearest one. Forts were already blowing out their smoke. Taxi procedure had begun.

Some clever character pointed, and cried, "Hey, there's a Mae West! Get one of those!" A couple of youngsters went streaking off to meet a crew which approached.

Far too frequently for satisfaction and comfort, we had to send green crews off on bombardment missions without giving them any further training after they arrived in our midst. But, whenever it was humanly possible, we had them fly out over The Wash, which is a shallow bay and marshland oozing in from the North Sea between Norfolk and Lincolnshire. Another plane would go along with them, to tow a sleeve target; and those fortunate gunners might have an opportunity to learn what it was like to shoot at another object also speeding through the air, before they had to encounter veteran pilots of the Luftwaffe. Maybe it didn't do a lot of good, but we used to believe it helped.

So this crew had been shooting sleeve over The Wash, and now were home, having been cleared by the tower to land just before the combat mission departed. They came trailing away from their aircraft, jingling their harnesses across the hardstand.

"Sergeant! Quick—"

"What is it?"

"Your Mae West. We need it!"

"*Who* wants my Mae West?"

They stabbed their fingers in General Anderson's direction. "*He* needs it, stupid. Quick—take it off!"

Obediently the sergeant-gunner slid off his Mae West and handed it over, and they dashed away. You could see that he was thinking, however: thinking hard. He looked narrowly in General Anderson's direction. Fred had his back turned to the new crew, and was already being adorned with the life vest, put on over that shabby field jacket without any stars. For all the sergeant knew, Fred might have been some mere war correspondent or photographer who was going to accompany the Forts, and hadn't gotten himself properly equipped beforehand.

The sergeant-gunner came running over through all the smoke and engine roar, to where the commander of Eighth Bomber Command was just about ready to boost himself up through the hatch of a noisy B-17. He slammed the flat of his hand on General Anderson's backside, so that he'd really know that somebody was talking to him. "Listen, bud!" yelled the sergeant. "I don't want to have some character coming around to me from 365th Supply and telling me that I owe them seventeen dollars and eighty-four cents for a life vest. The moment you come back from this mission, you be damn sure that you leave that thing up there at Supply!"

Everybody else was speechless with horror or else so amused that they couldn't have spoken anyway. Fred scarcely turned his head. He looked around just enough to see the stripes, and he nodded seriously. "O.K., Sergeant, O.K. Will do!"

Then a dozen of the sergeant's friends and fellow crew members converged on him from all directions—ground crew, flight crew and all. General Anderson paid not the slightest further attention. He moved toward the B-17 hatch, giving a few last-minute instructions to his aide. But behind him the populace unloaded the bitter truth upon that sergeant.

That sergeant's face went from stubbornness and self-assurance to an expression of utter disbelief. Then terror. Then complete collapse.

Everyone was gabbing at once—all his friends were—telling him *whom* he's just slapped on the rear, and *whom* he'd been laying down the law to. They had the poor unfortunate by the arms, by the shoulders, they were supporting him around the waist. He looked back once. Then his head lolled over, and he was borne away, seemingly reduced to hopeless and permanent imbecility.

. . . Not too long after the incident occurred, one of our people was back in the States—an old mutual friend—and he grabbed time in Washington to have lunch with Liz Anderson, the general's wife. With amusement he told her this story, but Liz wasn't even ruffled. She said serenely, "Fred can handle *any* situation."

2

Soon after I went to Offutt some of the newspapers and magazines quoted me, while on a tour of SAC bases, as saying, "Today I found a sergeant guarding a hangar with a ham sandwich." I was quoted correctly. That was par for the course in SAC at the time.

Lessons learned during somber days of World War II (in recalling the Fred Anderson anecdote, I keep thinking of January and February, 1943, amid the mud of Chelveston)— Those are what sparked me to make certain that *what we had* was going to be ready to go, *and could fight.*

As for the world situation: in 1948–49 we were standing on a loose, slippery, fragile pile of broken crockery. My determination was to put everyone in SAC into this frame of mind: *We are at war now.* So that, if actually we did go to war the very next morning or even that night, we would stumble through no period in which preliminary motions would be wasted. We had to be ready to go *then.*

Our people must be combat ready and combat wise. First one group, then another.

We spread it out, we amplified the program as rapidly as increasing resources permitted. We fathered a master war plan. Everyone knew, eventually, what he was going to do. Each crew was assigned an enemy target, and they studied those targets, following out my old Lead Crew policy. People working for us and with us invented and constructed training aids (especially a radar trainer) whereby a man, if he was assigned a target at Moscow, could bomb Moscow hundreds of times, merely by using his training aid. So when the time came, it would be just another of those training missions, far as he was concerned.

But the SAC which was would never have become the SAC which is if everybody had sat on the ground, diddling around with that radar trainer. We went out and—flying, going through each vital motion except for the physical act of releasing live bombs from the shackles—we attacked every good-sized city in the United States. People were down there in their beds, and they didn't know what was going on upstairs. By the time I left SAC, in 1957, every city in the United States of twenty-five thousand population or more had been bombed on innumerable occasions. San Francisco had been bombed *over six hundred times in a month.*

An organization which could accomplish things like this couldn't be cobbled together overnight. It took years, and it took a lot of personnel who believed the way I believed. They must be given credit, and will be as long as I'm alive.

We had to fight all conceivable sorts of conflicts along the tortuous way. More fusses and arguments such as we'd been through a hundred times before, and some previously unknown to us. We had to square off and slug, just to keep enough people to do the job. SAC was built to its present determinate state of efficiency by a few hard-core dedicated men who had been through the mill again and again.

I wouldn't even venture to estimate how many airmen have gone through that command. You'd have to go and dig out the statistics; they would be appalling. Our reënlistment rate in the Air Force—in fact throughout all the military Services—was abysmally low in 1948–49.

There was no place to live. We had to scrape around to get money for barracks—even money to put in the pay envelopes, if you could call 'em that. Nothing came easy. Battle for equipment, battle for non-obsolescent airplanes, battle to get tankers. Just to *get* the tankers . . . we might have to fight from the United States if our overseas bases were gobbled up. And right then it would have been mighty easy for the Russians to gobble them up.

One of our earliest challenges was in merely attaining the capability of moving overseas. We might need to go somewhere and fight immediately, instead of taking months to transport an unwieldy Army. By 1950 we had actualized—and demonstrated, in a shooting war—the skill of starting over there in *hours*. We did this by living out of suitcases, and developing our flyaway kits. In the end we could just slam the lids on the boxes when the whistle blew, and throw the boxes in the airplanes . . . boxes were all numbered, and each went into its own airplane, and the proper people went along with them. Incidentally, a flyaway kit of that period contained around 44,000 separate items. First things got there first. As soon as we landed we were ready to go.

Less than five days after General MacArthur requested SAC's assistance at the beginning of the Korean War, our B-29's were based in the Asiatic theater and were flying missions against enemy targets.

To reach this potent state took time and it took effort. It wasn't done without squabbling all over the place—fighting figurative flank actions and rearguard actions. I declare again: the feat was accomplished by people who had been ground right through those engines, and were willing to stay on the job. I don't think America would be alive today if it weren't for them.

Mention of a ham sandwich at the beginning of this chapter brings to mind something else that loomed as an ugly problem. This was the condition of the SAC messes. They stunk.

Let any reader think of one of the many bad messes he must have encountered during World War II, and apply that to SAC in 1948–49, and he'll know what is meant. The s-on-s was there all right, and it wasn't even good s-on-s. Steaks obviously came from the nearest shoe repair shop; potatoes had been cooked in the laundry; the spaghetti and macaroni might have interested an entomologist or a herpetologist, but not any hungry customers.

I thought of my old lieutenant-mess-officer days, and got rid of a lot of official discussion and handshaking along the way, and went behind the scenes. Just to see, "What about that food?"

I discovered that we had plenty of food—good quality supplies, the very top. It was just poorly prepared and presented. As I said Away Back When: second-lieutenants can't make much of an imprint on such a state of affairs. Generals can.

I rounded up our cooks and arranged to send them off to the best hotels in the area near their stations, and let them train there. (Guess I was the first commander to ever do this.) I didn't put them on leave; they were on regular duty at the hotels.

Believe me, this took a bit of doing. The unions jumped up on their hind legs and brayed. Their main idea was, "If this guy works here, he's occupying some union member's job." So I had to go to the heads of the unions and straighten things out. I explained what I was trying to do, and why. I told them we were trying to keep people in the military Service, where they were needed so desperately, and not carelessly let lousy meals be an additional inducement for them to return to civilian life. Food was one of the important items on the military man's horizon. We were trying to teach our cooks how to prepare food properly. I pointed out that the SAC personnel who worked in those kitchens and dining rooms were not dislodging any union members; they were being paid only their regular Air Force wages. If anybody was benefiting it was the hotel proprietor who was getting some extra free labor.

After presenting my case I won the reluctant consent of the union people to go along with us on the deal. And I mean reluctant. But actually they didn't bring up the problem again.

As for those cooks who had been ordered down there to learn the business which they should have known all along— They got the message loud and clear through their own private lines of communication. The grapevine had it, and very definitely, that they would learn to cook that food and present it in the very best style, or else. Or Else might mean a sudden and unhappy change of station. Alkali Air Base out on the Alkali Plains in the State of Alkali had never been regarded as real good duty. Nobody wanted to go there.

Instead they pitched in and learned how to bake a muffin, and how to season the goulash, and how to scallop the oysters, and how to make salad dressing out of something besides cough syrup and worm medicine; and not to slop the whole meal together when it was presented.

It didn't take too long either. Very soon SAC was eating a lot higher on the hog. In another year the messes were really terrific, and have remained at a more-than-creditable level ever since.

The fiasco of Wright Field and Dayton really shook everybody up. Very speedily we got back to training at altitude. We got the schools going, got target study going, got more people into the act who knew what they were doing. You couldn't move around the Command without stumbling over names like Atkinson or Preston or Armstrong or Mike McCoy or Buster Briggs. We got the equipment shaken down, and did a lot of detective work and found out where so much lost equipment had gone. Plenty of it had been lost. . . . We shuttled personnel this way and that way, and heaved out whatever no-goods we had inherited—the ones that didn't fit.

There was a stupendous building job to do right then, and a lot more building ahead of us. But it was easier, once the boys became convinced that *everyone needed training.* You train enough, and you can be practically unconscious, but your reflexes will pull you through.

Right now I'd like to hold a guessing contest, and determine whether the reader can guess what the accident rate was in those early SAC days. We figure our accident rates at so many, per hundred thousand hours flown by the planes. Here goes.

How many major accidents did we have per hundred thousand hours? Sixty-five.

In the end we got it down to about three major accidents per hundred thousand hours flown. You can compare that with the sixty-five, and discover that the accident rate was about twenty-two hundred per cent worse in 1948 than it is nowadays.

This happened because nobody was using SOP procedures. (According to the *Air Force Dictionary,* that's Standing Operating Procedure. But I think the word Standard is used even more frequently.)

Also it's difficult to believe that no one was using checklists for take-off. But it's true.

I made a new rule. Every time a commander suffered a major accident in his wing, he came to Offutt to see me about it. (The groups had been redesignated as wings.) We went into the matter from every angle. They didn't like the idea of coming up there and standing on that unpleasant piece of carpet in front of my desk, but it's what I made them do. We were going to find *how* that accident happened, and *why.*

There was time to operate in this manner. This wasn't World War II, when we were expanding in every possible direction, and sending crews overseas who were as green as leaf lettuce. Our crews in SAC were going to be seasoned. They were going to know their business.

. . . We lined up every chore in the Command, and found people who knew how that chore should be run.

"O.K.," I said. "Get down to business and write a manual. I want a manual for every soul who has a job to do."

They wrote a manual for bombardiers, a manual for navigators, a manual for mechanics. Therein were listed the things the man in that particular niche should be doing, every single time. New people coming into SAC could take these manuals— A man could sit down with his own book, the one which applied especially to his task, and learn from the start how he should be performing.

As a rule the fresh personnel received this with more enthusiasm than some of the old folks. The attitude on the part of those elder people was, "Well, this is fine for the novice. But I'm too experienced for this sort of thing."

Let's go back to the accident business again. A wing commander would come in, and say, "I can't understand that accident. This man was the best pilot I had in the outfit. He cracked up. I don't understand *why*."

All the commanders were telling me this. I can't say that I reacted very daintily each time I heard the familiar words again. . . . The stupid pilots *never* cracked up their airplanes. It was always the *best* pilot.

So there'd be a nice smearing terminal accident, and here would come the commander of the 999th Wing or whatever the outfit was. He'd had a very brief period of time in which to prepare his case and check up on the circumstances. He'd open his mouth, and I'd know just what he was going to say.

It got so that I would start the conversation myself: "For Lord's sake, don't tell me this is the best pilot you had. I'm sick and tired of *that*."

It came down to this: the stupid pilot followed procedures which had been outlined for him. The best pilot . . . that was *beneath* him, of course. *He* didn't have to follow these checklists. That was for the neophytes. So he went out and busted his butt someplace along the line.

It was the sort of education which was needed desperately, yet which wasn't come by popularly. It was a bitter, rigid process. Still, we made steady advances in every case when we started hacking away at the basic problem.

Generally speaking, I received the type of coöperation which I desired. You always find men who have a different idea of how things should go, and they're willing to stand up and say so. That's as it should be. It's bound to keep the commander on his toes as well.

I had an entirely different problem than General Kenney had in the immediate postwar SAC. There is no invidious comparison intended. What General Kenney was trying to do was to hold something together which was being torn down. (Our new Chief of Staff, General Vandenberg, dwelt in a different climate than the one which surrounded Tooey Spaatz.) So, by the time I took command, the situation was reversed. Folks in Washington had become scared; they were ready to help me start to build the thing back up again, and sharpen it to a point of proficiency never previously attained.

No longer did we stress cross-training. We did not dissipate our energies. We made every man concentrate on being as nearly perfect as possible in his own specific enterprise. Hell, we made every man concentrate on being *perfect*. So, if he had any time left over and he learned what the next man was doing, that was a little gravy.

A planned campaign where everybody knows everybody else's job? It's like wishing for Utopia. It doesn't exist.

We found gratification in watching individual commanders respond to the fever and vigor of this incitement to performance. Nor did I promulgate any campaign with a slogan such as, "Have every commander try to get back his key personnel." Didn't need to. It happened automatically. When you have men whom you *know* in the key slots once more, just as they've been in key slots *before*— When you get them back to work, they automatically reach for the people whom they knew who served them previously and effectively in subordinate positions. The thing just snowballs.

Pretty soon some guy is going to say, "I want to get my old crew chief back." Actually it got down into those echelons.

It was popular to build, popular to increase. The Personnel office in Washington began to say Yes a lot sooner than they had before. The whole Air Force rolled over and shook itself and began to expand. SAC was a part of that expansion and, I believe, necessarily foremost.

Stalin dictated the increase of our Air Force.

As I said, the 509th was the first to come up to strength and proficiency. They were in better shape to begin with. It didn't take us very long before we could dust them off our hands and start in on another outfit. We concentrated on the next unit—got the right personnel in there, got the training program going. And we were constantly building.

Some pretty dreadful incidents occurred along the way, naturally. I observed such matters with some apprehension, because this was the first time I had been even remotely connected with the budget process, etc. (except when in R & D. But I was on the staff there, not in command).

. . . You went through the normal process of putting your request into the top of the Air Force, when you needed something. Then the Air Force had to battle that out with the Secretary of the Air Force. Then the Secretary of Defense, the Bureau of the Budget, and the Congress.

For example, we simply had to have a Headquarters and Control Center whereby we could be in instantaneous control of SAC bases scattered all over the United States and elsewhere in the world. And be in instantaneous touch with every plane we had in the air. But the situation was elastic and changing. This was also the first time when we were beginning to see a way in which we could get some tankers, and perhaps fight successfully from home bases in the United States if we got pushed off the edge of other continents.

It took us exactly five years to get that Headquarters and Control Center.

Here's the way it went:

The atomic bomb was with us, and the atomic bomb was here to stay; it had replaced the horse and buggy. I talked the whole thing over with my clan. Headquarters and Control Center? Had to go underground. Just *had* to. We agreed on that; my staff were with me in this opinion.

So we went in for this program.

And back came the answer from Washington. "It's far too expensive for you to go underground. Don't be insane. You just can't have it that way."

O.K. Very wearily we had designed a building and all that we needed, above ground.

This was during the Truman Administration. Well, we got the design, got the plans. Every item was approved. We collected our money, and advertised for bids. And—

Say it's tomorrow that we're going to open the bids and let the contract. Suddenly it's January, 1953, and we don't have the Democratic Administration any longer. We have the Republican Administration. The Republicans say, "Stop everything! We're going to review all this stuff."

Well, they reviewed our HQ building program. And said, "How stupid can you get in this day and age, building a headquarters *above* ground? Don't you know that you ought to be *below* ground?"

They were telling that to *us,* now.

Groan. We say, "All right." Here we go again, kids. By this time the hydrogen bomb is with us—not only the atomic bomb. And going underground gets to be rather academic.

So we compromise, and decide to go underground *partially*. A direct hit will knock the place out; but near misses will not knock it out; and fallout won't bother us—we're going to be behind thirty inches of concrete—

(Fallout has been built into an all-pervading all-penetrating monster in people's minds. I've tried to explain many times before, "If you can get two or three feet underground, in a basement or something like that, and stay there for a while until the hot air cools off a bit—and the air does cool off rapidly—then you'll be able to get by without permanent injury." Tests have proved this. I'll have more to say about fallout later on.)

All the while the cost of living is going up like the traditional homesick angel, the cost of construction is swelling. We go through the motions all over again, and come up with our new plan. Then we have to get *that* through the works.

You can't lose patience under such circumstances. You can't lose your self-control. You can't blow your top as you might wish to do. That's a luxury beyond the grasp of any SAC commander or any man in a similar position.

But patience doesn't mean sloth, and control of temper doesn't mean the loss of force and drive. You can't command by sitting back on your can. You have to keep going ahead, even when every circumstance seems to deny and obstruct you.

3

ONE FACTOR contributed admirably to the rise of SAC, and that was our rating system. It is a bit complex. Let me explain.

We knew what it took to make a good bombing outfit. They had to be able to bomb, they had to be able to navigate, they had to be able to fly formation. It was essential that they keep their airplanes in commission, and that they have the proper supply setup.

In the overall picture we listed these things. We listed what you *had* to have. If you had all of these things, then you were a good outfit.

It was essential to establish a point system in each category. We'd just forget about what the overall was going to be: that could be weighed and balanced in, later. But you'd set a value on every item which was included in the whole scheme, and the total of points gave you your score. This system was elastic; the bracket of points could go up or down, as was necessary in order to achieve an honest picture.

. . . Let's say that we are particularly bad in Supply at the present moment. So we're going to weight Supply a little heavier in the sum total. We assign higher numbers to Supply, and automatically people work on that. Then we examine the master scoring system, where all the outfits are scored, and one outfit can be compared with another. "Hmm," we say. "The 1638th has a very low score. They're sorry. The 1368th has a high score. They're *good*."

Well, let's start looking around and learn why one is good and the other is poor, and discover where he fell down.

Inside the organization the commander examines his own score, and he can observe that in Supply—or Personnel or Operations—some particular phase—he made a lousy showing. So he swoops down into that area and fixes it. If not— New commander.

This may be varied and used in a lot of ways. For instance, one wing consistently receives a high number of points in Operations or some other activity. So we go over there and learn how they did it.

. . . Just see what they were doing that was *so right;* and then the word could be spread around to other outfits. People would be sent to visit that one model unit and observe for themselves.

By this system of reckoning and dissemination of information, and evaluation of skills and the situation and abilities involved, you not only *had* a good outfit. You could tell instantly *why* it was good. And then you picked out the valuable ideas and spread them across the Command.

When I first started this routine, all hell broke loose. No commander ever wants to be compared with his contemporaries—especially, you might add, to his own confusion. He doesn't like it one little bit.

He scrutinizes the report and he, Ralph Range, has been designated as a sad apple, and his wing designated as a sad apple wing. And over there two States away, old Tim Tonnage has come out smelling like a rose.

Ralph blows his top. "Of course Tim has got a good outfit! Just see what he's got: all those hangars, and beautiful barracks. He's got some fine machine shops; he's got all the tools he needs to make an outfit. Look at *me* over *here.* I have nothing. God damn it, I've got this little hole in the wall for a machine shop, and we've only got one hangar, and my men are sleeping in tents. So I *haven't* a good outfit! Well, how could I *have* one?"

It took a lot of convincing. You had to be long-suffering, and sit down with him and say, "Yeah, Ralph, I know the whole story. But if we have to go to take the Russians, it doesn't make one sick mouse's bit of difference to the Russians whether you're sleeping in tents or in a marble palace. What the enemy is concerned with is where you put your bombs, and how you fought your way in. And that's all I'm concerned with. Look, Ralph. When I evaluate these scores, don't you think I know that Tim Tonnage has all those hangars and machine shops and quarters and everything else? Don't you think I know that Ralph Range has all these holes in the walls, and only one hangar, and all the other lean-and-hungry resources? So I look at his score *compared with the resources he has*. That's what I look at, in determining his efficiency—not the overall score. And I look at the overall score to see what I should work on, away upstairs where I am, to get *more* resources in here, to raise your overall efficiency."

It began to percolate eventually. It finally worked when people understood it. But, oh God— To start with, it was awful.

. . . Tickled me to death later on—very much later on, just a while back. J. B. Montgomery had gone to work, after he retired, in a large industrial complex. He put the SAC rating system into effect there. The same identical flap occurred. Everybody screamed his head off, and it took a big selling job on J.B.'s part to make them understand. He had all those companies; he had put the SAC rating system in, to see which firms were doing well and which weren't. No, they didn't like it either . . . exactly the same in civilian life as in a military establishment. Human nature is human nature, in uniform or out.

Sometimes I have been asked whether the Air Inspector General's office took umbrage at the application of our rating system. They did not; we never had the slightest conflict with the AIG and his people. Actually we were teaching them lessons all along. In our rating system we employed a completely novel philosophy.

People who were on duty in the old days will remember the dread of the Inspector General's arrival. He was a bogeyman; he was going to come down once a year and inspect your outfit. Well, of course, everyone always knew he was coming. So everybody polished up the silver, swept all the dirt under the rugs, hid everything that was bad, trotted out everything that was good for the inspector to *see*.

And down he came. He was always looking for something to gig you about, and usually he could find it.

Now, permit me to introduce a more rewarding philosophy on the subject of inspectors. I had one, evolving through the years, and I was trying for a long time to build this up, not only in SAC but throughout the entire Air Force. (Again, human nature being what it is, this was rather difficult to get into a workable state.)

My philosophy is:

The inspector is down there to help the commander make a better outfit. With the experience that he possesses, he should be able to help the commander.

Therefore, the inspector should make his *first* report to the *commander of the inspected unit;* and make his *second* report to his own boss.

The commander should be begging for the inspectors' assistance, instead of shivering in alarm long before they have stepped over the horizon.

We had to dress things up with a different name. I said, "I'll form an Assistance Team that won't be in the AIG shop at all." Actually it was just another inspector, but run as I thought an inspection should be run.

Herein was the variation: the Assistance Team went down there and *stayed* with the outfit awhile, to help them fix the things which were wrong. Possibly this could follow on the heels of an initial report given by an inspector; but sometimes they went without that. You don't need an inspector's report, on many occasions, to recognize that a wing is in trouble. Your normal reporting system should show you that, long before you ever send an emissary down there.

Ultimately it worked out fine. Over the years our inspection system has changed gradually from one which concentrated on counting the number of blankets they had—the amount of canned goods on hand in the mess, and the number of cans of axle grease or bags of oats or what the hell ever they counted. This has changed just as surely as the last horses have moved to the ceremonial details at Fort Myer; just as surely as the air is full of airplanes, where before there were only warblers and herons and gulls.

Nowadays you check on their *combat capability*.

Our big effort is in what we call the ORI, the Operational Readiness Inspection or test. In this, the inspector arrives on the scene, utterly surprising everyone. He says, "Execute your war plan," and you either do it or you don't. He's not one bit interested in whether you are short ten blankets or not. What he wants to know is, "Can you fight? And with what? And how will you fight, and how soon?"

In other words, going back to the old March cadet days, he wants to see you all standing at attention, after he kicks the tent and comes plunging through the door. Only thing is, he *doesn't kick* the tent. You've got to be on an attentive basis every moment. Not only because you fear the inspector might come. Also because you know that *war* might come.

. . . Along about this time I became aware also that I could be just as obtuse as the next person, when it came to divining the motives of people who more or less seemed to have *me* on the carpet. I began to appear more frequently before Congressional committees, and with more at stake than I had ever owned before; and with more people dependent on me to present honest testimony, and present it in such a way that it would redound to the benefit of our cause.

At first I'd considered that some of the questions put to me by the Congressmen were captious or even silly. Were these people deliberately trying to pick at me, to needle me? Or, in more overt fashion, to beat my brains out? Why did they jab, why did they seem to repeat, and go over the same ground again and again, *ad nauseam?*

To begin with, I had been a little jolted by the impact of the necessity at hand. I was, you might say, *frightened* initially.

But not for too long. It soon became apparent that the members of that committee had been around for a long long time. It became apparent that, when they asked me questions of that nature, they weren't being captious or silly. They weren't making a deliberate attempt to attack me or the program or the Command which I represented. Not by any means. They were trying to be helpful, that's all there was to it.

As well as I, they had a responsibility to provide for the defense of our Country.

The Congressmen were trying to formulate a record which might demonstrate why the aircraft or the program under discussion was truly needed, or why it wasn't. They were bent on discharging their own responsibility just as sincerely as I was bent on discharging mine.

Each in his own task, they were as dedicated as I might ever be.

As soon as this fact penetrated my thick skull, the whole ordeal became easier. What supported me—indeed what supported all of us— was the realization that we were working for a common cause. Then we began to understand, then we began to trust.

4

To SCRUTINIZE the LeMay personal and home life for a moment, first thing to note during those SAC years is that I was gone away from Offutt just as much as I was there. Roughly half the time on the road.

Quarters 16 was an old-fashioned pile of cornices and bricks—with ceilings and windows so high, especially on the first floor, that Helen wailed about the curtains.

Janie was nearly ten when we went there, so those were her growing up years. As I think we've noted, I was almost nine years on that job. There we lived longer in one house than I have ever lived in my life. Our family was constantly on the move when I was a child. Then, in Army and Air Force days, there was the SOP gypsying around. In the Pentagon period, I was on the two jobs for a little less than eight years total; but we lived in more than one place during that time.

Recently at breakfast we were reminiscing with a friend about those Offutt days, and the following conversation ensued.

Friend: "I remember Janie used to go to school out there—"
Helen: "Brownell Hall."
Friend: "She had to take a bus."
Helen: "She went to Brownell Hall, which was a private school in town."
Friend: "I remember she was always losing her books in the morning."
Helen: "On purpose."
Friend: "And then she claimed somebody had stolen them."
Helen: "Just the way Curt always claims somebody's stolen something when he's lost it."

Friend: "Yeah."

LeMay: "No. Her mother had probably put them away someplace, and put them away so effectively that they couldn't be found by anyone."

Helen: "So you wouldn't fall over them when you walked in the front door."

When it comes to family life, generals don't live in any more rarefied atmosphere than other folks. We have the same strains and squabbles and laughter and guerrilla warfare which other families have. But I'm confident that, in our threesome, we've had a lot more downright fun than I ever enjoyed when I was a boy.

There were all the usual confusions and accusations and tolerations and intolerations. And generals' little daughters can drive their fathers to drink, just the way other little daughters can drive their fathers.

Somebody gave Janie a couple of ducks; maybe it was more than a couple. Sounded like a whole flock. We fixed a coop for them out in the backyard, and a place for them to paddle in, and so on. Janie thought the sun-moon-and-stars rose and set in those ducks. When I was at home I thought I'd go nuts every time they started quacking. Quack, quack across the backyard; march around the house; quack, quack across the frontyard. Quack, quack, quack; drive off a neighbor's dog; quack, quack, quack, back to their feeding place again.

One time there had been a lot of wild animals in those parts, and I used to wonder hopefully whether any of the predators were still around. Maybe a sly weasel or a mink or something, or maybe a skunk or fox, would come out of some surviving piece of creekland, and do those ducks in. . . .

I must confess that I prayed this would happen. It didn't.

A visitor might be coming for lunch, and we'd stand in my little library-den-bar and look out of the window at those ducks. Quack, quack, quack.

The visitor would say wistfully, and probably hungrily if lunch was late, "You know, Curt, they'd look just beautiful on a big platter with a lot of mashed potatoes and gravy and green peas—"

I'd groan, and tell him, "If I did anything in the world to those ducks, I'd be through. Absolutely through. Finished. I mean that."

Helen finally tumbled to my agony of mind. She loved her Janie; Janie loved her ducks; so Helen had to suppose that she loved the ducks, and I ought to too. But there was getting to be a wild light in my eye. And two or three times, when I thought I was only mumbling to myself, I quacked.

Helen scouted around and found a farm where the people were glad to welcome the ducks, and where, by a peculiar coincidence, there was a pony for Janie to ride whenever she went to visit her erstwhile pets. That did the trick. From then on she had a different image to love. As for the old man, there wasn't a quack anywhere on the landscape. Slept better, too.

Piled up in the attic alcoves of that house were a mass of crates and wicker hampers and strange old scuffed leather valises, all fetched along from Germany. These contained certain trophies and toys of mine, as well as a lot of motion picture film. I had looked forward to going through this stuff, sorting it all out, splicing the film together on appropriate spools, and all that sort of thing. I planned to devote every Sunday afternoon to this pleasant chore—and it *was* a pleasant prospect, because I like to putter. Guess I spent about the first three Sunday afternoons, after we had landed there, doing that kind of thing. And then there just wasn't any more time. Too much else going on. Got involved in too many other directions.

I did manage to keep my guns and handguns in shape (I've a fair collection of those) but that meant blood and sweat. I can never stand seeing a gun neglected; so those were oiled and sheathed and taken care of. But the other things, the old hampers and cases— They went along with us to Washington when we moved there in 1957. There were piles of them put away in our Quarters 7 at Fort Myer, and they went from there into storage, the same week when we went— Well, certainly not into storage. I couldn't stand that either. But into military retirement.

Before long, now, we plan to build or buy a home. Eventually this baggage will be delivered and, I trust, finally opened . . . stuff packed in 1948 at Wiesbaden, and now unpacked here in the United States after all these years.

That ought to be quite an archaeological excavation. Like the matériel that was dumped and sealed up in those receptacles, when our main Army got out of Germany at the end of the war. Then we had to open it all up, two or three years later, in order to see what was there. . . . Can of worms or can of dried orchids? Probably I'll find both.

One of the toughest trivial problems to contend with, was the business of getting a little recreation. Not unpacking and sorting, either. I needed recreation just as my personnel did. But how on earth to get it in?

. . . Tried going across town to play golf but that didn't last very long. There wasn't any telephone out at the 6th or the 16th hole, and those were just the times when somebody wanted me on the telephone in a hurry. It was impossible to leave Offutt except when traveling in my own airplane, which was a flying Command Post—or on some spe-

cial jaunt to downtown Omaha, riding in a limousine with telephones
in it.

. . . One night I got to yakking to Helen for about the hundredth
time about that car which Bob Kalb and I rebuilt up there in Bradford, Pennsylvania, and how exciting it all was. Then I went over to
the window and did a lot of thinking. I looked off up the street . . .
that ancient Commanders' Row of the old Fort Crook days, where
horses used to be tied to hitching-posts out in front. (And, long before
that, they had to issue an order forbidding the enlisted men to shoot
buffalo from the windows of their barracks.)

But I wasn't seeing any buffalo or hitching-posts in my imagination.
I was seeing cars . . . automobile engines, and an old chassis, and rebuilt transmissions and such.

In many ways recreation was more important to the men whom I
commanded than it was to me. I would stay on in the Air Force; it was
the only thing I knew how to do or wanted to do. But our reënlistment
rate was pretty pitiful. It was a knotty problem—one which we had
attacked from every conceivable standpoint. Suddenly it seemed to
me that if we fired up a new form of off-duty recreation, that might
help a bit.

So many of our people were very young, and very young men are
apt to enjoy fooling around with cars. They enjoy constructing model
planes or hot rods. . . .

We had our clubs, of course, but there had always been clubs in
recent years; clubs weren't the answer. The Officers' Club; the Non-
Com's Club; a Service Club for the airmen (on most bases the Red
Cross girls ran that). Oh, there was usually a baseball field, and there'd
be tennis courts, and adjacent golf courses at certain bases.

They'd tried to get things started down at the Service Club . . .
Who wants to join a photo group? Who's interested in leather working? Who's interested in skiing or plug-casting or whatever . . . ?

It seemed that I might have something this time. What about an
automobile hobby shop, where people could mess around with their
own cars—rework engines, build automobiles from scratch, and do
everything else along that line?

The very next morning we started running a survey. Had to find a
place for this experimental deal to be set up. Within hours we came
across a building not far from the flight line where a quantity of surplus property was stored. It would be excellent for a hobby shop. So I
gigged the Supply people but plenty, and they got that surplus property out of there—either disposed of or moved someplace else.

Now the problem was to revamp the premises in order to start the
auto hobby shop. We had to depend on volunteer labor for this: folks
all had their full-time jobs. No one could be taken off his regular duty
for such an enterprise. And long ago I had learned this: you can go out

and work valiantly at helping the men . . . usually they are glad to take advantage of anything which is handed to them. But it takes a little organizing to get people to come and *do something for themselves* so that, in turn, they will have something new to enjoy.

We broadcast a call for volunteer labor to prepare an automobile hobby shop. The first time the volunteer labor force assembled on the dot. LeMay and two sergeants. We were It. Not another soul turned up to do any work on the place.

Well, I was sore. I knew it was a valuable enterprise, and that the goldarn fools would recognize *that,* when once we had the thing in operation. So I got out a whip and cracked it around in a few places. Very soon, not to my too great astonishment, some other people volunteered.

Then the thing started snowballing. They discovered that this could be fun—even the preparation of the shop itself could be fun.

To begin with, it was a kind of do-it-yourself garage. A man might have something wrong with his carburetor and he wouldn't want to shell out money to a garage; but perhaps he could fix it himself? So he'd bring his own car down there to the hobby shop and start working on the carburetor—fuel pump, radiator, whatever was wrong.

Next thing he'd decide to reline his brakes. Then he'd start talking it over with another boy, and they'd get the notion of experimenting with a distribution of braking power by putting oversized drums on those wheels.

That was the way it went: people started building cars, making hot rods, sports cars, fiddling with the engines, souping them up, so on.

I guess it would be pretty difficult to mistake me for a professional do-gooder. But I wanted very much to make a go of that hobby shop, and was absolutely without shame when it came to getting handouts. There were always important civilian visitors at SAC: manufacturers, tool people, automobile people, airplane people by the dozen . . . top executives or stockholders or officers. And a few lathes or other gadgets— A firm like that could donate such stuff and never feel it. I'd always steer our visitors (or have them steered) right down to that hobby shop, and show them what we were trying to do. Pretty soon the gifts started coming in. Machine tools, automotive repair equipment, all sorts of things.

Before very long we had more of this stuff than we could use. We took it all, however; we wrote the warmest of Thank You notes. In no time we had Hobby Shop Number Two going, not there at SAC HQ, but out at one of the bases. Then Hobby Shop Number Three . . . Seven . . . Nine. The automobile hobby shop got to be a vital thing on our bases, as much identified with SAC as the B-47. We discovered also that we would be able to use some of the welfare money (our recreational funds) to buy materials which hadn't been donated and couldn't be donated.

Those shops were the busiest damn places on the base. We ran a careful check at Offutt. More people actually went into the hobby shop, and used it, than used the Service Club.

During the period when Tommy Power was with R & D, and Butch Griswold became my Deputy Commander, we lived for the time when we could get down to that shop. Grizzy enjoyed messing around cars just as much as I did. There's nothing like having an old friend (pursuing a friendship which goes back almost to boyhood) who can share an identical interest with you in later life. Jeff Griswold and Helen complained that they were hobby shop widows. I'm afraid this was true. Neither Grizzy nor I had much free time; but what little we had, we spent being hobbyists. During my years in that command I built two full-scale sports cars.

One dark and stormy night Grizzy and I were both working late, determined to finish up whatever ambitious project we had embarked on. Lord knows—probably trying to make a Ferrari out of an old Chevrolet. We tried just about everything—

The other hobbyists had all drifted off to their quarters, and we were still tooling away. Next thing some youngster called to us from the doorway, pathetic and appealing.

"Hey, guys—"

General Griswold and General LeMay turned around and looked. We were in ratty old coveralls, and liberally smeared with everything from grease to graphite.

"Hey, guys. Help me out, will you? My engine's gone dead, out here in the street."

"Well, what do you want to do about it—bring the car in here?"

"Naw. It's just battery trouble. I've had it before, and I'm going to pick up a new battery in the morning. But if you'll just give me a push, the thing'll start running. How's about it? Huh?"

"Sure," we said. We went out and pushed his car for him, and he waved his thanks and drove away, and we went back to finish up the job we were on. We hoped that the kid would never discover who had pushed his car. We were afraid that it would take more than an automobile battery to bring him back to life after he dropped dead.

. . . I remembered something we'd seen while going around peeking into corners, seeking some place to establish the original hobby shop. We found an airplane stashed away over in some remote dispersal area. I stopped and looked at it: a Taylorcraft or an Aeronca—something like that—Piper Cub type. And the whole thing was being recovered.

I asked at the time, "What's this?" Nobody knew a thing.

. . . Got to thinking about it later, and did a little detective work.

Discovered that ten people had gotten together, and each chipped in ten bucks. They'd bought that wreck which had been all beaten to pieces in a hailstorm (yep, Nebraska hail can run to the size of golf balls or hen's eggs or even larger). So these boys had the old hangar queen, but no hangar; and they were fixing it themselves and doing a right good job.

What I could see immediately was the genesis of Hobby Club Number Two: an aero club.

"What have you got this airplane sitting out here for? Plenty of room over in the big hangar. Why not haul it over there?"

Well, they had thought that it would be illegal and we wouldn't stand for it.

"Nonsense. Get the thing out of here and get it over *there*. If we're going to have an aero club here at Offutt, let's have an aero club."

When I left Offutt in the summer of 1957 to go to the Pentagon, our aero club owned at least a dozen planes . . . I should guess that the club was worth a hundred thousand dollars or more. And similar aero clubs have been born on certain other SAC bases.

It was in those years of the middle 1950's that we really got the hobby shops a-going. I noted this: in 1954 we had a twenty-nine per cent reënlistment rate, overall, in the United States Air Force. In 1955 it was thirty-four per cent: five per cent increase in one year's time. I think that quite possibly the hobby shops helped on this.

I used to feel sad because I didn't have enough time to spend on that sort of stuff. (Not only planning and organizing and getting the things started, but actually down there swinging a wrench myself.)

You have to go to work in the Big House on the Potomac to know how the other half lives.

During my later years on the job there, I discovered that I had enjoyed practically a life of leisure when I was at Omaha, compared with my experience as Chief of Staff. It wasn't a question of fooling around mechanically with a car; it was a question of merely being able to drive one.

My idea of utter relaxation was to get in my little Corvette and run along the Potomac parkways for a while, and breathe the cool air and feel the power working under my hands and feet, just the way any driver who loves to drive enjoys it.

The last autumn I was on the Chief of Staff job I took a friend for a ride. Then we came back to the garage there at Quarters Number 7, and I said, "It's a close fit, next to Helen's car here. You'll have to get out before I drive in."

So he got out and stood outside, and I eased the Corvette inside, and then squeezed from the seat and shut the door. I got my tarp, and the friend came to help me unfold the cover and put the car to bed. I said, "So there she'll sit until the battery runs down."

"Say again?"

"Damn thing sits in the garage until the battery runs down. Then I find it's down, and have to have someone give it a quick charge, so I can use the car *if* there's ever another chance."

Rank may Have Its Privileges, but Retirement Has Its Points. That's my own RHIP. I'm enjoying it more every day.

5

IN THOSE SAME early SAC years I began to make my first friends on The Hill (that's the way we refer to the Congressmen in Washington). I learned unmistakably that there were some people in the Military Affairs Committee, and elsewhere in our Congressional structure, who had been around a long time. They were keen and knowledgeable, yet pliant and willing to accept new ideas. It was truly an inspiration to be confronted with them. I refer to men like Vinson and Russell and Mahan, and some others: old pros who truly were apprised of military affairs, and could talk to a commander in terms he understood, and who would listen to a commander talking in terms they might understand.

But I was never able to get our whole Military Affairs Committee out to Offutt at one and the same time.

Individuals came to visit us, that is true. But if ever in subsequent days I felt like needling the Congressmen a little, I'd say, "Let me tell you a story about Norwegians."

I'll tell it now.

In Norway, their Minister of Defense, the Deputy Minister of Defense, and the entire Military Affairs Committee of the Norwegian Parliament expressed a desire to visit SAC and learn what it was all about. We were willing, naturally, to fly them to Omaha as soon as it was convenient for them to make the trip.

While we had briefing officers who could speak in German, French, Spanish and many other languages, it so happened that at the time we didn't possess any briefing officer who knew Norwegian. Some of the people in the delegation could speak English—most of them, I guess. But there were some who had no English, and we needed to rely on an interpreter. Their Deputy Minister of Defense served in this capacity.

The U. S. State Department was eager to have us convince the Norwegians that they weren't clear at the end of the line—which it seemed that they considered themselves to be, geographically speaking. When you consider that you can step directly from Norwegian territory into Russian territory, or vice versa, you'll understand why they felt that way. It takes about as long to fly from Leningrad to Norway's capital as it does from Chicago to the New York State capital.

I made a private plot of my own.

We assembled for the normal briefing at eight o'clock in the morning. Had to start early, because the Norwegians were only going to be there one day.

Well, we went ahead with the regular SAC briefing and then, about nine-thirty, enjoyed a coffee break. While we were drinking coffee and talking around in groups, an officer came in and handed me an envelope of photographs. There were fifteen or twenty prints in the envelope. So I gave everybody one of the photos. Didn't say a word, just handed them out. There was no annotation on the photographs, no legend to describe what they were seeing. It was a picture of a city, taken from the air: a very good print indeed, recognizable to anyone who knew what he was looking at.

For a few moments our visitors must have thought we were a little balmy, in suddenly putting such a photo into their hands. Then one of them exclaimed, "This is Oslo!"

From then on it was a riot. They recognized everything. Each man was trying to point out something else to his neighbor. There was the City Hall at the head of the Oslo Fjord, the airport out at Fornebu, the big Holmenkollen hill; everything else.

"Why, there's the Storting!" (Their Parliament building.)

"See, the cathedral—"

"Look here. Akershus Castle."

"Yes, yes! Here is Karl Johan Street—"

Well, about the time they had everything identified, I said, "That's Oslo all right. One of our B-47's took that picture this morning."

"This *morning?*"

"This morning."

That was when their faces really began to light up. They were receiving the message.

We told them what we'd done. I had a B-47 fly up from England early that same day—remember, there's the time difference—and take a picture of Oslo. There were a lot of clouds, but fortunately a hole drifted open at the right place. So they could happily pick out the identifying characteristics of their capital.

. . . The B-47 flew back to England immediately, and people put the picture on the wire, right into SAC HQ. So, all in the same morning, the 47 flew from England, got the picture, brought it back, sent it to SAC.

No wonder that there were now beaming faces among the members of the Norwegian Military Affairs Committee and the ministers. I could have gone over there to Oslo and talked until I was blue in the face, to try to get our SAC story across to them, and it wouldn't have packed the wallop that one picture did. They knew they weren't so far away after all. It meant a lot.

Also it gave me my chance to have a little fun with our Congressmen, whenever I wished. "I've never been able to get my own Military Affairs Committee out to Offutt, but I got the Norwegians to come."

. . . As I say, many of them did appear one time or another out at Omaha, but as individuals. Our Military Affairs Committee is larger than the Norwegian one, and thus more unwieldy. It would be difficult to get them there *en masse*.

But we were becoming acquainted. I'm proud that I developed a reputation for standing up and telling them exactly what I thought.

"General LeMay, what do you think about this . . . ?"

I'd tell them. Usually that was the answer to the question. I didn't say what someone else had told me to say.

Definitely the regard displayed by Congress has been the most satisfying experience of my entire career. I take joy in it. This is something that doesn't happen every day in the week, nor to every man. Set up the way we are, the backing of the Committee is the backing of the Congress itself; and the backing of the Congress is the backing of the Nation.

I have found it especially rewarding in considering that I had almost no experience in that sort of relationship before I took command of SAC. Still, the identical graph runs right through my whole service record . . . rising and descending lines are always the same. My pattern throughout thirty-five years was painfully similar: getting heaved into something in which I'd had no previous experience.

When it has to be done, you just dig in and do the best you can.

Repeatedly I tried to adhere to well-tested tactics. Get the best people you can, around you, who will help. Decide on the course of action. Get busy on it, and keep out of your subordinates' way. Actually, it seems like the simplest thing in the world: to be excruciatingly honest always with yourself, and with everyone who's working for you.

Never throughout my service was I in a position where I could say, "Well, next year I'm going to—" do this or that. "Therefore I'd better go and get a little schooling, and ready myself, and train for this specific task, so I'll be able to perform when the time comes." Never, never was I in a situation like that.

Again and again I was thrown into a job which was new to me—one in which I felt inexperienced and untrained. In advance I didn't know exactly what to do. Had to play it by feel.

. . . First off, assemble the team: you can't do everything alone. Our business was too damn complex for that, right from the start. I had to line up a good team in the 305th; had to do the same thing at Third Bomber Command; same thing with the 29's, and in R & D. And over at USAFE, and back again at SAC.

The public has had projected before it the image of a LeMay who always went his own gait, strictly a lone wolf, mind full of bombs (and maybe his pockets too). I'd like to correct this impression now, and eradicate it if I can.

Somewhere during the brief period of military schooling which I was able to enjoy, I heard a lecture wherein a veteran recalled talking to a German officer after World War I. The German officer says, "I don't see how you people won, because you have no discipline among your troops! First you have to give them the order, and then you have to explain *why*. That is not a good way. *Nein.* How did you ever get anything done?"

My notion has been that you explain *why,* and then you don't need to give any order at all. All you have to do is get your big feet out of the way, and things will really happen. Forever I took the same course. Get the team together. "There's the goal, people. Go ahead."

Certainly there were bound to ensue arguments among the tribesmen as to *how* they should go about the mission. Every now and then I'd need to get in and straighten things out. Even, unfortunately, sometimes I would be compelled to exercise my prerogative of command. *Get the axe. Chop him out of there.* That's if somebody really fell down on his part of the job. But mainly I was pretty successful in getting the right people in the right slots to begin with. *Very* fortunate indeed.

It was the only system whereby I could function.

There was always bound to be trouble ahead. There was always the strong feeling that I wasn't adequate for the job. Never a moment when I could honestly say to myself, "I've had plenty of training for *this.* I know just how to do it. It's merely a matter of going in and applying my past knowledge. Then everything's going to be fine." Never. Never. I've been *behind,* through all those thirty-odd years. And that's the reason I've emphasized training and military education so persistently.

Nowadays, in 1965, we finally have an Air Force where young men are being trained for the things they are going to do perhaps even three or four years hence. I've kept striving for this all the time. Get the people into school earlier. Get them to school before they are actually *in* the jobs which they're going to do.

Hell's bells. After World War II we started training people in school to do jobs they had *already done* in an outstanding manner. That just didn't make sense.

Take the first class we sent down to the War College. I think you could have tossed a nickel in order to determine who was going to be the student and who was going to be the instructor.

It's nice enough to have it on your record. Someone looks at your record and says, "*He's* gone to the War College." The man thinks that it enhances this individual's chances of promotion, and he's right. But it was utterly absurd, sending a lot of people to the War College after

the war, when they had already been through the mill. Now we're
sending folks to the War College when they're young enough to have
it do them some good.

6

IN 1958 a writer named Richard J. Hubler published a book called
SAC: The Strategic Air Command, and certain paragraphs from this
book still stick in my mind. I think especially of some lines concerning
the Korean War.

"As a new type of conflict—the 'fenced-in war'—the Korean imbroglio
was a frustrating experience for the SAC strategists. There were few
real strategic targets; there was not enough physical room to allow for
real deployment of nuclear arms. Even mildly lucrative targets were
rare—and those that did exist were soon masses of rubble. The real and
most inviting targets lay in China, just over the Manchurian Yalu
River, industriously turning out war goods for the enemy without the
slightest fear of reprisal."

That was pretty much the way it happened. The reader will remember that previously I told of my immediate suggestion that we go up
north and burn the principal cities, as we had done during World War
II in Japan. I believed that this would stop the war very quickly, with
minimal casualties, as compared with an attenuated war dragged out
through several years. Screams of horror arose when I made this suggestion. Needless to say, we didn't get anywhere with the idea.

There was one bomb wing out there in FEAF (Far East Air Force)
at the start of the war, in June, 1950. That was the 19th. When the
request for SAC assistance came, promptly we deployed the 22nd
Wing (James Edmundson) from March Air Force Base, and the 92nd
(Claude Putnam) from Spokane.

These two outfits were picked because they were low on the totem
pole. By that I mean they were low-priority wings in our conversion
program. They had not yet reached the stage where they possessed
much atomic capability. We still had to keep SAC at an instantaneous
readiness in case someone pulled the Big Switch, and the Big Blow
fell.

Remember our old schedule. "We'll get one wing ready, and then,
as we achieve more resources, we'll get another wing ready, and hold
that— Then get another one ready, and hold onto what we've got. . . ."

Before the end of July two more wings were requested from SAC.
I put up a little resistance. I didn't want too many splinters to be
whittled off the stick which we might have to wield. I felt that they
should have sent more TAC over there, and fewer medium bombers.
(Take note: where our B-29's had been designated as Very Heavy

Bombers in 1945, they were now Medium Bombers.) But the people in Washington decided to accede to this request, and I was directed to send the two extra wings.

We ordered over the 307th (Buster Briggs) from MacDill, and the 98th—Dick Carmichael's wing—from Spokane.

This was somewhat of a drain on SAC, because we had to keep rotating our crews through. It retarded some of our other programs. And there wasn't anyone over there who seemed to know how to use our B-29's. So we hustled Rosie O'Donnell to Japan, right at the start, to head Bomber Command.

They were using the 29's against troops. The ancient concept of flying artillery was reborn and reinstituted; but the B-29 was never intended to be a tactical weapon. Some exchange officer from the RAF, down at FEAF HQ, was credited with putting across his idea of using our planes as night intruders. That was the way the British employed the Beaufighters and Mosquitoes during World War II, and they were instruments which could be used ably for this work. B-29's were never primed for such a task.

The visionaries wanted to send them out with flares and mixed bomb loads, looking for Targets of Opportunity, chasing tanks down mountain roads. The idea was to drop flares over the landscape, discover a target, and come around and go after it with more flares. The bomb loads were mixed: frags, HE bombs, napalm, the works.

The bombardier was expected to perform an economic evaluation, and decide whether the target was worth the expenditure of ordnance. Meanwhile, if the target were sufficiently mobile, it had gone scuttling up one of the roads among the hills, and taken shelter along cliffs or in the woods.

Rosie O'Donnell practically blew his top at having to send people out on such frustrating missions. It was necessary for him to accede, however reluctantly: the orders were *there*. As for our aircraft commanders and crews who had trained long and hard on strategic bombardment from altitudes— Their opinions would be unprintable.

More infuriating than anything else was the sight, in daylight, of those masses of enemy tanks parked up there across the Yalu River. They could have all been burned up in one breath. But the Yalu was sacrosanct; and even a twenty-mile zone bordering the south side of the stream was proscribed for our aircraft. Then, during the night, when troops and individual vehicles and tanks filtered down into North Korea, the idea was to hunt them out and attack them.

Like hunting stray coyotes in the dark. Won't work.

Back home at Offutt we groaned, and thought of what had been suggested by us, and turned down by Washington. We could see clearly and painfully that more people were going to be wiped out in a protracted war of this sort—far more than ever would have disappeared beneath an incendiary attack on those northern cities. But we would have killed a lot of noncombatants at one fell swoop. That was not palatable. It was palatable to kill a great many *more* noncombatants, as well as soldiers, during the next three years.

We knew they were getting their supplies from China. We requested permission to bomb the Yalu bridges and stop the supply routes. No; couldn't do that. We were told to keep the roads closed and the bridges out, down *below* the line; and we did that successfully.

But enemy soldiers were able to carry enough stuff on their backs to keep things going. That's the eternal story about Oriental versus Occidental troops. Certain readers may recall that, at the start of the war, some of our former enemy Japanese commanders came to General MacArthur and volunteered their willingness to raise a couple of divisions for immediate service in Korea. This might have been the answer to war on the ground.

Our Administration shook its head at the notion. We had not concluded our treaty of peace with Japan as yet. It just couldn't be done, from a State Department or diplomatic standpoint. As for the South Koreans: they announced that they wouldn't have any part of Jap troops coming in there. So there we were. No dice.

Americans find it necessary to enter a conflict loaded so heavily that our logistic backs are aching to begin with. We go to war with elaborate hospitals, messes, recreational facilities, PX's—everything you can think of—to sustain our fighting men in the manner to which they have been accustomed, whenever and wherever possible. It certainly wasn't possible on that long retreat down from the Changjin reservoir, and I would not presume to minimize the sufferings of our troops out on those wintry ridges, then or any other time. (Or in the swamps of Viet Nam in 1965.) It would be an insult to the memory of boys who died there, often lopped off entirely from support and supply. That's not the point.

The point is: our conception of a program, and our *approach* to the whole idea of warfare. We break our logistic backs with all this impedimenta.

An Oriental enemy does nothing of the kind. In the Korean War, the North Korean or Chinese Communists marched into a village and lined up the men. They picked out Kim and Tim and Yim and so on. They put them in a rank, and said, "Tomorrow you will join your commands—" Over here or over there. "Here's your gun, here's your cartridges. You take a wad of rice or a chunk of fish in the pocket of your jacket. You be there at nine tomorrow morning. If you don't show up, you might as well say goodbye to your entire family right now. They won't be here when you get back."

So Kim and Tim and the others get the picture. They spend that whole night trotting across the mountain to an appointed rendezvous, and they show up bright and early. They haven't got anything in the world but their guns and ammunition and whatever rations may be stuck in the pockets of those dirty quilted jackets. And an undying Oriental philosophy and fanaticism.

Human attrition means nothing to such people. Their lives were so miserable here on earth that there can't help but be a better life for them and all their relatives in a future world. They look forward to that future world with delight. They're going to have everything from tea-parties with long-dead grandfathers down to their pick of all the golden little dancing girls in Paradise.

This is a prize frame of mind in which to approach combat. You're not risking much. You're only risking your life, and a better life awaits you.

But you don't want to see your own wife and mother and children massacred before their time. So you proceed under threat of their annulment. You just keep attacking.

The Americans have a machine gun down in that gully or up there on that hill, and you are ordered to destroy the machine gun. The Americans fire with attentive accuracy; they are well-trained troops. They have ammunition, they know what they are doing. They mow down the whole first wave of Kims. So then all the Tims rise up off their haunches, and they keep charging. The Americans shoot and shoot. But their gun heats up at this incredible expenditure of ammunition and rate of fire, and the piece begins to give them trouble. Furthermore, ammunition is getting low. About half the Tims may have been killed in that second charge; but there are the Yims behind them, still waiting to go; and over the hills comes a whole new covey of Bims and Vims.

They need to swarm over that machine gun nest and wipe out the Americans, and free that section of the terrain from the domination of enemy machine guns. So the Orientals keep attacking and attacking. Then the gun jams—permanently, this time—or else the ammunition runs out. Americans fight with their side arms; but there are too many Fims and Jims tumbling over them.

The machine gun nest is gone. So are the Americans.

It calls to mind an ancient wheeze which circulated around about 1930, when the Chinese and Japanese were locked in their warfare, long before World War II began.

There is a Chinese laundryman in the United States, and he can't read the newspapers because he doesn't know how to read English. He has a good friend, a customer who comes in every day. The Chinese always asks for the war news.

"Well," says the customer, "I'm afraid it's bad. This morning's headlines say that a hundred Japs were killed, but you people lost two thousand Chinese."

"Good, good," says the Chinaman, smiling broadly.

Next morning. "You have war news?"

"Yes, the paper announces this morning that ninety Japanese were killed, but you lost five hundred Chinese."

"Good, good."

Next day maybe it's two hundred Japs gone, and four thousand Chinese. But that information too is greated with smiles.

"For God's sake!" says the customer. "They kill off whole gangs of Chinese and only a few Japs, and you keep saying, 'Good, good.' "

"Good, good," says the Chinaman. "Pletty soon no more Japanese."

In the next year or so we learned some interesting things. We learned details concerning the Russian Migs which we hadn't known before.

At first the enemy employed only Yaks, and he didn't push their employment, either. On earlier missions which our people flew across North Korea (compelled to keep warily away from that twenty-mile interdicted zone south of the Yalu) they would look out and see a bunch of Yaks riding herd on them. Mostly the Yaks stayed out of range, and it was seldom that any shooting occurred.

In the meantime, however, the enemy was trying to build fields farther south of the Yalu. Apparently this was for future deployment of the Migs. Thus we came to believe that they didn't have the range to get from across the Yalu in Manchuria, all the way down to the front lines. The thing seemed to be to deter them from ever operating those airfields.

Our boys went up there at night and kept the airfield capability down. They'd go out about every third night and drop bombs on them; then, in two or three days the enemy would have that repaired; and we'd drop some more bombs. They never did get those fields finished. But actually we found out later that indeed the Migs possessed enough range to reach the front lines.

If I had been working for the other side, and had had all those Migs in Manchuria that the Chinese had, I would have run General Mac-Arthur right out of Korea.

Maybe they were afraid that if they did commit the Migs to any extent, we would go across and bomb them up there. But we weren't bombing in Manchuria; weren't allowed to.

With that Mig force, any energetic commander could have cleaned out all the airfields we had in Korea, and mighty soon. And I think he could have done it on the first mission; then they could have started working on the troops. Why they didn't do it I'll never know.

This may come as a surprise to the reader: *we never lost a single man on the ground to enemy air action in Korea.* Far as our Air Force losses were concerned, we lost all too many men in air-to-air action or ground-to-air action. But I am talking about the ground soldiers. No ground soldier is known to have lost his life during enemy air action. Not one.

The Migs never came down and fropped our troops when the soldiers were on the road or in their front line positions. The Migs never attacked barracks or camps, or any other variety of troop installations. They never bombed. They did not attack our ground forces, period.

Certainly we attacked theirs, again and again. Our tactical airmen, and Navy outfits as well, performed excellent duty in assaults on enemy ground forces.

The enemy didn't take any cue from our activities.

Even with B-29's, we sought out enemy troops in the field. Take that diversionary assault down there by the Naktong River, coördinated on the same day with the Inchon landings.

Our 29's were ordered to bomb a quadrangle immediately west of the Naktong. American troops were trying to break out of the Pusan perimeter where they had been contained. As a whole, our B-29 people didn't even know what the primary target actually consisted of. I guess Rosie O'Donnell knew well enough . . . seem to recall that he led the mission that day, and got his DSC.

Everyone was cautioned against attacking that primary target unless the visibility was just about perfect. Weather didn't promise much: looked like it might be seven- or even nine-tenths cloud, and they'd have to go on to their secondary, and leave the fatal rectangle safely unbombed.

Well, our Weather information was off just about a hundred and eighty degrees. By the time the 29's had left their Japanese bases and flown across the sea, and were coming up from those southern islands where they had formed, the clouds all broke away. The bombers went in there with perfect visibility, and when those three squadrons turned off the target there were the three blankets of smoke and vapor rising in three solid sections at different levels—so even that they seemed to have been marked out with a ruler in the sky. The crews said, "We don't know what we hit. But whatever it was, we certainly shot the s——t out of it."

When they got back to their base— Here was a case of man bites dog. A communication had just come in, signed by General Walton H. Walker, commander of our Korean forces, and General Hobart R. Gay, who bossed the First Cavalry Division. The message said to the B-29 people: "Our congratulations and our thanks. The First Cavalry Division is now across the Naktong River."

What they had done was to completely erase the enemy artillery concentrations on those hills west of the Naktong. With all their people and artillery either destroyed in that area, or rendered impotent, there was no possibility of the enemy's resisting or even much delaying the crossing by the First Cavalry Division.

This was the old Attack technique: the modern TAC technique, and the original dream of Army commanders who saw in the new-fangled airplane only an extension of ground firepower. "Flying artillery" once more. It worked in this case, because they had perfect visibility. There wasn't any necessity for smoke markers: the Naktong River could be identified. We didn't want to kill any more General McNairs and we didn't kill any.

But that wasn't what B-29's were trained for, nor was it how they were intended to perform. The B-29's were trained to go up there to Manchuria and destroy the enemy's potential to wage war. They were trained to bomb Peking and Hankow if necessary. They could have done so. The threat of this impending bombardment would, I am confident, have kept the Communist Chinese from revitalizing and protracting the Korean War.

The World Book, published in 1964 (Volume 11, page 297), calls the Korean War "one of the bloodiest in history. . . . More than a million civilian men, women and children were killed. . . . United Nations and South Korean troops suffered more than 1,460,000 casualties. About 2,000,000 Chinese and North Koreans were killed, wounded, or missing."

We Americans suffered a total of 157,530 casualties. That includes battle deaths, other deaths, and wounds not mortal. The great tragedy is that even these 157,000 casualties were mostly unnecessary. That war (its veterans don't like the term *police action*) could have been terminated almost as soon as it began. I will always believe this.

7

It doesn't mean a damn thing to Omaha, and it doesn't mean a damn thing to me.

As I've said, those weren't exactly the words employed, but some such thought was in my mind.

How little I knew Omaha.

There hadn't been any particular reason for the Strategic Air Command's moving out there—except that, frankly, we had no place else to move to. A centrally located area was essential. Every manner of communication and transportation would need to come in there. The middle of the country was the place for SAC.

So there we were, back in 1948–49, installed in that old bomber plant.

Almost immediately I called on the Omaha city officials, and they returned the courtesy. Not only the city officials: a committee of businessmen came, and not only businessmen—professional people as well. Also there were individuals whose years of active business or professional life were at an end, but whose interest in and affection for their community did not slacken in retirement.

In every municipality there's such a group of people behind the scenes, some of them seldom mentioned in the newspapers. Those are the folks who really run the town. And those were the Omaha folks with whom we had contact from the start. Never could there have been a greater benefit achieved.

A local citizens' committee for SAC was set up. They were ready with everything: advice, understanding, imagination. As it turned out, before very long they were ready with money too.

Right at the start I supposed that I was in for the same difficulties which had beset commanders all the way back to the Girl-I-Left-Behind-Me days. Offutt Air Force Base had been pretty well closed down since the war. Not many personnel needed to be around. Then here came SAC HQ, dumped down there. Very suddenly there were a lot of young airmen in a new environment, racing downtown after their working hours to have a look at the beer situation, the movie situation, and—above all—the girl situation. Promptly there came troubles with the local drugstore cowboys. The airmen started dating the girls; there was a fistfight here and a fistfight there . . . symptoms of that social conflict which, in places where there were colleges, used to be called a Town and Gown war.

. . . Well, the mayor welcomed me hospitably, and we discussed the situation.

He said, "This will be fixed immediately. Tell your boys that they are now locals."

And that was that. Word went around. There was to be no more such feuding. And there was no more.

Net result? We *never* had to declare a single place Off Limits in the city of Omaha. Outside of that first little flare-up, no menacing looks have ever been exchanged between the Air Force boys and the locals. Discerning citizens shouldered their responsibility. SAC was no longer a suspicious-looking and suspicious-acting furriner come to town. SAC belonged to Omaha, and Omaha belonged to SAC.

I am happy to add a pleasant word about the racial integration problems as well. We just didn't have any. Offutt was one of the first bases where Negro personnel were brought in after the disbanding of our colored units as such. We never had the slightest trouble in Omaha on that score.

Nor on any score.

Back and forth, give and take. The handshake, the welcoming smile. And the more-than-welcoming deed when it needed to be done.

We were gratified to bring the committee of citizens out to our head-quarters whenever they wanted to come, collectively or individually; and they wanted to come a lot. We offered them briefings on SAC, on the national situation, the international military situation. Before long they were a part of our lives in thought and in act, just as we were a part of theirs. We kept them up to date on what we were doing in SAC and—insofar as Security permitted—why and how. As fast as new equipment was unwrapped for public gaze, the Omaha folks saw the new stuff. Sometimes they were the very first to see it.

It's a good thing for citizens and military officers to mull over, to-gether, any problems which they both see, or which one or the other sees, coming up on the base or in the town itself, as a result of military activities in their midst. You can stop a lot of troubles before they ever begin. And the mere fact of having some keen and receptive people in the core of the community who know what the necessary require-ments are, is pure gold to any commander. It worked wonders there, and it's worked wonders in other SAC areas.

Such relationships may have been instigated and pursued before. If so, I just never happened to hear of it. And there must be many other places where the machinery described has functioned proudly, with the same method of liaison between. I believe, though, that in the Offutt-Omaha situation we really formalized this system. Lincoln, Nebraska, has been very good too; but I just don't know of any place where the people turned out, openhanded and hearty, and made the military feel as they did at Omaha.

Going back into the past, we found that there was a tradition of such kindness established long before we ever appeared. The Army and even the Navy had had units stationed there before we came along. Omaha folks always gave an annual party for the soldiers or sailors in their midst. In 1957, the year I left to go to the Pentagon, the citizens planned a novelty in the way of parties. They went off and dug around, and found a few of the old commanders of the Seventh Corps area which used to be there. These men were still alive, retired someplace; and Omaha brought them all back for the party. That's Hospitality with a capital H.

Admired civic leaders, some of them elderly—men such as Arthur C. Storz and others like him— They gave us practical help when we needed it most. I wish I could mention every name but I can't. They were all Americans in the best old-fashioned sense of the word, back-ing up the Armed Forces, and giving a colossal demonstration of in-terdependence and interfaith.

To cite one example, I'll have to get ahead of my story a trifle. Soon I'll tell about our fight to achieve decent housing, and what the Ne-braskans did for us along that line. But let us leave out all the *general*

(55) A very brief visit to the Navy

(56) The new Air Force Vice Chief of Staff is congratulated by Air Force Secretary Douglas, Chief of Staff White, and JCS Chairman Twining

(57) LeMay being interviewed by Argentine reporters

(58) LeMay leaving his KC-135 after record flight to Buenos Aires, November 12, 1957

(59) The swearing-in of the new Air Force Chief of Staff

(60) Awarding the U.S. Legion of Merit to General Takeshi Matsuda, Chief of Staff, Japan Air Self Defense Force, October 10, 1963

(61) In Tokyo, being awarded the First Class of the Rising Sun, December 6, 1964

(62) Inspecting Japanese industry, not destroying it

(63) The day
Butch Griswold
retired

(64) "I wish every future
Chief of Staff could possess
a wife like Helen, but that's
asking too much."

(65) President Johnson congratulates LeMay after decorating him at retirement ceremonies

(66) LeMay making his farewell address—Helen and Janie and Jim Lodge are seated on Vice President Humphrey's left

(67) "The music mingled with a roar and rush of jet engines upstairs."

housing problems for a moment, and concentrate on our need for what we called the SAC-type barracks.

Ordinary barracks are of the open bay variety, familiar in memory to every man who's been in the Service. A long echoing room, lined with cots and foot-lockers . . . clothes hangers, laundry bags and shelves . . . toilets and showers reached through a main doorway at the end of the room. That's all there is to an open bay barracks.

But our needs were peculiar. Our people had to go on duty at staggered intervals, not all together in a mass. In the old-time quarters, and existing under old-time service conditions, the alarm would go off, the bugle would blow; and all personnel got out of bed at once, or were supposed to. They washed, they shaved, they dressed. They marched off together.

Not so in SAC. Someone in each barracks was working every one of the twenty-four hours in a day and a night. Some were flying, some weren't. Some were performing other sorts of duty, some weren't. They were coming in at all hours, in daylight, in midnight, in dusk or dawn. Several tired men would come in, direct from their jobs, and they'd be showering or going to the toilet or trying to get to sleep. And an hour later, perhaps, other folks would be getting up. Boys and men became weary and annoyed, tempers grew frayed. Inevitably, efficiency and discipline suffered, especially the *individual* efficiency.

What we needed was a special SAC-type barracks. The building would be divided into rooms. Two men only to a room, with a bath between each room. This was not necessarily luxury: it was practical convenience, in order to conserve and even stimulate the energies of our personnel in the jobs they had to do.

At long last, and after more fussing and fuming than I'd like to review now, we got our first barracks of this type constructed. One barracks. There would be a lot more in the future, and not only at Offutt. The SAC-style barracks would be built and used on every base occupied by the Strategic Air Command. We hoped for this; we told ourselves that it would be true eventually. It came true.

But let's get back to that first lone structure.

In the growing intimacy of our conferences with Omaha citizens, they knew what we were after, and they applauded when the first barracks was built. But it wasn't just hand clapping. Omaha citizens raised the money to furnish the rooms. Several people in town got together and did the whole thing by public subscription. Those first lucky airmen didn't move into their barracks to sleep on GI cots and keep their clothes in foot-lockers. Instead they found Simmons beds, genuine innerspring mattresses, dressers, desks— Even table lamps and easy chairs. This was a gift from the people of Omaha.

Nor was it the last gift they gave. I could make a list of things which they did for us over the years—a list as long as your arm. I don't deny that other populations have done such things in other places; but I doubt very much that any group of civilians have done as much for the men of the Armed Forces in their midst as the people of Omaha have done, and over such a long period of time. They went "above and beyond the call of Duty" in their sense of responsibility for a military establishment in their American community.

. . . The young staff-sergeant and his wife came wearily back to their cheap motel, built smack up against the route of roaring trucks. They pulled down the broken Venetian blinds so the neon from signs wouldn't keep flashing in their eyes as they tried to go to sleep. Fifty yards away, huge oil trucks screeched with weight and speed; the building trembled every time another one went past. . . . We've got to find a place to live. We've just *got* to find a place. . . . Well, where? Bernice, we've looked all over the countryside. We've looked around the base, we've looked fifteen miles away from the Base. We just can't find anything. . . . But honey, we've *got* to find a place. Just *got to,* that's all. I'm six months along. We can't have a baby *here* in this motel. . . . Well, God damn it, I don't know what we're going to do.

. . . The thick-necked old master-sergeant, the crew chief to end crew chiefs, the flight engineer to end flight engineers— He stepped into a telephone booth at the gas station, and called his wife in Moline, Illinois. . . . O.K., hon, I found something. Come out as soon as you can. Think you can get here by the end of the week? I'll try to get a weekend pass. Well, I haven't found *much* of anything, to tell the God's own truth. Some people are living in chicken coops. I mean that: I've been in their homes, I've seen them. Actually there was a guy out here who used to raise white Wyandottes or some kind of hens; and then he went broke or something; and they've got all those long low buildings, and they sort of fixed 'em up. A lot of guys from the Base are living there with their wives. But I've got something better than that. It's a garage out behind a lady's house. Her husband just died recently, and she sold their car because she doesn't drive. It's only a block or two from the downtown district. Well, this garage— See, I'm going to get a loan, and we can fix it up. Guess it's got two windows . . . concrete floor . . . but there's plumbing installed, even a toilet back in the corner. Well, you come on out, and we'll fix it up.

. . . The young lieutenant went springing up the stairway of an old hotel a block from the railroad tracks. He raced down the long hall with its smells of diesel fumes and other smells from the nearby gas works. He knocked on the door of his room, using their own special knock, so his bride would know he was there, and she could let him in. . . . I think I may have something, Angel! . . . The little bride got back into bed and pulled the covers up around her bare shoulders, because it was cold in the room. In a quavering voice: You said that before, Tom. . . . Well, really this time I think we may have something. . . . What is it? . . . It's one of those kind of two-way trailer jobs. I mean— It *was* an old trailer, and then somebody built on an addition. It's out on the north side of town, next to a lumberyard. Course, that's about thirteen miles from the Base, but— See, we couldn't swing the whole thing ourselves. But the trailer's in two sections: actually a two-family trailer. Only thing is, we'll have to share the bathroom with the other family. And I don't think the plumbing's too hot. But we *do* have separate entrances. Aw, please, Angel, don't cry. You make me feel like crying myself, when you cry. Now *cut it out!* After all, it's a place to *live.*

. . . There was another room in another thin-walled motel far down the highway, and in this room the tall major with the soft voice, the major with the good wings and the good ribbons— He sat on the edge of the bed, and finally heard his wife say Hello in Lansing, Michigan. She was staying with her folks there. He said: Darling, here's the latest report from Shackle Air Force Base, located in the town of Shackle, in the State of Shackle. The answer is still strictly Negative. Oh, I know, I know, there must be a place, but I haven't found it yet. Everybody was there ahead of me. I heard about one place, and went out there. It was a series of old chicken houses, but every one had already been taken. Then there was a garage deal— Garage behind an old lady's house. She advertised that it could be made into housekeeping quarters. But some couple got in ahead of me. Then I got track of a deal on the other side of town: a remodeled trailer with an addition built on it, to be occupied by two families. Share the bath. Even *that* sounded wonderful. But it had just been rented, about half an hour before I got there. Darling, I've got a suggestion: why don't you go downtown to some sporting goods store, and see what they've got in the way of tents. I mean that seriously. I could promote a tent out here, but it would have to be on the Base. What are you laughing about, darling? Oh, you're not laughing. Quit crying. We've been through this before, we'll be through this again. Oh, thanks a lot!—you were kidding me. Of course I know *you* wouldn't cry. You're too good an Air Force wife for that. Matter of fact, as soon as I'm through talking with you, I'm going to take a great big drink, and then get into bed, and boo-hoo all by myself. Good night, darling. I'll let you know as soon as anything breaks. Good night.

A lot of our bases were built during the war for training purposes, and many of those were adjacent to small towns where practically no extra housing was available. Even if the town was larger, it wasn't enough to support our needs.

As for rents— It was believed that some of those landlords spent their off hours, in darkness, robbing graves. If they weren't ghouls then there have never been any ghouls. This happened all over the country. Even in Omaha. It would be as foolish for me to suggest that every land-owner and house-owner and chicken-coop-owner in the Omaha area was generous to a fault, as to insist that all Samaritans were good, simply because of what one did in the Bible. We had our share of rent-gougers, right there next door to Offutt.

We had hundreds and hundreds of young families at SAC HQ, all needing a place to live in. And more coming every week. We had thousands and thousands of young families throughout the extended areas of our Command, and they all needed the same thing. Homes.

Up to date the procedure had been that special funds must be appropriated to build housing on any base for your people. And we weren't receiving any such funds.

A group of us got together. We knew that we must figure out what we were going to do. Our people had to have roofs over their heads.

We came up with a very solid thought. Fact is, it was just about the only thought we *could* come up with.

We would build our own houses.

That was just when the prefabricated house was coming along. There were several companies building them at various places around the country. We investigated, and especially we looked up the situation regarding one company with a factory in a large mid-Western city. We'll make up a name, and call this house the Zeno house. The product was made out of steel—but enameled, almost like a bathtub. Our investigators scrutinized the Zeno house, from the cradle to the grave. Or perhaps *grave* isn't a very good word, because this was a pretty good house. We couldn't find where any of them had fallen apart. They sold for around forty-five hundred dollars, as I remember. But the Zeno company had borrowed a lot of money from the RFC: they were into RFC for about $27,000,000, as I remember. And they weren't doing very well.

So here was our plan:

We would buy these houses with a down payment, erect them on the base, connect up to the base sewer system and water supply and all other utilities. Everyone on the base, in spare time, would turn out to put those houses up, along with some technical help from the manufacturers.

That was it: erect the buildings, ourselves, in our spare time. Whoever was going to get any particular house would work full-time. He'd take a month's leave, and work on his house. Everybody else would work in their spare time.

It was like the plan for the build-up of SAC itself: get one wing in order, then concentrate all effort on the next wing. We'd do the same thing: get one house up . . . the family would move into it, the man would pay his rental allowance into the general fund . . . then we'd get the next house up, do likewise. We would pay off the entire debt on those houses by applying our personnel's rental allowances.

Our initial purchase was going to be about four thousand houses. That ran, then, in the neighborhood of an $18,000,000 order.

I went personally to see the RFC people about this. They didn't raise a single eyebrow; in fact, they were highly delighted. They said definitely, "This is just about the best deal we've ever had. Everything's sound, and will work out."

I told them, "We're going to be able to pay off the mortgage on these things in about four and a half years. Eventually we can give them to the Government, or to the Officers' Club, or the NCO Club, or give it all over to general welfare funds. We can do just about anything we choose to do, with the houses."

There was a lot of mutual congratulation about a workable plan, and I came home feeling great. We all felt great. We were truly exhilarated, and looking forward with ambition to the project. We wanted to roll up our sleeves and pitch in.

Well, there's always someone standing around, ready to muddy up the water.

In this case it was our Comptroller General. He labored, or his office labored, and brought forth the following: "Negative. If you live on a base, we can't pay you any rental allowance."

The Comptroller General had fallen back on an old hard-and-fast rule. If you live in Government quarters, you don't draw rental allowance. Very broadly he had interpreted this as: *You will be living on the base, you people. We can't pay you a thing.*

This despite the fact that we *had no quarters* on the base for our people to live in. This was the only way in which quarters could be made available, and the quarters wouldn't even belong to the Government at the time. But they would be *on* the base.

We complained to high heaven; but that was the ruling, and it stuck.

Fortunately for SAC, Senator Wherry of Nebraska was still alive at that time, and still active; and, as always, able and farseeing and courageous. If he hadn't embraced those virtues, he could never have been Republican Whip in the Senate, as he was. It was Kenneth S. Wherry who saved our bacon.

I told him about the whole case, and gave the Government hell for a narrow ruling which prevented us from doing something for ourselves. If SAC wanted to pull itself up by its own bootstraps, why shouldn't SAC do it?

Thank God, Wherry agreed with me wholeheartedly. "Maybe I can help you."

He got together with Senator Millard Tydings of Maryland, and they fostered a bill. This gave us the successful housing plan known as the Wherry Act. It was the same thing all over again, but with non-military considerations. The land on the base was leased to a contractor who then built the houses, and rented them back to the military.

The Comptroller would go for this. He had said that *we* couldn't do it; but when *private* contractors were involved— Oh, yes. Surely.

I still feel like clenching my fists and gritting my teeth every time I think of this. An outright solidly backed order for four thousand houses. Around $18,000,000 restored to the RFC, which they had already lost in subsidizing the Zeno company. And, don't forget— We would have bought many more houses than that, once we got the proposition going. Might even have wiped out the whole indebtedness incurred by Zeno.

Well, I was plenty irked at the time, and so was Senator Wherry. I knew him well enough to say what I thought in his presence, and I did say what I thought. So he got to work, and came up with that Wherry bill, and he got us our houses.

I'd like to say something for Omaha again. There wasn't enough land on the base for us to put our houses immediately within the confines. So the city of Omaha got together the necessary money, and bought land immediately adjacent to the base, and *gave* the land to the Government, and that was where the homes were built.

I don't think that in many ways the actual house finally selected was as good as the Zeno building. And—

Look at the payments. These we had to pay for on a thirty-year basis instead of on a four-and-a-half-year basis. Later we had to buy them from the operator, anyway.

So the contractors built the houses, and made a profit on them. The operator made a profit on them. Then we bought them back *again*, and there was another profit. They're all Government-owned now. But think of the cost.

Yes, the Comptroller changed his tune, after the Wherry bill was passed.

Of course I could be nasty and say: "It's all right for a civilian to make money off the military in this sort of deal; but it's not all right for the military to do something for themselves, and save themselves a little money, and get a decent place to live."

I could be nasty and say that. Probably I'd better not be nasty.

8

WHEN FIRST I went to Offutt the personnel of the entire Strategic Air Command numbered about forty-five thousand. There were fourteen bomb wings (on paper: not one at full strength) but only two of these were equipped with B-50's. The rest all had 29's. The very first B-36's had just come in, and new jet B-47's were in the offing.

By 1955 our strength had grown to almost two hundred thousand. Twelve hundred B-47's had come into SAC during the previous five years. And pioneer B-52's went to Castle Air Force Base during the early summer of that year.

The organization's tactical units broke down into twenty-three wings of B-47's, six wings of B-36's, and one—the new one, at Castle—of 52's. This was in addition to our refueling wings and squadrons. We had about 2,800 airplanes all told.

Take the B-36. It was in the works for exactly seven years and two months before the first of these aircraft was delivered. It took five more years before we ever made a mass flight of B-36's to the Far East.

It seems difficult for people who are not working in our profession (or busy in our art) to realize how long it takes to get an airplane which you need. Even if the program rolled smoothly (never does) it would take a very long time. Our B-36 was actually laid down early in World War II. It looked as if England might fall, and we would have to fight from the United States, and we required an instrument with a capability of crossing the ocean to bomb the enemy in Europe. But for immediate reasons a greater effort soon began to be expended on the B-29. Perforce the B-36 program crawled.

When you build airplanes, you grind out a few; then, while you're doing that, somebody gets ideas in the way of improvement. So you perform alterations on the aircraft, successively. You have first the B-model, C-model, D-model, so on. If I remember correctly, the B-50 was really a K or L model of the B-29; somewhere along in there.

Forever the process of innovation, forever the process of conversion. We started out, after I took command, with a force consisting almost entirely of B-29's. Within a few years at one and the same time we had ten different types of Very Heavy, Heavy, Medium and Light bombardment planes.

. . . Alteration, alteration. Change after change. With the 36 we needed to increase our altitude enormously, and we must lighten weight to get that altitude . . . take off some of our defensive armament in order to let the aircraft proceed longer in flight.

The B-36 was often called an interim bomber. For my dough, every bomber which has ever been or ever will be is an interim bomber.

Every weapons system is an interim system.

There *is* no ultimate weapon.

Common sense will require continually that industry combine with the military, in order to bring about development of a force which can meet the need for increased responsibility. This, in an age when technological advances are running right off the edge of the page.

Early in 1949 a lot of ugly rumors began to circulate concerning the B-36 program. There was an increasing series of whispers which finally grew into a mutter and roar—accusations against certain Air Force people and against certain industrialists. They reiterated mention of fraud, collusion, and a deliberate attempt to foist upon the American military structure an instrument unsuitable and ineffective: the B-36.

The result was a Congressional investigation. Dozens of people testified before the committee, including myself.

Sum of evidence revealed an ugly fact. Not one of the charges was true or could be substantiated in any form. The entire whispering campaign was born in the brain of a civilian employee—an assistant in the office of the then Under Secretary of the Navy.

Appropriately enough, the guilty man turned out to be a former Hollywood script writer.

From the official report by the Congressional committee:

"Where did you get this document?"

"I wrote it."

"You wrote it, yourself?"

"Yes, sir."

". . . Did the Assistant Secretary of the Navy or anyone in the Navy Department know that you were preparing this document?"

"No, sir."

"You did this all by yourself?"

"Yes, sir."

". . . You vouch for these as facts?"

"No, I don't."

"Well, you did in the document in writing."

"That is regrettable."

In analysis the chairman of the Congressional committee summed up the testimony:

"There has not been in my judgment—and, I am satisfied, in the judgment of the entire committee—one iota, not one scintilla of evidence offered . . . that would support charges that collusion, fraud, corruption, influence, or favoritism played any part whatsoever in the procurement of the B-36 bomber. There has been very substantial and compelling evidence that the Air Force selected this bomber, procured this bomber solely on the ground that it is the best aircraft for its purpose available to the Nation today."

From my own testimony:

"I . . . represent the people who flew our bombers in the last war. They are the ones who are going to fly the bomber missions if you call on us to fight. It is my job to know what they like in the way of equipment, and what they can do with it. . . . You must run a combat operation like you run a business. You are going to buy something; you are going to pay for it. You always assess the price against what you are going to buy."

I went on to give my opinion about the 36, its capability for delivering bombs on enemy targets, and the extent of its vulnerability to attack from ground or air.

". . . There will come a time when a fighter can shoot down eighty per cent of the B-36's—but by that time the B-36 will be obsolete."

Certain columnists in those days presented me to the public as being violently anti-B-47. That was not a correct interpretation of the attitude I held. I was asked which aircraft I would prefer to use, from the bases which were available to us at the time, and I said that I would choose the B-36. The reason for this was that our refueling techniques had not progressed to the stage where we could place whole-souled reliance on the B-47 as an instrument.

As refueling techniques progressed, and as the B-47 itself underwent improvement as an operational aircraft, so did my willingness to rely upon the B-47 increase.

In 1954 I would be quoted as testifying before another Congressional committee: "If I had my way, all the B-36's would be on the junk pile." I was quoted correctly. But that was five years later. Bomb delivery capability of the B-47 had increased to the stage where we could really rely on it for effective performance. Also, by that time, B-52's were being phased into our program.

It would be well to emphasize how much the American people owe to American industry—how much the airplane manufacturers have actually contributed to our air power. Take the KC-135 as an example. It has been around for quite a while now, and we are still (1965) depending on the KC-135's for much of our refueling. We have the Boeing Company to thank for this. It is perhaps the only airplane which initially was developed by an aircraft company *on their own*.

. . . We had a requirement for a jet tanker. We'd been using the KC-97's, but what we needed was a jet tanker to match the B-47 and the B-52. And there was always a shortage of money. We could never cram this oh-so-necessary tanker into the budget.

The Boeing Company understood our need. More than that, they saw our future need for a jet transport. So, completely on speculation, and employing the knowledge they had gained in the B-47 and B-52 projects, they built a jet transport. This was the father of the KC-135. We bought it as a tanker, making only a few basic changes.

This was a calculated risk taken by the industrialists, and a wonderful example of the value of free enterprise.

Normally it would have been the other way around. We would state our needs to the aircraft industry. The various companies would compete, each with its own design. We would then evaluate the designs from every angle—both a technical evaluation and an operational evaluation—to decide whether it was a good tool for the user. And we would evaluate the company, judging their capability to produce what we needed.

Then, and only then, would a development contract be let from the Air Force to the company, to develop that airplane. Once it was developed and tested, and it looked like it was going to be a success, we could offer them a *production* contract.

Almost every modern airplane was built according to that pattern. Quite frequently—perhaps even usually—a commercial version followed.

The whole story of the Boeing-707 was a reversal of manufacturing and procurement history. They used their B-52 and B-47 knowledge, and built a transport. We bought it for a tanker. Thus, leaning on Boeing's initiative, we were way ahead of the game.

It would be nice if things could always go as smoothly as that, but they seldom do. If a designer and a manufacturer and the key military aviation people involved— If all these knew exactly what they'd emerge with *eventually,* in that moment when they first start the project for a particular type of airplane— They'd be more than just aviation wizards. They would be the wizards at whom other wizards would scream, "Wizard!" the way the RAF types use it in their slang.

You feed an idea, together with its basic requirements, into a slot; and you all keep turning the cranks and just see what emerges in the end. . . .

Take, without any attempt at chronology, our various programs from time to time. The B-50 program was a makeshift affair: it came out only as a modification of the B-29. An improved B-29, that's all it was.

Our B-52 program was for a new airplane from scratch. And it started out as a propeller plane.

The B-47: as I remember, we had propellers on that for a while too. And it was started before the B-50. But the 47 was slowed down in the process, so we got the 50 first.

. . . And our modern B-52 was on the drawing boards away back in those years—1946-47—when I was in Research and Development.

This isn't even taking into consideration the troubles and pressures which come from other sources. This is only looking at the matter from the standpoint of a military need at a given time; and then that same military need, eight or sixteen or twenty-four months later.

Particular necessities have grown . . . some have been canceled out by technological progress. Folks in the office of the Department of Defense, or of the Navy Department, or War Department—whatever historical moment you select in our administrative structure— They've got ideas on the subject too.

Volunteers who couldn't land or take off in a Piper Cub are willing to state in elaborate detail their program for a complete remapping of the Fighter business or the Bomber business or the Missile business.

Leap ahead to the B-70. There was no difference in the case of this airplane; nothing any different than had happened with the B-36, the B-52, the B-17 or anything else. Remember, the B-17 was canceled three or four months before World War II broke out. Canceled completely, and we were told to get a smaller, shorter-ranged, cheaper airplane. After General Marshall became Chief of Staff, he managed to have this decision reversed; but still it took us a couple of years to get B-17's back into the inventory.

Our 52 was dead four separate times. I had to go to Washington and concentrate every effort to get the 52 back on the track. Even so, it came along two or three years after we should have had it.

Every bomber we ever built, we've had trouble in the getting. The story of the B-70 does not make history in this regard. It was delayed to begin with, slightly, under the Eisenhower Administration. But it wasn't until the Kennedy Administration came along that the B-70 was just flatly canceled.

They still contend that they haven't canceled it now, in the Johnson Administration.

By the late spring of 1964, when the first B-70 rolled out of its hangar at North American's plant at Palmdale, California, it was the world's only B-70. Secretary McNamara had cut the program to three experimental XB-70's in 1961, and the third of those was killed before the airplane was ever pulled out for public gaze.

Often people can't understand how it is that, when Congress can vote funds for such a program, the Secretary of Defense has the power still to defeat something which a Congressional majority has ruled and decided.

In the case of the B-70, I think that if the Secretary of Defense had put the matter to a test before the whole of Congress in the form of legislation, he would have lost. Congress was with us on the program— not with the Secretary, as was evidenced by that thirty-one-to-five committee vote mentioned in the first chapter of this book. (3-5 again.)

Eternally in our complicated Democracy we have every branch of the Government to consider: legislative, executive, judicial. Each has its own responsibilities; and they are apt to interpret those responsibilities in different manners and directions. Congress can vote the money for any project it wishes to vote for, but the executive branch of the Government doesn't have to spend the money.

On the other hand, they can't spend anything which *hasn't* been appropriated. But it doesn't mean that they have to spend money which *has* been appropriated.

It seems that there could be no more pressure put upon the opponents of any specific program, within the structure of legislative organization, than has already been employed after the thing has gone through a hearing before the Military Affairs Committee. The nearest might be possibly some form of political blackmail. The proponents of the program could say, "Well, if you don't do it, we won't put up the money for some other things which you *do* want."

Something of that sort *might* work. It would be persuasive, perhaps, but cumbersome. And might, in the long run, become dangerous.

I have not discussed the story of our missile program at SAC in this chapter, for a very good reason. We weren't—by the year 1957, when I moved to Washington—sufficiently developed in missile capability for the missiles to form an important percentage of our deterrent power. That came later, after I was in the job as Vice Chief and, later, as Chief. Technological advances when applied to SAC during the period 1948–57 did not permit such a reliance.

By far the greatest advances in missile potential and reliability have been gained during the past eight years, both by ourselves and by the Soviets. As scientific and industrial skills and capacities extend, so does the application of such force for military purposes extend itself. SAC in the early 1950's was not the missile-studded complex which it has become. There was a plan for a mixed weapons system, but the mixture was still in the recipe stage. Our reliance was on the manned bomber.

In 1954 Tommy Power had been sent back East to take command of ARDC (Air Research and Development Command). During that same year, Bernie Schriever was sent to California to establish and command the Western Development Division of ARDC. This was just the start, the getting-the-team-together phase. But, by 1957, the Air Force Ballistic Missile Division, with its civilian opposite numbers, was supervising over one hundred and fifty first-line contracts in this field.

According to Dr. Ernest G. Schwiebert, writing in *Air Force Magazine,* May, 1964:

"It has been estimated that the ballistic missile program in the late '50's was employing some 2,000 contractors with more than 40,000 personnel in a broad industrial base to accomplish the many tasks attendant upon the ballistic missile program, which had by that time grown to encompass the Atlas, its follow-up missile the Titan, the intermediate-range ballistic missile Thor, the solid-propellant Minuteman, initial operational capability for these missiles, and the advanced reconnaissance system. This composite program far exceeded, both in complexity and magnitude, the earlier Manhattan Project."

We didn't even begin to test the Thor missile until late January, 1957. SAC did not achieve an operational capability with the Atlas-D until September of 1959.

That was the same month when the Soviets successfully fired their Lunik II and hit the moon.

. . . Considering this missile gap, so unavoidably demonstrated, I couldn't help but think back to those days in 1946–47 when a few still small voices were crying in the R & D wilderness, and asking, "Look. Wouldn't it be possible to put a satellite into orbit?"

And we were told that such an idea would entail astronomical costs, and was not to be tolerated for a single moment.

9

THROUGHOUT THE COMMAND we played a lot of cops and robbers, but it wasn't for fun. It was for real.

Ever since that first ham sandwich episode, there had been concern about enforcing strict security at our bases.

In 1951 we got a special course in SAC security a-going. From that time forth, there was constant effort expended by picked penetration teams to effect "sabotage." Every trick in the deck was used, and more were dreamed up which had never been in the deck; and more are still being dreamed up at this moment.

The business of forged passes or identification cards is obvious. But, since those were first used, we have had "enemy agents" posing as SAC officers, posing as enlisted men working on the flight line, posing as people who serviced the soft-drink vending machines. Fake Government surveyors, fake uniformed chauffeurs of commanding officers— Phony mailmen, phony AP's, phony civilian contractors come to a conference, phony armorers and electronics experts— SAC penetration teams have worn every disguise which vivid imagination might produce.

People trained devotedly for the job, and people are still training. The job is dangerous. SAC bases are alive with armed guards, or dog-handlers walking their fierce trained dogs at night. Men from penetration teams have looked very closely at death when they found themselves under the muzzles of pistols or submachine guns. They have been severely wounded by the dogs. Yet there has never been a lack of volunteers for this program.

Spice of danger builds a kind of romance in the minds of young men, serious as the task may be. And it is exciting too, to pit your wits against the best armor of security which the Command can fasten into place. Our personnel serving in this capacity are not unaware of the fact that they are making a hard-and-fast contribution.

What they think of, in trying to simulate the destruction of a jet bomber on the ground, Russian agents can think of as well. What they dream up in the way of murder of key personnel— Enemy agents can dream the same thing up.

On the whole we've been able to maintain a pretty good record. In 1952 we put on a big exercise, along with the Air Defense Command and the RCAF, during which simulated bombing attacks were launched against forty major cities in Canada and the United States. There were two five-man penetration teams on the job—hand-picked, ten of our best men. We captured eight of them, although one got away with the "destruction" of a B-36 on the ground.

We have been able to tighten our security ever since 1952. I know that we tightened it a great deal before I left the job in 1957.

They had a story out about me . . . told how some telephone repairmen came into my office and started fooling with the lines. I got suspicious, grabbed an automatic, held the men up against the wall until the Air Police got there. . . .

Funny, but I don't remember a thing about this. I'm sure that I would have remembered it if it had actually happened, and I'd stood there with my finger on the trigger, not knowing whether those men were false saboteurs or real saboteurs.

No one *ever knows*. That's the point of the whole matter. The fellow who places the empty tin-can "bomb" under your desk could just as well be a bona fide enemy saboteur as a member of one of the penetration teams.

In a program like this there is bound to be a certain danger incurred. It is not so great a danger, however, as would be incurred if there were no such program.

On one hand you think of these skilled young people, literally risking their lives to show up our weak points and persuade us to rebuild them into strong points. On the other hand, you think of actual spies coming in to teach us the tricks. . . .

My guess is that by this time we have achieved the greatest security in SAC which has ever been achieved by any far-flung military organization.

That sergeant guarding the hangar with a ham sandwich wasn't worth a damn to us. Not even if the ham sandwich had been poisoned. Because he was eating it himself.

10

THERE WAS, definitely, a time when we could have destroyed all of Russia (I mean by that, all of Russia's capability to wage war) without losing a man to their defenses.

The only losses incurred would have been the normal accident rate for the number of flying hours which would be flown to do the job.

This period extended from before the time when the Russians achieved The Bomb, until after they had The Bomb but didn't yet own a stockpile of weapons.

During that same era their defenses were at low ebb. As for their offensive capacity: not one bomb or missile, in that day, could have hit the United States.

We at SAC were the first to perceive this potential. We had constructed it to that point, and had our weapons ready.

Certainly I never notified our President that we could do this. That wasn't my duty. The Chief of Staff of the Air Force could recognize the extent of our power, and before very long the Joint Chiefs of Staff knew it also.

It would have been possible, I believe, for America to say to the Soviets, "Here's a blueprint for your immediate future. We'll give you a deadline of five or six months"—something like that—"to pull out of the satellite countries, and effect a complete change of conduct. You will behave your damn selves from this moment forth."

We could have done this. But whether we *should* have presented such a blueprint was not for me to decide. That was a question of national policy.

All I can repeat is: at the time, we could have done the job as described. Whether we *should* have done it then or not, when you quarterback it— I don't know. You can discuss the pros and cons of such a situation from now until Doomsday. You might argue whether it would be desirable to present such a challenge to the Russians, even at this (1965) stage of the game.

That is not something for the military to say. It is for our Administration to say.

Repeat: the Soviets did not possess the might to affect us in retaliation at the time.

There are stories still current that on one occasion I called a meeting, and pulled in a number of key personnel who weren't even related to SAC, and closed the doors, and put this proposition up to them as a suggestion. The story goes that strong men trembled in their boots, and went quivering out of the place, white-faced at my bellicose statements.

I don't ever remember having called such a meeting. What I may have done was to say to some of my people at one time or another, "We've got this capability. Maybe the Nation ought to do it." I might have said that, off the cuff. But never did I make any such formal suggestion.

Always I felt that a more forceful policy would have been the correct one for us to embrace with the Russians, and in our confrontation of their program for world Communism. In the days of the Berlin Air Lift I felt the same way. I wasn't alone in that regard, either. General Lucius B. Clay concurred in the belief.

I can't get over the notion that when you stand up and act like a man, you win respect . . . though perhaps it is only a fearful respect which leads eventually to compliance with your wishes. It's when you fall back, shaking with apprehension, that you're apt to get into trouble.

We observed Soviet reaction during the Lebanon incident and during the Cuban incident. Each time when we faced the Russians sternly we've come out all right. It's only when we haven't stood up to these challenges that things went sour.

But our job in SAC was not to promulgate a national policy or an international one. Our job was to produce. And we produced. We put America in that situation of incipient power which she occupied at the time. It was an extremely fortunate and advantageous position.

Nobody used our preponderance as a lever.

We in SAC were not saber-rattlers. We were not yelling for war and action in order to "flex the mighty muscles we had built." No stupidity of that sort. We wanted peace as much as anyone else wanted it. But we knew for a fact that it would be possible to curtail enemy expansion if we challenged them in that way. Some of us thought it might be better to do so then, than to wait until later.

I never discussed the problem with President Truman or with President Eisenhower. I never discussed it with General Vandenberg when he was Chief of Staff. I stuck to my job at Offutt and in the Command. I never discussed what we were going to *do* with the force we *had*, or what we *should* do with it, or anything of that sort. Never discussed it with topside Brass, military or civilian.

All I did was to keep them abreast of the development in SAC. I told them what strength we had, as fast as that strength grew.

. . . And don't forget this: you know more about that football game when you read the Sunday morning papers— You know more about that game than you did on Saturday afternoon when the teams first came trotting into the stadium. You didn't know about the long pass or the fumble or the blocked punt, Saturday midday. You knew about it after the game.

11

As STATED, in SAC I was away from Offutt at least half the time. You can't know exactly what fat is in the fire, out at various bases, until you go there and see for yourself. I had to cover all of the United States, and occasionally visited foreign installations.

. . . If you happen to be gone over a weekend or a holiday, and have any chance for recreation, naturally you'll take advantage of whatever recreation is available in the area. Even out in the field, and with a tight schedule, it is possible to take a little time off now and then. In fact, you *have* to take a little time off now and then. So the golfers play golf, and the tennis players play tennis, and the fishermen fish, and the hunters hunt (they do, if there's any hunting in the region where they happen to be).

Readers went along with me on my first .22 rifle excursions when I was a child, but they haven't gone along on any hunting trips. Let's go.

It started with deer, in the early 1930's, when I was stationed at Selfridge. There were numerous eager deerslayers among the young lieutenants, and each of us would do his level best to get in a trip in the fall, up on the Northern Peninsula of Michigan. Trouble was, often you'd have everything set up . . . you could smell that woodsmoke and feel your cheek against the rifle . . . then somebody would pull the buckskin rug out from under your feet. You'd have to go and fly formation, opening up an airport at Podunk Falls.

In Hawaii there wasn't really very much to hunt . . . we used to go after wild hogs once in a while. Those hogs were descended from stock brought in by the first Polynesian settlers or, later, by Captain Cook. Actually domestic stock which had run wild for centuries.

After we returned to the States, down at Langley, it was mostly duck shooting and occasionally some quail. But from then on my hunting sorties were strictly limited. I never had much time to indulge myself. If you wish to hunt in the United States, it usually means going someplace other than the place where you are. It takes time to get there and time to get back, and the operation must occur during specific seasons. In most cases that has to be arranged beforehand.

Then, if something happens—as something usually *does* happen in the Air Force—you must cancel out at the last minute. Probably I scrubbed half-a-dozen or a dozen hunting trips for every one that I really got to take. This was true particularly in later years. You'd plan on it—you'd be invited hither and yon, to hunt everything from leopards to abominable snowmen. Then something would happen. No hunt.

Far as transportation goes: there's always an airplane flying someplace. MATS (Military Air Transport Service) has its regularly scheduled routes all over the map. Besides that, there's a certain amount of administrative flying which needs to be done. So a commander can almost always ride to some point near his eventual destination, within a reasonable length of time.

(You see, in the Air business we travel so much normally in our regular jobs that just *going someplace* on a vacation is not particularly attractive to us. But if we're hunters, going someplace *to hunt*— That's different.)

So we fly. Then, sure as death and taxes, some character who runs a newspaper column, or some politician who has a bigger mouth than he has a fund of correct information— He gets up and starts raving about AF people using AF airplanes on trips for their personal pleasure. . . . You shoot a moose. Yep, you went to Maine for your personal pleasure. . . . You shoot a big brown bear. Yep, you went to Alaska at the taxpayers' expense.

During my tour of duty at SAC they had a rumor running around for a while that I was commuting regularly between Omaha and San Francisco in order to attend the opera season. Quite a story. Well, I never went to an opera in my life; haven't gone to my first one yet. If there was one next door tonight, I wouldn't go.

In addition to that, San Francisco didn't *have* any opera operating at the time.

Point is, the person in public life is bound to receive a lot of half-witted criticism. He's a natural-born target for it. It is unnecessary to go to any extraordinary lengths to maintain a picture of lily-white purity and innocence. If you let things like that worry you, very soon you run out of worrying time. There are too many real problems up there on the board.

Whatever you do, somebody's going to criticize you. Forget criticism. . . . There was that tiny bit of bird shooting in Virginia when I was young. Then came the war. I believe I mentioned that a few of our 305th personnel, over in England, were killing off some local game with ammunition which had been issued to them for strictly defensive purposes. But I was not one of the guilty characters.

When I moved over to take command of the Third Division at Elveden Hall, I found myself on one of the most famous pheasant estates in all England. It had rather gone to seed, however. Lord Iveagh's ancient gamekeeper was a Mr. Turner. He'd been there for years and years. (To the best of my knowledge he's still alive in this year of 1965. Somewhere in his nineties.) Mr. Turner was most coöperative, but he was severely handicapped: young men and middle-aged men were all gone off to the war. There were just a few well-meaning old gaffers and some little boys left, and they couldn't keep the predators down. If there was much hunting, it was done persistently at night by foxes and stoats and rats which preyed on the nests and on all birds, old and young.

. . . No beaters or anything of that sort . . . only one tiny section of the whole estate where we could get in any real shooting. Occasionally, however, I was invited to other places over the countryside; and I did go out several times with the local minister, a retired RAF chaplain. He liked to shoot.

So did our Administrative Officer, Squadron Leader Lawson.

Despite his current RAF affiliation, most of Lawson's career had been spent as a sergeant-major in the British Army. He put in many years out in the Near East and Middle East and Far East, and I recall with glee the stories he'd tell about various outbreaks among the natives in those regions. That's how the British officers got in their shooting. A detachment would be ordered out into the hills or the wadis, to seek rebellious customers. They'd go searching for the rebels, prowling up ravines and dry watercourses, trying to flush enemies from their hiding places. Enlisted men, with rifles, would shoot it out with the rebel tribesmen . . . carry on the war. But the officers would be lugging shotguns, so they could shoot the birds which were stirred up by all this fuss.

Sounds so typically British. I don't think any other nationality would ever have had the resource to think of that.

There was a tiny bit of snipe hunting after I got out to India, late in 1943 . . . not much. But I groan every time I think of my tiger hunt . . . it had been so carefully arranged. The monsoon season was just ending when I arrived at Kharagpur, and December is a pretty good month; it starts to dry out . . . January and the early part of February: that's the dry season. That's when you do your shooting, and that was when I was invited on a tiger hunt by the Maharajah. Golly, I had been looking forward to that. I'd always wanted to shoot a tiger.

Well, the hunt was all set up; then suddenly I found myself en route to Guam; and then back with Roger Ramey again; and off once more to the Marianas to take command on the 19th of January, 1944. Sad, sad business. The tiger hunt went off with a whoop and hurrah, or whatever tiger hunts go off with. But it was Roger Ramey who slew the tiger—not I. I was in the Marianas. No hunting there. They said that once in a while somebody flushed out a real live Jap; but it was more or less the closed season on them too.

. . . First autumn I was home and busy in R & D, there came a chance to go to Alaska. While there I got loose and out in the bogs for a day, and managed to shoot a Kodiak bear. He made a fine rug and we had him on the floor, out in my den at Offutt, for years afterward.

The next year, 1947, we were off to Germany to command USAFE; and to my complete amazement I found myself shooting for the pot once more.

In the chapter about our tour in Germany, I described the prevailing meat shortage. We had that house full of servants, and we had to give them something to eat, and they were really starving for meat. In Germany you can hunt *something* every day in the year. Sometimes it may be only a pig; but the pig is awfully good to eat. It's a wild boar—*Wildschwein*—and there are a lot of mouth-watering recipes among German cooks for preparing those boars.

I swore that I was going to make up for lost time and go hunting every weekend. Well, I managed to make it about every other weekend for a couple of months. Then the Russians started kicking up their heels, and next thing I knew we had the Lift going, and so on. Thus I wound up by not carrying out my resolve very well. But still we had a lot of *Wildschweine* hanging in the refrigerators. It was the first time I'd been hunting especially for the pot since I was the Great White Hunter of English Sparrows for the cat's pot, out there in Emeryville, California. At five cents a throw.

But, for certain reasons, I reckon that the most memorable trip of this period was one down in French Morocco. I was invited there by my French liaison officer, and for a wonder I could go.

They had the hunt all laid on. They said that three thousand beaters were out, to chase game into our area and past the stands where we waited. The game was the *mouflon* or wild mountain sheep of the region . . . those rams carry pretty good horns. I had hunted sheep before, in the Rockies at home, but never anything like this. Three thousand beaters! I thought the game would be buzzing past us like tin ducks in a shooting gallery.

We got up there into wild mountains, and the weather turned really sour. They had me out on a stand with a couple of Arabs for company, and a wind began to blow to beat hell. Half rain, half sleet, horizontal visibility at zero . . . coldest wind I think I've ever been in.

My Arab companions couldn't speak any English, and I couldn't speak any Arabic. It may have been that they were able to speak a little French, but I didn't speak French either. So they didn't and couldn't explain anything to me. Apparently they decided that this was pretty awful weather to be hunting in. So, before long, they retreated and got down behind some rocks and bushes, and pulled their nightgowns up over their heads. They squatted there and peeked out at me. I could see what they were thinking: "Well, take a look at that silly bastard, standing up there, freezing to death."

I wouldn't have moved if I'd congealed into a statue. That's where they put me, by God, and that's where I was going to stay.

After a long while somebody in authority came by, and informed us that the visibility was down. Really? It turned out that I was standing on the edge of a sheer precipice. You couldn't see anything beyond, but thank the Lord I hadn't moved. If I'd moved any farther along, in the sleet and all, I would have gone over that cliff, and without any parachute either.

The game had all oozed past. Nobody had seen a thing. Not one *mouflon* had been shot. So the hunt was a miserable flop.

But not I. LeMay wasn't any miserable flop. It hadn't rained up there in *three years*. If it rains in French Morocco when a visiting fireman comes in, *he's* the one who gets the credit for it. So, on this big deal, I got credit for the rain.

I had a hard time keeping from being elected Sultan of French Morocco right then and there. The rain was *mine,* even though I nearly froze to death in it.

My especial French friend was Claude Boislambert, military governor of their Zone in Germany. There was a lot more game in the French Zone too, and those people regulated the management according to Old World custom. Up in the American Zone we just let everybody hunt, period. That's the way Americans are apt to do, and ruin the hunting accordingly. I hunted several times in the French Zone.

I'd like to tell a little about Boislambert. Before the war began he was in the Colonial service; and then, later, it was required by military exigency that the Allies take over French Equatorial Africa. Supposedly we had an arrangement with the Free French to go in there; but necessarily there must be some display of firearms to save the French honor.

Boislambert took French Equatorial Africa singlehandedly, as I understand it, by resorting to the simple expedient of putting a .45 against the temple of the Colonial Governor. Then he gathered up the troops who were in the region, and guided them across the desert. Eventually they joined up with the British in North Africa.

Claude Boislambert was and is a chunky apple-cheeked man a few years younger than myself, with sparkling eyes and a sparkling humor. Like other fabulous military figures whom I've met, especially in the Latin countries, he is one bundle of energy, as his record proves. After the French Equatorial deal, he was in and out of France during the war; busy with the Resistance, etc. He was in a couple of concentration camps, and escaped a couple of times. The last time he didn't manage to escape, but languished as a prisoner until the end of the war. Shortly thereafter he was made military governor of the French Zone in Germany, with headquarters at Coblenz.

Also he was elected president of the *Council International de la Chasse,* the international hunting organization. A very noted sportsman. He was the one who made it possible for me to have those *Wildschwein* hunts in the French Zone.

Shortly after I came back to take command of SAC, Claude gave up his task as military governor and returned to France. Later he ran for the Chamber of Deputies, and was elected.

. . . He flew to the United States for a visit and, to Helen's and my great joy, came out to Offutt. I managed to set up a little shooting for him—antelope and deer and so on—and also got him up to Alaska. I couldn't go along, but some other people took him out.

Boislambert was excited over our manner of hunting. Not like they have over there . . . luxurious hunting lodges, servants, beaters, game-keepers, all sorts of ceremonies and traditions. Here in the States and in Alaska you go out like a pioneer and carry your own pack. That's not exactly the way Boislambert was accustomed to hunt, but he was ready to try anything.

They started him out, up there in Alaska, on a river, with a guide and a small outboard motorboat. First thing they did was hit a snag and dump Claude into the drink, and lose all their supplies. But he came up smiling, and dried out and finished the trip. He got a grizzly bear, a caribou and a good moose. He declared also that he'd had one whale of a time. I was surprised that he didn't actually bring back a whale, since he brought back about everything else.

It was revealing to observe that Europeans look forward to shooting in Alaska the way we Americans look forward to shooting in Africa.

Before Claude left he told me, "If you ever have an opportunity to go to Africa, let me know and I'll go with you." I didn't think the opportunity would arrive, but it did.

Before we get off among the jackals and the elephants, I'll have to tell about Arthur Godfrey. We first met when I was out at Offutt, and he came there to take a look at SAC and see what it was all about. As all his widespread audiences know by this time, Godfrey was in the United States Navy when he was a kid. In fact, he was a high school dropout at sixteen. (Nowadays he would be supported by the Government, just because he *was* a high school dropout. But those were different times, and he was a quaint old-fashioned boy.) He believed that he ought to support himself.

One good way to do that was to join the Navy, so he did.

And it was that early experience which made him view the world through salt-covered glasses, you might say. In later years, as a successful performer and commentator on the air, he became acquainted with General Vandenberg. And Vandenberg said to him one day, "Why don't you come off all this Navy pitch you're putting out all the time? Put out a true story for a change."

Godfrey says, "Well, what *is* the true story?"

"Go out to SAC and they'll show you."

Godfrey flew his own airplane to Offutt, and began to look around. Then we showed him some other bases; and later I took him on a trip to some of the overseas places where I was going, and really gave him an indoctrination tour.

Result was that eventually he resigned his Reserve commission in the Navy and moved over to the Air Force—lock, stock and barrel. In the end we were able to give him a commission in the Air Force Reserve (Retired). I declare that it took him only a couple of days to come completely under the spell of the Air Force, right there at the start.

Early in 1957, Godfrey came around to me with Jim Shepley from *Life* magazine, and the late Dick Boutelle, president of Fairchild. They said, "We want to go on an African hunt. Could you arrange one?"

I told them, "Boislambert told me that if I ever came to Africa he'd fix it up. O.K. Let's lay one on."

It started like that. I sent off a note to Boislambert, telling him that I would like to go on a little hunt, and bring Boutelle and Shepley and Godfrey along, and could he arrange it?

He said, "Certainly," and went ahead and planned a modest hunt— commensurate with my salary, since I was the poorest of the bunch. I think originally it was going to cost us about five hundred dollars apiece.

Claude had hunted in French Equatorial Africa every year, except during the war, since he was nineteen. He had some equipment there —enough to suit moderate tastes and needs. He would be our outfitter and guide and everything else, and that was adequate . . . he knew all the tribes down there, all the local people.

Then the thing started growing like a puffball in the yard. First thing that happened was Jim Shepley. . . . "Look, we may not get to go to Africa again. We ought to have some good pictures of this hunt, and we all know that you can't shoot and take pictures at the same time. Why don't I take one of our *Life* photographers along? He can get the pictures; we can all have copies of them. Then, if we find anything good— Maybe I can do a spread in *Life*."

It was Arthur Godfrey who came up with the next bright idea. "If he's going to take still pictures, we ought to get some movies too. I might be able to use the movies in a television show."

So we borrowed some movie cameras, and planned to turn them over to the still photographer, who was a wonderful still photographer and had won many awards on his work. Just the same, he was an extra man—another man on the expedition.

Godfrey got his next notion. It was to save time by flying over the desert in his DC-3. We should send the airplane on in advance to Tripoli. With the weather the way it is in wintertime down there, you sometimes have to wait for favorable conditions, until you can start out with a DC-3. However, this grand plan was going to save us a lot of time, because we could go over to Tripoli in one of the big planes in a jiffy; and then fly the DC-3 straight across the Sahara to Fort Lamy in the Lake Chad area. That was just about the limit of range for a C-47, as I knew (a DC-3 is the civilian version of the military C-47).

"Arthur, if we're going to cross the Sahara Desert, we'd better have a single sideband radio put in that airplane. Then I can always get into the SAC net. If we should be so unlucky as to go down in the desert, we can tell them where we went down, and somebody will look for us."

So the high-frequency radio—the single sideband—was installed in the aircraft. After Arthur saw it— "Why, isn't this the same kind of thing we use in ham radio, on the ham bands?"

"Sure. Same set."

"Well, why don't we get a generator and take this along on the hunting trip? We can do some hamming in the ham bands."

I told him that we could do this, but it would call for more equipment, and I'd better check with Boislambert.

Next Godfrey idea. "Why can't I get a commercial show set up? Why can't I pipe radio shows out from Darkest Africa?"

I agreed that this would be possible; but for anything commercial of that sort, you'd have to get on the commercial frequencies. You'd have to arrange with one of the communications companies to do that. It would be just like sending a wire on a commercial telegraph. But if we did this, it meant a radio operator must go along. Also we'd require another truck for the generator. More extra men.

Godfrey owned a Bell helicopter. He says, "Why don't we take the helicopter? We ought to be able to get some good pictures that way, of game and things, and we could use it for transportation to un-get-at-able places."

So, check with Boislambert once more. Claude responded with enthusiasm. "This is superb! We can reach some remarkable locations, utterly unspoiled, where hunters have never been before. We couldn't get there otherwise, except in this helicopter."

O.K. on the helicopter. So we ship that chopper by boat to Douala on the African west coast, just off the Gulf of Guinea, and then have it flown up from the coast to Fort Archambault in the interior. That meant that we needed a mechanic to put the thing together up there. . . .

Then Godfrey decided that he couldn't hunt and fix up the radio program, and do all those other things related to his project, and still do all the flying on the helicopter. So we borrowed a pilot from the Bell company.

In the end it wasn't any modest little five-hundred-dollar-per-head hunt, such as Boislambert had originally projected. It was Godfrey's party, pure and simple, and I can't even estimate what it cost. He had taken over the financing of the whole thing. He shipped quantities of his sponsors' products into Fort Archambault via Air France. Fruit juices, Lipton's tea, Lord knows what. But we didn't use the DC-3 after all. Just the sideband radio.

Instead of being mobile and roving, we were compelled to have a static camp. We built one, on the River Aouk, a hundred and fifty miles or so northeast of Fort Archambault. Our static camp boasted a population of seventy-five people. Not much like Boislambert's original conception.

But we were enabled to camp in this untouched area solely because of the helicopter. We used it as a reconnaissance vehicle, and spied out a route which the trucks could travel. French officials had declared that it would be impossible to get any trucks in there. The helicopter pointed the way; and the trucks got in there after five days—and quite a lot of hacking of brush, in order to clear a path.

Then they set up the permanent camp on the river, with thatched huts and everything. There on the Bahr Aouk, not too far from the Sudanese border.

We were in Africa from March 4th to the 27th. We lived literally surrounded by herds of antelope and wildebeest, troops of wart-hogs . . . practically every other variety of good table meat, except zebra. Guess we could have stood up on camp stools and shot everything we needed, if we'd wished to do so.

Once again I found myself shooting for the pot. Sparrows would have done no good. Seventy-five hungry people, most of them healthy hard-working Africans, will eat a lot more meat than one Emeryville tomcat.

Butch Griswold was minding the manse at Omaha. Even when we were remotely in the bush, I would get on the radio at least once a day and talk with SAC Headquarters. Sometimes electrical conditions didn't permit me to reach them directly; but I could always get in to one of our North African bases, and then they would rebroadcast right to SAC HQ. If anything had come up, I could have flown out in the helicopter to Fort Archambault and been picked up there. There was plenty of runway. That's the way we came to the country, by Air France from Paris, via Tripoli.

I spoke of being out in the bush. Boislambert and I took one trip away from the camp, and we were gone eight days. We had a truck with half-a-dozen boys and two trackers, and our hunting car; and then we picked up a local native or two, to guide us.

Forever it was a gentle rolling plain, something like southwest Texas, quite dry at the time. Green grass still colored the river bottoms, and we could drive down those beds. Herds all around us . . . the antelopes and gazelles had never seen hunters before, had never seen a truck or a car.

They were never spooked, unless the wind was wrong; then they would go galloping off suspiciously. But normally, as long as we stayed in the car, they paid no attention. Actually we drove in the middle of huge mixed herds. They would open up as we came along, and let us by, and then close back in behind, grazing as they traveled.

We didn't see any rhino, although we saw tracks: there were a few around. A few lions . . . leopards galore. I got four buffalo on the trip, and two elephants.

In recollection I can still see Boislambert with his can of talcum powder in hand. That was when we would be going into a thicket after an elephant. You had to squeeze into the woods where the elephants had gone. Usually you knew how many there were in the herd; your tracker could tell you that. But you were never sure that they hadn't picked up a couple of volunteers at the last minute, in that very thicket. And you had to decide on a male, and you had to decide which end you were looking at. Sometimes the bush was so thick that you could see an elephant, but you didn't know whether you were observing his shoulder or his flank. There was no point in shooting one that wasn't shootable for a trophy. So it was a real stalking problem.

Boislambert was an old hand at this. Hence the can of talcum powder.

As we penetrated the thicket he would sprinkle a little powder . . . it was so light that it indicated the slightest variance in the breezes' direction. Within those thickets, wind was apt to be drifting toward any point of the compass. You could make all the noise you wanted to, and the elephant would pay no attention. But if he *smelled* you, that loused up the whole business.

Many people exclaim about the element of danger in a big game hunt. They wonder how much tension a human being can endure, standing up to a wild charging beast. I've read hunting stories of that sort, and must confess that I'd wondered about it too. I've heard friends declare that they'd rather go into a well-defended flak zone, than stand out in the weeds where a buffalo can rush at you.

But I learned this on the trip: if you get into a position where a buffalo is rushing you, then you haven't done things right. Or, perhaps, some freak of nature has occurred. For instance, I shot four buffalo during the expedition; three of them I killed with a single shot, each. The character just dropped in his tracks, and that was that. On the fourth one I went wrong, because I hadn't been expecting to shoot that one.

Boislambert directed me on the first kill, saying, "That one over there. Get *him*. He's the biggest one." So I shot him, and the rest of them ran and milled around to get away. And Boislambert says, "Shoot *that* one too," as the buffalo was running. I hadn't anticipated this; so, when I fired, my aim wasn't too sharp. That buffalo had to be shot a second time before he died.

Under certain circumstances my careless shot could have resulted in a perilous situation. Normally, if a buffalo charges, it's because he feels that's the only way he can escape. Or, if you wounded him, and he knows you've wounded him, he may charge in self-defense or even in revenge.

A number of anecdotes were related, either by Boislambert or by the native huntsmen, and translated by Boislambert— Anecdotes told also by game wardens who visited us in camp— Stories about wounded buffalo who stood patiently in ambush, to charge the unwary hunter and pound him into the ground. Stories about animals who became the aggressors instead of the aggressed, and circled around in order to trail pursuing sportsmen, and then crashed from hiding when least expected.

These tales had a familiar ring. It sounded like the Air business, it sounded like SAC. If you went over your checklist religiously, and followed every standard procedure in the manual, flying was a breeze. If you threw required steadiness and caution to the winds, and thought you were an Old Bold Pilot, you were apt to be in trouble. . . .

Think I might have suggested an SOP course in elephant or buffalo hunting for our airmen in the future, had such a thing been possible.

There were other values accruing besides the mere stalking and shooting of game which any hunter might enjoy. I found myself becoming acquainted with African people on their native heath. Through the years I had gained firsthand knowledge of a lot of different nationalities, including some extremely primitive Asiatics. But I hadn't known any genuine Africans before, except those few Arabs up in French Morocco.

Natives in our region were exceptionally friendly. True, they may have been bowled over by the fact that ours was the largest hunting expedition which had ever gone into French Equatorial Africa.

French holdings are now broken down into several independent states. The region where we hunted is part of the country of Chad. Niger is over to the west and north, and the Camerouns back to the southwest. But in those days none of the natives worried about being represented in the United Nations.

They visited our camp constantly, and we went down a couple of times to their villages, where we were entertained. They put on a dance, and so on. When anyone was sick or hurt, they would come to our camp; thus we all became doctors. I recall Godfrey's dressing, day after day, the hand of one of the chiefs' wives, where a severe cut had become infected. They were all very appreciative of attentions like that.

. . . Sometimes I think I could talk all day or all night about that trip, because it was fascinating, and so revealing in many ways. Wardens from the Colonial government came to stay at camp; indeed, one or another of those gentlemen was with us all the time. They considered that they were on a vacation and having fun. Because, while we were shooting, and shooting for the pot, and shooting for trophies too, it didn't make any difference to us from one day to the next whether we shot anything or not. We were there for a vacation as well. That rather endeared us to the wardens because they were arch conservationists. Unfortunately they had come across all too many so-called sportsmen who wanted to slay every animal in sight.

. . . As for the food we ate, I guess my favorite dish was wart-hog liver. I'd be overjoyed to have some for dinner tonight, but no use asking for it. Helen would look in the refrigerator, and announce that we were fresh out of wart-hog liver. . . .

About Godfrey: I think he counted the trip a success. Anyway, he did his shows, but his venture into the movie business was rather sorry.

Remember, we had this still photographer along; and he was a great still photographer, but somewhat inexperienced with motion picture cameras. On a Leica camera you twist the lens one way to go from close focus to infinity; and the photographer had become so accustomed to twisting the lens that way, to get infinity right off the bat, that he did this on the movie camera.

No go.

We flew and flew in the helicopter, pursuing game, taking pictures of the game. It ended up that the beasts were all out of focus, but there was a beautiful clear view of Arthur Godfrey's big feet.

12

You go down past the flight line and you walk along until you come to a place where the B-58's are dispersed in orderly fashion. You stop and look up at one of those silver arrows with the black arrowhead (nicknamed the Hustler) and you observe a maintenance crew at work.

I have never been checked off on the B-58, nor was I ever checked off on the B-36; just didn't have time in either case. According to my Form 5 File out at Norton AFB (not our old Norton at Columbus, but the modern Norton at San Bernardino, named for a World War II flyer) I have been checked off on, and have flown, exactly seventy-five different species of military aircraft used by the Air Corps, Army Air Forces, United States Air Force. All the way up from PT-1's and 3's to the KC-135, and the B-52, and the F-104; and back again to huge contemporary cargo planes, and late-model helicopters. In addition I have flown a lot of foreign and domestic civilian types, and foreign military types.

So I hold natural curiosity concerning the innards of any flying machine, especially one where I've never sat in the left-hand seat.

. . . The chief of the ground crew and one of his men are up on the dock, engaged in removing a metal plate from the fuselage of the aircraft. We stand and watch.

Off comes the plate, and there is exposed a labyrinth of silver and wire and plastic . . . tiny colored blobs and shreds. That's a meager crumb, a mere sample of the electronic equipment which is stuffed and geared throughout the stiff flesh of the B-58.

. . . Something like the business of that old-fashioned jack-in-the-box you had as a child, or one of those snake devices which bad little boys used to aim at good little girls. Say the thing would be in the shape of a camera; you'd pretend that you were taking the little girl's picture; then you'd release the catch, and out would leap a toy snake. The little girl would scream and run (usually she liked to be scared). Then ensued the labor of stuffing that spring-bodied snake back into his cell. Sometimes this was hard to do.

. . . You look up at that plate, and the fuselage aperture, and vaguely you wonder: *how are they going to get that snake back in there?*

They'll get it back. And every tuft and every peg and every thread-like wire, and every infinitesimal jewel of the complex array will have been tested and found to be functioning, before that slice goes back on the aircraft—with reptiles arranged in designated position, before the plate is locked. The B-58 is crammed with those thousands and thousands of working warming cooling bits of metal and wire and tubing. Every available cubic inch within the body is occupied by such little monsters and treasures.

Not much like Kelly in 1929.

All had the same thing: a stabilizer, a stick, a rudder, a throttle, a spark control. That was it. You just got in and flew. . . .

And in that beautiful devilish pod underneath, the baby of the fuselage—half-size, but still of the same shape and sharpness, clinging as a fierce child against its mother's belly—the B-58 carries all the conventional bomb explosive force of World War II and everything which came before. A single B-58 can do that.

It lugs the flame and misery of attacks on London . . . rubble of Coventry and the rubble of Plymouth. . . . Blow up or burn up fifty-three per cent of Hamburg's buildings, and sixty per cent of the port installations, and kill fifty thousand people into the bargain. Mutilate and lay waste the Polish cities and the Dutch cities, the Warsaws and the Rotterdams. Shatter and fry Essen and Dortmund and Gelsen- kirchen, and every other town in the Ruhr. Shatter the city of Berlin. Do what the Japanese did to us at Pearl, and what we did to the Japa- nese at Osaka and Yokohama and Nagoya. And explode Japanese in- dustry with a flash of magnesium, and make the canals boil around bloated bodies of the people. Do Tokyo over again.

The force of these, in a single pod.

One B-58 can load that comprehensive concentrated firepower, and convey it to any place on the globe, and let it sink down, and let it go off, and bruise the stars and planets and satellites listening in.

Every petard, every culverin, every old Long Tom or mortar of a naval ship in the eighteenth or nineteenth centuries, every turret full of smoky cannon at Jutland . . . Big Bertha bombarding Paris . . . musketry of the American Revolutionary battles or the Napoleonic ones. Spotsylvania and Shiloh and the battles for Atlanta. All the paper cartridges torn with the teeth, and all the crude metallic cartridges forced into new hot chambers. . . .

Firepower. All the firepower ever heard or experienced upon this earth. All in one bomb, all in one B-58.

The B-58 was and is symbolic of SAC, as is the B-52, as could be the B-70 if we had them standing on the line (where they should be stand- ing this minute. Maybe their advanced prototypes will stand there in the future).

If you removed that plate from the body of SAC, you could look in and see people and instruments. They would be as the intricate elec- tronic physiology of an airplane today: each functioning, each trained, each knowing his special part and job—knowing what he must do in his groove and place to keep the body alive, the blood circulating. Every man a coupling or a tube; every organization a rampart of tran- sistors, battery of condensers. All rubbed up, no corrosion. Alert.

"Peace is our profession," say the folks in SAC. Couldn't be more cor- rect, either.

The able cop on the beat is the one who keeps the peace. There isn't much peace on a beat where there isn't any cop. I remember seeing a revival of the old Charlie Chaplin picture, *Easy Street,* not long ago. There was every kind of mayhem and murder on Easy Street, occurring every minute, until Charlie finally functioned as a kind of one-man SAC.

In other words, he effectively demonstrated his resource and his might, without actually killing anybody.

Result: he had all the folks going to church, escorting their wives tidily, whereas before they'd been belting women over the head with gin bottles, and kicking children out of the windows. Now the children were sleekly clad and cleaned up, and dancing on their way to Sunday School. Everybody happy.

Perhaps Mr. Chaplin might not be delighted at this comparison—not when one considers his alleged political views, and his withdrawal from participation in American life. But we are talking about Charlie Chaplin, the figure and the figment on an ancient screen; not a sour old man who preaches the virtues of Communism. We can still learn a lot from his rerun pictures.

SAC staged the first nonstop around-the-world flight in late February and early March of 1949. An overgrown B-29 (which came to be designated as the B-50) was the aircraft employed.

The A/C, Captain James Gallagher, and his crew racked up 23,-452 miles from start to finish. B-29 tankers took off from Carswell Air Force Base in Texas, and made four refueling contacts with the B-50 at various points around the globe.

A few days later a B-36 flew 9,600 miles in forty-three hours and thirty-seven minutes without refueling in flight.

A third world record was set, also in 1949, by one of the new B-47's. They flew from Moses Lake in the State of Washington, back to Andrews, just outside Washington, D.C., in three hours and forty-six minutes.

In 1953 one of our B-47's flew from Maine to England in four hours and forty-three minutes: a distance of 2,886 miles. In the same year two B-36's took off from our old Bomber Command HQ base in Japan —Yokota—and went from Japan to Loring Air Force Base in the State of Maine. Time: twenty-eight and one-half hours. Distance: slightly over 10,000 miles.

Speaking of Yokota again, we sent three B-47's from March Air Force Base in California to Yokota (the next year, 1954). A fifteen-hour flight, covering 6,700 miles, nonstop.

Same year, a B-47 took off from our base at Sidi Slimane in French Morocco, intending to fly up to England. They got up there and found impossible weather conditions . . . couldn't land. Like the words in the old World War II song which we used to sing to the tune of "Bless 'em All"—

> The fog was, at seven, ten-ten on the deck,
> And sometimes a bloody sight more. . . .

They flew back to North Africa, but didn't land. "Let's go back to

England, where we're supposed to go." Accordingly a tanker came up and gave them a cargo of fuel, and back they went to England again. Couldn't land.

Down to Sidi Slimane once more; mid-air refueling once more. This began to be a stunt, and it ended up that way. The B-47 remained in the air, fueled repeatedly, for forty-seven hours and thirty-five minutes. Total distance traveled: 21,163 miles.

In 1955 we sent two whole wings of B-47's from our Sixth Division at MacDill Air Force Base, Tampa, Florida— Sent them over to Europe to simulate an attack on certain targets there; and then they landed at an African base. All ninety airplanes were refueled twice en route— first over Bermuda, and again over the African coast.

Let's move up to 1956.

Says Hubler, in *SAC: The Strategic Air Command:*

"Within two weeks in December, twenty-one B-47 wings supported by eighteen tanker squadrons flew simulated missions over the North Pole—for a total of 8,000,000 combat-ready miles covered in a single exercise. A non-stop refueled flight went around the northern perimeter of North America: Castle Air Force Base [that's at Merced, California] to Goose Bay, Newfoundland, to the North Pole, to Anchorage, Alaska, to Seattle, to San Francisco, swinging across the United States to Baltimore to cover 13,500 miles in 31 hours and 50 minutes. It displayed the increasing ability of SAC to fly hard and long with combat loads."

In 1957, the year I left SAC, three B-52's were ordered out from California to make a simulated attack on a target in the Malaysian neighborhood, and then on around the world back home. Quoting from *SAC: The Strategic Air Command* for the final time: "The elapsed estimate for the globe-girdling trip was scheduled to be 45 hours and 6 minutes by the closest kind of reckoning. The three B-52's missed making their time schedule for the whole trip—with all its intricate possibilities of failure—by just 13 minutes. As far as the on-target arrival was concerned, they were only 60 seconds late—halfway around the world."

And at that time SAC airplanes were doing more than one million hours annually in the air. They were burning up 1,500,000,000 gallons of jet fuel in a single year; and more than 200,000,000 gallons of this fuel were being exchanged in refueling operations. Refueling operations occurred, at that time, every three minutes of the twenty-four hours, day and night.

No use in citing any more statistics, either directly from SAC files or from articles and books written about the Command. Probably I've been overgenerous already. Statistics tend to bog a reader down if too many are thrown at him. (I don't use too many statistics in any speech I make. The picture as presented is apt to dissolve into a mess of numerals.)

Do not fail to recognize, however, that the people in the Command have been grateful for interest and coverage awarded them by the press, nationally and internationally. It would seem now that the world at large is more familiar with operations and growth of SAC than with any other part of the United States Air Force or any other air force.

SAC became a blanket, a bulwark. It was winning that Big War—the One Which Didn't Have to Be Fought—purely because of the existence and might of SAC.

Even the circulation of certain novels and the presentation of motion pictures which maligned the organization or offered an entirely false picture of what went on within our structure, could not undermine the solid confidence which, I'm glad to say, the bulk of civilian population has in SAC.

It is a good thing for dedicated personnel to know that they are appreciated.

Well, those were some of the accomplishments in my own time. During Tommy Power's years in the left-hand seat, SAC demonstrated a thousand more. Now the responsibility is Jack Ryan's. We look ahead hopefully to increased exhibition of military capability by the greatest air-powered organization which the world has ever seen.

. . . It was a morning in October, 1963. I was Chief of Staff, long departed from SAC. I was busy at my desk in the Pentagon, when an aide came in with several red-letter high velocity Mach 10 types of papers which I had to go over immediately.

"Also I have some good news, sir."

"What's that?"

"A B-58 from the 305th Bomb Wing has just flown nonstop from Tokyo to London. Eight thousand and twenty-eight miles. Major Sidney J. Kubesch, Major John O. Barrett, Captain Gerald R. Williamson. . . .

"Of course they could have made it sooner and more directly if they'd violated Soviet territory. But they didn't. They went up over our own Arctic regions, and then across the polar cap to England. Eight hours and thirty-five minutes. They refueled five times in flight. The refuelings were accomplished without incident."

I took time out for a long drag on my cigar. Somehow the smoke tasted even better than it had tasted a few minutes before.

"You said that was the 305th, from Bunker Hill Air Force Base, Indiana? Frank O'Brien's wing?"

"Yes, sir."

The 305th. They were bounced like a tennis ball. *Inactivated* December, 1946. *Activated* again in July, 1947. *Inactivated* again in September, 1948. *Activated* once more in January, 1951 (that was after I was on the SAC job); but *inactivated* once more in June, 1952 . . . *activated* again subsequently.

They were the first wing in SAC to be equipped completely with B-58's. This wasn't a case of teacher's pet or anything like that. According to performance borne out in repeated examination and inspection, the 305th was ripe for the transition to this equipment.

May I say that, as SAC commander and later Vice Chief and Chief of Staff, I didn't put any stones in their path.

But I have the sort of mind which pounces on numbers, and fiddles around with 'em. I gestured toward the aide, and settled down to go over those papers.

Interpreting my gesture correctly, the young officer was already halfway through the door when I called him back.

"What did you say that time was, on the Tokyo-London flight?"

"Eight hours and thirty-five minutes, sir."

. . . Couldn't help lingering over those numerals for a few seconds. The record time made by that 305th Hustler wasn't eight hours and thirty-four minutes; and it wasn't eight hours and thirty-six minutes. Not at all.

Eight hours and *thirty-five* minutes. Those 3-5 numerals were still kicking around.

BOOK VIII

USAF: The Pentagon

(1957 – 1965)

1

IN THE SPRING of 1957 General Thomas White informed me that he would become Chief of Staff of the Air Force on July 1st of that year, by President Eisenhower's appointment. He asked if I would choose to serve under him as Vice Chief. I said Yes.

. . . Could be that this came as something of a surprise to certain people in the Air establishment. There were those, especially in other commands, who had held to the opinion that I would never be called upon to serve in such a capacity, because I was considered to be strictly a bombardment man. It wasn't true, but newspaper columnists reaffirmed this belief from time to time.

They continued to do so right up to the termination of my active career.

They'd say, "LeMay's a bomber general. Just like the old battleship admirals." They blandly ignored the fact that I labored to get additional missiles during the same time that I battled for a manned system. I battled for interceptors to bolster up our air defenses in the same hours when I strove to get us the new manned strategic system.

I concentrated as firmly as possible on my particular job at the time, whatever it was. That may have given the impression to some undiscerning souls that I didn't think about anything else. But I did.

I'd received my fourth star away back in 1951, so there wouldn't be any advance in rank attached to the new job.

As I climbed up out of the pilot's seat at SAC and gave over the wheel to Tommy Power, I mused about what the situation might have been if I'd gone in for a civilian career instead of a military one.

. . . Yes, I'd always wanted to fly. When I was young, it became obvious that the best flying instruction—in fact the only flying instruction I could afford—was to be found in the military service. So I went into the military and got my training.

Often during cadet days the thought recurred that if I ever wished to resign I always could. Surely I was interested in the military: ROTC activities at Ohio State were proof of that. But, once trained as a pilot, there would always be that other civilian avenue open to me.

After I reached Selfridge there was a lot of talk among us new lieutenants about civilian versus military careers, pro and con. New airlines were starting up on every side. Pilots were in high demand, and they were excellently paid. They earned infinitely more money than we did in the Air Corps. That was attractive in itself; I couldn't help but be tempted.

About 1931 I decided that I might take the plunge. Ford was making those famous old tri-motors, and they were hiring pilots right along with them. If you went down to work for Ford a few months in the factory, you were actually undergoing a special training course on the tri-motor plane. It was something like the Rolls-Royce program of educating chauffeurs: you became familiar with the aircraft, and were thoroughly checked off on it, right there at the factory. A huge advantage: you had a job as well as made. When Ford sold an airplane he usually sold the pilot along with it. The pilot was delivered along with the plane.

So, when I could take my next leave, I actually went down and got a job with Ford. That is— I didn't resign my commission yet, or go to work. But the job was available.

I told the man, "Just let me have a few days to think this over." I returned to Selfridge and did a lot of pondering. Must have considered it from every angle, dozens of times during the next few days and nights.

. . . On the commercial side there was the advantage of an excellent income, with a possibility of working into something much better in a higher civilian echelon. That would mean more and more money in the future. I had been poor all my life. The rustle of paper money sounded very pleasant to my ears.

Also there was this business about being your own boss, living a life not hedged in and restricted by regulations . . . going where you wanted to go, whenever you wanted to go . . . living where you wanted to live. No one could tell you that you had to dress for dinner when you didn't want to dress for dinner. There wasn't any Uniform of the Day. If you decided that you didn't like the man who was your immediate superior, good enough. Go off and find another immediate superior whom you did like to work for. You were a free entity.

Case for the military side:

There was a pride in being an officer in the United States Army. This was by no means limited to the folks in my branch.

Some of us in the Air Corps may have considered ourselves among the elite, as pointed out before. The Army was small in those days, compact; there were stern and grinding demands, and the people who emerged from the mill were generally much the better for it. I couldn't face down the fact that during those several years as a flying cadet and then as a Regular officer, I had come in contact with the finest group of people I'd ever met in my life. They had an integrity, a sincere belief in what they were doing.

This integrity extended across the border into civilian life as well.

An Army officer was an *Army officer,* and that was important to the world at large. You, as an officer— If you found yourself in need of money during some emergency, you could walk into the nearest bank and sign your name to a note drawn for any reasonable amount of money which was commensurate with your salary. You could deposit that note without a single co-signer—no pledge of personal property, nothing but your name and status as an Army officer. Borrow the money, write checks on it . . . your credit was gilt-edged, anytime, anyplace, with no further questions asked.

You didn't get to be an officer in the Army easily; or in the Navy either, for that matter. Advancement in grade was pitifully slow. It was not uncommon—in fact, it was very common—to take seventeen years to make captain. Innumerable people had been in much longer than that, before they ever rose to field grade.

Readers whose experience has been limited to a comparatively brief tour of duty during World War II or the Korean War may raise their eyebrows about this. But it's true; it was true for the time and the condition. We expanded during war years from about twelve hundred officers and perhaps ten thousand men, to two and a half million in the Army Air Forces. Boys went from the status of high school track captains to being United States Army Air Force captains in maybe two years.

The old code did not prevail. It couldn't, with that sudden expansion. We had to build up a vast establishment, and work that establishment, and fly it and fight it. There were bound to be a lot of sad apples in the barrel.

This is when that old crack found wide circulation: "Yeah. He's a gentleman—by *Act of Congress.*"

But in 1931— There was the officers' code, the officers' and gentlemen's code. If anyone violated that code— If a man made a false official statement, for instance— In other words, if he told a lie, that was *the end* for him. If he didn't pay his bills, or if he wrote a bad check, or if he were guilty of any transgression in that vast hodge-podge of morals and ethics covered in the statement "conduct unbecoming an officer," he was finished. (Nowadays, I am proud to say, we are building back to our original reputation. We have now a military organization where there is prevailing respect and integrity.)

So I beat the thing to death when my head was on the pillow. I beat it to death in the back of my brain while I was flying. Waking or sleeping, I hammered the matter out.

And I listened to what other people had to say on the subject . . . talked with a number of Regular officers who had been in for years. Once again I couldn't get past the obvious fact: *I have come in contact with the finest group of people with whom I've ever been in contact before.*

That did it. My mind was made up. I was going to stay in.

. . . Here came a friend, Sidney Nelson. He said, "All along, I've had no definite plans on staying in the Military. I think I'll get out and find a civilian job."

Well, there was one ready for him. So Sid Nelson went down and took my job instead of my taking it. He was in the factory for a couple or three months, and then he went with the airplane to the company who purchased it . . . they were the predecessors of United Air Lines. Later United took over, and Sid remained with them. He had a distinguished commercial career, and has just recently retired.

As for myself: somehow I owned the feeling that I'd burned a great big long bridge. It had been there behind me, but now I was glad to burn it. I would give the best I had to my military career.

Never have I regretted that decision.

Still, to the best of my observation, the military man is about the only professional expert who is apt to be scorned *for* his experience—not for the lack of it. A lawyer, a doctor, a teacher, a clergyman: these are awarded a trusting respect which adds and even multiplies as their years of duty are augmented. It has become increasingly the fashion, however, to regard the veteran military professional with gravest suspicion—a suspicion which deepens and darkens as his term of duty extends. There are sneering whispers about "Colonel Blimps" and "horse-cavalry concepts."

I suspect that this is true because most of the active journalists and politicians have had a turn at Army or Navy life, or perhaps have picked up some flying time. They tend thus to dress themselves with a technical wisdom they do not truly possess. And they go on to deride *The Military Mind* because once, as enlisted men or youthful officers, they were compelled to defer to higher authority, and did so with reluctance.

In later civilian life they assume a military sophistication wholly unwarranted by the limitations of their careers. Commonly we don't meet up with laymen who have firsthand knowledge of the lives led by priests or obstetricians; but the self-appointed military savants are a dime a dozen.

There is a danger in this. It becomes obvious when these men are projected into positions of national influence or power.

2

THE RELATIONSHIP between the Vice Chief and the Chief of Staff is much more the relationship of a team than it is that of a commander and his subordinate.

This may come as a surprise to the reader. Certainly it came as a surprise to me.

Even viewing the Pentagon situation from my position as Commander of SAC (as I had done previously on many occasions) I did not realize how the exact apportionment of labor and liability went, until I was installed up on that fourth floor myself.

For this reason we'll present my review of the Pentagon years as a single episode rather than making distinction between the 1957–61 stint as Vice Chief of Staff, and the 1961–65 span as Chief of Staff.

During the first phase, General Thomas D. White and I pulled away in double harness. After General White retired and I went into the main office, General William F. McKee became Vice Chief of Staff. Again we were a team, just as Tommy and I had been.

The reason for this: *somebody* has to run the Air Force.

We conducted a minute time check every now and then. Each of those checks bore out the same testimony: the Air Force Chief of Staff has to spend from seventy to seventy-five per cent of his time on JCS activities.

Repeat: *someone* has to run the *Air Force*.

The Vice Chief of Staff isn't just sitting around waiting to succeed the Chief of Staff if he drops dead. The Vice Chief is working every damn minute.

(No pun or any other form of humorous allusion to the Vice Chief will be tolerated. That wore thin long ago.)

. . . First time I met Tommy White was down in South America, away back in 1941. Remember, I flew with C. V. Haynes in a B-24, along with General Brett and his party, surveying a proposed route for fighter planes to be taken into the Middle East.

We had to go in to a field at Belém in Brazil in order to get gas. (We're going on to Natal and thence to Africa.) When we landed at Belém, here was Tommy White. Belém is on the Pará River, maybe a hundred or a hundred and fifty miles southeast of the various mouths of the Amazon.

I didn't know Tommy, but C. V. Haynes knew him well. He sings out, "What on earth are you doing here? I thought you were down in Rio."

Rio was where White really belonged—he was chief of our Air Mission down there. As such, we younger people stood a little in awe of him.

Tommy said, "I'm on leave. I've been busy with tropical fish, hunting for some new species."

"Where you been?"

Oh, he'd been along the Rio do Pará or the Rio Tocantins . . . I think also up the Amazon. . . .

"Find anything?"

"Yes," says Tommy White. "I found a fish which can swim backward as well as forward."

I'll never forget C.V.'s face. C.V. gasped, "Oh my God, you've missed too many boats!" The old tropical expression for declaring that some-one has gone soft in the head.

Tommy says, "I'll show you."

We went and looked into a five-gallon can of water, where a fish was nicely penned. The critter had only one dorsal fin down its back, and this worked something like an auger. Sure enough, it could go either backward or forward with equal speed and agility.

Also Tommy had a lot of other fish he'd caught, up those rivers.

I would hazard a guess that General Thomas D. White is the only ex-Chief of Staff anywhere in the world who has several fish named after him.

It is a benefit to the Nation at large, and to the Air Force itself, if the Chief and the Vice Chief can complement each other. And I don't mean *compliment* (although they do that sometimes too, if they happen to feel in a courteous mood).

Of late we have been fortunate in this regard. General White and I had almost no friction when we teamed together. After I was Chief, Bozo McKee and I suffered very little wear-and-tear.

I anticipate that in the regime which succeeded mine there will be no abrasion, either, between General McConnell and his Vice Chief, Butch Blanchard.

If a Chief has strong points in his makeup, and certain points where he is not so strong— Even weak points— If the Vice Chief is *strong* in those areas, the complementing factor is apparent.

Take my years with Tommy White. I always wanted to go ahead and push, regardless of what the obstacles were, to try to force a pro-gram through. Sometimes it was going to be a difficult job, if not nearly impossible, to get the thing done.

Tommy, on the other hand, talked about "the Art of the *Possible.*" In other words, if a thing is impossible to perform, don't even try it. Just try to get done what you think it *is* possible to do.

But my natural inclination was to believe, "Well, hell. I'm sure you're not going to get anything done if you don't try to do it." My tendency is to feel that if people constantly assayed a plan in advance, and decided that it was obviously unfeasible, men wouldn't have got-ten a lot of things done which they *have* gotten done.

For instance, people said that it was impossible to fly. But there were a lot of others who didn't believe that to be true. So they went ahead, and they flew.

I admit that some of them didn't fly too successfully. They weren't all Wright brothers. Mythology tells us that Icarus flew too close to the sun. His father had fastened on his wings with wax, and the wax melted, and the wings came off, and Icarus ended up in the drink.

Then, somewhere along the line, we recall that boy Darius Green, who didn't fly so well either.

Sometimes the full-speed-ahead philosophy has ended in disaster. Not invariably, however.

. . . Tommy White would say, "Out of the question! We'll never get that done." Sometimes I could still convince him that we should try. . . . We never succeed if we don't try. Maybe it will be all to the good, in the end. Maybe not. . . .

But there were many incidents wherein General White was exactly the kind of brake which should have been applied to keep me from battering myself to death.

Again, I could get him off the ground when, without being sparked, he might have continued to sit on the runway.

That's what I mean by complementing.

Same way with Bozo McKee.

Bozo and I had never met during the war. He wasn't even in the Air Force then. He had spent the bulk of his military career in the Coast Artillery, and came over to the Air Force only after the war. He happened to have an assignment in the Pentagon, and that was where we met.

I guess Bozo had decided that he would get more out of life by concentrating his energies on the airplane business instead of the anti-aircraft business (which had been his particular addiction during World War II in the Army). He told me with relish, a couple of years ago, about all the headshaking which went on among his fellow members of the Class of '29 at West Point.

They said, "Bozo, you're absolutely crazy. It's absurd of you to go over to the Air Force. . . . Oh yes, we admit that since the Air Force became a separate Service, you might feel that there was more room for you to get ahead in a new organization than in your own establishment. But look at the facts, Bozo. You're nonrated. You've never worn wings, and you're too old to qualify for them now. You haven't even been a navigator or a bombardier or an air crew member, let alone a pilot. Every officer who ever got to first base—let alone third—in the Air establishment, has been a pilot. It's SOP. You go over there, nonrated as you are, and they'll cut your silly throat."

Actually those volunteer advisers had something on their side. They were thinking back to the old Langley days. At Langley we operated on a different principle than we operate on now. We *knew* then that we were merely a nucleus of the force which would be formed after a war started. So, naturally, we didn't have any paddlefeet (nonrated officers). I don't think that any nonrated officer ever came into the Air Corps or the GHQ Air Force. The only people we had who didn't fly were a few unhappy pilots who degenerated into a condition where they couldn't pass their physical examinations. They were kept on, in order to apply some other skills they had learned.

Everybody else was a flyer. That meant that flying people did most of the nonflying jobs too.

Then, when World War II came along, we couldn't afford that. We had to take in paddlefeet, immediately, to do those jobs. And we did. That was according to the original plan; for, with flyers relinquishing their nonflying jobs, we had a broader base of flying skill to build upon.

All we'd had before the war was a platform on which we were *going to build* our fighting force.

Today our contemporary fighting force is *in existence.*

And it's symptomatic of a trend toward greater proportionate dependence on nonrated people. General McKee was the first Vice Chief of Staff, ever, who was a nonrated officer.

A Vice Chief of Staff is not necessarily heir-apparent to the throne of Chief. We've had a number of Vice Chiefs who didn't become Chief. Also, General McKee came up for retirement while he was still on the job as Vice Chief.

But I don't think that you're ever going to find a *Chief of Staff* of the Air Force who is a nonpilot. No one wants to feel that the boss of a flying outfit can't fly.

Admittedly the Vice is doing about half the work of the Chief. I had expected a little flap on this, and there might have been, except that Bozo is an exceptional character.

Just how exceptional was demonstrated only a few months ago (June 1965). McKee was out in Los Angeles, and President Johnson called him up and asked him to become the new administrator of the Federal Aviation Agency. We old-timers were delighted when he agreed to take the job. Couldn't get a better man.

. . . To get back to Bozo and his 1929 class. Shortly before he retired, he went up to his thirty-fifth class reunion at the Point. He came in to say goodbye to me before he left, and he was grinning from ear to ear.

"Boy, have I been looking forward to going up there! Because all those old fuds in my class used to cry havoc at the notion of my transferring to the Air Force. 'You're not a pilot. They'll carve your throat from ear to ear.' Ha. I just want to walk around and show off my four stars."

Here's the way the JCS business was conducted, both during White-LeMay days and LeMay-McKee days.

Let the reader imagine that he is Chief of Staff of the Air Force, and that he lives in that brick quarters number 7 at Fort Myer, and he must go to work on Monday morning, like any other working stiff.

You kiss Mrs. Reader goodbye, and go out of the door and down the steps. It's anywhere from 0745 to 0815, depending on the urgency of the moment or on how much gumption you, General Reader, can feel crawling around within your weary old frame.

Maybe an aide will be along in the limousine, maybe not. It depends. The aide or the chauffeur will pick up a telephone and inform communications that General Reader is now in his car and en route to the Pentagon. It's essential to do this, because someone may want to get hold of you during the next few minutes, while you're en route.

It doesn't take long to get down there. So, in a matter of minutes, you drive in under a roofed area at the entrance (looks a good deal like a garage in a big hotel) and you get out and walk to the elevator, and use your key, and go up to the fourth floor.

This, we said, is Monday, and it's a JCS day. Meetings of the Joint Chiefs of Staff are held on Monday, Wednesday and Friday. Those are regularly scheduled meetings. If something big is going on or shaping up, you get together oftener.

But first there's a gathering of the Air Force staff. That will be at 0830, and it takes from half an hour to an hour. Happens every morning. Then, at 0930 on Monday, there is usually a conference with the Secretary of Defense, down on the third floor. That takes an hour or so.

Then you go back to your own office and start your briefing for the afternoon JCS meeting. You run through what the staff has done on various papers which are going to be discussed by the JCS. You get up-to-date on all the information and recommendations, and decide what you are going to do about them. That takes until noon.

If you're lucky, you have time for lunch. You're not always lucky.

. . . So it's Monday . . . there isn't any meeting of the Operations Deputies on Monday. You go to the JCS meeting at two o'clock; and get out of there anywhere from five to seven in the evening. Once again: it all depends.

Let's explain about the Operations Deputies. These are called, in Pentagon parlance, the Ops-Deps. They are staff officers of the three Services. It's very like a small Joint Staffs meeting. They come from Personnel, from Plans and Operations, from Logistics, from the Comptroller; besides these, we have Intelligence and all the Special Staff.

Those latter people aren't called Ops-Deps, but they act like Ops-Deps.

Ops-Deps meet on Tuesdays, Wednesdays, Thursdays, Fridays. Their chief function is to try to get some of the work done for the Chiefs. The Chiefs would have far too much to manage otherwise; there just wouldn't be time. Ops-Deps have the Chiefs' authority to handle many matters. As always, and as in the case of the Vice Chief— The Chief of Staff can delegate *authority,* but he can't possibly delegate his *responsibility.*

If they all agree on subjects under consideration, they go right ahead and put the stuff into the works, and we don't even have to look at 'em. (Not *then.*)

They know our feelings on many important questions. They can't know our feelings on *all.*

But, if one Op-Dep is seriously convinced that the decision which the others have arrived at is a mistaken one, he holds up this particular matter in order for it to be presented to his Chief. It is his duty to do this. It applies both to items which are destined for JCS consideration, and to other topics peculiar to his own branch. Because the Chief is forever responsible.

Same thing applies where the Vice Chief is concerned. He has the authority to make decisions when the staff cannot agree on the solution of a problem, and often he comes to the final conclusion. Still, if any Deputy feels that the Vice Chief has judged erroneously, and he can't live with it, then he is obligated to wave his hand and say so.

. . . Soon as it is possible for them to come in and meet with the Chief about this knotty problem, the Chief will settle the matter. He'll either support the Vice Chief, or he'll say, "No, you were wrong. Do it *this* way."

Everyone is aware that this is SOP. Nobody feels aggrieved when the objection is raised. "Vice Chief, Negative. I think you're wrong. Let's go see the Chief about this."

If the eventual resolution goes along with the Vice Chief's ideas, O.K. And if it doesn't, O.K. also. To tell the truth, there have been very few cases where it has been necessary for the Chief to override the judgment of a Vice Chief. I know that there were instances wherein Tommy White didn't agree with me or else I didn't agree with Bozo McKee. But they're forgotten now. I can't recollect just what they were.

. . . Every time you're free for a moment, the Vice Chief will stick his head in at your door, and tell you what he's been doing and what's going on in the staff. "What do you think about *this?*" Whether you have anything pertinent to discuss or not, usually he's sticking his head in just the same. You're yakking together perpetually.

There must exist utmost confidence and faith between Chief and

Vice Chief. The Vice Chief gets to know what's going on in the intricacies of the Chief's brain. It is very nearly possible, after you two have been working together for a while, for the Vice Chief to come up with the identical answer which you will give on almost every subject.

Let's move from Monday to Wednesday, now. Wednesday is another JCS day. You had your staff meeting at 0830, and you start your briefing at nine o'clock. As a rule that eats up the rest of the forenoon, getting ready for JCS in the afternoon. But meanwhile, this being a Wednesday, the Ops-Deps have assembled, and they can clear up quantities of routine detail. Then, at one o'clock, after you've had lunch, in they come to sit down with you. But if the Ops-Deps have run off the edge on time, somebody else has to come in and scrub up the agenda instead.

". . . *This* has been taken care of. . . . *That* has been taken care of. . . . Here's the discussion held on this paper, down at Ops-Deps . . . here's where we are on it now. Here are the main issues which have to be resolved. . . . You've got to get a little more up-to-date on *this*. . . ."

This may occupy an hour or at least half an hour, prior to going down to JCS. If you're a lucky duck you'll get out of JCS by six p.m.

Same thing goes for Friday.

Accordingly, you will find that your Mondays, Wednesdays and Fridays are completely taken up by JCS work. If there's some kind of international flap occurring, you'll also meet with the rest of the JCS over weekends, or Saturday, or on Tuesdays and Thursdays. You'll be constantly on call, like a cop or fireman, where that flap business is concerned.

Tuesdays and Thursdays you'll try to catch up with what's happening in the Air Force. On those days the Vice Chief lays on briefings and talks with the staff. Then he comes in to keep you informed of what's going on. He asks for a final settlement of sundry questions, and he makes various new recommendations as well.

Sometimes, if heat and pressure aren't turned on too hard— If there is no important problem claiming your attention immediately, you two can sit down and talk together, in comfort and in mutual confidence. A random easygoing conversation, touching on all sorts of unrelated subjects—even in a desultory fashion—has extreme value. In this process you're getting to know each other more and more. And the better your Vice Chief gets to know you, the smoother future operations will be. He learns what you are really thinking about. He discovers what you *want*.

Your Vice Chief—your General LeMay or General McKee or General Blanchard—may at some future time succeed you, General Reader, in your role as Chief of Staff. Whether or not he succeeds you makes no difference insofar as your current relationship is concerned.

You, for instance, are not Chairman of the Air Council. You haven't time to get down to all the Air Council meetings. Your Vice Chief is Chairman of the Air Council.

Whenever possible, of course, you get down there. Divers sections of the staff will offer propositions for Air Council approval. (Mostly to keep them abreast of what's going on within the organization.) Then the Council makes a recommendation which you, General Reader, will either approve or disapprove. If you're familiar essentially with the subject, chances are that you'll approve right off—if you comply with what's being done, as usually you do.

But sometimes you don't confirm. Sometimes you say, "I don't agree with this. But maybe I haven't got the whole story? Get up here and give me some more dope."

So they'll lead you all through the thing again, and point out how they arrived at their conclusions. You may agree with them at last, or you still may be contrary-minded.

Let's say a problem arises which the Air Staff must solve. They refer it to one of their sections, to monitor. Everybody is interested in the eventual solution, everybody has to be in on it. Often there will be arguments about how to get the deed done. "Are we going to do it this way or that way or the other way?" If you have a hung staff, as in a hung jury, then there must be an authority who'll say Yea or Nay. And General Reader can't get into all these fusses and still spend seventy-five per cent of his time down in the JCS. So your Vice Chief is going to settle the thing. He will make a decision in your name.

They *call* him a Vice Chief but actually he's a deputy, because you have deputized authority to him. (Also we call the senior staff officers "deputies" because they do a lot of things on their own too.)

The Vice Chief has rendered his verdict in your name. If the staff says, "That's fine. Go ahead and do it," why, we'll go ahead and do it. But if any member of the group says, "No. I still think this is *wrong*. I can't *stand* this," then it's his duty to come in and tell you.

In a case like that, you get into it in sufficient detail to understand the difficulty, and ultimately you give the nod—or the axe.

Everybody knows there are different ways of doing things, but in final conclusion it's in your own lap.

. . . And then it will be up to you to clear the air in the family. "This is the procedure I wish carried out. I haven't got time to pick all the berries in the patch myself. That's why we *have* a Vice Chief."

Pretend that a new staff officer is coming into the organization. He's not widely experienced in this field, he doesn't know just how you've been operating. Therefore it's always wise to explain the situation in detail.

. . . Give him a little lecture. Say, "Look. This is the way we're going to operate. Now, I fully expect my Vice Chief, now and again, to make a decision which I won't agree with. Whenever he does that, I'm surely going to tell him about it. You'll probably hear about it too. . . . Now, I may or may not annul his decision. It depends on how important it is, and what the ramifications are. But if I *do* rescind it, I'm not going to be at all embarrassed. And I don't want *him* to be embarrassed because I happened to countermand one of his orders. It's a perfectly natural chain of events. And I don't want *you* to be embarrassed, if you should happen to object to one of his decisions."

Tell him firmly, "It's your duty to object, if you feel strongly about the situation. Without embarrassment. Without repercussions. Without vendettas."

You, the Chief of Staff, may not dwell in an ivory tower or an iron tower or any other kind of tower. You've got to be down there on the flight line, talking with your crew.

3

A FEW MONTHS after I became Vice Chief of Staff, it was decided that I should fly a KC-135 down to Buenos Aires in an endeavor to set some records, and deliver in this dramatic fashion a letter from President Eisenhower to President Aramburu, during the celebration of Argentina's Aviation Week.

"General LeMay's flight is a graphic demonstration of how rapidly technology is reducing the once formidable barriers of time and distance in communication between countries," President Eisenhower would say in his letter.

This was, in the main, a propaganda flight; but not necessarily any demonstration to impress solely the Argentinians. Point was, the folks in Washington wanted me to make a flight which would be much longer than the distance from New York to Moscow. That's the reason we took off from Westover Air Force Base, Massachusetts, and didn't proceed on a geographical straight line to Buenos Aires. Instead our route on the downward trip took us first over Fortaleza, which is far out on the bulge of Brazil, almost to Natal; and then on to Buenos Aires. That's about like flying from Los Angeles to Moscow. On the upward trip, returning, we would head directly from Buenos Aires to Washington, D.C.

(For purposes of speed it would have been better if we'd reversed the procedure, and gone down direct and come back the other way. Tail winds would have helped us, with the then-existing weather conditions. But we did it the hard way.)

You might crystallize our purpose and say that we were out to set a record for large jet aircraft—a Stratotanker like the KC-135. As the

Associated Press said, ". . . In its utility role as a jet speed high-altitude global transport."

In most respects it was a routine flight, but we did have a little trouble shortly before takeoff. While checking the aircraft out, up there at Westover, one of the mechanics lost his hat. It blew off and went right through the Number Two engine, so we had to change the engine. They did that in less than four hours, and we got off on schedule.

Takeoff time: 4:48 p.m., Eastern Standard Time. 11 November, 1957. KC-135. (3-5 once more. Well. . . .)

We had our normal crew, plus a civilian official, Mr. Charles Logeston. As described, we went over a thousand miles out of our way on the trip down. Flew a total of 6,322.85 miles without refueling. Elapsed time: thirteen hours, two minutes, fifty-one seconds. They didn't publish that right away, but it was a record for the time.

Coming back we set another record for a nonrefueling jet flight of 5,204 miles, which took us almost eleven hours and four minutes, with a speed of around 471 mph.

Going down, I spent about eight of the thirteen hours at the controls, which was what I liked to do. Once again the pilots could complain that I wouldn't let them get in enough flying time. . . . We did have some cross winds as high as one hundred and twenty-five knots, and those slowed us down a little.

We were welcomed at the Ezeiza Airport, about an hour away from downtown Buenos Aires. A lot of USAF types were around, who had come down to participate in the aviation week. Our Thunderbirds were there, using F-100's and doing all their precision tricks in the sky. During the show, President Aramburu climbed into one of the Super Sabres, and thus became the first Chief of State to fly faster than sound.

I remember that he was astonished at our speed coming south in the KC-135. He said it had taken only as long as a train ride might take from Buenos Aires to their city of Córdoba, five hundred miles inland.

There were some newspaper and magazine people from the United States around too, and they asked for a ride back. This would all depend on the temperatures and winds, early the next morning, when I planned to take off on the return trip. That would be Wednesday, November 13th. I thought that the length of the runway (only 8,300 feet) was somewhat critical for the enormous fuel load we'd be carrying. If it were necessary, to insure a safe takeoff, I might even leave behind some of the men who had accompanied me south. In fact we did so, but for another reason. Two of the personnel stayed behind to supervise the return of some heavy radio equipment which we'd unloaded there.

I did bring Vern Haugland back with me, and some other magazine writers. Especially I wanted to take Haugland if I could, because I had known him back in the 21st Bomber Command days on the Marianas. He was a war correspondent; and General MacArthur pinned a Silver Star on Haugland's pajamas, after he was hurt during a B-26 mission, down in the South Pacific in 1942.

Well, he came along home, as did a few others, and Haugland wrote a nice story about the flight in *Air Force Magazine* a couple of months later.

On the return trip I didn't spend as much time at the controls as I did on the way down. I was fiddling with the radio. I couldn't figure out why we had the interference which we suffered. We were flying above thirty-five thousand feet in a very queer mist. Visibility restricted: you couldn't say that it was cloud, but it was a heavy cirrus. We had one spot in that high cirrus where we got most peculiar interference, and we were almost out of radio contact for a while. Not completely out of contact, but it was difficult to get anything through. Later the situation cleared up.

President Eisenhower had wished us to come in at Washington National Airport, and there we did land by special dispensation of the Civil Aeronautics Administration—the first time a jet had ever landed there. People in the region voiced their usual noise complaints at the idea, and the CAA considered gravely the "general safety hazards and airline interruptions," but finally they concluded that the flight was of sufficient importance, and gave permission for us to land at National.

Tommy White came to meet us, along with the then Secretary of the Air Force, Mr. James H. Douglas.

Before we let down I had an opportunity to do a little kidding with my passengers. It was announced that we had taken aboard a large supply of that morning's Buenos Aires newspapers. I said, "I'm going to have them delivered this afternoon in Washington—to the White House, the Pentagon, the Argentine Embassy, and the National Press Club. I'm surprised that some of you writers didn't think of that one."

We made a pretty smooth landing too. Haugland describes it in his *Air Force Magazine* article:

"The descent was so gradual, so unlike that of most jet approaches, that in the windowless interior of the plane there developed an uncanny feeling of suspended animation. The engine throb was so steady and low, and the plane itself so free of vibration, that it seemed as if the craft had already landed and come to a stop. I unfastened my seat belt and went to the porthole, and was amazed to see clouds drifting by. We were still in the approach pattern. I sheepishly returned to my seat, but I noticed that others too had left their seats to glance out, thoughtfully. I was not alone in my confusion.

"At last there was the slightest touch of movement underneath, and then the throbbing sound of turning wheels. We were home."

So our passengers thought they were on the ground, but they weren't on the ground at all. This reminded me of something which took place long before, when I was up at Selfridge.

There's a girl mixed up in this story.

One Friday night we were to have a party at the Officers' Club. This was in the BH days (Before Helen). There was a girl back at Columbus whom I considered to be pretty sharp, and she *was* pretty sharp. Her name was Marion Thompson. I invited her up to Selfridge, and thank goodness she was willing to come, and she stayed for the week-end with a married pair—officer friend and his wife. That was what the out-of-town girls always did.

And we went to the dance.

Being the usual smart cookie young show-off, I desired most awfully to give my girl a ride in an airplane. Every now and then a stunt like that could be managed. The base commander (who was, you'll remember, Major George Brett) had the authority to grant permission for such a flight. Somewhere in Regulations it said something about giving select civilians a ride. This was interpreted as an indoctrination flight —good for the Air Corps, teach civilians what was going on, etc. Well, it had to be stretched a good deal in order to give your gal friend a ride. But it had been done before, and I was not behindhand in approaching Major Brett with the idea.

He hemmed and hawed a little bit, and finally says, "All right."

So the dance was on Friday night, but I kept thinking of taking Marion up in an old dual-control PT-1 the next morning. Yes, I could dance; but like a lot of other young men I didn't especially like to. Seemed like a kind of waste of time. My little friend was humming happily along with the orchestra, "Embraceable You" or "Star Dust." But in my imagination we were already up there in the air, and I was showing the beautiful Marion Thompson everything I knew about the fly business.

She still looked beautiful the next morning, even when bundled up in one of those old horsehide flying suits which everybody thought they had to wear.

. . . Take a look at the weather. Stinko. By ten o'clock we still didn't have more than about a five or six hundred foot ceiling.

I was brokenhearted at the thought of canceling the whole thing out. I said, "Well, we can't do the kind of flying which I wanted to show you. But we can buzz around within a couple of miles of the airdrome here, at low altitude." The terrain was flat in that region; no tall buildings to interfere. "We'll take off for ten or fifteen minutes at low altitude."

. . . We were buzzing along at about four hundred feet, when the engine quit. She was just *out,* that's all there was to it.

Well, I looked ahead . . . nothing but high-tension lines, and I didn't want to go fooling around with those. But there appeared to be a little flat tree-less spot over there to the right. The only thing I could do with that PT-1 was to drop it into the flat spot, which was on a farm.

I just mushed the aircraft in there, and deliberately banged it down for the last twenty feet so that we would wash out the landing gear, and thus slide to a stop.

We did that all right: washed out the landing gear, and eased through a barbed-wire fence. It wasn't much of a fence . . . I remember one post broke off, and a couple of wires. That post wounded the leading edge of our wing, but the entire airplane wasn't damaged greatly. We coasted ahead, and finally stopped without much of a shock.

Now, here's what made me think of this incident when I read the writer's account of approaching National Airport on the flight from Buenos Aires. It was just the reverse:

Those people thought they were *on the ground* when we were still up there in the approach pattern. And in the case at Selfridge— Marion knew that we had *landed,* I guess, but she didn't know that we had *pranged.*

I still consider that quite a stunt. Crack up an airplane, and never have your passenger realize that she's been in a smash.

And we had landed on— Wait.

I leaped from the airplane in order to gallantly lift the gal out, and she was looking very big-eyed and incredulous. But, as I say, I assisted her chivalrously to step *right into the middle of a huge manure pile.* We'd ended up there.

Main trouble: the manure was awfully fresh.

. . . We went to the farmhouse, and called Selfridge on the phone, and they sent a car and picked us up. I had been wondering if inadvertently Marion had cut the switches in her cockpit, and thus turned the magneto off. But that was still on . . . not much to check, in those days. . . . Is the mixture on? Is the spark full advanced? Is the gas on? Are the switches on? . . . That was all you could check.

It turned out that the magneto shaft had broken. Also the carburetor was pretty dirty: there was a lot of guck in there, probably decomposed gasket material. That in itself might have clogged up sooner or later.

This seemed to be about the most unkind prank which Fate could play on me. The word got around pretty fast. "Did you hear about Curt taking that cutie for a ride? And did you hear where they *ended up?*"

I've never been too fond of manure piles since.

Although, thinking back about it, it was just the sort of cushion we needed at the moment.

A soft sweet-smelling clover stack would have been better.

At a reception which they gave us in Buenos Aires on the evening of November 12th, I was pleased at meeting several people who remembered our first flight down that way, when the B-17's came chugging, away back in 1938. But the most interesting conversation which I had was with a retired Argentinian Air Force general, one Ángel María Zulaga.

He was an extremely fine-looking man: very elderly, but not looking his age. General Zulaga had made the first flight across the Andes, and he did it in a balloon. That was forty-one years before our KC-135 flight, on June 24th, 1916. General Zulaga, with a companion, Eduardo Bradley, flew in their balloon from Santiago, Chile, to Uspallata in the Argentine.

Imagine what that was like in those days. You will remember, from my description of the B-17 flight, that we had to be at seventeen thousand feet to get through that pass; and the peak of Tupangato, right next door, looms up to 21,284 feet. Winds are tricky and violent. And they went up over the mountains, in a balloon, *without oxygen;* and they made it.

If I was to get any thrills out of meeting Early Bird flyers—and believe me, I get those thrills—my excitement didn't terminate in Buenos Aires. Shortly after returning from that trip, I had to go up to Canada to make a speech. Forget what the occasion was, but I can never forget a man I met there. He was Mr. J. A. D. McCurdy; and on the 23rd of February, 1909, at Baddeck, Nova Scotia, he flew an aircraft called the Silver Dart. It was the first heavier-than-air flight in Canada, or the first made by a Canadian. That happened when I was twenty-seven months old, long before I'd grown tall enough to go chasing airplanes across the backyards of Columbus, Ohio.

On the way home to Washington, I meditated on my good fortune in having met both General Zulaga and Mr. McCurdy. But another big thrill was to follow. Soon I had a visitor, there at the Pentagon: a very old man. He was Yoshitoshi Tokugawa. As a young Japanese captain, he had been the first of his nationality to pilot a heavier-than-air aircraft. He flew Henri Furman's biplane for four minutes to an altitude of seventy meters; and that was in 1910.

Then I sat back and realized that even General Frank P. Lahm, who had given the introductory remarks at our Kelly graduation in 1929, was still alive. And he had been taught to fly by the Wright brothers. It seemed that old flyers never died, nor did they even fade away.

I considered this most encouraging.

4

BEGINNING IN 1957, the Soviets' unexpected rate of technical progress in the missile and Space field brought a shift in the power balance.

This new capability, in the hands of a potential enemy, placed in question both the *direction* and the *pace* of our military effort.

As a fundamental step in maintaining an effective deterrent posture, it was necessary to enhance our counterforce capability. This counterforce strategy had been designed primarily to confront the enemy with certain destruction of his military force in case he attacked the free world. This was essential to effective deterrence. In turn, the objective in event of a nuclear war was—and is today—to limit damage to the United States and our allies, and terminate the war on terms favorable to our Nation.

Alternatives to the counterforce concept have been proposed, from time to time, in the form of the finite-deterrence and minimum-deterrence approaches to strategy. These alternatives are unacceptable because they are based on the assumption that we can deter a resolute aggressor by reducing our capability to the point where we could only target "hostage" cities. I do not believe this would provide an efficient deterrence or a war-winning capability, should war occur.

Today we hear much discussion about "overkill." The people who are talking "overkill" knowingly or unknowingly support the adoption of a minimum-deterrence strategy. In advocating that strategy, they are addressing the *wrong* problem. Instead of belaboring our ability to destroy the population of an aggressor nation, they should consider what we require to save American lives and property by preventing war, or by gaining a decision as quickly as possible if war occurs. That is the proper and traditional task of United States armed forces. The counterforce strategy which we are pursuing and analyzing today provides our best prospect for success in that task.

To carry out a counterforce strategy, we have consistently advocated the development and maintenance of a mixed strategic force. The pace of our programs has been impressive. We have been able to bring several versions of the Atlas, the Titan, and the Minuteman into operation, and at the same time to maintain the known capability of our manned-bomber force. This was accomplished in about one-third of the time period that elapsed between the B-17 and the B-52.

Since 1961 we have also increased our tactical forces' capability to perform their missions of airlift, close air support, interdiction, counter-air, and counter-insurgency.

When the Cuban crisis occurred, it was clear that our intensified efforts to broaden and improve our deterrent position had produced a major dividend.

Our mixed strategic force at that time included about six hundred B-52's, more than four hundred of which were equipped with the Hound Dog missile. We also had about seven hundred B-47's, nine hundred tankers, and one hundred and seventy ICBM's. That force was meshed closely with NORAD's warning system, manned-interceptor units, and missile squadrons. Our tactical forces included twenty-five hundred fighters and five hundred transports, augmented by fifteen Reserve troop carrier wings, eleven Air National Guard reconnaissance squadrons, and five communications squadrons.

Our always-alert SAC and NORAD forces, during that crisis, held a decisive margin of Strategic advantage. The National will to employ those forces was clear and unequivocal. This combination of capability and determination imposed a stern restraint against a conflict of higher intensity. Under that protection, strong United States tactical forces were able to provide a decisive margin of local advantage. Acting from our overall margin of military superiority, we successfully supported our National policy in that major crisis. . . .

In our Space program we are taking positive action to assure that, if the Soviets pose a threat in Space, we will be ready. The Soviets have already made intensive efforts in the low-orbit, near-Space area where military applications will most likely first occur. We must, therefore, begin acquiring now the military Space capabilities to defend against hostile actions that could be directed against us from Space.

With these points in mind, the Air Force has proposed efforts in Space over the ensuing years which are aimed at two objectives. First, in our move to augment terrestrial forces, we can expect programs such as Space-based communications to improve the reliability and scope of command-and-control systems. Surveillance of atmospheric weather from Space can provide information regarding cloud conditions in target and refueling areas.

Space systems may also furnish a means of active defense against ballistic missiles, and of warning that a missile attack is under way. These, and other Space systems which we are considering, could enable us to posture and employ our forces more effectively.

Our second objective in Space is to be able to determine at all times whether there is a threat present, and to deal with it if necessary. To accomplish this, we have a requirement for an improved detection and tracking system, a means of inspecting unidentified Space devices, a means of disabling hostile satellites; and, finally, a system for continually monitoring such Space phenomena as radiation and solar flares—a capability that would be essential in supporting prolonged operations.

The basic research components already in development in our Space program are the Titan III booster and the X-20A (Dyna-Soar) research reëntry vehicle. Provisions have also been made for Air Force participation in the Gemini program, and we are investigating the potential military utility of an orbital test Space station.

In advancing these efforts, we are convinced that man's skill and experience will contribute to the reliability and effectiveness of military Space systems. Experience in the Mercury flights has supported that view, and the Air Force role in the Gemini program will provide an early source of new information on man's usefulness in Space. Certainly the X-20A type of vehicle, by enabling the pilot to select a preferred landing site from the many available over a spread of thousands of miles, may have significant advantages over ballistic reëntry.

We should remember that it was the technical superiority of our forces that provided the basis for our strategic advantage in the years following World War II. For that reason we strongly advocate the continuation of an intensive technical effort to insure that we preserve the qualitative edge in weapon systems.

Looking at our efforts, past and present, all across the board, I think it is obvious that our direction toward broadening our deterrent base has been wisely selected. It can be measured by the success we have experienced in preventing a full-scale war. It has also contributed by deterring conflicts of lesser intensity. And it has protected United States interests when this latter type of conflict occurred.

In an absolute sense, our progress has been impressive. Relative to the Soviets, it has been good enough to maintain a clear though greatly reduced margin of strategic advantage.

What we accomplish or fail to accomplish, over the months and years ahead, will swing the balance either way.

The foregoing section of this chapter is taken from a speech which I delivered about fifteen months before my retirement.

Now we'll try to give away some horrid details about the speech-writing and speech-speaking business. Of course no member of the intelligent public should be deluded into the notion that the Chief of Staff of the Air Force, or even the boss of a major command, would ever find time to sit down and write his own speech. No more could the President of the United States; no more does he.

(A hundred and two years ago, Abraham Lincoln could make notes here and there on the back of an envelope, some have said, or on a rumpled piece of blue paper, others have said; and try it out, first on his secretaries, then on whoever happened to be around. That was a hundred and two years ago.)

With the wide dissemination of immediate information which goes on nowadays through every medium available—press, radio, TV, films

—there are simply too many demands on the speechifier if he happens to be in a position where he is scrutinized constantly, and where his opinions on all current matters are not only sought but angled for.

I'm afraid that there were some pretty dismal exchanges which took place in my recent past. Witness:

Public Information Officer: "Here's the speech which you will deliver, sir, next Friday in—" Chicago, Minneapolis, Edinburgh, Vienna, Montevideo.

Chief of Staff, perusing speech: "Good Lord. I don't want to say *this*."

PIO: "Well, that's the current policy. I'm afraid you've *got* to say it."

Chief of Staff, groaning: "O.K. I'll say it."

A public address can be a masterpiece of community effort and human coöperation and a general pooling of resources, a general getting-together of ideas— A masterpiece of those things, if not a masterpiece of speech-writing or speech-giving. Everybody gets in on the act. Sometimes it seems that too many people do so. Every now and then the boss man must put his foot down and keep it down.

On the whole I think I've been extremely fortunate, since I got into the echelons where the Address and the Lecture were of paramount importance. During the something-over-sixteen years when I was either commanding SAC or filling one of the higher slots at the Pentagon, the preparation of a particular speech went along somewhat in the following manner.

To begin with, my Exec was not in the speech-writing business; he merely assigned the tasks. He surveyed the occasion and the circumstances and the audience as they were projected, and then—

"Chief, it would seem that—" In Paris, Boston, Copenhagen, Seattle. "You ought to say this. I think it would be appropriate, and so does so-and-so and so-and-so and so-and-so."

Then they'd start to prepare the speech. Various sections of the staff might cook it up, or on rare occasions one individual might write the whole thing himself. Meetings would be held on the subject if necessary. But our speech-writing officer— It's his job to get the thing written, and no one cares how it's put together or by whom, as long as the proper effect is obtained.

They all sit down and judge this solemnly. Sometimes matters of a highly technical nature might be included, along with facts and figures which not even a Von Braun or a Dornberger could have at his fingertips at any given moment. These facts and figures have to be checked and double-checked. There may be historical references, quotations from the past, and details which might have strong international implications; and thus, if poorly handled, lead to international *complications*.

Whatever the subject, and no matter how many cooks have been stirring this particular bowl of broth, eventually the thing is brought to me.

I take a look at it. I say, "Well, I don't like it. Change this. Change that. Change this."

Or I look at it and say, "That's O.K."

(Actually I fear that usually I said, "Well, it's lousy. But I don't know what else to say, so I'll take it.")

There were times when the whole process was reversed. There were times when I believed sincerely that I was the only person who knew enough about what I was intending and intended to talk about, to say it properly. In that case, in a discussion with the Exec or whoever it was, I'd say, "Now, this is what I think I should say to those people in—" San Francisco, Rome, Ottawa. "Get hold of the speech-writer for me."

The speech-writer would come in. I'd tell him, "Look. Here's what I want to say out there." I'd talk with him, directly, informally, in my normal colloquial phraseology.

"Yes, sir," and he'd go away thinking hard. He'd have his notes, and he'd have the other ideas which I had put into his mind, and he'd go ahead and write the speech. Sometimes that was the very best way to do it.

It was pleasing to save lost motions before they were made.

There occurred rare and satisfactory episodes where an individual might seek me out beforehand. He'd have a very clear notion about what I should say in the speech . . . yes, there were many times when those people *knew*. They'd declare, "This is exactly what the Chief should say. I'm positive that he'll approve this." And then they'd come to me with the manuscript. Bang. The thing was as good as made.

I think that, when a man heads a large organization, this is just about the only conclusive manner in which his public utterances may be prepared. It must be give and take: the shuttling of ideas back and forth between the Chief and his subordinates, between the word-artisans and that Unfortunate who must eventually stand up there surrounded by those microphones. The interchange should be free-flowing, sincere. There can be no pretense on either side, no mouthing of words for words' own sake . . . no pointless oratory which might sound well in the uttering, and yet could cause the auditors to wonder, in the end, just what they'd been listening to.

. . . I always recall that old colored lady who was so disgusted with her grandchildren for wasting their nickels on the merry-go-round. "You got on there, and you rid and rid and rid. And where you been, when you gets off?"

Just as, in the case of future bombardment missions, we kept a list of priorities and targets—subjects which needed to be stressed. "In the next speech you make, you should say *this*." And constantly the list was being revised and brought up-to-date.

The procedure led to odd inversions every once in a while. Perhaps we'd start out with an idea around which my next address should be constructed. The thing would gain and gain and grow and grow . . . long before the speech was ever written or delivered, an entirely different treatment might be offered to the public. A lecture by the commander of SAC or the Vice Chief of Staff? Instead there appeared eventually a series of magazine articles. Or maybe it might be possible to achieve more valuable coverage through a series of syndicated pieces in newspapers. The originally intended lecture might eventually become a jam-packed journalistic story, to be translated into a dozen languages or distributed on TV screens.

Let's go back to that regular speechifying business again. I've got a script in my hand which I've approved, and now I must prepare myself. . . . I am perfectly awful at giving speeches, especially when I have to read them. When I have a chance to offer a short comment, more or less off the cuff, then I can do a lot better. (The day I retired, and when I went to the White House to be decorated by the President, I spoke in response exactly six sentences. Helen still insists that was the best speech I ever gave in my life.) Trouble is, you can't always do this. In fact, you are presented with the opportunity or the inspiration to do so very seldom.

. . . So I'd have a forty-minute discourse on which I needed to be checked off. Soon as I got the opportunity (usually at home) I sat down and read the whole thing aloud. Also I would mark it for emphasis before delivering it. That was the only way in which I could remind myself exactly *how* I should deliver the utterances.

I've been assured by experienced speakers—and have observed the same thing— Audiences don't resent a speech which is read to them if it is delivered with sufficient verve and enthusiasm. A *read* speech which is delivered in a listless monotone is one thing; a *read* speech which is presented with a keen awareness of the audience's interest and response, is quite another. Frequently those people are beguiled into the impression that the man is speaking to them directly and extemporaneously. I have heard folks argue that a speech which was read to them was *not* read to them at all. That was when the fellow up there on the rostrum was just about as good with the spoken word as Robin Hood was with a bow and arrow.

Not among my skills. Can't make it sound that way.

And the speeches have to be read for two reasons. First, if you don't read from a prepared manuscript, you are apt to say something which, from a political standpoint, should not be said at all. By that I don't mean politics in the vernacular. I mean a consideration of National policy and statesmanship. We've had all too many unhappy examples of just what should be avoided in the way of public utterance by persons

whose only refuge, in the end, was to squeal that they had been mis-
quoted.

Second (this goes especially for military people): you're very apt to
say something which you should not say from a Security standpoint.
You'll forget whom you're talking to . . . something will slip out. You
yourself will violate that Security which you have been bending every
conscious effort to achieve.

In retirement I still have to make occasional speeches. There are
certain responsibilities which must be discharged, and which you can't
shuck off even when you've peeled loose from that ape-suit for the
last time in Grade. But I'll say this: a retired man may pick and choose
a little, where sometimes he couldn't before. The obligations are not so
immediate or so intense. In rare moments I can actually find a little fun
in standing up there and saying more or less what I want to say, and
what I wanted to say all along.

5

Just like always, throughout our later Washington years, Helen was
up to her ears in every sort of Air Force wives' activity. Also in work
sponsored by the SSM & A Club. That's the Soldiers, Sailors, Marines
and Airmen's Club. It's run by a board of officers' wives from the joint
Services.

One very fine thing these girls did: they took an old house in central
Washington, at 11th and L Streets, N.W., and renovated it into a hostel for transient personnel. Later they added a fifty-five-bed annex.

Because it is our Capital, and has several bases adjacent, Washington sees thousands and thousands of young servicemen shuttling back
and forth, going through the city, either on leave or bound to take up
new duty nearby. Anyone who knows Washington knows that the
transient housing problem is pretty sticky, in any bracket of living.
There are many times when you can't get a room in a single hotel in
town, for love or money. Cheap hotels are crammed to overflowing,
as well as the big expensive ones out northwest.

So this hostel filled a dire need. The wives designed, budgeted, let
contracts; they pitched in, and they made an overnight home for those
kids. Youthful seamen and soldiers and gyrenes and airmen headed
for the place like homing pigeons. Price is one dollar per night, with
food at cost. You can buy a good dinner for forty or forty-five cents.
And free Open House cookies and coffee and such, and free dinners
on holidays. The figures are impressive: between twenty-five and
thirty thousand men were entertained in that place last year.

As to the LeMay personal housing problem— We started in at Fort
Myer, just next door to Tommy White's house. But before long it

seemed to me that we ought to be at Bolling, where so many of my staff people lived. So we trekked down across the river. Then, in 1961, after I became Chief of Staff, it was back to Fort Myer again, and Quarters 7. We returned from there to Washington when I retired, and the McConnells moved in that same weekend. *The C of S has gone. Long live the C of S.*

Janie wasn't with us all the time, nor had she been with us all the time at Offutt. She attended Brownell Hall until she was fifteen, then went East to the National Cathedral School for girls in Washington. I regret to state that Miss Janie's study habits weren't of the best. But she was up against a handicap. Like quite a few other kids, it was discovered late in the game that she was a mirror reader, so that had to be corrected. Her ability at study improved decisively.

. . . She's a tall gal, as Helen is tall. You take one look at her and you see a lot more Maitland than LeMay. She has the same dancing eyes and very similar golden-brown hair. I assert, in proud fatherly fashion, that if I had been a boy of her own age group, and had met her at some kind of doings when I was in Columbus, Ohio, I would have thought that she was quite a dish.

Janie wanted to return from National Cathedral back to Brownell Hall in Omaha, however, for her senior year. That began in 1956. I heard her telling Helen, "Don't you realize, Mother, that pretty soon —next year, in fact—I'll be going to college? And you go away to college and then, probably, you get married. . . . Don't you see? I won't ever really be *home* anymore."

So she came back to Brownell for her senior year, and graduated in 1957. It was a good year for her: she had her own little car, and a lot of friends. Our place was always running over with young people.

Janie said, "You're supposed to have *fun* during your senior year." She had fun.

It was almost a full decade since we'd lived in Germany in the old Henkell house. If I shut my eyes I could think back and see the whole thing again. That troop of Brownies, for instance. Helen had been eagerly active in the Brownie business when we lived in Arlington, while Janie was still pretty small. She'd taken the training course for Brownie leaders, and knew how to handle younguns; although I can't believe that her patience didn't get a little frayed at times. Mine would have.

Well, when we arrived at Wiesbaden and moved into that mansion, there was a third-floor playroom for children. It was about the size of a ballroom in a hotel. It had everything to bring joy to kids. Small fry of the Henkell family had left their mark through successive generations. There were mild forms of gymnasium apparatus; there was a puppet theater, and gay mural paintings all over the walls, and a stage, and even a place to show movies.

This had to be Brownie HQ, because apparently none of the other American mothers knew the first thing about Brownie operations, logistics, etc. The normal troop, as I understand it, goes maybe up to sixteen or eighteen in number. Before Helen got through she had thirty-eight or forty of the little goblins. It was comical to see her, along with a German butler and a German governess, running that aggregation. Course, I didn't witness much of it firsthand; but every now and then we'd hear the noise, and see them swarming in or out of the place.

It wasn't all play by any means. That's one of the great things about Brownies and Girl Scouts as well as Boy Scouts. The kids have to work. They do things themselves.

In Wiesbaden was a *Kinderheim*. That was sort of a sanitarium for undernourished children. (I think that actually it had been a sanitarium for tubercular people, before the war.) They would come, boys and girls alternately, for a matter of weeks . . . thinnest and spindliest kids, the ones who really were in need of dietary attention. Brownies must have projects, so the local *Kinderheim* became the local Brownie project.

They constructed toilet kits for the German children. Quite a kit, I remember: they were made out of regulation khaki material. The girls put in all the conventional items: toothbrush, comb, toothpaste, nail file, scissors, needles and thread and buttons. The boys got these too . . . they tell me practically any German gentleman can sew (there've been times when I wished that *I* could).

Also the Brownies entertained the little Jerries from the *Kinderheim* . . . gave parties for 'em. We've still got a picture somewhere around, showing the Brownies giving a party. All the German girls with their hair twisted up in buns, and funny old-fashioned dresses . . . all the American Brownies with hair in pigtails or curls. Janie with her curls. . . .

So Janie was long since retired from her *Kinderheim* career and her Brownie career, and she was now going into the college business. . . .

We said, "Where do you want to go?"

"Stephens."

That's at Columbia, Missouri, and she'd be close to us. Could drive home for holidays, and so on. Stephens has long been a girls' college very much respected in the Middle West. Elsewhere too, for all I know.

Janie was primed and set for Stephens, and duly entered. Then, suddenly, just about the time of her graduation from Brownell, the Old Man found that he wouldn't be at Offutt anymore, next fall. He'd be in Washington.

The usual feminine flap when a situation like this develops. . . .

I heard a wise old fellow say one time that if he had his way there'd be a law that all children would have to go at least a thousand miles away from their parents, to attend college. Not a bad idea on the whole, either.

But I think he had reference to a family who enjoyed the so-called normal home life. They've lived in one place through all the child's growing-up days, or maybe a couple of places at the most. The youngster wasn't constantly jerked from here to there, trying to adjust himself or herself to a new environment. In the military, that's the eternal fate which befalls.

When I think of all the moves Helen and Janie had to adjust themselves to, trudging along after me, I get kind of dizzy. And even they were more fortunate than most of the Service folks. At least they had Helen's home in Ohio for a port-in-storm while I was gone overseas. But still, in that little girl's background, there was everything from the Henkell mansion to the State Line Hotel out on the salt flats. No matter how you slice it, it's an adjustment to be made.

Therefore in policy we were compelled to disagree with the wise old man quoted above. Children who've always had to move hither and yon— It's natural for them to feel the urgency for, and the dependence on, an intimate family circle. Even during college years. They couldn't cling to a *place,* ever. They could cling only to Mom and Pop, and brothers and sisters, if any. There was always a new little girl in the next yard, and a new little boy across the street, and a new teacher whose eccentricities you'd better damn well find out about.

That explains why Janie wished to transfer from Stephens to the University of Maryland as soon as she could. We went along with her on that. We liked having her close to us. The gay young voice is a good thing to hear as it keeps echoing around the premises.

6

IT SHOULDN'T SURPRISE anyone to learn that there are bound to be essential differences of opinion between the Chiefs of Staff of the various Services, with regard to an approach which should be made toward almost any problem in the world.

For more than a century and a half the Navy was the first line of defense for our Country. It had to be, due to the weapons systems of the time, and due to our geographical position.

The John Paul Joneses became accustomed to receiving the bulk of the military budget, to having the most important spot in the councils of the land. They were used to having the most important commands.

It is not astonishing that they still fight for those same advantages.

For instance, the Navy even today has succeeded in arranging the world-wide command situation so that no Naval units serve under anyone except Naval officers.

The top man in the Pacific, where there is a joint command of the Services, was (during my term as Chief of Staff) a Naval officer: Admiral Harry D. Felt. He came up for reappointment a while back, and the JCS recommended someone else for the job. But Secretary McNamara felt that he had to appoint a Navy man.

Actually it seemed to some of the rest of us that the Yo-Heave-Ho tradition in the Pacific was a little faded and weed-grown. We now have other considerations, particularly Air. In fact, we are certain that Air has become the predominant factor.

In Europe it's arranged that we have a small fleet in the Mediterranean. But they only report in time of war. And in their normal capacity they are under a Naval commander: CINC-SOUTH. That's true all over the world.

The bulk of our Atlantic forces? CINC-LANT. Navy commander.

They are always perfectly willing to join the team in a national effort if they can be captain. Any other way, they appear uninterested, or else willing to fight it down to the last notch. When I say this, I intend no criticism of certain U. S. Navy officers whom personally I admire and respect, and with whom I have had every sort of profitable contact—all the way from working together to having a swell time socially. I refer to the Naval policy: *their creed and attitude toward the non-Naval Services.*

The bulk of us old-timers consider that there should be some specified commands, as we call them, which are completely functional—Commands which should always be commanded by *one* Service. SAC is an example. So is CINC-LANT. Assuredly the Atlantic fleet should always be under the Navy, from a functional standpoint. But in Europe, and out in the Pacific, and in some other areas where it is essential to have a joint effort—and most military operations *are* joint efforts— Then you should have joint staffs, joint commands. You should rotate the commands in peacetime throughout the Services. It must be a joint effort *in fact* as well as on paper. Everyone should be able to participate, and everyone should have a chance to command. Otherwise—

If you're going to put any single Service in a subordinate role, you're not going to produce anything good in that particular Service. When a man doesn't have a chance to get to the top, he is robbed of incentive.

I discovered that there were a surprising number of other people who felt as I did about this, both in and out of the Congress. We should assume that all the Services have equal talent, and they should have equal opportunity to bring people forward for the command. I think it's better for the Country that way.

During the Kennedy Administration, much of our future effort was parceled out to the Polaris submarines. A big point in Polaris' favor was their so-called invulnerability—the idea that the submarine couldn't be attacked when it was on station.

And also this was another example of a mixed system, and its resulting profit in diversity and flexibility.

But there are several contrary factors here. Consider the fact that the men who manage a land-based missile *know their exact position to the nth degree.* A submarine commander cannot reckon his position to such hair's-breadth accuracy. Thus a missile fired from a silo can, we must assume, achieve a target precision which Polaris is incapable of attaining.

Then there is the question of cost. Only about one-half or two-thirds of a submarine missile force can be kept on station: the rest necessarily are coming or going, or are back in port for overhaul. Such gadding about is expensive.

In the end, it would cost *seven times as much* to bring about the destructive effect on specific targets by employment of Polaris missiles, as it would to do the same job with missiles shot from silos on land.

Distinctly we went overboard on the Polaris.

The people who were interested in bringing this about, and eager to see us place increased reliance on the Polaris, just came up with the wrong assumptions. And on whether your assumptions are correct or not depends the outcome of the battle or the war. If you have bad assumptions to start with, you get a bad answer.

We must remember that it is impossible to find in peacetime exactly the wartime conditions under which you are going to fight. Certainly you need to train, train, train, out into infinity. You should, insofar as is possible, proceed in peacetime identically as you plan to proceed in war.

But, in terms of realism, it is impossible to tell exactly what the enemy *is going to do.* Very often the enemy, in a war, does something which you didn't expect him to do. Let us say that you are always going to be *surprised.* So you must have the flexibility to react to that surprise.

One Service doesn't run a war. Not any longer. It must be a team of all Services which will handle any fighting we get into. Very seldom will you see a case, now or in the future, where only the Army is involved—or only the Air Force, or only the Navy.

We should strive for bigger and better maneuvers. By that I mean inter-Service operations, joint exercises. We must practice working together as a team.

Well, we're making some headway on this. We have been doing so, ever since STRIKE-COM came along. That was our first attempt to put together the very best air-ground team which we could.

STRIKE-COM will have an overall commander of every task force which goes out to do a job. That force will have its air components and its ground components, and they will work together under that overall commander.

The more practice we can achieve in this, the more ideas we will have for improving our coördination. And the more ideas you have— correct ideas, with respect to your tactics— The more rapidly will your functional abilities improve.

But forever you must be extremely chary of the assumptions you hold. Especially when you attempt a competitive maneuver—one side against the other. If you're not careful, you'll be very apt to come up with the wrong answers.

Example:

Long before World War II began, the Navy was certain that it had the capability to do all the antisubmarine work which would be necessary. That was the reason we air people were told not to fly more than a hundred miles out from shore.

Along came the war. And the Army Air Forces found themselves involved promptly in flying antisubmarine patrols, just as the RAF did in the seas around Britain. The British Fleet Air Arm just wasn't up to the job, either.

Matter of fact, over here in the States, they even got the Civil Air Patrol into the act. Had to.

There had been an incorrect assumption to begin with.

Away back in this book we made it clear that the proponents of air power always had a battle on their hands with the Army as well as with the Navy. The Army nourished a lot of wrong assumptions too.

I would say that the main difference between the Air Force attitude and the Army attitude at this time is on the question of *who is going to do a particular job.*

We agree on a great many things. We agree that there are certain chores which have to be performed with airplanes on a battlefield, and that these are an integral part of a well-equipped Army and a well-conceived battle plan.

A good question might be: how large *is* a battlefield? Where does the battle zone end, and the non-battle zone begin?

If the commander of a ground force of whatever size is going to operate with efficiency, he has to *see*. The farther he can see, the more information he has available, and the better position he is in to make his own moves and take his own actions.

Let's start with the front line, and say that you're in a foxhole, and you need to see out a little way ahead.

You raise your noggin up out of that foxhole, and look. That doesn't cost one cent. But if you want to see a little farther than that, you raise up your noggin again, and you have binoculars clamped against your eyes. Now, this costs more: you must *buy* the binoculars.

. . . You need to see out there, three or four miles ahead, behind that hill? Then it's going to cost even more. Because you're going to have to *send* somebody out there; and that might cost a life or lives, and the Government has invested a lot of money to train those men. Omitting all human grief and suffering—if you *can*—the Government loses money on every man killed.

. . . But you wish to see what's going on, on the other side of that mountain, over beyond that range of hills? The bill is going to be considerably higher, because this time you'll send an airplane over to look. You have to buy the airplane, and you have to train the men, and it costs more to train men in airplanes than it does to train men to shoot on the ground.

And, if you desire to observe what's happening two or three or five hundred miles back in enemy territory, you'll require an even more sophisticated airplane—one which can penetrate the enemy defenses. That costs a lot more yet.

Same thing is true when we consider firepower. Our ground commander needs to deliver firepower. This starts off with rifles, hand grenades, automatic small arms; and then you get into the realm of mortars, artillery; and, finally, tactical fighters. The farther you go behind the lines, striking the enemy, the equipment becomes more sophisticated and more expensive.

This also applies away back at your own rear, with the supply function. Speed is what you need. You must deliver your supplies with speed, and the greater the speed, the greater the expense. If you only want to lug some ammunition from one foxhole to another, you can carry it on your shoulder. But, next step onward, you get into the business of trucks. And now they're using a lot of airplanes to move their stuff around.

The Army's belief is that the battlefield is *theirs*.

They theorize by drawing a line, out *in front of the front,* say X number of miles . . . and to the rear, X number of miles. They say: "This is the battlefield, and this is *ours*. We'll do all these chores in our battlefield area." And immediately they add: "We'll do our own chores *beyond* the battlefield area."

Contrary-minded, we in the Air Force say: "It's wrong. We will always find more things to do with airplanes than we have money with which to buy the airplanes. And you're going to be performing many of the same tasks. The identical reconnaissance equipment with which you are taking pictures five hundred miles behind the front lines, will serve very nicely for front-line purposes, generally speaking. The same type of fighting it is necessary to do in order to win air superiority— You could do that over the front lines as well as farther back.

"Don't you see? Can't you understand this? There'll be duplication of effort, if we have the Army doing the battlefield, and the Air Force doing the rest. We'll wind up, because of this duplication, in getting a lot less for our money."

We say: "Instead, assign the command to the Task Force Commander. Thus you'll achieve the best organization to produce the best air-ground team."

I affirm that the mere existence of STRIKE-COM today is a gigantic stride in the right direction.

7

DURING ALMOST the whole of my Pentagon experience, the subject of Space obtruded with increasing importance.

We are exploring a subject and an entity completely new to us. Might say that today in Space science we're about where we were in aeronautical science, say, in 1910.

In 1910 no one could possibly foresee the weapons systems which would evolve from the then crude flying-machine. Nor, where civilian usage was concerned, could anyone possibly foretell the vast transportation systems which would come into being. Man, in his exploration and management of this new field, brought incredible benefit to his brothers and his sons—in the same moment when he effected his capability for wholesale eradication of the human race.

There is a certain shame in recognition of the fact that in the United States the flying-machine was laughed at as an impractical instrument. Other nations really scored in the initial development of aircraft.

However, I don't believe that nowadays, in our own Country or anywhere else on the face of the globe, people are pooh-poohing our immediate attempts at probing Space. Folks are too bewildered and too impressed and too admiring.

We have fabulous media for instant communication and observation which we did not possess fifty-five years ago. A TV program is bounced off the satellite, and myriads of viewers are able to observe an astronaut whipping about at the end of his tether.

We watch people living in Space and—grim thought!—inescapably we shall, by the law of averages, watch some of them die there. There can be no decisive advances in a new field without a certain percentage of catastrophes. . . . How many unmarked burials were there along the Oregon Trail?

During preliminary phases we Americans have been extremely fortunate, thus far. It is related that the Russians have had some hard luck on the way.

But we've learned very little as yet, and we're still rattling along in a comparative 1910 condition, far as our unassailable knowledge of Space is concerned. We just don't know what we're going to find.

We will go forward, we will delve extensively, because that is the eternal reaction to the Unexplored. We must go forward, or perish. Throngs of people now alive will participate in what is probably the greatest adventure of Mankind.

No more did the voyagers of the past know what they were going to glimpse. Columbus was seeking a western route to India. Henry Hudson was searching for a northwest passage, and Sebastian Cabot for a southerly one. Continents of the Americas loomed in between, but the explorers didn't know that when they left their home ports.

In this moment we can only ponder on the surprises which await. I'm confident that we will find a great deal of useful work in Space, and I'm equally confident that there are going to be military tasks to perform up there.

What are they?

Don't know yet. We've got to get up there, to ascertain.

Journeying to the moon *per se* may turn out to be utterly unimportant. By the same token, it may be *all important*. My recommendation is that we be not behindhand in our discussion and penetration of this problem which we have elected ourselves to solve.

We should not desire to carry out any military task in Space—any task at *all* in Space—just because it is a glamorous challenge at the moment, and will be named as a tremendous achievement when we do it. Serious-minded leaders wish instead to carry out military tasks in Space only when the tasks can't be done better in any other manner. It may be cheaper to work at a specific job there, than it is to perform that same job by more conventional means in the atmosphere of the earth.

We have a lot to learn. We have *almost everything* to learn.

Our manned orbital laboratory program is of paramount importance. That's not under the NASA; it's under the Air Force. We are planning to send up a small laboratory, and we will have people working in that laboratory. The successful multi-orbital trips made by our astronauts White and McDivitt in the early summer of 1965 were a part of this scheme.

Consistently we shall be able to increase the intricacy of experiments, and thus our knowledge will grow apace. Before long we'll be able to go aloft and take the old crew off, and put a new crew aboard. We'll *supply* in Space, just as we refuel airplanes in the atmosphere.

And this is one phase of the program of landing on the moon. We must make rendezvous on the moon. I have no doubt whatsoever that we will achieve this capability, and shortly. We must gamble lives and equipment, and we'll have to accept the misery of an occasional failure; as well as clap our hands and whistle and shout and throw the ticker tape, and dish out the medals, when any successful portion of the Great Adventure has been concluded.

I repeat: No doubt whatsoever that we'll be able to go to the moon. And we'll be able to get back.

We may lose some astronauts. (Written in June, 1965. Haven't lost any yet.) There are a lot of bones in the Arctic ice too.

Right now a great many people are *seein' things at night* and in the daytime as well. A less-than-lunatic portion of the public seems to react to the whole moon notion as follows:

"The moment the Soviets land some people on the moon (if they do it before we do) they're probably going to set up some sort of death ray, and inform us, 'Join the Soviets, or else we'll kill you from the moon.'"

I did say a *less-than-lunatic* portion of the population, because such a feat and such a challenge are not beyond the realm of possibility.

But I cannot conceive of anything in the way of a military threat which could be posed from the moon which couldn't be posed down here. Judging from the sum total of our contemporary knowledge (and, I shall hazard the opinion, the Soviets' as well) it would be much more efficient and less costly to fire off ordnance *from* the surface of the earth *to* the surface of the earth. When a capacity for wholesale destruction has already been achieved, the question of the manner of delivery of firepower becomes rhetorical.

Attacking an enemy from the moon's surface is perhaps more glamorous from the Flash Gordon or comic-book or science-fiction point of view, but I can't see any professional military people going into a state of twitters over the idea. We have to keep our feet on the ground, as at the same time we apply our gaze to the planets and satellites and stars.

By-products of Space projects are many and various. New ideas, new products and new technology are literally gushing out of the satellite programs, the missile programs, the manned-Space-flight programs.

As early as June, 1962, the Denver Research Institute isolated one hundred and forty-five separate examples where industry was already manufacturing products or using processes which had originated in Space science. I don't think it requires a great deal of imagination to see how this fresh knowledge will benefit the American economy.

The field of physical materials is undergoing changes by the hour. Miniaturization has already affected such diverse applications as weather forecasting, improved packaging techniques, self-contained power supply units, and communications. Even medicine and education are undergoing significant alterations as a result of our persistent inquiry.

Let us permit ourselves the luxury of rose-colored glasses for a moment, and observe that this still fledgling science has the potential to create an order of magnitude— A fund of economic cultural and scientific wealth which might significantly change the whole fabric of society in a few short years, and change it for the better. Conceivably it might affect this world more than all the break-throughs of history— The work of men like Copernicus and Archimedes and Newton and Galileo and Darwin. Each had a share in altering the world of his day.

The alterations can be more rapid and more widespread, simply because already we possess the machinery for such acceleration and dissemination.

But—

Take off the rose-colored specs, and consider something else. Space is also a brand-new dimension in the dangers confronting Man.

This chill unpenetrated void begins only a few miles above whatever portion of the earth's surface we happen to be standing upon. It is a medium through which and from which enormously lethal machines, such as intercontinental ballistic missiles, can move even now. There is no basis for doubt that future Space developments may threaten us with even greater dangers than these. We might even be threatened, not merely with new Space-born weapons, but also with an entire unperceived region of additional possibilities for aggression.

In the United States and certain other Western nations, some politicians and editors prate about a curriculum in which the Americans and the Russians should go hand in hand, shoulder to shoulder, into those voiceless realms—pooling all their knowledge, giving a hand up over the rough spots—tied together like mountaineers with a life-rope of mutual admiration and sharing.

This picture strikes me as being a little like the paintings done by Edward Hicks, that primitive American artist who painted one "Peaceable Kingdom" after another.

It is estimated that Hicks may have done a hundred of those paintings, or more. There are different backgrounds, different groupings, and different approaches. But the personnel remains in each "Peace-

able Kingdom" essentially the same: a little child—one version or another of the Christ Child—beaming happily with an aggregation of wolves, lions, lambs, serpents and panthers. They're all picnicking together, and everybody loves everybody else.

I direct your attention to a telegram of congratulation, sent to the Vostok cosmonauts by Soviet Defense Minister Malinovsky.

He said, "Let our foes know what technology and what militance are in the possession of Soviet power."

The implications are obvious.

Our National Space Program consists of two parts. One portion—that of scientific exploration into Space—is the function of NASA, the National Aeronautics and Space Administration. The other portion—that of providing necessary military capabilities in Space—is the function of the Department of Defense.

These two sections work in coördination. Indeed, all the Space shots so far attempted have been lifted by rockets developed in the USAF program. And all the astronauts have been Service personnel.

NASA's Space operations, however, are not *intended* to develop military Space capabilities. NASA does not bear military obligation. They have all they can do to perform their own nonmilitary exercises.

There are many possibilities to concern the Air Force. Interception and inspection of unidentified or noncoöperating Space objects—the operation of weaponry, observation— A multitude of others. But the basic Space science which is revealed by NASA activity is and will continue to be useful in respect to military application.

We welcomed the opportunity to participate with NASA in the Gemini program. Certain items of military equipment which might ultimately be destined for application to unmanned Space vehicles were and are much easier to test, in their earlier phases, when we have intelligent technically trained men to facilitate these tests.

This might not necessarily be true if we were compelled to develop a manned vehicle especially for the purpose of conducting these tests. But, given a manned vehicle already achieved—such as the Gemini Man-in-Space program, which is proceeding for other reasons anyhow—we can do collateral testing.

At this time a significant threat to the United States lies in the existence of ICBM's. These missiles pass through Space en route to their targets. As a fact, in the overall flight of a ballistic missile, much the greater part of its trajectory is through Space.

Could be that the threat of offensive missiles can be dealt with only by utilizing defensive systems which involve Space orbiting or rendezvous operations. And that, in turn, raises the question of the in-flight survivability of *our own* missiles. We must know whether Space can provide to an aggressor some means of intercepting them.

To seek such defensive opportunities as may be afforded, it is logical for us to learn to operate militarily in the Space medium. There are afforded, for instance, unparalleled opportunities for observation and communications. These are extremely critical factors. Yet the threats of Space are perhaps most profound and most deadly in those aspects which cannot yet be described, for the lack of accurate data. Our military knowledge is sketchy, to say the least.

The medium of Air, in which military operations have been conducted for less than fifty years, provides a warning to him who would discern. When an airplane was first seen in flight, no man visualized wave after wave of B-29's pouring their destruction into the inferno which was Tokyo. The military implications of Space may prove to be even more hazardous and more revolutionary than those which have evolved along with the airplane.

For our own safety we must take the lead and remain in the forefront of developments. Constantly we must remind ourselves that any medium—land, sea, air *or* Space—where Man can function and operate a military system for either offensive or defensive purposes, can become a region fairly crawling with threats to our peace and security. And, if an unforeseen peril emerges in this new medium of Space, months or even years may be required to devise, develop and render operational whatever defense it is necessary to apply.

Don't forget: a military capability of defense is the product not only of technology, but also of training and operational experience.

For this reason the USAF Space Program is directed toward both the development of hardware and the training of men. I don't believe that the preservation of peace in Space can be relegated to any little black box, no matter how fascinating the buttons and the switches.

. . . This vast complex which we call America is by far the most advanced achievement which the world has ever seen. Yet it was a marvel contrived not by computers, but by men. Americans who are now living have helped to bring this achievement about, have defended it in painful wars, and still execute for our Nation the task of sharing its continued growth and security.

This should be enough to ask of one generation. Yet the same generation and the one which follows on (and the one looming, smooth-faced and youthful and resilient, behind that) must combine in a breath-taking feat: the opening of the door into Infinite Space.

These people will be required to make decisions which will affect

the future of every living soul upon this earth, and every soul who might spring into being in the years ahead.

These people will be concerned with unpredictable events. They will garner benefits and meet strange menaces. They will go where, throughout billions of years, earthly Man has never been able to venture before.

Thank God, Americans have always been professional pioneers. I think that the covered wagon will still be able to roll, and the riflemen to ride alongside.

It will be no surprise to the public to hear that I am asked about flying saucers all the time.

"Did you ever see a flying saucer, General LeMay?"

"Nope."

Here, for what they are worth, are my own comments on the subject. Naturally I am not quoting any Classified information. I am giving the straightest answers I can give.

In the modern age, reports on UFO's coming in from individuals who sighted them or who claimed to have sighted them seemed to have appeared in a rash at various times. A big contemporary flap started in 1947, when it was alleged that nine disk-shaped objects chased each other around over Western mountains.

Immediately the Air Force was asked what it thought about this business; and gradually machinery for investigation was set up, as other reports continued to pour in. Project Blue Book was instituted at Wright-Patterson Air Force Base about 1951, while I commanded SAC. Some very good people—technical people—got a complete team together to make an investigation of every one of these reports.

The bulk of them could be run down. Some natural phenomenon might usually account for those sightings which had been seen and reported, and thus explain them. However, we had a number of reports from reputable individuals (well-educated, serious-minded folks—scientists and flyers) who surely saw something.

There is no question about it: these were things which we could not tie in with any natural phenomena known to our investigators.

Many of the mysteries might be explained away as weather balloons, stars, reflected lights, all sorts of odds and ends. I don't mean to say that, in the unclosed and unexplained or unexplainable instances, those were actually flying objects. All I can say is that no natural phenomena could be found to account for them.

Let's try to add it up. Thousands or perhaps millions of readers have read the books by Charles Fort. He assembled fascinating accounts of weird events which had happened throughout history—not only UFO's, but all sorts of seemingly fantastic occurrences. I think he said that the first UFO was reported back around 3000 B.C. or somewhere in that ball park. And people have been seeing them ever since. Remember, in Biblical times, "Ezekiel saw the wheel, 'way up in the middle of the air."

Ezekiel didn't have any radar insofar as is known. But even if his flying wheel had appeared on a screen, he might have been mistaken in assuming that it was an actual UFO. Even radar can be fooled.

. . . I've forgotten exactly where this occurred, but I think it was down in the Carolinas. It's not important where it happened; but what did happen was important. . . . All sorts of strange objects appeared on a radar screen. The Air Force checked and checked . . . definitely there were no planes flying in the area. Yet these blips had shown up on the screen. . . .

Here's what actually occurred: some time later we discovered that, out at a dump, workmen were burning masses of pine needles which had been used in a filtering system. When the pine trash burned, a chemical was given off which actually would show up on radar.

The investigators did a creditable job in tracking that matter down. These were UFO's which we *could* explain.

Unfortunately there is a current belief, on the part of the public as a whole—the intelligent public—that the United States Air Force has made and is still making a deliberate effort to discount all reported sightings. Furthermore, if they couldn't actually discount a certain case by referring to hallucination, inexperience, or mass hysteria— To disregard it completely.

It is alleged also that there have been attempts, by word of mouth or by directive to newspapers from the Air Force, to hush the whole thing up. To muzzle the press.

This is an unpleasant and sometimes embittering state of affairs. What undermines the confidence of the public in the Air Force in one direction is most certainly going to assist in undermining it in another.

People who believe these rumors are clinging to a falsehood. It is absolutely untrue that any such directive was ever put forth. I never heard of it in 1947, when the first saucer accounts were published; I never heard of it after I came to command SAC; never heard of it when I was in the Pentagon. Ever since Project Blue Book began there has been a complete investigation of every report which came through channels. Many viewers were mistaken in what they saw, or what they thought they saw. Some of the viewers and reporters turned out to be the fathers of a deliberate hoax or even an attempted fraud.

It is regrettable that there were a lot of people wearing the Air Force uniform who scoffed consistently at any mention of UFO's. They knew enough about the program—or thought they knew enough—to be convinced, each in his own mind, that there wasn't anything to it. In many instances, doubtlessly, they tittered a little too gaily when a serious individual came forward and really wished to know the answer to his question. Instead of going through the matter in detail, and explaining to him, so he would have as much knowledge as the explainer did— They brushed it all off.

Certainly that smirk, in itself, would convince other folks that we were hiding something.

We must have had a bad public relations program in this particular area, to let such an impression get out.

Major Edward J. Ruppelt, former head of the United States Air Force's Project Blue Book, wrote "The Report on Unidentified Flying Objects," published in 1956. His book is interesting reading to anyone who believes in flying saucers or, I should think, anyone who doesn't.

On pages 239 and 240, Major Ruppelt reports the instance of an RB-29 which took off from Wright Field (one of the two airfields that make up Wright-Patterson Air Force Base) about eleven a.m. on 24 May, 1954, and while in flight photographed a round blob of light which several crew members declared to have been a UFO.

". . . Working with people from the photo lab at Wright-Patterson, Captain Hardin from Project Blue Book carried out one of the most complete investigations in UFO history. They checked aircraft flights, rephotographed the area from high and low altitude to see if they could pick up something on the ground that could have been reflecting light, and made a minute ground search of the area. They found absolutely nothing that could explain the round blob of light, and the incident went down as an unknown."

Many people who worked in the program were convinced that there just wasn't anything to this UFO business. Anybody who thought there was— He was the type of person who saw pink elephants.

Let me repeat: to my knowledge, there's never been any directive or effort from the top, in the Air Force, to control the public attitude toward UFO's.

And repeat again: there were some cases we could not explain. Never could.

8

I ACCUMULATED two huge, loose-leaf volumes with black covers. These were kept under lock and key, and they weighed about a ton. They were tantamount to a daily diary of my work during the C of S years. Wish I had gotten such a record together for the Vice Chief period, but we just didn't do it.

There are exactly seven hundred and twenty-eight items in those folders, ranging from Top Secret to Unclassified. By far the largest portion, naturally, are Classified documents. It is likely that the bulk of these won't be downgraded for years to come. Therefore they may not be used in this book.

Nor can a great deal of the testimony and presentation before Congressional committees be included. We'll show an example of extensive deletion in a moment. But since the material relates to the Nuclear Test Ban Treaty, let me discuss briefly the JCS attitude on that treaty.

The Administration was eager to effect such an agreement. It was maintained that there were incalculable political and diplomatic gains to be made. We in the military couldn't see these; but we have to work on the Government team, and we accepted the conclusions which came out of the State Department, that there *were* gains to be made. Reluctantly, we agreed that we would support a test ban treaty, *provided* certain safeguards were set up to reduce the risk.

One of the safeguards was that we would maintain the capability of conducting a full-scale atmospheric test program in the shortest possible time, once the decision was made to do so. We were to continue an extremely active underground test program within the restrictions of the treaty, so that we might accumulate as much as we could in additional knowledge on atomic subjects. We would maintain a laboratory, completely staffed, so that—in case the treaty blew up on us —we could immediately get into a full-scale program. There were other conditions which I don't recall. But, by and large, all of these conditions have been met. The Joint Chiefs reviewed this subject from time to time, and were satisfied that the safeguards are there.

We have been asked frequently, however, if it's possible for the Russians to sneak ahead of us, even with these safeguards.

There's a difference of opinion on this. Some people would say No —they can't do it without our knowledge.

I don't believe this. I think it's possible.

We are aware that the Russians are conducting a vigorous underground test program. Matter of fact, one of their test shots vented into the atmosphere and they actually violated the treaty, and the fallout *did* come down beyond the borders of the country. Newspapers reported that the State Department sent a note on this subject, but I've never seen anything as to what the answer to the note was. Now, we don't *know* whether this was a deliberate ignoring of the treaty or whether it was an accident. But in any case, they are conducting an ardent program.

Perhaps they're getting more out of it than we are out of ours. We really don't know.

An impression was given that I was the sole member of the JCS to oppose the nuclear test ban treaty. Untrue. I think the reason may well have been that I went into more detail in outlining military disadvantages of the treaty than did other members. But we all concurred in a formal agreement in favor of the treaty.

Somebody asked me the other day, "Well, in the light of three years' experience, what do you think of the treaty now?" Answer is: it's probably still too early to tell. First of all, I think the safeguards are being taken care of. But there is still a lot we don't know, in the way of Intelligence.

I mentioned the shot that vented. The Russians may be conducting a more vigorous program than we are, and may be getting a little ahead of us.

On the other hand, I have seen none of those tremendous political and diplomatic gains which were supposed to be forthcoming. Perhaps it's too early for them to materialize. But I haven't seen them.

We quote from *Military Aspects and Implications of Nuclear Test Ban Proposals and Related Matters. Part 2, published in 1964.* This paper-bound book, running in page numbers from 541 to 996, relates as much of the "Hearings Before the Preparedness Investigating Subcommittee of the Committee on Armed Services, United States Senate" as might be put into print.

We'll make this in small type; it won't take up so much room.

Senator JACKSON. . . . What disturbs me, General LeMay, is that in the high-yield area the Soviets appear to have a lead, as you have indicated. (Deleted.) the Soviets are concentrating on high-yield weapons. We are concentrating on lower yield weapons with many different delivery systems. Looking ahead, however, we are concentrating primarily on ballistic missile delivery systems. Where is this going to leave us from a strategic standpoint?

General LeMAY. Well, the Air Force has always been interested in higher yield weapons, in the earlier days because of the economy of fissionable material. You could get more megatonnage out of the big explosions than you could the smaller ones. It was more costly to build the smaller weapons.

Lately, we have been interested in higher yield weapons (deleted). I think that we probably can get by with what we can do in the high-yield field now, although I personally would like to go up to 100 megatons or more, or have the capability of getting there rapidly.

This we don't have, but the Atomic Energy Commission people tell me that we can have a 50-megaton bomb without further testing (deleted).

Senator Jackson.	(Deleted.)
General LeMay.	(Deleted.)
Senator Jackson.	(Deleted.)
General LeMay.	(Deleted.)

Senator Jackson.	(Deleted.)
General LeMay.	(Deleted.)
Colonel Moss.	(Deleted.)
Senator Jackson.	(Deleted.)
General LeMay.	(Deleted.)
Senator Jackson.	(Deleted.)
General LeMay.	(Deleted.)
Senator Jackson.	(Deleted.)
General LeMay.	(Deleted.)
Senator Jackson.	(Deleted.)
General LeMay.	(Deleted.)
Senator Jackson.	(Deleted.)
General LeMay.	(Deleted.)
Senator Jackson.	(Deleted.)
General LeMay.	(Deleted.)
Senator Jackson.	(Deleted.)
General LeMay.	(Deleted.)
Senator Jackson.	(Deleted.)
General LeMay.	(Deleted.)
Senator Jackson.	(Deleted.)
General LeMay.	(Deleted.)
Senator Jackson.	(Deleted.)
General LeMay.	(Deleted.)
Senator Jackson.	(Deleted.)
General LeMay.	(Deleted.)
Senator Jackson.	(Deleted.)
General LeMay.	(Deleted.)
Senator Jackson.	(Deleted.)
Senator Stennis.	(Deleted.)

I don't think any reader would consider this to be very informative.

Sometimes people are curious to know just how far we have to go in trying to accumulate the necessary figures and other statistics to support our testimony.

The committees have always been very lenient in this respect, at least within my own experience. Congress doesn't expect you to know everything. I try only to commit gross figures to memory, never detailed figures. It's just too involved, and you might go wrong.

So it's perfectly orthodox for you to look in your little book or your big book, to find the information which you want. And you carry great stacks of material along with you.

(Actually you can't lug every bit of information that's pertinent to the Air Force, on every subject affecting the Air Force or *affected by* the Air Force.)

It pays also to arrange for some backing in the shape of a few experts who have intricate knowledge of the field in which you're testifying. It's perfectly all right for you to turn around to them, and ask for the answer. Then they look in their notes, and come up with the proper dope.

Congress doesn't care where the answer comes from, so long as they get the correct information.

It is permissible, then, to say, "Well, I'll ask my expert in this field." Or to say, "Let me refer to my notes," and then come out with the answer. That's O.K.

Also at times you'll have to admit frankly, "I don't know." But you don't want to say that too often, or somebody's liable to think that you don't know very much about your business.

Long long hours of homework will pay off when you sit there in that chair—testifying, presenting, answering questions. You need to retain those gross figures in your mind, and you must have the programs outlined. The committees have always seemed very tolerant. Again, they know that you can't *know everything.*

. . . Let's say that we are going up there for a posture hearing. The Military Affairs Committee needs to know just how we stand; they want an overall picture of what we're doing, and how we're going about it, and what the state of the forces actually may be. They're demanding, "Give us a picture of what you've got."

I had to be generally familiar with all the programs . . . had to be briefed on them, long before going over to The Hill. It was necessary to review and rehearse, elaborately.

I can't possibly estimate how many times I've gone before those committees. It would be in the dozens of times, or probably even in the scores of times. It was work, it was often very exhausting work. I think that some of the toughest missions I've ever flown, I flew right there in the committee rooms, chair-borne as they come.

And the greatest *satisfaction* in my entire life was afforded when I knew that the Congress backed me up by a top-heavy vote. The reader was told about that in the first chapter. But I mention the circumstance again—now—because it is a matter of pride which I don't wish to relinquish and never shall relinquish.

Congress represents the people. The people are the Nation.

I knew that my Nation was behind me. Our Awards & Decorations folks don't have any special gong for that sort of feeling, but none is needed.

Always I found it a pleasure to work with Congress. They were trying to do the same thing I was trying to do: produce the best defense for the Country.

There's one thing the public has had a hard time in recognizing. That is the fact that I am in complete agreement with the need for an effective ballistic missile force as an important element of our deterrent posture.

A secure ICBM system, *in concert with other survivable strategic forces,* would provide the strongest possible influence on the USSR to refrain from any attack on population centers of the United States. I made this clear in an expanded statement submitted for the House Committee record.

But remember: the employment of ballistic missiles places warfare at its highest and most indiscriminate level. We cannot know the precise nature of the next war until the shooting starts. No forecast could be completely accurate.

In my judgment, a strategic force posture which placed *sole or principal* reliance on ballistic missiles would deny to our future leadership the ability to respond in a flexible manner to a wide range of minor provocations.

For instance, let us assume that new peripheral aggressions are going to be employed in the attempt of Communism to dominate the world. It would be incredible for the United States to employ a total ballistic missile response in such cases.

In the opposite fashion, a strategic force composed of *both* ballistic missiles *and* manned aircraft would give us the capability to retain the initiative at all levels of confrontation or conflict. It would decrease the danger of enemy miscalculation. We could then control or contest, in any conceivable predicament, without the risk of a missile exchange and the inevitable wiping out of enormous segments of our population.

I do not think that I'm overly optimistic when I say that eventually we will get—or continue—the mixed force which we want and need. At the moment we still have a mixed force. Our B-47's aren't all phased out, although they will be soon. B-52's can suffice for another five years at least. The B-58's, although fewer in numbers, are still far from obsolescent.

A couple of years ago, when he was still commanding SAC, Tommy Power said to General Bernard Schriever, "This is the first time in the history of the USAF that we have not had some type of bomber in production. Why doesn't the Systems Command, with so many advanced aircraft concepts under consideration, light on one bomber and build it?"

General Schriever turned aside for his reply. "General Power left the impression that *I* am doing all the considering, and *I* ought to light on something. He knows where the lighting is done."

As *Air Force Magazine* commented, "General Schriever's remark was assumed to refer to the Defense Department."

There used to be a saying on the fourth floor of the Pentagon (Air Force floor) that a plane or a plan could *take off* on the fourth floor, but would get shot down on the third (that's the Department of Defense).

That sounds as if the opinions are all unanimous, down there on the third. They're not, by any means.

First off, those in the Air Force and all of the others who are really working on the problem outside the Air Force— I'm talking about the scientific advisory board and folks of that sort— These came up with the answer that we needed a mixed force.

Then some men on the third floor began adhering to the same opinion. Naturally I wasn't able to quiz each individual; but *the bulk* of folks with whom we've had contact, down there in Defense, have definitely been for the mixed force.

Some were against it, to start with. Many of them have now been won over to the mixed force concept. So far this does not include Secretary McNamara, who of course has final responsibility and authority in the Defense Department.

Here's a reason for optimism on this point:

Congress, and throngs of people in the Department of Defense, and (I'm convinced) a preponderance of people all over our Country, want a mixed force. With the checks and balances which exist in our Government, just a few men—regardless of whether they head the Administration or not—cannot stop what the bulk of the public wants. The majority of our citizens prefer a mixed force, and I think that we'll get it eventually.

Of course, a delay could conceivably be disastrous. This is one of my main worries.

In any future conflict we will need air power which can respond quickly to a wide variety of unforeseen and rapidly changing conditions. Ballistic missiles were designed to be and to remain a single shot. They are weapons which, once fired, are committed irrevocably.

We have had repeated demonstrations of the valuable effect which can be achieved when in possession of a mixed force. Such evidence came clearly into being during the Lebanese and Cuban incidents. In moving airplanes, dispersing them here and there, it became obvious that we were *getting ready*.

Such activity is more than a gesture. It is an actual prevention of conflict. If an incipient enemy starts shoving you around, and you show strength, and in this show of strength he observes that you've *got the strength*— He backs off.

The manned element of a mixed force would have the capability to react immediately to redirection. They could exploit fleeting advantages, and thus execute a broad range of missions.

Observe also how a mixed force will complicate defensive problems for any enemy of the United States. The targets are widely scattered, simultaneously on land and in the air. A foe would have to dilute and divide his defensive effort.

Offer Cuba as an example once more. Had we possessed only ballistic missile systems at that time, there would have been two choices: to shoot, or not to shoot. But our manned aircraft system permitted us to provide visible evidence of resolve and determination. The other side observed that we could have brought about an early termination of hostilities at the lowest practicable level of conflict.

Shall we assume that ten years have passed, and it is now 1975, and we have achieved the perfect missile? (Considerable guesswork here: our missile reliability at the moment is based on relatively small statistical samples. We haven't had any substantial opportunity to test the force in its operational environment.)

Go ahead. In imagination, we have the perfect missile. It's perfect in that you never have a mechanical failure. It has such fantastic accuracy that every time you press the button you automatically destroy a target.

(I don't think we're ever going to get this; but we'll assume that it comes to pass.)

I still insist that you're in a *muscle-bound position*. You are endangering the defense of the Country by depending on this weapon system *alone*. You have no flexibility. You have only those two choices. You're off the button and we are at peace; or you're on the button, and we are at war.

What I have been looking for all along is the most efficient method of carrying out the tasks which confront us. And all of our studies to date, all of our experiences to date, indicate the most efficient way to do this. It is with a mixture of manned and unmanned systems.

Our primary purpose in maintaining a force *in being* is to prevent a war. With that flexibility which you possess in the manned system, you have a greater opportunity to prevent war than you have with a sole reliance on any missile system. In that latter condition you either shoot off the long-range Roman candle or you don't.

I've said this before, and now I say it again and always will:

We have quite a few devices and procedures nowadays which seem to dwarf their human creators. As missiles and electronics have progressed, so too has it become increasingly popular to make derisive comments about humble mankind's abilities. Cynics have declared that silo-sitting will replace flying—that all our voyages into deep Space will be led by unmanned satellites. Those fellows seem to believe that the computer thinks quicker and deeper than any mortal.

Last year or the year before, there was quite a stunt at one of our colleges, when a computer picked out just the right pair of students who should get married. So they got married. Perfectly sound . . . cards had been fed into a computer, and the boys were told which girls they should call up and bring to the party, and the girls were told which boys they should agree to go with. And one of those computer-selected blind dates led actually to a marriage.

Big day for their side.

Seems to me that I've observed a great many happy marriages resulting when boys picked out girls and girls picked out boys, and no computer ever got into the act. Didn't people have dates and get married, before there were any computers? Looks like.

Years ago in the Army Air Forces they used to have a lot of wise-cracks. They'd say, "Commission the Norden bombsight, not the bombardier." They'd say, "Promote the computing gunsight. Give the stripes to him—not to the air gunner." They'd say, "Don't congratulate the pilot for bringing his airplane home. Congratulate George, the autopilot. *Let George do it.*"

And George did it? Stuff and nonsense. Aerial victory in World War II was won by men—men who had the daring and the intelligence to master the machines, and to improve upon the procedures, and thus achieve a winning combination.

Nothing has changed. The conquest of Space will be won by men with wings.

I repeat: won by *men.*

I shall say this with full conviction until someone convinces me that the airplane invented the Wright brothers.

In our own LeMay household, when it came to courtship and romance, no computers were involved.

I suppose that every mother of a daughter who ever lived would say to her friends, "Who's that? . . . Why, he sounds very nice. . . . What did you say the young man's name was? . . . Well, why don't you bring him around?"

Any mother who was worth her salt.

Women are born matchmakers, anyway, or *would-be* matchmakers.

By this, I don't mean that Miss Janie LeMay sat in a corner at every ball when she should have been sweeping in the waltz on a wave of music. She wasn't allowed to sit still very long, any time. When she transferred to the University of Maryland from Stephens, she was going into a coeducational school for the first time in her life. And she had a very good time up there at the university, a very good time indeed.

But still, Helen was always in the market for new young men. Thus it was that, when Ollie Neiss and his wife started talking about a youthful pediatrician—Army type, named Jim Lodge—Helen said, "Let's have him come around." (Ollie Neiss . . . Major-General Oliver K. Neiss, Surgeon General of the Air Force, who is now retired.)

Jim Lodge called Janie in due course, after the Neisses gave him her telephone number. So that introduction was made over the phone. But I guess you'd still have to call it a blind date.

Girls are funny. If I'd heard about a handsome gifted pediatrician, and I was a girl, and he called me up and asked me for a date, I think I'd be enthusiastic as all hell.

Know what Janie said? She said, "Oh, I guess he's called two or three times. And I don't know . . . he must be an awful dope. Why can't he get his own dates?" She didn't care how enthusiastic Ollie Neiss was about him. Didn't mean a thing.

Well, I don't pretend to understand girls. Never have.

Along about that time, a friend of ours lent us his Potomac yacht for a month. Helen was delighted, although we didn't get to do much voyaging on the boat. But one night it looked like I'd be free for dinner, so we invited General and Mrs. Neiss; and we invited the as-yet-unseen Jim Lodge, to cruise on the Potomac and have dinner.

Better let Helen tell this one.

". . . Janie wasn't too enthusiastic about going out with him, any-way, because she thought this was just another blind date, you see. She came tripping down the stairs on this fatal night. She was ready dressed for the yachting trip; and just about the time she got on the stair landing, she looked down and saw Jim drive up to the outside porch. Here he was, in a beautiful dark-blue Jaguar. She thought, 'Boy—' and then again—'He must be an awful dope, if he can't get his own dates.'

"I guess, as a matter of fact, that's what women usually think about a blind date. Well, then Jim got out, and I remember how he looked that night. Just like something out of *Esquire*. He had on a black turtle-necked sweater and black pants, and the whitest shoes you ever saw. And you know— This black curly hair of his, and blue eyes, and that ready grin on his face. And you know what? Janie wanted to run right back upstairs, and dress all over again. But it was too late by that time."

. . . LeMay to Helen (after Jim and Janie were engaged or married, or somewhere along the line there): "You know, you're always talking about Janie first seeing Jim outside, down in the driveway. Seems like I remember a couple of girls out at Ann Arbor, standing at an upstairs window, and looking out when a couple of lieutenants came on a blind date."

Helen: "Uh-huh. And I said, 'I think I'll take the fat one.'"

LeMay: "You don't need to rub it in."

Helen: "I don't seem to remember anything about your gorgeous little Jaguar."

LeMay: "Chevrolet."

Helen: "A little less of the sporty type, shall we say?"

LeMay: "You mean me, or the car?"

Helen: "The car, of course."

LeMay (stubbornly): "It was a *damn good* Chevrolet."

9

AT THE TIME the announcement was first made in the press (February, 1965) that this book would be forthcoming, a few columnists seemed to know a lot more about the book than I did. The manuscript was by no means complete; yet those commentators, or whatever you call them, seemed possessed of full information. They announced that "glum cigar-chewing General LeMay" was going to blast Secretary McNamara right off the face of the earth. And probably President Johnson too.

I had no intention then of triggering such a holocaust, either by arson or bombardment. Nor do I intend to do so now.

It shall suffice to say that I did not hold many of the same views held by Secretary McNamara with regard to our military posture, and do not agree with many of the acts or attitudes of the Administration.

In the Pentagon I carried out every order issued to me to the best of my ability. There never occurred an instance in which I rebelled. I am a professional soldier and airman, and professional soldiers and airmen obey orders.

At the same time, there was another obligation inherent in the job. It was required that I give my candid opinion to the Congress when asked to do so. This I did. I gave my candid opinion to the Secretary of Defense, or to the President himself—all *three* Presidents under whom I served during those years. Any time they asked me for a straight answer, they got it.

Sometimes my answers did not happen to coincide with the opinions held by the Administration. Often, in such cases, various writers who turned out to be foes of the Air Force, or personal detractors of LeMay, would contrive many paragraphs in which I was accused of bearding Mr. McNamara in his lair, or going all-out to scuttle the White House policies in order to achieve, perhaps, personal vainglory; or even to put myself into candidacy as a future military dictator.

The military will never take over the Government in the United States. Not unless we lose a war. Then the *foreign* military will take over.

Civilian control is part and parcel of our Democratic system. The only nations without civilian control of the military have been notorious dictatorships. Civilian control is essential to a Democracy.

At this point I should like to bring to the attention of the reader an editorial written by Mr. Claude Witze, senior editor of *Air Force/Space Digest*, which appeared in the May, 1964, issue of that magazine.

"Gen. Curtis E. LeMay believes that if war starts he has failed in his mission as Chief of Staff, United States Air Force. And he is convinced 'you have a better chance of preventing a war happening with manned systems than you do with unmanned systems.'

"General LeMay has at no time held a press conference, released previously classified information, or made any kind of public statement in support of his opinion that did not go through DOD clearance. He has, as the law requires, appeared on Capitol Hill to answer questions from Congressional committees. It has been before these committees, and on no other platform, that he has explained his viewpoint, and admitted, usually under questioning, that he disagrees—to a certain extent—with his civilian superiors.

"Here at mid-April the exigencies of headline-making appear to have put the Chief of Staff in a position he does not want or deserve. His term of office extended for a single year by President Kennedy, has been extended again for less than a year by President Johnson. The date for his severance now is set for next February, which will be early in the new Administration to be chosen by the voters in November.

"The release at this moment of his testimony of last February before the House Subcommittee on Defense Appropriations is entirely routine. It had been anticipated, and the contents of that testimony have been known to the Executive branch of the government ever since the General answered the questions. The content was known to President Johnson and Secretary McNamara when General LeMay's term was extended, and long before it was seen by the press and public. The White House, in fact, knows more than the public because it has access to all the classified material deleted from the released transcript.

"What controversy has resulted came not from the General's statements on the Hill, but from Mr. McNamara's sudden release of previously restricted intelligence estimates. General LeMay holds that the margin of our military superiority over Russia is narrowing. The Secretary says it is increasing. What probably is more important is that the General is not questioning our superiority today. He is questioning the relative status a decade from now.

"There is a good deal of material in the General's released testimony that has been inadequately covered in the rush of the news in this politically charged atmosphere. Careful reading discloses that he did not advocate a hundred-megaton bomb merely for the sake of having a bigger bomb. General LeMay argued that war is full of surprises; he never has seen a battle without them. He says it could be that one of these surprises would require a big bomb. If the enemy has it and we do not, a war could be lost, or one occur that could have been avoided."

Inevitably during the last month or so of my service, folks were asking a lot of questions. Everybody was guessing how I felt about retirement. There was some mention in the newspapers as well; a few editorials were brought to my attention. The idea seemed to be that everyone thought that I would be furious at what was happening.

I wasn't.

Even some of the people closest to me didn't understand how I felt about the matter in advance or at the time or—in some cases—afterward. . . . Prevailing notion seemed to be that I was comparatively young, and still energetic in body and in mind, and that my experience was the most preponderant of any individual who had ever served in this field. Supposedly I would be consumed with rage and bitterness because I was going out of the job.

Here's the way my reasoning went:

We've had for many years a basic law requiring colonels and brigadier-generals to retire after thirty years' service. Major-generals retire at thirty-five years' service or after five years in grade—whichever is the longest. And major-general is the highest permanent rank we have, except by special act of Congress.

Therefore, all of us have always expected to retire after thirty or thirty-five years' service.

It so happens that some people don't do this. Repeat: the law says five years in grade. Well, in the Army and the Navy particularly, officers aren't apt to be promoted to the rank of brigadier-general or rear-admiral until rather late in their careers—after about twenty-eight or twenty-nine years' service, usually. Then, instead of retiring at thirty years as brigadier-general or rear-admiral, they serve five years in grade. That would give them about thirty-three or thirty-four years' service. Then, before they are retired after *that* five-year span, they are promoted once more. And they serve five extra years in that advanced grade before actually retiring at last.

Therefore we find people in both the Army and Navy serving anywhere from thirty-seven to forty years. That is normal retirement in those branches.

In the Air Force, those who get into the upper brackets have been permanent major-generals for years. So, customarily, they have been retiring after thirty-five years. But, in the same law, the Secretary of Defense has the authority to keep some people on beyond this thirty-five-year point—at least up until they're sixty-two years of age . . .

some small percentage, if he wishes to. This has seldom been done with Air Force personnel. It's been the policy for everybody to retire at thirty-five years.

Only two exceptions: Nate Twining stayed beyond thirty-five years, to finish his tour as Chairman of the JCS. Tommy White stayed a little beyond thirty-five years, in order to finish his tour as Chief of Staff. No one else in my recollection ever served more than thirty-five years.

I think that's a pretty good rule. There are a lot of people my age, of course (hope I'm one of 'em) who are still vigorous enough to go on and do a great deal of work—who still have ambition, and wish to accomplish something valuable. This despite any Service-incurred disabilities.

But we can point to some other old fogies who are definitely slowed down by the mere aging process, in thought and in deed, and really need to retire.

How is the law going to differentiate? The law says something, and it's got to stick. And aside from any physical failings, the majority of professionals feel that they are still pretty good, even when they're shoving the gray age of sixty.

It's a natural attitude of mind. However, it's one which changes with the generations.

I remember going to a retirement ceremony when I was a very-very second-lieutenant. I remember looking at that old fud up there, and saying, "What on earth has he stuck around so long for? He should have retired years ago."

Nowadays, in attending the same sort of ceremonies, I look at the subject on display, and think, "Good heavens. What's this fine young fellow retiring so early for?"

. . . Certainly there are exceptions; but how are you going to pick the exceptions and be fair, without engendering hard feelings on the part of the others?

There's another angle too. We have an enormous hump of people in the establishment who came into the Army Air Forces during World War II. We've been trying desperately to weed that hump down. For the simple reason that if we *don't*, half the Air Force will be leaving their jobs all at once, and that will happen within a four-year period. A huge mass of them will go out into civilian life. We've all been trying to smooth off this hump as the work went along, to prevent a damaging breakdown and dislocation when the thirty-year retirement time came for all.

Another thing: there's a multitude of people who are eligible for promotion to general officer. They are good people, they've worked hard. They've earned promotions which cannot be given them simply because *there aren't any vacancies*. I have a lot of friends in that position and condition, and it has galled me to see them stuck there.

Now, as to my own retirement date: I'd been a general officer for twenty-one and a half years, and a four-star general since 1951. That's a mighty long time. Fortunately we had a number of people well trained, steeped in experience, qualified in every way for the job of Chief of Staff. It was just a question of who would be appointed.

I think there's always a demand for a new approach and new ideas. New people bring these in with them.

Both the present (summer, 1965) Air Chief of Staff and the Vice Chief of Staff are men I've known a long time. I've watched them, worked with them, had them work for me. They are aware that they have my unqualified endorsement, my respect and good wishes.

Mac McConnell I met first when he was with the 20th Pursuit Group, and that's over thirty years ago. I had him working for me in SAC as a field commander, and later made him my Director of Plans at Offutt, where he served in that capacity for four years. He was Tommy Power's deputy commander of SAC, after I went to the Pentagon.

As for Butch Blanchard, now Vice Chief of Staff— I've mentioned him frequently in this book. He worked for me when I was out in the Marianas, worked for me at Offutt. I grew to trust and depend on Butch, and the Nation can well do the same.

We have a very fine system of training replacements for their first military duty.

I wonder if we'll ever get around to setting up a training deal for wives? Thus far we've never done so. There's no program for training wives.

I might wish that every future Chief of Staff would possess a wife like Helen, but that's just asking too much. I never saw another woman dig into the job all along, the way she has.

She did that back when we were second lieutenants, even though she complained about holding the flashlight when I was trying to do that celestial navigation during our honeymoon on the Hawaiian shore. Air Corps and the Army Air Forces and the United States Air Force became her life, just as much as they became mine. She gave every ounce of her zeal and energy and humanity, and she had quite a lot to give. I'm not talking this way just because Helen is my wife. I'm doing it because she's *Helen*.

Funny thing: I remember something I said at the time we were married. I was very serious, and looking into the future, and I explained to her all about how I'd been in the Air Corps as a bachelor for five years. There were things which she must understand. She must understand that I was dedicated completely to the Air Corps.

"There'll be plenty of times," I warned her, "when the Army is going to interfere with our married life. You've got to realize that in advance, and make up your mind to accept it. The Army will have to come *first*. You'll come second."

She didn't howl too loud. She accepted this.

Now for the funny thing. Through all the years, there have been more times when the Air Force came *first* with Helen, and I came *second*, than ever occurred the other way around.

I've suffered about this, and I've complained. Had to. I felt like Tail-End Charlie. Helen and the Air Force were out somewhere ahead, and they were there together. I came trotting along behind.

10

THERE WERE some folks I had to see and some things I had to look after, out in California. That was how I came to be in the San Francisco area.

My plane was sitting on the ground at Hamilton Air Force Base, ready to fly back to Washington; but the crew wouldn't show up for a couple of hours. Even my aide was gone on an errand. And the Air Force business hadn't taken as long as I'd thought it would take. Here I was, all alone (astonishing) with time on my hands.

So I had the driver run me over to Emeryville, across the bay from San Rafael. I got out of the car and just strolled around . . . went and looked. Yep, our old apartment building was still there: the tenement type, into which we first moved when we arrived from Montana.

Went down to the ball park. One of the houses we'd lived in was right beside the ball park; but that park was no more, and the house was no more. I looked for the race track where we children used to play. Gone.

The same schoolhouse was still standing, and a lot of other buildings which I recognized . . . went down to the fire house. There were several old men and a couple of younger ones sitting out in front. Maybe they were a bit surprised when a four-star general in full uniform came wandering over to chat with them.

It had been almost fifty years since we LeMays were residents of Emeryville. Fifty years is a lot more than a minute, except to geologists and paleontologists.

"Afternoon, General."

"Good afternoon."

"Looking for somebody. Can we help you?"

"Oh, I was just strolling. Used to live here when I was a boy."

"You did, huh? What's your name?"

I told them, and they shook their heads; they didn't remember any

LeMays. Well, we weren't exactly what you'd call a prominent family in the community.

But one of the white-haired men began to speak with considerable interest, as elder folks do when you start recalling the past. It turned out that he was still a fireman; and he had been a fireman fifty years ago, when he wasn't much more than a boy.

. . . We went on, discussing Emeryville. They remembered people whom I'd long since forgotten . . . the woman doctor. She had an office right over there across the street. I asked about her. Of course they remembered: the woman's husband was a doctor too. And she was the one who took care of Lloyd when he came down with lockjaw, after that bad wound received in falling among the broken glass.

They all remembered, even the men who were about my age. They could recall Lincoln Beachy soaring overhead in his aer-o-plane. They remembered the day Beachy went down in the bay.

I said, "I've got to get along now. Certainly enjoyed talking with you."

"We enjoyed it too, General. Whereabouts are you stationed? Over at Hamilton?"

"No," I said, "I'm stationed in Washington now."

"Well, take it easy."

"Goodbye." I went away through sunshine and shade of the street.

Some sparrows fluttered down. I looked at the sparrows speculatively, but there wasn't any old fat tomcat around. Anyway, I didn't have a .22 with me. Or any BB caps.

11

IF THERE'S going to be any change for the better in this world, you have to provide it by doing something.

Generally speaking, I'd like to see a more aggressive attitude on the part of the United States. That doesn't mean launching an immediate preventive war . . . although some people believe it to be poor policy to let the enemy know that you will *not* start a preventive war. It may be to your advantage to let them be aware that there exists this possibility. The enemy may take the hint.

China desires to accelerate the world revolution. The Soviets are for slowing down. But neither of them has said, "Let's abandon our goal of world domination."

That is a thing which the majority of free men cannot understand. A free man declares, most unrealistically, "Well, *we* are happy with our form of government *here*. If *they* wish to have some other form of government, why— Let them have it."

That's the genial generous philosophy of the free soul. In addition, he assumes that everybody else should feel the same way. He assumes further that they *will* feel the same way and do the same thing, if given half a chance. Or maybe even if awarded only a pleasant smile and a grasp of the hand.

When any speaker gets up and says, literally or in essence, "I would say to the people—and to the leaders—of the Communist countries, to the Soviet Union, to the nations of Eastern Europe, and Southeast Asia, 'We extend to you our invitation: come now, let us reason together,'" I'm afraid that such remarks are appreciated by home consumers only.

Communists don't think in those terms. They don't think, "We are happy with Communism—" those who *are* happy with it; a lot of them aren't; they've had it stuffed down their throats.

Those who are ardent in embracing the Communist ideal don't say, "Observe. We are happy with our form of government. Let others, in the Capitalistic world, have whatever they wish."

What they do say and what they have demonstrated repeatedly is: "*You* have to accept Communism. *We* are going to make you take it." That is the basic doctrine of the Communists. They have been reiterating this ever since the day of Karl Marx.

Many a dreamer dreams a dream which is founded on a basic falsehood. And no dream is of value when it comes into its evanescent being in such a manner. Your Parlor Pink, your Self-Appointed Crusader, grinds a column out of his typewriter—one in which he proves glibly that there is little to choose from in comparison of the two ideologies now opposing each other on this planet. A benign minister prays a prayer in which he ignores every assembled fact of history. Another person stands up on a platform and says, "Today, in both the open world of freedom and the curtained world of Communism, men and their families are enjoying the comfort and contentment of a life none have known before."

If this were true, there would be no reason for assembling and maintaining an armed force capable of resisting the Communist threat.

". . . For men know today, as they have not been able to know before, that war serves no necessary end for any nation on earth."

Conceivably war might serve a necessary end if it prevented our enemies from moving into the White House, the Capitol and the Supreme Court building, and kept Soviet firing squads from rat-tat-tatting in every city and hamlet of the United States. That's our reason for maintaining an Army, a Navy and an Air Force. We can't just ignore Communism and expect it to go away like a child's Halloween ghost. We have to be ready to take positive action against it.

. . . Native annalists may look sadly back from the future on that period when we had the atomic bomb and the Russians didn't. Or when the Russians had acquired (through connivance and treachery of Westerners with warped minds) the atomic bomb—and yet still didn't have any stockpile of the weapons. That was the era when we might have destroyed Russia completely and not even skinned our elbows in doing it. We could have pushed them back within their own borders, and freed some other smaller nations from a hideous infliction.

China has The Bomb. They are now going to be able to manufacture an arsenal of bombs. They evince extreme hostility. They avow an intention to fasten basic Communism upon the rest of the world, and they have millions and millions of people to implement such a program.

Some time in the future—twenty-five, fifty, seventy-five years hence— What will the situation be like then? By that time the Chinese will have the capability of delivery too.

That's the reason some schools of thinking don't rule out a destruction of the Chinese military potential before the situation grows worse than it is today. It's bad enough now.

It is not for a professional military man to select the course which we follow. That is a decision which the Government must make. It is a decision which in a Democracy should be sacred to the people of the Nation itself, through the act of their duly-elected and delegated officials.

My creed is that you don't get anything for nothing. If you want your freedom it may be necessary to fight for it some time. We should keep ready and able—"Rugged but Right." Strong—stronger than anybody else, so that we won't *need* to fight for our freedom. If you can destroy him who would attack you, he will not attack.

We can do this even now, even when our affirmed enemies have gone as far as they have. In this moment we still have the strength.

Let me cite one of the main differences between my way of thinking, and the notions held by certain theoretical types who have *all* the answers to our defense problems. They open their briefcases, and get out the graphs. . . . "Well, you need only X amount to do this. You need only a thousand missiles. You don't require any air defense . . . maintain the capability of fighting small wars, and that is all. That's enough. It will deter our enemies."

They sit with pencil and paper and all their charts spread before them, and total up what the enemy has, and what we have. "Very well. This is enough to deter them. We don't need enough to *win*. Just enough to *deter* them."

Who can say what is enough to deter an enemy? And *when* will it deter him? An armament which might deter an enemy today may prove ineffectual day after tomorrow. It may be a drop in the bucket. The situation changes with unruly and unholy speed, and you can't change your force levels that fast.

So I say, "We must have more than enough to deter them. *More* than you *think* is enough to deter them. You will need a mixture of weapons —so that, in the event there's a break-through which nullifies one variety of weapon, you're not lying there absolutely helpless."

That's the reason I'm frightened to death at the notion that we might wind up with a strictly deterrent force. Or a strategic force with a thousand missiles and nothing else.

I've emphasized to the reader that, with what little schooling for combat I had— When I got out where the lead was flying, I found that in many cases my instruction was about a hundred and eighty degrees off course.

We may think we know the way in which a war is going to start, and the way it's going to be fought. What we think *now* may be entirely erroneous when the fighting starts. Tactics and techniques are altered briskly as the war progresses. In our last trip down the pike we couldn't even keep our Training Command caught up with us.

You must accept the premise that you're going to be surprised. The enemy is not going to do what you *thought* he would do. He's going to do something different. But, if you possess a flexible system, you will be able to react competently to surprises.

An elder axiom must prevail. *No weapon is really a weapon until it is battle-tested.* When the firing starts, that popgun may be not as good as you thought it was. It doesn't function properly. There are modifications which must be made.

Right now we haven't had sufficient testing on the missiles, and to my mind we'll never get enough testing, because it's *too expensive to test missiles.* Certainly we have a test program in progress, and it's going to offer us some data; but it will never equal the data which can be secured by study of a manned system. In that case you go off and fly, and test the thing. If something breaks, you can come in and land and fix it.

If a missile breaks, all you know is that it didn't *get there.* Sometimes it's extremely difficult to determine what the basic problem really is. Sometimes it's impossible. And you are never going to bring that missile *back.*

Every time you fire one, there's a monstrous bill to be paid. We're never going to be able to get the thousands and thousands and thousands of flights out of missiles which we get out of our manned systems.

Also, the manned system can do many things *before war starts* which will give clear evidence of our determination. It will offer more options to the Nation's leaders in averting war. This is the most important characteristic which can be attributed to manned systems.

Just as I believe that individuals have to work, or should have to work, if they wish to live well in this world, so do I believe that countries have to work for the same reward. To any person who desires to argue this basic philosophy, I would say, "Show me just where, in the past, we got something for nothing." We must make sure in this unsteady world that our defenses are sound—and more than sound. We dare not lower the bars. Repeatedly we neglected our defenses too long in the past.

We are maintaining muscular protection at present. But we must make sure that we do so in the future as well. That's what I've been worried about.

We started out, years ago, to build a decisive power tailored around our possession of atomic weapons. So the enemy has the same ordnance now. Thus there are too many people saying, "Well, they've got them. We've got them. We're at a stalemate. Neither of us can do anything. Let's just *set*."

That sounds like a Maginot Line complex. Because this so-called stalemate *can be broken*. To harness or saddle. It isn't even the stablemate of a stalemate.

At the present time we hold an overwhelming advantage. But if we loll around and do nothing, we won't have the advantage for very long. We must keep that overwhelming superiority, and I believe that it will be possible *to keep* that overwhelming superiority.

Another old axiom: the greatest defense is the capability for offense.

It means work and more work. It means preparation and planning. It won't come from sitting around and crying *stalemate,* in a rocking chair or out of it. Wryly let it be said that we've demonstrated, in the past, a national characteristic for doing just that.

Oh, once we Americans are aroused and really want to do something, we go out like we're killing snakes. . . . Full speed ahead! To hell with everything else! . . . But in that way we spend more money than we should. And, regrettably, spend more lives. We dissipate a plenitude of our resources just to do the job. Because we want to go *bang*, now, on the instant, and get it done. Then, once we're no longer worried, we sit back on our fat cans and do nothing.

We've got to mend our ways or we're going to be in trouble.

In midsummer you can't possibly prophesy what will be happening next fall. There are going to be four or five moons in between, and a lot of weather fronts as well. We expect to have this book reach the public in the autumn of 1965, so there has to be a time lag. I can mention the situation in Viet Nam only as it was in July, 1965.

(Reminds me of my foundry days, working with molds and sand cores at Buckeye. You poured in the metal, and it cooled and hardened . . . pretty soon you couldn't change it at all. Time pours the same sort of metal. Castings molded in October or November, 1964, have

long since solidified; and metal shaped yesterday or the day before is
cooling.)

We may be engaged in an all-out war by the time this book is
published. I don't think we will be. But it could happen.

All along I said that if we were going to get anywhere in Viet Nam,
we'd have to attack in the north. I advocated that policy for about
three years in the Joint Chiefs, and I was all by myself. Then the
Marines came around to agreeing with me, and we were together in
the opinion. Then, two or three months before I retired, the Army and
the Navy began to see what we were talking about. Finally the entire
JCS recommended the northern approach.

Political and religious winds of Viet Nam blow in every direction.
Those people have been fighting for a long time; they are extremely
weary of fighting, but they can't see any end in sight. They don't especially wish to become Communists. Many rustics up in the backwoods
probably don't know the difference between Communism and Capital-
ism. They just want to be left alone, in peace.

But the people who *do* know the difference are still tired of the war,
and they've been looking to their government to try to do something
about ending the carnage. It is essential to show them a ray of light
somewhere along the line, and make them know that they have a
chance of winning, and getting the war over with. If any government
would show them that ray of light, assuredly they would support it.

But voices have been saying repeatedly, "No, we must recognize a
stable government, down there in the south, before we dare carry the
war to the north."

I don't believe that. If you carry the war to the north, and really
carry it there, you'll get your stable government.

The United States finally began attacking in the north last February.
This was assuredly a step in the right direction. I have not met anyone
conversant with the true situation in Southeast Asia who is not behind
the Administration's resolve to stay in Viet Nam.

The Russians now say that they will permit "volunteers" to go in
there. Chinese Communists are already installing the latest defensive
devices which they possess. I fear they will use them, maybe even before these words get into print. You allow the North Vietnamese to
build up an adequate protection, and it becomes harder and harder
to perform the military task which we need to perform. And it costs
more lives.

The military task confronting us is to make it so expensive for the
North Vietnamese that they will stop their aggression against South
Viet Nam and Laos. If we make it too expensive for them, they *will*
stop. They don't want to lose everything they have.

There came a time when the Nazis threw the towel into the ring.

Same way with the Japanese. We didn't bring that happy day about by sparring with sixteen-ounce gloves.

My solution to the problem would be to tell them frankly that they've got to draw in their horns and stop their aggression, or we're going to bomb them back into the Stone Age. And we would shove them back into the Stone Age with Air power or Naval power—not with ground forces.

You could *tell* them this. But they might not be convinced that you really meant business. What you must do with those characters is convince them that if they continue their aggression, they will have to pay an economic penalty which they cannot afford.

We must throw a punch that really hurts.

For example, we could knock out all their oil. They don't have oil of their own; it has to come into the country; so there are rich targets, in storage areas sprinkled around.

Knock them all out. This immediately brings a lot of things to a halt: transportation and power particularly. It would be the simplest possible application of strategic bombardment, and you could do the job with conventional weapons. You wouldn't have to get into a nuclear fracas.

. . . Or you could bottle up the harbor at Haiphong. That's their main port, fifty-odd miles east and a little south of Hanoi, the capital. One way to do it would be to knock out the dredges which keep the channel open. They have to keep dredging, or that particular channel will close up within a very short period of time, and ships can't get in or out. Take advantage of a local phenomenon: kill off the dredges. No dredges, no ships.

Or knock out the dock areas, the port itself. Or mine the harbor, the way we mined waters around Japan with our B-29's.

So— Choke off all supply by water routes. Or hit the few industries they have. Or knock out *all* their transportation.

Successful prosecution of this war would not necessarily require the introduction of nuclear weapons. But you won't get anywhere until you do go in there and really swat the Communists. This could be done with conventional weapons.

Maxim:

Apply whatever force it is necessary to employ, to stop things quickly. The main thing is *stop it*. The quicker you stop it, the more lives you save.

Once you are in a position where you are compelled to use military force, or in a position where you decide that military force is the only solution to the problem, then you *resort to military force*. The quicker you complete that military action, the better for all concerned.

THE 8th to 11th of October, 1964, we had ourselves quite a time out at the Air Academy in Colorado. That was the thirty-fifth reunion of our old class from Kelly Field.

I mentioned the thirtieth reunion before. But this was five years later, and nobody was growing any younger, and we'd paid the usual toll. There were a number of people who could be around in 1959 who just weren't there in 1964 . . . men like Roger Ramey and Bobbie Burns, for instance. We enjoyed a fine turnout of old-timers nevertheless.

Many names have appeared in this book . . . I was busy with a lot of those people along the way. Anderson, Egan, Harbold . . . Put Mundy, Blondie Saunders, Louis Vaupre. . . . John Gerhart drove over from NORAD, and Stuart McLennan, with his shining rebuilt face, came out from Washington to go high-tailing around as usual, and run practically everything, and be the busiest and most lighthearted person present. Chip West was telling all his best stories, and so was Bill Kennedy, and so was Howard Bunker, and so were Roe and Woodley.

To me one of the nicest things about the whole business occurred on the second or third evening when I was with Butch Griswold in a tiny suite which we shared at the visitors' quarters. We were enjoying just sitting there with another friend, drinks in hand, looking out at the mountains with the sunset behind them.

I think it was Grizzy who started the thing off with a positive assertion. He'd only retired the previous summer; and meeting companions of his youth, with all the reminiscences and memories evoked, he was really in a philosophical mood.

Grizzy says, "Know something? If I had it all to do over again, I'd do it exactly the same way. I'd entertain the ambition about flying, and I'd go in the Service, and I'd go out there to March. I'd be willing to live my whole life over again if I could."

He looked at me almost accusingly. "Wouldn't you?"

I nodded.

"Wouldn't you?" he asked the third member of our triumvirate. And the man said Yes. . . . Oh, there might be a few things he'd done which he wouldn't do . . . and certain things undone. . . .

Grizzy says, "But I mean in *essence*. I mean the program as a whole. If I had a choice, I'd live my life right over again. I'd do the same job. And I'd marry the same woman."

I said, "So would I."

Our friend said, "Me too."

We sat and grinned at each other. One of us (I don't remember which) said, "What a wonderful world! Three elderly characters willing to live their lives over again. You know, that's not *bad*."

We had another drink in honor of the occasion, or accomplishment, or whatever you want to call it.

The last morning, everybody was preparing to go down to Peterson, the Air National Guard installation which serves the Academy. They were awaiting buses and cars; and Bob Warren, then the Superintendent, came down to see us off. We were thanking him for the entertainment which the Academy had given us.

I really began to wonder whether everybody was there. Because it had been quite a party the night before, and—

Well, we'd lined up for a group photograph during the festivities, and I knew that that picture didn't look much like the one taken in '29 when we graduated at Kelly. Thirty-five years can alter the contours and countenances considerably.

I told General Warren, "If you find any old fuds around here after the airplanes have gone, just mail 'em back home, parcel post."

He said he would.

Guess he did so, for no one was reported MIA (Missing In Action).

13

AT NOON on February 1st, 1965, a few hours before retirement, I went over to the White House, where the President presented me with my fourth Distinguished Service Medal.

I had to make some sort of speech, and made a very brief one. It might be appropriate to quote it (completely) at this point:

"I wish I could say I was leaving and retiring with a world free of problems. Unfortunately that is not true. A great number of these problems rest on your shoulders, Mr. President, and you will have to solve them. I'm sure a goodly number will require participation by the Air Force. Hopefully—not combat participation, but possibly some of the humanitarian things that we can do. I leave behind the best Air Staff that I have ever seen assembled, and the best group of commanders in the field that can be possibly procured. They are at your call, Mr. President."

Some of the boys and gals complained about a cold wind that afternoon, out at Andrews Air Force Base where we had the actual ceremony. Somehow I didn't feel the chill. I didn't even wear any gloves, although probably I should have.

The President's airplane had been rolled out of its hangar to make room, and there were a lot of other airplanes sitting around. I had to pose for news photographers and TV men beside some of those. They had one B-17, and I enjoyed posing beside that. Somebody'd painted my old bomb group triangle-G on the stabilizer, and that pleased me very much.

We went into the hangar. Bagpipes had just been playing, and then the commanders took position, and troops fell in.

Well, they offered the usual ruffles and flourishes, and the nineteen-gun salute. The Colors were brought forward.

There was quite a crowd at the festivities . . . several former Chiefs of Staff were present, and my own military family from the Pentagon, and a lot of other people with whom I'd served, or who'd served under me in the past. Helen and Janie and Jim were up there on the platform, and there were many friends' faces in the background. Secretary Mc-Namara was ill and couldn't attend. . . . A message from President Johnson was read aloud, and then the retirement orders were, as they say, "published."

I don't remember thinking about anything in particular during the ritual, except I was glad that they were keeping the thing short.

. . . Yes, Secretary Zuckert; and General Wheeler, Chairman of the JCS . . . Chief of Staff of the Army, General Johnson . . . Chief of Naval Operations, Admiral McDonald . . . Commandant of the Marine Corps, General Greene. And our own Air Force folks—the incoming Chief, Mac McConnell; and his Vice Chief, Butch Blanchard. All in all I guess there were about fourteen hundred guests.

This was definitely a Joint Service ceremony. The personnel who paraded the Colors and presented arms were ceremonial troops from every branch.

So the commander reported: "Sir, this concludes this portion of the ceremony," and I realized that a particular portion of my life had been concluded as well. We walked outside to the reviewing stand, and the band kept playing, and here came the flyover.

There were forty or fifty planes in that cold sky, moving in procession at low altitude, and the B-17 came first. SAC had B-47's, B-52's, B-58's, and of course the KC-135's. Air Defense Command sent over four each of the F-101's, 102's and 106's. Air Training Command sent over some T-38's, and TAC flew their F-104's, 105's and F-4C's. And Thunderbirds went sweeping up and down the sky, very high overhead, their precise contrails curling like feathers. . . .

The band played our traditional, "Off We Go, into the Wild Blue Yonder," but on this day I was going off into the Wild Gray Yonder. The music mingled with a roar and rush of jet engines upstairs, and the droning of that ancient B-17.

In the current season, and dressed in civilian clothes, and with a civilian's problems confronting me, often it is essential to travel quickly to distant cities or even to other countries. I fly through those same strata of our atmosphere where for some thirty-six years I flew in military aircraft and on other sorts of missions. Nowadays I am not at the controls. Some other younger man is salaried by the airlines to do that little job instead. We go at a considerably higher speed than was attained by that old Waco three-seater over east Columbus, Ohio, in the early 1920's; and we progress at stranger altitudes.

Even now I am not so old as to have nothing left but my memories. I hope never to reach that condition. When a man becomes stagnant he is through—just as surely as if an enemy fighter had drilled him with 20-millimeter shells.

True living is a process of being keenly aware of challenges. I know that I am still staunchly alive because I can recognize certain problems which loom, and find a kind of tonic in considering them.

The entire world dwells in confusion, but this is not the first time that such a condition has prevailed. We had our puzzles and our frights back in the Napoleonic era; and long before that, in the age of the Caesars. Or when mid-Eastern or Asiatic hordes came galloping and marching. Without doubt some obscure cave dweller was appalled the first time he heard a mastodon bellow outside his cranny.

Yet the challenge of the modern day hits swiftly across our consciousness like a stroke of lightning.

General Douglas MacArthur was speaking to the Cadet Corps at West Point in 1962. He said, "The thrust into outer Space of the satellites, spheres and missiles marks a beginning of another epoch in the long story of mankind."

We have to brace ourselves to this.

"In the five or more billions of years the scientists tell us it has taken to form the earth, in the three or more billion years of development of the human race, there has never been a more abrupt or staggering evolution."

This, then, is for the moment a form of adversity. But any struggle against the adverse generates in a human being his surest power.

A couple of years before I retired from the Air Force, I recall addressing the Executives Club in Chicago. My speech writers and I had an earnest and profitable conference when the speech was in the making. I wanted to stress the point that our Governmental Space program was offering a lot of valuable by-products which would work to the eventual advantage and enrichment of all the world. The writers went along very capably on this . . . *concentrating our best scientific and engineering brains in the largest-scale attack on new knowledge in man's memory.*

But knowledge is never wisdom. Many people with a vast store of learning behave in a manner palpably unwise. A sense of morality and a decent judgment must function along with whatever new facilities we acquire or else all the effort is in vain.

. . . A man can look out of his airplane window at a dark and mostly sleeping landscape, and see the vague glow of cities, and make his exalted pronouncement about the people who live in them. If he is consciously disappointed or embittered, he'll say, "Most people walking around or in their beds down there— Most people are damn fools."

In a way he'll be correct. Many people are persistent idiots in the conduct of their lives or in their mismanagement of the gifts which nature and history and science have awarded them.

Every one of us is a fool at one time or another. In this failing we demonstrate a common and sometimes painful humanity.

Thus it is good to continue looking out of that same airplane window, but to turn the eyes upward instead of against the ground. Beyond the altitude where ordinary passengers can fly—and very close, at that—is Space.

Already men have gone hastening through Space, and more will hasten there immediately. Soon they will have definite destinations. We must pray that they will possess spiritual destinations as well as physical ones.

When I was living in uniform, I had necessarily to delve into these matters and to study whatever rudimentary findings we could come upon. I had blood upon my hands as I did this, but not because I preferred to bathe in blood. It was because I was part of a primitive world where men still had to kill in order to avoid being killed, or in order to avoid having their loved Nation stricken and emasculated.

I spent my life as a professional military man, and am not apologizing for having done so. We had to have professonal military men. Still have to.

But, quite contrary to trivial opinion, all professional military men do not walk blind and brutal. I have known some who demonstrated as much pity as they did courage, and they showed a lot of that.

When you're dealing constantly firsthand with the quivering elements of life and death— When you are trying to figure out the best manner in which to save certain lives as well as to take others, and in the same operation— You do not necessarily become calloused. Neither does a surgeon.

Now it is still night, and we are flying along a resounding path above the sea. I look down once more and think of the first B-17's fumbling their way to South America. I think of a B-24 picking up clear ice somewhere between Gander and Prestwick. Or I imagine B-29's growling toward Japan.

And there lives a recollection of the 305th, chugging ahead across the North Atlantic. That memory is every bit as persistent as the sound of engines which will always be in my ears.

It was the first and last time a lot of those boys ever crossed the Atlantic.

> Take down your service flag, Mother,
> And turn the blue star into gold.
> Your son is an aerial gunner;
> He'll die when he's nineteen years old.

Some of my boys did just that. Died when they were nineteen years old.

It's good comfort to go probing into the Past, hunting for the words of men who had something to say and could leave us their words. Abraham Lincoln had something to say about all this:

"We cannot escape history.

"The fiery trials through which we pass will light us down, in honor or dishonor, to the latest generation."

We have endured our fiery trials and, inescapably, will suffer others in the future. Space or no Space, we are still barely emergent from savagery. The weapon and the man who wields it will still determine who is to live and who is to die, and which nation is going to walk erect and sturdy, and which nation is going to lie among the maggots.

Recently it was announced that a poll of American high school and college juniors had been conducted by Northwestern University, Purdue University, the University of Wisconsin, and *U. S. News & World Report*. The findings were, among other opinions stated, that "eighty-four per cent denied that patriotism is vital and plays an important part in our lives."

I do not know how that poll was conducted, or how numerous were the segment of our youth who were interviewed. I do not know just how that question of patriotism was put to them. Young folks like to give startling answers, and they like to have their tongues in their cheeks.

If I believed that this finding was perfectly correct, I'd believe also that the America of the immediate future would not be worth saving.

I hope that the United States of America has not yet passed the peak of honor and beauty, and that our people can still sustain certain simple philosophies at which some miserable souls feel it incumbent to sneer. I refer to some of the Psalms, and to the Gettysburg Address, and the Scout Oath. I refer to the Lord's Prayer, and to that other oath which a man must take when he stands with hand uplifted, and swears that he will defend his Country.

None of those words described, or the beliefs behind them, can be sung to modern dance music. But they are there, like rocks and oaks, structurally sound and proven. They are more than rocks and oaks: they are the wing and the prayer of the future.

Whether we venture into realms of Space in our latest vehicles, or whether we are concerned principally with overhauling our engines and loading our ordnance here on the ground, we will still be part of a vast proud mechanism which must function cleanly if it is to function at all.

. . . Crank her up. Let's go.

Index